STUDIES AND DOCUMENTS

Founded by Kirsopp and Silva Lake

EDITED BY

IRVING ALAN SPARKS

in collaboration with

J. NEVILLE BIRDSALL   ELDON JAY EPP
SEBASTIAN P. BROCK   GORDON D. FEE

VOLUME 45

STUDIES AND DOCUMENTS, founded by Kirsopp and Silva Lake, is a monograph series devoted to basic research in the manuscript tradition of the New Testament. It promotes the publication of primary sources and critical studies that advance the understanding of the history and transmission of the text of the New Testament. Although chiefly concerned with palaeography, codicology, and textual criticism, the series seeks to illumine the way in which Western culture has preserved and appropriated a major element of its literary legacy. While the series concentrates on the investigation of the direct and indirect traditions of the text, this primary focus is interpreted broadly to embrace certain cognate subjects, such as the textual criticism of the Septuagint and the pseudepigrapha, as well as the history of linguistic and theological reflection upon biblical materials.

STUDIES IN THE THEORY AND METHOD OF NEW TESTAMENT TEXTUAL CRITICISM

BY

ELDON JAY EPP and GORDON D. FEE

WILLIAM B. EERDMANS PUBLISHING COMPANY
GRAND RAPIDS, MICHIGAN

Library of Congress Cataloging-in-Publication Data

Epp, Eldon Jay.
   Studies in the theory and method of New Testament
  textual criticism / by Eldon Jay Epp and Gordon D. Fee.
     p.   cm. — (Studies and documents ; v. 45)
  Includes bibliographical references and indexes.
  ISBN 0-8028-2430-7 (cloth)
    1. Bible. N.T. — Criticism, Textual. I. Fee, Gordon D.
II. Title. III. Series: Studies and documents
(London, England) ; 45.
BS2325.E66 1992
225.4'8 — dc20   93-1224
                                              CIP

To our younger colleagues in the
Society of Biblical Literature
New Testament Textual Criticism Section,
who must represent North America
in carrying the discipline
into the twenty-first century.

041132

CONTENTS

PREFACE

The present volume brings together a variety of studies on the textual criticism of the NT published or read before learned societies over the past twenty-five years, which reflect the authors' several areas of special interest, especially theory and method, the significance of the papyri, and the use of patristic citations. Since these studies for the most part have continuity with one another, and since some of them originally appeared in publications not immediately accessible to all scholars, it is hoped that their appearance in a single volume might be useful to the larger scholarly community.

It is also hoped that the collection might serve a somewhat broader audience, for example, as a supplementary text in courses in NT textual criticism, both as reading additional and complementary to the standard manuals and at the same time as a kind of hands-on experience with some of the more fundamental issues currently facing this discipline. Hence, some of the studies are more introductory in nature, while others trace the history of special aspects of the discipline. These, we hope, will be of interest to specialist and generalist alike.

Although we agree on much — indeed, these various essays tend to complement one another — the perceptive reader will also recognize that there are several areas in which there is some measure of disagreement. At the least, some of our emphases tend to go in slightly different directions. That too, we trust, will serve as good pedagogy for those who are being introduced to this field of study.

We need to say just a few introductory words about the authors and these various articles. Our common interest in NT textual criticism began at the University of Southern California in the Spring of 1964, where Professor Fee was at that time enrolled as a student in a seminar on this subject taught by Professor Epp. A seminar paper on the corrections of P[66] resulted in two publications and eventually evolved into a Ph.D. dissertation. Shortly after graduation in 1966, the same year in which Professor Epp's revised dissertation on the theological tendencies in Codex Bezae in Acts appeared as volume 3 in the SNTS Monograph Series, Professor Fee was invited to join the "work force" of the IGNTP for the "mopping up" of some of the patristic materials for the Luke volume. That began a long association as junior members on that project which continues to this day, now as senior members (Professor Fee currently serves as chair of the North American Committee of the IGNTP, looking toward the publication of John). There have been other associations in this field as well: as members of the steering committee of the NT Textual Criticism

Seminar/Section of the SBL (which Professor Epp served as chair for many years); as collaborators in editing the Festschrift for Professor Bruce Metzger (1981); and as members of the editorial board on the newly constituted Studies and Documents, in which series these essays now appear.

The idea to gather some of his essays into a single volume was first put to Professor Fee a few years ago by two students of Professor Metzger at Princeton — Michael W. Holmes (now of Bethel College, and currently the American editor for the IGNTP John) and Bart D. Ehrman (now of the University of North Carolina/Chapel Hill and currently chair of the SBL NT Textual Criticism Section). Although they persisted in encouraging such an enterprise, a long period of delay set in, brought about by a large number of other commitments. In the meantime, the suggestion was made, and finally has now been acted upon, that Professor Fee's collection might by shortened to those that are more methodological in nature and be joined by several of the same kind from Professor Epp. Hence, the evolution of this volume, which is both an expression of our interests in this field of study and something of a symbol of many years of friendship and cooperative labor.

All of these studies except for Chapter 4 have appeared elsewhere. They have all been reset to a common format, but apart from Chapter 10 they appear substantially as before. Chapter 4 was first read before the NT Textual Criticism Seminar of the SBL in 1975; it appears here in considerably revised form, basically as a complement to Professor Epp's Chapter 3 (which originated in the same Seminar). Chapter 10 is a collation and rewriting of three different studies that appeared originally as (1) "Modern Textual Criticism and the Revival of the *Textus Receptus,*" *Journal of the Evangelical Theological Society* 21 (1978) 19-33, plus "A Rejoinder," 157-60; (2) "A Critique of W. N. Pickering's *The Identity of the New Testament Text,*" *Westminster Theological Journal* 41 (1979) 397-423; and (3) "The Majority Text and the Original Text of the New Testament," *The Bible Translator* 31 (1980) 107-18.

The sources of the other chapters are as follows (and herewith we acknowledge our gratitude to the various editors and publishers for permission to republish):

Chapter 1 is from *Biblical Criticism: Historical, Literary and Textual,* by R. K. Harrison, B. K. Waltke, D. Guthrie, and G. D. Fee (Grand Rapids, MI: Zondervan Publishing House, 1978) 127-55.

Chapter 2 is from *The New Testament and Its Modern Interpreters* (ed. Eldon Jay Epp and †George W. MacRae; Philadelphia: Fortress Press/Atlanta, GA: Scholars Press, 1989) 75-106, where its title was "Textual Criticism."

Chapters 3 and 7 are from *Studies in New Testament Language and Text: Essays in Honour of George D. Kilpatrick on the Occasion of His Sixty-Fifth Birthday* (ed. J. K. Elliott; Leiden: E. J. Brill, 1976) 153-73, 174-97.

Chapter 5 is from the *Journal of Biblical Literature* 93 (1974) 386-414.

Chapter 6 is from the *Harvard Theological Review* 73 (1980) 131-51.

Chapter 8 is from the *Harvard Theological Review* 69 (1976) 211-57.

Chapter 9 is from *J. J. Griesbach: Synoptic and Text-Critical Studies 1776-1976* (SNTSMS 34; ed. Bernard Orchard and T. R. W. Longstaff; Cambridge: Cambridge University Press, 1978) 154-69.

Chapter 11 is from *Studies in the History and Text of the New Testament in Honor of Kenneth Willis Clark, Ph.D.* (SD 29: ed. Boyd L. Daniels and M. Jack Suggs; Salt Lake City, UT: University of Utah Press, 1967) 27-38.

Chapter 12 is from *New Testament Studies* 15 (1968/69) 23-44.

Chapter 13 is from *New Dimensions in New Testament Study* (ed. Richard N. Longenecker and Merrill C. Tenney; Grand Rapids, MI: Zondervan Publishing House, 1974) 19-45.

Chapter 14 is from *Gospel Traditions in the Second Century: Origins, Recensions, Text, and Transmission* (ed. William L. Petersen; Christianity and Judaism in Antiquity, 3; Notre Dame, IN: University of Notre Dame Press, 1989) 1-32.

Chapter 15 is from *Biblica* 52 (1971) 357-94.

Chapter 16 is from the *Journal of Biblical Literature* 90 (1971) 163-73.

Chapter 17 is from *Aufstieg und Niedergang der römischen Welt* (ed. Hildegard Temporini and Wolfgang Haase; Berlin/New York: Walter de Gruyter, 1992) II/26/1.246-65.

A special word of thanks is due to Peter Dunn, Professor Fee's teaching assistant, who retyped the majority of these papers into their present format, and who also gathered and typed the bibliography. Above all, we are grateful to Irving Alan Sparks, editor of Studies and Documents, for inviting us to publish the collection in that series, and to Dr. Edgar W. Smith, Jr. of the Wm. B. Eerdmans Publishing Co. for seeing the volume through the press.

Eldon Jay Epp
Case Western Reserve University

Gordon D. Fee
Regent College

ABBREVIATIONS

Note: Abbreviations follow the "Instructions for Contributors" in *JBL* 107 (1988) 579-96. For text-critical symbols see the Introduction to NA26.

AJP	*American Journal of Philology*
AnBib	Analecta Biblica
ANRW	*Aufstieg und Niedergang der römischen Welt*
ANTF	Arbeiten zur neutestamentlichen Textforschung
ATR	*Anglican Theological Review*
AUSS	*Andrews University Seminary Studies*
AUSSDS	Andrews University Seminary Studies Dissertation Series
BAC	Biblioteca de autores cristianos
BAGD	W. Bauer, W. F. Arndt, F. W. Gingrich, F. Danker, *Greek-English Lexicon of the New Testament and Other Early Christian Literature* (2d ed., Chicago, 1979)
BARev	*Biblical Archaeology Review*
BBB	Bonner biblische Beiträge
BETL	Bibliotheca ephemeridum theologicarum lovaniensium
BEvT	Beiträge zur evangelischen Theologie
Bib	*Biblica*
BibOr	Biblica et orientalia
bis	twice
BSac	*Bibliotheca Sacra*
BT	*The Bible Translator*
BZ	*Biblische Zeitschrift*
BZNW	Beihefte zur *ZNW*
c.	century
ca.	*circa*, about
CBQ	*Catholic Biblical Quarterly*
CChr	Corpus Christianorum
cf.	*confer*, compare
chap(s).	chapter(s)
ConBNT	*Coniectanea biblica, New Testament*
CSCO	Corpus scriptorum christianorum orientalium
CSEL	Corpus scriptorum ecclesiasticorum latinorum

EBib	Etudes bibliques
ed.	editor, edited by
e.g.	*exempli gratia,* for example
esp.	especially
et al.	*et alii,* and others
ETL	*Ephemerides theologicae lovanienses*
EvQ	*Evangelical Quarterly*
EvT	*Evangelische Theologie*
ExpTim	*The Expository Times*
GCS	*Die griechischen christlichen Schriftsteller*
GNB	Good News Bible
HTR	*Harvard Theological Review*
IB	*Interpreter's Bible*
IDB	*Interpreter's Dictionary of the Bible*
IDBSup	*Interpreter's Dictionary of the Bible, Supplement*
i.e.	*id est,* that is
IGNTP	The International Greek New Testament Project
Int	*Interpretation*
JB	The Jerusalem Bible
JBL	*Journal of Biblical Literature*
JBR	*Journal of Bible and Religion*
JETS	*Journal of the Evangelical Theological Society*
JSNT	*Journal for the Study of the New Testament*
JTS	*Journal of Theological Studies*
KJV	King James Version
LD	Lectio divina
LTP	*Laval théologique et philosophique*
LXX	The Septuagint
MajT	The Majority Text
mg.	margin (the reading found in the margin)
MS(S)	Manuscript(s)
n. (nn.)	note (notes)
NA^{26}	E. Nestle, K. and B. Aland, *Novum Testamentum Graece* (26th ed.)
NEB	New English Bible
Neot	*Neotestamentica*
NICNT	New International Commentary on the New Testament
NIV	New International Version
NovT	*Novum Testamentum*
NovTSup	Supplements to *Novum Testamentum*
ns	new series
NT	New Testament
NTGF	The New Testament in the Greek Fathers [see SBLNTGF]
NTS	*New Testament Studies*
NTTS	New Testament Tools and Studies
OL	Old Latin
OS	Old Syriac

OT	Old Testament
p. (pp.)	page(s)
PG	*Patrologia graeca* (J. Migne)
PO	Patrologia orientalis
POxy	The Oxyrhynchus Papyri
PTMS	Pittsburgh (Princeton) Theological Monographs
q.v.	*quod vide,* which see
RB	*Revue biblique*
repr.	reprint(ed)
ResQ	*Restoration Quarterly*
RevThom	*Revue thomiste*
RSR	*Recherches des science religieuse*
RSV	Revised Standard Version
SBL	The Society of Biblical Literature
SBLDS	Society of Biblical Literature Dissertation Series
SBLNTGF	Society of Biblical Literature New Testament in the Greek Fathers Series [see NTGF]
SBLSP	Society of Biblical Literature Seminar Papers
SC	Sources chrétiennes
SD	Studies and Documents
SE	*Studia Evangelica*
SecCen	*Second Century*
SNTSMS	Society for New Testament Studies Monograph Series
TextsS	Texts and Studies
TLZ	*Theologische Literaturzeitung*
TR	The Textus Receptus
tr.	translation, or translated by
TrinJ	*Trinity Journal*
TS	*Theological Studies*
TSK	*Theologische Studien und Kritiken*
TU	Texte und Untersuchungen
TZ	*Theologische Zeitschrift*
UBS³	United Bible Societies Greek New Testament (3d ed.)
v. (vv.)	verse (verses)
VC	*Vigiliae christianae*
vol.	volume
WH	Westcott and Hort, *The New Testament in the Original Greek*
WTJ	*Westminster Theological Journal*
ZNW	*Zeitschrift für die neutestamentliche Wissenschaft*

PART I

GENERAL AND HISTORICAL OVERVIEW

CHAPTER 1

TEXTUAL CRITICISM OF THE NEW TESTAMENT

Gordon D. Fee

Textual criticism, commonly known in the past as "lower" criticism in contrast to the so-called "higher" (historical and literary) criticism, is the science that compares all known manuscripts of a given work in an effort to trace the history of variations within the text so as to discover its original form. Textual criticism is, therefore, of special significance to the biblical interpreter in at least three ways: (1) It attempts to determine the authentic words of an author. The first question the exegete asks is, What does the text say? before one asks, What does it mean? (2) The majority of Christians have access to the NT only in translation, and the basic consideration in choosing a translation is its accuracy in representing the original text of the author. Before deciding what any of the words meant, a translator's first concern must be that he or she is translating the actual words the author wrote. (3) A knowledge of the history of textual variation will also help the interpreter to see how a passage was understood during the early history of the church. In many instances variant readings are a reflection of a scribe's or a church's theological interests, and sometimes such changes put one in direct contact with historical exegesis.

I. The Need

The need for NT textual criticism results from a combination of three factors: (1) The originals, probably written on papyrus scrolls, have all perished. (2) For over 1,400 years the NT was copied by hand, and the copyists (scribes) made every conceivable error, as well as often intentionally altering (probably with the idea of "correcting") the text. Such errors and alterations survived in various ways, with a basic tendency to accumulate (scribes seldom left anything out, lest they omit something inspired). (3) There are now extant, in whole or in part, 5,338 Greek MSS, as well as hundreds of copies of ancient translations (not counting over 8,000 copies of the Latin Vulgate), plus the evidence from the citations of the NT in the writings of the early Church Fathers. Moreover, no two MSS anywhere in existence are exactly alike.

      The task of the textual critic, therefore, is (1) to sift through all this material, carefully collating (comparing) each MS with all the others, in order (2) to detect the errors and changes in the text, and thus (3) to decide which variant reading at any given point is more likely to be the original.

II. The Sources

The sources for finding the original text are the Greek MSS, the ancient versions, and the citations by the early Fathers. Although many of the extant MSS (both Greek and versional) are fragmentary and the majority do not contain the whole NT, there is such a quantity of material that even the most poorly attested NT book, the Book of Revelation, has been preserved in over three hundred Greek MSS, while the Gospels are extant in over two thousand copies.

The Greek Manuscripts

Primacy of position in the quest for the original text belongs to the Greek MSS, partly because they are copies of copies in the original language of the biblical authors, and partly because the oldest ones are generally earlier than the other evidence (though age is no guarantee of better quality). The MSS are of four kinds: papyri, uncials, minuscules, and lectionaries.

The original documents of the NT were probably written on papyrus scrolls. The scroll, however, was cumbersome both for reading and for finding specific passages. As a result, Christians very early began to use the codex, or leaf-form of book, to copy their sacred writings. All extant fragments and copies of the NT, therefore, are codices; no copies on scrolls have ever been discovered.[1]

The book form also allowed Christians to include more than one document in a single codex, though it was not until the development of the canon and the emergence of large parchment codices (fourth century AD) that copies of the entire NT were made.

1. *The Papyri.* The earliest codices were written on papyrus leaves in uncial (capital letter) script, with no separation of words and little or no punctuation. Because papyrus is naturally perishable, few of the early copies have survived except in the dry sands of Egypt. So far, fragments or large sections of eighty-eight different papyrus MSS have been discovered. These range in date from approximately AD 125 (P^{52}, a single small fragment of John 18:31-34, 37-38) to the eighth century (P^{41}, P^{61}), though the majority belong to the third and fourth centuries. Every NT book except 1 and 2 Timothy is represented in these MSS. Several of the papyri are well preserved and present the earliest significant witness to the NT text. For example, P^{45} (ca. AD 250) has substantial sections of the Synoptic Gospels, P^{75} (ca. AD 200) contains more than half of Luke and John, P^{66} (ca. AD 200) about two-thirds of John, P^{46} (ca. AD 225) substantial portions of Paul's letters, P^{72} (ca. AD 275?) large sections of Jude and 1 and 2 Peter, and P^{47} (ca. AD 280) about one-half of the Revelation.

2. *The Uncials.* About the beginning of the fourth century, vellum (or parchment) began to replace papyrus as the primary writing material. These prepared animal skins had the advantage both of greater durability and larger size, so that

---

1. Father José O'Callaghan suggested that some Greek fragments of scrolls in Qumran Cave 7 should be identified as parts of the NT (*Bib* 53 [1972] 91-100; trans. by W. L. Holladay and published as a supplement to *JBL* 91 [June, 1972]; however, his "find" did not hold up under careful scrutiny (see, e.g., Fee 1973b; see now Epp 1993).

from the sixth century to the fourteenth almost all literary efforts of all kinds were written on parchment.

The scribes of the earlier of these codices (from the fourth to the ninth century) continued to use the uncial script. There are currently 274 known uncials, many of them preserved without blemish. Only one, however, Codex Sinaiticus (‭א‬, ca. AD 350), preserves the entire NT. (It also contains the Epistle of Barnabas and the Shepherd of Hermas.) The great Codex Vaticanus (B, ca. AD 325) includes everything except 1 Timothy to Philemon and Hebrews 9:14 through the Revelation of John, while the majority contain NT sections, such as the Gospels or the Pauline letters. These MSS are designated in two ways: by capital letter and by Arabic numeral with a zero prefixed. The earlier known MSS have two designations (e.g., D-05), while the later ones simply have the number (0268).

3. *The Minuscules.* At the beginning of the ninth century a script of small letters in a running hand (called "minuscule" or "cursive"), which stands in contrast with the uncial (capital letter) script, was created. The advantages of minuscule texts both in speed and economy were quickly recognized, so that by the end of the tenth century, uncial texts were no longer produced. The vast majority — 2,795 to date — of extant MSS are these late minuscules. They are designated by Arabic numerals from 1 to 2795.

4. *Lectionaries.* The second largest group of MSS of the NT are the lectionaries. These are texts written not in regular canonical sequence, but in accordance with the designated daily and weekly lessons from the Gospels and Epistles — lessons that had been developed in very early times.

There are presently 2,193 known lectionary MSS, the earliest fragments dating from the sixth century and complete MSS from the eighth. They are, therefore, both uncial and minuscule and contain either the Gospels or Epistles, or sometimes both. The lectionaries are designated by Arabic numerals prefixed with an italicized or cursive *ℓ* (e.g., *ℓ* 2193).

The Versions

Because of the broad missionary outreach of the early church, copies of most of the NT documents had been translated by the end of the second century into Latin, Syriac, and Coptic. In the following centuries other translations followed: Gothic, Armenian, Georgian, Ethiopic, Slavonic, and Arabic.

Because the Old Latin, Old Syriac, and Coptic versions were made very early and because their geographical location is fairly well fixed, they are particularly important in the recovery of the original NT text. Their use, however, is complicated by several factors. In the first place, certain features of Greek syntax and vocabulary are difficult or impossible to convey in translation. One can never be absolutely certain, therefore, what their Greek text looked like. For example, Latin has no definite article and the Syriac cannot distinguish between the Greek aorist and perfect tenses. Furthermore, it is highly probable that more than one translation was made in each of these languages by different persons, in different places, using different Greek texts. Finally, the earliest extant MSS of these versions are copies nearly two hundred years later than the original translation. Consequently they have very likely suffered their own fate of textual corruption.

In spite of these complications, however, the ancient versions are a valuable source not only in the quest for the original text itself, but also in the attempt to trace the history of textual transmission and corruption. These older versions are variously designated: some are identified by small Latin letters (a, b, c, or it[a], it[b], etc.) for the OL, while the others are identified by a superscript designation after an abbreviated form of the version (syr[c], syr[pal], cop[bo]).

The later versions and the "authorized revisions" of the older versions, namely, the Latin Vulgate and the Syriac Peshitta, are of more limited significance. Scholars, of course, make use of all evidence. But the bewilderingly complicated history of the Vulgate, which makes it a textual study in its own right, tends to give it a place of secondary importance even among the versions.

Patristic Citations

The final source of data for the textual critic is from the citations and allusions to the NT found in the writings of the early Church Fathers. As with the versions, their usefulness is complicated by several mitigating factors.

Most often the Fathers cited the NT from memory, so one can not always be sure that their memory reflects the actual wording of their Greek text. Moreover, a Father may have used several — and differing — copies of the NT. Finally, the available texts of the patristic writings also are copies, usually very late ones, and in some cases have suffered extensive corruption.

Yet when the painstaking work of reconstructing the NT text cited by one of the Fathers is done, it is of great value. For it gives us a datable and geographically identifiable witness to the NT available to that particular Father. Although such a witness is often considered tertiary to the Greek MSS and the versions in the recovery of the original text, nonetheless when one has certainty with regard to a Father's text, it is of the same value as the MSS themselves. Moreover, the texts of the Fathers are of primary importance in tracing the history of textual transmission.

Manuscript Relationships

The immense amount of material available to NT textual critics, exceeding all other ancient documents by hundreds of times, is both their good fortune and their problem. It is their good fortune because with such an abundance of material one can be reasonably certain that the original text is to be found somewhere in it. Quite in contrast to those searching for other original texts (including the OT), they scarcely ever need to resort to textual emendation, though the possibility must always be kept open that the very first copy of the original MS, from which all others derived, had some uncorrected errors.

However, the abundance of material is likewise the textual critic's problem, because no two copies are exactly alike, and the greater the number of copies, the greater the number of variants among them. Even in this day of computer technology, sifting through such an immense amount of material is a formidable task. This is especially so in light of the ideal that each piece of evidence must be used in order to identify the original by detecting possible corruption of the NT text.

The task, however, is not quite so formidable as it might at first appear. Although it is true that no two MSS are identical, it is equally true that many are so much alike that they tend to group themselves into three (some textual critics think four) major families of texts (text-types). Such text-types are identifiable on the basis of (1) the percentage of agreement certain MSS have with one another over a total area of variation and (2) the amount of agreement these MSS have in variant readings peculiar to them.

There is, first of all, a group of MSS that have all the appearances of being "local" texts, since they derive basically from Alexandria in Egypt. The group is headed by P75 and P66 (ca. AD 200) in the Gospels, P46 (ca. 225) in Paul, P72 (ca. 275?) in Peter and Jude, Codex B (ca. 325), and the citations of Origen (225-250). It is also supported to a lesser degree by several other MSS (e.g., ℵ C L W 33) and the later Alexandrian Fathers (Didymus, Athanasius, Cyril).

For many years textual critics have considered this text-type to be a carefully edited recension dating from the third century, created by the best Alexandrian scholarship on the basis of good ancient MSS. But the combined evidence of P75, P72, P46, and Origen has placed this text in all of its particulars squarely in the second century, or, so it seems, as early as Christianity was known in that city.

Although this text-type has occasional "sophisticated" variants, it commonly contains readings that are terse, somewhat rough, less harmonized, and generally "more difficult" than those of other text-types, though on closer study they regularly commend themselves as original. Furthermore, it is consistently so across all the NT books, with a minimal tendency to harmonize an author's idiosyncrasies with more common Greek patterns. All these facts give the impression that this text-type is the product of a carefully preserved transmission.

A second group, equally as early as the Egyptian, is commonly called "Western," because variants peculiar to it are firmly established in texts found in North Africa (Tertullian, Cyprian, some OL), Italy (Novatian, some OL), and southern France (Irenaeus). "Western," however, is something of a misnomer, for many of the variants peculiar to the text-type are also found in the East (Tatian and the OS) and occasionally in Alexandria (some quotations in Clement, in John 6–7 in P66, in John 1–8 in ℵ, and in Mark 1–5 in W).

In spite of this early and wide attestation to such a text, these various witnesses lack the homogeneity found in the Egyptian and later Byzantine witnesses. The textual relationships are not consistently sustained over large portions of text. On the contrary, "Western" describes a group of MSS headed by Codex D, obviously related by hundreds of unusual readings, sometimes found in one or several, sometimes in others, but apparently reflecting an uncontrolled, sometimes "wild," tradition of copying and translating. This text-type is particularly marked by some long paraphrases and long additions, as well as by harmonistic tendencies and substitutions of synonyms. In fact, the Western text of Acts is about ten percent longer than other texts and almost certainly reflects an early revision.

One must be careful, however, not to dismiss a variant reading out of hand simply because it is Western. There are several instances, especially in some striking "omissions" but in other places as well, where scholars have cogently argued that

7

the Western text preserves the original NT text. Moreover, the very antiquity of this text, and its wide distribution, should always gain for it a full hearing.

The third text-type, the "Byzantine" or "majority" text, is made up of over eighty percent of all the MSS. As a text-type it does not appear in history until AD 350, but even then its origins are shrouded in mystery. Readings peculiar to this text first appear in a group of writers associated with the church of Antioch: the Cappadocians, Chrysostom, and Theodoret of Cyrus. These Fathers had a NT about ninety percent along the way to the full Byzantine text of the Middle Ages. The earliest MS to reflect this text is from Alexandria (Codex A; ca. 475 — in the Gospels only), while the earliest full witnesses to it are MSS from the eighth century (E and Ω).

Does this text, therefore, represent a revision effected in Antioch in the fourth century? Most textual critics think so, but they do so on the basis of the secondary nature of its peculiar readings, not because of firm data. There are no early MSS from Asia Minor or Palestine. The earliest writers from these parts reflect a Western text, but there was no Origen or Tertullian in Antioch in the early third century to give us a large amount of data to study. Later in the century the scanty evidence from Methodius of Lycia and Tyre and, still later, from the texts of Eusebius of Caesarea and Cyril of Jerusalem seldom reflects the peculiarities of this text-type. Thus, the nature of the text in Antioch over many years is virtually unknown.

What is known is that such a text was available by AD 350, that it had partially begun to influence the text of Alexandria and Rome (Jerome), that it was carried by Chrysostom from Antioch to Constantinople, and that probably through his influence it became the dominant text in the Eastern church.

Most of the readings peculiar to this text are generally recognized to be of a secondary nature. A great number of them smooth out grammar; remove ambiguity in word order; add nouns, pronouns, and prepositional phrases; and harmonize one passage with another. Its many conflate readings (e.g., Mark 9:49), where the Byzantine text-type combines the alternative variants of the Egyptian and Western texts, also reflect this secondary process.

Some scholars also find a "Caesarean" text-type in the Gospels, supported sometimes by P45, W, Θ, family 1, family 13, and the citations of Origen (in Mark), Eusebius, and Cyril of Jerusalem. There is indeed some obvious textual relatedness among these witnesses (especially in Mark), but whether they constitute a separate text-type, rather than some unusual mixtures of the other three, remains doubtful.

Although there is general agreement that making such groupings is both a possible and a necessary task, the significance of such groupings remains contested. It is surely dubious procedure to accept or reject a reading solely because it is found in a certain text-type; on the other hand, such grouping, especially of the later (Byzantine) MSS, greatly reduces the work of sifting a multiplicity of MSS.

III. The Text in History

In order to understand the "how" of NT textual criticism, it is necessary to understand something of the history of the transmission of the text, as well as to have some knowledge of the history of textual criticism itself.

Period of Confusion (to AD 400)

The vast majority of the errors in the NT MSS occurred during the period that is also the most difficult to reconstruct — the first four Christian centuries.

Much of the difficulty stems from the work of the earliest Christian copyists. In a time when the majority of people were illiterate and when Christianity periodically underwent severe persecution, there were probably few professionally trained scribes in the service of the church. Moreover, seldom were the scribes possessed by the spirit of the scribes of later times who worked according to the instructions of the Lord given in Deuteronomy 12:32: "Thou shalt not add thereto, nor diminish therefrom." In fact, the opposite seems to have been true of the scribes in the first two centuries. They introduced thousands of changes into the text. To be sure, many of their errors were unintentional and are easily discernible slips of the eye, ear, or mind. Hundreds of changes in the text were, however, made intentionally. Yet we should not think of these scribes as having acted from evil motives. If they often took many liberties in copying their texts, apparently they did so in most cases in an attempt to "help out." They were more interested in making the message of the sacred text clear than in transmitting errorless MSS.

Thus, early scribes (and sometimes later ones) often "smoothed out" the Greek of the biblical writer by adding conjunctions, changing tenses of verbs, and changing word order. They also tended to clarify ambiguous passages by adding nouns or pronouns, by substituting common synonyms for uncommon words, and sometimes even by rewriting difficult phrases. One of the most common causes of error was the tendency to conform one passage to another. This harmonizing tendency is particularly frequent in the Gospels. It also occurs in parallel passages in Paul and Acts. There are also some instances — and these are usually very important ones — where scribes have added (or less often, subtracted) whole sentences or narratives in the interest of doctrine or completeness.

During the second century in particular, when each NT book was being transmitted independently of the others and when there was wide geographical distribution of these documents with little or no "controls," such scribal errors proliferated. Once an error was introduced into the text, it was then copied by the next scribe as his "received" text. Quite often a scribe "corrected" what he thought to be errors and in doing so created errors of his own. If, as did the scribe of P66, he had a chance to check his copy against another, he may then have "corrected" his text by adding still other variants from that copy. So errors were created and compounded and so they tended to accumulate.

Period of Transmission (400-1516)

Two significant events affected the history of the NT after AD 400. The Egyptian text, which by 450 was already greatly influenced by the Byzantine, generally disappeared from use. The major causes for this were the demise of the patriarchate in Alexandria and the subsequent rise and spread of Islam.

On the other hand, Latin had meanwhile become the predominant language in the West, so that production of Greek texts ceased there. The great number of discrepancies found in the OL MSS had finally resulted in an "authorized" translation, the Latin Vulgate, made by Jerome from ca. 384. But it took about two hundred years before it superseded the more popular older translations. Meanwhile, as it was being copied and carried from one part of the West to another, the Vulgate was variously conformed to the OL and developed local textual histories. Several attempts were made throughout the Middle Ages to purify Jerome's text, but each of these recensions eventually resulted in further corruption. As a result, the more than 8,000 extant Vulgate MSS reflect an enormous cross-contamination of text-types.

The result of these two factors was that the transmission of the Greek NT was generally limited to the Eastern church, where the majority of copies reflected the standardized text used at the capital, Constantinople. Thus, the history of the Greek text during this period, with a few notable exceptions, is simply the history of a thousand years of copying MSS of the Byzantine text-type.

Establishment of the Textus Receptus (1516-1633)

Johannes Gutenberg's invention of printing by use of movable type was the next major factor in the history of the NT text. Although the first Greek NT actually to be printed was edited by Cardinal Ximenes in 1514, the first text to be published appeared in 1516 and was edited by the great Dutch humanist, Erasmus.

Unfortunately, these first editions, which were to serve as the base for all subsequent editions until 1831, were themselves based on late medieval MSS of inferior quality. In fact, Erasmus's only MS of Revelation lacked the final leaf, which had contained the last six verses. For these verses Erasmus used the Vulgate, translating its text into Greek, with the result that his Greek text has readings that have never been found in any Greek MS.

Of the subsequent editions, three have special significance for the history of the NT text: (1) Robert Stephanus's third edition (1550), which was based on Erasmus's third edition, became the standard text in England and served as the base for the KJV of 1611. His fourth edition (1551) is also noteworthy in that it is the first text to be divided into numbered chapters and verses — the system still in use today.

(2) Theodore Beza, John Calvin's successor in Geneva, published nine editions between 1565 and 1604, and this tended to stamp an imprimatur on the text of Erasmus. His editions of 1588-89 and 1598 were also used by the King James translators.

(3) A Greek text very much like those of Erasmus, Stephanus, and Beza, edited by Bonaventure and Abraham Elzevir (1633), became the standard text used on the continent. The term Textus Receptus (TR = "received text") derives from the preface of this edition, in which the editors declared, "You therefore have the text which is now received by all, in which we give nothing altered or corrupted." This boast was to hold good for over two hundred more years.

Period of Discovery and Research (1633-1831)

The next period in the history of the NT text was one in which scholars made great efforts to amass new information from Greek MSS, the versions, and the Fathers.

Yet the texts published during this period continued to print the time-honored TR; the new evidence, especially that from much earlier MSS, was relegated to variant readings in the apparatus (i.e., the critical notes). Among the large number of scholars who made contributions during this period, especially noteworthy are J. A. Bengel (1734), who was the first to suggest a classification of MSS into text-types and to devise a system of evaluating variants according to merit; J. J. Wettstein (1751-52), who set forth extensive principles of textual criticism and began the device of designating MSS by symbols; and J. J. Griesbach, whose editions from 1774 to 1807 laid the foundation for all subsequent textual criticism. Griesbach modified Bengel's classifications of textual groups into the basic three, which are still recognized. He elaborated and carefully defined the principles of textual criticism and showed great skill in evaluating the evidence for variant readings. Although his own text was not so divergent from the TR as those that would follow, his pioneer efforts paved the way for what was to come.

Period of Constructive Criticism (1831-81)

The period that followed Griesbach was to see the overthrow of the TR and the rise of new critical editions based on the more significant manuscript finds and the principles of criticism pioneered by Wettstein and Griesbach.

The first important break from the TR came in 1831 with the Greek text published by the German classicist Karl Lachmann. His was the first systematic attempt to produce a text using a scientific method rather than the mere reproduction of the text of the Middle Ages.

More significant still was the voluminous and monumental work of Constantin Von Tischendorf. Besides bringing to light many hitherto unknown MSS, he published eight critical editions of the Greek NT, the last of which (1872) contained a critical apparatus giving all the variant readings of the known uncials as well as the reading for many cursives, the versions, and the Church Fathers. This volume is still an indispensable tool for NT textual criticism.

Although many others made contributions during this period (especially S. P. Tregelles), the Greek text edited by B. F. Westcott and F. J. A. Hort (WH 1881) was to supersede all others in significance. So thoroughly and well did they do their work that almost all subsequent textual criticism is defined in relationship to it. Their forte was the refinement and rigorous application of a scientific methodology to the NT text. The result was issued in two volumes as *The New Testament in the Original Greek.* Volume 1 contained their resultant Greek text; volume 2 comprised a lengthy Introduction, written by Hort, and an Appendix, in which certain problem passages were discussed.

In the Introduction Hort set out in full detail what has become a classic statement of the methodology of textual criticism. Especially significant are his careful analyses and evaluations of the relative merits of the various text-types and their leading representatives. Above everything else, Hort forever laid to rest the TR. He offered three main arguments against the Byzantine text-type (he called it Syrian), which subsequent discoveries and researches have generally validated: (1) The Syrian text-type is filled with conflate readings, i.e., readings that combine the elements

11

found in the earlier two text-types; (2) the readings peculiar to the Syrian text-type are never found in the ante-Nicene Fathers, neither in the East nor West; and (3) when the readings peculiar to this text-type are compared with rival readings on the principles of internal evidence, "their claim to be regarded as the original readings is found gradually to diminish, and at last to disappear" (1881: 2.116).

Westcott and Hort were thus left with a choice between the two earlier text-types. At this point internal considerations became the final arbiter, and they felt that a careful analysis of variants over many pages of text revealed the text of Egypt, or Alexandria (which they presumed to call "Neutral"), to be far superior in almost every case. Thus, their resultant text was an edition of the Neutral text-type, except in those instances where internal evidence was clearly against it.

Since Westcott and Hort (1881 to the Present)

As one might expect, such a radical departure from the "received text" was not immediately accepted by all. This is particularly true of the English-speaking world, where the TR had long been in the hands of the majority of Christians through the KJV. The reaction to Westcott-Hort was led especially by J. W. Burgon, Edward Miller, and H. C. Hoskier. Unfortunately, much of the reaction, especially that of Burgon, took the form of rhetoric rather than argument; and what argument one does find is basically theological and speculative, but seldom supported by the actual textual data.

This is not to suggest that all subsequent scholarship has followed Westcott and Hort. Most scholars found their affirmation of the Egyptian MSS as neutral to be too ambitious. In spite of disavowals, however, all subsequent critical texts look far more like WH than like the TR or the Western MSS. Therefore, it is fair to say that, whether intentionally or not, the mainstream of NT textual criticism since Westcott and Hort has moved toward modifying and advancing their work. In this brief survey it is possible to sketch only some of the more important advances.

1. *New Discoveries.* Probably the most important advance since Westcott-Hort is the discovery of large quantities of new textual data of all kinds. Among these, the most significant are the papyri, because for the most part they represent evidence earlier than that available to Westcott and Hort.

Many of the first discoveries of earlier evidence showed such a textual mixture that Westcott and Hort's theory of text-types was seriously called into question. But later discoveries, especially P[46], P[72], and P[75], have tended to verify the basic positions of Westcott and Hort. Furthermore, the papyri have generally confirmed their opinion as to the late character of the Byzantine text-type. One does find an occasional variant in the early papyri which supports the later text-type, but none of the early papyri is even remotely related to the Byzantine MSS.

2. *Other Researches.* Besides the discovery of new MSS, other researches of various kinds have also greatly advanced the science of textual criticism since Westcott and Hort.

Especially noteworthy has been the work done that sheds more light on the versions and on Tatian's Diatessaron (an arrangement of the four Gospels to form a single narrative) and the collecting and editing of the citations of the early Fathers. The usefulness of this work is now far greater than in 1881.

In recent years, methodology in establishing textual relationship has also been greatly improved, not only for text-types in general but also for clearer definition of relationships within the great mass of Byzantine MSS. This greatly increased the ability of textual critics to group MSS into their proper families and text-types.

Of particular interest to the exegete has been the work of such scholars as C. S. C. Williams (1951) and E. J. Epp (1966a), who have studied the theological tendencies of certain groups of variants. Such studies have made clear that not all textual variation is accidental or theologically unbiased. They further aid the exegete by throwing light on how certain passages were understood, or misunderstood, in the early church.

Two projects of large dimensions involving broad international cooperation are also of interest both to the scholar and to the interpreter: (1) The International Greek New Testament Project, composed of a team of American and British scholars, is preparing a critical apparatus of the Gospels that will include all known papyri and uncials, extensively representative cursives and lectionaries, all early versions, and citations of all Church Fathers to AD 500. (2) A team of German and French scholars, under the auspices of the Institut für Neutestamentliche Textforschung in Münster, is at work on a new major critical edition, including a full critical apparatus. The General Epistles are the first scheduled for publication.

3. *Critical Editions.* These discoveries and researches have resulted in a spate of critical texts since Westcott and Hort. A few should be noted because of their broad significance.

In 1913 H. von Soden published a long-awaited and massive work that included a critical text, a large and complicated apparatus, lengthy descriptions of MSS, and his own textual theory. This work, however, turned out to be a great disappointment. His textual theory never gained acceptance, his classifications of MSS have often proved to be wrong, and some of his collations are completely untrustworthy. Nevertheless, his accumulation of evidence goes beyond that of Tischendorf and is helpful to the expert when used with care.

More important to most exegetes are the smaller "pocket" editions. The most common of these is a series of editions begun by Eberhard Nestle in 1898. A twenty-fifth edition of this text was published in 1963, now under the supervision of Kurt Aland. This text was not a new critical text, but was rather based on the majority reading of the critical texts of Tischendorf, Westcott and Hort, and B. Weiss. The great usefulness of this edition has been its extensive, but abbreviated, textual apparatus.

In 1966 the United Bible Societies published a new "handbook" edition, edited by K. Aland, M. Black, B. M. Metzger, and A. Wikgren (C. Martini was added to the editorial board for the second edition [1968]). This text has been prepared especially for Bible translators and therefore has the following distinctives: (1) The critical apparatus is restricted primarily to meaningful variants, i.e., variants that may make a difference in the translation of the text; (2) each variant adopted in the text is given a notation as to the degree of certainty the editors felt it had; (3) each variant has a full citation of carefully selected representative evidence; and (4) there is a second apparatus giving meaningful alternatives in punctuation. A commentary on each variant, written by Metzger, was published in 1973. [This text was also used for the 26th edition of Nestle, now Nestle-Aland.]

A comparison of this text with WH and TR shows where a significant consensus of modern scholarship stands. For example, in Luke 10 the UBS edition varies from WH only eight times (plus six spelling differences), while it differs from the TR fifty-six times (plus twenty spelling differences). The reason for the differences between WH and the UBS, or among any of the modern texts, is fundamentally a matter of emphasis in methodology.

V. The Method

For a full discussion of the method and practice of NT textual criticism one should consult the manuals by Greenlee or Metzger. Certain basic considerations may be noted here.

One criterion above all others superintends the scholar's choice at any point of textual variation: the variant that best explains the origin of all the others is most likely original. In order to "best explain the origin of the others," there are two factors that scholars must consider: external evidence (the MSS themselves) and internal evidence (having to do with the authors or scribes).

External Evidence

The first thing one must do at any point of variation is to weigh the manuscript evidence supporting each variant. Thus, one usually asks the following questions: How old are the witnesses supporting each variant or how old is their text? How good is the general quality of the MSS? How wide is the geographical distribution of the witnesses? This latter question is especially important, because early and widespread geographical distribution of a reading points to an original parent much further back before the document in question was widely scattered throughout the early church. With few exceptions, however, scholars are agreed that knowing the age or the geographical distribution of early witnesses in no way guarantees finding the original text.

Internal Evidence

Internal evidence is of two kinds: transcriptional probability (what kind of error or change the scribe probably made) and intrinsic probability (what the author was most likely to have written).

1. *Transcriptional probability* has to do with scribal errors and is based on certain inductively derived criteria. For example, it is usually true that the more difficult reading is probably the original one, because it was the tendency of scribes to make the text easier to read. Again, the shorter reading is often the original one, because the scribes tended to add to the text. This criterion must, however, be used with great caution because scribes sometimes made omissions in the text either for smoothness or to remove what might be objectionable. Finally, a textual variant differing from quoted or parallel material is almost always original, since the tendency of scribes was to harmonize.

2. *Intrinsic probability* is the most subjective element in the methodology

of textual criticism. It has to do with the style and vocabulary of the author, his ideas as they are elsewhere known, and the probabilities based on the immediate context.

Not all the criteria mentioned above are equally applicable in every case; in fact, in some instances they oppose one another. For example, the longer reading may be the more difficult one, or the reading most in accord with the author's style may be a harmonization with that style. In such stalemates the textual critic is usually forced back to the external evidence as a final arbiter.

It is noteworthy that for most scholars over ninety percent of all the variations to the NT text are resolved, because in most instances the variant that best explains the origin of the others is also supported by the earliest and best witnesses.

The Debate over Method

With the rejection of Hort's genealogical method, by which the reading of the Egyptian witnesses was adopted except where internal evidence proved it secondary, there has emerged a method that may properly be called "eclectic." Essentially, this means that the "original" text of the NT is to be chosen variant by variant, using all the principles of critical judgment without regarding one MS or text-type as necessarily preserving that "original."

Despite a few notable exceptions, most of the differences that remain among critical texts result from a varying degree of weight given the external evidence.

On the one hand, there is a kind of eclecticism that, when all other criteria are equal, tends to follow Hort and to adopt the readings of the Egyptian witnesses. This may be observed to a greater degree in the UBS edition and to a somewhat lesser degree in the Greek texts behind the RSV and NEB, where early Western witnesses are given a little more consideration.

Another kind of textual theory was advocated by M.-E. Boismard and was used in D. Mollat's translation of John in the Jerusalem Bible. This is a kind of "eclectic Western" method in which great emphasis is placed on preference for the shorter readings as they are found in various Western witnesses, especially early versions and citations from certain Fathers. The difficulty with this method seems to lie in the preference for the versions and Fathers over against the whole Greek tradition, especially since many shorter readings may be shown to be translational paraphrases or untrustworthy citations apparently made from memory.

On the opposite side is the method of "rigorous eclecticism" practiced by G. D. Kilpatrick and his student J. K. Elliott. They advocate placing no weight on the MSS at all, but making every choice solely on the basis of internal principles. The difficulty with this method is that the results depend on the scholar's preference of internal criteria, which in the case of Kilpatrick and Elliott seems to be for variants in an author's style as over against the questions of transcriptional probability.

While, as has already been said, we may grant that not all of the principles of textual criticism are applicable to each variant, contemporary critics generally agree that questions of internal evidence should usually be asked first and that the weight of the manuscript evidence should be applied secondarily. What becomes obvious, however, is that on the grounds of internal evidence certain MSS tend to support the "original" text more often than others and that those MSS are the early

Egyptian. Therefore, when internal evidence cannot decide, the safest guide is to go with the "best" MSS.

VI. The Significance

What significance does all this make to the expositor? Much in every way. On the one hand, it provides one with confidence that for the most part the text being interpreted, whether it be from a modern Greek text or a contemporary translation, truly represents what the biblical author actually wrote.

Nevertheless, and more significantly, there are places where the original text is not so certain. At such points textual criticism becomes an integral part of exegesis. In some instances, such as in John 7:1, whether the original text says that Jesus "did not wish" to go about in Galilee or "did not have the authority" to do so, or as in v. 8, whether Jesus said he was not, or was not yet, going up to the feast, the textual choice will affect the interpretation of the passage.

In other instances, exegesis and textual choice go hand in hand. In John 1:34, did John the Baptist say, "This is the Son of God" (KJV, RSV) or "This is God's Chosen One" (NEB, JB)? The manuscript evidence is divided, even among the early text-types. "Son" is found in the key Egyptian witnesses (P66 P75 B C L copbo) as well as in several OL (aur c f l g) and the later Syriac Witnesses, while "Chosen One" is supported by the Alexandrians P5 א copsa as well as the OL MSS a b e ff2 and the Old Syriac.

The question must finally be decided on internal grounds. As to transcriptional probability, one thing is clear: the variant is intentional, not accidental. But did a second-century scribe alter the text to support a kind of adoptionist christology, or did an orthodox scribe sense the possibility that the designation "Chosen One" might be used to support adoptionism, and so alter it for orthodox reasons? In terms of probabilities, the latter seems far more likely, especially since "the Son" is not changed elsewhere in the Gospel to fit adoptionist views.

But the final decision must involve exegesis. Since what John the Baptist said was almost certainly intended to be messianic and not a statement of Christian theology, the question is whether it reflects the messianism of such a passage as Psalm 2:7 or that of Isaiah 42:1. In light of the suffering, or paschal, lamb motif of v. 29, it is arguable that "Chosen One" fits the context of the Gospel.

What finally points to "Chosen One" as original is the use the evangelist makes of the many confessions in the Gospel. All of them pick up different messianic motifs (1:29, 41, 49; 4:42; 6:14; 6:69; 11:27) and all of them "fit" their specific context (e.g., the "true Israelite" confesses him as "King of the Jews"; in the bread [manna] from heaven context he is called the Mosaic "prophet who is coming into the world"). Since "Chosen One" fits the context and gives the evangelist yet another messianic confession of Jesus, it seems to be preferred as the original. But in either case, the interpreter must also do textual criticism.

Thus, textual criticism, rather than being simply an exercise for the expert preceding exegesis, is also an integral part of the interpretation of the Word of God.

CHAPTER 2

DECISION POINTS IN PAST, PRESENT, AND FUTURE NEW TESTAMENT TEXTUAL CRITICISM

Eldon Jay Epp

New Testament textual criticism, like every other area of academic inquiry, is always in process. Its history is a record of various discoveries, insights, methods, and distinctive achievements that provide the basis for further investigation, but with fewer definitive conclusions or final resolutions than might be expected. A periodic assessment of the "state of the discipline," or of one segment in its long history, can be enlightening both with respect to understanding those accomplishments of the past and in facing the tasks of the future. Though history is eminently instructive, obviously it is more urgent for us to understand the unfinished tasks and to seek ways to accomplish them. Any assessment of such decision points in current NT textual criticism, however, almost of necessity requires at least a brief review of decision points in past NT textual criticism. If the "past is prologue," such a review will provide, at the very least, the necessary perspective for understanding the current and future issues, and at best will contain the basis for their resolution. This chapter,[1] therefore, includes those two aspects — past turning points in NT text-critical study and decision points in the current discipline of NT textual criticism — with an intervening section on specific developments since World War II that assists us in grasping those current issues that require our attention.

I. Past Decision Points in New Testament Textual Criticism

It is a curious but intriguing fact that if the past is divided roughly into fifty-year periods, starting in 1980 and moving backward through time, many of the major landmarks or turning points in NT textual criticism appear or find their impetus at such fifty-year intervals — give or take a few years — and most of them are landmarks in text-critical methodology. This will provide a convenient framework for our quick review of the major factors in the development of the discipline as we know it today.

One should begin at the beginning — some 1750 years ago — with Origen of Caesarea, who undoubtedly was the first to apply critical canons to the NT text.

1. Sections I and III of this paper draw upon presentations at the annual meetings of the SBL in 1980 and 1981 and of the Eastern Great Lakes Biblical Society in 1983, though with much revision. Some portions utilize material from Epp 1980 [now Chapter 6], and others overlap with material presented in the Kenneth W. Clark Memorial Lectures at Duke University in 1986.

His *Commentary on John* was written in the few years before and after AD 230, followed by commentaries on Matthew and Romans, and these works contain most of his references to variant readings in the NT that have the support of "few," "many," or "most" MSS accessible to him, as well as applications of such canons as suitability to context and harmony with parallel passages (Metzger 1963a: 81-92; Pack 1960: 144-45; cf. Epp 1976a: 216). Origen's lack of sophistication and consistency in applying such "rules" hardly qualifies him as a model of text-critical method, but his use of these embryonic guidelines does suggest that he was the discipline's founder. One hundred and fifty years later, beginning with his *Commentary on Galatians* in the late 380s, Jerome noted variant readings and was employing canons such as an older MS carries more weight than a recent one and a reading is preferable that fits the grammar or context of its passage (Hulley 1944: 91-93 *et passim;* Metzger 1980: 199-208).

These first, rudimentary "landmarks" of text-critical method bore little fruit prior to modern times, though 1050 years later Lorenzo Valla, in his "Neopolitan period" (1435-48), produced two editions of his *Collatio novi testamenti,* for which he collated several Greek MSS of the NT and in which he pointed out both involuntary and conscious scribal alterations, including variants due to homonyms and assimilation (Bentley 1983: 34-46). Though these early efforts were but adumbrations of modern critical approaches, the modern period does begin somewhere in the century between Valla's work on the NT text and Erasmus's final edition of his *Annotations* in 1535, which — in a much less developed form — had accompanied his 1516 *editio princeps* of the Greek NT and which rather fully explained the use of MSS and methods employed in his NT text. Of interest in this transition to modernity is the fact that Erasmus published Valla's second edition of the *Collatio* (which Erasmus called *Adnotationes*) in the very year (1505) that Erasmus himself began studying and collating NT MSS and observing thousands of variant readings in preparation for his own edition (Bentley 1983: 35, 138). In the middle of this transitional century, that is, in 1481 (500 years ago), the first publication of any portion of the NT in Greek took place, the Magnificat and the Benedictus, printed in Milan and appended to a Greek Psalter (Darlow and Moule: 2.574) — not a methodological landmark, of course, but the very beginning point of a stream of editions of the NT in its original language.

As the development of the new discipline of textual criticism continued, a few other early milestones can be identified in that formative period before variant readings in NT MSS were systematically sought and published. One such event occurred 400 years ago, when around 1582 the Reformation theologian Theodore Beza presented two important uncial MSS to Cambridge University, Codex Bezae and Codex Claromontanus. Beza himself apparently made little, perhaps no, use of these in his own editions of the Greek NT, nor did other editors until Brian Walton some seventy-five years later, but Beza's gift meant that these important and early codices became part of the accessible sources for critical study.

Similarly, one could look back 350 years to a pair of more noteworthy landmarks in the period of the 1630s, the first of which also consisted of the placing of an important MS in the public domain, when the fourth-century Codex Alexandrinus was presented in 1627 to King Charles I by the patriarch of Constantinople.

The variant readings of Alexandrinus first appeared at the foot of the pages of the Greek NT portion of Brian Walton's *Polyglot Bible* (1655-57), and his was the first report of these variants; in addition, Walton was the first to use a capital letter as a siglum for an uncial MS, employing "A" for Alexandrinus. More important, however, is the fact that the availability of the very ancient Codex Alexandrinus around 1630 and the recognition and use of this fourth-century MS by Walton represented, as K. W. Clark described it (1962a: 666), "the beginning of a fundamental critical process." This was not the beginning of genuinely modern or scientific NT textual criticism, for that is more likely to be identified at our next fifty-year interval with John Mill, but it is of more than passing interest to note that Codex Alexandrinus figured prominently in Mill's work.

The second milestone of the 1630s is the occurrence in the second edition of Elzevir's Greek NT (1633) of the instantly famous phrase, *textus receptus,* in the declaration "You have the text, now received by all," a marker not particularly noteworthy in itself, but one that two centuries later was to have special significance in the pivotal work of Karl Lachmann and the great modern textual critics who followed. Indeed, without this arrogant — though not unrealistic — generalization, challenges to this sweeping claim might have been even slower in coming.

Looking back 300 years to the period around 1680 brings into view two important figures from the beginning of a very lengthy period during which textual critics collected variant readings and printed them in various editions of the *textus receptus* (TR). The two figures are John Fell and John Mill. In 1675 Fell produced the first Greek NT printed at Oxford, an elegant octavo volume that presented variants (so he claimed) from more than one hundred MSS and versions and provided an important stimulus for seeking and assembling additional variants. Edward Miller (1894: 2.200) refers to Fell's small Greek NT as "the legitimate parent of one of the noblest works" of this type, John Mill's large Greek NT. It was Mill, our second figure, who began almost precisely at this time (1677) his thirty years of "labours nearly Herculean" (as Mill himself describes them; see A. Fox: 60, cf. 61-64) that were to lead to the publication of his impressive Greek NT of 1707, which was important not for its text (since he printed the 1550 text of Stephanus) but for its extensive apparatus (containing evidence on more than 21,000 variation-units and comprising more than 30,000 various readings; A. Fox: 64, 105) and for its prolegomena, where some interesting principles of textual criticism were enunciated and where "a foreshadowing of the genealogical method in noting relationships between manuscripts" appears (Vincent: 68). Mill, of course, was not without his opponents (see A. Fox: 105-15; Parvis 1962: 604), yet both his innovative, massive apparatus (which, by its very presence and its size, raised disturbing questions about the TR) and his rudimentary canons of criticism were to affect all succeeding work. As a matter of fact, M. R. Vincent, in his 1903 *History of the Textual Criticism of the New Testament* (67), asserts — not unjustly — that John Mill "marked the foundation of textual criticism," that is, of the genuinely modern discipline.

The next fifty-year stopping place, around the 1730s — 250 years ago — brings to light an event that is more a curious and fortunate occurrence than a methodological marker, for in October 1731 Richard Bentley, at the age of sixty-nine, rescued the four-volume Codex Alexandrinus (so important in this period of textual criticism) from a fire in the Cottonian Library (A. Fox: 125). For much of twenty years prior to this event, Bentley had been planning and collecting materials for an edition of the Greek and Latin NT that would present the text of the time of Origen ("the true exemplar of Origen") and thereby supplant the TR (A. Fox: 118-19; Ellis: xvii), a project never brought to completion but one significant nonetheless for the very fact of its proposal and for the text-critical principles that were intended to form its basis.

Another event of 1730, however, was more properly a milestone, though it too had its curious aspect. In that year, one of Bentley's collators, J. J. Wettstein, published (anonymously) the *Prolegomena* for his proposed edition of the Greek NT, an edition that was only to make its appearance twenty-one years later in 1751-52. Wettstein's *Prolegomena* listed nineteen principles of textual criticism, including such items as the more ample reading is not preferable to the shorter (no. 9), the Greek reading more in accord with the ancient versions is preferable (no. 13), and the more ancient reading is preferable (no. 17) (see Epp 1976a: 224 [now Chapter 8]), principles (especially the last two) closely akin to those of Bentley before him (which is not surprising) and to those of J. A. Bengel, who was shortly to follow. What is curious, however, is that Wettstein backed away from these canons in the interval before his edition appeared, and the text he printed was the TR of Elzevir, rather than a text based on Codex Alexandrinus, as had been his original intention. Hence, neither did the methodological breakthrough that Bentley might have made come to fruition, nor did Wettstein put into practice his stated principles of 1730.

It is for these reasons that we take notice, next, of the genuine landmark of 250 years ago, the publication of J. A. Bengel's Greek NT in 1734. His printed text was still the TR, but in at least three respects his work was to have far-reaching effects nonetheless. One was his pioneering division of the extant manuscripts into groups; another was his system of signs in the text, showing how close or far from the original he judged variants to be; and the third involved the canons of criticism that he enunciated and practiced, including his insistence that textual witnesses must be weighed and not merely counted. In these and other ways Bengel greatly accelerated the notion that the oldest MSS — rather than the most numerous or smoothest — were the best MSS, and the negative impact of this principle upon the TR would show itself increasingly as time passed.

These developments by Bentley (A. Fox: 122-24), Wettstein (Epp 1976a: 223-25), and Bengel (Metzger 1968a: 113) were to bear fruit roughly at the next fifty-year landmark, namely, J. J. Griesbach's Greek NT of 1775-77, which — along with its subsequent editions and his influential canons of criticism — constituted the first daring though measured departure at numerous points from the TR. Thus, it was with Griesbach that a decisive break with the TR had arrived in theory — but only in theory — for by no means had it yet been achieved in clear and thorough practice. In fact, however, the preceding one hundred years (from Mill's work in 1677 until Griesbach in 1777) and the fifty years following Griesbach comprised that lengthy period of exploration and experimentation in text-critical method that effectually laid the foundation for the final overthrow of the TR — which so long had dominated the field.

The decisive departure from the TR in actual accomplishment and practice arrived with the next fifty-year landmark, now 150 years ago: Karl Lachmann's Greek NT of 1831. A classical scholar like many editors of the Greek NT before him, Lachmann made a proposal that actually was quite modest, for he sought only to establish the text as it had existed in Eastern Christianity just prior to AD 400. Lachmann's method of achieving his goal, however, was anything but modest or reserved. Rather, it was both innovative and bold, for he relied for his NT text on no previous printed edition, but, laying aside the whole established traditional text, he devised a text entirely from the most ancient witnesses known to him, including, of course, the oldest Greek uncials (though no minuscules), but also the OL and Vulgate versions and some early Fathers, such as Origen, Irenaeus, and Cyprian (see Kenyon 1926: 286-88; Metzger 1968a: 125-26). Lachmann's 1831 edition contained fewer than one hundred words describing his principles for selecting the readings of his text; his first principle of selection was that he followed "nowhere his own judgment," but "the usage of the most ancient eastern churches"; when this evidence was not consistent, he preferred the reading on which the "Italian and African" witnesses agreed. Worth emphasis again is the fact that he gave no consideration to the "received readings," and in this respect Lachmann, the first scholar to make such a clean break with the TR, had taken a giant step forward by backing away 1200 years from the "received text" of the sixteenth century and seeking to establish that of the fourth.

The period from Lachmann to Westcott-Hort, 1831-81, undoubtedly constitutes the single most significant fifty-year period in the history of NT textual criticism, for important new materials appeared and significant new methodologies were implemented. Together these would bring us fully into the modern period. This fifty-year period opened with the beachhead by Lachmann against the TR — a beachhead that was fiercely resisted, just as were the earlier assaults upon the TR by Bentley and Bengel. But Lachmann represents more than a beachhead; his edition stands for the decisive battle — it was D-Day — and now it was only a matter of time until the territory hitherto held by the TR would be fully occupied by the triumphant forces led by a vanguard of the earliest NT witnesses. If this military imagery can be tolerated a bit longer, one of the leading "generals," soon on the scene, was Constantin Tischendorf, whose eight editions of the Greek NT between 1841 and 1872 and whose nearly two dozen volumes publishing new MSS were major factors in the occupation of the newly won territory. Codex Sinaiticus was, of course, the most prominent of these discoveries.

Tischendorf's second edition in 1849 provided the rationale for his text — a basic principle similar to Lachmann's:

> The text should be sought solely from ancient witnesses, and chiefly from Greek codices, but by no means neglecting the testimonies of the fathers and versions. Thus, the whole arrangement of the text is bound by necessity to arise from the witnesses themselves . . . , not from the edition of Elzevir, which is called "received"; however, to be placed first among disagreeing witnesses are those regarded as the oldest Greek codices, i.e., written from the fourth to about the ninth century. Again, among these those that excel in antiquity prevail in

authority, and this authority increases if testimonies of the versions and fathers are added, nor is this authority surmounted by the disagreement of most or even of all the recent codices, i.e., those written from the ninth to the sixteenth centuries.[2]

Tischendorf's terse and quotable dictum, witnesses "that excel in antiquity prevail in authority," no longer required defense, for Lachmann had already firmly established the point.

Another "officer" in the campaign — perhaps a brigadier general — was S. P. Tregelles, who announced his text-critical principles in 1854, unaware of Lachmann's similar principles. Tregelles's aim was "to form a text on the authority of ancient copies without allowing the 'received text' any prescriptive rights" (1854: 152; see Epp 1976a: 233). The occupation of the ground formerly held by the TR was occurring at an increasing pace.

If D-Day belonged to Lachmann, V-Day — fifty years later at our next landmark — belonged to the undisputed "general of the army," F. J. A. Hort, and his "first officer," B. F. Westcott. The Westcott-Hort text (WH) of 1881 — just about one hundred years ago — resulted from a skillful plan of attack and a sophisticated strategy for undermining the validity of the TR. Hort, the strategic expert, outlined in the introductory volume to the edition certain guidelines that were crucial in the plan. Some of these were old, others new, such as:

1. Older readings, manuscripts, or groups are to be preferred.
2. Readings are approved or rejected by reason of the quality, and not the number of their supporting witnesses.
3. A reading combining two simple, alternative readings is later than the two readings comprising the conflation, and manuscripts rarely or never supporting conflate readings are texts antecedent of mixture and are of special value.
4. The reading is to be preferred that most fitly explains the existence of the others.
5. The reading is less likely to be original that shows a disposition to smooth away difficulties.
6. Readings are to be preferred that are found in a manuscript that habitually contains superior readings as determined by intrinsic and transcriptional probability. (Westcott-Hort: 2.55, 44, 49-50, 22-23, 28, 32-33, respectively)

The application of these (and other) principles effected a thorough and dramatic rout of the TR (which Westcott-Hort called the "Syrian" text), for its chief witnesses could not withstand the charges concerning (1) their recent date, (2) their conflated readings and smoothening of difficulties, (3) the inability of their readings to explain the other readings, and (4) the fact that they kept company with numerous other

2. Quoted in Gregory's Prolegomena to Tischendorf's 8th ed., 1894: 3.47-48.

MSS sharing these same characteristics. This strategy pushed to the forefront the oldest and "best" MSS and the "best" groups of MSS, those witnesses which — they said — had virtually escaped corruption and contamination, and which they called — understandably — the "Neutral" text. Accordingly, this Neutral text was acclaimed by Westcott-Hort and accepted by many others as "The New Testament in the Original Greek," as the title of their edition reads.

What was most surprising in this final campaign in the overthrow of the TR was the last point, the audacious move by Westcott-Hort radically beyond the kind of modest proposal of Lachmann — to establish the text of the fourth century — to the unqualified claim to have established the text of the NT "in the original Greek." Would it not have been adequate for Westcott-Hort to have sought the text of the second century, for they were able with some assurance (based primarily on patristic quotations) to trace important portions of the text to that period? As it turned out, their final daring thrust — to identify the Neutral text with the original — represented an overkill (something not uncommon in a final military drive). It is the more understandable, then, that the strategy that had led to this result was itself quickly attacked at its vulnerable points. Some of these vulnerable points, as is well known, concern (1) Westcott-Hort's overly negative valuation of both the Byzantine text and the so-called Western text; (2) questions about their assessment of the components of the Western text and of what they termed the "Alexandrian" text; and, of course, (3) whether the Neutral text was really as pure and neutral and stood in so close and direct a relationship to the original as they claimed. The discussion of these and other questions was quick to be undertaken and ranged from the measured criticism of F. H. A. Scrivener and George Salmon (see Metzger 1968a: 137) to the vehement attacks by J. W. Burgon.

What was far more significant than such immediate responses, however, was the fact that Westcott-Hort's edition and the hypotheses behind it provided an incentive for text-critical investigations that led directly to many of the major opportunities and problems that face us currently in the discipline. Such discussions occupied the succeeding fifty-year period until the next landmark was reached in the 1930s and when an unexpected development at that point infused new life and new directions into the older discussions and brought fresh issues into view. These developments will occupy our attention momentarily, but some of the investigations most obviously stimulated by Westcott-Hort deserve mention. For example, Hort's staunch defense of the three most prominent text-types of their theory (Syrian, Western, and Neutral) evoked two major branches of studies. One concerned the Syrian or Byzantine text, and investigations took at least two directions: efforts were made to redeem Byzantine readings (if not the entire text-type) from the low status accorded them by Westcott-Hort, and attempts — most notably by H. von Soden — were made to classify the massive body of Byzantine MSS into manageable groups and to assess their respective character. Another major branch of studies concerned the so-called Western text. Here Hort's judgment — that Western readings, though very ancient, evidenced extensive corruption — provided a challenge to defend their originality at many points and, for example, encouraged Friedrich Blass to develop fully the view that Luke wrote two versions of his canonical books, one represented by the Neutral and the other by the Western text (Blass 1895, 1896, 1897, 1898:

96-137). (Such a view had been mentioned and rejected by Hort himself, but is now being revived — in the 1980s — by E. Delebecque 1980, 1982a, 1982b, 1982c, 1983, 1986; Boismard-Lamouille.) In addition, Hort's assignment to the Western text-type of witnesses soon recognized to be disparate and divergent rather than homogeneous converged with a series of new manuscript discoveries (such as codices Washingtonianus [W] and Koridethi [Θ] and the Sinaitic Syriac) to quicken studies that would lead to the identification of a separate text-type, the Caesarean. All of these developments are well known to us, and numerous analyses of the Western, Byzantine, and Caesarean text-types occupied textual critics for fifty years and longer.

It was, as a matter of fact, just fifty years after the WH edition that the next landmark appeared, for in 1930-1931 Chester Beatty acquired the famous papyri that bear his name, notably — for our purposes — P[45], P[46], and P[47], and the London *Times* of 19 November 1931 carried the first public announcement of the discovery. These were the first early and extensive NT papyri to come to light, and a whole new era of NT textual criticism suddenly unfolded. This discovery is a landmark not because NT papyri had not been found before but because the Chester Beatty papyri effected not merely a *quantitative change in the materials* available, but a *qualitative change in the discipline.* The Oxyrhynchus papyri, of course, had been discovered and published already beginning in 1898, providing many fragments of NT text, and the Bodmer papyri from 1956 and following were in some significant ways to over-shadow the Chester Beatty, yet the Chester Beatty papyri were so extensive and so early in date that they rightly demanded a restructuring of NT text-critical theory and practice. Such a restructuring, of course, did not actually take place; for example, when P[45] in the Gospels was aligned with the Caesarean text, critics still called that text Caesarean rather than the P[45] text or the Chester Beatty text (either of which would have been an appropriate and natural designation). Nevertheless, the ultimate effects of these papyri upon critical editions — both text and apparatus — and as stimuli to studies across the entire discipline were enormous and lasting, and the landmark quality of the discovery is indisputable. When the Bodmer papyri, most notably P[66] and P[75], are recognized also as ingredients of the period since 1930, it is quite appropriate to refer to the fifty-year period from 1930 to 1980 as the "Period of the Papyri," for, given the high valuation placed upon these and the other papyri, we seem to have reached a new stage — perhaps "plateau" is the word — which provides a new and refreshing vantage point for viewing the NT text, but a plateau from which, for the moment at least, we have not been led to an obvious higher plane.[3]

All of us share this high valuation of these extraordinarily early and significant NT witnesses that have rightly received such close attention during the fifty-year "Period of the Papyri," and perhaps our newest fifty-year landmark — that of the 1980s — has now made its appearance in the "Introduction" to the NA[26] (1979), where the editors affirm that for this new "Standard Text" of the NT the forty earliest papyri (and the four earliest but fragmentary uncials) are "of automatic [*automatisch*]

---

3. On the historical impact of the papyri on NT textual criticism, see now Epp 1989b.

significance, because they were written before the III/IV century, and therefore belong to the period before the rise of major text types" (K. and B. Aland 1979: 12*, cf. 49*; see Epp 1980: 144-50). Whether this is a legitimate claim, or a plausible claim, or a claim much overdrawn is a highly complex question to which we shall return, yet — unless significant new papyrus discoveries are made — it seems clear that the fifty-year "Period of the Papyri" from 1930 to 1980, that period of the discovery, analysis, and utilization of the earliest and most substantial papyri, may have to give way to a fresh period of the *re*assessment of the papyri and perhaps of their *re*application to the history and theory of the NT text. This, however, brings us up to date and leads directly to that part of our discussion concerned with current challenges in the discipline. Before joining these issues, the post–World War II period requires finer scrutiny.

II. The Post–World War II Setting

New Testament textual criticism was a quiet discipline as the scholarly community regrouped and reemerged following World War II. How text critics viewed themselves and their work can be garnered from any of the numerous "state-of-the-discipline" reports that appeared in the first decade of the period. An interesting contrast appears, however, when one takes a prewar status report from one of the most prominent textual critics and compares it with the postwar reports. Sir Frederic Kenyon, when asked in 1938 to contribute an article on "The Text of the Greek New Testament" for the *Expository Times* series "After Fifty Years," describes in glowing terms the astounding manuscript discoveries since 1888, refers to "much progress" in textual theory, and, with reference to the confidence of scholars in the Alexandrian text [Hort's Neutral, or the Egyptian], concludes with a statement which — while cautious and modest on the surface — exudes that same high confidence in what has been achieved: "We shall," he said, "do well to recognize that complete certainty in details is not obtainable, and that there may be something yet to be learned from discoveries still to be made" (1938: 71). In contrast, Merrill Parvis, in *The Study of the Bible Today and Tomorrow* — a 1947 collaborative volume like the present one — affirmed that "no great advance has been made in the method of textual study since the days of Westcott and Hort" (58); several years later K. W. Clark, in a 1956 status report, echoed the same sentiments in referring to "how little, and how tentatively, textual criticism since 1930 — and much earlier — has altered the New Testament text we study" and in positing that "any substantial effort to improve the basic critical text must 'mark time' until the whole complex of textual studies reveals a new integrating pattern" (41-42); and — as a third example — in 1962 H. H. Oliver's status report indicated that "so far, the twentieth century has been a period characterized by general pessimism about the possibility of recovering the original text by objective criteria. This pessimism has persisted despite the appearance of new materials" (308). The change in mood is of more than passing interest, for this same lack of progress — attributed to an even broader portion of the discipline — could be claimed by at least one person in the field as recently as 1973 (Epp 1974 *passim*). We shall return to these issues after a brief survey of post–World War II efforts under three categories: critical editions, discoveries, and methods.

Critical Editions and Studies

Editions of the Greek NT

The critical apparatuses of Mark and Matthew produced by S. C. E. Legg just prior to and during the war (1935; 1940) were not highly acclaimed either for their conception, accuracy, or usefulness. One by one, however, the various hand-editions of the Greek NT reappeared after the war. That of H. J. Vogels first appeared in 1920 (then with the Vulgate in 1922), with a fourth edition in 1955; A. Merk's originated in 1933, with a third edition in 1938, followed by a postwar sixth edition completed in 1948, and a current ninth edition, 1964. J. M. Bover's was a wartime product, appearing in 1943, with several postwar editions through the fifth of 1968, and revised by J. O'Callaghan for inclusion in the 1977 *Nuevo Testamento Trilingüe* (Bover-O'Callaghan). A. Souter's Greek NT (original, 1910) made a postwar appearance in a revised form in 1947. G. D. Kilpatrick revised the 1904 *British and Foreign Bible Societies Greek New Testament* to produce its second edition in 1958. In 1964 R. V. G. Tasker published "the actual Greek text, of which *The New English Bible* is a translation" (ix). In the same year K. Aland (1964) issued his *Synopsis quattuor evangeliorum*, with text and apparatus of the four Gospels, and in 1981 H. Greeven produced a new critical text of the four Gospels (with apparatus) for his *Synopsis*. Finally, in 1982, Z. C. Hodges and A. L. Farstad edited a "majority text" NT, based on the Byzantine MSS. (For earlier attempts to rehabilitate the TR, see Hills; Fuller 1972, 1973, 1975; Pickering.)

But the most widely used hand-edition of the Greek NT, at least in Europe, was that of Eberhard Nestle, which had passed through sixteen editions prior to the war (by 1936) and made its first reappearance after the war in a photographic reproduction by the American Bible Society in New York sometime prior to 1948 (when I purchased my copy), though it bears no publication date. The Nestle edition had been edited, beginning with the thirteenth edition of 1927, by Nestle's son, Erwin, but Kurt Aland appears as coeditor after the twenty-first edition of 1952, and later as sole editor until Barbara Aland became the second editor of the twenty-sixth edition of 1979. The text of this latest edition is, by agreement, identical with that of the third edition of the United Bible Societies' *Greek New Testament (UBSGNT)* of 1975, and this Greek NT text (contained in these two hand-editions) has recently been designated the "Standard Text" by Kurt Aland.[4] As the most readily available and most widely used Greek NT text, it may justly be called the "Standard Text," though claims made for it as a text universally accepted as the "best" or "original" NT continue to be debated (e.g., Moir 1981a; Elliott 1983b; Bartsch, and K. Aland's reply, 1982).

The WH text of 1881, some three or four generations in the past by the outbreak of the war, perhaps retained more status as a modern TR than any other critical text, at least in English-speaking scholarship. The ground swell, however, for a new major critical edition or apparatus was beginning to form in the period

---

4. In K. and B. Aland 1989, the term "Standard Text" has been replaced by "new text" (e.g., pp. 25, 34-36 as compared with 1987: 25, 34-36, respectively).

between the wars, prompted more than anything else by the new manuscript discoveries of the twentieth century. A push for a "new Tischendorf" based on the Nestle text had emerged already in the mid-1920s in a British-German group, but the German group withdrew when no agreement could be reached on the textual base to be utilized; it was at this point that the British group carried on, producing the ill-fated Legg volumes. Recognition of their inadequacy led to a British-American undertaking, the so-called International Greek New Testament Project (IGNTP), whose goal was a new critical apparatus of the NT — that is, the provision of the *data* essential for a new critical text of the NT, though not proposing to create that *critical text* itself. This project was conceived on a large scale but began where Legg left off — with the Gospel of Luke — though envisioning a vastly enlarged manuscript coverage as compared with Legg. Its collation base was the TR, employed on the correct assumption that the most economical way in which to display the variants in the apparatus was against this "fullest" of texts. The choice of the TR was misunderstood and, indeed, ridiculed by Kurt Aland (1966b; see the replies by Suggs [in Duplacy and Suggs: 196-98, 204-6] and Epp 1974: 402-3), but the British-American project persisted through nearly forty years of cooperative efforts and discouraging delays until the first — and perhaps only — results appeared in 1984 and 1987, an apparatus to the text of Luke's Gospel (*The New Testament in Greek: The Gospel according to St. Luke, Part One: Chapters 1-12* [1984]; *Part Two: Chapters 13-24* [1987]). Users and critics will have to judge its usefulness, but the economical display of vast amounts of material seems to be a self-justification for the principles on which this critical apparatus of the Greek NT [it is not really an edition] was constructed.

The IGNTP's long history began in 1948 with a large British committee, chaired successively by R. H. Lightfoot, H. I. Bell, G. H. C. McGregor, and J. M. Plumley; J. N. Birdsall served as executive editor from 1968 to 1977 and was succeeded by J. K. Elliott. A somewhat smaller American committee was organized, chaired from 1949 to 1970 by E. C. Colwell, who was succeeded by B. M. Metzger. K. W. Clark served as executive editor of the materials prepared by the American committee (Parvis 1950; Colwell et al. 1968; Robinson et al. 1970; Elliott 1983a).

The current British committee (now a committee of the British Academy) consists of H. F. D. Sparks, G. D. Kilpatrick, J. M. Plumley (chm.), S. P. Brock, M. Black, T. S. Pattie, J. L. North, J. K. Elliott, and W. J. Elliott, and the present American committee consists of B. M. Metzger (chm.), A. P. Wikgren, M. J. Suggs, E. J. Epp, G. D. Fee, I. A. Sparks, and P. R. McReynolds (American and British Committees: 1: xiv-xv). Whether the IGNTP will carry forward its original plan to provide next a critical apparatus for the Fourth Gospel is unclear at this time.[5]

The division of work provided that the British committee assemble most of

---

5. A new phase of IGNTP was launched during 1987-88, whose purpose is to produce an *apparatus criticus* of the Gospel of John. The British Committee is now composed of J. K. Elliott, W. J. Elliott, J. L. North, D. C. Parker, and T. S. Pattie [with G. D. Kilpatrick until his death in 1989]; and the North American Committee consists of J. Brooks, B. D. Ehrman, E. J. Epp, G. D. Fee, T. C. Geer, M. W. Holmes, P. R. McReynolds, C. D. Osburn, and W. C. Petersen. The latter functions under the auspices of the Society of Biblical Literature.

the patristic and versional evidence, while the American committee was to oversee the collation of the Greek MSS and Greek lectionaries and obtain the textual evidence for most of the Greek Fathers and for the Armenian, Ethiopic, Georgian, Gothic, and Old Church Slavonic versions. Two hundred and eighty-three scholars, mostly from North America, participated in the collection of data from the Greek MSS and Greek Fathers, and many other scholars from Great Britain, America, and other countries assisted in collecting the versional evidence (American and British Committees: 1: v, xiv-xvi).

Several methodological issues were faced in connection with the American assignments, resulting in the Claremont Profile Method for quickly assessing the character of minuscule MSS — permitting the selection of a relatively small number of MSS for inclusion in the apparatus that would adequately represent the various manuscript types in the minuscule mass (Colwell et al.: 191-97; Epp 1967: 27-38; Wisse and McReynolds 1970: 67-75; McReynolds 1972, 1979; now esp. Wisse 1982). A considerable literature is developing around this Profile Method (e.g., Richards 1977a, 1977b, 1979, 1980). In addition, criteria were devised for choosing appropriate representatives of the complex lectionary text (Colwell et al.: 188-91; cf. Duplacy 1970), and, finally, precision was introduced into the process of differentiating patristic "citations," "allusions," and "adaptations" (Colwell et al.: 187-88; Suggs 1958; Metzger 1980: 167-88; but esp. Fee 1971a [= Chapter 15], 1971b [= Chapter 16], Chapter 17; cf. R. M. Grant in Parvis and Wikgren: 117-24; P. Prigent in K. Aland 1972: 436-54; H. J. Frede in Aland 1972: 455-78).

The Greek text that appears in NA[26], which seems to have replaced all the hand-editions and which (as indicated above) has been proclaimed recently as the "Standard Text" by Kurt Aland, was produced, beginning in 1955, by an international team working under the sponsorship of the United Bible Societies. Titled simply *The Greek New Testament,* it is referred to as the *UBSGNT.* Eugene A. Nida of the American Bible Society initiated and administered the project, and the editorial committee for the first edition was composed of K. Aland, M. Black, B. M. Metzger, A. Wikgren, and A. Vööbus; for the second and third editions, C. M. Martini replaced Vööbus. The first edition appeared in 1966, the second in 1968, and a more thorough revision in 1975 (UBS[3]), which — by design — is identical in text to that of NA[26]. A revised fourth edition is in preparation; meanwhile, in 1983 an interim corrected third edition was issued. Assistance was provided all along by the Münster Institut für neutestamentliche Textforschung. An accompanying *Textual Commentary,* written for the committee by Bruce M. Metzger and published in 1971, comments on hundreds of variation-units in the NT and provides explanations for the choice of one reading over others. A torrent of reviews and assessments of both the *UBSGNT* and the companion *Commentary* have been published since these volumes appeared, and the flow has resumed as each new edition has been issued.

Finally, it was the leading critic of the IGNTP, Kurt Aland, who spearheaded several projects involving NT editions and other text-critical work at his Institut für neutestamentliche Textforschung (just mentioned above). The NA hand-edition and the cooperative *UBSGNT* have already been described. In addition, Aland and his Institut produced the monograph series, Arbeiten zur neutestamentlichen Textforschung (see K. Aland 1963, 1967, 1969, 1972, and 1975-83). The first volume (1963) is the *Kurzgefasste Liste der griechischen Handschriften des Neuen Testaments,* which, with a supplement in volume 3 (1969: 1-53), provides the official list of the Greek MSS of the NT, covering the papyri, uncials, minuscules, and lectionaries. The numerous essays in volumes 2, 3, and 5 (1967, 1969, 1972) are of great importance for the study and research of the NT text, with volume 5 devoted to NT versions, patristic citations, and lectionaries. Volume 4 of the series is the now standard *Vollständige Konkordanz zum griechischen Neuen Testament* (K. Aland 1975-83), an indispensable tool for NT exegetes as well as textual critics (see the reviews, e.g., by Fitzmyer 1976-85; and Epp 1979-84). The Institut continues to work toward its *editio maior critica* — its major critical edition of the Greek NT — which began with the Catholic Epistles (see K. Aland 1970, 1987). All of these projects are carried through with meticulous care and thoroughness, and the discipline owes much to Professor Aland and his Institut. (For reports on the status of various projects, see Kunst.)

Critical Editions of Versions and Fathers

Limitation of space permits reference only to post–World War II monographic works and not to periodical literature.

The study of the Latin NT has been greatly assisted by two projects. The first is *Itala,* an edition of the OL Gospels begun by A. Jülicher but later edited by W. Matzkow and K. Aland. The second is the *Vetus Latina,* a large-format edition of the OL Bible with a detailed critical apparatus, carried out at the Beuron monastery under the supervision of Alban Dold until his death in 1960 and then directed by Bonifatius Fischer under the auspices of the Vetus Latina Institut. Currently Walter Thiele oversees the work, and, to date, the Catholic Epistles have been completed (Thiele 1956-69), as well as Ephesians, Philippians, Colossians (Frede 1962-69), and 1-2 Thessalonians, 1-2 Timothy, Titus, and Philemon (Frede 1975-83). In addition, an index of the Fathers has been compiled by Frede (1981, 1984), and an accompanying monograph series provides specialized studies (Frede 1961, 1964, 1973; Thiele 1965; Fischer 1985; Hammond Bammel 1985). On both projects, see Metzger 1977: 320-22.

The Old Georgian version of the Gospels has been edited for Mark and Matthew by Robert P. Blake (1974, 1976), for John by Blake and Maurice Brière (1950), and for Luke by Brière (1955). The Georgian version of Acts was edited by Gérard Garitte in 1955. The Ethiopic of the Apocalypse was edited by Josef Hofmann in 1967-69, and the Coptic of John by Rodolphe Kasser in 1966.

Among numerous studies of the versions are the comprehensive manuals by Vööbus (1954) and Metzger (1977) and the masterful survey edited by Aland (1972), which contains studies by B. Fischer and W. Thiele on the Latin, M. Black on the Syriac, G. Mink on the Coptic, L. Leloir on the Armenian, J. Molitor on the Georgian, J. Hofmann on the Ethiopic, E. Stutz on the Gothic, and C. Hannick on the Old Church Slavonic, as well as chapters on the NT citations in the Greek Fathers by P. Prigent and in the Latin Fathers by H. J. Frede. Lists of versional MSS are provided by Metzger (1977), by Clemons for the Syriac of the Epistles and the Apocalypse, and by Rhodes (1959) for the Armenian. Monographs on the Latin versions have been authored by Zimmermann (1960), Tinnefeld (1963), Frede (1964), Nellessen (1965), Thiele (1965), and Fischer (1985); on the Old Syriac Gospels by Vööbus (1951a) and on the Old Syriac Paul by Kerschensteiner (1970), on the Syriac of the Gospels by Vööbus (1951c) and Strothmann (1971), on the Harclean Syriac by Zuntz (1945; see now Brock 1981), and on the Peshitta by Vööbus (1948); on the Diatessaron by Lyonnet (1950), Messina (1951), Leloir (1962), Henss (1967), Ortiz de Urbina (1967), Quispel (1975), and Petersen (1985); on the Coptic Acts by Joussen (1969); on the Ethiopic Gospels by Vööbus (1951b) and the Apocalypse by Hofmann (1969); on the Armenian by Lyonnet (1950) and Leloir (1967); on the Old Georgian Gospels by Vööbus (1953) and Molitor (1965); and on the Gothic by Friedrichsen (1961).

Regarding patristic quotations of the NT text, the postwar period has provided us with a four-volume index of citations (Allenbach 1975-87) and a number of studies: Muncey (1959) on Ambrose (but see the warning in Metzger 1980: 172); Baarda (1975) on Aphrahat; Mees (1970) and Zaphris (1970) on Clement of Alexandria; Greenlee (1955) on Cyril of Jerusalem; Ehrman (1986) on Didymus the Blind; Leloir (1953-54, 1958, 1962, 1963, cf. 1967) and Petersen (1985) on Ephrem; Eldridge (1969) on Epiphanius of Salamis; Blackman (1948) on Marcion; Frede (1961) and Borse (1966) on Pelagius; D. J. Fox (1979) on Philoxenus; Hammond Bammel (1985) on Rufinus; Vogels (1955a, 1957) on Rufinus and Ambrosiaster; Quispel (1975) on Tatian; and Lo Bue (1963) on Tyconius.

Discoveries

New materials are the "grist" of the text-critical "mill," and the premier discoveries of the post–World War II period are the Bodmer papyri, notably P66, P72, P74, and P75 (Martin 1956, 1962; Testuz; Kasser 1961; Martin and Kasser 1961a, 1961b). These discoveries brought the Chester Beatty papyri into renewed discussion, and a large literature developed on the NT papyrus MSS. In addition to the three Bodmer papyri mentioned above, the other papyri numbered from P55 through P88 came to light after World War II. P58 was found to belong to P33; P64 and P67 were parts of the same MS; and P73, P83, P84, and P87 remain unedited. Place of publication may be found in the handbooks by Metzger (1968a: 247-56) and by K. and B. Aland (1982: 106-11; Eng. 1987: 96-101; 1989: 106-12).

This is not the place to attempt a summary of other manuscript discoveries since World War II, but the following texts were published in monograph form: a Greek fragment of 1 Peter by Daris (1967); the Greek portions (with parts of the Gospels) of Codex Climaci Rescriptus by Moir (1956); a Greek papyrus of Matthew by Roca-Puig (1962). Latin texts were published by Vogels (1953) and Frede (1973); Syriac by Vööbus (1978); Coptic by Browne (1979), Hintze and Schenke (1970), Husselman (1962), Kasser (1958, 1962), Orlandi (1974), Quecke (1972, 1977, 1984), and Schenke (1981); and an Arabic MS of Paul by Staal (1969). Publication of other texts can be found, for instance, in K. Aland (1969, ten items by various editors); Birdsall and Thomson (1963: 33-63); Elliott (1976: 235-38, 262-75, 301-12); in *New Documents Illustrating Early Christianity*, treating papyri and inscriptions (Horsley, 1981-87), and in other scholarly volumes and periodicals too numerous to record here.

Additional studies of Greek MSS were contributed by Davies (1968) and Fee (1968b); studies of the Greek lectionary text by Bray (1959), Buck (1958), and Harms (1966) were provided in the Chicago series on Studies in the Lectionary Text of the Greek New Testament, and another by Cocroft (1968) in Studies and Documents, and chapters by Metzger and Junack can be found in K. Aland 1972; monographs appeared on Greek uncials by Cavallo (1967), on Greek catena by Reuss (1957, 1966, 1984); Treu (1966a) published a list of NT MSS in the U.S.S.R.; and Voicu and D'Alisera (1981) furnished an index of facsimiles of Greek NT MSS. Current lists of all uncials and important minuscules can be found in K. and B. Aland (1982: 113-66; Eng. 1987: 106-55; 1989: 107-58). Surveys of discoveries, not only of Greek MSS but also of versional materials, have been offered by Metzger in various articles (1955b, 1959, 1963b: 145-62; 1965: 347-69).

Methods

The postwar period was a rich one for text-critical methodology. This evaluation may be placed in context by recalling the basic (though not the only) task of NT textual criticism — recovery of the original text — and by reviewing the fundamental methods employed to accomplish that task. In view of our earlier survey of its history, NT textual criticism obviously is a highly complex discipline, yet in conception it really is relatively simple. Actually, the same circumstance accounts for both descriptions — both its complexity and its simplicity — and that circumstance is the vast quantity of raw material available to us: For the NT — a rather small volume of writings — we possess some 5,355 Greek MSS alone (86 different papyri, 274 uncials, 2795 minuscules, and about 2,200 lectionaries [K. and B. Aland 1982: 106-11, 113, 137, 172; Eng. 1987: 95-105, 128, 160; 1989: 96-106, 128, 163]), plus thousands of versional documents and an untold number of patristic citations. The point is that we have so many MSS of the NT and that these MSS contain so many variant readings that surely the original reading in every case is somewhere present in our vast store of material. In theory, then, that should make the task of recovering the original text relatively simple. Incidentally, this vast number of MSS is the reason that conjectures — which play so large a role in the textual criticism of classical literature, and also in that of the OT — are rare and almost nonexistent in NT textual studies (see, e.g., Elliott 1974: 352; Kilpatrick 1981; Rhodes 1981; but to the contrary, see, e.g., Strugnell 1971).

We have, therefore, a genuine embarrassment of riches in the quantity of MSS that we possess, and this accounts, on the one hand, for the optimism in the discipline and for the promise of solid results, but also, on the other hand, for the extreme complexity in the study of the NT text. The writings of no Greek classical author are preserved on this scale. Among the most popular ancient authors, Homer's *Iliad* is found in fewer than 700 Greek MSS, Euripides's tragedies in somewhat more than 300, but other ancient writings, such as the first six books of the Latin *Annals* of Tacitus, are preserved only in a single MS (see Metzger 1968a: 34-35).

The riches in NT MSS, however, are not only in their *quantity* but also in their *quality*. Here I refer primarily to age. As is well known, the interval between the author and the earliest extant MSS for most classical writings is commonly hundreds — sometimes many hundreds — of years, and a thousand-year interval is not uncommon. In the examples given a moment ago, that single MS of Tacitus dates from the ninth century, and most of Euripides's MSS are from the Byzantine period (Metzger 1968a: 34-35). Of course, most of the NT MSS are also of late date, but what is striking is that so many others are early and that the interval between the NT authors' times and the transmission dates of a sizable number of extensive MSS is only a century, more or less. In at least one case, P[52] of John's Gospel, the interval may be as brief as twenty-five years. In addition, we have two elegant parchment MSS from about the year 350, codices Vaticanus (B) and Sinaiticus (א). This aspect of quality stands in sharp contrast to much other ancient literature. By the way, for the most part the oldest MSS of the NT have been found most recently, for the Chester Beatty and Bodmer papyri turned up in the 1930s and 1950s, respectively.

We must not exaggerate the NT manuscript materials, however, for the vast majority of the early papyri are highly fragmentary, and among the earliest uncial MSS only Codex Sinaiticus (א) contains the entire NT — though about fifty later MSS also provide complete coverage. The Apocalypse of John is the least well preserved, being found in only 287 Greek MSS — still a rather lavish scale of preservation for a writing of modest size (K. and B. Aland 1982: 91; Eng. 1987: 78-79; 1989: 78-79). Far more numerous are the witnesses to the Gospel of Luke, for which the IGNTP's elaborate apparatus has recently been published (as referred to earlier). The new apparatus presents the textual evidence from eight papyri that contain portions of Luke; from sixty-two uncial MSS (out of sixty-nine that contain Luke); from 128 minuscules (scientifically selected from the nearly 1700 extant minuscule MSS of Luke); and from 41 lectionary MSS (scientifically selected to represent the hundreds that contain Luke); as well as evidence from the Latin, Syriac, Coptic, Armenian, Georgian, Ethiopic, Gothic, and Old Church Slavonic versions, from the Arabic and Persian Diatessaron; and from all Greek and Latin Church Fathers up to AD 500, as well as evidence from selected Syriac Church Fathers. And that is just the Gospel of Luke as it has come down to us in the process of transmission!

These are some indications of the riches in MSS that we possess for determining the original text of the NT; the embarrassment is that we have not often been able to agree on solutions or, in fact, to find satisfactory solutions at all for some of our leading problems.

If, then, the original reading in virtually every case is somewhere present in our raw material, the only problem is how to find that original reading — and, by extension, how to find the original text of the Greek NT as a whole. There are essentially three ways to identify the most likely original reading:

1. *Historical-documentary method.* A first method attempts to reconstruct the history of the NT text by tracing the lines of transmission back through our extant MSS to the very earliest stages and then choosing the reading that represents the earliest attainable level of the textual tradition.

It is not, of course, that simple, but the theory is that we should be able to organize all of our extant MSS into groups or clusters, each of which has a very similar type of text. Then, as a result of this process of reconstruction, we would or should be able to identify some clusters of MSS — or ideally one such cluster —

that represent the earliest known group, and therefore to identify other groups that fall into an identifiable chronological succession — groups, that is, that are later. Further, this method attempts to reconstruct the streams of textual transmission that have brought our extant MSS to us, conceiving of each MS as a point of a trajectory of textual transmission. If these clusters and streams can be reconstructed with any measure of certainty, then we shall have isolated the earliest stages of those streams or the earliest points on those trajectories, and we shall have isolated also the earliest clusters, that is, the earliest types of text in the transmission process. If this were to result in the identification of only one very early cluster, succeeded by one or more later clusters, then readings belonging to that earliest cluster might legitimately be identified as those closest to the original and as most plausibly the original readings.

Ideally, then, when faced with a variation-unit — that is, a NT passage in which the manuscript tradition presents two or more differing textual readings — the reading would be chosen that comes from the earliest cluster or stream of textual tradition. This is the traditional method of external or documentary textual criticism, so-called because it emphasizes external criteria — such as the age and provenance of a document or MS, as well as the general quality of its scribe and its text (on scribal habits, see Colwell 1967: 9-11; 1969: 106-24; Fee 1968b; Royse 1979; Junack 1981). It might, therefore, be called the "historical-documentary" (or even the "historical-genealogical" method, though strict genealogical method has never been feasible in NT textual criticism, for there is too much textual mixture in the complex array of MSS [Colwell 1969: 63-83; Birdsall 1970: 317; cf. Zuntz 1953]).

The earliest papyri, as well as the early uncial MSS, play a significant role in this historical-documentary method. These early MSS have the highest possible value, which is even more greatly enhanced in proportion to their age, and the reason for this high value is just as obvious: the early papyri offer for the first time a realistic hope of reconstructing the history of the NT text in the 150- to 200-year period preceding the great parchment codices Vaticanus (B) and Sinaiticus (ℵ) and the other great landmarks of textual history, such as codices Alexandrinus (A), Bezae (D), Washingtonianus (W), and a grand host of others. We shall explore these possibilities in Section III, below.

There are, of course, complications of enormous complexity in pursuing this historical-documentary model, some of which will be discussed later (see also Birdsall 1970: 309-17). Yet many textual critics, particularly those in this country who were inspired by recent scholars like Kenneth Clark (see 1980) and Ernest Colwell (see 1967, 1969), are convinced that this is the path that must be followed and that the isolation of the earliest text-types must be our goal. We are convinced that only in this way can a solid foundation be laid for understanding the history of our NT text and that only in this way can we secure a large measure of confidence that we are genuinely in touch with the actual, historical origin of the NT writings. It was in this spirit and with these goals that the IGNTP was developed and that much postwar text-critical work was pursued, including the extensive studies in quantitative measurements of manuscript relationships.

The development of quantitative measures to establish relationships between and among MSS by comparing the extent to which they share significant readings has an extended history, as demonstrated by Duplacy (1975), but E. C.

Colwell, with E. W. Tune, provided (in 1963) the recent inspiration for the methods currently in use (reprinted in Colwell 1969: 56-62). Important refinements were provided by Fee (1968a, 1968b, 1971a); see also Hurtado (1981a), McReynolds (1979), Griffith (1969, 1973), Wisse (1982), the discussion above on the Claremont Profile Method, and cf. Zuntz (1953), Dearing (1959, 1974a, 1974b). For surveys of such methods, see Wisse (1982: 19-32), Epp (1974: 407-10), but above all the comprehensive treatment of the entire history of quantitative methods by Duplacy (1975).

Even the assessment of textual variation for theological motivation arose out of this approach, for the aim of the historical-documentary method has always been the better understanding of MSS (à la Hort). If theological or ideological bias could be identified in any MS, that would aid in placing it in its proper position in the textual streams or clusters — or identifying it as an aberrant member of a cluster. The postwar period witnessed much discussion and some controversy in this area, primarily related to the Western text: see Menoud (1951); Fascher (1953); Epp (1966a, 1981); Barrett (1979); Martini (1980: 103-13, 165-79, 181-88); Rice (1980a, 1980b, 1984, 1985); Eshbaugh (1979); Globe (1980); Black (1974, 1981); Pervo (1985); Witherington (1984); Delobel (1985); also Williams (1951); Clark (1980: 90-103, 104-19).

E. C. Colwell (1967: 5) referred to the working out of this external method of textual criticism as "the task of the next generation," and some of its leading problems and possible ways toward solutions will be explored in Section III, below.

2. *Rigorous eclectic method.* At the opposite extreme stands a second method, which examines all the variants available to us in a given variation unit and selects the reading that makes the best sense in terms of the internal criteria. That is, we select the variant reading that best suits the context of the passage, the author's style and vocabulary, or the author's theology, while taking into account such factors as scribal habits, including their tendency of conformity to Koine or Attic Greek style (Kilpatrick 1963b; see the caution by Martini 1980: 145-52), to Semitic forms of expression, to parallel passages, to OT passages, or to liturgical forms and usage. This method, therefore, emphasizes internal evidence and is called "rigorous" or "thoroughgoing" eclecticism, and also "rational" or "impartial criticism" by its proponents (Elliott 1978: 95; Epp 1976a: 251-55; Fee 1967: 174-76).

Actually, this is a method of recent vintage that is practiced primarily by two fine and persistent British scholars, George D. Kilpatrick [who died in 1989] and J. Keith Elliott. It stems largely, however, from C. H. Turner's famous "Notes" on Marcan usage published during the 1920s, on the first page of which Turner altered Westcott-Hort's famous dictum "Knowledge of documents should precede final judgement upon readings" to "Knowledge of an author's usage should precede final judgement" (see Epp 1976a: 250). Kilpatrick's views appeared during the war, beginning in 1943 and 1944, and a few phrases quoted from him and Elliott will clarify the method further. Kilpatrick says: "The decision rests ultimately with the criteria as distinct from the manuscripts, and . . . our evaluation of the manuscripts must be determined by the criteria" (1943: 25-26); or "Each reading has to be judged on its merits and not on its [manuscript] supports"; or "Readings must be considered severally on their intrinsic character. Further, contrary to what Hort maintained, decisions about readings must precede decisions about the value or weight of manuscripts" (1965: 205-6). Elliott says: "The cult of the best manuscripts gives way to the cult of the best reading"; and the method "devotes its main attention to the individual variants themselves and very little attention to external evidence" (1972c: 340), for "we are concerned with which reading is likely to represent what our original author wrote. We are not concerned with the age, prestige or popularity of the manuscripts supporting the readings we would adopt as original" (1974: 352); or "The thoroughgoing eclectic would accept the reading which best suited the context and would base his reasons on exclusively internal criteria" (Elliott 1978: 99); or, finally, "It seems to be more constructive to discuss as a priority the worth of readings rather than the worth of manuscripts" (1978: 115).

From these quotations it is at once apparent that to these rigorous eclectics the NT MSS are repositories of raw material and have independent importance only to the extent that they may furnish textual variants or readings that may commend themselves as original by the application of internal criteria: Does a new reading conform to the author's style and vocabulary, to his theology, to the context? Can it explain the origin of the other readings? If so, it may well be judged the original reading. The fact that many of the papyri and the great fourth-century uncials are extremely early does not, in this method, lend to them any special consideration or authority, nor does it account them as possessing any special character or value. It is well known that rigorous eclectics diligently search the late Byzantine MSS for readings that might be original and that they have accredited scores of such readings, for — as Kilpatrick put it — "the outright condemnation of the Byzantine text by Westcott and Hort was one of the main errors in practice of their work" (1963a: 76). So, for "rigorous" eclectics, readings are readings are readings, whether early or late.

The challenge of this view is discussed in Section III below.

3. *Reasoned eclectic method.* A third approach combines these two procedures. It is essential to have this third method if — as is realistically the case — the criteria for making decisions on the basis of the first method (the historical-documentary) are not obvious or clear, and if — as many textual critics think — the second method (rigorous eclecticism), though valuable for its numerous insights, is — in isolation — a one-sided and less than adequate method. On this third procedure, when faced with any variation-unit, we would choose the variant reading that appears to be in the earliest chronological group *and* that also makes the best sense when the internal criteria are applied. Moreover, if no one cluster or type of text can be identified unambiguously as the earliest, then we would choose the variant reading in any given case that is in *one* of the earliest clusters *and* that best fits the relevant internal considerations. This method, therefore, utilizes both external and internal criteria and is called "reasoned eclecticism" or "moderate" or "genuine" eclecticism, or simply the "eclectic" method (Fee 1976: 174-76; Epp 1976a: 212-14, 244-45), for it utilizes the best available methods from across the methodological spectrum. In this method it is recognized that no single criterion or invariable combination of criteria will resolve all cases of textual variation, and it attempts, therefore, to apply evenly and without prejudice any and all criteria — external and internal — appro-

priate to a given case, arriving at an answer based on the relative probabilities among those applicable criteria.[6] As Kenneth Clark said of the method in 1956:

> It is the only procedure available to us at this stage, but it is very important to recognize that it is a secondary and tentative method. It is not a new method nor a permanent one. The eclectic method cannot by itself create a text to displace Westcott-Hort and its offspring. It is suitable only for exploration and experimentation. . . . The eclectic method, by its very nature, belongs to an age like ours in which we know only that the traditional theory of the text is faulty but cannot yet see clearly to correct the fault. (1956: 37-38)

This is to say that if we had worked out the early history of the text, as prescribed under the first method, neither rigorous nor reasoned eclecticism would be necessary. Until that is accomplished, however, most textual critics will rely upon the latter — a genuinely eclectic method that pays careful attention both to the documentary evidence from the history of the manuscript tradition and also to the internal criteria of readings. Together they can help us with the urgent textual decisions that we must make until the time when the historical-documentary method has been fully worked out. And, if the reconstruction of the early textual history cannot be achieved, the eclectic method will continue to be the method of choice — and of necessity.

The text common to the NA[26] and UBS[3] was formed in accordance with this kind of eclectic method, though placing emphasis, wherever possible, on the reading that explains the other readings and treating that as the most likely original. This latter procedure is what Kurt Aland calls the "local-genealogical method" (K. and B. Aland 1979: 42*-43*), which is discussed further in Section III below.

It will already be recognized from the very mention of these several optional methods that the situation in NT textual criticism is not ideal and that neither automatic formulas nor easy decisions are readily forthcoming. The challenges emerging from the postwar discussions of method will be treated in Section III below.

Regrettably, our survey of editions, discoveries, and methods cannot begin to cover the hundreds of contributions made by scholars worldwide to these important areas of research.

III. Current and Future Decision Points in New Testament Textual Criticism

The decision points in current and future NT textual criticism all arise out of this lengthy, productive, and yet largely inconclusive past history, and they present us with a degree of difficulty and with a measure of urgency that are disquieting. I wish to focus on three turning points or issues currently under investigation. Certainly there are others, but these seem to me the most critical. The three items have a common characteristic: each constitutes a distinct "battleground" in the discipline;

---

6. Birdsall (1970: 316-18) in his masterly survey of NT textual criticism in *The Cambridge History of the Bible* uses the original term "rational criticism," from M.-J. Lagrange, for this method, but the co-opting of this term by "rigorous eclectics" suggests that a more specific term, such as "reasoned eclecticism," is now preferable to the less precise, generic term "eclectic."

that is, they represent disputed areas that recently have been or shortly will be contested not only with vigor but even with some vehemence. The three conflicts that face us are the following.

The Struggle over the Text-Type

Perhaps the word "struggle" is too strong, yet there is a continuing and genuine disagreement, if not contention, as to whether or not "text-types" existed in the earliest centuries of the transmission of the NT text. That question in itself may not seem to involve a significant issue, but the answer to it does affect rather directly the obviously important issue of whether or not — and if so, how — we can trace the history of the earliest NT text, which — in turn — is related directly to the ultimate goal of recovering the original text. The validity of these steps is, at any rate, the conviction of many of us, with the result that the question of early text-types deserves close attention.

When J. A. Bengel long ago placed MSS into classes or groups, the development of text-types was under way in the textual critic's mind, reaching its classical formulation in the system of Westcott-Hort, though the more elaborate classifications of von Soden were still to come. As new MSS were analyzed, they were placed into a Westcott-Hort or a von Soden framework; this was appropriate enough if the MSS in question were generally later in time than the cornerstone MSS of each text-type. When, however, much earlier MSS — primarily papyri — began to appear (particularly those well beyond the fragmentary stage), we began to recognize the anachronism of placing these earlier MSS into groups whose nature had been determined on the basis only of the complexion of later MSS (see Birdsall 1960: 8-9, 17; Klijn 1969: 33-38, 50).

The identification of text-types and of the MSS comprising them was a controversial matter for two centuries from Bengel to the discussions about the Caesarean text (roughly 1735 to 1935), but it was the analysis of papyri like P[45], P[46], P[66], and P[75] that brought a new dimension to the controversy, namely, whether the established text-type categories any longer made sense or were even useful for the earliest period, or — to push the question even further — whether there were, in fact, any identifiable text-types at all in that period.

Discussions of papyri in relation to text-types during the 1950s and 1960s led to statements like that of E. C. Colwell in 1961 that "very few, if any, text-types were established" by AD 200 (Colwell 1969: 55), or the more radical statement of Kurt Aland in 1964 that one can speak of an Alexandrian [or Egyptian] and of an Antiochian [or Byzantine] text-type, but:

> These are, it seems to me, the only text-types which may be regarded as certain, and that only since the fourth century. Everything else is extremely doubtful. It is impossible to fit the papyri, from the time prior to the fourth century, into these two text-types, to say nothing of trying to fit them into other types, as frequently happens. The simple fact that all these papyri . . . did exist side by side . . . in Egypt . . . is the best argument against the existence of any text-types, including the Alexandrian [Egyptian] and the Antiochian [Byzantine]. (1965)

P[75] had been published when these statements were made, and perhaps its close affinity with Codex Vaticanus (B), pointed out in 1966 by (the now archbishop of Milan) Carlo Martini (see Fee 1974), should have acted as a restraint on this all-too-rapidly developed view that there were no entities in the first centuries that can be called "text-types." Yet it is clear enough that the study of the early and extensive papyri constitutes the turning point from confidence to skepticism about early text-types.[7]

These varying skeptical opinions about early text-types were not, however, the only judgments on the subject in the 1950s and 1960s. A. F. J. Klijn, for example, argued that two text-types existed side by side in Egypt, a Western text and a Neutral text (to use Hort's terms) (1969: 39-40). It seems to me, therefore, that we should not yet withdraw from this battlefield, as though the matter were settled or as though we ought to abandon hope that the early papyri can be classified according to varying textual complexions ("individual manuscripts can be characterized" [Colwell 1967: 5]) or that they can be linked with later MSS that can be said to possess a similar textual character ("manuscripts can still be grouped and the group characterized" [Colwell 1967: 5]).

I am reluctant to repeat suggestions that I have made over the past several years and which still await development, but it seems clear to me, first, that differing *textual complexions can be identified* in the various papyri, even in the fragmentary ones — and many textual critics assign them to textual categories, including Aland himself. Second, if this is so, it seems clear to me that the *grouping of early witnesses is possible* (and such groups or clusters might very well be designated "text-types"). Third, it seems clear to me that *lines of connection or trajectories can be traced* from early to later witnesses of similar textual character or complexion. When such an exercise is carried out, we may find that a text-type labeled "P[75]" appears for the Gospels in the earliest period (third century) and has later representatives in Codex B in the fourth century, in Codex L in the eighth century, in Codex 33 in the ninth century, in MS 1739 in the tenth, and so on. In addition, we may find that a less-well-documented but still adequate trajectory can be traced for Acts from a type of text found in P[29] and P[48] in the third century, with later representatives in P[38] around AD 300, in Codex D in the fourth or fifth century, and in MSS 614 and 383 in the thirteenth century; or that another type of text of the Gospels (and Acts), to be named for P[45], appears in the third century and follows a line to Codex W in the fifth century, though it seems to stop there (see Hurtado 1981a: 63-66; Epp 1974: 395-98; on manuscript trajectories, Epp 1974: 397-400; 1980: 147-49).[8]

Much more work, admittedly, is required in this area, but we should not so easily capitulate to those forces that contend that no text-types existed or can be identified in the pre-fourth-century period of NT textual transmission. We need answers; we need them soon; and I think that — by diligent effort — they can be found for this important issue. As will be obvious, it is precisely the papyri that can lead the

---

7. It is one thing, of course, to say that the traditional text-types are not useful as pigeonholes into which the early papyri may be placed, which — as his context shows — is the force of Colwell's statement, and something quite different to affirm that no text-types existed in the earliest period, which seems clearly to be what Aland means.

8. See now Chapter 14 = E. J. Epp 1989c, esp. 84-103.

way, for they extend the textual streams or trajectories much further back than was previously possible, and they assist us in identifying the earliest textual clusters.

Reference to a debate over the text-types, however, is only another way of saying that we face a crisis over *methodology* in NT textual criticism. Identifying early text-types is one means — or at least one aspect — of reconstructing the earliest history of the transmission of the NT text. Such a history of the text — if indeed it could be written for the earliest period — would provide a rather firm methodological track back to a point very close to the original text. Thus, to the extent that all Greek MSS of the NT can be classified according to types of text, or at least placed on a continuum in accordance with their differing textual complexion, and to the extent that a history of the text can be reconstructed, to that extent we can speak of having formulated a theory of the NT text (or at least a portion of such a theory). To state it differently, we need to devise a plausible and defensible hypothesis that explains how the original NT text issued in our thousands of extant MSS, with their varying textual complexions. We seem not to have such a theory, though most of the great figures of the past ventured to formulate one. Westcott-Hort surmised that two early text-types were in competition in the second-century church, one corrupted by paraphrastic expansions (the Western) and the other virtually untouched in its course of transmission from the original (the Neutral) (see Epp 1974: 392). Von Soden and B. H. Streeter and a host of others announced and defended their theories of the NT text, but none has stood the tests of criticism or of time. Yet the task is not to be abandoned, for it is a correct and proper task if significant progress is to be made in NT textual criticism. Though a hundred years have passed, it is still prudent to keep in mind the two — and the only two — principles that Hort printed in large type in his chapter on method: "Knowledge of documents should precede final judgement upon readings" and "All trustworthy restoration of corrupted texts is founded on the study of their history" (Westcott-Hort: 2.31, 40). So the decision point over text-types becomes a broader and more significant decision point about basic textual history and theory and about fundamental methodology in the discipline of NT textual criticism. To resolve the issue of early text-types, therefore, would have far-reaching theoretical implications. For one thing, it would fulfill the hope implied in K. W. Clark's 1956 statement that "we know only that the traditional theory of the text is faulty but cannot yet see clearly to correct the fault" (37-38).

The Crisis of Criteria

The second area of conflict is the present crisis over the criteria for determining the originality of readings, or the "canons of criticism," as they were known in earlier times. This is a significant decision point, for NT text-critical methodology — though more on the practical level now than the theoretical — in its essence and at its very heart is concerned with the criteria employed to choose the most likely original reading wherever the textual tradition presents two or more readings at a given point in the text. To be quite blunt — if also a bit cynical — it is this simple-sounding matter of how to choose the "right" or "best" reading that is not only the major interest, but (I fear) often the *only* interest that exegetes have in textual criticism. Yet this attitude — whether widespread or not — is actually a compliment to textual criticism, for it points to the important practical application and utility that the discipline has, as well as to the high expectations that our colleagues hold for it and for us. They may care little for our theories and disputations, but they do care greatly about how they shall make those decisions between and among competing readings that exegesis so regularly demands.

These critical canons or criteria have been of concern to NT textual critics since Origen and Jerome in ancient times, since Gerhard von Mastricht's formal list — the first such attempt — in his Greek NT of 1711, and particularly since they were given prominence by such notables as J. A. Bengel, J. J. Wettstein, J. J. Griesbach, K. Lachmann, C. Tischendorf, S. P. Tregelles, and Westcott-Hort. Throughout this lengthy period, during which the criteria were evolving, the clash (as is well known) was between reliance on the numerous later MSS, or on the growing — but still relatively small — number of older MSS, or, to put it differently, the struggle was between *quantity* of the MSS and "weight" or *quality* of the MSS supporting a reading, culminating in the triumph of the few earlier MSS over the many that represented the TR. Though this period concluded with bitter conflict, complete with the acrimonious language of J. W. Burgon, it is not this skirmish that interests us.[9] Rather, what does interest us is that, following Westcott-Hort but beginning particularly with C. H. Turner (1923ff.), M.-J. Lagrange (1935), G. D. Kilpatrick (1943ff.), A. F. J. Klijn (1949), and J. K. Elliott (1972ff.), a new crisis of the criteria became prominent and is very much with us today: a duel between external and internal criteria and the widespread uncertainty as to precisely what kind of compromise ought to or can be worked out between them. The temporary "cease-fire" that most — but certainly not all — textual critics have agreed upon is called "moderate" or "reasoned" eclecticism (for the terminology, see Fee 1976: 174-77, and the discussion above) or what I have designated the "eclectic generalist" approach (Epp 1976a: 244-48), in which it is recognized that no single criterion or invariable combination of criteria will resolve all cases of textual variation and which, therefore, attempts to apply evenly and without prejudice any and all criteria — external and internal — appropriate to a given case, arriving then at an answer based on the relative probabilities among those applicable criteria (Epp 1976a: 244-48). We are all familiar with this method, for we all — or nearly all — employ it, as did the committee who prepared the UBS[3], and abundant examples of the method at work can be observed in the pages of that edition's *Textual Commentary.* This "reasoned" eclecticism is not recognized as appropriate by those "eclectic specialists" who practice a "rigorous" or "thoroughgoing" eclecticism that emphasizes the internal criteria, notably (as described earlier) George D. Kilpatrick and J. Keith Elliott. Even a "reasoned" eclecticism is accorded only a temporary "victory" by many of us who feel strongly that it is indeed a method for our time but not the ultimate method. As J. Neville Birdsall put it already a quarter of a century ago:

> Although for the present we must utilize these diverse criteria and establish a text by an eclectic method, it is impossible to stifle the hope that, at some future

---

9. In spite of the present-day revival of the TR by some who take Burgon's side against the rest of us — e.g., the recent edition by Hodges and Farstad (1982); see their Introduction: ix-xiii.

time, we shall find our methods and our resultant text justified by manuscript discoveries and by the classical methods . . . which Hort exemplified so brilliantly in his work. (1957a: 199)

Many of us share this hope that the eclectic method can be replaced by something more permanent — a confidently reconstructed history and a persuasive theory of the text — and we are working actively toward that goal. In the meantime, all of us need to recognize, first, that the crisis of the criteria is real; second, that the literature of the past two or three decades is replete with controversy over the eclectic method, or at least is abundant with evidence of the frustration that accompanies its use; and, third, that we must devote our best and most serious efforts to refining the eclectic method in any and all appropriate ways, for it is likely to be our only guide for some time to come.

How can we refine the eclectic method? An important first step (which will not be necessary for all) is to understand the criteria themselves, their history, development, and use; I attempted such an assessment in some fifty pages in the *Harvard Theological Review* for 1977 that proved to be instructive for me.[10] Second, we need to analyze critically each of the fifteen or so external and internal criteria as to their validity and relative worth. Is it really incontrovertible that the shorter or harder reading is to be preferred? Does wide geographical distribution of a reading or its attestation by several established groups give it added weight? Does antiquity of documentary evidence outweigh everything else? Is fitness to the context or with the author's style or theology automatically decisive? As a matter of fact, can our various criteria be placed in some hierarchic order, so that some are consistently more decisive than others? These and many other questions require continued and conscientious attention, and they need to be addressed both at the theoretical level and at the level of practice. Naturally, the trial and error of the laboratory and the give-and-take of everyday application can lead to significant insights and subsequent refinements in method. In addition, we can learn much from those who elevate one category of criteria or even a single criterion to a dominant position, as have those, for example, who practice "rigorous" eclecticism. Very recently a new challenge of this kind has come from Kurt Aland through the published definition of his "local-genealogical" method, which appears to be a refinement or a very special form of eclecticism, though he vigorously denies that it can properly be called "eclectic" (K. and B. Aland 1979: 43*; 1982: 44; Eng. 1987: 34, 1989: 34). This method arrives at the most likely original text by selecting that variant which best explains all the other variants in the variation-unit, and in the process Aland employs the various criteria or canons of criticism as possible ways of explaining how each secondary reading might have arisen. Professor Aland will surprise some — perhaps many — by his forthright statement that "from the perspective of our recent knowledge, this local-genealogical method . . . is the only one which meets the requirements of the New Testament textual tradition" (K. and B. Aland 1979: 43*); and it is, he claims further, the method that produced the new "Standard Text" (as he calls it) in the UBS[3] and NA[26] (see also K. Aland 1979a: 10). Testing his claim that this local-

10. See now Chapter 8.

genealogical procedure has exclusive validity can be a further avenue for refining the eclectic method — an urgent decision point for current NT textual criticism. All the while, however, many of us will continue to hope — but more than that, to work — toward those more objective methods (like the historical-documentary method), based on better knowledge of the history of the NT text and its transmission, which will enable us to surmount the "crisis of the criteria."

The Approaching Battle over the Papyri

I referred earlier to three fields of conflict, and the third is the approaching battle over the papyri. This represents our final, but doubtless most critical, decision point in current text-critical discussion. I emphasize the word "approaching" for good reason. Since the discovery of the early NT papyri, but particularly since the nonfragmentary P[45], P[46], P[66], P[75], and others have come to light, there has hardly been anything that one could call strife or conflict in this area, for each new papyrus, whether extensive or fragmentary, has been welcomed with rejoicing and analyzed in anticipation of positive and constructive results. When, for example, P[75] was shown to possess a text virtually identical to that of Codex B (Martini 1966; Fee 1974), yet two centuries or so earlier in date, the long-standing conviction of a fourth-century recension of what had been called the B-text was freely given up — no struggle, no strife.

My suggestion of an *approaching battle* over the papyri refers to something else: it concerns primarily two issues. The first of these is the *worth* of the papyri as textual witnesses, though this — as all will recognize — is merely a question of *relative* worth, for it goes without saying that the NT papyri are of exceptionally high value and will be thus esteemed by all textual critics (with the possible exception of the few "rigorous eclectics," who tend to view even the earliest MSS — along with all others — merely as sources for potentially original readings). The question, rather, is whether these papyri, or at least the earliest ones — those dating up to about AD 300 — are to be accorded what might be characterized as a rightful status one or two rungs above that of our great uncials of the fourth century, or are to be accorded a considerably or even vastly higher status than that, one that raises them in significance far above our other eminent witnesses and that elevates them to a position somewhat akin to that accorded the relics of the saints. I am alluding here, of course, to the extraordinary status afforded these earliest papyri by Kurt Aland, who (in his "Introduction" to the NA[26]: 12*, 49*) not only affirms their "automatic significance" as textual witnesses, but in a later article makes the astounding claim that in the forty papyri (and uncials) prior to about AD 300 the early history of the NT text "can be studied in the original," and that all other efforts to get a glimpse of the early text "must remain reconstructed theories" (K. Aland 1979a: 11).

Such an exceptionally high valuation of the earliest papyri has its problems, and included among these is the second issue over which conflict is inevitable, namely, the question of how *representative* of the earliest history of the text these early papyri are. If his statement means what it seems to mean, Professor Aland is virtually identifying the text of the pre-fourth-century papyri with the "original" text. If this seems incredible or unlikely, it may be added that, in a still more recent article on "the new 'Standard Text' in its relation to the early papyri and uncials," Aland employs these pre-fourth-century papyri and uncials as the "touchstone" of originality, for he states that the common text of the NA[26] and UBS[3] "has passed the test of the early papyri and uncials. It corresponds, in fact, to the text of the early time," and he then goes on to a more startling conclusion. Speaking of the text of NA[26], he asserts: "A hundred years after Westcott-Hort, the goal of an edition of the New Testament 'in the original Greek' seems to have been reached" (1981: 274-75). It is, of course, the unique value ascribed to the papyri that is the key to this remarkable claim.

It seems clear to me that a struggle over the papyri — about their relative worth as textual evidence and about their representative nature — has in fact begun, will increase in intensity, and is a crucial decision point requiring our serious attention. Can such high claims as Aland makes be sustained? I for one wish that they could be readily accepted and be as easily substantiated, for that would constitute a breakthrough in both method and practice that would be highly significant and warmly welcomed. Yet some disturbing questions arise and call for answers before we rush to embrace such claims about the papyri.

To begin with an obvious question — yet one too rarely discussed or even raised — how representative, really, of the earliest history of the NT text are these earliest papyri? What assurance do we have that these randomly surviving MSS represent in any real sense the entire earliest period of the text? Subsidiary questions appear: First, all of these documents come from one region, Egypt. Can we be satisfied with Egypt as the exclusive locale for viewing this earliest history of the text? Was Egypt in the third century AD representative of the NT text for *all* of Christianity at that period? Was any NT book written in Egypt? Probably not. Does not Egypt then represent at best a secondary and derivative stage in the history of the NT text? After all, is it not merely an accident of history (though a most fortunate one) that papyrus almost exclusively survives only in the dry sands of Egypt?

If textual witnesses, then, are to have "automatic significance" (to use Aland's phrase), should there not be a basis for so significant a role that is more substantive than merely their early age? And, before we claim that in these papyri the history of the NT text "can be studied in the original" (again to use Aland's words), should we not assure ourselves either that these earliest witnesses present a unitary text (which, of course, they do not), or — lacking that assurance — should we not require a guarantee (or at least some persuasive evidence) that they are genuinely representative of the earliest history of the text, representative, that is, of the various textual complexions that existed in the earliest period? As a matter of fact, as suggested earlier, certain "types" of text or textual complexions do seem to be represented by the various of the early papyri, including (1) the Alexandrian or Egyptian (Hort's Neutral) text, (2) the so-called Western text, and (3) a text somewhere in between (now usually designated pre-Caesarean) (see Epp 1974: 393-96; cf. 1980: 146-47; Hurtado 1981a: 88-89).[11]

We are faced, then, with a puzzle, for there is one rather clear sense in

11. See now Chapter 14. For new directions in pursuing the question of how representative of the entire NT text the papyri of Egypt might be, see now E. J. Epp 1991, "New Testament Papyrus Manuscripts and Letter Carrying in Greco-Roman Times," esp. pp. 52-56; the study's conclusion is quoted below, Chapter 14, n. 25.

which the early papyri seem *not* to be representative — and that is their restriction to a single geographical segment of Christianity — and another sense in which they *may* be representative — and that is their presentation of textual complexions characteristic of what have previously been identified as the major early text-types. For these reasons, it seems that we have been thrust into a period of the *reassessment* of the papyri. Certainly it is more than mere curiosity or coincidence to find that fifty years ago, after his preliminary analysis of the Chester Beatty papyri, Sir Frederic Kenyon made the following provocative statement in his Schweich Lectures of the British Academy for 1932: "There remains what is perhaps the most perplexing problem of all, the problem of the Biblical text in Egypt" (Kenyon 1933a: 80). And in 1949, before the Bodmer papyri came to light, A. F. J. Klijn said, "Egypt appears to be more and more important for the history of the text" (Klijn 1949: 145). How much closer to solving that puzzle have the past fifty years brought us? Certainly we have more abundant materials for the task than Kenyon and Klijn had — notably the Bodmer papyri — and we may hope that we will not have to wait for another fifty-year landmark to see these questions about the significance of the papyri resolved. After all, there is virtually unanimous agreement that the NT papyri not only are textual criticism's greatest treasure but also its best hope for "cracking" the textual "code" and breaking through to the original text.

Despite confident claims to the contrary, however, we have not yet reached the point of readily and assuredly identifying any MS, any group of MSS, or any critical text with that elusive "original," but the papyri most certainly will be the instruments that we shall use to settle the struggle over the text-type, to resolve the crisis of the criteria, and to push toward a "standard text" acknowledged by all. The difficult question that remains, of course, is exactly *how* we are to use them to achieve these urgent goals.

IV. Conclusion

New Testament textual criticism is a vigorous and stimulating discipline, in which — as history demonstrates — new discoveries are always possible (though not assured) and in which many theoretical decisions — fundamental to the discipline — remain to be made on the basis of the materials we have. Since World War II new discoveries have come to light and new methods have been devised (or old ones refined), and there has been much progress. On the other hand, as we have noted, major issues still require resolution. In these cases textual critics and not the discoveries or theories themselves will lead to further progress, and in this connection the words of Georg Luck (1981: 166), a prominent classical textual critic, are discomfiting but nonetheless true: "Part of the problem is that our critical texts are no better than our textual critics." If competent textual critics can be rallied in NT studies, our new materials and refined methods can be utilized to solve the critical problems, and the discipline can move toward the ideal of a critical text that closely approximates the "original" NT text.

PART II
DEFINITIONS

CHAPTER 3

TOWARD THE CLARIFICATION OF THE TERM "TEXTUAL VARIANT"[1]

Eldon Jay Epp

Professor George D. Kilpatrick's text-critical studies, spanning more than thirty years and treating myriad NT passages and countless textual variations, have been particularly instructive and indeed provocative in their attention to the so-called internal criteria for deciding between or among variant readings in the NT manuscript tradition; by these contributions he has placed all of us much in his debt, and it would be in no way an overstatement to say that he has brought the whole question of text-critical criteria to the forefront of our current discussion. All textual critics, whether they pay more attention to internal evidence or to external, are concerned with textual variants — they are their stock-in-trade — and the careful definition of "textual variant" and its associated terms is not only important but fundamental to the entire discipline. This study attempts such definitions, for, surprising though it may seem, some of the basic terminology of NT textual criticism has been used much too loosely in the past.

The perspective and thrust of this essay admittedly are quite different from the major emphases of Professor Kilpatrick's own text-critical work; whereas he has emphasized increasingly the stylistic, linguistic, and scribal factors in textual variation, the writer and his several American colleagues mentioned in this paper have emphasized the rôle of so-called external evidence, including the possible reconstruction of the earliest history of the NT text, the grouping of MSS and the quantitative measurement of their relationships, and the relative weight to be given to such groups and to individual MSS in text-critical decisions. To those by whom variants are treated much more as independent entities, that is, as readings in isolation from any presumed text-type or any other particular textual tradition or history, some of the discussion which follows will appear to be inconsequential. In this respect, a number of differences with Professor Kilpatrick doubtless can be anticipated, but the following treatise is presented with the direct aim and with the sincere hope both of clarifying the terminology used by all of us and of stimulating discussion on those crucial points where differences remain.

---

1. This paper received its first hearing on 25 October 1974 in the Textual Criticism Seminar of the SBL, Washington, DC, and it appears here with revisions that were prompted by the Seminar discussion. [Publication of the paper in a Festschrift for George D. Kilpatrick accounts for the introductory remarks.]

I. Introduction: The Problems

The clarification, definition, and delimitation of the term "textual variant" are vastly more complex and difficult matters than at first would appear. The common or surface assumption is that any textual reading that differs in any way from any other reading in the same unit of text is a "textual variant," but this simplistic definition will not suffice. Actually, in NT textual criticism the term "textual variant" really means — and must mean — *"significant"* or *"meaningful* textual variant," but immediately this raises the further question of the meaning of "significant" or "meaningful." For example, a clear scribal error is certainly a variant in the common sense of the term, but is it a significant variant? A nonsense reading clearly is a variation, but is it meaningful? A singular reading, particularly when it can be construed grammatically or gives a new denotation, is even more clearly a variant in the everyday sense, but is it significant?

Involved in these questions is a further one: significant for what? Here the complexities multiply. For instance, a *clear* scribal error is a textual variation, but it is not a significant textual variant for recovering the original text, nor is it significant for determining manuscript relationships — unless, of course, the error has been copied and reproduced in an uncorrected form by a later scribe, but even then coincidence in a commonly committed scribal error cannot easily or often be utilized as *proof* of a direct manuscript relationship. The scribal error, however, may be a "significant" variant reading for the study of scribal habits and characteristics even though it is not "significant" for broader text-critical tasks. Orthographic variations are similar in nature and pose similar problems. A further example is the nonsense reading, that is, one that cannot be construed grammatically; it is a textual variant in the ordinary sense, but in almost no conceivable way is it a meaningful or significant variant. Singular readings are more complex than these other examples and raise the question of "significance" in even sharper ways. A distinction must be made, therefore, between "reading" and "variant" — where the latter term means "significant variant," and it becomes clear that textual critics must raise the question of when a textual *reading* is also a textual *variant*.

There are other aspects to the problem of defining a textual reading or variant. One such issue is, What are the limits of a textual variant? That is, what grammatical unit or other measure is to delimit a textual variation when two or more MSS differ? Another issue — a large and complicated one — concerns readings in ancient versions of the NT; how are they to be understood as "variants" to the Greek NT? And, by extension, how are patristic quotations, whether Greek, Latin, Syriac, or other, to be treated in terms of variants?

Like most aspects of life and learning, the seemingly simple turns out, upon analysis, to be complex and to veil a multitude of uncertainties and ambiguities. In the present case, a fresh scrutiny of that irreducibly basic entity in NT textual criticism, the "textual variant," is essential, first, to alert those who use the term simplistically to the serious terminological and methodological issues involved and, in the second place, to push toward the clarification and definition of the term and of related expressions.

II. Colwell and Tune on the Classification of Insignificant Variants

The problems posed above by way of example must, today, be approached with reference first of all to the brief 1964 article of Ernest C. Colwell (1901-74) and Ernest W. Tune on "Variant Readings: Classification and Use."[2] Like all of Colwell's articles, this is a terse presentation which offers a penetrating analysis of the problems and then moves rapidly, by a series of programmatic statements, toward the solution of those problems. Accordingly, the article was quickly and properly recognized as a methodological milestone, particularly on the path toward the successful quantitative measurement of manuscript relationships. Its weaknesses are its brevity and the consequent lack of detail and of attention to further implications of the principles there established. It is evident, however, that Colwell and Tune's apposite term, "variation-unit," has become standard, referring to each section or "length of the text wherein our manuscripts present at least two variant forms" (97). The "length" or extent of a variation-unit, they said, is determined according to "those elements of expression in the Greek text which regularly exist together" (99). The two examples they give are clear enough: when an alteration of an initial conjunction in a sentence is accompanied regularly by a change in verbal form, the unit includes both the conjunction and the verbal form; when a transposition in word order affects the presence/absence of an article, all the words involved constitute a single unit. What is not so clear is whether this understanding of the limits of a variation-unit is formulated with adequate precision or what problems emerge in actual practice. For one thing, at times a multitude of readings will be clustered within a single grammatical or syntactical unit and, upon analysis, will group themselves into two or more sub-formations of variants, with the sub-formations bearing no relationship to one another. In such a case the delimitation of a variation-unit in terms of "elements of expression which regularly exist together" is not adequate to the complexities of the actual situation, and the question arises, are the various sub-formations of such a "variation-unit" to be understood as variation-units in themselves?

Colwell and Tune, however, have provided a simple but fundamental — and therefore important — clarification that a "variation-unit" is not the same as a "variant," for "a variant . . . is one of the possible alternative readings which are found in a variation-unit" (99-100). It is of considerable importance to note, furthermore, that Colwell and Tune actually — though much less directly — defined "variation-unit" in more precise terms than found in the statements quoted above; for them a variation-unit, as is evident from the full discussion in the article, is that length of text (1) where our Greek NT MSS present at least two variant forms *and* (2) where each variant form is supported by at least two Greek MSS (103-5). This further qualification arises out of and depends upon their analysis of "singular readings," a matter to be discussed at length presently. In reality, however, a still further qualification would have to be added — based on their assessment of other

---

2. Reprinted under the title "Method in Classifying and Evaluating Variant Readings," in Colwell 1969: 96-105. References are to the latter.

"insignificant" readings (also discussed below), so that the full definition of a variation-unit, according to Colwell and Tune, would be something like this: that length of the text (1) where our Greek NT MSS present at least two variant forms, (2) where each variant form is supported by at least two Greek MSS, and (3) from which all "insignificant" readings have been excluded (viz., nonsense readings and clear scribal errors of the homoeoteleuton type). Somewhat simplified and arranged more suitably, the definition might read: *In NT textual criticism, a variation-unit is that segment of text where our Greek manuscripts present at least two variant forms and where, after insignificant readings have been excluded, each variant form has the support of at least two manuscripts.*[3] Several aspects of this conception of the variation-unit, as held by Colwell and Tune, will figure prominently in the discussion to follow.

These basic clarifications of the terms "variant" and "variation-unit" — at least in their broad strokes and leaving aside for the moment the details — may seem self-evident to us now, but they were timely and requisite; already they have aided considerably the refinement of quantitative measurements of manuscript relationships[4] and should allow for greater precision in text-critical work generally. For one thing, a NT textual reading or variant is no longer to be defined (as so often in the past) in terms of variation from a printed text (such as the TR, WH, or NA), but the term refers only and should be limited to variations among actual NT MSS.[5] Furthermore, Colwell's work would imply that only a variation involving *Greek* NT MSS deserves the designation "textual variant," but this is an issue requiring further discussion below.

Colwell and Tune proceeded to classify readings that in their judgment were insignificant for purposes of isolating the original text, tracing the history of the text, or determining manuscript kinship and that — for this and other reasons — were to be excluded from the critical apparatus and, for the most part, excluded also from further text-critical tasks. These classes include, first, the *Nonsense Reading,* "that variant reading which does not make sense, and/or cannot be found in the lexicon, and/or is not Greek grammar." Why is it to be excluded both as the original reading and from the critical apparatus? Because, say Colwell and Tune, it is highly unlikely

3. From Colwell's work in the IGNTP, it is clear that he considered as "insignificant" also those readings that consist of orthographic differences, particularly itacisms and the presence of the movable nu.

4. See, e.g., Fee 1968b: iv-v et passim; 1968a: 25-31.

5. This limitation need not preclude the often useful comparison of manuscript variation with the text, e.g., of the TR, which in such cases is used as the general representative of a vast number of late MSS, nor should it preclude the use of the TR as a base or standard, as in the IGNTP, where it serves without prejudice as the collation base, or in a process like the Claremont Profile Method, where it serves as a fixed, neutral reflecting board. In both instances the TR actually facilitates the comparison of MSS with one another, and in both cases true "variants" and "variation-units" as defined above are easily derived or formulated from the data provided. Yet, technically speaking, the readings of the TR or any other constructed text are not "variants" as here so far defined; they only become variants when they are identified as readings of particular Greek MSS. Nor are the readings of a particular MS "variants" when they are isolated by comparison with the TR; they also become variants only when the TR readings in question are identified as actual manuscript readings.

that either the author or scribe wrote nonsense, except as an error, and moreover, because it is more likely that a scribe would write nonsense than that the author would; also the nonsense reading is excluded from the apparatus because "agreement in error" has not commended itself as a method for establishing manuscript relationships; rather, "agreement in readings" has emerged as sound method (101-2). This category, the nonsense reading, is clearly established, and the arguments for excluding such readings are sound; few will argue for their originality or even for their retention in the critical apparatus, though the grounds for this exclusion may be variously formulated.

The second class of reading to be excluded is the *Dislocated Reading,* which is Colwell's term for the unintentional deletion of a passage (haplography) or the unintentional repetition of a passage (dittography) because of similar or identical words in a narrow context. Usually such an error is clear and demonstrable (102-3). The brevity of this discussion in Colwell's work, as well as the tentative terminology that is employed, suggest that further analysis of the Dislocated Reading category is warranted. For one thing, are not harmonizations — particularly within the Gospels, but also involving OT quotations and epistolary material in Paul — really dislocated readings? Very often readings of this kind can be demonstrated to be harmonistic additions or conformations, and very often — though this is more difficult to document — they were unintentional, almost unconscious alterations, though inevitably they would yield sense, not nonsense. Should they be designated as insignificant, meaningless readings? One would be inclined to say "yes" if their secondary character were unambiguously demonstrable, but this is unlikely to be the case.

Furthermore, so-called errors of the ear, involving the alteration from one letter or word to a similar-sounding letter or word, might be included in the Dislocated Reading category, for such readings often can be identified as clear errors, though occasionally (especially in the case of the plural personal pronouns) it is difficult to determine the direction in which the alteration moved (see examples in Metzger 1968a: 190-92). If such alterations produce nonsense, both the direction of the change and the certainty of an error will be clear; when the result makes sense, however, it will become much more risky to exclude it as a dislocated reading, for not always will it be an indisputably demonstrable error.

Finally, the transposition of letters within a word or changes in the sequence of words (see examples in Metzger 1968a: 193) might be called dislocated readings and thereby be excluded if nonsense is produced; but again, when sense is maintained in the variant reading, exclusion from the apparatus or from other text-critical tasks would be dangerous and unwarranted.

None of these further candidates for dislocated readings figures in Colwell and Tune's discussion, but it will be apparent, I think, that their Dislocated Readings and any extension of that category to other kinds of readings along the lines suggested above will isolate insignificant readings with a measure of certainty only when those readings produce nonsense or when the process of error can be clearly recognized; however, the category is plagued by considerable uncertainty when alleged dislocated readings yield sense, for then it is difficult to tell whether some form of haplography or dittography has occurred, whether without any doubt harmonization has taken

51

place, whether a hearing error was in fact the cause of a variation or which of two similar-sounding but construable words came first in the textual tradition, or whether or not the transposition of a letter or word resulted from error and, if so, which reading occasioned the other. These uncertainties suggest that perhaps this classification, the Dislocated Reading, should be abandoned and that those readings that constitute nonsense simply should be relegated to the first category, that of nonsense readings. If, however, there are some readings that make sense and yet can *with certainty* be traced to scribal error, they should be grouped under a new category discussed below (i.e., clear and demonstrable scribal errors).

The third kind of reading that Colwell and Tune suggested for exclusion from the critical apparatus is the *Singular Reading,* of which some will be nonsense or may be dislocations (to use their term), while others will make sense; all, however, stand alone in the (known) Greek manuscript tradition, for a singular reading is a variation of text within a variation-unit that is supported by one Greek MS but has no other (known) support in the Greek tradition. This category bristles with problems, some of which Colwell and Tune acknowledge (e.g., that future collations or discoveries may eliminate the "singular" status of a reading, or that singular readings may be of value in assessing scribal habits and thereby in evaluating the non-singular readings of a particular MS — opening to question their exclusion) (103-5), though other problems are not discussed (e.g., is a singular reading in the [known] Greek manuscript tradition still a "singular" reading when it has the support of MSS of the ancient versions? This is an issue of considerable importance in connection with a textual stream like that of the "Western," in which relatively little attestation is available in Greek, though relatively much more is available in certain ancient versional MSS).

Some researchers in recent attempts at the quantitative measurement of manuscript relationships have eliminated singular readings from their tabulations and tacitly, if not always explicitly, have defended this point in Colwell's methodology (e.g., Wisse and McReynolds in Colwell et al. 1968: 193); of course, Colwell and Tune themselves excluded singular readings (referred to, at that time, as "unique readings") from their tabulations in another programmatic and subsequently influential essay, "Method in Establishing Quantitative Relationships between Text-Types of New Testament Manuscripts" (1963 = Colwell 1969: 56-62). Other recent researchers in this area have included singular readings in their first assessment of manuscript variation, but — utilizing conscious and careful refinements of Colwell's method — have removed such readings from their final tabulations when these were designed to reveal manuscript relationships, thus supporting, essentially, Colwell's point. In these cases the singular readings have been employed for other, more restricted text-critical purposes (see Fee 1968a: 28-34, 42-43; Hurtado 1981a: 67-84, 86-88[6]), following methods elaborated elsewhere by Colwell himself (1965 = 1969: 106-24). The usefulness of singular readings in discerning scribal patterns, purposes,

---

6. A revised and augmented version of Hurtado's 1973 Ph.D. dissertation at Case Western Reserve University, "Codex Washingtonianus in the Gospel of Mark: Its Textual Relationships and Scribal Characteristics." See pp. 50-54, 194-201 and ff., 231-39.

and characteristics, both in recent and older studies, should caution us against the simple or premature exclusion of singular readings from all text-critical tasks other than, to use Colwell's phrase, "the initial appraisal of the work of the scribe in a particular manuscript" (Colwell-Tune 1964: 104). Colwell and Tune, however, seem to have made two valid points: (1) singular readings are not genetically or genealogically significant and should not be counted in quantitative measures of manuscript kinship, and (2) in a textual tradition as rich as that of the NT, the high probability is that no original reading has survived solely in a singular reading (104). Not all readily will grant the validity of these points, especially the latter one, but they form two rules that may be affirmed generally, though — as with all rules — allowance will have to be made for noteworthy exceptions.

In addition, there are some terminological problems with respect to the designation, "singular reading." Gordon D. Fee, for example, speaks in one of his articles of "singular agreements" of ℵ and D (1968a: 38, 42-43; cf. 31-32), by which he means that ℵ and D alone among the Greek MSS have a particular reading. It is quite clear what he means by this, but the juxtaposition of "singular agreements" with the term "singular readings" perhaps complicates unnecessarily an already confusing terminological situation; surely a term such as "dual agreements" or, better, "peculiar dual agreements" would relieve the ambiguities encouraged by the use of similar language when referring, on the one hand, to a reading with single and solitary support (a genuinely singular reading) and, on the other, to a reading with dual, but only dual, support.

Just as understandable perhaps, but more problematic are terms such as "nearly singular" and "subsingular."[7] The latter term apparently was introduced by Westcott-Hort, who defined subsingular readings as those having "only secondary support, namely, that of inferior Greek MSS, of Versions, or of Fathers, or of combinations of documentary authorities of these kinds" (2.230). Obviously, for Westcott-Hort "subsingular" involved more of a qualitative judgment than a quantitative measure. Today in the quantitative measurement of manuscript relationships, the term "inferior" would not be applied to any Greek MS or to any other textual witnesses, for qualitative judgments (and especially pre-judgments) have no place in this phase of text-critical methodology. Subsingular, therefore, never should be employed in Westcott-Hort's sense of readings with relatively narrow support, for in such a loose use of the terms "nearly singular" and "subsingular" the singularity aspect is lacking completely. To be sure, in these cases the self-contradictory nature of the terms themselves could be overlooked, for language demands ways of expressing — if colloquially — "almost unique," hence "almost singular"; yet it is difficult to know where to draw the line on a spectrum that, at one end, has singular, singular-plus-one, singular-plus-two, etc., all of which still are referred to by using some form of the term "singular."

Gordon D. Fee has given a new and different sense to the term "subsingular

7. For the former, see, e.g., Fee 1968a: 34, 43; for the latter, see Westcott and Hort 1881: 2.230, 238, 246-50; Wisse and McReynolds 1968: 193; and Fee in an unpublished paper presented to the Textual Criticism Seminar of the SBL, Washington, DC, 25 October 1974, entitled, "Toward the Clarification of Textual Variation: Colwell and Tune Revisited" [now Chapter 4].

reading"; he defines it as "a non-genetic, accidental agreement in variation between two MSS which are not otherwise closely related,"[8] and here "related" refers to a tested quantitative relationship. The difficulty with this use of "subsingular," of course, is that at least plausible grounds must be established in each case for the *accidental* or *coincidental* nature of the agreement between two readings that are in reality two independent "singular" readings; not always will this be easy to do, though Fee's presumption is that the lack of relatedness as judged by quantitative tests is itself sufficient evidence of their independence. Thus, if the independence of the two readings is reasonably certain, the term "subsingular" in Fee's sense is an apt and useful term, for "singular" in the term actually is intended to specify *singular,* but the coincidence in the singularity of reading in the two MSS warrants the qualification *sub*singular — less than completely singular, nevertheless still within the category of singular.

Finally, even more complex is the use of the term "singular" for a reading of a Greek MS that is a reading unique in the (known) Greek manuscript tradition, but that has some additional support from ancient versional MSS — a problem alluded to earlier. To cite an example again from Fee's indispensable treatise on quantitative method, he speaks at one point of Codex Bezae's "twenty-three singular readings in this chapter [John 8], nine of which have Old Latin and/or Old Syriac support" (1968a: 43). All of these are, as far as we know, singular readings in the *Greek* manuscript tradition, and in Colwell's terms that is the proper framework and appropriate limitation for defining singular readings. But are the nine with OL or OS support really singular readings in any final sense of that term? Logic would seem to require an answer in the negative, but such an answer, if acted upon, would multiply vastly the complexity of quantitative methods now so successfully employed for determining manuscript groupings, for not only would the versional evidence have to be fed into the process at *all* points (not only in cases of alleged singular readings), but this evidence would have to come from full collations of numerous versional MSS in several languages and, what is more problematic, would have to be stated in terms of its Greek equivalent at every variation-unit.[9] Even a cursory acquaintance with the versional evidence will expose the difficulties, the uncertainties and ambiguities, and the inconveniences of such a procedure. Would the benefits that might flow from such added labors be commensurate with those efforts? A superficial guess would be that in a book like the Fourth Gospel, with its rich and extensive Greek attestation, the results would not repay the efforts; yet a procedure that would utilize a fuller range of versional evidence has interesting implications for the application of quantitative methods, for example, to the "Western" text of Acts, where often only one "clearly" "Western" witness in Greek is extant for a given variation-unit, but where several additional "Western" witnesses in Latin or Syriac offer the same or a similar reading.

---

8. Fee, "Toward Clarification," 10 [now Chapter 4: 67].

9. Critical apparatuses, unless they include *all* significant variants (however that is defined) in the MSS treated, cannot be used in such a process, for sound method demands that *total* agreement and disagreement among witnesses be measured.

As a matter of fact, a major source of disquietude about the Colwell-Tune definition of a singular reading — singularity defined by taking into account only the Greek tradition — is Codex Bezae. As so often in NT textual criticism, this troublesome codex and the "Western" text in general have a way of ruining standard procedure and neat distinctions. The leading principles that Colwell and Tune enunciated with reference to the utility of singular readings are basically sound and acceptable: singular readings are not genetically or genealogically significant, and in a rich textual tradition like that of the NT an original reading is not likely to have been preserved only in a singular reading; hence, singular readings are "insignificant" for the text-critical tasks related to these two principles. Yet, the obvious importance of Codex Bezae in tracking the early history of the NT text and the early and widespread nature of the "Western" text in general should caution against any procedure that would rule out of court, almost without a hearing, a large body of early, interesting, and unmistakably important evidence: this indeed would be the fate of a great many of D's readings if singularity is to be defined with reference solely to the Greek manuscript tradition, for these numerous singular readings of D, particularly in Acts, then could play no rôle in questions of the original text of Acts when in reality the greater number of the "unique" D-readings have support — sometimes broad support — from MSS of one, two, or more of the most ancient versions of the NT. Presumably some accident of history stunted the preservation in Greek of this rich and colorful "Western" tradition and confined its transmission largely to Latin and Syriac. Furthermore, the determination and measurement of textual relationships *within* the "Western" tradition of the Gospels and Acts is entirely excluded if quantitative methods are to be limited to nothing but Greek witnesses; yet, the alternating claims to cohesiveness and to diversity in that "Western" tradition need to be tested by such methods, and this can be done only on the basis of a more restrictive criterion for the identification and subsequent exclusion of "singular readings" — that is, fewer singular readings must be allowed to succumb to exclusion if quantitative methods are to function in the sphere of the "Western" textual tradition.

Acts 3:17, with its four variation-units [though the term is used loosely here for the sake of illustration], represents a typical case in the "Western" text of Acts and serves to illustrate the problem (see Fig. 3.1, p. 56).

In this example, D and its versional and patristic allies have the support of a Greek MS only in variation-unit (1), in this case Codex E. Accordingly, the lower readings in variation-units (2), (3), and (4) would be singular readings if only the Greek tradition were taken into account. The D-reading in variation-unit (3), because of the uncertain reading in the text of *h,* may have to be taken as a singular reading in any event, since only Codex Bezae (D and d) supports it; in variation-unit (2), D is supported by two of the rather primary "Western" witnesses to the text of Acts; and in variation-unit (4), containing the obviously most striking and important of the textual divergences in the passage, the D-reading would be a singular reading if only Greek witnesses were consulted, but it has strong support from *h* and sy[hmg], two primary "Western" witnesses, plus the widespread support of mixed or secondary "Western" witnesses (though the latter all add the demonstrative, "this," to form an additional reading not found in the Greek tradition).

Fig. 3.1

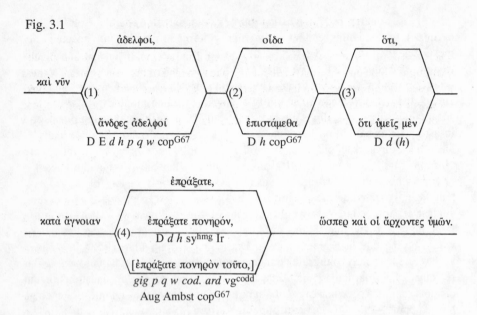

Note: The reading on the top line is that of the entire manuscript tradition with the exception, of course, of the witnesses attesting the readings on the lower line or lines.

The point is a simple one, though clear: on the Colwell-Tune definition the most interesting and widely-attested alternative reading in this passage fails to achieve the status of "variant," with all the rights and responsibilities attached thereto, for it — and two of the other three D-readings — are relegated to a kind of textual Sheol, a shadowy textual existence, by the failure of the term "singular" to mean singular.

Beyond the complexities already enumerated, any alteration of the category, "singular reading," by taking into account versional manuscript evidence opens up also the further vexing question of whether Greek and other *patristic evidence* should be accounted when verifying singular readings. The additional difficulties that accompany the use of this kind of testimony are well known, and the total, monumental task of coping with the masses of material — Greek, versional, patristic — and with the several sublevels of complexity that they entail staggers the imagination and surely will be a deterrent to what otherwise commends itself as a desirable goal, namely, the casting of the text-critical net as widely as possible in the sea of apposite witnesses to the NT text.

The ten-page article of Colwell and Tune has provided us, either directly or upon our further analysis, with several fundamental clarifications of basic terminology in textual criticism, such as "reading," "variant," "significant reading," "insignificant reading," "singular reading," and "variation-unit." Some of these clarifications are definitive just as Colwell and Tune formulated them; others challenge us to reach for definitive formulations that will add greater precision and self-confidence to our practice of NT textual criticism.

III. Recommended Definitions and Limitations

The preceding discussions quite clearly demand an attempt at formal and precise definitions of the major terms related to the phenomenon of textual variation. If these proposed definitions and limitations serve only to alert us to the issues involved, they will have served one of their chief purposes; if, in addition, they should lead to or commend themselves as standard formulations, they will have fulfilled their further goal.

1. Reading

The term "reading" is a general term designating a textual difference or a varying text-formulation and refers to any divergence of text in a passage or segment of text in one MS as compared with the same segment of text in any other MS. The term "reading," therefore, may designate any kind of textual disagreement, whether it is later to be classified as nonsense or meaningless error, as an orthographic difference, as a singular reading, as a correction, as a significant reading, or as falling into any other category. "Reading" is the broadest term for a dissimilarity disclosed by the comparison of two or more MSS or even by the comparison of two or more hands in the same MS. It may be used also to designate the text-formulation in any segment of a constructed text (e.g., such recognized texts as the TR or WH) or of any critical edition of any part of the NT. Moreover, any textual divergence is always a "reading" before it is anything else, and the term should be distinguished from the narrower term "variant"; as we shall see, a "reading" may remain a "reading" permanently, or, depending upon its nature, may become a "variant." This leads to the remaining and more specific terms requiring definition.

2. Significant and Insignificant Readings

"Readings" fall into two large subdivisions; they are either "significant" readings or "insignificant" readings, and in this context "significant" means meaningful or useful for the broad tasks of NT textual criticism, including the determination of a MS's relationship with all other MSS, the location of a MS within the textual history and transmission of the NT, and the ultimate goal of establishing the original text. By the same token, "insignificant" means inappropriate, inadequate, or inconclusive for those broad tasks of textual criticism, but it does not mean insignificant in any absolute and final sense. Both "significant" and "insignificant" readings — that is, all readings — may be useful for understanding the nature and characteristics of an *individual manuscript* and of the scribe or scribes of that MS (see esp. Colwell 1965 = 1969: 106-24), and for this reason it is essential that an edition of any MS isolate and analyze thoroughly all of its readings prior to separating the "insignificant" readings from the "significant." (This isolation of a MS's readings ideally must employ a quantitative measure, utilizing adequate representatives of all major groups of NT MSS.) "Insignificant readings" may be subdivided into four classes, and any reading that is identified as belonging to one or another of these classes should be eliminated from the data employed for the broad tasks of NT textual criticism, as these have been described above. "Significant readings," on the other hand, are "textual variants" in the technical and restricted sense; they alone are accorded the designation "variants" and are treated separately below under the heading "Significant Readings or Variants."

a. *Insignificant Readings.* Insignificant readings, as described in general terms above, may be subdivided adequately under four headings:

i. *Nonsense Readings.* The "nonsense reading" is a reading that fails to make sense because it cannot be construed grammatically, either in terms of grammatical/lexical form or in terms of grammatical structure, or because in some other way it lacks a recognizable meaning. Since authors and scribes do not produce nonsense intentionally, it is to be assumed (1) that nonsense readings resulted from errors in transmission, (2) that they, therefore, cannot represent either the original text or the intended text of any MS or alert scribe, and (3) that they do not aid in the process of discerning the relationships among MSS. The one exception would be the slavish, overly scrupulous scribe who would reproduce an uncorrected error, but — as pointed out earlier — agreement in a *common* (i.e., commonplace) scribal error certainly could not be taken as demonstrable proof of manuscript kinship, nor would the copying of an *uncommon* error be easily or certainly demonstrable as proof for such a relationship between MSS. The "nonsense reading," accordingly, is an "insignificant reading" and should never be called a "variant."

ii. *Clear and Demonstrable Scribal Errors.* A second class of "insignificant readings" is comprised of readings that can be construed grammatically and make sense but can be demonstrated with reasonable certainty to be scribal errors. (Any scribal errors that produce nonsense are placed in the preceding classification.) Candidates for scribal errors that make sense would be certain instances of haplography and dittography, cases of harmonization with similar contexts, hearing errors producing a similar-sounding word, and the transposition of letters or words with a resultant change in meaning. The snare in this category, naturally, is the phrase "clear and demonstrable," for no reading that makes sense should be consigned lightly to the "insignificant" category; on the other hand, if the process of error can be recognized and traced with reasonable certainty, there is no reason to retain the erroneous alteration among the "significant readings." A reasonably certain recognition of error may be possible in some instances of each type mentioned above, such as certain cases involving homoeoteleuton, but the use of this classification of "insignificant readings" will by its nature require caution lest some "significant" variant be cast aside prematurely.

iii. *Orthographic Difference.* Mere orthographic differences, particularly itacisms and nu-movables (as well as abbreviations) are "insignificant" as here defined; they cannot be utilized in any decisive way for establishing manuscript relationships, and they are not substantive in the search for the original text. Again, the exception might be the work of a slavish scribe, whose scrupulousness might be considered useful in tracing manuscript descent, but the pervasive character of itacism, for example, over wide areas and time-spans precludes the "significance" of orthographic differences for this important text-critical task. Nor is "correct" spelling a material issue when establishing the original text, provided, of course, that no ambiguity in meaning results from the alternative spelling formulations. There is, however, a genuine area of exception, and that concerns the spelling of proper nouns; some classic text-critical and historical problems turn on the forms of names for persons or places, and both experience and prudence suggest that, other things being equal, these particular orthographic differences be preserved in the critical apparatus and as part of the "significant" data of textual criticism.

iv. *Singular Readings*. A "singular reading" is a "reading" found in one NT MS but with the support of no other; it is a unique reading as far as our knowledge of NT MSS extends. "Singular readings," more so than the other classes of "insignificant readings," may be especially useful in assessing the nature and characteristics of an individual MS and its scribe, but "singular readings" are not genetically or genealogically significant, nor is an original reading to be expected among them. Hence, they are to be utilized in the study of individual MSS and scribal habits, but should be excluded from those procedures in textual criticism that attempt to determine manuscript kinship or to establish the text of the NT.

Singular readings are of two major kinds, "nonsense singular readings" and "singular readings that make sense."[10] Nonsense singular readings should be treated (and classified) as nonsense readings in general, for they will contribute almost nothing to text-critical study, except perhaps a general insight as to the carefulness/carelessness of a particular scribe. Singular readings that make sense, including certain orthographic differences, scribal corrections, harmonizations, and various alterations of a historical, descriptive, ideological, theological, or generally editorial nature, will aid in understanding the particular MS under consideration, both in terms of the habits of its scribe and in terms of any stylistic peculiarities or ideological biases.

Whether the term "singular reading" should be applied to a reading that stands alone when only the straight-text Greek manuscript tradition is taken into account (resulting in many singular readings) or should be further limited to a reading that stands alone when not only the Greek MSS, but also the ancient versional MSS and perhaps the early patristic quotations are taken into account (resulting in fewer singular readings) is a difficult but nonetheless urgent issue, as is evident from our earlier discussion. Exploration of this question is desirable, if not mandatory, in the near future, but for the present, if only for practical reasons, the former limitation — a reading in the Greek manuscript tradition that is found in one MS only — should govern the term "singular reading" (1) when quantitative methods are used to search out manuscript relationships and to locate a Greek MS within the NT textual tradition and (2) when the establishment of the original text is in view. However, for purposes of discerning, for example, the ideological bias of a NT MS, it will be prudent, if not essential, to adopt the more restrictive view of "singular readings," that they must be unique — without support — in the *entire* (known) textual tradition before they can be excluded from consideration. Under the latter principle many previously "singular readings" will lose that status by their support, for example, from OL or OS MSS; particularly, for instance, this will be the case in the text of Acts, where Codex Bezae has numerous "singular" readings when judged solely in terms of the Greek manuscript tradition, but most of

10. Colwell (1969: 111-12) employs the terms "Nonsense Singular Readings" and "Sensible Singular Readings."

these have early versional or patristic support and no longer would be "singular readings" under a more severe policy for establishing singularity. Actually, such an • assessment of ideological bias in a MS — to extend the example — falls within the scope of the study of an individual MS, for which otherwise "insignificant readings" are employed anyway, and the suggestion made here does not, therefore, go beyond the basic Colwell-Tune principles for the use of singular readings. What is essential, however, is that the criteria for singularity be reassessed along the lines suggested earlier to determine whether the singular readings hitherto confined to the analysis of an individual MS might not be liberated by their versional support for use both in establishing manuscript kinship and in seeking the original text.

We are left, then, with the definition of a "singular reading" as a textual divergence within the Greek manuscript tradition that is attested by one Greek MS only, and we are left also with a challenge whether that definition ought to be restated so that the term "singular reading" applies only to a textual divergence not merely without other Greek support, but also without ancient versional support or support in the patristic quotations of the NT.

b. *Significant Readings or Variants.* The term "variant" or "textual variant" should be reserved for those readings that are "significant" or "meaningful" in the broad tasks of NT textual criticism, as specified in 2 above. It is easier to define "variant" in this proper sense of "significant reading" by indicating what it is not than to specify what it is. To state the obvious, a "significant variant" is any reading that is not determined to be "insignificant," that is, a reading that is not a nonsense reading, not a demonstrable scribal error, not an inconsequential orthographic difference, and not a singular reading. "Variants," then, will constitute a distillation from the "readings" of a MS, though "readings" — including "variants" — can emerge only by comparison with one or more other MSS; normally, a wide range of MSS, which together represent adequately the major manuscript groupings in the NT textual tradition, must be employed in the comparison and distillation process so that the isolation and subtraction of the "insignificant readings" and the consequent determination of the "variants" of the MS in question can be achieved with a reasonable measure of confidence, thoroughness, and definitiveness. These "variants" — the distillate — then are utilized in text-critical tasks reaching beyond the study of a given MS itself, including, of course, that MS's relationship with all other MSS and ultimately the quest for the original text of the NT.

Subclassifications of "significant readings" or "variants" require exploration, for they will provide the means for describing and understanding "variants" from a more positive standpoint; this, however, is beyond the scope of the present discussion.[11]

3. *Variation-Unit*

A "variation-unit" is that determinate quantity or segment of text, constituting a normal and proper grammatical combination, where our MSS present at least two variant

---

11. Such classifications have been proposed by Fee in the paper now published as Chapter 4 in this volume.

readings and where, after insignificant readings have been excluded, each variant reading has the support of at least two MSS. Of course, if the technical definition of "variant" (2.b above) is clearly understood and carefully applied, the definition of a variation-unit can be stated much more succinctly as *that segment of text, constituting a normal and proper grammatical combination, where our manuscripts present at least two "variants."* Whether the word "Greek" should be specified and inserted before the word "manuscripts" in the definitions above involves those same issues explored in connection with singular readings; again, for the present let us assume that "manuscripts" means "Greek manuscripts" in the definitions, but at the same time let us face the challenge of broadening the term "manuscripts" to include ancient versional MSS and perhaps also early patristic quotations.

The attempt to define the limits or extent of a variation-unit by the phrase "constituting a normal and proper grammatical combination" may lack precision when it comes to actual practice, for what may appear to be a single variation-unit in the sense just described often will contain, in fact, more than one set of separate and genetically unrelated variants.[12] This complicates matters, for is such a "variation-unit" really more than one unit, or should such a variation-unit be said to consist of several inner sets of variants, each of which is tabulated separately in a quantitative analysis? Gordon D. Fee, who calls attention to this problem, suggests from extensive experience that "a count of agreements in variation-units alone will reveal clear patterns of relationships, while a count including sets of variants refines the details of agreements within major groups" (Chapter 4: 66). The delimitation of "variation-unit" as constituting a normal and proper grammatical unit lacks precision also in another respect, for there are larger and smaller "proper grammatical combinations"; a suggested refinement, which still will depend on the peculiarities of each situation, is that in every case where a variation-unit is being defined the *shortest* or *smallest possible* grammatical unit be selected, that is, the shortest grammatically related segment of text that still will encompass all the variants from across the manuscript tradition that present themselves at that point. .

IV. Conclusion

When is a "reading" a "variant"? When the reading is a "significant" reading by virtue of its fitness for genetic and genealogical tracking and by virtue of its appropriateness as a possibly original reading. And how is a variant thus fit and appropriate? By virtue of its character as a reading that makes sense, that is not an indisputably demonstrable scribal error, that is not a mere orthographic difference, and that is not a singular reading. And, because a "reading" in general and a "variant" in particular exist only over against another and divergent reading, a variant to be a variant must be a member of a "variation-unit," that entity which brings into direct confrontation two or more variants and thereby constitutes the basic and indispensable factor in the discipline of textual criticism.

---

12. See Fee [Chapter 4] and the exhibits appended. This phenomenon is referred to as the "nesting" of variants by Dearing 1974b: 22; see the entire essay for a somewhat different approach to the analysis and identification of textual variation.

CHAPTER 4

ON THE TYPES, CLASSIFICATION, AND PRESENTATION OF TEXTUAL VARIATION[1]

Gordon D. Fee

During the past twenty-five years significant progress has been made in the development of an adequate methodology for the establishing of textual relationships among Greek MSS. Several of the studies in the present volume are a part of that enterprise. Since the new methodology is a quantitative analysis of textual variants, it is especially important that the concept of textual variation become more precise than was true in the past.

Pioneering studies of both of these areas — a quantitative method for establishing textual relationships and the classification of kinds of textual variation — were made by E. C. Colwell, in collaboration with E. W. Tune (1963, 1964). This present study is an attempt to build upon their foundational work by offering some further refinements both in the presentation and in the classification of textual variation, the results of which are reflected in several of the following studies.

Colwell and Tune began their study on textual variation by arguing for a term other than "variant." In its place they offer "unit-of-variation" or "variation-unit." This is not merely a new nomenclature; rather it involves a totally new conceptual frame within which they attempt greater precision in establishing manuscript relationships. The term "variant" implies "a deviation or change from something else taken for a norm" (1964: 253), that is, it implies a relationship of one MS or a group of MSS to an external standard. The abiding contribution of Colwell-Tune is the laying to rest forever of such a methodology in favor of one in which MSS are first compared directly with one another.

Thus, they define a variation-unit as "that passage or section of the Greek NT where our MSS do not agree as to what the Greek text is." It refers to "a length of the text wherein our MSS present at least two variant forms" (254). Within this new frame the term "variant" is retained to refer to "one of the possible alternative readings which are found in a variation-unit" (256).

The two methodologies are illustrated in Exhibits A and B, in which the opening words of John 7 are diagrammed. Exhibit A gives the text of the TR and

---

1. The substance of this paper, heretofore unpublished, was originally presented at the NT textual criticism seminar of the SBL, Washington, DC, 25 October 1974, entitled "Toward the Classification of Textual Variation: Colwell and Tune Revisited." It has been slightly revised and updated for publication in this volume.

shows how variants (in the former sense of the term) are understood in relation to that standard. In this piece of text there are five variants from the TR. Exhibit B gives the same information in terms of variation-units. Here there are two variation-units, with two variants in the one and four in the other.

The advantages of the presentation in Exhibit B are readily apparent: (1) The reader has immediate access to manuscript agreements and disagreements as well as to manuscript relationships to two (or possibly more) external standards (in this case the TR and NA[26] [always the top variant]). In fact, such a diagrammatic presentation of textual variation is an almost indispensable tool for determining quantitative relationships. (2) It provides an invaluable way to collate new MSS, as well as Patristic texts, quickly and efficiently. (3) It offers immediate visibility of the problems of variation in the quest for the original text. (4) It is readily adaptable to computerization.

This pioneering work by Colwell and Tune is an extremely valuable refinement of the concept of textual variation. The rest of this paper offers further and more careful refinement in two additional areas: (1) determining the extent of a variation-unit, and (2) the classification of variants.

I.

Colwell and Tune recognized the problem of determining the extent of a variation-unit and noted that "one scholar may subdivide what another scholar regards as a single unit" (255). Their suggested solution is empirical: "The general rule for the recognition of a total variation-unit is by noticing those elements of expression in the Greek text which regularly exist together" (255). A little further they repeat: "It is what goes together in the individual witnesses that establishes the unit-of-variation" (255). This is perfectly sound; and their illustrations are good examples of "what goes together."

Such a definition and its subsequent diagram, however, may overlook another significant empirical factor, namely that within one variation-unit where the elements of expression go together there is sometimes a second or a third set of variants which also belong together. That is, a single variation-unit may contain more than one set of variants, which are (or may be) genetically unrelated.

Before examining some illustrations of this problem as set forth in Exhibits B through H (see pp. 69-79), it is appropriate first to comment on the nomenclature being used to describe sets of variants — for one of the criteria that has emerged for recognizing possible sets of variants within any unit-of-variation has to do with relatedness of variants in terms of *types* of variation.

First, all variation is one of four *kinds:* addition, omission, substitution, transposition. However, when variation is being described objectively, that is, when the variation between any two or more MSS is being described in terms of their relationship to each other and all others, the kinds of variation narrow to three: (1) add/omit (A/O), in reference to other textual data; (2) substitution (SUB), including whole clauses or phrases, individual words, or variant forms of the same word (e.g., number/case of nouns; tense/voice/mood of verbs); and (3) word order (W/O). In some cases, of course, any two or all three of these may occur in combination in any set of variants.

63

Second, most variation involves a single part of speech; the exceptions are major add/omits (e.g., the bloody sweat in Luke 22:43-44) or longer transpositions (e.g., 1 Cor 14:34-35, or variation-unit 4 in Exhibit D[a]).

Thus, most sets of variants may be isolated as involving one or more of the three kinds of variation in relation to a given part of speech. It might be noted in passing that all of this could be easily adapted to a computer, with a basic two-column, five-digit code that could classify all variation among NT MSS:[2]

Column I	Column II
A/O = add/omit	Aj = Adjective
SUB = substitution	Ar = Article
W/O = word order	Av = Adverb
AOS = add/omit/substitution	Cj = Conjunction
AOW = add/omit/word order	Cm = Compound word
SWO = substitution/word order	Nn = Noun
ASW = add/omit/substitution/word order	Pn = Pronoun
	Pp = Preposition(al phrase)
	Pt = Participle
	Vb = Verb
	Vo = Vocative
	L = Large add/omit
	M = Major rewriting
	(s) = singular reading
	(ss) = subsingular reading

Now to return to the examination of variation-units that contain more than one set of variants. The problem may be illustrated initially from the second variation-unit in Exhibit B, where Codex Vaticanus has a singular "omission" of the article with Ἰησοῦς. The basic unit is a combination of add/omit/substitution/word order of a prepositional phrase (ASW-Pp). But the variant "add-omit the article" (A/O-Ar) is quite *unrelated* to the basic variation-unit. In fact, had Codex B been joined, let us say, by P[66] and P[75] in this "omission," one may have diagrammed the whole unit thus:

(a) μετὰ ταῦτα περιεπάτει ὁ Ἰησοῦς
(b) μετὰ ταῦτα περιεπάτει Ἰησοῦς
(c) περιεπάτει ὁ Ἰησοῦς μετὰ ταῦτα
(d) περιεπάτει μετ' αὐτῶν ὁ Ἰησοῦς
(e) περιεπάτει ὁ Ἰησοῦς

But in such an instance, whatever one may call the larger unit, there are

---

2. If one wanted still further refinements, which are sometimes useful for "weighing" variation after counting, a third column could be devised, indicating either further variant information (Hm = possible homoeoteleuton; As = possible assimilation), or further defining of the part of speech (for nouns, O = object; S = subject; etc.).

two clear and basically unrelated sets of variants; and in a quantitative analysis one would want two sets of manuscript agreements: (1) add/omit/substitution/word order μετὰ ταῦτα/ὁ Ἰησοῦς, where the agreements in variants *a* and *b* are counted together, and *c, d,* and *e* separately; (2) add/omit the definite article, where the MSS in variant *b* would be in agreement against all the rest.

Exhibit C offers another example of the same problem, this time with three sets of basically unrelated variants: add/omit/word order of γύναι, a substitution (tense of verb), and add/omit μοι. Such a unit-of-variation is difficult to diagram in any other fashion than that shown in the exhibit. The tense substitution, however, and the transposition (or omit altogether) of γύναι do not necessarily go together; therefore they must be treated as two *sets of variants* (1 = *ab, cdg, ef;* 2 = *ace, bdfg*), even though they diagram as one unit. Furthermore, one should note that the basis of subdivision is relatedness. For example, one could argue that variants *ab* and *cd* constitute a set based on word order, and that *abcd* and *ef* constitute another based on add/omit γύναι. But these two sets are *related,* and therefore constitute one set of add/omit/word order of γύναι.

Exhibit D is a still more complex unit, with the same information being set forth in the two separate diagrams *(a)* and *(b)*. In D*(b)* there are three units: (1) A/O οὖν; (2) a combination of four sets of variants (AOW τοῦτον; A/O τῶν; A/O τριῶν; A/O all three words); (3) a major W/O. The difficulty here is raised by Codex Bezae, whose variant is a major rewriting of the entire sentence. The whole complex, therefore, is better diagrammed as in Exhibit D*(a)*, not *(b)*. The latter diagrams the data as presented in von Soden's apparatus, where the information is quite misleading. Codex Bezae at this point has one major singular reading — not three smaller ones — which is unrelated to the other variation-units, except for the οὖν in unit 1, which may be validly included in the count for that unit.

Exhibit E*(a)* shows another group of variants complicated by the text of D and Itala. In this case the complexity of the unit has played havoc with the apparatus of the UBS, whose information may be diagrammed as in Exhibit E*(b)*. But we have here three variation-units, not one; and each is quite unrelated to the other two. Unit 1 is the large add/omit of all or most of the whole clause; unit 2 is a substitution (of two kinds: the word itself and the mood in codex 69) — the reading of D is rightly included in the count for this unit; and unit 3 is a major add/omit/word order (presence and place of ὀλίγων or ἑνός). In this last unit codex B joins the witnesses in variant *a* in the count of agreements, since its variant is a singular reading of the word order χρεία ἐστίν.

Exhibits F*(a)* and *(b)* illustrate the complexity of deciding "what goes together" in a Johannine formula introducing direct discourse. On one hand, there are four different types of variation: (1) add/omit/substitute a conjunction (οὖν/δέ); (2) add/omit/word order of αὐτοῖς; (3) add/omit the article with Ἰησοῦς; (4) add/omit Ἰησοῦς. On the other hand, the Johannine formulae for direct discourse often reflect multiple variation in such a way that one is tempted to regard the entire unit as a single set of variants. Variant *h* is John's usual style; the presence of the conjunction with ἀπεκρίθη is particularly rare, as is the word order αὐτοῖς (ὁ) Ἰησοῦς καὶ εἶπεν. Since I have shown elsewhere (1970a) that the presence or absence of the article with Ἰησοῦς in John is partly a matter of word order, it is highly unlikely that variants *a* and *h* are *related* (= reflect common parentage) in the "omission" of the article. Therefore, Exhibit F*(b)* tries to isolate those sets of variants which appear most likely to have relatedness. Unit 1 is easily isolated from the rest (as AOS-Cj). Unit 2 has two sets of variants (AOW-Pn and A/O-Ar) and a singular reading (codex 660 add/omit Ἰησοῦς).

Exhibits G and H illustrate one further kind of complexity. Unit 2 in Exhibit G may be regarded as having one set of variants or two. Most likely it should be regarded as two: a variation in the number of the noun (SUB-Nn); and an add/omit/substitution/word order of the demonstrative/possessive (ASW-Pn). Likewise with Exhibit H. One is tempted simply to regard this as a single set of variants. However, variants *e, f,* and *g* lack the very words (πολύς or περὶ αὐτοῦ) which are involved in the two sets of word order variation. Therefore, these should probably be regarded as AOW-Av and AOW-Pp.

The final question is whether, in a quantitative analysis, one should count agreements in variation-units or in sets of variants. My experience is that a count of agreements in variation-units in itself will reveal clear patterns of relationships, while a count including sets of variants refines the details of agreements within major groups.

II.

Another area in Colwell and Tune's study that needs further refinement has to do with the classification of variants. In their discussion they suggest the advisability of devising some classifications "so as to make possible the elimination of insignificant variant readings from the subsequent stages of this study" (257). Thus, they propose the classes "Nonsense Reading," "Dislocated Reading," and "Singular Reading" and argue that these are irrelevant in the study of the history of transmission.

To these classifications, several additions may be suggested. For example, the "Orthographical Reading" is generally irrelevant for studying manuscript relationships, except for the closest kinds of relationships, such as those between P[75] and B (see Martini 1966: 91-122). Otherwise such variation merely reflects scribal idiosyncrasies.[3] However, their judgment as to the disregarding of singular readings needs to be qualified. The earlier judgment of Hort with regard to the singular readings in Vaticanus should warn us not to dismiss totally all such readings. Hort distinguished between those singular readings which he judged to be "clerical errors" by the scribe of B itself and those which "must be reasonably supposed to have belonged to the text of its exemplar" (Westcott-Hort 1881: 2.230-46). The implication of this is clear: In the time of Hort some of B's singular readings were solecisms of the scribe (therefore, truly singular readings), while others he judged to belong to his Neutral text-type, and if earlier (or other) MSS of this text-type were ever found, the readings of B would no longer be singular. The subsequent discoveries of P[45], P[66], P[72], and P[75] not only have shown Hort to

3. Cf., e.g., Appendix D in Fee 1968b, 128-38, where I have listed all the orthographical variations by this single scribe.

be right but also have demonstrated the extraordinary skill with which he made his judgments.[4]

It appears, therefore, to be only a matter of prudence that singular readings be included in a diagrammatic presentation, but outside the regular presentation of variation-units (such as in Exhibits B and C where they are above the line, except when a MS has a singular variant amid other instances of variation among the MSS, as in variants *e* and *g* in Exhibit C).

But what happens when a newly discovered MS, collated against the text in Exhibit C, agrees with Koridethi in omitting the article with Ἰησοῦς? And especially what does one do when a full analysis of manuscript relationships reveals a very low overall percentage of relationship between these two MSS? It is such a phenomenon that suggests the use of the term "Sub-singular Reading," which can be defined as "a non-genetic, accidental agreement in variation between two MSS which are not otherwise closely related." In other words, two (or a few) MSS accidentally agree in a singular reading of the clerical error variety.

To make such judgments, however, requires first of all the preliminary step of establishing manuscript relationships on the basis of all variation-units where two or more MSS agree against the rest. But more significantly it involves a process of "weighing" variants, as well as counting. That is, it moves us toward a classification which considers the degree (or lack of it) of the possible genetic significance of agreements in variation. In fact, Colwell and Tune disregarded the singular reading precisely because "it is not genealogically significant" (261). But the "weighing" of variants with reference to their genealogical significance leads one to make the following observations.

1. The basic problem, of course, has to do with the degree of dependence or independence two or more MSS have where they share a common variant. It is a truism of our discipline that some agreements in variation by their very nature are just as likely to be the result of independent scribal activity as others are almost impossible to explain apart from some kind of dependence on exemplars from the same family or text-type. One cannot make hard-and-fast rules here, inasmuch as it must be assumed as *possible* that an error which one scribe committed could have been committed by any other scribe as well. Not all possible things, however, are equally probable. Therefore, some agreements of readings seem to demand textual relatedness, either by immediate ancestry or by ultimate relationship with a text-type parent or the original text itself.

In the classifications noted above, the vast majority of variants fall into the category of textual trivia. Genetic relationships must ultimately be built on firmer ground than on agreements, for example, in the addition/omission of articles, possessives, conjunctions, or the tense change of verbs (usually), or certain kinds of word order, or in many instances of harmonization. On the other hand, major rewrit-

---

4. For example, in Luke and John, where both P[75] and B have extant text, B currently has 47 singular readings. Only one of these (a word order variant at John 10:32) is found in the WH text. On the other hand, there are many instances where WH included in their text a reading of B that was singular in 1881, but which is now supported by P[75], and sometimes by other subsequent discoveries.

ings, some large addition/omission variants, certain kinds of substitutions, as well as several kinds of word order variants, must certainly be recognized as the basic data from which to construct stemmata of textual relationships.

2. Very often in a unit with three or more variants which are otherwise textual trivia, one variant may be so clearly the *lectio difficilior,* or in any case the clear cause of all the other variation, that that variant will have genetic significance for its manuscript agreements. At the same time the other variants may or may not have textual relatedness. That is, the very fact that two or more independent attempts have been made to relieve the difficulty may mean that any two MSS with the same variant independently relieved the difficulty in the same way.

3. The closer MSS are to one another in actual point of origin, the closer will usually be the textual relatedness between them in *all* the classifications of variation. Therefore, at the highest level of manuscript relationships (over ninety percent agreement in total variations) all variants take on genetic significance. This may also be stated in reverse: The closest relationships between MSS exist not only when they agree in a majority of genetically related variants, but also when they agree in the vast majority of trivia.

Until scholars work out a complete classification of variants in the manner suggested here, it is not likely that progress will be made in the writing of the history of the NT text. And even then, the problems of independence of error and unknown cross-fertilizations will make much of our work in this area only tentative. But in any case, the adoption of the suggestions made in this paper may help to make our continuing work in this discipline a bit more precise.

Exhibit A — John 7:1

και	περιεπατει	ο Ιησους	μετα ταυτα	εν τη Γαλιλαια

(1) omit
P66 ℵ* C² D
248 314 892 1010 1279 1293
a aur b c e f ff2 r¹ sa sy

(2) omit
Γ Ψ 713

(3) μετ᾽ αυτων ο Ιησους
N

(4) μετα ταυτα περιεπατει ο Ιησους
P66 P75 ℵ CDGKLWX Θ
f1 f13 16 33 213 265 280 291 348 477 482 892
945 990 1010 1071 1207 1216 1219 1223 1241
1293 1321 1346 1355 1579
a aur b c e ff2 r¹ vg sa bo sy^cp arm eth

(5) μετα ταυτα περιεπατει Ιησους
B

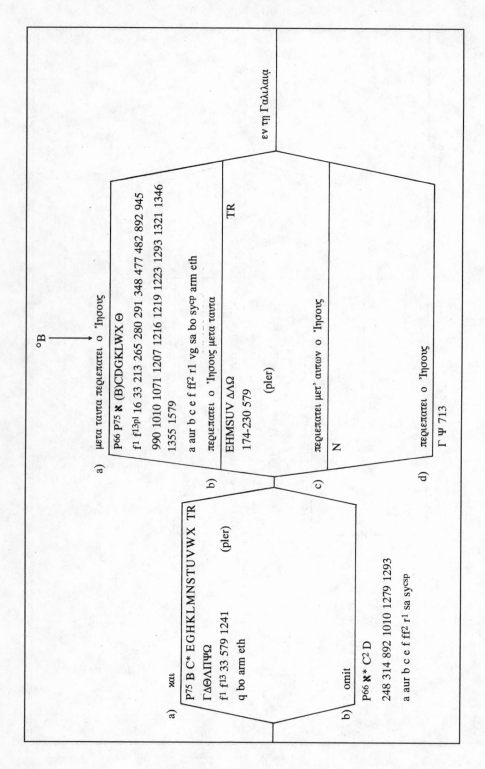

Exhibit C — John 4:21

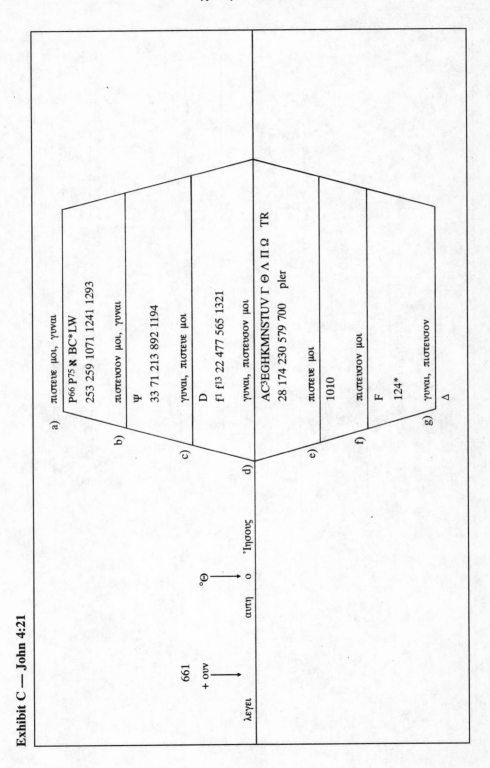

Exhibit D (*a*) — Luke 10:36

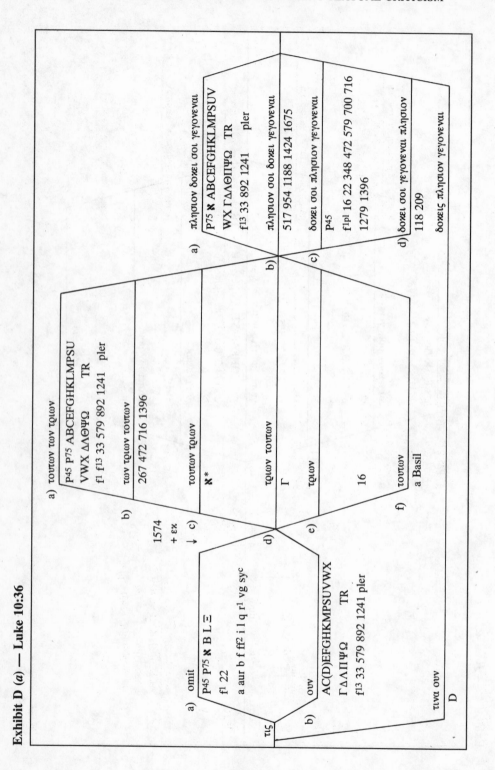

Exhibit D (b) — Luke 10:36

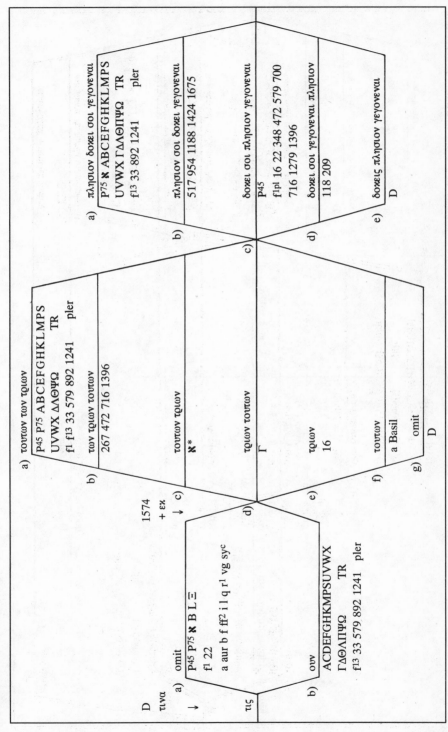

Exhibit E (*a*) — Luke 10:41b–42a

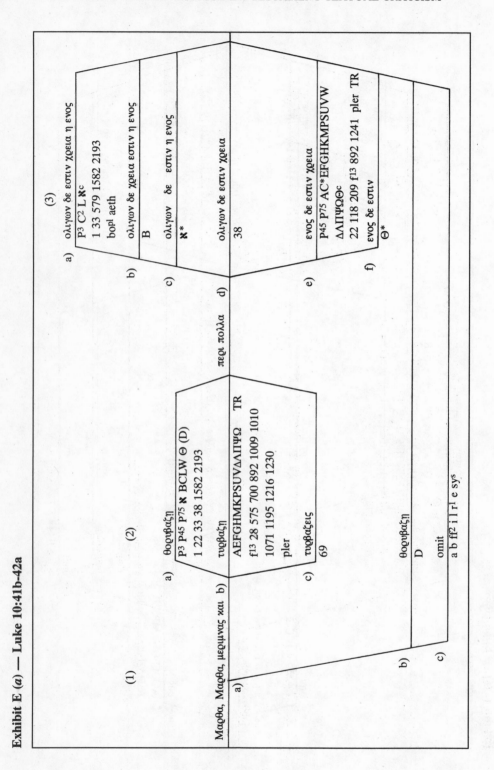

(1)

Μαρθα, Μαρθα, μεριμνας και

(2)

a) θορυβαζη
P3 P45 P75 ℵ BCLW Θ (D)
1 22 33 38 1582 2193

τυρβαζη
AEFGHMKPSUVΔΛΠΨΩ TR
f13 28 575 700 892 1009 1010
1071 1195 1216 1230
pler

c) τυρβαζεις
69

b) θορυβαζη
D

c) omit
a b ff2 i l r1 e sys

περι πολλα

(3)

a) ολιγων δε εστιν χρεια η ενος
P3 C2 L ℵc
1 33 579 1582 2193
bopl aeth

b) ολιγων δε χρεια εστιν η ενος
B

c) ολιγων δε εστιν η ενος
ℵ*

d) ολιγων δε εστιν χρεια
38

e) ενος δε εστιν χρεια
P45 P75 AC*EFGHKMPSUVW
ΔΛΠΨΩΘc
22 118 209 f13 892 1241 pler TR

f) ενος δε εστιν
Θ*

Exhibit E (*b*) — Luke 10:41b-42a

Μαρθα, Μαρθα,

a) μεριμνας και θορυβαζη περι πολλα, ενος δε εστιν χρεια
   P45 P75 C*W Θ

b) μεριμνας και τυρβαζη περι πολλα, ενος δε εστιν χρεια
   AEFGHKMPSUV Δ Λ Π Ψ Ω   TR
   f13 28 565 700 892 1009 1010 1071 1079 1195 1216
   1230 1241 1242   pler

c) μεθιμνας και θορυβαζη περι πολλα, ολιγων δε
   P3 ℵ BC2L
   1 33 579 1582 2193

d) μεθιμνας και θορυβαζη περι πολλα, ολιγων δε εστιν χρεια
   38

e) μεθιμνας και (θορυβαζη) περι πολλα
   c

f) (θορυβαζη) περι πολλα
   Augustine

g) θορυβαζη
   D

h) omit
   a b e ff2 i l r1 sys Ambrose Possidius

η ενος

εστιν χρεια
P3 ℵc C2L
1 33 579 1582 2193

χρεια εστιν
B

εστιν
ℵ*

Exhibit F (*a*) — John 7:16

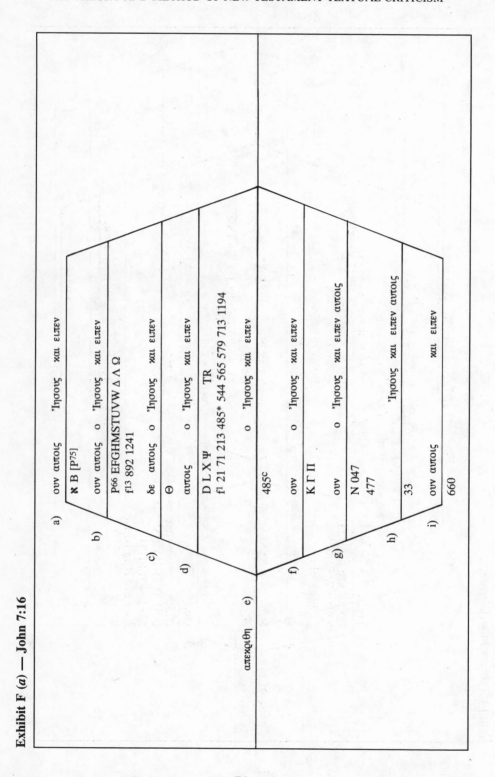

a) ουν αυτοις Ἰησους και ειπεν
  א B [P75]

b) ουν αυτοις ο Ἰησους και ειπεν
  P66 EFGHMSTUVW Δ Λ Ω
  f13 892 1241

c) δε αυτοις ο Ἰησους και ειπεν
  Θ

d) αυτοις ο Ἰησους και ειπεν
  D L X Ψ   TR
  f1 21 71 213 485* 544 565 579 713 1194

e) απεκριθη   ο Ἰησους και ειπεν
  485c

f) ουν αυτοις ο Ἰησους και ειπεν
  Κ Γ Π

g) ουν αυτοις ο Ἰησους και ειπεν
  N 047
  477

h) Ἰησους και ειπεν αυτοις
  33

i) ουν αυτοις Ἰησους και ειπεν
  660

Exhibit F (b) — John 7:16

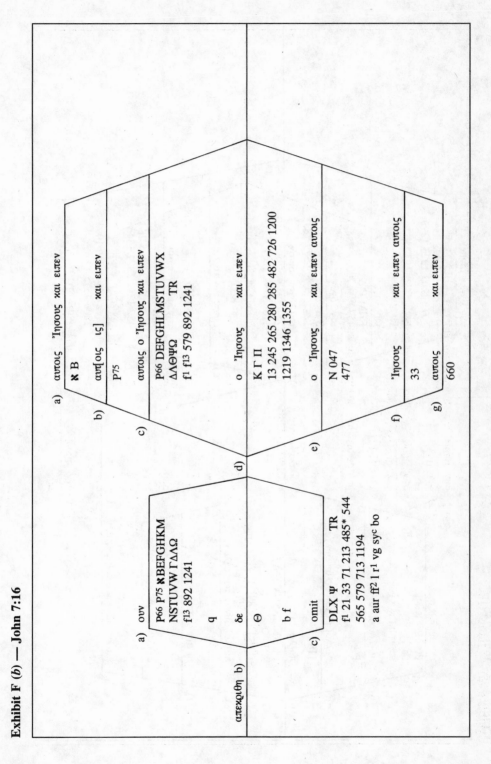

a) ουν

P66 P75 **ℵ**BEFGHKM
NSTUVW ΓΔΛΩ
f13 892 1241

q

δε

Θ

b) απεκριθη

b f

c) omit

DLX Ψ   TR
f1 21 33 71 213 485* 544
565 579 713 1194
a aur ff2 l r1 vg syc bo

a) αυτοις Ιησους και ειπεν
ℵB

b) αυτ[οις ις] και ειπεν
P75

c) αυτοις ο Ιησους και ειπεν
P66 DEFGHLMSTUVWX
ΔΛΘΨΩ   TR
f1 f13 579 892 1241

d)

e) ο Ιησους και ειπεν
ΚΓΠ
13 245 265 280 285 482 726 1200
1219 1346 1355

ο Ιησους και ειπεν αυτοις
N 047
477

f) Ιησους και ειπεν αυτοις
33

g) αυτοις και ειπεν
660

Exhibit G — John 7:40

εκ του οχλου ουν

a) εκ του οχλου ουν
P66c P75 א DLTWX
f1
a aur b l r1 vg

b) πολλοι εκ του οχλου οι
P66*

c) πολλοι εκ του οχλου ουν
118

d) πολλοι ουν εκ του οχλου
EGHKMNSUV Γ Δ
ΛΠΨΩ   TR
f13 33 579 892 1241   pler

e) πολλοι ουν εκ των οχλων
053

f) οι ουν εκ του οχλου
Θ

g) οι ουν εκ του οχλου πολλοι
124

h) πολλοι ουν ακουσαντες εκ του οχλου
047

ακουσαντες

των λογων τουτων

a) των λογων τουτων
P66c P75 BLNTU Ψ
f1 22 33 565 892 954
1071 1207 1223 1293

b) τουτων των λογων
G

c) των λογων

d) τον λογον
EHMΓ Δ*
157 604 700
S Δc Λ Ω   TR
124 230 399 579 783

e) τον λογον τουτον
213 291 945 990 1010
1188 1194 1241

f) αυτου των λογων τουτων
P66* א D

g) αυτου των λογων
Θ
498 1355

h) των λογων αυτου
KW Π
122 127 229 265 280 473
482 1219 1321 1346

i) τον λογον αυτου
f13 270 544 726 1093
1200 1375

j) αυτου τον λογον
124

Exhibit H — John 7:12

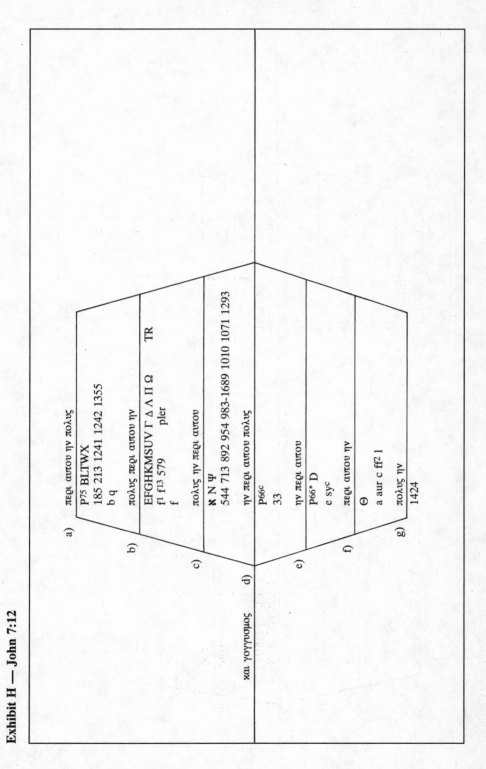

και γογγυσμος

a) περι αυτου ην πολυς
   P75 **BLTWX**
   185 213 1241 1242 1355
   b q

b) πολυς περι αυτου ην
   EFGHKMSUV Γ Δ Λ Π Ω   TR
   f1 f13 579   pler
   f

c) πολυς ην περι αυτου

d) ην περι αυτου πολυς
   ℵ N Ψ
   544 713 892 954 983-1689 1010 1071 1293

   P66c
   33

e) ην περι αυτου
   P66* D
   e syc

f) περι αυτου ην
   Θ
   a aur c ff2 l

g) πολυς ην
   1424

PART III

CRITIQUE OF CURRENT THEORY AND METHOD

CHAPTER 5

THE TWENTIETH-CENTURY INTERLUDE IN NEW TESTAMENT TEXTUAL CRITICISM[1]

Eldon Jay Epp

I. Introduction

At the time of his death, William Henry Paine Hatch (2 August 1875–11 November 1972) had been a member of the Society of Biblical Literature for sixty-seven years — longer than any other living person — and doubtless was the oldest current member of the Society. When he served as president of SBL in 1938, he already had been on the membership rolls for 33 years. Our purpose here, however, is not to recount or to assess the life and work of this distinguished American textual critic,[2] instructive as that approach might be; but Professor Hatch's long life coincides almost exactly with the period of NT textual criticism which I wish to examine, for he was born within a year of Tischendorf's death (which occurred 7 December 1874); in the same year as the death of S. P. Tregelles (1875); and at the time when Westcott and Hort were in the late stages of their nearly thirty-year project to produce the text of the NT "in the original Greek," which finally was published in 1881 — when Hatch was just six years old. As all will recognize, Tischendorf, Tregelles, and Westcott-Hort were among the foremost figures in the final overthrow of the tyrannical *textus receptus* (TR) in favor of older and better NT MSS (though, as a matter of fact, Karl Lachmann some fifty years earlier — in 1831 — had effected the first clean break with the TR). Simply stated, an old era had come to its end, the era of the TR, and a whole new era of NT textual criticism had been fully established in the last decades of the nineteenth century, culminating in the work of Westcott-Hort; and the lifetime of our distinguished — and lamented — contemporary, W. H. P. Hatch, bridges that period between the self-confident, optimistic, and resolute textual criticism of the late nineteenth and early twentieth centuries and the diffuse, indeterminate, and eclectic NT textual criticism of our own present and recent past. Indeed, I have

---

1. The W. H. P. Hatch Memorial Lecture, The Society of Biblical Literature, 11 November 1973, delivered at the Palmer House, Chicago, Illinois.
2. Nearly all of Hatch's published volumes dealt with MSS of the Greek NT or with Syriac MS studies, as did many of his articles. A bibliography of his writings appeared in the Festschrift for his seventieth birthday (Shepherd and Johnson 1946: 179-82). Something of the significance of Hatch's work for NT textual criticism may be indicated by the index to Metzger 1968a, for here Hatch is referred to 15 times, while no other scholar, including the great figures of the field, is referred to more than 11 times.

ventured to call this period the twentieth-century interlude in NT textual criticism, and I use the term "interlude," not in its everyday sense as a period of waiting between two events, often with the implication of merely marking time or of inactivity, but in its classical meaning in theater and music as a performance between the acts of a play or the parts of a composition.

To characterize twentieth-century textual criticism as an interlude is, on the one hand, to suggest something negative: it affirms that the critical work of the period is not a main feature, but a subsidiary or a secondary and minor performance following a portion of the main event. On the other hand, there is a positive aspect, for interlude implies — if not demands — that another major act is to follow, and it is this to which the interlude leads and for which it prepares. It does not mean inactivity, but if it is a pause or an interval, it is a meaningful and preparatory pause.

Certainly for NT textual criticism the twentieth century has been anything but a period of inactivity. To attempt here a survey of this period in terms either of its rich yield of new MSS or manuscript studies or its extensive bibliographical contributions not only would be inappropriate but would be too easy a way out and would fail to strike at the central issues. Yet the productivity of the period is obvious from mere mention, for example, of the Oxyrhynchus papyri (1896ff.), the Chester Beatty papyri (1930-31), and the Bodmer papyri (1956ff.), which together represent a 600% increase over the number of NT papyri known at the turn of the century; this productivity is evident also in the isolation of the lectionary text and the wide-ranging work on the versions, and by recalling the tedious labors expended in the production of new critical editions. All of this amounts to a sizable achievement, involving the tireless efforts of hundreds of scholars, not the least of whom were W. H. P. Hatch and other members of our own Society past and present. Clearly, it is not my intention to minimize or to denigrate these numerous and worthwhile accomplishments; yet the twentieth century, as far as we have lived and worked in it, has been an *interlude* between the grand achievement of Westcott-Hort and whatever significant second act is to follow. What that succeeding act might be or ought to be will occupy us presently, but that it has not occurred in the years since Westcott-Hort must be established first.

II. Evidences of the Interlude

A. *Lack of Progress in Popular Critical Editions*

The first and clearest indication that we have passed through and still find ourselves in an interlude is found in the critical hand-editions of the NT produced since WH. There have been many, but nine or ten stand out as the most widely known and used, and they are the following, listed in the chronological order of their first editions:

1. R. F. Weymouth, 1886.
2. B. Weiss, 1894-1900.
3. Eberhard Nestle, 1898; 25th ed. by Erwin Nestle and K. Aland, 1963.
4. British and Foreign Bible Society, 1904 [= Nestle, 4th ed.]; 2d ed. by
    G. D. Kilpatrick, 1958.

5. A. Souter, 1910; revised ed., 1947.

[6. Hermann von Soden, 1913 — not a hand-edition, though such a smaller edition of the text with a short apparatus appeared the same year.]

7. H. J. Vogels, 1920 (+ Vulgate 1922); 4th ed., 1955.

8. A. Merk, 1933; 9th ed., revised, 1965.

9. J. M. Bover, 1943; 5th ed., 1968.

10. United Bible Societies' Greek New Testament, 1966; 2d ed., 1968; 3d ed., 1975.

Most would agree that, besides the WH text, the various editions of Nestle (and NA) have received the greatest use in the past generation, though Souter has had wide usage in England and in Anglican circles, and the editions of Vogels, Merk, and Bover have served Catholic scholars; in our own day, NA and the recent UBS *Greek New Testament* are the leading critical hand-editions of the Greek NT.

When these most popular editions are analyzed and compared, the first surprise is that two of them, Vogels and Souter — even in their later editions — side with the TR in textual character rather than with WH (or with NA) and belong, therefore, to the old era of the TR rather than to the current period of textual criticism. This is shown, for example, by K. W. Clark's test of Mark 1–5, where Souter showed 191 differences from WH, of which 168 were TR readings, and where Vogels showed 103 differences from WH, of which seventy-five were TR readings. It is shown also by J. Harold Greenlee's comparison of five current critical texts with the TR in eleven chapters from various sections of the NT; the differences from the TR were as follows: NA = 233; Merk = 160; Bover = 111; Vogels = 67; and Souter = 47, showing Vogels and Souter strikingly close to the TR when compared with NA.[3] Other tests show similar results.[4] Thus, we may safely disregard the texts (though not the apparatuses) of Souter and Vogels, for they show insufficient signs of having participated in the Lachmann/Westcott-Hort overthrow of the TR.

The NA, Merk, and Bover editions form a group fairly close to WH in textual character, and among them NA is the closest to WH. This is demonstrated, again by K. W. Clark, in a comparison throughout Mark of the 21st edition of Nestle (1952) with WH, which revealed only eighty-nine variants between the two texts; yet of these only thirty-two were "substantial" and only twelve involved a difference in meaning. He reports, curiously enough, that of the seventy-five changes made in the text of Mark through twenty-one editions of Nestle (1898 to 1952) thirty-five

---

3. Clark 1956: 31-33. Clark reports a more recent test, with similar results, in 1968: 158-60. Greenlee's study is reported by Aland 1959: 719-20. (It should be noted that a simple counting of gross differences from the TR, or any standard, is considered now a questionable procedure; rather, the variation-units common to two or more of all the members in the comparison must be determined and total agreement and disagreement taken into account — see below.)

4. Aland (1969: 720-21) compares the Marcan text in four current editions with WH, and — counting significant variants — the differences from WH are as follows: Vogels = 239; Bover = 160; Merk = 128; and Nestle = 65, implying that Vogels is significantly closer to the TR than, e.g., Nestle (on the reasonable assumption that WH and the TR are at opposite poles). Another comparison reported by Aland (1967: 59-61) shows that throughout the NT WH has 558 variants from NA, while Vogels has 1996 variants from NA. (Bover shows 1161, and Merk 770 variants from NA.)

were restorations of WH readings. Clark's conclusion, on the basis of Mark, is that the 1952 Nestle "still rests heavily upon Westcott-Hort" (1956: 34-35). Kurt Aland made a similar comparison of NA[25] with WH and with the latest editions of Merk and Bover, and he reached a similar result: when NA[25] is compared with texts such as those of von Soden, Vogels, and even Tischendorf, the texts of Bover, Merk, and WH are markedly closer to NA[25] than are the others, and of the group consisting of Bover, Merk, and WH, it is WH which is the nearest to NA[25] in its textual character. The statistics show that throughout the NT von Soden is farthest from NA[25], with 2047 variants; then Vogels with 1996; Tischendorf with 1262; Bover with 1161; Merk with 770; and finally WH with only 558 variants from NA[25] (1967: 59-61). An earlier comparison of significant variants in the Marcan text of WH with those of the NA[25]/Merk/Bover cluster yielded the following results: Bover showed 160 differences from WH; Merk 128; but NA[25] only sixty-five differences from WH [Vogels showed 239 variations and may serve as a control].[5] The conclusion is clear: These three most widely used Greek New Testaments of the mid-twentieth century (NA, Merk, and Bover) "show little change from Westcott-Hort and only rarely present a significant variant" (Clark 1956: 36).

If one now considers the recent and increasingly widely used UBS *Greek New Testament,* it will be observed at once that its editors began their work on the basis of WH (Preface to 1st ed., v) and that the text of the UBS edition is close to the text of Codex Vaticanus (B) — Westcott-Hort's primary MS — and close, therefore, to Westcott-Hort's text (Moir 1967-68).

What all of this means is that none of the currently popular hand-editions of the Greek NT takes us beyond WH in any substantive way as far as textual character is concerned, for two of them stand — anachronistically — with the TR, which was the WH opposition, and the others stand with WH. What progress, then, have we made if "even the modern editions which claim to break new ground still in general present the text of Westcott-Hort" (Aland 1959: 721)? We are compelled to face the simple but pointed question: Is it adequate to have as our best NT text one which, in essence, is more than ninety years old? Westcott-Hort's text was based (a) on no papyrus MSS, whereas more than eighty of these early witnesses now are available; (b) on perhaps forty-five uncials, whereas nearly 270 of these important documents now are known; (c) on about 150 minuscules [though more were known], whereas now the number is approaching 2800; and (d) on an unknown, but small, number of lectionaries, whereas more than 2100 have now been catalogued. Moreover, since Westcott-Hort's day, our knowledge of ancient versions and patristic quotations has been advanced significantly.

Some of us were startled at the one-hundredth meeting of the SBL in 1964 when Kurt Aland employed what seemed to be an overly dramatic conclusion to his paper on "The Significance of the Papyri for Progress in New Testament Research." His final sentences were: "*None* of us would entrust himself to a ship of the year 1881 in order to cross the Atlantic, even if the ship were renovated or he was promised

5. Aland 1959: 721. The same cluster (NA[25]/Merk/Bover) emerges when distance from the TR is tested; see the statistics of Greenlee, cited above.

danger money. Why then do we still do so in NT textual criticism?"[6] The question, however, *was* appropriate then; unfortunately, now — nearly a decade later — it is still both a valid and an embarrassing question.

B. Lack of Progress toward a Theory and History of the Earliest NT Text

One response to the fact that our popular critical texts are still so close to that of WH might be that the kind of text arrived at by them and supported so widely by subsequent criticism is in fact and without question the best attainable NT text; yet every textual critic knows that this similarity of text indicates, rather, that we have made little progress in textual *theory* since Westcott-Hort; that we simply do not know how to make a definitive determination as to what the best text is; that we do not have a clear picture of the transmission and alteration of the text in the first few centuries; and, accordingly, that the Westcott-Hort kind of text has maintained its dominant position largely by default. Günther Zuntz enforces the point in a slightly different way when he says that "the agreement between our modern editions does not mean that we have recovered the original text. It is due to the simple fact that their editors . . . follow one narrow section of the evidence, namely, the non-Western Old Uncials" (1953: 8). This lack of progress toward a theory and history of the earliest NT text is a second strong indication that the twentieth century has been an interlude in NT textual criticism.

The quest for the early history of the text of the NT has its own and surprisingly inconclusive history. The process of sorting and grouping the thousands of manuscript witnesses to the NT text is fundamental to the discovery of its history and development, and such groupings have been attempted ever since J. A. Bengel in 1725 proposed a classification of the textual witnesses into "companies," "families," "tribes," and "nations" so that MSS could be "weighed" for their evidential value rather than merely counted. As new manuscript discoveries were made, particularly discoveries of early uncials, the grouping of MSS led to the separation of the relatively few early MSS from the mass of later ones, and eventually the process reached its climactic point of development and its classical statement in the work of Westcott and Hort (1881-1882), and particularly in their [actually Hort's] clear and firm view of the early history of the NT text. This clear picture was formed from Hort's isolation of essentially three [though he said four] basic textual groups or text-types. On the basis largely of Greek manuscript evidence from the middle of the fourth century and later and from the early versional and patristic evidence, two of these, the so-called Neutral and Western text-types, were regarded as competing texts from about the middle of the second century, while the third, now designated Byzantine, was a later, conflate, and polished ecclesiastical text. The lateness of the Byzantine text-type was established from test passages in which the Byzantine variants represent a conflation of the Western and the Neutral [i.e., Alexandrian/Egyptian] variants and from the fact that the Greek and Latin Fathers up to the middle of

---

6. 1965: 346. The article was updated in "Die Konsequenzen der neueren Handschriftenfunde für die neutestamentliche Textkritik" (Aland 1967: 180-201), though without this concluding illustration.

the third century support one or another of the pre-Byzantine texts, but do not support the conflate Byzantine variants or any other distinctively Byzantine readings; the logical conclusion was that the Byzantine text had not yet been formed by the middle of the third century.[7] This left essentially two basic text-types competing in the earliest traceable period of textual transmission, the Western and the Neutral, but this historical reconstruction could not be carried further so as to reveal — on historical grounds — which of the two was closer to and therefore more likely to represent the original NT text.

Actually, Hort made it quite clear that "the earliest readings which can be fixed chronologically" belong to the Western text and, moreover, that "the most widely spread text of Ante-Nicene times" was the Western (2.120; cf. 126). Now when he argues that the text-groups which can be documented as pre-Byzantine are closer to the original than is the Byzantine, his argument is convincing; however, it requires some elaborate gymnastics in argumentation to move then, as he does, to the contention that the earliest attested text, the Western, is *not* closer to the original than is the Neutral, whose documentation is in fact later. Anyone who looks again at Hort will observe that he presents his case in such a way as to prejudice his readers against the Western text (by describing it as given to paraphrase and as otherwise corrupt) well before he discusses the "pure" or Neutral text from the standpoint of its historical reconstruction. Hence, when Hort has worked back to a situation sometime in the second century when an early Western text was competing with an early Neutral text, and when historical reconstruction fails to yield a solution, subjective (or "internal") judgments enter to render a decision as to whether the Western or the Neutral is superior in the quality of its text and therefore closer to the original. The same test of "prevailing internal excellence" (2.193) which was used negatively to discredit the Western is now applied to the Neutral, with the result that "certain peculiar omissions excepted, the Western text is probably always corrupt as compared with the Non-Western text" (2.194). What we see, then, is that Westcott-Hort's text is (a) based partly on a clearly delineated view of the history of the NT text — two early texts competing in the second-century church,[8] one corrupted by paraphrastic expansions and the other virtually untouched in its course of transmission from the original — and (b) based partly on subjective judgments about the respective quality of those earliest texts.

The pointed question for us is, What methodological advance have we made over this scheme? Tedious and impressive labors have been expended since 1881 on the great Neutral uncials, B and ℵ; a small library has been produced on the Western centerpiece, Codex Bezae (D), and on its OL and OS allies; vigorous and lengthy debates have focused on the originality of Neutral versus Western variants; and

---

7. Westcott-Hort 1881: 2.91-119. The Westcott-Hort terms "Neutral" and "Western" are used throughout this paper for convenience, though in full recognition of their inadequacy. The most common alternatives for "Neutral" are "Alexandrian" and "Egyptian," though "Beta" is preferred by some; "Delta" has been proposed in place of "Western," but neither it nor any other term has been successful in supplanting the only partially accurate "Western." [See now chapter 14.]

8. See Westcott-Hort 2.112-13, 222-23, where the 2d, and at times the early 2d, century is in view.

numerous new discoveries have been brought to bear on these several questions. Yet, nearly a century later we still affirm the general superiority of the Neutral text-type and the generally secondary character of the Western, and we do so largely on the same grounds as did Hort: a similar picture of the early history of the text and a similar subjective judgment about the respective quality of the two early text-groups.

If these statements appear too sweeping and somewhat oversimplified, it should be added at once that even the discovery of P75, so extraordinarily significant in several respects, does not — as many seem to think — solve this puzzle of Neutral versus Western, nor does it in this respect carry us beyond Westcott-Hort. P75 takes us back to about AD 200 and shows us a text — as much of it as we have — which is virtually identical with the mid-fourth-century Codex B. To be sure, we have no extant Greek or versional MSS of this early date on the Western side, though we do have quotations from some of the Fathers of this period, which — with all their complications and without getting into the vexing complexities of the OS and OL as witnesses to an early Western text — are perhaps evidence enough of a second-century Western text. Even with P75, then, we still can move no farther back with a historical reconstruction than Hort did. We can say with confidence, of course, that B faithfully represents a text extant, not only in 350, but already around 200, but P75 does not answer the question whether this B-type of text (now including P75) does or does not represent a recension; twentieth-century scholarship had viewed B as the product of a fourth-century recension (see Clark 1956: 37), and P75 rules this out; yet the B-text may represent a late second-century recension — or it may not. The question is pushed back, but not settled by P75. We are still faced, as were Westcott-Hort, with two early, competing texts whose epicenters are represented in B (or now P75) and in D.[9] How is this in any essential and substantive way an advance beyond Westcott-Hort?

Someone will remind us, however, that a fourth-century major text-type, the Caesarean, was isolated two generations after Westcott-Hort and will suggest, first, that this provides further material for reconstructing the early history of the NT text and, second, that its discovery represents significant progress not only in the history but also in the theory of the text. Certainly the studies in and around the Caesarean text have contributed immensely to our knowledge of individual MSS and of some families, but it is my contention that the Caesarean text affair is another and rather striking evidence that the twentieth century has been an interlude in NT textual criticism.

This was indicated already in 1945 by Bruce Metzger in his concise and incisive survey of the development and criticism of the Caesarean text when he concluded that "it must be acknowledged that at present the Caesarean text is disintegrating."[10] A major reason for such a conclusion was the growing recognition — encouraged most notably by Ayuso's work — that what had been called the Caesarean text by Streeter, the Lakes, and others must be divided into (1) a primitive, pre-Caesarean text and (2) a recensional, or properly Caesarean text, each of which

---

9. Metzger (1966/67: 374) remarks that "the general lineaments of the textual theory of Westcott and Hort have been confirmed rather than weakened by the discovery of P75."

10. Metzger 1945: 483; reprinted, with some updating to about 1960, in 1963b (see p. 67).

shows cohesion and homogeneity within itself, as well as a close relationship with the other.[11] This, essentially, is where the matter has rested for the past thirty-five years. Most recently, however, a 1973 dissertation by Larry W. Hurtado[12] seems to demonstrate that at least in Mark (where most of the work on the Caesarean text has been done) the validity of this earlier or pre-Caesarean text as a distinct text-type is seriously — and I think convincingly — called into question. This, of course, is not a new view, for two decades ago C. S. C. Williams, for example, offered his opinion that "any hopes . . . that here [in the Caesarean MSS] we should find a pre-Byzantine textual type independent of and as valuable as the 'Western' and the Alexandrian [or Egyptian = Neutral] seem now very remote" (1953: 389); furthermore, a decade ago, before this very Society, Kurt Aland expressed his judgment that no Caesarean text-type existed (1965: 337). Nevertheless, Hurtado's more cautious conclusion is based not only on the latest quantitative methods for determining manuscript relationships, but also on collations and analyses *throughout* Mark and not merely in sample chapters; therefore, the negative conclusions concerning the Caesarean text receive both a broader and firmer basis than previously possible. Hurtado's study focuses on the Washington Codex (W) in Mark, which traditionally has been classified as Caesarean in 5:31–16:20 and has been taken, along with P[45], fam. 1, and fam. 13, as a leading witness to the pre-Caesarean text. At the same time, Codex Koridethi (Θ) has been taken as the leading member of the later or Caesarean text proper. His thorough quantitative analysis shows that W and Θ, assessed chapter by chapter in Mark, have an average agreement in chapters 5 through 16 of 40%, far below the 70% established norm for significant intra-text-type relationship,[13] which means that if Θ is a good representative of the Caesarean text, then W cannot be a Caesarean witness. Furthermore, the element common to Θ and W is mainly Western in its character, with the result that both show considerable affinity with D, the leading Western witness: W and D show an average agreement through all the chapters in Mark of 40% (36% in chapters 5–16), while Θ and D show an average agreement of 48% (51% in chapters 5–16). This means that if W, with its 39% average agreement with Θ throughout Mark (and 40% in chapters 5–16), were to be classified as a Caesarean witness, D would be a better Caesarean witness![14] Moreover, the nearly 50% agreement between Θ and D might suggest that Θ should be taken as a secondary witness to the Western text.[15]

Second, the quantitative relationships among W, P[45], and fam. 13 are such that, in 103 variation-units where P[45] is extant in Mark 6–9, W and P[45] show a 68% agreement; W and fam. 13 show a 60% agreement in these same variation-units, and for P[45] and fam. 13 the figure is 59%; no other control MS shows more than 42%

11. I rely on Metzger 1963b: 63-64, 124-26.

12. "Codex Washingtonianus in the Gospel of Mark: Its Textual Relationships and Scribal Characteristics," Ph.D. dissertation, Case Western Reserve University, 1973. [Hurtado 1981 represents a substantially revised version.]

13. Hurtado relies on the general quantitative method and criteria of Colwell 1969: 56-61, 163.

14. Hurtado 1973: 130-31. The percentages have been recalculated from his charts (267-74). [See now Hurtado 1981: 43-45 and 24-45 generally; cf. 90-94 for the charts.]

15. Hurtado 1973: 245, 249. [See now Hurtado 1981: 44-45.]

agreement with either W or P[45] in this section of Mark. In chapters 5–16 of Mark, W and fam. 13 show a 55% agreement; but notice that fam. 13 also shows a 55% agreement with the TR — 56% over all of Mark; but only a 46% agreement with Θ; 33% with B; and 32% with D.

All these figures suggest that W and P[45] are primary members of a text-group (since their agreement approaches the 70% norm), while fam. 13 is (at best) a loose third member.[16] These figures mean, furthermore, that W and P[45] (and fam. 13) do not have a significantly close relationship with the so-called Caesarean text of Θ, that they represent "in no way an early stage of the text of Θ,"[17] and that the term "pre-Caesarean" is inappropriate and should be abandoned. In short, the so-called "pre-Caesarean" witnesses are neither pre-Caesarean nor Caesarean at all.[18] It has, of course, been argued by others that the Caesarean text was not Caesarean (cf., e.g., Colwell 1969: 54), but our concern is not with the name or its geographical appropriateness; rather, Hurtado's point — and ours — is that the so-called "pre-Caesarean" witnesses are not related significantly to the so-called "later Caesarean" witnesses, with the result that the P[45]-W line of text has no continuity with the Θ-line of text and, furthermore, that the P[45]-W line stops with W and leads no farther.

If, however, these former Caesarean witnesses are not Caesarean, what are they? Codex Θ, as we have seen, drifts off toward the Western camp; fam. 13 drifts off distinctly toward the Byzantine text when compared with the leading Neutral and Western representatives; and W and P[45] constitute a textual group with no close relationship (a) to the Neutral text (P[45] and B have a 42% agreement; W and B show a 34% agreement in Mark 5–16, 32% overall), or (b) to the Western text (P[45] and D have a 38% agreement; W and D 36% in Mark 5–16, 40% overall), or (c) to the Byzantine (P[45] and the TR have a 40% agreement; W and the TR show a 38% agreement in Mark 5–16, 36% overall), though Hurtado thinks he can argue that the P[45]-W kind of text is basically and was originally — that is, in its early stages of development — nearer to the Neutral, and that it later developed toward the Byzantine type (as evidenced by fam. 13).[19] Regardless of this last point, the result in broad strokes reveals, first, a disintegrating Caesarean text, with its presumed components falling back into place among the other established text-groupings, and shows us, second, an early kind of text (P[45] with W) which is almost equidistant in its agreement from those textual types designated Neutral and Western. Every contemporary textual critic knows that to locate a MS or a text-type by describing it as "midway" between Neutral and Western is no way to determine a MS's relationships or to define a text-type; if any did not know this, Colwell made the point in a forceful manner fifteen years ago in his much used article on "Locating a Newly-Discovered Manuscript" (1959; repr. 1969: 26-44; see 36-37). Nevertheless, the quantitative demonstration of this midway position of P[45]-W — a distinctive textual pair — does support in a rather striking way the 1961 proposition, also of Colwell, that the so-called "pre-Caesarean" text is "a proto-type, an early stage in the process which produced

16. Hurtado 1973: iii. [See now Hurtado 1981: 86-89. He does not treat fam. 1.]
17. Hurtado 1973: 251; cf. 191-92, 248. [See now Hurtado 1981: 88; cf. 89.]
18. Hurtado 1973: 191-92, 251. [See now Hurtado 1981: 88.]
19. Hurtado 1973: iii, 250. [See now Hurtado 1981: 87, 88-89.]

the mature Beta [= Neutral] and Delta [= Western] text-types" (Colwell 1969: 54). This observation undoubtedly is correct; the mistakenly designated pre-Caesarean witnesses attest one kind of text — a "midway" text — which existed in that early period when the Neutral and Western texts represented the competing extremes of a spectrum of texts whose intervening members in varying degrees shared the characteristics of each extreme.

What, then, is our picture of the earliest documented century or two of the NT text? Were there text-types or not? Kurt Aland denies that *any* text-types existed in that early period in Egypt, where all the papyri were found, because he thinks that the NT papyri show that *numerous* distinctive texts existed side by side in the same area in the same period. Hence, Aland views P45, P46, P66, P75, and the other early papyri as representatives of these numerous individual texts — but not text-types — which were to be found in the second and third centuries.[20] Such a view would seem to take us beyond, or perhaps behind, Westcott-Hort in the sense that Hort's two early text-types have been replaced by many texts. But is Aland correct in this view, and does it really move us beyond Westcott-Hort, as Aland claims? As is often the case, we are indebted once again to Ernest Colwell for pointing out that Hort, in his basic theory of the text and its history, allowed for a range of early texts by his insistence on an early ancestor for the Neutral text (something perhaps like our P75), an archetype of an early revised form of the Neutral text (perhaps like our P66?), and an early ancestor for the Western text (maybe something like our P45?) (Colwell 1969: 156-57; Westcott-Hort 1881: 2.122, 220-23). It seems clear, then, that Aland's claim[21] that the discovery of early papyri invalidates Westcott-Hort's whole scheme and places us in an entirely new situation is not well founded; rather, the papyri provide hard documents to replace, roughly speaking, a number of Hort's theoretical ones.

What picture emerges, then, of the first two centuries of NT textual transmission? It can be argued, I think, that text-types, as Hort conceived them, surely were in the process of development and did exist, for when we survey this period from AD 200 to 300 we find a series of papyri, notably P45, P46, P66, and P75, but also fragments of many others, to which should be added some early uncials, such as 0171, 0189, 0212, and 0220, all dated within the third century.[22] Actually, there are thirty-one papyri of the Gospels, Acts, or Epistles which quite certainly can be dated 300 or earlier, thirty-seven if those of the third/fourth century are included; and four uncial fragments from the second and third centuries.[23] It would be unwise

---

20. Aland 1965: 334-37; cf. Colwell 1969: 55, who says that ". . . very few, if any, text-types were established by that time [AD 200]."

21. Aland 1965: 336-37; contrast his earlier view (1959: 721-22, 730-31), implying that little if any progress had been made and that we stand within the Westcott-Hort era.

22. 0171 is now dated 300; in addition to the fragments containing Luke 21:45-47, 50-53; 22:44-56, 61-63, additional portions of this MS have been identified, containing several verses from Matthew 10 (see Aland 1969: 8); the MS was published by Treu 1966b, who dates it ca. 300. MS 0189 has been redated 2d/3d century by C. H. Roberts (see Aland 1969: 8).

23. The dates are those accepted by Aland 1967: 104-6. Papyri of the Apocalypse, of which two are from this early period, are not included, nor is the Apocalypse taken into account in any of our preceding discussions.

to claim definitive identifications of textual character on the basis of a few variants in a dozen lines of text, which themselves are often incomplete, yet most of these papyri have been identified variously as Neutral (notably P75, but also the fragmentary P1, P4, P13, P15, P16, P20, P23, P28, P39, P40, P49, P52, P64, P65, and P67), or as Western (the fragmentary P5, P29, P37, P38, P48, and also 0171), or as midway between (notably P45, P46, and P66, and the fragmentary P22, P27, P30, P32, P53, P69, and P72) in terms of their textual character.[24]

Although we are told that text-types, subsequent to the discovery of these early witnesses, should no longer be classified according to the much later codices B and D, it is true nonetheless that our extant materials and our much enhanced hindsight reveal *only two clear textual streams or trajectories* through all of our material from the first four centuries or so of textual transmission, and these two trajectories are what we have long called the Neutral (or Alexandrian/Egyptian) and the Western text-types. The Neutral line is the clearest, plotted first from P75, then perhaps through P23, P20, 0220, P50, etc., to Codex B and thence on through the centuries, e.g., to Codex L (eighth century), MSS 33 (ninth century), 1739 (tenth century), and 579 (thirteenth century). The Western line takes us, for example, from P5 and P29 through P48, P38, P37, and 0171, then to codices D and D_p, and thence on through the centuries to F_p and G_p (ninth century) and MSS 614 and 383 (thirteenth century). The other extensive and early papyri (P45, P46, P66, and also the others in the "midway" category) stand between these extremes and, as far as we know, develop no "midway" trajectories of their own, except for P45, which leads abortively to Codex W, but that line leads no further (as we have seen). Rather, beginning perhaps in the general period of Codex W (ca. 400), the two extremes of the early spectrum, namely the Neutral and the Western, became confluent, producing a form of text represented in the gospel portion of Codex Alexandrinus (A; fifth century) and forming the Byzantine line which carries on through the centuries, for example, in the uncials Ω, V, H_a, H, L_{ap}, S, and most of the minuscules. Naturally, this rough sketch should not be understood to mean that the MSS mentioned under each of the three categories above necessarily had any *direct* connections one with another; rather, they stand as randomly surviving members of these three broad streams of textual tradition. Moreover, this sketch does not include the versions or the patristic witnesses, which — as suggested earlier — could reasonably locate some additional early points, especially on the Western textual trajectory.

Now, to argue as we have in terms of recognizable textual streams or trajectories, which can be plotted from known points and also point backwards from them, may not in any way *prove* that text-types (as we commonly define that term) existed in the period of 200 to 300 or so, but the perspective which is provided by these extended trajectories (and the lack of them) is a valuable aid to sorting out the wide range of texts in the earliest documented period and in determining (albeit by hindsight) the extent to which these various early texts were utilized and the relative degree of influence which they brought to bear on the developing lines of NT textual

---

24. I simply have taken over the classification of Metzger 1968a: 247-55, though I have held to H. A. Sanders's judgment (1926: 223) that P37 is Western.

transmission. Is it mere accident that our spectrum of the earliest texts, comprised of some forty papyri and uncials from around AD 300 and earlier, issues in *only two* distinct lines of development, each at one extreme of that spectrum? Some will say "yes," but I would suggest, rather, that the sorting process, of which only a portion remains open to our view, functioned as though it were under some centrifugal force and resulted in the concentration and consolidation of textual masses at the outer — and opposite — edges of the textual spectrum. The reasons for this may be obscure, but the phenomenon itself is visible enough.

To be sure, the question of originality is not aided materially by this approach, for we cannot move easily behind the series of earliest papyri to the situation in the first century or so after the writing of the Gospels, Acts, and Epistles, although the citations in the sub-Apostolic Fathers may be of some help in that direction. Hence, the question which faced Westcott-Hort remains for us: Is the original text something nearer to the Neutral or to the Western kind of text? And what about the development of these two competing text-types? Did the range of early texts now available to us develop laterally, starting from something like P^{75}, then undergo changes toward texts like those in P^{45}, P^{46}, and P^{66}, and finally yield a Western text (through, e.g., P^5, P^{38}, P^{48}) like that of Codex D? Or was the original text at the Western extreme and did it then move laterally in the other direction toward something like P^{75}? Or, as a third model, was the original one of those "midway" texts something like P^{45} or P^{66}, and did it develop in two lateral directions — toward the Neutral on the one hand and toward the Western on the other? This is where we stand, and this is precisely where Westcott-Hort stood; Hort resolved the issue, not on the basis of the *history of the text,* but in terms of the presumed *inner quality* of the texts and on grounds of largely subjective judgments of that quality.

Actually, the extension of the trajectories backwards to include the earliest Fathers available for any extensive NT textual evidence (Justin Martyr, Tatian [= Diatessaron], Marcion, Irenaeus, Clement of Alexandria, Tertullian, Origen, and Cyprian) would prompt us to say — as Westcott-Hort did — that the earliest text known to us is Western in its character and, furthermore, that most of these earliest patristic witnesses attest that Western kind of text; again, we are left in the company of Westcott-Hort, and in this respect the extraordinary papyrus discoveries of the past three quarters of a century do not alter our basic dilemma as to whether Neutral or Western better represents the original NT text — at least they provide no new objective criteria to bear on the solution.

This approach in terms of developing streams or trajectories in the earliest period is quite a different approach and involves a different conception from that of Kurt Aland, who has written so frequently of the significance which the papyri have for modern textual studies. It may not be entirely fair to Aland to say that he views the earliest documented period of textual transmission in somewhat *static* terms, yet this is the impression made, for example, when he says: "The simple fact that all these papyri, with their various distinctive characteristics, did exist side by side, in the same ecclesiastical province . . . is the best argument against the existence of any text-types" (1965: 336-37). Aland does, in another passage, speak of the early papyri as evidence that "the NT Greek text had been circulating in many and divergent forms, proceeding in different directions, at about the same time, in the same ecclesiastical province" (334); hence, it might be more accurate to say that Aland sees the period of the early papyri as a slice of time largely isolated from the preceding and especially from the subsequent period, for he states that "it is impossible to fit the papyri, from the time prior to the fourth century, into these two text-types [i.e., the Egyptian (= Neutral) and the Byzantine], to say nothing of trying to fit them into other types" (336). The period of the early papyri, it seems, is viewed as an archipelagic phenomenon and one insulated from the period of the great uncials which followed, for Aland finds no continuity between those early papyri and the fourth-century and later textual developments. The term "static" still may be appropriate, then, if one considers that he sees the phenomenon of the early papyri as failing to interact in and with the subsequent developments.

In contrast to this conception, my major concern is with the *dynamic* situation of the text in those first centuries, as it can be observed by looking at the papyri, not in isolation, but in their broad historical context and especially from the larger perspective provided by the manuscript situation in the succeeding century or so. In other words, the tracing of textual streams or trajectories shows us that something was happening between 200 and 300; the trajectory approach sets the constellations in motion, and the patterns of textual movement become visible to us. The feeling is akin to that of gazing at the projections of the stars and planets in a planetarium before the machinery is engaged, and then, when it is set in rapid motion, observing the regular paths, the orderly directions of movement, and the shaping of constellations. The vast spectrum of early but diverse papyri does present a formidable barrier to our understanding of NT textual history before 300 or 400, but look at the dynamic situation, set the machinery in motion, start moving the gears of historical development and the lenses of historical perspective, and perhaps there will be some chance of charting that early history of the NT text.

Professor Aland, furthermore, seems always to be emphasizing the *number* of early witnesses, especially papyri, which now are available in the quest for the earliest attainable NT text. He can point, for example, to seventeen papyri of the Fourth Gospel alone, and certainly the papyri discovered in our century represent a striking advance in the *quantity of papyri* as compared with the time of Westcott-Hort. Yet, most of the NT papyri are extremely fragmentary, and what net gain we have in actual *quantity* of text comes almost entirely from seven papyri (P45, P46, P47, P66, P72, P74, and P75). It must be noted — as Aland correctly emphasizes — that our distinction between "papyri" and "uncials" is an artificial one, since both are uncials and differ only in the material on which they are written; hence, papyri have an "automatic significance" only when they take us back behind the great uncials of the fourth century (1967: 93). With this in mind, P74, of the seventh century, should be eliminated from the "automatically significant" papyri, and this leaves us with six papyri which are both early and extensive. As a group, these MSS contain a quantity of text perhaps equivalent to about one-third the amount of text in Codex B, and these early and extensive papyri provide almost complete coverage of the Fourth Gospel, about three-fourths of Luke, about one-half of Acts, much of the Epistles, and about one-third of the Apocalypse of John. (All of the papyri together contain perhaps half the amount of text in B and include some portion of every NT book except 1–2 Timothy.)

It is obvious, then, that in spite of the many lacunae, large and small, the textual gains from the papyri are impressive and highly prized. But is it the *number* of early papyri or even the quantity of their text which is significant? If so, the text-critic might well reach the point of saying — as I sometimes, perhaps unjustly, imagine Aland saying (if we may paraphrase Ignatius, *Philadelphians* 8.2), "Unless I find it written in the *papyri,* I do not believe it in the gospel." Merely counting papyri when assessing variant readings may very well be as wrongheaded as counting witnesses was in the days of the TR, for the crucial question for any textual witnesses, whether early or late, is — as Colwell states it: "Where do they fit into a plausible reconstruction of the history of the manuscript tradition?"[25] Certainly Colwell's question is precisely the correct one, and it is another way of stating that the text of the NT cannot be established on the basis of an array of early papyri, even if the entire NT should be contained in them; rather, the establishment of the NT text can be achieved only by a reconstruction of the history of that early text and by extracting the earliest text from MSS which have been clearly located in that reconstruction and found to be integral parts of a stream of tradition which flows continuously from the earliest points which can be documented (or which can be recognized or established on adequate and reasonable grounds). Obviously, doing this is harder than saying it, and for this reason we have suggested the trajectory approach as a way of seeing this early history in more dynamic terms than perhaps previously has been the case; naturally, the recent emphasis on text-types as process (see Colwell 1969: 15-20, 53) plays into this, but we need to find ways of observing the entire early textual movement or flow and of drawing firm conclusions from such observation.

Yet, all of our past discoveries and also these present suggestions, as far as they concern the methodology and early history of the text, still leave us largely in the position of Westcott-Hort and within a twentieth-century interlude in NT textual criticism, and, what is more, they leave us with the major and decisive tasks still ahead.

C. Lack of Progress in Major Critical Editions/Apparatuses

We began by referring to the popular hand-editions of the Greek NT as one evidence that we had not moved beyond Westcott-Hort; the similarity between these popular texts and that of WH was seen as symptomatic of the lack of progress toward a theory and history of the text. Now we return — though in a different way — to the editions of the Greek NT to show how this lack of progress in textual theory has led to an extended debate and a serious difference of opinion as to how a *major* critical edition or apparatus should be constructed. When it is observed that this debate about basic procedures goes back to post–World War I times, it will be clear again that the twentieth century has been an interlude.

---

25. Colwell 1969: 156-57. Colwell speaks of Aland in a rather cutting fashion regarding the counting of papyri, though this is modified slightly a few paragraphs later; these remarks may not be fair, for I do not find statements in Aland which are explicit concerning his attitude toward and treatment of papyri as textual evidence; cf., however, Aland 1967: 93.

It is disheartening to discover that nearly fifty years ago now, when a number of British and German scholars were considering the compilation of a new critical apparatus to the Greek NT, the German group withdrew when no agreement could be reached on the text to be used.[26] At that point the British carried on, but — ignoring the sound advice of B. H. Streeter to employ the Byzantine text as a base (1924: 147) — they used the WH text and produced the two volumes edited by Legg (1935; 1940). A similar impasse exists now between the so-called International Greek NT Project (IGNTP) and the Münster Institut für neutestamentliche Textforschung: these two projects and the collations produced for them have, in each case, a different base or standard text. On the one hand, the recognition of the inadequacy of Legg's volumes had resulted, for one thing, in compelling arguments for the adoption of some form of Byzantine text as a collation base in any future apparatus,[27] and accordingly the Oxford 1873 edition of the TR was selected by the IGNTP. The Münster Institut, however, has followed the views put forward by the German group earlier mentioned — views which found expression, for example, in 1926 by Stählin and von Dobschütz — that the Nestle text should form the basis for a "new Tischendorf." Thus, Münster is employing the NA text as a base and will display the resultant apparatus against the new critical text derived from the apparatus (Aland 1969/70: 166, 172). Both projects have persisted in their divergent ways, with the British and North American group presently involved in the final editing of the critical apparatus for the Gospel of Luke[28] and the German group working, with the aid of computers, on the General Epistles (see Aland 1969/70: 163-77; cf. Ott 1973).

This is not the place to debate the merits of these different approaches; rather, we wish merely to point out that the selection of different collation bases by the two projects and the persistence in these judgments over a period of forty years implies far more than appears on the surface, for it veils two basic but differing attitudes concerning the status of text-critical theory. This is revealed most sharply perhaps in Kurt Aland's 1965 critique of the IGNTP's specimen page when he spoke of the use of the TR for a base as, in view of our advanced knowledge, an "anachronism" (1966b: 184; also in 1967: 89-90), almost as if the printing of TR at the top of the page implied that it represents a good critical text. It is not only curious but striking to discover that von Dobschütz in 1926 used precisely the same term — anachronism — in reference to Streeter's proposal that the TR be used as a collation base at that time (1926: 318). In 1967 Professor Aland remarked that, in the IGNTP's edition, the original text of the NT would have to be sought from the apparatus by subtraction from the printed TR (198),[29] a statement suggesting that he now understood the purpose of the British/American project, for Professor Aland, even though he may not agree, knows well, of course, that the purpose of the IGNTP is to produce

---

26. Parvis 1950: 301; see Stählin 1926; von Dobschütz 1926: 171-72, 318.
27. See, e.g., the reviews of Legg by Kilpatrick 1942 and by Manson 1942; cf. Zuntz 1953: 28-30.
28. See now American and British Committees of the IGNTP, 1984-87; cf. Chapter 2: n. 5.
29. Printed also in *NovT* 9 (1967) 103. This paragraph was not in Aland's English version (1965).

an *apparatus criticus* and not a new critical text of the NT; this purpose had been specified and emphasized in every printed description of the Project from its very beginning, and it had been made just as clear that this critical apparatus was understood to be only a halfway house to a much needed new critical text. The reason for stopping halfway rather than pushing immediately to the principal destination was simply that there existed no theory of the text which would allow for the establishment of a definitive critical text; the assumption, rather, was that both the theory and the text must be determined from an adequate display of textual evidence, and the IGNTP was modest enough to recognize that this could not be done in one sitting. It was not modesty alone, however, which brought the British and North American participants to this view, but the hard facts and the actual situation in which our text-critical discipline found — and still finds — itself: we simply do not have a theory of the text. What Kenneth W. Clark wrote in 1956 is as true today; he spoke of "a day like ours in which we know only that the traditional theory of the text is faulty but cannot yet see clearly to correct the fault" (37-38). Professor Aland and the Münster Institut prefer to move immediately and decisively to the construction of a critical text; certainly this aim, the boldness with which it is pursued, and the courage which lies behind it are all commendable, but the pointed question remains: On what theory and history of the text is it based? If no clear and adequate answer is forthcoming, then the more cautious and methodical approach of the IGNTP may be taken as justifiable and, indeed, as mandatory in the present circumstances.

The single, simple point which stands out and which is our interest here is this: the lack of progress toward a theory and history of the earliest NT text has seriously hindered and extensively delayed the production of those major critical editions which would provide the detailed apparatuses required for the determination of that history and theory. We are caught in a vicious circle of long standing, and it constitutes another dimension of that twentieth-century interlude in NT textual criticism in which we find ourselves.

D. Lack of Progress in the Evaluation of Readings

The lack of definitive theory and history of the early text and the lack of progress in critical editions have caused, during the twentieth century, a chaotic situation in the evaluation of variant readings in the NT text. The result has been the almost universal employment of the "eclectic" method, and this is perhaps the most visible evidence that we are in an interlude. The "eclectic" method is, in fact, *the* twentieth-century method of NT textual criticism, and anyone who criticizes it immediately becomes a self-critic, for we all use it, some of us with a certain measure of reluctance and restraint, others with complete abandon. Those in the latter category seem to assume that the eclectic method is, for all practical purposes, fully legitimated and acceptable and represents a final method, a permanent procedure, while others of us find K. W. Clark's 1956 judgment the only acceptable assessment of eclecticism:

> It is the only procedure available to us at this stage, but it is very important to recognize that it is a secondary and tentative method. It is not a new method nor a permanent one. The eclectic method cannot by itself create a text to

displace Westcott-Hort and its offspring. It is suitable only for exploration and experimentation. . . . The eclectic method, by its very nature, belongs [and here we pick up the quotation referred to a moment ago] to a day like ours in which we know only that the traditional theory of the text is faulty but cannot yet see clearly to correct the fault.[30]

Actually, those who employ the eclectic method with the greatest abandon seem to be the least eclectic, for they tend, usually, to emphasize not a selection of various principles and canons of textual criticism — as the term would imply — but only the principles from one small corner of criticism, particularly the intrinsic principle, with heavy emphasis on harmony with the author's style or suitability to the context. What is worse, they tend to de-emphasize, sometimes drastically, the historical factors in textual criticism, including the date and provenance of MSS, and they generally eschew the task of reconstructing the history of the text (see Colwell 1969: 154-56). It probably is not unfair to say that when historical factors (external evidence) and judgments about the quality of given MSS and text-types are disregarded, then the numerous variant readings become little more than detached pieces of a puzzle which must now be selected entirely on the basis of their shape and fitness for the space to be filled. This kind of "eclecticism" becomes the great leveler — all variants are equals and equally candidates for the original text, regardless of date, residence, lineage, or textual context. In this case, would it not be appropriate to suggest, further, that a few more conjectural readings be added to the available supply of variants on the assumption that they must have existed but have been lost at some point in the history of the textual transmission?

All this is not to say that even the "thoroughgoing" or "rigorous" eclectics, as they have been called,[31] have not made important contributions to text-critical method. For instance, G. D. Kilpatrick's emphasis on the non-Atticizing reading as the more likely original reading yields a canon of criticism which may find a place among the older canons of Bengel and Griesbach, but — like those older canons — it too has limited applications and serious shortcomings.[32] Beyond this isolated example, the broad utilization of an eclectic methodology by numerous scholars throughout the twentieth century has helped us to sharpen our critical senses, to evaluate the traditional canons and principles of textual criticism, and to maintain a plausible critical text for use in the exegetical and historical studies in the general NT field. In short, eclecticism is a holding action, a temporary and interim method with presumably equally temporary results. It is, however, what the twentieth century has produced and worked with, and, as a twentieth-century emphasis, it evidences again our twentieth-century pause in NT textual criticism.

30. See his similar, but later statement in 1968: 166.

31. E.g., by Fee (1966: 4-6, 264-65), who distinguishes "rigorous" eclecticism from "reasoned" eclecticism. [See now Chapter 7 of the present volume.]

32. For dangers and difficulties, see Metzger 1968a: 177-78 and Colwell 1969: 154-55. Kilpatrick's main treatment of this matter is in 1963b.

E. The Return of the Textus Receptus

Perhaps the most curious and certainly the most ironic evidence that we stand in the situation of Westcott-Hort is the revival in our own generation of the view that the TR represents the best NT text. In 1956 Edward F. Hills published a work entitled *The King James Version Defended! A Christian View of the New Testament Manuscripts,* and only months ago David Otis Fuller (1973) edited a volume called *True or False? The Westcott-Hort Textual Theory Examined,* both of which defend the TR.

I suspect that no one of us will or need take these books seriously, but that they could be written at all and published in our own day is, in a way, an indictment of our discipline. These works not only attack the theories of Westcott-Hort, but they attack us as representatives of Westcott-Hort's views; in a striking way they return us to the days when Dean Burgon made his vehement, acrimonious, and abusive attacks upon Westcott and Hort and upon their malicious intentions and corrupt MSS (1883, 1896a, 1896b). I am being facetious only to a limited extent when I ask, If the TR can still be defended, albeit in merely a pseudo-scholarly fashion, how much solid progress have we made in textual criticism in the twentieth century?

III. The Post-Interlude Performance

We have described the first major performance or act of modern NT textual criticism as the destruction of the tyrannical TR during the last half of the nineteenth century. The TR and its precursor, the Byzantine ecclesiastical text, had maintained a position of dominance for as long as a millennium and a half when the mortal wound was inflicted by Westcott and Hort. A brief death struggle ensued in the 1880s and 1890s when Dean Burgon, to whom we have just referred, and his allies attacked the attackers in a desperate but unsuccessful attempt to reverse the issue; but the verdict held, and the twentieth century opened with the newly found optimism that, by excluding the mass of late MSS from the search, textual critics had extracted the original text of the NT from the best of the earliest uncials, or that at very least they were now in the immediate neighborhood of the original text. Challenges arising from the Westcott-Hort scheme were tackled quickly and enthusiastically within this same spirit of optimism. One of those challenges was to carry further the search for the history of the text, and the extraordinarily ambitious and well-provisioned project of Hermann Freiherr von Soden faced that problem broadly and on all fronts; the first fascicle of his three-volume prolegomena appeared in 1902, and the last, after 2200 closely packed pages of fine print, came out in 1910, followed by his critical edition of the text in 1913. Something of the magnitude of labor involved can be grasped by noting that von Soden classified as to their textual character some 1260 minuscule MSS out of the 1350 known to him — an astounding 93%. Yet his great work, the scale of which has not been matched again in the twentieth century, was as deep a disappointment to the scholarly world as the expectations for it had been high. His comprehensive history of the text was only partially satisfactory, his classification of manuscript groupings had questionable — and largely unknown — methodological bases, his new system of manuscript sigla was complex and calamitous, and (as

Kenyon says) "his resultant text was no advance on its predecessors" (1933a: 44). I employ this reference to von Soden to show the magnificently grand fashion in which the twentieth-century interlude in NT textual criticism was inaugurated!

For me to bring upon my own discipline so sweeping an indictment as I have is no pleasant undertaking. Surely some will dispute its necessity, and others its justification; and none will like it. I dislike it as much as anyone, but both the popular and major critical editions and the state of research in both the theory and history of the text stand as vivid evidence of its reality.

If we have been in an interlude, what are the prospects of moving from it into a new phase — a second major and significant act? On balance, and in view of some rather recent developments — some of which I have already mentioned — the chances are considerably better than they were a generation ago. Naturally, the papyrus discoveries have contributed to this hopeful situation, but I refer more directly to developments in method which will aid in the reconstruction of the early history of the text, for it is this task — as urged above — which is basic to progress in NT textual criticism.

A. *Quantitative Measurement of Manuscript Relationships*

The first reason for optimism is found in the methodological advances which have been made during the past decade in the quantitative measurement of manuscript relationships.

Throughout the twentieth century (and also earlier) analyses of manuscript relationships have been based, generally, on a comparison of the number of agreements which two or more MSS shared in their variation from an external standard, usually the TR. For example, a given MS, let us call it x, in three sample chapters from Mark, would be collated against the TR, showing fifteen variants; then these fifteen variants would be checked, for example, against Codex B, showing that in ten of these fifteen variants MS x and Codex B were in agreement — in agreement, that is, against the TR. More than likely a conclusion was drawn that MS x was a Neutral witness. If, however, Codex B in these three chapters should show fifty additional variations from the TR, which MS x does not share, would MS x have any claim to be classified as Neutral when its ratio of agreement to disagreement with B against the TR was 1 to 5? Hardly, but frequently, if not normally, this comparison of *total agreement and disagreement* was not taken into account. Suppose, using the same example, that MS x showed that in five of its variants from the TR it agreed with Codex D, as compared with ten of the fifteen in which it agreed with B; it would, as before, be called Neutral. But what if D differed from the TR in these sections of Mark a total of only two additional times, leaving MS x agreeing with D against the TR five out seven times, or roughly 70% of the time; should it not then be classified as Western rather than Neutral? To extend the example, if MS y were found also to have fifteen variants from the TR in the same sample chapters and ten of these were the same readings as ten of the fifteen variants in which MS x differed from the TR, what conclusions would be drawn? Older methods would have claimed, perhaps, that MSS x and y are closely related, and perhaps they are. But how close a relationship is it? Actually, the two MSS being compared have between them a total of twenty variations from the TR; x and y agree in ten of these, but they also fail to agree in the other ten, resulting in only 50% agreement with one another in their total variation from the external standard. That is quite different from the implication that they are closely related because they agree with one another 67% of the time against the TR. Sometimes even more superficial comparisons and more careless conclusions were made. For example, two or three MSS might be shown to have a similar number of variants from the TR, even though they are not the same variants; therefore, the argument would go, the two or three MSS are related textually because of their supposedly similar distance from the common standard. There were other ways in which these long-standing methods were inadequate. For example, variants involving obvious scribal errors, nonsense readings, singular readings, and insignificant variations (such as orthographical changes) were not evaluated for their usefulness (or lack of it) in tracing manuscript relationships. The result, to put it mildly, was inexactness, inclusiveness, and miscalculation in the determination of manuscript relationships.

At least two developments which have achieved a certain measure of maturity only during the past decade have changed all of this, and shoddy, indecisive, and misleading methods for establishing manuscript relationships can no longer be tolerated. The first development stems from an eight-page article by Ernest C. Colwell and his collaborator, Ernest W. Tune, on "The Quantitative Relationships between MS Text-Types," which appeared in 1963.[33] Building on some earlier suggestions (by H. S. Murphy 1954: 167 and B. M. Metzger 1945: 489),[34] they devised a quantitative method in which "the total amount of variation" is taken into account among all the MSS of a wide-ranging panel of MSS employed in the comparison, rather than merely tabulating agreements against an external norm. This means that each MS in the study must be measured against every other one in the study, including a carefully selected list of control MSS which represent the major points on the broad textual spectrum of the NT, and this measurement must be made in terms of the total number of variation-units which occur among all the MSS involved in the study — a variation-unit being defined as every point where two or more of the witnesses agree in a variation from the rest. Moreover, all variants are "classified as either genetically significant or not," with the result that scribal errors, alternative spellings, and especially singular [they use the term "unique"] readings are eliminated, since they "tell us nothing about manuscript relationships" and seriously distort the tabulations of other manuscript agreements. An important final suggestion is that "the quantitative definition of a text-type is a group of MSS that agree more than 70 per cent of the time and is separated by a gap of about 10 per cent from its neighbors" (1969: 59). It should be pointed out that, as Colwell and Tune conceived it, this method was still a *sampling* method; sound method, however, requires that total variation of numerous MSS throughout entire books of the NT be analyzed, though it should, at the same time, be done section by section or chapter by chapter. The

---

33. Reprinted with some revisions in Colwell 1969: 56-62. References are to the latter.
34. To these might have been added the points made, mostly against K. Lake's methods, by Hills 1949: 153 and the method employed by Porter 1961.

fullest utilization and the most thorough exposition of the method to date are by Gordon D. Fee, who has devised and employed some refinements as he investigated the text of the Fourth Gospel in P66, P75, ℵ, and in Origen and Cyril of Alexandria.[35] Hurtado, in the study referred to above, also applied the method in a thoroughgoing fashion to the Caesarean witnesses. In addition to the original Colwell article, Fee's study of "Codex Sinaiticus in the Gospel of John: A Contribution to Methodology in Establishing Textual Relationships" (1968a: 25-31) is essential for understanding the method and for some account of its history.

This quantitative method is not for the indolent; endless hours of tedious manuscript collation, of careful isolation of variation-units, and of meticulous tabulation of results are required over large areas of text, but the method yields those precise quantitative measures of manuscript relationships and textual character which are mandatory for reconstructing the textual history of the NT. Hence, there is vibrant new hope if scholars can be found and enlisted to carry out these procedures. Moreover, the computer program in use at the Münster Institut yields data for this kind of measurement (see below).

The second development in quantitative method is the so-called Claremont Profile Method for grouping NT minuscule MSS. This approach was developed by Frederik Wisse and Paul R. McReynolds for the IGNTP as a means of assuring that the Project's *apparatus criticus* would contain a selection of truly representative minuscule MSS — representative, that is, of all the identifiable groups in terms of textual character. Since only about 150 out of more than 1700 minuscules of Luke could be included in the apparatus, and since the majority of these Lucan MSS had never been collated, a highly efficient yet sufficiently sophisticated means had to be devised to locate the desired 9% without unduly over- or under-representing any identifiable group.

It would not be practicable to describe this method in detail here; this has been done several times already, though the full exposition and justification has not yet appeared.[36] In short, a series of test readings in three chapters of Luke were isolated from collations of 550 MSS; when a MS was checked for its agreement or disagreement with these test readings, a certain pattern or profile of its own readings in these variation-units resulted, and MSS with the same or closely similar profiles fell into groups showing a similar configuration of characteristic readings. Hence, each group revealed a distinctive profile, and new MSS could quickly be checked in the test passages and fitted — according to its profile — into one of the groups established by the method. The Profile Method is applicable particularly to the location of Byzantine sub-groups, which previously were identified through "unique group readings," but such unique or distinctive group readings are rare in Byzantine groups. The Profile Method relies, rather, upon *characteristic* group readings which

35. Fee 1968b, 1968a, 1971a. [The latter two appear as Chapters 12 and 15 in the present volume.]

36. Wisse and McReynolds, in Colwell et al. 1968: 191-97; 1970; McReynolds 1972; Epp 1967 [now Chapter 11]. The method has now been described fully: see McReynolds 1979; esp. Wisse 1982. It also has evoked a body of critical literature, e.g., Richards 1977a, 1977b, 1979, 1980; Ehrman 1987.

yield a distinctive group profile, and it replaces an older instrument with one of higher fidelity, encouraging correspondingly high hopes that some measure of order can be brought to the chaotic mass of NT minuscule MSS. Finally, it is important to note, however, that the Profile Method is still a sampling method, thereby sharing the general weaknesses of sampling methods, but it operates with rigid principles in the determination of its test readings, and it has perhaps as many safeguards as can be worked into a sampling method. Furthermore, it will bring to the surface those relatively few MSS which deserve thorough and detailed study.

These two quantitative methods have come to us out of the twentieth-century interlude, the latter taking its departure largely from von Soden's attempts to group the Byzantine MSS, and the former arising largely from the efforts to quantify the relationships among the Caesarean witnesses. Both, however, stem more immediately from Colwell's work on locating new MSS within the textual tradition, on grouping MSS, on determining text-types, and, of course, on his actual proposal for a quantitative method. Perhaps the coincident appearance of the extensive papyri, with their textual material of great intrinsic significance, gave the whole enterprise a measure of cogency and heightened the strategic import of quantitative analysis which could now offer such precise and confident results. In any event, it is these exact and assured results in determining manuscript relationships which hold rich promise for a movement out of the interlude into a new phase of NT text-critical achievement.[37]

B. Homogeneity and Recension in Early NT Text-Types

The twentieth century appears to have created and then destroyed the Caesarean text-type, returning us once again — as in the days of Westcott-Hort — to two major textual streams traceable from the earliest period. It is clear, however, that the witnesses which can be identified as on or in the vicinity of these two textual lines are of varying textual character, especially many of the fragmentary papyri. This means that two old, difficult, but important problems remain for resolution: the problems of homogeneity and recension in the Neutral and Western traditions. Positions on these issues have come full circle since Westcott-Hort, and little progress has been made. Hort viewed neither text as the product of a recension, but took both, apparently, to be homogeneous in their textual character (though the Western showed evidence, he said, of "homogeneously progressive change" [Westcott-Hort 1881: 2.122]). Subsequent scholarship, however, soon argued that both the Neutral (Bousset 1894; von Soden 1911; Kenyon [see, e.g., Kenyon 1933a: 67-69, 81-83; 1940]) and the Western (Blass 1895-98; Ropes 1926 [see Epp 1966a: 4-6]) text-types were the products of systematic revision. More recent scholarship has often viewed the Western as "the uncontrolled, popular text of the second century" (Colwell 1969: 53, 166; cf. Riddle 1936: 230), hence unrevised and lacking homogeneity, while the close relationship of P75 to B has suggested to some that any view of the Neutral text as the result of recension should now be reversed [see above].

37. Reference may be made also to Vinton A. Dearing's method of "textual analysis" (1959, 1967; see now also 1974a, 1974b), for which he utilized the computer and has recently made further applications to NT texts.

These two questions, homogeneity and recension, may or may not be closely related: homogeneity may imply — but need not require — a recension; evidence of recension may lead to the expectation — but not automatically to the discovery — of homogeneity. Clearly, however, these questions press themselves most critically upon the Neutral and Western texts, if only because they represent the earliest of the recognized textual traditions and because, therefore, the further issue of the original text of the NT is encountered more immediately in these textual streams. As the history of scholarship shows, these are problems of extreme complexity and difficulty, but decisions about either homogeneity or recension in these texts would aid significantly in the required reconstruction of the history of the text.

Obviously, the newly developed and refined quantitative method provides a means for investigating these issues afresh and with precision. As for the Neutral text, its homogeneity and recensional nature have been touched anew by the discovery of P75: Was there an early recension in Egypt of this Neutral text-type, which seems to bear the marks of a recension when compared with the more problematic and divergent Western witnesses, or does the striking agreement of P75 and B reflect accurate transmission of an early, smooth, but unrevised text? The homogeneity of witnesses placed in the Neutral text-type has been tested rather widely, though only recently by adequate quantitative methods; still, one of its leading members, ℵ, continues to show interesting and puzzling deviations.[38]

It is in the Western text, however, that the questions of homogeneity and recension are the more problematic, for here one is faced with a relatively small number of witnesses — which is advantageous methodologically — but with an unusually fragmentary set of witnesses in several ancient languages — which is disadvantageous both for developing a methodology and for an easy solution. Whether or not the Western text of the Gospels and Acts has passed through a recensional process and whether or note it has a homogeneous character are questions which have resisted resolution primarily, perhaps, because of the lack of extensive Greek witnesses to this textual tradition; actually, there is only one such witness, Codex Bezae (D), though some may wish to add MSS 614 and 383 for Acts; the other important witnesses are the OL and OS MSS, which not only are few (about thirty-two of the Gospels and twelve of Acts in Latin; only two of the Gospels and part of a single leaf for Acts in Syriac) and fragmentary (all of the above are mutilated), but date from the fourth through the thirteenth centuries, on the average quite far removed from the presumed origin of this textual tradition in the second century. Patristic quotations and commentaries and a few other MSS offer additional testimony with a Western flavor. When, however, all of the available witnesses are compared, for example in Acts, a number of variation-units emerge as points where two, three, or more of these witnesses can be compared; this is a hopeful sign for the use of quantitative methods to probe the issues of homogeneity and recension. On the other hand, it is not a little discouraging to discover, from preliminary checks, that not often are three or more of the "hard-core" Western witnesses available for any given

---

38. See Fee 1968a. Fee argues, on quantitative and other grounds, that the early P75-B text-type is not a recension in his forthcoming "P75, P66, and Origen: The Myth of Early Textual Recension in Alexandria" [now Fee 1974; Chapter 13 of the present volume].

variation-unit; this may place a critical strain on methodology if extensive demonstration of uniform results is required.

The degree of success which can be expected in these investigations of homogeneity and recension is not yet clear, but during the past two decades the dual factors of (1) improved quantitative methods (which may prove applicable even to the more fragmentary witnesses) and (2) the discovery of strategically significant new witnesses for both of the earliest textual streams may tip the scales toward a successful resolution of these old and intractable problems.

C. Computers in Textual Criticism

The expectations from new technological developments and applications tend at times to be greatly underestimated and at other times to be vastly overrated. How the computer's application to textual criticism should be evaluated is not entirely clear, for many assertions as to how it can or should be utilized differ markedly from more sober statements about its actual use and present limitations.

The latest, most extensive, and most direct application of computers to NT textual criticism is that utilized by the Münster Institut for its major critical edition of the Greek NT. Under the expert hand of Dr. Wilhelm Ott, information derived from its collations of MSS of the General Epistles — which must be done in the traditional way by hand (Fischer 1970) — is carefully coded and punched on tape. Ott makes very clear what can and what cannot be done by the computer: it cannot make judgments on the truth or falsity of readings; it cannot restore the text or reconstruct the history of its transmission (Ott 1973); nor can MSS be collated by the computer, though presently this limitation is a technical and economic limitation rather than a theoretical one; there are not now — nor will there be in the foreseeable future — optical scanning devices capable of reading the kind of MSS with which NT textual criticism works.[39] Accordingly, one recent estimate is that "to encode the available manuscripts by hand on punched cards or tape would demand the resources of 200 man-years."[40] On the other hand, the computer *can* classify witnesses and define the relationships among them, and it can "guarantee consistent and error-free execution of the more mechanical part of the work," namely, the compilation of the *apparatus criticus* and the printing of the text and of the apparatus (Ott 1973: 200; cf. Fischer 1970: 306).

These are significant gains, which already can be demonstrated in a partial way through actual accomplishment, and are not mere dreams of what might be done. Those who are working with these techniques — Ott, Fischer, Aland — are careful to emphasize, again, that this by no means implies that they have approached anything comparable to automatic textual editing or "automatic textual criticism." And there are other cautions here for the incurable dreamer whose confidence in modern hardware knows no realistic bounds, for Ott points out that these new tools

---

39. I rely on a letter from Mr. George Nagy of IBM (dated 17 March 1970) who said of several samples of NT minuscule MSS that their Greek text "is beyond the capabilities of any mechanical systems now in sight." Cf. Morgan 1970.

40. Reported by H. Greeven to SNTS, 1970; see *NTS* 17 (1970/71) 478.

may mean that the costs for critical editions may be even higher than in the days when these tools were not available (201). Much of this expense will be for the labor of providing the coded collation data to the computer, and — as one observer put it — scholars will still be "doing much drudgery, but a new kind" — hence, "it seems less accurate to say that they are freed from drudgery than to say that their drudgery can handle a much larger volume per human drudge-hour."[41]

Certainly even this realistic assessment of the computer in NT textual criticism is a hopeful sign, but it hardly has been touched by North American scholars.[42]

IV. Conclusion

The few areas broached here do not exhaust the hopeful signs for the post-interlude period; a further example, and one quite different from those presented earlier, is the recent development of more precise methods for the radiocarbon dating of parchment MSS.[43] Yet the items we have discussed may be harbingers of a movement out of a long, though not inactive, pause in NT textual criticism and into a fresh and qualitatively different phase of our discipline. Unfortunately, however, any such hopes must be balanced, at least in North America, by a somber reflection. Any one of us who faces the present status of NT textual criticism with some reasonable measure of honesty and detachment will recognize that changes of a kind very much unlike any mentioned to this point have forced themselves upon us. In 1955, the very first volume of *New Testament Studies,* itself a symbol of a new era in international and ecumenical scholarship, carried a lecture by W. G. Kümmel on "New Testament Research and Teaching in Present Day Germany"; there were five lines devoted to textual criticism, including the statement that:

> Textual criticism has virtually ceased to be a subject of active research in present day Germany, that is to say so far as the investigation of textual families, relationships between texts, etc. are concerned. This kind of research requires a great deal of time and money, so that it has almost entirely been transferred to America. (1955: 231)

If Kümmel's assessment, which came just ten years after World War II, was correct for the middle 1950s, quite the reverse is true today. Given the ironic twists of national economies, one now has to say — to change the wording slightly — that since textual criticism requires a great deal of manpower and money it has almost entirely been transferred to Germany. To cite only a few points of support for this dispiriting

---

41. J. Leed, *Computers and the Humanities* 1 (1966/67) 14.

42. Gains in computer use since 1974 obviously have been enormous. One example is the Institut für NT Textforschung in Münster; another is the convenient and sophisticated program developed for the Johannine phase of the IGNTP, accommodating efficient entry and accumulation of data and the easy reproduction of any collated MS.

43. R. Berger, N. Evans, J. M. Abell, and M. A. Resnik, "Radiocarbon Dating of Parchment," *Nature* 235 (1973) 160-61. So far, however, "the best periods for dating . . . are the thirteenth and fifteenth centuries."

statement, the grand tradition of textual criticism at the University of Chicago from Goodspeed through Willoughby, Colwell, and Wikgren apparently has ended with the latter's recent retirement, and other text-critical centers, such as Emory and Duke, no longer seem to be active in graduate studies in the field. It is, in fact, difficult to name more than one or two recognized graduate institutions in North America where doctoral studies in the textual criticism of the NT can be pursued under some established specialist. It is disheartening to say that I doubt whether the working and publishing NT textual critics in all of North America are equal in number to the post-doctoral researchers in the Münster Institut. To speak of the lack of personnel in the present is one thing; what is more worrisome is the dismal prospect for specialists in the future, particularly on this side of the Atlantic. In short, NT textual criticism is an area seriously affected by decreasing attention, diminishing graduate opportunities, and dwindling personnel. It is ironic that this state of affairs — a situation contrasting sharply with any during the long life of W. H. P. Hatch — obtains just at the time when methodological advances warrant a renewed optimism for the discipline and offer fresh challenges which, if met, would carry NT textual criticism beyond its twentieth-century interlude to a new and distinctive period of achievement.

CHAPTER 6

A CONTINUING INTERLUDE IN NEW TESTAMENT TEXTUAL CRITICISM?[1]

Eldon Jay Epp

The following reassessment of present-day NT textual criticism requires, by its very nature, a brief statement of the circumstances that occasioned it. Seven years ago, in the W. H. P. Hatch Memorial Lecture at the 1973 Annual Meeting of the Society of Biblical Literature, I attempted in fifty minutes an adventuresome — if not audacious — assessment of the entire scope of NT textual criticism during the past century. Though this was an instructive exercise for me and one that others report as instructive also for them, it was inevitable that so bold an undertaking would elicit sharp criticism. The first hint of this came from Münster in 1976,[2] but more clearly within the past year or so in an invitation to subscribe to a Festschrift for Matthew Black containing an article by Kurt Aland of Münster with an announced title — appearing as it did in English — that had a highly familiar ring: "The Twentieth-Century Interlude in New Testament Textual Criticism," obviously the title of the Hatch Lecture, which, following its presentation, had been published in the 1974 volume of the *Journal of Biblical Literature*.[3] When the Festschrift itself appeared, it seemed obvious from Professor Aland's article[4] that some reassessment of the course and significance of twentieth-century NT textual criticism was in order. Late in September 1979, Aland's article was reprinted in the annual report of his Münster foundation for NT textual research, now under the title of "Die Rolle des 20. Jahrhunderts in der Geschichte der neutestamentlichen Textkritik."[5]

The introduction to this reprint claims that in the *JBL* article I "take the floor as spokesman for American textual criticism" (28), a claim I would renounce emphatically. It indicates also that only occasionally has Professor Aland "let himself be lured out of his reserve" to reply to views that disparage the way the Münster Institut für neutestamentliche Textforschung has assembled the data of NT research

1. A paper presented originally in the New Testament Textual Criticism Section, Society of Biblical Literature, New York City, 17 November 1979, now considerably revised for publication.
2. B. Aland 1976: 5.
3. Epp 1974; a major portion was translated into Japanese and published in *Studia Textus Novi Testamenti* 103-9 (1975) 856-60, 866-68, 875-76, 890-92, 898-900, 907-8.
4. Though the title is English ("The Twentieth-Century Interlude in New Testament Textual Criticism"), the article is in German in Best and Wilson 1979: 1-14.
5. The first two paragraphs and the last few lines of the original article were omitted in the reprint.

or that go (as he phrases it) in an impossible direction. Thus, quite explicitly the *JBL* essay was seen as a challenge both to the views of Professor Aland himself and to the work and significance of the Münster Institut, for which he undeniably is the spokesman. Certainly his reply is negatively — and, in its intent, destructively — critical, sometimes harshly so, yet no one could welcome this response more than I, for the primary purpose of the Hatch Memorial Lecture was to evince responses that might help us all to see where we — as late twentieth-century NT textual critics — stood. More particularly, its major thrust was to raise questions (as well as to offer some answers) as to where we stood *methodologically,* that is, where we found ourselves with reference to a *theory* of the NT text and with respect to an *understanding of the history* of the earliest NT text. In precisely these respects, I submit — perhaps with no less arrogance and audacity than in 1973 — that little could have been more disappointing than the lengthy response from Aland, for his argumentation at point after point seems to confirm the selfsame conclusions at which the Hatch Lecture arrived and which he is attempting to refute. This observation is presented, not with any sense of self-satisfaction, but out of deep regret, for the response (while it does enlighten us as to Aland's own method of establishing the original NT text and does refer to methodological procedures employed in the important computer applications at the Münster Institut) tells us little that is either new or constructive concerning the issues raised in the Hatch Lecture, though it does strongly imply that discussion of many of those issues is misguided. I, for one, regret also that this solitary negative response to the Hatch Lecture has been so long delayed, for even with its negative bent it earlier could have provided an appropriate stimulus for our discussion of the important issues upon which it touches. Presently I shall attempt to show, however, why I still persist in the views defended earlier and why I remain unrepentant in the face of Professor Aland's stinging and at times sarcastic criticism.

This lengthy introduction may suggest that what follows will be merely a personal defense on a point-by-point basis or a personalized polemic. Certainly Aland's response scored some "debating points" against the Hatch Lecture, and just as surely some could be scored against him. Such an approach, however, would be basically unproductive; rather, the focus here will be on the issues that are, I think, important for all of us — Professor Aland and his Münster colleagues included — and whose open discussion and clarification could provide significant stepping stones to progress in our knowledge of how the original text of the NT has been transmitted to us and of how it might be recovered.

A further prefatory word is appropriate and essential. Apparently the Hatch Lecture's repeated emphasis on "little progress," "no progress," and "little or no progress" has led to a misunderstanding, and that must be corrected. Let there be no mistake about this: the twentieth century has been an extraordinarily rich period for NT textual criticism; never have I suggested otherwise (see 1974: 387), nor would anyone else find a defensible basis for claiming that nothing has been done or that little has been accomplished during the last eighty years. For example, if NT papyri are considered — an area of crucial interest to Aland and to every textual critic — all of the most important papyri have been brought to light during this remarkably productive period (the Oxyrhynchus, 1896ff.; the Chester Beatty, 1930-31; and the Bodmer, 1956ff.) and have been edited and published; very recently the impressive Münster Fragment Identification Program has been developed, which employs a computer concordance to place independent papyrus fragments back into their proper places in larger papyrus MSS of the NT (Aland 1979b); and for some time the Münster Institut has been in the process of producing a study of "The New Testament on Papyrus" (announced at least as long ago as 1965),[6] a display of all the texts of the papyri with an apparatus indicating the results of full collations. Depending upon how one counts, the quantitative increase from the one papyrus (P^{11}) evaluated for an edition of the NT in the nineteenth century to the papyri presently available may be as much as 9000% (to use Aland's figures [1979a: 3]). Furthermore, as a second example, known Greek MSS as a whole have increased significantly in the twentieth century, by 1000 in number or 25% in our generation (to use Aland's figures [2]). As is well known, over the years the industrious Münster Institut has collected microfilms and photographs of about 5000 of the known 5300 Greek NT MSS and, in more recent years, has begun the computer collation of these MSS, first by comparing them in approximately 1000 test-passages selected throughout the NT, resulting to date in some two million items of information in computerized form, with more work proportionately being done on the Catholic and Pauline Epistles than in the four Gospels (Aland 1979b: 74-75). As a final instance of twentieth-century accomplishment, the new "standard text" (as Aland is wont to call it) common to the third edition of the UBS[3] (1975) and the NA[26] (1979) has become a reality.

This list of attainments could go on at length, but let us simply recognize the prominent contributions made to these and other areas of achievement, not only by the Münster Institut, but also by the United Bible Societies, the Vetus Latina Institute at Beuron, the Centre d'Analyse et de Documentation patristiques at Strasbourg, and many other groups and individuals in the twentieth century. Let us celebrate these accomplishments and give due credit to those whose names are prominently associated with them, including Kurt Aland as one prominent among the most prominent, and also to others who contribute to such projects but whose names may not be well known or remembered. Their labors have produced the "grist for our mills" and will continue to do so into the future. Without these resources, our scholarship could not function productively or efficiently — if at all — for they furnish us the materials and data required for progress in NT textual criticism. What is more, these twentieth-century projects at Münster and elsewhere — as Aland is so intent on pointing out — do themselves represent progress, something I have never denied. Yet, and here is the crucial point — indeed, the only point in this respect — that the Hatch Lecture was trying to make: all of these exemplary advances in our accumulated materials, in the tools of research, and in our control of the data have not yet resulted, it seems to me, in decisive progress in certain critical areas of NT textual criticism, namely in the textual character of the critical editions of the twentieth century; in the theory and history of the earliest NT text; or in the evaluation

---

6. Aland 1967: 213. The article cited was first published in 1965. [See now, Grunewald 1986.]

of readings.[7] These points need to be reexamined, if only briefly, to see whether Aland has — as he supposes — refuted the claim that the twentieth century has been an interlude in NT textual criticism, though only two matters can be treated here.

I. Progress in Popular Critical Editions

The claim in the Hatch Lecture that little progress has been made in establishing the text or altering the textual character of the most popular hand-editions of the Greek NT, says Aland, "causes surprise to cease and astonishment to begin" (1979a: 3). What chiefly causes astonishment, it seems, is the employment of the descriptive term "Westcott-Hort" in attempting to characterize the text presented in the NA edition (the 25th edition was referred to at the time) and insisting that substantial progress had not been made in this area in the twentieth century because the text of that 25th edition was closer to WH than was the text of any of the other popular hand-editions. Yet, it is not so much that Aland disagrees with this characterization of the NA text, for — after all — his own analyses and statements had been used (apparently properly) in the Hatch Lecture to support the point (Epp 1974: 388-90). Rather, it would appear that what is actually astonishing to him is the claim that the new "standard text" of the UBS[3] and (now) NA[26] represents no substantive progress over WH (or, as Aland prefers to call it, Westcott-Hort-Weiss),[8] for whom Codex B was the primary MS, in spite of the fact — as Aland sees it — (1) that the new "standard text" almost always departs from the B-text when only an ℵ versus B attestation is in question; (2) that the "standard text" has followed B only after a full external and internal criticism of B's text shows its reading to be "correct"; and (3) that the new Münster collations of the papyri and parchment fragments up to the third/fourth century provide "emphatic corroboration" that the "standard text" is correct because these early witnesses seldom deviate from it, and if they do, they do so "incorrectly" (1979a: 4), a somewhat curious statement!

Now, simply because the UBS[3] and the NA[26] text (i.e., the new "standard text") is still close to that of WH, that is, close to B, will lead no one — certainly not me — to suggest that nothing has happened in NT textual criticism since 1881. Quite the contrary; much has taken place, and yet the question remains — the only question that the Hatch Lecture raised at this point — as to what progress has been made in nearly a century if our standard critical texts today are so very close to those of a hundred years ago, in spite of the fact that our present critical texts have or could have utilized more than eighty papyri, more than 200 additional uncials, more than 2600 additional minuscules, and perhaps 2000 additional lectionaries that were

---

7. The Hatch Lecture mentioned two other areas in which progress was not evident: (1) major critical editions/apparatuses of the Greek NT (in addition to popular critical editions), but these can be treated together since the major editions/apparatuses that have been announced have not appeared as yet; and (2) the return to the TR as the best NT text by a few, but this requires no additional comment, though there are continuing attempts to provide a scholarly basis for that viewpoint. Treatment of the evaluation of readings has been incorporated into point 2, below, but see also Epp 1976a [now Chapter 8].

8. Aland 1979a: 3. The Weiss text, which highly valued B, held the deciding vote for the older Nestle editions.

unavailable to or were not utilized by Westcott-Hort. Furthermore, this close similarity between the text of our best hand-editions today and that of WH does not mean — as Aland wants to make the Hatch Lecture say — that Westcott-Hort "return with their theories, as if 100 years had not passed since the appearance of their edition" (1979a: 5), for the similarity of texts does not validate Westcott-Hort's theories (as Aland misunderstands me to advocate), nor should it be thought that to arrive at a critical text concurrent with that of WH is necessarily intrinsically undesirable — or that it is necessarily desirable. That is not the issue. What this textual resemblance does, however, is to raise the question of progress; this was and still is my argument: With all of our new manuscript materials and the many valuable research tools produced in the twentieth century, where is the *methodological* advance if our critical text still approximates that of the late nineteenth century or if we still cannot clearly trace its early history? This is a complicated but not unimportant question. Certainly the apparatuses of present-day editions, when compared with their predecessors, are laden with more abundant and more accurate information from earlier and more numerous Greek MSS and also contain improved data on the versions and Fathers, all of which represent a century's rich harvest; but if exegetes still use a text only moderately different from what they used a hundred years ago, what have our vastly increased manuscript discoveries and analysis done for us? Do they confirm the methods and theories that produced the text of a hundred years ago? All of us would quickly answer "Certainly not!" Do they show that new methods and theories coincidentally yield a generally similar result? That would be a clear possibility and represents the answer that we would like to give, but it would be a possible answer only if we happened to possess distinctly new methods and theories. Or have we perchance arrived at a text roughly similar in character to that of the past by somehow circumventing the whole methodological question? I would venture the suggestion that it is more by default than by reason and design that our best critical text today bears the image of the best nineteenth-century text, and in this connection it is not adequate to affirm, as Aland does, that "the New Testament can have possessed only *one* text" [a truism] and therefore hand-editions are not likely to deviate radically from one another, for each is likely to have a close relation to the *Vorlage* upon which its text is built (1979a: 4-5). That is too easy an avoidance of the methodological issue, and surely we should be able to offer a better explanation than that for the close concurrence of present and past texts of the NT. To recall again Aland's 1964 comparison of the NT text to a ship (Aland 1965: 346),[9] we seem still — whether we like it or not — to be crossing the Atlantic in an 1881 vessel, although its hull seems to have been strengthened with additional, recently discovered materials, its superstructure has been adorned with new furnishings, and therefore we launch out on it with a certain increased sense of confidence. Yet, if the ship has not been redesigned and reconstructed in accordance with new technological theories and engineering principles, which in turn utilize an advanced knowledge of the new and better materials, where is the progress? This point in the Hatch Lecture was as

---

9. The article was updated for publication in Aland 1967: 180-201, though without this comparison.

simple as that: Where is the substantive advance if the "standard" texts of the Greek NT then and now are so close in character and if, at the same time, we possess no comprehensive and generally accepted theory to support and justify that form of the text? All of this, however, leads directly into the next area of concern.

II. Progress toward a Theory and History of the Earliest New Testament Text

Nearly forty percent of the Hatch Memorial Lecture was devoted to the methodological issues just alluded to, issues that I considered (and still do) to be both among the most difficult and also the most crucial in NT textual criticism, namely, (1) the formulation of theories or hypotheses to explain both the striking diversities and the positive relationships between and among the NT manuscript witnesses and groups of witnesses, especially in the earliest period of their transmission, and then, if possible, (2) the reconstruction of the history of the earliest NT text. Aland in this general connection speaks of the "naïveté" and of the "fundamental error" of anyone who still hopes to find ways to trace back through our manuscript tradition in some kind of objective fashion and to recover the pathways of early textual transmission, hoping thereby to isolate the original text. Moreover, he says, to hope for the recovery of early exemplars or to envision "lodestar" MSS (like Westcott-Hort's B or Tischendorf's ℵ, or even P[75]) that would point the way directly to the original text is "to dream the impossible dream."[10] Above all, says Aland, textual theories and historical reconstructions such as those of Westcott-Hort must be laid to rest, for "the age of Westcott-Hort and of Tischendorf is definitely over!" (Aland and Aland 1979: 43*).

Now, as is well known, the genealogical method of classical philology, which established a stemma for the manuscript transmission of a literary work, has been almost entirely abandoned by NT textual critics, though its validity for establishing relationships within a smaller group (a "family") of MSS (though not in a "tribe" or "text-type") has been generally recognized.[11] As is also well known, Westcott-Hort and others, such as von Soden and Streeter — to take some random examples — advocated various, often discrete theories to explain how the textual tradition developed as it did in its early history, and how it has left to us the manuscript remains that we possess, and — as is equally well known — we have rejected, in whole or in part, these particular theories. For example, we no longer think of Westcott-Hort's "Neutral" text as neutral; we no longer think of their "Western" text as western or as uniting the textual elements they selected; and, of course, we no longer think so simplistically or so confidently about recovering "the New Testament in the Original Greek."

The pertinent question raised seven years ago was what progress have we made in the twentieth century in this broad area of theory and history, for we seem

---

10. Aland 1979: 11; cf. Aland and Aland 1979: 43*. His phrase is "the unfulfillable dream," but I have taken the liberty of using the language of the popular song "The Impossible Dream," from Dale Wasserman, *Man of La Mancha* (music by Mitch Leigh, lyrics by Joe Darion), which conveys, of course, the same meaning.

11. Colwell 1947; reprinted in Colwell 1969: 63-83; see esp. p. 82.

to have been unable to formulate a theory of the NT text that would explain and justify the modern critical text, which, coincidentally or otherwise, still stands so close to that of the preceding century, and, in addition, we remain largely in the dark as to how we might reconstruct the textual history that has left in its wake — in the form of MSS and fragments — numerous pieces of a puzzle that we seem incapable of fitting together. Westcott-Hort, von Soden, and others had sweeping theories (which we have largely rejected) to undergird their critical texts, but we seem now to have no such theories and no plausible sketches of the early history of the text that are widely accepted. What progress, then, have we made? Are we more advanced than our predecessors when, after showing their theories to be unacceptable, we offer no such theories at all to vindicate our accepted text? Hardly! As a matter of fact, our failure becomes all the more glaring in juxtaposition with the abundance of newly found textual materials and fresh knowledge.

In precisely this connection, however, Aland seems now to call into question the whole search for a theory and history of the NT text. He does so in two ways: first, by his recent, though very brief, statement of his own text-critical method, and second, by his long-standing but recently reemphasized position on the importance and role of the NT papyri. As to the first, in two places recently Aland has furnished a thumbnail sketch of his method — put forward as the only proper and only possible method — in NT textual criticism, and he has even ventured (though reluctantly) to give it a name: the "local-genealogical method." These descriptions are found in the "Introduction" to NA[26] (43*) and in the article in the Matthew Black Festschrift (10); elsewhere he is referred to already as the method's "champion" (in the reprint of 1979a: 42). He describes his method as follows, stating first, however, that:

> It is impossible to proceed from the assumption of a manuscript stemma, and on the basis of a full review and analysis of the relationships obtaining among the variety of interrelated branches in the manuscript tradition, to undertake a *recensio* of the data as one would do with other Greek texts.

He then goes on to say:

> Decisions must be made one by one, instance by instance. This method has been characterized as eclecticism, but wrongly so. After carefully establishing the variety of readings offered in a passage and the possibilities of their inter-pretation, it must always then be determined afresh on the basis of external and internal criteria which of these readings (and frequently they are quite numer-ous) is the original, from which the others may be regarded as derivative. From the perspective of our present knowledge, this local-genealogical method (if it must be given a name) is the only one which meets the requirements of the New Testament textual tradition. (Aland and Aland 1979: 43*)

The designation "local-genealogical" is more clearly explained elsewhere. Following the collection of the variants and their attestation in the Greek MSS, the versions, and the Fathers, the method involves " — just as in classical philology — the appli-cation of the genealogical method, only with the distinction that the stemma drawn up is valid, not for the entire writing, but only for the places under discussion (and their surrounding text!)" (1979a: 10). Aland justifies this independent treatment of separate variation-units by saying that the "living" text of the NT — continually influenced as it was by various, strong forces — follows other laws than does the "dead" standard text of a classical author transmitted by scholars and schoolmasters; the result is that a NT MS "almost from place to place may have a different value" (10). In each locale, then, the genealogy of variants is constructed so as to isolate that variant reading from which all the others successively are to be explained, at the same time taking into full consideration all applicable internal criteria (such as the writing's style, vocabulary, and theology); this process, says Aland, "must yield the original text" (10) and, as he emphasizes, it is the process that was employed by the editorial committee that produced the new "standard text" to be found in the UBS[3] and NA[26].

Although the name is new, naturally this "local-genealogical" method is not itself new, but in the formulation that Aland gives it the method both affirms and rejects text-critical method as practiced in classical philology, for it accepts and applies the genealogical method to NT MSS, but in a most important way it also rejects it, for — as mentioned earlier — the stemma drawn up is valid, not for an entire literary work, but only for the particular variation-unit under discussion, and one acknowledged result is that a given MS may have a varying value from reading to reading and, accordingly, may be expected to reflect a multifarious textual character or complexion. This application of the genealogical method means that Aland has amended the almost universal agreement among NT textual critics regarding the classical genealogical method — namely, that while it is not applicable at the level of "text-types," it may be useful at the level of textual "families" — for Aland now goes one step further by claiming that the method is applicable only at the level of the individual variation-unit. Furthermore, although Aland in a very recent study speaks of the formation (by computer) of manuscript groups and "large complexes" of MSS (1979b: 80-82), his "local-genealogical" approach really seems to represent a rejection of the whole enterprise of grouping NT manuscript witnesses for the purpose of tracing the history of the text. Perhaps that is why he finds my pleading for a theory and history of the NT text to be "dreaming the impossible dream" (see n. 10).

It is curious that precisely in the context of explaining the "local-genealogical" method Aland interjects a striking statement that would seem to invalidate not only that method — which he is in the course of describing — but every objective method in NT textual criticism, a statement that might be said to leave us nearly speechless: in referring to the "expert practitioner," whom he describes (in a footnote) as one who stands "in contrast to 'amateurs,' who in general live on theory," he defines the "expert" textual critic not only as one who cares not for theory, but also as one:

> who himself has carried out countless collations and interacts constantly with the variants and the variation possibilities of the NT tradition, from which he gains judgment as to the value of the statements of individual manuscripts, [and who] at sight of the variants and their attestation at a given place generally will very soon be clear as to where the original text is to be sought. (10)

Now, while all of us recognize the strategic importance of practiced experience, this statement — appearing as it does in the very discussion of method — could be understood, on the one hand, as advocating something akin to what has been called "the cult of the best MS," for it suggests that the expert learns to look upon certain individual MSS as time and time again possessing a certain positive (or, conversely, negative) value. It is clear from this immediate context and elsewhere, however, that this is not what Aland means, for he consistently rejects any single MS as "a guideline we can normally depend on for determining the text."[12] On the other hand, his statement might more easily — though more shockingly — be understood as advocating textual criticism by *intuition*. Could he be suggesting that NT textual criticism is entirely art? — that the practiced expert knows almost instinctively where the original lies? To be sure, some have tried to make textual criticism entirely *science*, but certainly Metzger is correct when he begins his standard manual by characterizing it as *both science and art* (1968a: v). All things considered, however, it is doubtful that Aland really intends to advocate textual criticism by intuition, for in the immediate context he simultaneously affirms the "local-genealogical" method, thereby ruling out intuition; yet his statement remains an anomaly — and a somewhat disturbing one — to those many scholars who search for text-critical methods that are based in some way on knowledge of the broader history of NT textual transmission and who consciously affirm the value of theory (something Aland seems to denigrate) as the supporting foundation upon which the practiced expert might base his work.

It is worth probing another point arising from the discussion of the "local-genealogical" method, namely, Aland's suggestion that a NT MS may have a different worth virtually from variation-unit to variation-unit. From one perspective, this statement is, of course, not surprising, for we all recognize the extraordinary degree of "mixture" (if that is the proper term) to be found in NT MSS. From another perspective, however, the statement might be understood to mean that separate NT MSS do not possess or manifest a particular textual character or stamp. That view would, I think, fly in the face of much demonstrable evidence; for example, Codex Bezae possesses and evinces something that can only be called a "textual character" or "complexion," and it is evident, not merely at an occasional or isolated locale, but at point after point, at reading after reading; P[38] in a striking fashion shares with Codex Bezae numerous textual features, revealing a distinctive textual "character"; P[66] has a textual "character," both in its text and in its corrections (see Fee 1968b, esp. 76-83); various profiling methods suggest that MSS (often in common) show distinctive textual "patterns"; and many Byzantine MSS show (and share) a "quality" of fullness — and these are merely random and rather obvious examples. If, however, as Aland's statement implies, MSS may not be described in terms of something we are permitted to call their textual character, then the traditional way of grouping MSS does become problematic, and that, in turn, would call into question any reconstruction of the history of the NT text that proceeds through identification of texts similar in character. I sincerely doubt that we have reached the point of abandoning the claim that textual character can be identified in and for entire MSS, though it must

12. Aland and Aland 1979: 43*, where the "local-genealogical" method is also discussed.

be emphasized again that the construction of a stemma is *not* what is envisioned in a reconstruction of the history of the NT text, but something considerably looser, for the NT was indeed a "living" text.

To summarize, Aland does seem to allow for a "theory" of the text and for a sketch of its "history" at the level of the individual variation-unit, but he states directly and in other ways implies that a broader theory of the NT text is neither necessary nor possible and that the search for a history of the text beyond that of the individual variation-unit has little validity and even less likelihood of success. The Hatch Lecture clearly acknowledged the immense difficulty of establishing such a theory and history of the NT text, but unambiguous responses from numerous NT textual critics in Great Britain, Europe, and North America suggest that few would support Aland's implication that the search for a broad theory and a comprehensive history of the text is invalid, unnecessary, or — in the final analysis — impossible. As suggested below, rightly understood and conceived, it is a difficult but not an impossible dream.

The second way in which Aland seems to call into question the search for a theory and history of the earliest NT text is through the prominence that he gives to the NT papyri. The Hatch Lecture devoted nearly three pages to his views on this matter (1974: 399-401), which need not be covered again here, and Aland's otherwise hypercritical response contains no complaint that these particular views have been misunderstood or misrepresented, though he does take strong exception to what he sees in the Hatch Lecture as a severe undervaluing of the papyri. For example, he objects to fixing the increase in known papyri since the turn of the century at 600%; rather — using a different basis of comparison — he states that the increase in the use of the papyri in critical editions since then amounts to 9000%, and he insists that *qualitatively* the increased significance of the papyri is a "multiple" of that very high figure (1979a: 3). This prime importance of the papyri is reinforced in the recent "Introduction" to NA[26], where Aland claims that the forty earliest papyri and the four earliest (but fragmentary) uncials are "of automatic [*automatisch*] significance, because they were written before the third/fourth century, and therefore belong to the period before the rise of the major text types" (K. and B. Aland, 1979: 12*; cf. 49*). Among these, the most significant of all, he says, is P[75], followed closely by P[45] and P[66]. (These, of course, are the three early papyri with the greatest *quantity* of text [only P[46] and P[47] come close in amount of preserved content], but if a textual "character" can be observed in a fragment like P[38], who is to say that it is *qualitatively* less significant because an accident of history allowed only a dozen of its verses to survive?) Aland, then, views the papyri as having changed everything, for "the manuscript basis for Westcott-Hort's work dates from the IV century. . . . Today the early papyri provide a wide range of witness to the text of about 200 A.D., and these are Greek witnesses" (ibid., 43*). It comes as no surprise, therefore — as a response to a claim in the Hatch Lecture that, while papyri discoveries will contribute to positive text-critical developments in the future, recent methodological developments (such as certain quantitative methods) will more likely aid in the reconstruction of the early history of the text (Epp 1974: 407) — to find Aland exclaiming that "great astonishment strikes once again." Why? Because, he explains, "if this 'early history of the text' is visible anywhere, it is directly and immediately [visible] only in the nearly forty papyri and uncials from the time up to the third/fourth century. Here it [the early history of the text] can be studied in the original [!]; all other efforts must remain reconstructed theories" (1979a: 11).

In view of what is known about NT textual transmission, this is an extraordinary — an astonishing — statement of the importance of the papyri, though not inconsistent with Aland's previously expressed viewpoints on the subject. When seven years ago, with some admitted reservation, I applied to him the paraphrase of a well-known passage from Ignatius (*Philadelphians* 8), I thought that I perhaps was going too far with what might well be seen as a "smart alecky" remark, but it appears, after all, that Professor Aland really does embrace the view, "Unless I find it written in the papyri, I do not believe it in the gospel" (Epp 1974: 401).

The NT papyri *are* extraordinarily significant, and the earliest ones even more so; that we can all freely acknowledge, and it may be strictly correct to say that the early history of the text is *directly* and *immediately* visible *only* in these earliest papyri and uncials. Yet, can we really be satisfied with so limited a view of that early history? Can we really be content with Egypt as the exclusive locale for this glimpse into the earliest textual history? Was any NT book written there,[13] and does not Egypt therefore clearly represent only a secondary and derivative stage in textual history? Is the accident of circumstance — that papyrus survives almost exclusively in the hot climate and dry sands of Egypt — to dominate and determine how we ultimately write our textual history? Can we proceed with any assurance that these forty randomly surviving earliest MSS are in any real sense *representative* of the entire earliest history of the text? Actually, as a logical principle of proper procedure — as well as common sense — there must be a substantive and defensible basis if something is to have "automatic" significance. But if the only basis that can be established for even this select group of treasured papyri is their early age, it is doubtful that the phrase "of automatic significance" will or ought to be so readily accepted. Should we not seek to assure ourselves — if it can be done — that these most precious earliest monuments of the text constitute, not merely "a wide range of witness to the text of about 200 A.D." (as Aland characterizes them [NA[26]: 43* = K. and B. Aland 1979]), but a genuine representation of discrete forms of the text current in that earliest period — and not only in Egypt. If that cannot be done, nothing is lost and we still have numerous very early Egyptian witnesses that have significance for understanding that period of textual history in Egypt between AD 200 and 300, but we would have witnesses that — in spite of their age — are not necessarily of "automatic significance" for *the* original text of the NT. Yet even this limitation would in no way deny their very great importance. If, however, the earliest papyri can be shown to be representative in a larger sense, much might be gained.[14] To carry the point a bit farther, is it appropriate to hold, as Aland seems to do, that the earliest text circulated in "many and divergent forms, proceeding in different directions, at about the same time, in the same ecclesiastical province" (1965: 334) — a

---

13. Some scholars past and present have suggested that the Fourth Gospel may have been written in Alexandria, but the view has meager support; see the standard commentaries on John. No other NT writing has even a plausible claim to authorship in Egypt.

14. See now Chapter 14 and Epp 1991.

quite acceptable statement — and yet to say (as he does) that these earliest papyri do not fit into the text-types identified from later MSS, suggesting thereby that there is no continuity between those early papyri and the fourth-century and later textual developments? My question, earlier and now, is: Can we not do better than this? Can we not perhaps draw some connections between these earliest papyri and the later points of textual transmission as represented in the more extensive early uncials, the exceptional minuscules, the early Church Fathers, and the earliest versions as far as these can be isolated? Following that, can we not attempt to trace the history of the text and formulate some theory as to how the text developed? The earliest papyri and uncials can furnish the starting point for this process, which in turn can provide a substantive basis for describing their significance with respect to ascertaining the original text, though it is doubtful even then that all of them equally will come to be described as "of automatic significance" for establishing the original NT text.

The "trajectory" model (borrowing a term from Robinson-Koester 1971, who employ that designation) that I earlier proposed, obviously with the tentativeness of a suggestion, was an attempt to draw the earliest papyri into some appropriate relationships with the later textual history and to show the continuity between the earliest witnesses and the massive tradition that followed. The model involved plotting a loose and tentative series of textual steams or trajectories, beginning with those forty earliest papyri and uncials and — based on an assessment of their textual "character" or "complexion" — drawing the appropriate connecting lines with later MSS of similar textual "complexion." The result was the disclosure of only two basic textual streams from that earliest period, one that emerges later as the B-text and one that coalesces later as the D-text.[15] It is this restriction to only two textual streams in the earliest period that leaves Professor Aland, as he puts it, "finally speechless,"[16] implying that at best an incredible naïveté must lie behind such a simplistic and foolish view. I am inclined, however, to persist in this foolishness at least a little longer (as will many other NT textual critics), for with the increase of very early manuscript witnesses — and I fully agree with Aland that these have increased dramatically in the twentieth century — we are in a vastly improved situation for tracing these connections. Moreover, as we refine current methods and as we develop more sophisticated methods for assessing the textual "character" or "complexion" of MSS, we shall be able to make such assessments more confidently. Yet, even our *present* judgments as to the textual character of the earliest papyri and uncials (upon which Aland rightly focuses) permit us to trace textual trajectories *forward* from them to further points on the same line represented by major (and still early) uncials, such as codices B, D, A, and W, and still further to later uncial and minuscule codices. This results, to take some obvious examples, in a trajectory traced from P[75] (third century) through Codex B (fourth century) to Codex L (eighth century), 33 (ninth century), 1739 (tenth century), and 579 (thirteenth century); or (in Acts) from P[29]

15. Epp 1974: 397-400; the reader is directed to the Hatch Lecture for details, for they cannot be repeated here. [Now also see chapter 14.]

16. Aland 1979a: 6. Actually — and unfortunately — he quotes my description of West-cott-Hort as my view, but the point about two early textual streams is made later by me, though not in Westcott-Hort's terms.

and P48 (third century) through P38 (ca. AD 300) to Codex D (fifth century) to 614 and 383 (thirteenth century). With admitted caution, these lines of trajectory also may be extended *backwards* behind (i.e., earlier than) the earliest papyri and uncials to show presumed lines of development, though considerable speculation is involved in such an exercise. Merely connecting the *known* points — based on the identifiable textual character of the extant witnesses — can, however, be instructive for understanding the earlier history of the NT text and may constitute the basis for a broader theory of the text. That was the point that the Hatch Lecture was making, as well as pointing out (I think indisputably) that looking at the forty earliest papyri and uncials *in isolation* (as Aland seems intent upon doing) cannot enlighten us very much as to how the NT text developed in the early generations of Christianity; rather, we need to draw the trajectories and mark the appropriate connections between these earliest witnesses and the later witnesses of similar textual character so as to show thereby the direction and movement of the text in that early developmental period. It was for this reason that I referred in the Hatch Lecture — perhaps somewhat ungraciously — to Professor Aland's view of the early papyri in isolation from the later witnesses as a "somewhat *static*" view and attributed to him a portrayal of the period of the early papyri as "an archipelagic phenomenon and one insulated from the period of the great uncials which followed" (1974: 399). Yet that is the image that he continues to project. We can, on the contrary, show that there *is* continuity between the earliest papyri (or at least many of them) and the fourth century and later textual developments, and we can and ought to utilize these connections as the basis for formulating a theory and for tracing the history of the NT text in the earliest periods of its transmission. It would be uneconomical to repeat here the preliminary proposals — already alluded to — on textual trajectories (i.e., that only two distinctive *and continuing* streams of text — at opposite edges of a spectrum — emerge from our textual history, which we designate the B-text and D-text, with a third stream leading abortively to Codex W) or to rehearse the issues raised in this connection in the Hatch Lecture (390-401), but this is an area that continues to impress me (and many of my colleagues) as both an obvious and a legitimate field of inquiry, as well as one with renewed possibilities in the wake of the unprecedented papyri discoveries of the twentieth century.

Finally, in connection with Aland's high valuation of the NT papyri, we are confronted with an additional claim from him that will astonish many. In a forthcoming article on "Der neue 'Standard-Text' in seinem Verhältnis zu den frühen Papyri und Majuskeln" (1981), which — as its title indicates — raises the question of how the "early text" contained in the earliest MSS is related to the new "standard text" of UBS3 and NA26, Aland renders his judgment that:

> The new "standard text" has passed the test of the early papyri and uncials. It corresponds, in fact, to the text of the early time. . . . At no place and at no time do we find readings here [i.e., in the earliest papyri and uncials] that require a change in the "standard text." If the investigation conducted here in all its brevity and compactness could be presented fully, the detailed apparatus accompanying each variant would convince the last doubter. A hundred years after Westcott-Hort, the goal of an edition of the New Testament "in the original

Greek" seems to have been reached. . . . In the framework of the present possibilities, the desired goal appears now to have been attained, to offer the writings of the New Testament in the form of the text that comes nearest to that which, from the hand of their authors or redactors, they set out on their journey in the church of the 1st and 2d centuries. (1981: 275)[17]

With this striking announcement that in and through the new "standard text" found in UBS[3] and NA[26] "a hundred years after Westcott-Hort the goal of an edition of the NT 'in the original Greek' appears to have been reached," we seem to have come full circle. On the one hand, we are told in no uncertain terms that the Hatch Lecture was misguided even in invoking the Westcott-Hort categories in a discussion of the history and theory of the NT text and was naïve in demanding that some broad text-critical theory ought to be sought to justify the form of the NT text that scholars and exegetes use, for "the age of Westcott-Hort . . . is definitely over!" (K. and B. Aland 1979: 43*). On the other hand, the same audacious claim that Westcott-Hort made in the title of their 1881 work — that their textual method had yielded "The New Testament in the Original Greek" — is made now for a text not greatly dissimilar from that of WH and one that disclaims any comprehensive textual theory as its basis and justification except a "local-genealogical" assessment of each variation-unit and the "automatic significance" of the earliest papyri and uncials. Lest I be misunderstood again, emphasis must be placed on the fact that both the UBS[3] and the NA[26] editions are monumental achievements of twentieth-century NT textual criticism, for both their common text and their differing but extensive apparatuses will well serve textual critics and exegetes for some time to come; and our gratitude to Professors Aland, Black, Martini, Metzger, and Wikgren and to the United Bible Societies for the former volume (as well as the accompanying *Textual Commentary*) and to Professor Aland and Dr. Barbara Aland and to the Münster Institut for the latter can hardly be overemphasized — we are grateful beyond measure. Yet, an edition of the NT "in the original Greek" cannot, it seems to me, be made a reality by fiat or proclamation, nor can the validity of such a claim be so easily pontificated. Rather, textual critics at large will require a more comprehensive and convincing rationale for the text they accredit as the nearest possible approximation to the original — a rationale that reaches beyond the highly valuable but severely limited assessment of individual variation-units *in isolation* and a rationale that seeks and finds a broader historical base than the early and precious but narrowly restricted and clearly derivative manuscript witnesses of Egypt. Naturally, to state these *desiderata* is much easier than to fulfill them, but that difficulty does not relieve the scholar of his or her obligation to evaluate critically the methods employed by NT textual critics down through the years and the claims they make for the NT texts

---

17. This (with some omissions) is the last paragraph of the essay. Aland gives in English the words "in the original Greek," quoting from the title of Westcott-Hort's edition. He does qualify his statement to the extent of acknowledging that it is not made with the "self-certainty of Westcott-Hort," for the "standard text" has an extensive apparatus that will alert scholars to numerous "thoughtful considerations" (whereas Westcott-Hort presented no apparatus to suggest that other options were viable — although vol. 1 has a ten-page list of rejected readings and vol. 2 has an "Appendix" containing 140 pages of "Notes on Select Readings").

produced on the basis of their methods and principles of criticism. It is in that spirit that this evaluation is presented.

In conclusion, then, we may very well be able to live for the present on a "practitioner" approach to NT textual criticism, employing a "local-genealogical" method that includes the application of the appropriate external and internal criteria variation-unit by variation-unit, but in the long run we shall want — and I think need — to have something better, something that rests more firmly on the solid rock of historical reconstruction and less upon the shifting sands of a serviceable but tentative and sometimes slippery eclecticism[18] or a myopic variant-by-variant assessment, even though it is in the hands of an expert practitioner. It is to be freely confessed however, that thus far we have failed to reach down to that desired bedrock and that we also are not entirely sure of the procedures that will bring us to it. Nevertheless, I am confident that we should and must press on toward that goal; perhaps we should dare even to "dream the impossible dream."

18. See Epp 1976c [now Chapter 8].

CHAPTER 7

RIGOROUS OR REASONED ECLECTICISM — WHICH?

Gordon D. Fee

The following paper is a critique of the NT text-critical methodology used by Professor Kilpatrick and J. K. Elliott, his former student and the editor of this Festschrift. However, it is offered as an expression of sincere appreciation for Professor Kilpatrick's many contributions to scholarship and for his warm personal friendship.[1]

I.

There can be little question that the currently reigning method in NT textual criticism is eclecticism. It is the method openly espoused by the translators of the RSV (Grant 1946) and the NEB (Tasker 1964: vii-x), and used, if not by that name, by the editors of the UBS[3] (Metzger 1971: xiii-xxxi). Not all scholars, to be sure, are pleased with this state of affairs. Some have even suggested that it is only a provisional method, belonging "to a day like ours in which we know only that the traditional theory of the text is faulty but cannot yet see clearly to correct the fault" (Clark 1954: 37-38). Nonetheless, eclecticism is the currency of the realm and will undoubtedly be so for years to come.

The term "eclecticism," however, is an umbrella term, and not all who stand under it mean the same thing. On the one hand, it refers to a method such as that used by the translators of the NEB and the editors of the UBS[3], where the age, weight, and diversity of witnesses to a variant play a significant role in textual decisions. This method, called "rational" or "reasoned" eclecticism,[2] has been defined by Vaganay as one where there is "no shutting up of the different branches of the science into watertight compartments; verbal criticism, external and internal criticism, all have their parts to play, and they must give each other mutual support" (1937: 91-92).

In contrast Professor Kilpatrick and Dr. Elliott have advocated a "rigorous" eclecticism (sometimes called "thoroughgoing" or "consistent"),[3] in which intrinsic

---

1. [The original publication of this paper in a Festschrift for George D. Kilpatrick accounts for the introductory remarks.]
2. The term comes from Lagrange 1935.
3. See the following significant studies by Professor Kilpatrick: 1943, 1963a, 1963b,

and transcriptional probabilities ideally are the sole criteria, irrespective of the date and nature of the external evidence which supports a given reading. Kilpatrick has repeatedly affirmed that "readings must be considered severally on their intrinsic character" (1965: 205-6); they must be "accepted or rejected, each and all, on their merits" (1963a: 65). This means further that since no MS or text-type has escaped corruption, textual decisions must not be made on the basis of which MSS support a reading, and further that the variant of any single MS has as much authority as does the combined witness of all the rest.

Elliott has spelled out this method in greater detail and has offered a Greek text of the Pastoral Epistles based on internal evidence alone. More strongly than Kilpatrick, he inveighs against "the cult of the best manuscript" and repeatedly condemns a methodology which uses "exclusively documentary criteria" (1968a: 1-14).

At issue between "rigorous" and "reasoned" eclecticism is the weight, if at all, one gives the external evidence in making textual choices. The editors of the UBS[3], for example, often appeal to "the age and diversity of text-type of the Greek witnesses" (Metzger 1971: 27 *et passim*). Kilpatrick and Elliott reject such appeals out of hand. But this is not the only difference. Also at issue are the internal criteria which Kilpatrick and Elliott tend to emphasize, sometimes to the exclusion of others.

Over the years Professor Kilpatrick has offered several studies in which two primary emphases have emerged: Atticism[4] and author's style.[5] Elliott has put these propositionally: (1) "When faced with a straight choice between an Attic and a non-Attic expression, the latter is more likely to be what the original author wrote" (1968a: 9). (2) "A variant consistent with the author's style and usage elsewhere, is more likely to be original than a variant out of character with the general usage, other things being equal" (1968a: 8).

This methodology has from time to time been called into question. E. J. Epp (1965: 172-73), E. C. Colwell (1969: 154-55), and B. M. Metzger (1968a: 177-79) have each cautioned against the short-sightedness of seeing Atticism as the basic kind of stylistic change occurring in the second century, and Metzger in particular has warned against decisions which place undue confidence in variants reflecting an author's style (1968a: 178). Furthermore, E. C. Colwell has argued convincingly that to neglect the external evidence is to run the risk of default as an historian.

The purpose of this paper is to spell out in greater detail the inadequacy of rigorous eclecticism as a total method, an inadequacy which is essentially twofold: (1) It assumes a faulty theory of textual corruption and transmission, and therefore an unrealistic — and unhistorical — attitude toward the various textual witnesses. (2) Having abandoned the evidence of the witnesses, it leaves textual judgments to the whims of the

---

1965, 1967a, 1967b, 1969, 1970. And by Dr. Elliott: 1968a, 1968b, 1969, 1970, 1972a, 1972b. Dr. Elliott (1973: 300) has recently called the results of this method a "radically eclectic text." This is a useful article in that he has brought together the resultant text of a great many of the studies listed in this note.

4. E.g., Kilpatrick 1956, 1963a, 1963b, 1965: 202-4, 1967a, 1967b.

5. E.g., Kilpatrick 1943: 30-34, 1956, 1960a, 1960b, 1963a, 1969.

individual practitioner. This problem is especially acute whenever variation can be shown to have two equally plausible explanations. In such cases rigorous eclecticism will tend either to become monotone, that is, to lock in on one possibility of error to the exclusion of others, or else it will simply be cast adrift amid a welter of options, wherein the choices are made in a most random and arbitrary fashion.

II.

Since Professor Kilpatrick has repeatedly expressed disapproval of Hort's methodology, he also of necessity has rejected Hort's theory of textual transmission. For it must be remembered that Hort did not use genealogy in order to discover the original NT text. Whether justified or not, Hort used genealogy solely to dispense with the Syrian (Byzantine) text. Once he had eliminated the Byzantines from serious consideration, his preference for the Neutral (Egyptian) MSS was based *strictly* on intrinsic and transcriptional probability. That is, he applied the canons of internal criticism *first* to the documents, then to the "original" text. In his own words:

> Where then one of the documents is found habitually to contain these morally certain or at least strongly preferred readings, and the other habitually to contain their rejected rivals, we can have no doubt, first, that the text of the first has been transmitted in comparative purity, and that the text of the second has suffered comparatively large corruption; and, next, that the superiority of the first must be as great in the variations in which Internal Evidence of Readings has furnished no decisive criterion as in those which have enabled us to form a comparative appreciation of the two texts. (Westcott and Hort 1881: 2.32)

His judgment that Codex Vaticanus (B) best represents the text which has been "transmitted in comparative purity" is well known:

> It will be evident . . . that B must be regarded as having preserved not only a very ancient text, but a very pure line of very ancient text, and that with comparatively small depravation either by scattered ancient corruptions otherwise attested or by individualisms of the scribe himself. (Ibid.: 2.250-51)

Kilpatrick, on the other hand, not only rejects any MS or tradition as having a relatively pure transmission, but also almost altogether disregards questions of manuscript relationships. He thereby also discards one of Hort's basic principles: "All trustworthy restoration of corrupted texts is founded on the study of their history" (ibid.: 2.20).

In place of a careful study of documents and their history, Kilpatrick has tended to relegate that history to the period *before* the documents — the second century. He has frequently cited with approval the contention of Vogels that, "apart from errors, the great majority of variants in the New Testament text have come into being before AD 200." He has further argued that "by the end of the second century A.D. Christian opinion had hardened against deliberate alteration of the text," a hardening which was "connected not with the canonical status of the New Testament but with the reaction against the rehandling of the text by the second century heretics" (1963b: 128-31; cf. 1965: 190).

The importance of this argument for Kilpatrick's methodology cannot be overestimated. The assumption that all textual corruption derives from the second century, plus the general disregard for knowledge of individual MSS, textual relationships, and the citing habits of individual Fathers allows him to posit that the original text may be found *anywhere* in the later witnesses. It is as if the original text were scattered during the second century as pieces of a puzzle, to reappear in the most random geographical or chronological fashion — even in a single MS from the medieval period, although *all* of that MS's hundreds of relatives do *not* have the reading. As Colwell has put it, "Such an editor relegates the manuscripts to the role of supplier of readings" (1969: 154).

But there are some serious criticisms which may be leveled against this theory of textual corruption. In the first place, the relegation of textual corruption to the second century and a hardening against deliberate change thereafter does not seem to accord with the actual data. P66, for example, which was copied at the *end* of the second century, underwent a considerable deliberate revision. But that revision, made chiefly by the original scribe, shows no reaction to heresy, nor does it manifest a concern for the original wording per se (Fee 1968b: 57-75). Furthermore, if Colwell is correct that singular readings are clues to the scribe's fingerprints upon the codex (1965: 372-76), then the plethora of such readings in some MSS as over against others (e.g., P66 ℵ D W) indicates that more than mere carelessness is involved in the copying process. Finally, the complete disregard for the wording per se that one finds in such "orthodox" Fathers as Tertullian, Epiphanius, and Chrysostom suggests that hardening against deliberate change is scarcely a trademark of the third and fourth centuries.

The problems with this theory, however, lie deeper still. Rational eclecticism agrees in principle that no MS or group of MSS has a *prima facie* priority to the original text. Furthermore, it agrees in principle that every variant should be considered on its own merits. Hort's famous, and surely correct, dictum — "Knowledge of documents should precede final judgement upon readings" — may *not* be turned into "Knowledge of documents shall prejudge judgments upon readings."

Rational eclecticism, however, in the words of Duplacy, will plead "donc la cause de l'histoire et surtout, au nom de l'histoire, la cause des documents" (1965/66: 125). For it is both illogical and unhistorical to imply, as both Kilpatrick and Elliott do, that because no MSS have escaped corruption, therefore all MSS are equally corrupt, and no MS(S) may be judged better than others. In fact, the very internal considerations for which Kilpatrick and Elliott argue as a basis for the recovery of the original text, Hort used *first* for the evaluation of the existing witnesses. And if his evaluation of B as "neutral" was too high a regard for that MS, it does not alter his judgment that compared to all other MSS B *is* a superior witness.

This has been confirmed by recent studies which have applied the principles of intrinsic and transcriptional probability to several of the papyrus discoveries. For example, Günther Zuntz subjected P46 to a most rigorous analysis as to its quality in preserving the original text of 1 Corinthians and Hebrews in various types of variation (word order, interpolations, LXX quotations, features of style and grammar). His conclusions:

> The excellent quality of the text represented by our oldest manuscript, P46, stands out again. As so often before, we must here be careful to distinguish between the very poor work of the scribe who penned it and the basic text which he so poorly rendered. P46 abounds with scribal blunders, omissions, and also additions. In some of them the scribe anticipated the errors of later copyists; in some other instances he shares an older error; but the vast majority are his own uncontested property. Once they have been discarded, there remains a text of outstanding (though not absolute) purity. (Zuntz 1953: 212-13)

I have subjected P66 and P75 to a similar investigation with similar results (1968b: 36-56; 1974: 31-44). The singular and subsingular readings of P66 are all of secondary character precisely because they reflect the scribe's wildness in copying and his tendency to "smooth out" the text. With regard to certain clearly discernible features of Johannine style, P66, in nonsingular variants, more often preserves the Johannine original than the Western and Byzantine witnesses, but whenever it varies from its close relatives, P75 and B, it picks up predominantly secondary readings. Such judgments will affect the value of its witness in variant after variant.

As to P75, it can be shown to be precisely what Hort considered B to be: a very pure line of very ancient text. For example, when tested along with all other witnesses in Luke 10 and 11 for variants reflecting possible harmonization to Matthew, Mark, or the LXX, P75 and B stood alone in their "comparative purity." Codex D, for example, had thirty-six such harmonizing variants, the Byzantine majority had twenty-seven, while P75 and B had six, and some of theirs were more likely the result of other factors than harmonization. The results were almost identical when the tests were made against certain features of Johannine style (asyndeton, anarthrous personal names, "vernacular possessives," and ὅτι-*recitativum*), which were chosen because there were *both* Johannine *and* generally unidiomatic Greek, thus bringing them also under the principle of *lectio difficilior*.

The point is that MSS *may* be evaluated as to their scribal characteristics and their general worth in preserving the original readings. And such judgments *must* play their proper role in textual decisions. This verdict will be noted at several points, but it is nowhere more demonstrable than in the way that Hort, on the one hand, and Kilpatrick and Elliott, on the other, evaluate singular and subsingular readings.

III.

It is well known that Hort often adopted singular readings of B because of his evaluation of the general superior quality of this MS. But he was no blind follower of B; he opted for its singular readings *only* when internal considerations merited it. He therefore distinguished between those singular readings which he judged to be the "clerical errors" of B itself and those which "must be reasonably supposed to have belonged to the text of its exemplar" (Westcott and Hort 1881: 2.230-46). The implication of this is clear: In the time of Hort some of B's singular readings were solecisms of the scribe (therefore, truly singular readings), while others really belonged to the "Neutral" text-type, and if earlier (or other) MSS of this text-type were ever found, the readings of B would no longer be singular. The subsequent discoveries of the Egyptian MSS P45, P46, P66, P72, and P75 have demonstrated the

128

extraordinary skill with which Hort made his judgments. For example, in Luke and John, where both P[75] and B have extant text, B now has forty-seven singular readings. Only one of these (a word order variant at John 10:32) is found in the WH text. On the other hand, there are many instances in WH where B was singular in 1881, but now is supported by P[75], and sometimes also by other subsequent discoveries. In other words, Hort did not consider these as solecisms of B but as belonging to the "Neutral" (therefore for him, "original") text; and subsequent discoveries have proven him right.

This does not mean, of course, that Hort was correct in following B or that such readings are indeed original because they have additional support. What is suggested rather is that Hort was aware of the tenuous nature of the singular reading, and that he adopted such readings only when they occurred in a MS which, according to his theory of textual transmission, was found to be generally superior.

Kilpatrick and Elliott, on the other hand, on the basis of their theory of "random transmission," are prepared to opt for singular and subsingular readings wherever their principles lead them. Elliott does indeed recognize the problems involved and briefly speaks to them in his presentation of the case for rigorous eclecticism (1968a: 10-11). He argues in principle that "a reading can be accepted with greater confidence, when it has stronger support" (11). But he also argues, and cites Aland and Tasker in support, that in principle "there is no reason why an original reading should not have been preserved in only one ms." (10). He does note that here especially (or only) one needs to be aware of manuscript idiosyncrasies, and concludes (rightly): "When a weakly attested reading is accepted as the true reading, it must be shown why and how the variant came about, and why it was so widely accepted" (10).

But surely the opposite is equally necessary. That is, when one opts for singular readings in such witnesses as P[66], ℵ, D, 1241, or Eusebius (!) in the Gospels, as Kilpatrick does, or 88, 440, 1908, D, F, or Ψ in the Pastorals, as Elliott does, must it not be shown that these MSS have a generally overall reliability that would cause one to side with them *even when they depart from their own relatives,* not to mention the entire textual tradition? In these instances such readings are not necessarily condemned because they are singular, but, as is the case with P[66], ℵ, D, and 1241 in John, because they are singular in MSS whose texts abound in singular readings of patently secondary character.

Furthermore, in practice such choices not only reveal a faulty theory of text, but in almost every case there is a better explanation as to why the singular reading is the variant rather than vice versa. For example, in a discussion of diminutives in the NT, where it is argued that the elimination of diminutives is a feature of second-century Atticizing, Elliott says:

> More significant is the noun νεανίας which occurs in the New Testament at Acts vii 58 and is the only firm example of the noun in the New Testament. The diminutive form νεανίας occurs as a variant for νεανίσκος at Matthew xix 20; Mark xvi 5; Acts xx 9, xxii 17, 18, 22. The noun νεανίας has been substituted for the diminutive form by scribes influenced by Atticism. In all these places the diminutive form should be read. (1970: 392)

Both the strangeness and weaknesses of this argument can be seen once the variants and manuscript data are grouped as follows:

A) Acts 7:58	νεανίου	no variation	
B) Matt 19:20	νεανίας	Θ 700	
	νεανίσκος	Rell	
Mark 16:5	νεανίας	2145	
	νεανίσκος	Rell	
C) Acts 20:9	νεανίας	P74 rell	
	νεανίσκος	614 1108 1245 1518 2147	
Acts 23:17	νεανίαν	P74 rell	
	νεανίσκον	2147	
D) Acts 23:18	νεανίαν	B D Ψ Byz pler TR	
	νεανίσκον	P74 ℵ A C E 33 81 1175 pc	
Acts 23:22	νεανίαν	D Ψ Byz pler TR	
	νεανίσκον	P74 ℵ A B C E 33 pc	

Groups A and B alone fit within Elliott's appraisal of things. Group C, especially the singular reading of 2147 in Acts 23:17, seems to suggest just the opposite. To say here that "νεανίας has been substituted for the diminutive form" is a most peculiar way of looking at textual variation. This seems to ask too much of a single eleventh-century minuscule whose textual relatives all have νεανίαν. How is one to explain how this "original" reading is completely missing in all earlier stages in the transmission of the text?

Furthermore, the question I have asked elsewhere applies here as well. Should not "thoroughgoing eclecticism" lead to "thoroughgoing emendation" (1970b: 506)? For if Elliott had written this article *before* von Soden had collated codex 2147, then he would have had two "firm examples" of νεανίας; and contrariwise, if a MS of any kind were ever found to have νεανίσκου at Acts 7:58, then even this "firm example" would yield to the variant. With tongue in cheek, one wonders what would happen if such a MS were "discovered" similar to that given Erasmus with the *Comma Johanneum* included.

Group D further demonstrates the weakness of this method. Here alone one has substantial support for both variants; and the cause of variation is not related to Atticism at all. As NA26 and von Soden both note, it is a simple case of assimilation to the text of Acts 23:17.[6]

This, of course, does not necessarily condemn *all* singular readings in *all* MSS. The fact that P75 (sometimes with P45) and P46 have eliminated what were once singular or nearly singular readings of B at some points where these MSS in combination seem to preserve the original text, and the fact that each (P46 P75 B) has

___

6. With this one might compare Kilpatrick's siding with a single citation from Eusebius (*d.e.* 10.8; Kilpatrick 1956: 156) in reading μνημεῖον at Mark 16:2, or Elliott's opting for μεταλαμβανόμενον (*cum* 81 2005) at 1 Tim 4:4, and many others, all of which can be better explained as singular assimilations, rather than all other witnesses as having been corrupted by Atticism.

been judged as a careful preservation of a very early type of text, should cause one to allow the *possibility* that any of them in a singular reading best represents this text-type. It does not necessarily follow, of course, that the "best representative of the text-type" also preserves the original text, but it does mean that the original reading may have survived only in the "best" representative of a type of text, not necessarily in the entire group of MSS.

However, all of this is to say that if P[46], P[75] or B does preserve the original text in a singular reading, consideration given to such a reading (besides its best answering the questions of internal criticism) rests chiefly on the judgment as to the generally excellent quality of these MSS. And it must be granted even then that singular readings by their very nature are suspect, which means that there must be *decisive internal evidence* in favor of such a reading before it is considered as original.

IV.

If one is going to take each reading "on its own merits," then the fullest range of intrinsic and transcriptional probabilities must always be kept in view. Professor Kilpatrick himself recognizes this principle and skillfully employs it in some of his arguments against Westcott-Hort (some alleged conflations may be due to omission by homoeoteleuton [1965: 190-91]). However, both Kilpatrick and Elliott appear oblivious to other alternatives whenever Atticism is seen as a possible cause of textual corruption.

Atticism may indeed be a cause of some corruption in the second century, but it is hypothetically equally probable (to this writer, *far* more probable historically) that a Christian scribe in the second century altered a less common form (= the alleged Atticism) to a more common, if less literary, form. This is especially true when the more common form is also septuagintal. One may *not* assume that scribes always to have gone in one direction; and in the second century one may suppose scribes just as often to have preferred a biblical to a nonbiblical idiom. After all, these scribes were Christians, whose spiritual life — and therefore perhaps stylistic idioms — were thoroughly nurtured on the LXX. Kilpatrick, however, does not seem to consider this possibility. He has averred, without supporting evidence from the MSS themselves, that "the tendency of scribes was to eliminate or moderate Semitic features rather than introduce them" (1963a: 69). But the evidence from the MSS and the Church Fathers points to the contrary. This can be demonstrated by a detailed examination of three of Kilpatrick's alleged Atticisms: the case of the object of προσκυνεῖν; ζήσω/ζήσομαι; ἀποκριθεὶς εἶπεν.

A. Kilpatrick has noted that with προσκυνεῖν "the grammarians condemned the dative construction and recommended the accusative"; and therefore he has argued that "we should expect it to be changed to the accusative and not the other way about" (1967a: 154-55). That such may have happened seems likely. In fact, Kilpatrick fails to note the variant in Mark 15:19 where this *is* the likely explanation of the reading of Ψ 4 213 273 440 472 579.

However, his discussion of the variations of this idiom in John and the Apocalypse seems to be crippled by his view of the alleged Atticizing tendencies of the second-century scribes. For example, there are six (possibly seven)[7] occurrences of προσκυνεῖν with an object in John. In two instances the object is τῷ πατρί *without* textual variation (4:21, 23). In two others (4:22 *bis*) the object is a noun clause begun with the relative ὅ (which Kilpatrick suggests "may well be for τούτῳ ὅ"). The other two instances occur with some textual variation of the personal pronoun:

4:23	αὐτόν	P66c P75 B ℵc rell
	αὐτῷ	P66* ℵ* 124c 238 (pc known to Tisch)
4:24	αὐτόν	P66 P75 B ℵc rell
	αὐτῷ	251 (pc known to Tisch)[8]
	omit	ℵ* D* ff2 Herac Novat

Although Kilpatrick is properly hesitant, he favors αὐτῷ as the Johannine original in both cases. His conclusion: "Αὐτόν is probably an Atticising correction, but should we read αὐτῷ with so few witnesses or nothing? Opinions differ, but in any case we have probably no example in John of προσκυνεῖν with the accusative" (1967a: 155-56).

I demur — on two grounds. (1) If the αὐτόν read by the preponderance of witnesses from every geographical and chronological stratum is an "Atticizing" correction, how does one explain how this form so thoroughly replaced the other at these two places while not a single "Atticistic" correction is known anywhere for the two occurrences of τῷ πατρί in the same passage? Surely the more likely explanation of the data is that the author, for some reason unknown to us, wrote αὐτόν and that a few scribes *independently* conformed it to the more common αὐτῷ, either because of the immediately preceding τῷ πατρί or especially because this is the thoroughgoing idiom of the LXX.

(2) An evaluation of the witnesses to αὐτῷ confirms this judgment. The singular reading of codex 251 is of the same kind noted in the preceding section. The αὐτῷ in 4:23 appears to have more support, but the appearance is illusory. Codex 238 is unknown to me, except to note that it is unrelated textually to P66 and ℵ. Furthermore, P66 and ℵ are *textually* unrelated in John 4; therefore the variant does not go back to a common early ancestor. Nor does it go back to the Johannine original. Rather, these MSS are related as to their scribal characteristics — many wild, singular readings, often corrected, usually made in carelessness or conformation to more common expressions, and almost always secondary. In any case, a glance at the photograph of P66 suggests that the scribe made an immediate correction of a careless slip and his αὐτῷ is therefore not a copy of a MS with this reading at all. That is, his αὐτῷ begins and ends with him and is in no way related to ℵ*, nor to the original text of John.

The problem of variants with this idiom in the Apocalypse is more complex; however, Professor Kilpatrick's statement of the problem seems to be somewhat

---

7. I agree with Porter 1966/67 that John 7:38-39a is an interpolation by a later hand.

8. Tischendorf incorrectly includes Eus. *Marcell.*, which reads αὐτόν with the majority; see *GCS* 4 (1906) 5.

misleading. He indicates that προσκυνεῖν occurs with the dative in eighteen instances (actually nineteen; he omits προσεκύνησαν τῷ δράκοντι in 13:4) and that there is a variant with the accusative in ten of the eighteen (variation occurs in fact in thirteen of nineteen), thus implying that the variation is always from the dative to the accusative. But such a presentation is prejudicial.

There are indeed six instances of the dative without variation (τῷ ζῶντι, 4:10; τῷ θεῷ, 7:11; 11:16; 19:4, 10; 22:9), as well as seven others where the dative is read by the majority, and one or a few MSS have the accusative (τῷ δράκοντι, 13:4; τῷ θηρίῳ, 13:4; τῷ ποιήσαντι, 14:7; αὐτῷ, 19:10; τῇ εἰκόνι, 13:15; 16:2; 19:20). But there are also five places where the accusative is found in all but a few late MSS (τὰ δαιμόνια καὶ τὰ εἴδωλα κτλ., 9:20; τὸ θηρίον, 13:12; 14:9, 11; 20:4), as well as one where the early evidence is fairly evenly divided (αὐτῷ/αὐτόν, 13:8).

It would seem that factors other than Atticism should be taken into account. The evidence suggests that neither John *nor* scribes were consistent. If in some cases a few MSS reflect "Atticizing" tendencies where John had the dative (and one always wonders why such scribes were not consistent to change *all* such datives), there seem to be cases where John is the "Atticist" and scribes conformed to the *more common* dative. Rather than run roughshod over the data, perhaps the MSS can be used to determine the author's tendencies: e.g., τῷ θεῷ is always dative without variation; neuter nouns are usually accusative, especially τὸ θηρίον (thus, the τὸ θηρίον of A 296 1876 2014 2043 2066 is perhaps original at 13:4, where it was conformed to the preceding δράκοντι). In any case, such possibilities seem far more probable to explain the manuscript evidence than Atticism alone.

B. Professor Kilpatrick says of the future of ζῆν that ζήσω is the Attic form, ζήσομαι the non-Attic. This being the case, "we would expect the NT writers to use ζήσομαι" (1963b: 132). He then illustrates his argument from the Gospel of John by setting out, with the manuscript evidence, the six occurrences of the future of ζῆν.

The heart of the Egyptian tradition (P⁷⁵ B L) reads the active four times (5:25; 6:57, 58; 14:19). In three of these they are joined variously by D, Θ, fam 1, fam 13, and members of the Byzantine tradition.

On the basis of the witness of P⁴⁵, P⁶⁶, and P⁷⁵ (the former two read the active once each), Kilpatrick notes that the active occurs in MSS which are older than AD 200. He therefore concludes:

> As the variation came into being in the second century, the century of Atticism, it is more probable that the evangelist at the end of the first century used the non-Attic middle which was later corrected to the Attic active future. That the evangelist should go out of his way to introduce an Attic form into his *Koine* Greek which the second century scribes then changed to the *Koine* forms seems most unlikely. We may accordingly regard the middle-future as what the evangelist wrote and the active as an Atticist correction of the second century. (1963b: 132)

Kilpatrick further notes four places in the Epistles where the future active occurs, in three of which he finds Atticism at work (Rom 6:2, ζήσομεν/ζήσωμεν; 2 Cor 13:4, ζήσομεν/ζησόμεθα; Jas 4:15, ζήσομεν/ζήσωμεν). Only at Heb 12:9 does he allow that the almost universally attested ζήσομεν is original.

Of these last four readings, however, two things should be noted: (1) They all occur in the first person plural, and these are the *only occurrences* of the first plural of the future of ζῆν in the NT. (2) Only one of these readings (2 Cor 13:4) reflects a variation between the "Attic" active and the "koine" middle. The variation at Rom 6:2 is between a deliberative future indicative and deliberative subjunctive,[9] both of which are classical *and* koine forms (see Smyth 1956: 428, 596; N. Turner 1963: 98); likewise in Jas 4:15 the choice is between a future indicative and an aorist subjunctive. It would seem, therefore, that the future *active* of ζῆν in the first person plural is the fixed form, and it was this that was being resisted in favor of a koine form at 2 Cor 13:4, not *vice versa* as Kilpatrick suggests.[10]

But the real weakness in Kilpatrick's argument is that he fails to note the other ten occurrences of the future of ζῆν in the NT (Matt 4:4; 9:18; Luke 4:4; 10:28; Rom 1:17; 8:13; 10:5; Gal 3:11, 12; Heb 10:38), all of which occur, as in John, in the second and third person. In every instance but one (Luke 10:28 where D and 28 read the active) ζῆν occurs in the future middle without textual variation.

Furthermore, the future middle is the septuagintal form. Of over 105 occurrences of the future of ζῆν in the LXX, the active occurs only in Ps 137:7; 142:11; and Prov 9:11, all three in the second person singular. One might well ask why the same Christian scribes, who allegedly introduced Atticisms into John, did not do so also in the LXX?

The fact that in John the future middle is universally attested (except for P[45]) at 11:25, and the active attested by the majority of uncials at 6:58, plus the universal attestation of the future middle (apart from the first person plural) outside of John, seems to point to a conclusion directly opposite that of Kilpatrick. The question which Kilpatrick must answer is, why *only in John* do the Alexandrians, and others, reflect Atticist tendencies? For whether or not the evangelist "went out of his way" to do so, the future active of ζῆν is strictly a Johannine phenomenon in the entire Greek Bible. Furthermore, the combined evidence of 6:58 and 11:25 indicates that the Fourth Evangelist was not consistent. What we have then in John is not P[66] and later MSS resisting "corrections" toward Atticism, as Kilpatrick argues, but P[66] and later scribes resisting the "Atticism" of the Fourth Evangelist in favor of the more common biblical idiom.

C. Kilpatrick has also argued that the ἀποκριθεὶς εἶπεν idiom, where there are variations, is to be preferred to either of the verbs occurring by itself; for "no Greek of any period, left to himself, would say or write ἀποκριθεὶς εἶπεν." He therefore concludes:

---

9. Interestingly, von Soden cites two MSS (1245 104 [? von Soden has H[013], which is presumably a misprint for H[103]]) as reading ζησόμεθα. Yet this is *not* the original text for which Kilpatrick argues, but rather the aorist subjunctive (which is *not* necessarily non-Attic). Kilpatrick is therefore agreeing that in this instance at least the koine ζησόμεθα is the secondary form toward which these scribes were correcting.

10. In his evaluation of UBS[3], Dr. Elliott (1973: 299) has quite missed the point here. He has stated that "the middle form should be printed at Romans vi 2, II Corinthians xiii 4, James iv 15, where UBS follows ℵ A B which read the active form." Even Kilpatrick does not argue for the middle at Rom 6:2 (see preceding note), and the middle at Jas 4:15 would be a case of thoroughgoing emendation!

Hence we are not surprised when we find that often where ἀποκριθεὶς εἶπεν and the like occur in our Greek text there are variants designed to mitigate or remove this unGreek expression. We may even suspect that sometimes the attempt to improve the language has been successful and that the more Greek expression is in our text and the original unGreek wording in our apparatus. (1963b: 126)

However, an analysis of this idiom in John seems again to point to the opposite conclusion, namely, that the author himself had a basic un-Greek idiom, ἀπεκρίθη ['Ιησοῦς] καὶ εἶπεν [αὐτῷ], which he himself altered occasionally toward the "more Greek" ἀπεκρίθη ['Ιησοῦς]; the scribes, on the other hand, tended not "to mitigate" the author's un-Greek idiom, but tended rather to conform to that idiom where the author himself had used the "more Greek" form.

The following evidence substantiates this conclusion:

(1) The full idiom occurs without manuscript variation nineteen times in John.[11] On nine other occasions a *single* MS "mitigates" this un-Greek form.[12]

(2) The "more Greek" idiom (less καὶ εἶπεν) occurs twenty-one times without MS variation.[13]

If one may trust the manuscript evidence at all, these two sets of readings clearly indicate that the author of the Gospel himself used both the "Attic" and the septuagintal forms. Moreover, the nine instances where a single MS reads the "more Greek" for the "un-Greek" idiom indicate that there is very little tendency in the manuscript tradition to mitigate the un-Greek form.

(3) On the other hand, on seventeen other occasions, where the majority of MSS read ἀποκρίνομαι without καὶ εἶπεν, one or a few MSS read the full idiom. The manuscript evidence for those which read the full idiom at these points is given below:

3:5	L K M Θ Π 053 69 124 174 213 230 579 1093 1241 pc
6:70	ℵ (D) N 1187 a ff² sa
7:46	544 C bo
8:19	ℵ D 27 78 543 700 713 1093 1188 1241
8:33	D 1 7 291 565 658 660 1293 1354 1582 2193
8:49	ℵ G Θ λ φ 291 440 565 1093 1170
8:54	1093 1170 1242 1555 e bo
9:3	053 λ 565 e b
10:32	33
10:34	P⁶⁶ (D)
13:8	1071 r¹ eth sy^pal

11. 1:48, 50; 2:18, 19; 3:9, 27; 4:10, 13; 7:16, 21, 52; 8:38, 48; 9:30, 34; 14:23; 18:25, 30; 20:28.

12. 3:3 (ℵ* om. καὶ εἶπεν); 3:10 (083 om. ἀπεκρίθη 'Ιησοῦς); 4:17 (ℵ* om. καὶ εἶπεν); 5:19 (ℵ* ἔλεγεν . . . ὁ 'Ιησοῦς); 6:43 (053 om. καὶ εἶπεν); 6:26 (N om. καὶ εἶπεν); 8:14 (ℵ εἶπεν αὐτοῖς ὁ 'Ιησοῦς); 12:30 (ℵ om. καὶ εἶπεν); 13:7 (33 om. καὶ εἶπεν).

13. 5:7; 6:7, 68; 7:47; 8:34; 9:20, 27; 10:25, 33; 11:9; 12:34; 16:31; 18:8, 20, 23, 34, 35, 36; 19:7, 15; 21:5.

13:26	ℵ D 13 346
13:38	D aur c ff[2]
18:5	X 213 f
18:37	P[66]
19:11	φ a c ff[2] sy[pal]
19:22	1170 1242

(4) On only four occasions do the Egyptian MSS (always with several others) read the shorter form against the majority (1:49; 7:20; 9:11, 25).

From these sets of figures the conclusion is unmistakable that the MSS tend not to become "Atticist" against the author, but rather that they tend to conform to the more characteristically biblical idiom. The fact that the MSS which do have variations at this idiom are not necessarily "superior" witnesses seems to confirm this conclusion. Codex Sinaiticus (ℵ), for example, whose tendencies to be "wild" in John make it suspect, "mitigates the un-Greek idiom" five times, but it also reads the full idiom against most of the rest at four other places. The fact that P[66] (almost alone) conforms to the more characteristically Johannine idiom at two places indicates that even in the second century the tendency to "conform" is at least as great as any tendency to "Atticize," as far as this idiom is concerned.

Finally, while it may be true that "no Greek, of any period, left to himself, would say or write ἀποκριθεὶς εἶπεν," the point is that biblical scribes and Church Fathers were *not* "left to themselves." They were steeped in the biblical idiom, as even a Greek of unquestioned rhetorical and literary powers such as St. John Chrysostom bears unexpected witness. For in two separate citations of John 5:7, where all known witnesses have ἀπεκρίθη (or λέγει) αὐτῷ ὁ ἀσθενῶν, he writes ἀπεκρίθη αὐτῷ ὁ ἀσθενὴς καὶ εἶπε (*anom.* 12.2 [PG 48.804]) and ἀπεκρίθη αὐτῷ καὶ λέγει (*hom.* 36 *in Jo.* [PG 59.204])!

All of this is not to exclude Atticism as a *possible* cause of corruption. But it is only one possible cause, and in all of these cases *not* the most probable one. Textual criticism simply cannot afford a "hardening of the categories."

V.

But if rigorous eclecticism is likely to lock into one possibility of error to the exclusion of others, it also runs the risk of making choices in a most random and arbitrary fashion. Hort long ago warned of this possibility: "The uses of internal evidence are subordinate and accessory: if taken as the primary guide, it cannot but lead to extensive error" (Westcott-Hort 1881: 1.543). The following sampling (among scores of examples) from Dr. Elliott's study of the text of the Pastoral Epistles illustrates the soundness of Hort's judgment.

A. In 1 Tim 1:1 Elliott has argued that the τοῦ added before σωτῆρος in D 81 104 is original because it gives balance to the opening sentence (κατ᾽ ἐπιταγὴν θεοῦ *τοῦ* σωτῆρος ἡμῶν καὶ Χριστοῦ ᾽Ιησοῦ *τῆς* ἐλπίδος ἡμῶν) and conforms to the appositional use of σωτῆρος elsewhere in the Pastorals (Χριστοῦ ᾽Ιησοῦ τοῦ σωτῆρος ἡμῶν, Titus 1:4; 3:6).

But one may ask whether this is a correct use of "author's style." In the first place, the appositional use of the article with σωτῆρος in Titus is probably irrelevant; for in each case it occurs with the compound name Χριστοῦ 'Ιησοῦ, which *always* has the article in the Pastorals when an appositive is added. On the other hand, the true stylistic equivalent of θεοῦ σωτῆρος is the often repeated anarthrous θεοῦ πατρός (1 Tim 1:2; 2 Tim 1:2; Titus 1:4; and Paul *passim*). Furthermore, the similar phrases in the salutations of these Epistles do *not* have the "balanced" construction (ἀπὸ θεοῦ πατρὸς καὶ Χριστοῦ 'Ιησοῦ *τοῦ* κυρίου ἡμῶν).

B. In 1 Tim 1:2 Elliott says that the ἡμῶν after πατρός found in the Byzantine tradition is probably original. He argues: "The possessive was omitted here on stylistic grounds: ἡμῶν occurs 4 times in verses 1 and 2." Yet in identical variations in 2 Tim 1:2 and Titus 1:4 he argues that the ἡμῶν was *added* to conform to 1 Tim 1:2! But is not this the explanation for all three variants? The Pastor consistently wrote πατρός; scribes variously conformed it to the more Pauline πατρὸς ἡμῶν (Rom 1:7; 1 Cor 1:3; 2 Cor 1:2; Eph 1:2; Phil 1:2; Col 1:2; Phlm 3; cf. the TR on 1 and 2 Thessalonians).

C. In an extensive — and helpful — discussion of all variants involving the *nomina sacra,* Dr. Elliott states, of word order, that "for the author of the Pastorals $\overline{ΙΣ}$ $\overline{ΧΣ}$ was the most natural order. He kept this order wherever possible, but when $\overline{ΙΣ}$ did not unambiguously show the case in the genitive and dative, he inverted the words" (1968a: 201). This is a remarkable statement, given that even in Elliott's resultant text "the most natural order" occurs but five times (in the nominative at 1 Tim 1:15, 16; 2:5; accusative at 2 Tim 2:8; genitive at Titus 3:6) out of twenty-nine occurrences of the double name, and that there is textual variation in twenty-two of these. Elliott's "rule" seems altogether arbitrary; for in fact, discussion of case aside, the most common order in the Pastorals is Χριστὸς 'Ιησοῦς. There is only one instance (Titus 3:6) of the more "natural order" occurring without significant textual variation, and in that case it occurs in the genitive! And when this order occurs with scattered but insignificant support in 1 Tim 1:15 and 2:5, one wonders again how such choices can be made without consulting the manuscript evidence, since there simply are no unambiguous internal grounds on which to establish the "rules."

D. In 1 Tim 2:9 Elliott adopts the reading of τάς before γυναῖκας with the Byzantine majority. In the discussion he notes that γυνή elsewhere as well as other general nouns are anarthrous in the Pastorals. "Nevertheless," Elliott argues, "we should be inclined to add τας here, which parallels τους ἄνδρας." Indeed, is this not precisely what *the scribes* were inclined to do? Far more so, one would think, than that as early grammarians they "omitted the article to conform to other and similar uses of the anarthrous generic noun."

E. At 1 Tim 4:6, 10; 5:5; and 6:17 there is a series of four variants where five, two, one, and three witnesses respectively have another tense than the perfect of the majority. Elliott has opted for the variant in each case on the grounds of "the rarity of the strict perfect in the Pastorals" (although he acknowledges that it does occur in no less than seven instances without variation). That this is another case of an argument turned on its head may be seen from his choice of ἐλπίζειν at 6:17 (*cum* F G John Damascus) for the ἠλπικέναι of the rest. Elliott grants that the perfect infinitive is rare in the NT (which makes it the *lectio difficilior*), although it *is* found without variation at 2 Tim 2:14 and Titus 1:16 (which makes it a known Pastoral usage). Yet in spite of this Elliott says: "[The immediately preceding] παραγγελλε and ὑψηλα φρονειν are present. So ἐλπιζειν agrees naturally." But this is precisely what the ancestor of F G and John of Damascus both sensed, and they altered the text accordingly!

F. At 1 Tim 2:12 Elliott prefers the word order of the TR, γυναικὶ δὲ διδάσκειν, because a somewhat similar word order occurs at 1 Tim 5:1 and because it is unusual for an infinitive to stand first in a sentence in the Pastorals. Since γυνή stands first in the preceding sentence, Elliott argues that "the variant διδασκειν δε γυναικι arose on stylistic grounds to prevent two consecutive sentences beginning with the same noun." But Elliott's "variant" is the more difficult reading on all counts, especially since the reading of the TR puts διδάσκειν and ἐπιτρέπω in more logical juxtaposition.

G. At Titus 1:2 Elliott opts for the προεπηγγείλατο of 1908 against the ἐπηγγείλατο of all others, despite the fact that ἐπαγγέλλω is a Pastorals' word. Elliott says: "[προεπηγγείλατο] was altered (a) because it was not Classical, (b) scribes objected to verbs compounded with and followed by the same preposition, (c) scribes preferred simple to compound forms." But all of this is arbitrary, for scribes can be shown to go either way in all three of these situations. (Cf., e.g., the singular readings of D and M in Mark 3:20 for εἰσέρχονται εἰς and [συν]-έρχεται.)

All of these illustrate the tenuousness of choices made on internal grounds alone. If textual criticism is going to approximate a science — or at least be considered a discipline — it must avoid both the heavy-handedness of seeing only one cause of corruption and the whims of the individual critic. In each of the cases noted above, the alternative option also has the better support. Surely that factor tips the scales of probability.

VI.

The final dilemma of rigorous eclecticism is related to the preceding problem, namely that very often internal questions either are indecisive or sometimes collide.

This dilemma may be illustrated best by noting the three criteria of rigorous eclecticism offered by F. C. Grant for evaluating variants (1946: 41):

1. No one type of text is infallible, or to be preferred by virtue of its generally superior authority.
2. Each reading must be examined on its merits, and preference must be given to those readings which are demonstrably in the style of the author under consideration.
3. Readings which explain other variants, but are not contrariwise themselves to be explained by the others, merit our preference.

The problem for rigorous eclecticism here is, on what grounds does one choose when rules 2 and 3 point to directly opposite conclusions? It would seem that when such happens — and it often does — rule 1 must be laid aside; for "the generally superior authority" of a given MS or type of text may be the *deciding* factor.

One may note, for example, the following set of variations in John 5:17. Without regard for the moment to the external evidence, there are these four variants:

1.   απεκριθη αυτοις
2. ο δε απεκριθη αυτοις
3. ο δε απεκρινατο αυτοις
4. ος δε απεκριθη αυτοις

The readings are here listed in the order of preference according to Grant's rule 2. Reading 1 is preferred because it is the *only* reading in accordance with Johannine style. The use of ὁ δέ for the continuation of narrative is so uncommon in the Gospel of John as to make the rigorous eclectic suspect it at any point; and ὅς δέ at such a point is found in the NT only here and in a reading of ℵ B N Σ 33 579 pc in Mark 15:13.

On the other hand, according to Grant's rule 3, the exact opposite is the order of preference. The ὅς δέ is the only reading which explains the other variants, and is not contrariwise itself to be explained by the others. The ὁ δέ is easily explained from ὅς δέ as the preference for a more common form of expression; the omission of either reflects a preference for a more characteristically Johannine mode of expression. If the omission were original, one can scarcely explain the addition of either ὁ δέ or ὅς δέ — especially with a form of ἀποκρίνεσθαι in the Fourth Gospel. If ὁ δέ were original, one can explain the omission as a conformation to Johannine style, but ὅς δέ defies explanation except as an inadvertent scribal error.

It would seem, therefore, that either Grant's rules must be transcended, or else a choice must be made between rules 2 and 3.

However, when external evidence is added, a decision in favor of ὅς δέ seems well founded. The external evidence is as follows:

1.   απεκριθη αυτοις   D E F H M S U V pler TR
2. ο δε απεκριθη αυτοις   P[66] C G K L N Δ Λ pm
3. ο δε απεκρινατο αυτοις   ℵ* W
4. ος δε απεκριθη αυτοις   P[75] A B

The textual relationship between P[75] and B means that theirs is a single witness. The reading of A is unexpected support, inasmuch as it more often reads with the Byzantine MSS than with P[75] B, where these two types of text differ. Moreover, my recent study on the alleged recensional character of the Egyptian text-type demonstrated that the text of P[75] B, although by no means pure, is indeed a witness to the faithful preservation of a given type of text (Fee 1974). On the other hand, P[66] has been noted frequently to differ from P[75] B in favor of an easier reading (Fee 1968b: 56), and thus it does here. Furthermore, D, the only early witness to the more "characteristically Johannine" reading, has been shown often to conform to a "later" text (1968a: 33).

When, therefore, the earliest and "best" MSS have the reading which best explains the others, this combination would seem to overrule the choice dictated by rigorous eclecticism.

Similarly, the introductory formula at John 11:12 has the following variants:

1. ειπαν ουν αυτω οι μαθηται	ℵ D K W Π 579 b ff²
2. ειπαν ουν αυτω οι μαθηται αυτου	251 254 a c
3. ειπαν ουν οι μαθηται αυτω	P⁶⁶ P⁷⁵ B C X Θ pc
4. ειπαν ουν αυτω	A 44 122
5. ειπαν ουν οι μαθηται	7 116 314 1200 *l*
6. ειπαν ουν οι μαθηται αυτου	L Ψ Byz aur e f TR

The most characteristically Johannine reading here is (1) (see Fee 1970a). The combination of verb-object-subject (VOS) is far more common than the combination VS in (5) and (6) and VO in (4).

But the only reading which explains all the others and is itself explained by none is (3). This is easily the *lectio difficilior* inasmuch as in the some 120 occurrences of this idiom in John the order VSO occurs without variation only where the object is a noun (e.g., 2:5; 6:67; 18:11) or where the prepositional phrase προς . . . replaces the dative (e.g., 4:48; 8:57; 11:21). The order VSO where the pronoun is in the dative occurs only here and at 11:44 (P⁷⁵ B C L W sa bo e vg) in the Gospel of John.[14]

Therefore, reading (2) may be dismissed as a modification of (1), and readings (1), (4), (5), and (6) all represent various attempts to remove the difficulty of the word order of P⁶⁶ P⁷⁵ B et al. The fact that this reading is supported by the earliest and "best" MSS, as well as by various others which do not necessarily have Egyptian proclivities, seems to indicate that the "more difficult" and "best supported" reading is to be preferred.

Such judgments are *not* expressions of a genealogical method, nor do they suggest a full-scale return to Hort. The fact that external evidence serves as a final arbiter is precisely where rational eclecticism parts company with Westcott-Hort. They started with one text-type as superior and followed its readings except where it had clearly discernible clerical errors or, in a few cases, where internal principles dictated the superiority of the Western text (as in the so-called Western noninterpolations). Rational eclecticism starts with readings, noting first the various intrinsic and transcriptional possibilities, and where such questions are indecisive, then appeals to the relative value of the witnesses.

Rational eclecticism is indeed the currently reigning method, and it appears to be a valid one, for it takes seriously both internal questions and the manuscript evidence. Rather than search for a new method as some propose, or jettison historical study as rigorous eclecticism tends to, the present methodological task would seem to be the implementation and refinement of rational eclecticism. It is here that the labors of Professor Kilpatrick and Dr. Elliott should prove to be most useful. Their contributions as to various stylistic features of the NT authors as well as their isolation of the variants where Atticism might be a possible factor have not only increased our knowledge but also widened our perspective when asking the internal questions. For this we express unqualified appreciation.

14. This unusual order also occurs in three singular readings (6:32 [579]; 7:33 [1241]; 9:41 [D]).

CHAPTER 8

THE ECLECTIC METHOD IN NEW TESTAMENT TEXTUAL CRITICISM: SOLUTION OR SYMPTOM?[1]

Eldon Jay Epp

I. Problem and Purpose

The "eclectic method" in NT textual criticism is one of several disguises for the broad and basic problem of the "canons of criticism" or of the "criteria for originality" as applied to the various readings in the NT textual tradition, and in a real sense eclectic methodology — in its several forms as currently practiced — is as much a *symptom* of basic problems in the discipline as it is a proposed and widely applied *solution* to those problems. By the same token, perhaps every methodological approach and even every discussion of methodology in NT textual criticism could be described as symptomatic of the problems; yet the eclectic method seems in a particularly pointed way to veil the problems of the discipline, for by its very nature it tries in one way or another to utilize all available approaches to textual problems, and in a single given case of seeking the original text it often wishes to apply to the problem several established text-critical criteria, even if these criteria have the appearance of being mutually exclusive or contradictory. If indeed basic problems are disguised by the eclectic approach, perhaps they also can be disclosed by a careful scrutiny of the eclectic method.

The eclectic approach to the recovery of the most likely original text of the NT is, in its broadest definition, a method (1) that treats each text-critical problem (normally a single "variation-unit") separately and largely in isolation from other problems, (2) that "chooses" or "selects" *(eklegomai)* from among the available and recognized text-critical criteria those that presumably are appropriate to that particular text-critical situation, and (3) that then applies the selected criteria in such a way as to "pick" or "choose" *(eklegomai)* a reading from one or another MS and thereby arrive at a text-critical decision for that particular variation-unit. (Incidentally, it is not clear whether the term "eclectic" refers primarily to the *selection of readings* from here and there or to the *choice of criteria* from among the many and

1. A paper prepared originally for the Textual Criticism Group of the SBL, Chicago, 30 October 1975, and printed in SBLSP 1975: 2.47-82; it appears here by permission and with revisions prompted by the seminar discussion. This study was made while the author was a Fellow of the John Simon Guggenheim Memorial Foundation, 1974-75; the support and generosity of the Foundation are gratefully acknowledged.

various ones available. It is clear, however, that both kinds of choice are prominent in the eclectic approach.)

The term "eclectic," as applied to NT textual criticism, not only is comparatively recent in its use but also varied in its meaning and emphasis, as the succeeding pages show. Its earliest occurrence in this context may have been in L. Vaganay's text-critical manual of 1934, where he employed "eclectic" to describe an evenhanded method that took into account the analysis of error in textual transmission as well as the assessment of both documentary evidence and intrinsic quality of readings; a decade later the term "eclecticism" (with certain restrictive adjectives, such as "rigorous," "impartial," and "consistent") was used by G. D. Kilpatrick to refer to a decidedly one-sided approach, which emphasized stylistic rather than documentary considerations and which earlier had been designated "rational criticism" *(critique rationnelle)* by M.-J. Lagrange in 1935.[2] "Eclecticism," then, has been applied not only to the proposal for a balanced text-critical method that would utilize critical principles drawn from both external and internal criticism, but also — strangely enough — to a method emphasizing only one of these, namely, internal criticism; still more recently, "eclecticism" has been used to designate a method that actually gives the deciding voice to external evidence. Whether a single term is appropriate for such a wide range of emphases is open to question, but that "eclectic" is used currently in these varied ways is a matter of fact.

The terms "eclectic" and "eclecticism" may have appeared only recently in NT textual criticism; yet in a real sense the eclectic method, taken in its broadest meaning, is as old as the formulation and application of the traditional "canons of criticism," such as those promulgated by J. A. Bengel in 1725, by J. J. Griesbach in 1796, by K. Lachmann in 1842, and others, for if it is axiomatic that "the harder reading is to be preferred," and that "the ancient and weighty witnesses" are to be given priority, then one is forced to choose between or among conflicting criteria when the shorter reading is the easier or the harder reading is the longer, or the shorter or harder reading is attested only by late MSS. It is at this point that the delicate and ingenious phrase "the balance of relative probabilities" comes into play, for when two or more conflicting criteria seem applicable to a given variation-unit, then both the choice of the most appropriate criterion (or criteria) and the textual decision itself become increasingly complex and problematic. In precisely such a situation (logically at least) the eclectic method was born, for at this juncture factors on the external, historical, and documentary side of the transmission of the text are thrown into the balance with factors on the internal, contextual, and stylistic side, and an eclecticism that takes into consideration all conceivably applicable criteria — though always within a "balance of relative probabilities" context — is applied to each case to isolate the most "suitable" criteria or criterion, which then becomes the basis for the selection of the one variant reading that is to be accredited as the most likely original.

---

2. Vaganay 1937: 91-94; French original, Paris: Bloud & Gay, 1934. For Kilpatrick see 1943: 33-34, 36; 1944: 65; 1963b: 136; 1965: 205. For Lagrange see 1935: 27-40; cf. Klijn 1949: 170-71. Further on the designation and use of "eclectic," see Metzger 1968a: 175-79; and the references to the works of Grant and Birdsall in the following note.

Difficulties are multiplied, however, when different values are placed upon different sets of criteria (e.g., on the "external" criteria as opposed to the "internal") by different schools of thought; for instance, when the criterion of the "oldest and best manuscripts" is valued more highly than the criterion of "conformity to the author's style," then textual decisions will vary markedly from those made when these relative valuations are reversed. Such differing valuations represent, in fact, not only a general problem faced by contemporary textual critics, but also a very special crux in text-critical methodology, for among practitioners of an eclectic approach there is a distinction to be drawn between what might be called *eclectic generalists* (true eclectics), who in each case of textual variation try to employ the appropriate criteria without prejudice as to their relative weight or value [Do any such "true" eclectics exist?[3]], and *eclectic specialists* (biased eclectics), who tend to fall into two distinct subgroups, (1) those who quite obviously value external criteria above the internal and who utilize the latter mainly to clarify cases plagued by an ambiguous array of external evidence, and (2) those who forthrightly value internal criteria above the external and who rely almost exclusively on grammatical, stylistic, and contextual factors in their textual decisions. The issues underlying these distinctive eclectic approaches determine and constitute the subject matter of the discussion to follow.[4]

The problem of eclectic methodology, then, has at least two aspects. First, integral to the eclectic method — in all its forms — are the criteria for originality of readings, and these need to be described with some care and assessed, for they are the stock in trade of eclecticism. In the second place, the various eclectic approaches need to be examined, not only to see whether what we have called the eclectic-generalist method is viable, but particularly to scrutinize the relative merits and usefulness of the two competing eclectic-specialist approaches. It has been said often before (recently by Epp 1974: 403-5), but bears repetition, that all of us — except the genealogists — employ an eclectic method, for it is *the* contemporary procedure both for handling separate cases of textual variation and for formulating

---

3. Vaganay 1937: 91-95 would appear to qualify on the basis of his description of "proper" method; F. C. Grant's description of the procedures adopted by the RSV commission may fit this category (1946: 38-41); also, the combination found in J. N. Birdsall (1970: 316-18, 374-77) of an extensive treatment of the history of the NT text in its earliest period and of a strong emphasis on "rational criticism" to achieve, by this twofold approach, the goal of an "eclectic text" suggests that his method fits the category of "true" eclecticism.

4. These broad classifications (eclectic generalists and specialists), it should be noted, encompass all contemporary NT textual critics with the exception of the genealogical scholars; the latter construct stemmata for NT textual transmission and thereby affirm the feasibility either of reconstructing the archetype or of isolating the earliest "state" of the NT text (or, better, of each major segment or transmissional unit of the NT text). The older, simplistic genealogical approach (stemmata and archetypes) has been abandoned almost entirely by NT textual critics (except in connection with small "families" of MSS) because it is both inapplicable to the massive and disparate NT data and ineffectual in tracing sure developmental lines through MSS with such complex mixture as those of the NT textual tradition (Colwell 1969: 66-70, 82-83, 164; Kenyon 1975). An approach known as "textual analysis," which (somewhat more modestly) determines the genealogical relationship between and among the various "states" of a text (though not the genealogy of the documents containing them) with a view to identifying the "state" from which all the others have descended (see Dearing 1974a: 1-2), has not as yet been widely assessed — and certainly not definitively so — by NT textual critics in general.

critical texts of the NT. Yet, recent handbooks and other technical literature of the discipline all too seldom engage in serious self-criticism of this central and basic matter of the methodology employed in isolating the most likely original NT text. Above all, our aim in this present discussion is the clear definition and description of the eclectic method and of attendant issues, and beyond that our purpose is the critical evaluation of the eclectic approaches currently in use. In fulfilling these goals it will be instructive, as is so often the case, to employ a historical approach, attempting to show whence and why current eclectic methods developed; accordingly, a history of the criteria for originality of readings will form the first step in our analysis of the eclectic method and will provide the context for its evaluation.

II. Criteria for Originality of Readings

The traditional "canons of criticism" are in reality, of course, criteria for determining the originality of variant readings in a textual tradition, that is, they are principles devised to countervail the corrupting processes attendant to the manuscript transmission of ancient texts and are based both on knowledge of the documents transmitting the texts and on acquaintance with the scribal habits of those who copied them.

A. Use of the Critical Canons in Antiquity

Undoubtedly the first application — rudimentary and unsystematic as it was — of such canons of criticism to the NT text was made by Origen, who, for example, could characterize certain variant readings as found in "few," "many," or "most" MSS known to him (Metzger 1963a: 81), an adumbration of the much more modern canon underlying the sixteenth-century phrase *textus receptus* (TR), or "text received by all," a canon that in reality declares that the reading supported by the largest number of MSS is to be accounted original. Although Origen does not always follow the majority reading and at times even rejects a reading of the entire known manuscript tradition (ibid.: 91-92), yet the canon of the majority reading is latent in his comments. Moreover, at other times Origen employs etymological and theological canons (ibid.: 82, 85, 87), and he preferred readings that suited the immediate context (once he uses the phrase "inner probability") and that were harmonious with parallel passages (Pack 1960: 144-45). A century and a half later, Jerome evidences the use of the canons of age (old MSS are given more weight), of scribal quality (the care in writing and in correcting a MS affects its reliability), of a reading's suitability to its context, of a reading's grammatical appropriateness (Hulley 1944), and of harmonization from parallel passages (Lagrange 1935: 37). Though it would be useful to pursue such early uses of critical canons down through the Middle Ages, in the final analysis it is their formulation and utilization in modern NT textual criticism that will be most instructive for us.

B. Use of Critical Canons in Modern Times

It was only in modern times that canons were drawn up in formal fashion, ranging from the first such attempt by Gerhard von Mastricht in his 1711 edition of the Greek

NT (11-16, 48-68), who lists forty-three canons and comments at length on most of them, to the terse *proclivi scriptioni praestat ardua* ("the harder reading is to be preferred") of Bengel, to Griesbach's fifteen canons and Lachmann's six, and to the various lists of critical principles found in manuals of NT textual criticism.[5]

It is instructive to peruse these lists of critical canons, especially those given and employed by various editors of the Greek NT down through the years. JOHN MILL of Oxford listed no canons of criticism for his edition in 1707, but he appears to have relied primarily on two canons, that smooth and easy readings are not necessarily genuine and that the united testimony of different kinds of authorities carries more weight than mere numerical preponderance of authorities, though at the same time he does not regard as important the mere number of MSS attesting a reading. In addition, he considered patristic quotations decisive and highly valued the Latin versions, particularly the OL, in textual decisions (see Tregelles 1854: 44-45; Fox 1954: 70-71). Mill's own formulations of Bengel's later canon concerning the "harder" reading are of interest: ". . . In proportion as a [reading] is more obscure, it is generally speaking more authentic, and among various readings that occur, those that seem clearer are justly suspected of falsification by having crept in from the margins of a MS in place of other more obscure ones." Or, "I consider this reading [in Rom 7:23] to be genuine, as also almost all that are somewhat hard and look absurd"; also, Mill at one point describes a variant as "clearer [*argutius*] rather than correct."[6]

The canons of GERHARD VON MASTRICHT,[7] referred to earlier, were designed to disparage the value of those variant readings that he had taken from the 1710 edition of Mill and Küster's Greek NT and had reprinted in his own 1711 edition. His forty-three canons are no longer important in themselves, though extolled by some at the time; they take on significance, however, when it is observed that both Wettstein (b. 1693) and Bengel (b. 1687), very soon after 1711, encountered these canons and the text that accompanied them and apparently were rather profoundly affected by them. Bengel became acquainted with the canons in Heidelberg about 1713, and he published three separate refutations, first in the *apparatus criticus* attached to his edition of 1734 and finally, with considerable detail, in his preface to *Gnomon Novi Testamenti* in 1742.[8]

Many of von Mastricht's canons are concerned with scribal habits and the causes of variant readings, such as the "negligence, listlessness, haste, and . . . malice" of scribes (Canon I), the repetition of words or sentences from the context

---

5. See, as examples, Michaelis 1802: I.1.328-29, who lists about twenty canons; Hug 1836: 301-7; Tregelles 1860: 4.343-45; Hammond 1880: 93-99; Scrivener 1894: 2.247-56; Nestle 1901: 239-41; Schaff 1903: 202-5; Jacquier 1911: 2.328-35; Metzger 1968a: 209-10; Metzger 1971: xxiv-xxviii; cf. also Warfield 1907: 82-87; 107-27; Lagrange 1935: 17-40; Vaganay 1937: 64-89 [now Vaganay-Amphoux 1986: 98-127]; several canon lists are reproduced in Colwell 1952: 32-33, 73-75, 111-15; also now see B. and K. Aland 1989: 280-82.

6. Adapted from Fox 1954: 147, where the pertinent Latin texts may be found.

7. On the name, which has been the subject of controversy, see Abbot, "Gerhard von Mastricht" (1888: 184-88).

8. Bengel 1855: xiv-xxi. The detailed refutation has been omitted from the English ed. of *Gnomon* (Philadelphia, 1864) and from its recent reprint, *New Testament Word Studies* (2 vols.; Grand Rapids: Kregel, 1971); cf. xx-xxi, xxxiv (= reprint, vol. 1).

(II, III), the substitution, addition, omission, or alteration of letters, syllables, words, and the like (V, VI, VII, XXVI, and XXVII), and the growth of variant readings from gospel parallels (XVI, XXIV); moreover, variations recognizable as due to the presumption or impudence of a copyist are not "variant readings" (XXVI, XXVII, cf. IX) and are to be rejected in favor of the "received readings" (cf. VIII), as are "absurd" readings (XXII). Moreover, copyists as well as MSS can be observed and described as prone, for example, to add or to omit (XV, XXX, XXXI). More specifically, especially in cases involving omission, one codex does not make for a variant reading (IX), nor do two codices in agreement against a received reading that makes sense (X), nor do three or four codices produce a viable variant against twenty MSS (XI), for "a great number of manuscript codices, for instance twenty or more, establish and approve a received and common reading of good sense, above all in a case of a variant involving an omission" (XII), nor does a reading of three or four codices that does not alter the sense — whether consisting of addition, deletion, or change of construction — command attention, for "certainly no reason is compelling that will prefer a variant reading to a received reading" (VIII). Finally, Canon XXIV indicates that a variant reading commonly disappears when the origin of that variant reading is discovered.

RICHARD BENTLEY, in his 1720 pamphlet on proposals for printing a Greek and Latin NT (which task, as is well known, was never completed), made it clear that the criterion of the antiquity of MSS (". . . the most ancient and venerable MSS, in Greek and Roman capital letters") was primary (Proposal I), with the corollary that readings chosen for the text must be confirmed by the use of "the old versions, Syriac, Coptic, Gothic, and Aethiopic, and of all the fathers, Greeks and Latins, within the first five centuries," adding that any reading intruding upon any copies since that time is "of no value or authority" (Proposal IV). Bentley's overriding concern appears to be with what are now called external criteria rather than with internal evidence.

J. A. BENGEL, in a 1725 "Prodromus" to his proposed edition of the Greek NT (which appeared in 1734), stated his leading and classic canon, "the harder reading is to be preferred," a principle already utilized with some frequency by Mill in his lengthy prolegomenon. In this celebrated canon, Bengel was responding to his own urgent question as to which reading (in a given case) is likely to have arisen out of the others (Kümmel 1972: 48; cf. 414 n. 45), and actually he was reducing all of von Mastricht's forty-three canons "to one comprehensive rule of four words" (Nestle 1901: 16-17, 239): *proclivi scriptioni praestat ardua.* Since Bengel's time, this canon often has been expressed as *difficilior lectio potior.* Akin to this canon are some others issued by Bengel and relating also to internal considerations: readings representing obvious scribal errors or scribal elaborations are inferior (cf. his numbers 13 and 14 below), as are readings showing alliteration, parallelism, or lectionary adjustments to the text (number 14) (1855: xiii; Eng. ed. 1.xvii):

> 13. A reading which does not allure by too great facility, but shines by its native dignity, is always to be preferred to that which may fairly be supposed to owe its origin to either the carelessness or the injudicious care of copyists.

14. Thus, a corrupted text is often betrayed by *alliteration, parallelism,* a modification for the beginning or end of a church lesson. The recurrence of the same words suggests an *omission;* too great facility, a *gloss.* Where various readings are many, the *middle* reading is the best.

Though Bengel's "harder reading" canon is not in this list in so many words, it is presupposed (and actually contained) in both 13 and 14 where the word "facility" occurs.

For text-critical decisions, Bengel also valued highly, as did Mill and Bentley before him, the oldest Greek MSS and the Latin versions; this is clear from the preface to his *Gnomon* (1742), where he gives his list of twenty-seven "canons" (he calls them *monitis* — "admonitions" [xii-xiv; Eng. ed., 1.xvi-xx]), two of which we have quoted above and many of which range well beyond what normally would be designated as text-critical canons. Admonition 12 is by far the most telling of his rules:

> . . . More witnesses are to be preferred to fewer; and, which is *more important,* witnesses which *differ* in country, age, and language, [are to be preferred] to those which are closely connected with each other; and *most important of all, ancient* witnesses [are to be preferred] to modern ones. For, since the original autographs (which were in Greek) can alone claim to be the Fountain-head, the highest value belongs to those streams which are least removed from it; that is, to the most ancient codices, in Greek, Latin, &c. (xiii; Engl. ed., 1.xviii [italics in original]).

Two other canons are closely related to this one: number 9, which refers to versions and patristic quotations as carrying little weight when they differ from Greek MSS of the NT, but "where Greek manuscripts vary, those have the greatest authority, with which versions and fathers agree"; and number 10, which commends the Latin Vulgate, when supported by Latin Fathers, because of its singular "high antiquity" (xiii; Eng. ed., 1.xvii).

Just at this point it is essential to emphasize that no discussion of critical canons dare overlook Bengel's greatest contribution to this aspect of NT text-critical methodology, namely, his pioneering division of the extant MSS into classes or groups (syzygies, he called them), for a fundamental and far-reaching "canon" or principle emerges from (or perhaps underlies) this methodological procedure. For Bengel, all NT MSS fall either into the *African* "family," consisting of the most ancient Greek MSS and the most ancient versions (Codex A, the Greco-Latin codices, and the Ethiopic, Coptic, and Latin versions), or into the *Asiatic* family, made up of the more recent Greek MSS and versions. He then speaks of the readings of the African family as "always ancient" and states that those of the Asiatic family, "many as they are, have often but little weight. . . ."[9] Though there were adumbrations of these views, particularly in Mill — who recognized the greater importance of certain combinations of witnesses (such as A and the Latin versions) than of mere numbers

9. See Tregelles 1860: 4.69-70; he also gives Bengel's Latin text of these statements.

of witnesses — and in Bentley — who viewed the Greek MSS as transmitted from three areas (Egypt, Asia, and the West) and who gave preference to the more ancient readings — yet here in Bengel's classification of known sources of the NT text was enunciated for the first time in a systematic formulation the significant and fundamental principle that *textual witnesses must be weighed and not merely counted.* It is noteworthy, too, that in Bengel's text-critical system the internal and external criteria are counterparts, though it is sufficiently clear nonetheless that for him the external considerations have both the first and the decisive voice. This is evident from his Admonition 12 (quoted above), but also by implication from the very phrasing of his summary statement on text-critical principles (Admonition 15):[10]

> There are, therefore, five princip[al] means of judging the Text. The *Antiquity* of witnesses, the *Diversity* of their extraction, and their *Multitude;* in the next place, the *Origin of the corrupt* reading, and the *Native* appearance of the *genuine.*

Obviously, the first three items here involve external criteria, the other two internal, and Bengel — significantly — separates the categories with a semicolon and *tum* ("then," "in the next place"). The last two items refer to Bengel's 13th and 14th Admonitions (see above), covering scribal errors, elaborations, and improvements. Since the first three items of Admonition 15 correspond to the three criteria in Admonition 12 (reversed in order of listing, though not in their order of importance, as the different phrasing will show), we know precisely how Bengel valued these criteria: antiquity of witnesses was most important, then their geographical, language, and age distribution, and last — though still significant — their number. When Bengel in his summary statement then lists, both in a separate category and as "in the next place," matters involving internal considerations, we may be sure that these are subsidiary to the external criteria first listed, and this indication of the superiority of external criteria is supported also by the system of classification that he applied to the textual witnesses.

Bengel, therefore, suggests that text-critical criteria are of two distinct and separable kinds, external and internal, and that the external are superior to and more decisive than the internal. Bengel implies, moreover, that an eclecticism becomes operative when the evidence or the canons are in conflict: he says of his five principles for judging the text, "Where these concur, none can doubt but a skeptic; when, however, it happens that some of these favor one reading, and some another, the critic may be drawn now in this, now in that direction; or, even should he decide, others may be slow to agree with him" (Admonitions 16 and 17 [xiii; Eng. ed., 1.xviii]).

To what extent did Bengel's canons of criticism shape his text of the NT? Actually, his text was hardly affected when measured against the effects that would naturally have been expected to flow from his theories, for he chose to retain the TR except when readings judged by him to be original had appeared already in some

---

10. Bengel 1855: xiii; Eng. ed., 1.xviii. I have added "in the next place" *(tum)* from Bengel's Latin text, quoting otherwise the English ed.

printed edition of the NT. He did, however, impose his judgment on the text in a more direct way by rating variant readings (placed under the text, without reference to supporting witnesses) according to their closeness to the original and according to their relative merits in comparison with the reading of his printed text; there were five categories, each indicated by a Greek letter: (α) the genuine reading, in Bengel's judgment; (β) a reading whose genuineness was not entirely certain, but which was preferable to the reading in the text; (γ) a reading equal in worth to that in the text, but the choice was unsure; (δ) a reading of less value than that in the text; and (ε) a spurious reading.[11]

Despite his failure to carry through consistently on his principles, Bengel effectively set in motion two processes, each of which was destined to have far-reaching effects upon the establishment of the NT text and upon NT textual criticism as a discipline. One of these processes would involve the increasing recognition that the oldest MSS, rather than the most numerous or smoothest, were the best MSS; the other process would involve the alternating cooperation and tension between external criteria and internal considerations in determining the most likely original NT text. These processes had only the dimmest beginnings in Mill and Bentley, but with Bengel came the basis for their swift development. The former process would lead, through Griesbach and then Lachmann, more than a hundred years later, to the decisive overthrow of the TR in favor of a NT text based solely on ancient witnesses; the latter process would lead through many editors of the NT text — and their editions — to the problematic juxtaposition of external and internal criteria and to the current ambivalence and ambiguity in their application. It would seem not too far from the truth, then, to say that the origins of eclecticism can be traced with some assuredness to Bengel's formulary intermingling or conjoining of external and internal canons and that, in terms of our earlier definitions, Bengel appears to be an eclectic specialist and one on the side of those who consider external evidence decisive but who employ internal criteria to settle matters for which the external evidence is conflicting or ambiguous.

J. J. WETTSTEIN, whose two-volume *Novum Testamentum Graecum* appeared in 1751-52, took an interest in variant readings before he was twenty years old (in 1713), following the appearance of G. von Mastricht's Greek NT of 1711 — published by Wettstein and Smith of Amsterdam, whose senior partner was Wettstein's relative. During the several years of direct preparation for his own Greek NT and during the nearly twenty years of delay (due largely to theological issues — his Arian views), Wettstein's critical principles were altered from a generally high view of the oldest MSS to quite the opposite, a change based on his acceptance of the latinization theory — that all of the oldest Greek MSS had been corrupted by interpolation from Latin MSS; consequently, he said, the textual critic must move several centuries beyond the oldest Greek MSS to more recent ones if a pure text is to be found. Yet, in his 1751-52 edition, Wettstein enunciates many of the critical canons that he had published separately in 1730, before his views on the oldest Greek MSS

---

11. Cf. now the ratings in the UBS[3], which "indicate the relative degree of certainty . . . for the reading adopted as the text" (xii-xiii).

had changed, and the result is curious: his approved readings (over against the Elzevir text printed in Wettstein's edition) often stand in opposition to his stated principles or canons of criticism. Among those principles are the following: the reading in clearer or better Greek is not necessarily preferable; more often the contrary (item 7); among readings equally suitable to the context, that which employs an unusual expression is preferable (8); the fuller, more ample reading is not preferable to the shorter (9); the reading found in the same words elsewhere is not preferable to one that is not (10); a reading conformable in every respect to the style of the author is preferable (11); the more orthodox reading is not necessarily preferable (12); the Greek reading more in accord with the ancient versions is preferable (13); patristic testimony has much weight in attesting the true reading, and silence in the Fathers on readings of importance in the controversies of their times renders such readings suspect (14 and 15); the more ancient reading is preferable, other things being equal (17); and the reading of the majority of MSS, other things being equal, is preferable (18).[12]

Obviously, many standard — if sometimes mutually exclusive — criteria are to be found in this list; it is equally obvious, however, that Wettstein abandoned many of them in establishing his final textual theories and in printing his own preferred readings for the NT text. Some of Wettstein's theories and canons and particularly the contradictions among them can be explained by his change of views between 1730 and 1751, especially his growing opposition to the views of Bengel, who (as noted earlier) held to a high view of the oldest Greek MSS and of the Latin versions, and whose views Wettstein combated by pushing further than anyone else the theory of the latinization of the oldest Greek MSS of the NT. Wettstein's inconsistencies become obvious when, for his edition, he prefers later, presumably unlatinized, codices to the earlier ones — against his canon 17 that the more ancient reading normally is preferable, and when he can state in the same work that any division of readings into groups with more or less weight is useless (canon 6) and also can affirm that "codices are to be appraised by weight, not by number."[13]

Our interest here, however, is not in Wettstein's consistency or his lack of it, but only in the formulation of criteria for the recovery of the most likely original readings; his list of canons, whether he followed them or not, represents a thoughtful approach at a time now judged by all to precede a genuinely scientific understanding of NT textual criticism; as such, they are as worthy of our attention as any other list of critical canons from this general period. Finally, for our purposes it is of interest to observe that the external and internal criteria are undifferentiated in Wettstein's canon list.

J. J. GRIESBACH published three editions of the Greek NT between 1775

---

12. Selected from nineteen items in chap. 16 of Wettstein's [anonymous] *Prolegomena* of 1730, which appear as eighteen items in the appendix to his 1751-52 edition of the NT, "Animadversiones et cautiones ad examen variarum lectionum N.T. necessariae," 2.851-74. Cf. Tregelles, 1854: 80; Hulbert-Powell 1938: 114-21. If not otherwise available, the text of Wettstein's 1752 "Animadversiones" can be found in Wrangham 1828: 1.511-12.

13. Metzger 1968a: 114. Note that Wettstein, in his 1752 appendix, has dropped the original 18th canon — that the reading of the majority of MSS is normally preferable.

and 1807, and the second edition of 1796-1806 contained his canons of criticism, fifteen in number. These canons are concerned with internal criteria for determining the originality of readings, and they include numerous points made earlier by Bengel and Wettstein. Griesbach's first canon,[14] judging both from its primary position in that list and from the detailed attention accorded it by Griesbach, must have been regarded by him both as first in importance and fundamental in nature. The canon states that "the shorter reading . . . is preferable to the more verbose"; this, says Griesbach — quite correctly — is based on the principle that scribes are far more prone to add to their texts than to omit.[15] He qualifies the canon carefully and in several ways, noting, for example, (1) that the canon applies only when the reading in question has some support from "the old and weighty witnesses"; and (2) that the originality of a shorter reading is more certain still (a) if it is also a harsher, more obscure, ambiguous, elliptical, hebraizing, or ungrammatical reading, (b) if the same matter is expressed differently in various codices, (c) if the order of words is inconsistent and unstable, (d) if the reading stands first in a pericope (or church lesson), or (e) if the fuller reading shows evidence of a gloss or an interpretation, or is in accord with words in parallel passages, or appears to have been taken from a lectionary. He continues, however, that the shorter reading would *not* have a strong claim to originality (unless supported by *many notable* witnesses) (1) if the missing portion of the longer reading (a) can be attributed to homoeoteleuton, (b) would have appeared to scribes as obscure, rough, superfluous, unusual, paradoxical, an offense to piety, an error, or inconsistent with parallels, or (c) does not, by its omission, destroy the sense or the word structure, or (2) if the shorter reading (a) is less suitable to the author's character, style, or goal, (b) makes no sense at all, or (c) probably represents an intrusion from a parallel passage or a lectionary. In these qualifications and elaborations of his first canon, Griesbach has anticipated many of his succeeding canons, thereby providing an instructive illustration of how the various critical canons overlap and intertwine in actual practice.

Griesbach's fourteen other canons specify that:

2. "The more difficult and more obscure reading is preferable to that in which everything is so intelligible and cleared of difficulties that every scribe is easily able to understand it."

3. "The harsher [or rougher] reading is preferable to that which flows pleasantly and smoothly." "Harsher" refers to readings that are elliptical, hebraizing, ungrammatical, contrary to normal Greek usage, or offensive to the ears.

4. "The more unusual reading is preferable to that which constitutes nothing unusual." "Unusual" means rare words, words with rarely used meanings, and uncommon phrases and constructions. Scribes seized on the

---

14. The canon in its entirety may be seen conveniently in Metzger 1968a: 120. The Latin text of all of Griesbach's canons — should the 2d ed. of his Greek NT not be available — will be readily accessible to most in Alford 1883: 1.81-85.

15. Though this is a well-established principle, see now the questions raised about its validity by Royse 1979: 154-55; cf. Kilpatrick 1978: 7.

more customary expressions rather than the more exquisite, and for the latter they substitute glosses and explanations (especially if these are provided in the margin or from parallel passages).

5. "Expressions less emphatic [rhetorically], provided that the context and goal of the author do not demand emphasis, are closer to the genuine text than readings possessing, or appearing to possess, a greater vigor, for polished scribes, like commentators, love and seek out [rhetorical] emphases."

6. "The reading, compared with others, that produces a meaning suited to the support of piety (especially monastic piety) is suspect."

7. "Preferable to others is the reading that conveys [at first glance] an apparently false meaning, but which meaning, upon thorough examination, is found to be true."

8. "Among many readings in one place, that reading is rightly considered suspect that clearly suits the opinions of the orthodox better than the other readings," for it was impossible for a scribe who was a monk devoted to the church to overlook any reading that appeared strongly to confirm any catholic doctrine or to destroy a heresy.

9 and 10. These canons treat homoeoteleuton and related phenomena, and readings arising from this "symmetry" of language are of "no value" and are "rightly rejected."

11. "The reading is preferable, among many in the same place, that lies midway between the others, that is, the reading that, as it were, holds together the threads in such a way that, if this reading is admitted as original, it becomes obvious how or, better stated, by what origin in error all the other readings have arisen from it."

12. "Readings having the odor of a gloss or an interpretation may be rejected."

13. "Readings that have been introduced into the text from ancient commentaries or scholia of the Fathers are to be spurned."

14. "We reject readings appearing originally in lectionaries."

15. Finally, "readings introduced from the Latin versions into the Greek books are disapproved."

These internal criteria supplemented Griesbach's theory of the history of the text that was evident already in his first edition of the Greek NT in 1775-77. He divided the extant MSS of the Gospels into three groups (following J. S. Semler's 1764 expansion of Bengel's two-family scheme): two ancient "recensions" or families (the Western and Alexandrian, dating to the beginning of the third century) and one more recent (the Constantinopolitan, dating to the late fourth century and following). One of Griesbach's critical principles, arising out of this understanding of the early history of the text, was that a reading had high claim to originality when supported by two of these three "recensions"; more particularly, (1) a reading was accounted genuine when supported by all three of these old "recensions" ("Prolegomena," sec. III, item e); (2) a reading attested by the Western and Alexandrian against the Constantinopolitan was the most ancient reading — and was, indeed, to be regarded as genuine if at the same time its "internal excellence" shone forth (item g); (3) a reading supported by the Alexandrian and the Constantinopolitan "recensions" but not by the Western (or by the Western and the Constantinopolitan but not by the Alexandrian) was examined to see whether faults characteristic of the Alexandrian (or, in the other case, of the Western) "recension" were apparent; if so, the reading was suspect; accompanying the evaluative process in these cases, however, was the careful weighing of internal evidences (items h, i); and, finally, (4) when different readings were found in the "recensions," they had to be judged, not according to the greater number of supporting witnesses, but by weighing "internal criteria of excellence." Even then, however, any such "remarkably good reading" (on internal evidence) had to be attested first as a "primitive reading of an old recension" if it were to be esteemed (item k).[16]

It becomes clear, then, that Griesbach's *external* criteria for establishing the original NT readings, as these criteria arise out of his theory of the early history of the text, take precedence over the *internal* criteria in the entire text-critical task. That the internal criteria are subsidiary to the external appears already in the first dependent clause of his first canon, where he indicates that this most basic of the internal criteria does not even apply to a shorter reading should that reading lack the support of all "old and weighty witnesses." Notice, furthermore, that the "weight of internal evidence" comes into play when there are differing readings in the two oldest groups of MSS or when different readings occur in all his groups; in other words, when the external evidence is inconclusive, then the internal canons become decisive, but normally external evidence alone should be sufficient for a confident decision. This is not essentially different from Bengel's understanding of the interrelationship between external and internal criteria, but this relationship — including (1) the differentiation of the two categories, (2) the precedence of the external criteria and their superiority, and (3) the decisive role of the internal criteria *only* when the external criteria are ambiguous or in conflict — becomes more explicit in Griesbach. It is self-evident, of course, that Griesbach, like Bengel, relied on a basic rationale of weighing rather than counting witnesses, and this principle becomes well established with Griesbach's work, though by no means does it yet become universal. Griesbach's contribution in this area was considerably greater than may appear from the present summary, for when Griesbach began to formulate his views, particularly those on the great worth of the oldest MSS, Wettstein's denigration of all the older MSS (and his latinization theories) were highly influential and dominant. Griesbach's reestablishment of the principle put forward by Bengel was, therefore, neither a natural direction in which to move nor an easy task to accomplish.[17] This context of Griesbach's work also makes more understandable his failure to abandon the TR to a greater extent than he does and to the extent that his text-critical theories would seem to require; the time for a decisive break with the TR had arrived in theory, but the time for putting good theory into practice still lay in the future.

16. Griesbach 1796: 1.lxxiii-lxxxi; reprinted in later eds. See also Tregelles 1860: 4.76.
17. See Tregelles 1854: 91-92; witness also the views of J. M. A. Scholz, whose Greek NT text (1830-36) followed the Constantinopolitan "recension," and who relied on *numbers* of MSS (Tregelles 1854: 92-97).

The foregoing discussions should alert us again to observe closely the pattern of interrelationship between the external criteria and the internal whenever text-critical methods and principles are under consideration, for the development of modern eclectic approaches is related to this interplay and to the incipient polarity between them, as pointed out earlier in connection with Bengel.

KARL LACHMANN published a Greek NT in 1831, the fruit of five years of work, whose purpose was to present the text of the NT as it existed in the fourth century. The only statement in this edition giving Lachmann's principles for selecting the readings of his text was a paragraph of fewer than one hundred words,[18] indicating that he followed "nowhere his own judgment," but "the usage of the most ancient eastern churches" as a first principle of selection; when the evidence was not consistent, he preferred the reading established by the agreement of the "Italian and African" witnesses. When these principles did not lead to the resolution of a textual issue, Lachmann employed brackets in the text and alternative readings in the margin to indicate indecision and other possible readings. His entire work, however, gave no consideration to the "received readings" (i.e., the TR), but sought, from the older MSS and by his stated principles, to establish the text of the fourth century.

Lachmann states his text-critical principles in a more systematic fashion, though still concisely, in the preface to his second edition of the Greek NT (1842-50) as follows:

1. Nothing is better attested than that on which all authorities agree.
2. If some of the authorities are silent or defective, the weight of evidence is somewhat lessened.
3. When the witnesses are of different regions, their agreement is of more importance than when those of some particular locality differ from the rest, either from negligence or from set purpose.
4. When witnesses of different widely separated regions disagree, the testimony must be considered to be doubtfully balanced.
5. When readings are in one form in one region and in another form in another region, with great uniformity, they are quite uncertain.
6. Lastly, readings are of weak authority when not even the same region presents a uniform testimony.[19]

These are all external criteria, for it was Lachmann's aim to reconstruct the *transmitted text* of the fourth century, and for this purpose external criteria seemed sufficient. The *transmitted text* of a certain period is, after all, recognizably different from the *most likely original text,* yet the transmitted text of the fourth century obviously was, for Lachmann, a step on the way toward the most likely original text (and a giant

---

18. The Latin text is given in Gregory 1900-1909: 966-67, and in Tregelles 1854: 98n. Lachmann also refers the reader of his first edition to his article of the preceding year (Lachmann 1830) for the rationale and plan of the edition. This article, however, contains neither a list nor a discussion of critical canons.

19. Translation adapted from Tregelles 1860: 4.135-36 and 1854: 103; the Latin text may be found in Gregory 1900-1909: 968, or in Gregory, *Prolegomena* to Tischendorf 1869: 3.260.

step of twelve hundred years away from the "received text" of the sixteenth century, which was accorded no authority by Lachmann, the first scholar to make such a clean break with the TR), and accordingly we may assume with some justification that external criteria would have held the same dominant — though perhaps not exclusive — position whether Lachmann were seeking the fourth-century transmitted text or the original text itself. This assumption is, in fact, confirmed to some extent in Lachmann's second volume (1850), which contains notes with occasional conjectures as to the original text, and here he uses "the traditive readings of the oldest documents as his basis of argument" (Tregelles 1854: 111). Clearly, then, with Lachmann the weight in text-critical decisions shifts heavily to the side of external criteria.

There is no need for a detailed description of the criteria used by the many succeeding editors of the Greek NT until the time of Westcott and Hort. Brief notice, however, should be given to the critical canons of such notable figures as Tischendorf and Tregelles.

CONSTANTIN VON TISCHENDORF, in his second edition of the Greek NT in 1849, gave as his rationale for his text the basic principle, much like Lachmann's, that:

> The text should be sought solely from ancient witness, and chiefly from Greek codices, but by no means neglecting the testimonies of the versions and the fathers. Thus, the whole arrangement of the text is bound by necessity to arise from the witnesses themselves . . . , not from the edition of Elzevir, which is called "received"; however, to be placed first among disagreeing witnesses are those regarded as the oldest Greek codices, i.e., written from the fourth to about the ninth century. Again, among these, those that excel in antiquity prevail in authority, and this authority increases if testimonies of the versions or fathers are added, nor is this authority surmounted by the disagreement of most or even of all the recent codices, i.e., those written from the ninth to the sixteenth centuries.[20]

This fundamental external criterion is supplemented by Tischendorf's further canons, some external, some internal:

1. Readings wholly peculiar to one or another [ancient] witness are suspect, as are readings, in a class of documents, that appear to have originated from critical, scholarly correction.
2. Excluded are readings, no matter what their attestation, that clearly or very probably have originated from a copyist's error.
3. Witnesses with passages parallel to the OT, the NT, and especially the synoptic gospels, when they attest disagreements, are preferable to witnesses that show agreement, for the ancients paid particular attention to parallels.
4. More probable than others is the reading that appears to have occasioned the other readings or that still contains within itself elements of the other

20. Quoted by Gregory in his *Prolegomena* to Tischendorf 1869: 3.47-48; also in Tischendorf's 7th ed., 1859: xxvii-xviii.

readings. Taken broadly, says Tischendorf, this is the foundation of all rules.

5. Readings should be studiously retained that are in accord with the Greek language and style of the individual authors of the NT.

Both the basic principle and the five canons of Tischendorf are repeated in C. R. Gregory's *Prolegomena* to Tischendorf's eighth major edition of the Greek NT (1869-94) and may be taken as those governing all of Tischendorf's efforts to establish the text of the Greek NT.

The combination in Tischendorf of a dominant external criterion — the oldest Greek MSS are the most authoritative — and of further, intermingled external and internal criteria means that the basic reliance on the oldest witnesses cannot be carried through consistently, for the further internal criteria force the modification of the basic principle at point after point and thwart its comprehensive application; the result is that at numerous points the "balance of probabilities" formula must be invoked. This is evident from the illustrative passages discussed by Tischendorf, where, as examples, he prefers a reading in Mark 2:22, attested by only two ancient witnesses, to another reading, better attested (on his principles), that shows evidence of harmonization to Matthew (1869: 3.54-55); and in Matt 24:38 he prefers a shorter reading, rather sparsely attested, to longer forms that are better attested but that are due, according to Tischendorf, to scribal expansion and are explicable as occasioned by the shorter (original) reading (1869: 3.63-64). Yet Tischendorf's basic approach to textual decisions is by way of an external criticism that in each case invokes any internal criteria especially appropriate to that particular situation.

S. P. TREGELLES published his text-critical principles in 1854 (174-226; cf. 151-74), summarized them in his rewriting of the text-critical portion of T. H. Horne's *Introduction* in 1856 (342-45), and published his edition of the Greek NT between 1857 and 1872. Unaware of Lachmann's principles, Tregelles arrived at a similar view, that is, "to form a text on the authority of ancient copies without allowing the 'received text' any prescriptive rights" (1854: 152).[21] This basic principle, consisting of an external criterion of reliance upon the oldest documents, was supplemented by a general statement on the decisive role of internal criteria whenever the old witnesses are in disagreement:

> In confining the examination to the ancient documents, all care must be taken rightly to understand their testimony, and to weigh it in all its particulars.
>
> Authorities cannot be followed mechanically; and thus, where there is a difference of reading amongst the more trustworthy witnesses, all that we know of the nature and origin of various readings, and of the kind of errors to which copyists were liable, must be employed. But, let it be observed, that discrimination of this kind is only required when the witnesses differ; for otherwise, we should fall into the error of determining by conjecture what the text *ought* to be, instead of accepting it as it is. (1854: 186; 1860: 4.344 [item 6])

21. Cf. Tregelles 1860: 4.140-41: "The ancient MSS. should be the authorities for *every word*"; "the ancient authorities should be allowed a primary place"; "the general principle in the formation of the text is that of following [external] evidence."

When Tregelles is forced to move to internal considerations so that a decision may be made between or among readings with ancient attestation, factors such as the following determine which way his "balance of probabilities" turns: favor the reading that appears to have occasioned the others (1854: 191-92, 222, 230); reject readings that clearly involve scribal errors, such as homoeoteleuton (194-96, 205-6, 220-21); prefer the reading that at first glance is incongruous but that makes good sense upon further scrutiny (196-200); reject harmonizations (206-7, 220-21, 224-25), marginal intrusions into the text (221, 245-46), and dogmatic alterations (222-23);[22] prefer the reading that accords with the author's style (256-57); and, more generally (since they encompass some of the above), prefer the harder reading (201-2, 221-22), and prefer the shorter reading (220-21).

Tregelles thought it impossible to classify MSS in any definite fashion, though he recognized that they fall into two large groups of documents, the Alexandrian or more ancient and the Constantinopolitan or more recent witnesses (1860: 4.104-7). As in the case of Tischendorf, however, manuscript grouping does not affect Tregelles's text-critical principles in any material way, except, of course, to place together in a convenient category those early witnesses that form the basic materials for his recovery of the most likely original text.

Once again, like Bengel, Griesbach, Lachmann, and Tischendorf before him, Tregelles operates with a fundamental external criterion, supplemented when necessary by subsidiary criteria of an internal kind.

The twenty years of prodigious labor by B. F. WESTCOTT and F. J. A. HORT in preparing their edition of *The New Testament in the Original Greek* of 1881-82 and the text-critical insight and theory that accompanied this influential critical text bring to a climax the entire development and interaction of external and internal "canons of criticism." Westcott and Hort do not give a list of canons in any traditional fashion, and they do not even like the term (2.23),[23] yet their "canons of criticism" are easily enough compiled from their direct statements or by inference from them; however, any abstraction of "rules" from their carefully drawn contexts or any formulation of simple principles by epitomizing Westcott and Hort's full discussions will invite both oversimplification and possible misrepresentation. Nevertheless, if Westcott and Hort's canons were to be formulated for such a list, it would include the following:

1. Older readings, MSS, or groups are to be preferred. ("The shorter the interval between the time of the autograph and the end of the period of transmission in question, the stronger the presumption that earlier date implies greater purity of text.") (2.59; cf. 2.5-6, 31)
2. Readings are approved or rejected by reason of the quality, and not the number, of their supporting witnesses. ("No available presumptions

---

22. Tregelles allows these as "occasional" occurrences, such as alterations in the interest and support of asceticism, but he says that it would be "an entire mistake to suppose that there was any evidence of doctrinal corruption of the sacred records . . ." (223); cf. 222-25.

23. As is well known, Westcott and Hort's vol. 2, *Introduction, Appendix* (1882; 2d ed., 1896), was authored by Hort, though both are fully responsible for the "principles, arguments, and conclusions set forth" (2.18).

whatever as to text can be obtained from number alone, that is, from number not as yet interpreted by descent.") (2.44)

3. A reading combining two simple, alternative readings is later than the two readings comprising the conflation, and MSS rarely or never supporting conflate reading are texts antecedent to mixture and are of special value. (2.49-50)

4. The reading is to be preferred that makes the best sense, that is, that best conforms to the grammar and is most congruous with the purport of the rest of the sentence and of the larger context. (2.20)

5. The reading is to be preferred that best conforms to the usual style of the author and to that author's material in other passages. (2.20)

6. The reading is to be preferred that most fitly explains the existence of the others. (2.22-23)

7. The reading is less likely to be original that combines the appearance of an improvement in the sense with the absence of its reality; the scribal alteration will have an apparent excellence, while the original will have the highest real excellence. (2.27, 29)

8. The reading is less likely to be original that shows a disposition to smooth away difficulties (another way of stating that the harder reading is preferable). (2.28)

9. Readings are to be preferred that are found in a MS that habitually contains superior readings as determined by intrinsic and transcriptional probability. Certainty is increased if such a better MS is found also to be an older MS (2.32-33) and if such a MS habitually contains readings that prove themselves antecedent to mixture and independent of external contamination by other, inferior texts (2.150-51). The same principles apply to groups of MSS (2.260-61).

The extraction and tabulation of such canons do not, however, enlighten us as to the real significance of Westcott and Hort's treatment of text-critical principles. Rather, their contribution (and our major interest) rests in the fact, first, that they combined in a unique fashion the internal and external criteria as they had evolved and had been used over the years and, second, that they utilized the resulting combination in a new way — with far-reaching effects on NT text-critical theory and method.

Westcott and Hort had the highest regard for Griesbach — "a name we venerate above that of every other textual critic of the New Testament" — with respect to his historical reconstruction of the "genealogical relations of the whole extant documentary evidence" (2.185-86), that is, Griesbach's scheme of two ancient and one more recent group of MSS. Westcott and Hort's own reconstruction followed this general pattern, though with well-known modifications. On the other hand, they complain that Griesbach's two great weaknesses were, first, his use of the TR as a basis for correcting the NT text and, second and chiefly, his propensity "to give a dangerously disproportionate weight to internal evidence, and especially to transcriptional probability, on which indeed for its own sake he placed excessive reliance" (2.184). This criticism of Griesbach by Westcott and Hort will be perplexing to anyone who knows Westcott and Hort's own text-critical theory; although they claim that genealogy is primary (2.63-64; cf. 2.17), thereby leaving the impression that external evidence provides the solid foundation for their text-critical theory, yet a closer reading shows that Westcott and Hort employed genealogy only on a broad scale and in a generic and almost loose fashion to separate the pre-Syrian lines of text from the Syrian line and that they never worked out their genealogical method (at least as far as we know) in terms of specific stemmata of actual NT MSS;[24] moreover, when the crucial question of deciding between the two earliest text-types (Neutral and Western) is broached, they admit that genealogical method cannot lead to a decision (2.41-42). At this point, the whole range of internal considerations comes into play, as Westcott and Hort elaborated them (2.19-39, 60-66): (1) the Internal Evidence of Readings, that is, consideration of individual readings in terms of (a) Intrinsic Probability (what the author most likely wrote) and (b) Transcriptional Probability (what the scribe most likely wrote), yielding great certainty about the most probable reading when both methods certify the same reading, but with transcriptional probability decisive when the two methods are in conflict; (2) the Internal Evidence of Documents, that is, consideration of each single group of readings that constitutes a MS so as to acquire "knowledge of documents," that is, knowledge of that MS's general quality and reliability, so that the weight of its readings can be assessed when the Internal Evidence of (individual) Readings is unclear; and (3) the Internal Evidence of Groups, or consideration of a single group of MSS to determine its overall character in relation to other groups as a bearer of generally reliable documents.

Westcott and Hort's *quantitative* use of internal considerations adds up, in the final analysis, to a *qualitative* judgment on internal evidence as superior to and more decisive than external (genealogical) evidence. In fact, for all practical purposes, it is internal evidence alone that is determinative for them in virtually all text-critical decisions once the early text-types have been separated from the later Syrian type, and, moreover, internal criteria are thereafter utilized to support this basic distinction between the early and the later types of text.

This qualitative judgment on the superiority of internal evidence is obvious from Westcott and Hort's descriptions of the basic text-types; though the Syrian and pre-Syrian texts ostensibly were isolated and differentiated in the first instance by objective, genealogical procedures (2.90-117), it seems clear enough from Westcott and Hort's characterization, for example, of the Syrian type (a text that is smooth, eminently readable, complete, and conflate, filled out by harmonization, assimilation, and appropriate connecting tissue [2.134-35]), that reliance on internal evidence alone would have yielded the same result — that the Syrian text is a relatively late derivative text, posterior to, built upon, and incorporating numerous elements of its antecedent texts (the Western, Neutral, and Alexandrian).

What actually develops for Westcott and Hort, then — to be more specific — is a theory that leads, first, to a division of MSS and groups of MSS into early and later text-types presumably by an external, genealogical method, and, second

---

24. Colwell 1969: 65; cf. the section on "Genealogical Evidence" in Westcott-Hort 2.39-62, also 90-119, 178-79.

(though concurrently), to an assessment of the relative quality or reliability of these various MSS and groups of MSS. The result is their well-known judgment (1) that the later Syrian (or Byzantine) MSS are conflate and therefore furthest removed both chronologically and qualitatively from the original text; (2) that MSS like C, L, and 33 (the Alexandrian text) are individually and as a group good but refined and polished texts and thereby removed somewhat from the original; (3) that MSS like D and D[paul] (the Western text) and their group are ancient but corrupt texts and thereby removed in quality though not so much in date from the original text; and (4) that MSS B and ℵ are the "best" MSS and that their group (the Neutral text) is the "best" group because they are at once close in time and closest in quality to the original NT text.

It will be obvious that this distinctive textual theory and these confident judgments of Westcott and Hort were produced by a unique *synergism of external and internal evidence*. This coaction of the two kinds of criteria involved two separate but concurrent processes. On the one hand, the earliest and least mixed (and thereby presumably the purest) readings and also the groups of manuscript witnesses supporting such early, unmixed readings were isolated; this process utilized external data (the date or relative antiquity of the MS, the age of the reading as determined by patristic support, etc.) and employed genealogical-like methods (locating pre-Syrian readings and text by analysis — primarily — of conflate readings) to achieve its goal. Second, and concurrently, the anterior (in the sense of logical rather than temporal priority) and "best" readings and groups of witnesses (and thereby presumably the purest readings and groups) were isolated; this was accomplished by utilizing the Internal Evidence of Readings (both Intrinsic and Transcriptional Probabilities) to assess variation-units that included, again, conflate readings, thereby permitting the "superior" readings and texts to be separated from the "inferior" (2.90-119).

The first result of these processes was that Westcott and Hort's synergism of external and internal evidence separated the later Syrian (or Byzantine) text and its readings from the earlier texts and readings of the three other groups, the Western, Neutral, and Alexandrian. Furthermore, the Alexandrian text was shown, by the same cooperation of external and internal evidence, to be posterior (both in terms of time and logical sequence) to the Western and Neutral groups because its readings were shown to have been derived from one of these two other pre-Syrian text-types (the Neutral) and could be dated externally to about the beginning of the third century (2.130-32). The further result of these processes was Westcott and Hort's characterization of these groups or text-types: the Syrian text is a late, critically edited, and polished text, incorporating the bulk of available readings to form a full text; the Alexandrian is a somewhat earlier, inventively interpolated, and philologically refined text; and the two other, still earlier texts, the Western and the Neutral, are rather drastically different from each other in character, for the Western is judged, on internal grounds, to have "a love of paraphrase" and "a disposition to enrich the text at the cost of its purity," and a "fondness for assimilation" (2.122-26), while the Neutral text is "a relatively pure Non-Western text" (2.128; cf. 178). Hence, the Neutral text emerges as the "best" NT text.

From these conclusions, the synergism of external and internal evidence proceeds, in Westcott and Hort, to the identification, not only of the "best" (i.e., the purest) text or group of witnesses (the Neutral), but of the "best" (i.e., the purest) MSS. Their well-known assertion is that Codex Vaticanus (B) "holds a unique position" since "its text is not only Pre-Syrian but substantially free from Western and Alexandrian adulteration" (2.150-51); moreover, "B very far exceeds all other documents in neutrality of text . . . , being in fact always or nearly always neutral" (2.171), and this conclusion is based both on genealogical or external evidence and on internal evidence (2.150-51, 170-71, 210-71, esp. 210). The corollary to this assessment of B is that Codex Sinaiticus (א) is next in purity among all other MSS (2.171, 210-13, 222-23), and Westcott and Hort can speak of "the preeminent excellence of the Vatican and Sinaitic MSS, which happen likewise to be the oldest extant Greek MSS of the New Testament" (2.212). Again, this judgment on א arises from the coaction of external and internal evidence.

As is common knowledge, Westcott and Hort go on from these settled points to make use of the Neutral text generally, but particularly of codices B and א, as the lodestar for locating and establishing the original NT text.

It is precisely at this point of determining the single best text, however, that the synergism of external and internal evidence in Westcott and Hort's scheme suddenly breaks down to reveal instead — and quite unexpectedly — a tension between the external and the internal criteria. This tension turns out, upon examination, to be a genuine *polarity of external and internal evidence* and it comes to light as these two methodological procedures and their resultant data are employed by Westcott and Hort in building their text-critical theory. It is the so-called Western text and its leading representative, Codex Bezae (D), that bring this polarity to view, in the following way: the combination of external and internal evidence had led Westcott and Hort to the "best" readings (the pre-Syrian); thence to the "best" text or group of MSS (the non-Western pre-Syrian Neutral text), since this "best" text consistently contained these "best" readings; thence, finally, to the "best" MSS (B, with א), since they are the "constant element" of those groups that are "found to have habitually the best readings" (2.212).[25]

This line of argumentation established, in effect, a new "objective" standard for originality, namely, the *criterion of the best MS* or best MSS, and this canon then could be invoked for a decision between or among readings in cases where the evidence was otherwise ambiguous or where other criteria were inconclusive. (Critics have called this Westcott and Hort approach "the cult of the best manuscript."[26]) That this new criterion was established by the coaction of external and internal evidence is not to be disputed, but an inconsistency is soon disclosed in Westcott and Hort's scheme when their treatment of D and the Western text is investigated,

25. Cf. 2.210: "Every group containing both א and B is found, where Internal Evidence is tolerably unambiguous, to have an apparently more original text than every opposed group containing neither."

26. Elliott 1972c: 339, 340; 1974: 345-46, 349; cf. 1973: 278-300, esp. 297; and 1975c: 15. A view similar to Westcott and Hort's — the championing of a "best MS" as an almost "external" criterion but one based essentially on internal judgments — can be seen in the work of M.-J. Lagrange and would be worth exploring as another possible step that brought us on the way to the current chaos in NT text-critical method; cf. Colwell 1969: 6, 80-81.

for Westcott and Hort's external evidence isolated *two* "earliest" texts or groups, the Neutral *and* the Western, and suddenly it becomes apparent that the criterion of the best MS(S), which focuses on B (with ℵ), was not the exclusive fruit of Westcott and Hort's genealogical and external considerations; actually, and by their explicit admission, external evidence shows that the Western text, in fact, has the earliest documentation:

> The earliest readings which can be fixed chronologically belong to it. As far as we can judge from extant evidence, it was the most widely spread text of Ante-Nicene times; and sooner or later every version directly or indirectly felt its influence. (2.120)

And of Codex Bezae they say:

> . . . When every allowance has been made for possible individual license, the text of D presents a truer image of the form in which the Gospels and Acts were most widely read in the third and probably a great part of the second century than any other extant Greek MS. (2.149)

On what grounds, then, do Westcott and Hort strain and apparently violate their presumably basic genealogical principle by an unequivocal preference for the Neutral text rather than the Western? On grounds of internal evidence, for "any prepossessions in [the Western text's] favour that might be created by this imposing early ascendancy are for the most part soon dissipated by continuous study of its internal character" (2.120). The harmonious synergism of external and internal evidence may have enthroned B as the best MS on both grounds (perhaps, in isolation, a reasonable conclusion), but the case made at the same time by Westcott and Hort for the dethronement of D cannot with consistency be based on the external evidence admitted by them for D and the Western text. In other words, to accept the readings of B in virtually all cases as practically identical with the original text and to utilize B as the standard of excellence because it represents the purest and an extremely ancient text, and at the same time to reject possibly even older readings (in terms of demonstrable evidence) simply because they are found in a MS like D, containing (according to Westcott and Hort) a "prodigious amount of error" (2.149), or in a "licentious" (2.178), "corrupt" (2.124, 127, 131), and "aberrant" text like the Western (when judged by internal evidence), not only violates their genealogical principle, thereby placing a strain on logic, but also is a clear capitulation to the primacy of internal evidence, and it effects a shift from a cooperative role between external and internal evidence to a situation of polarity. Now the rather clear external evidence concerning D and the Western text is pushed aside and stands in opposition to internal considerations, forcing upon critics a choice between them; in fact, the two kinds of evidence have been separated to the extent that they assume a dualistic posture, breaking once and for all Westcott and Hort's harmonious synergism of external and internal evidence and highlighting the ambiguity of both the external testimony and the internal judgments. When there is conflict of evidence, as is so often the case, are basic text-critical decisions to be made (or able to be made) on the basis of historical-development and documentary (external) considerations or on the assessment of contextual, stylistic, and scribal (internal) factors? When the evidence fails to point to a single conclusion, one or the other — but never both — must assume the determinative role, and it will not immediately be clear to most textual critics whether it is the external evidence or the internal considerations that should play that decisive role. What is clear, however, is that the failure of Westcott and Hort's synergism of external-internal evidence precisely at the crucial point of the earliest demonstrable fork in the NT textual stream (the separation of the Western and Neutral traditions) has evoked, in large measure, the uncertainty, the bewilderment, and the virtual anarchy of recent and current NT textual criticism, and — to be more specific — has occasioned the entire eclectic movement as presently practiced in the textual criticism of the NT.[27]

This inordinately lengthy "survey" of the "canons of criticism" and the accompanying assessment of their formative role in text-critical theory and practice hardly would be complete without a summary list of canons that have survived the test of time and that are recognized generally as viable principles. These canons fall, of course, into the two major categories that have been discussed above, (1) criteria appealing to *external evidence,* that is, to documentary and historical-development factors in the textual transmission process, and (2) criteria appealing to *internal evidence,* that is, to factors relating to scribal habits, the contexts of passages, and the author's style, language, and thought. In the following outline, which aims to be comprehensive but could never be exhaustive, each criterion is phrased in such a way that, if it accurately describes a textual variant, there would be a presumption (other things being equal) to regard that variant as the most likely original reading.

    A. Criteria related to external evidence
        1. A variant's support by the earliest MSS, or by MSS assuredly preserving the earliest texts
        2. A variant's support by the "best quality" MSS
        3. A variant's support by MSS with the widest geographical distribution
        4. A variant's support by one or more established groups of MSS of recognized antiquity, character, and perhaps location, that is, of recognized "best quality."
    B. Criteria related to internal evidence
        1. A variant's status as the shorter or shortest reading
        2. A variant's status as the harder or hardest reading
        3. A variant's fitness to account for the origin, development, or presence of all other readings
        4. A variant's conformity to the author's style and vocabulary
        5. A variant's conformity to the author's theology or ideology
        6. A variant's conformity to Koine (rather than Attic) Greek.[28]

27. These ideas, in compressed form, were first developed for my article, 1976b.
28. This canon is based on the suggestions of Kilpatrick 1963b. Cf. now the compelling cautions of Fee 1976 (which was preprinted in *SBLASP* 1975: 2.36-41) [now Chapter 7], and of Martini 1974.

    7. A variant's conformity to Semitic forms of expression

    8. A variant's lack of conformity to parallel passages or to extraneous items in its context generally

    9. A variant's lack of conformity to OT passages

    10. A variant's lack of conformity to liturgical forms and usages

    11. A variant's lack of conformity to extrinsic doctrinal views.

This list does not include those further criteria for originality that must be applied to readings at an earlier stage in the text-critical process to determine whether readings are "significant" or "insignificant" for the establishment of the most likely original text. Hence, readings that obviously are (1) nonsense readings, (2) clear and demonstrable scribal errors, (3) mere orthographic variations, and (4) singular readings will be assumed to have been excluded from the process, for they are not "textual variants" in the proper, restricted sense of that term[29] and therefore do not constitute appropriate raw material for the actual determination of the most likely original NT text.

C. Use of Critical Canons in Current Eclecticism

The categories earlier specified as including all contemporary NT textual critics (except the genealogical scholars), namely, *eclectic generalists* and *eclectic specialists,* will provide an appropriate framework for a brief assessment of text-critical methodology in the present, post-Westcott-Hort situation — a situation characterized by a polarity of external and internal evidence. That "all of us" employ an eclectic approach in NT textual criticism may stand as a fair generalization; it is also a fair generalization that eclecticism is of two distinct kinds, variously designated, on the one hand, as "moderate" or "reasoned" eclecticism and, on the other hand, as "thoroughgoing" or "rigorous" eclecticism, though the more descriptively accurate and less question-begging terms used here, eclectic generalists and eclectic specialists, perhaps are preferable. As will appear presently, eclectics in both groups attempt to break down or neutralize the polarity between the external criteria for originality and the internal, some by ignoring it, and others by emphasizing one pole to the diminution or even the banishment of the other pole. All, however, stand within the dualistic situation created by the conflict of text-critical criteria that has issued from Westcott and Hort's failure to hold the external and internal canons together.

1. Use of Critical Canons by Eclectic Generalists

An *eclectic generalist* is a textual critic who recognizes that no single criterion or constant combination of criteria will adjudicate all text-critical cases and who tries, within this acknowledged limitation, to apply with evenness and without prejudice any and all criteria appropriate to the given case and who attempts, further, to arrive

---

29. These not uncontroversial matters have been treated by the present writer (Epp 1976a) in a paper presented to the Society of Biblical Literature's Textual Criticism Seminar, Washington, DC, 1974 [now Chapter 3].

at a reasonable solution based on the relative probabilities among those applicable criteria.

Eclectic generalists acknowledge the validity, for the appropriate situations and with other things being equal, of the various canons of criticism or criteria for originality that have emerged in the history of textual criticism and have demonstrated their worth, such as those in the formal list above, including both kinds — external and internal. Accordingly, the eclectic generalist would overcome the polarity of these external and internal criteria by ignoring that polarity or by attempting to ignore it. This is easily possible when, for example, one variant reading among several is the hardest reading from the perspective of scribal habits, is also in accord with the author's ascertained vocabulary and style and with his theology as critically determined, and happens at the same time to be attested by "excellent" MSS and by ancient versions or early Fathers of wide geographical distribution. In such cases, where textual decisions are easy, the eclectic generalist (and every other textual critic!) will be oblivious both to the dualistic framework of two distinct classes of criteria for originality and also to the ambiguities so often attendant upon the application of those criteria. When, however, as is so frequently the case, several "strong" criteria do not favor a single reading but variously approve one or another reading, and when — also a frequent occurrence — there is a further bifurcation of evidence between the external and internal poles, then the critic finds himself or herself in a dilemma as he or she faces the difficult "crisis of criteria." If the reading that better suits the author's style is found only in later MSS, while the rival reading is found in codices B and ℵ (cf. Matt 6:33 [Metzger 1971: 18-19]), which is to be chosen? If one of five variant readings is attested by B and D, but two other similar readings most adequately account for the origin of all the others (cf. Matt 15:14 [Metzger: 39]), which is to be selected? If a wide variety of textual types attest a reading that is clearly "easier" than its alternative (cf. Matt 15:38 [Metzger: 40-41]), which should be preferred? If a variant that quite possibly arose from a parallel passage is omitted by the "best" witnesses (cf. Matt 16:2-3 [Metzger: 41]), should it be admitted into the text? If a longer reading that is almost certainly explicable as a scribal addition due to the influence of the immediate context is supported by B and ℵ (cf. Matt 16:21 [Metzger: 42-43]), should it be approved? If the vast majority of MSS, including the "best" MSS, attest a shorter reading that could easily be explained as a doctrinal modification of an original longer reading (cf. Matt 27:16, 17 [Metzger: 67-68]), which is to be chosen? If the majority of witnesses support a reading that appears to be original on grounds of transcriptional probability, but a few of the earliest and "best" MSS have a shorter reading (cf. Acts 3:6 [Metzger: 307]), which reading is to be approved?

Examples of this kind easily could be multiplied, but it will be obvious that textual problems involving the conflict of external and internal criteria are common. Of course, many textual problems are even more complex than these examples, for at the same time they may involve, on the one hand, evenly divided external evidence and, on the other hand, conflicting but balanced internal factors. These situations not only demand considerably more refinement in all of the criteria and call for ways to weigh them against one another, but they also highlight the vexing ambiguities to be found in both the external and internal aspects of text-critical criteria.

Most contemporary NT textual critics, if asked to classify themselves, probably would affirm that they belong to this eclectic generalist class, for most textual critics today, recognizing the inconclusiveness of modern text-critical theory, would profess to have adopted this evenhanded employment of the available means for judging between and among textual variants, that is, a balanced and impartial application of the relevant external and internal criteria to each case of textual variation. To take an example, certainly this was the intention of the distinguished editors of the UBS[3] (Aland et al. 1975), as evidenced by the careful delineation of the criteria in the report of their textual deliberations and decisions (Metzger 1971: xxiv-xxviii). This intention comes to the fore time and again as the editors, for example, go against a variant supported by Westcott and Hort's lodestar, Codex B (with א), when other evidence — external or (perhaps more often) internal — suggests the originality of an alternative variant; it appears also in the scrupulous and judicious evaluations of relevant criteria in those numerous cases where the evidence is very closely divided. Yet, a perusal of *A Textual Commentary on the Greek New Testament* by the editors of the UBS[3] strongly suggests that the steady repetition of such phrases as "the preponderant weight of external attestation," "the overwhelming weight of manuscript evidence," and "superior manuscript support," along with such expressions as "the earliest and best witnesses," "the oldest and best attested reading," and "attested by inferior authorities," all signal a predilection for an external principle along the lines of "the readings of the oldest and best manuscripts are to be preferred," and most often this means B with א and, where applicable, the early papyri, such as P[75], P[66], P[45], and P[72].[30] This assessment, based as it is on impressions from extended interaction with the *Textual Commentary,* just possibly could be an unfair generalization; more likely, however, it is a reasonable and fair judgment, and, if so, it signifies that the editors of the UBS[3] in the final analysis are not eclectic generalists after all, nor in fact are there many among contemporary NT textual critics who could be so classified, despite the good intentions of most of them to follow this balanced approach (cf. n. 3 above). Rather, contemporary textual critics for the most part are to be classed as eclectic specialists, whether on the right wing of that subdivision or on the left.

---

30. That B played this decisive role in the UBS[3] is confirmed by the statement in Metzger 1971: 295: ". . . The possibility must be left open that occasionally the text of B represents a secondary development." The fact that this comment occurs in connection with an Acts passage makes it all the more significant, for Metzger reports (272-73) that the editors recognized that in the text of Acts "neither the Alexandrian nor the Western group of witnesses always preserves the original text, but that in order to attain the earliest text one must compare the two divergent traditions point by point and in each case select the reading which commends itself in the light of transcriptional and intrinsic probabilities," and that, therefore, the editorial committee "proceeded in an eclectic fashion." The clear implication is that, for the UBS committee, B was indeed the lodestar of the original text, for if in Acts — where there is the greatest uncertainty as to whether B and its group or its early rival, the Western text, represents the original — if here in Acts the *possibility* must be allowed that B *occasionally* represents the *non*-original text, then elsewhere B must surely stand as the most reliable guide. Incidentally, the statement from pp. 272-73 quoted above does not mean that in Acts the editors gave primacy to internal evidence, for what they sought, as stated explicitly, was "the earliest text" — an external criterion, though internal criteria were employed, as part of an overall eclectic process, to determine which of the two rival texts or which of the various alternative readings was in fact the earlier or earliest.

2. Use of Critical Canons by Eclectic Specialists

The *eclectic specialist* recognizes quite clearly the polarity between external and internal evidence, and he or she tries to overcome it by *specializing* in or by *emphasizing* one of the poles to the minimizing or even exclusion of the other. Whether one can escape the dualistic dilemma by this one-sidedness remains to be seen, but such a critic is aware that a *major* choice between text-critical criteria (in addition to and quite different in character from the innumerable minor choices) must be made in order to solve the textual problems that one faces, and the choice — when the chips are down — is between *final reliance* either on evidence from the historical-development and documentary side of textual history (external evidence) or from scribal, stylistic, contextual, and ideological factors in manuscript transmission (internal evidence).

At least two subgroups are to be found among the eclectic specialists. On the right hand are those textual critics who permit external evidence to cast the decisive vote in cases where there is equiponderance of evidence, but the utilization of historical-documentary evidence in this way requires that the critic first shall have accepted as valid a particular historical-development scheme for the earliest transmission of the NT text; usually the scheme adopted will follow the general lines of Westcott and Hort's understanding of a twofold Syrian (or, better, Byzantine or Koine) and pre-Syrian textual history, including their further demarcation of a "Neutral" (or, better, Alexandrian or Egyptian) text-type and a "Western" text-type as the earliest (and competing) texts, but also the recognition of a third early text, the Caesarean type.[31] For critics of this kind, normally a reading strongly attested by widely diversified witnesses from all of the early groups would be preferred, as would a reading very strongly attested by the Alexandrian (Westcott and Hort's Neutral) group. When the probabilities are more evenly balanced (such as divided support among the Alexandrian witnesses or among the early text-types), then other criteria will come into play, particularly internal considerations (hence, the designation, *eclectic* specialists), such as the search for the reading that best explains the origin of all the others, or any other applicable criteria. The complicating factors attending textual decisions can be severe and vexing, but the point is that in the final analysis an eclectic specialist, as one who emphasizes external criteria, *characteristically* will flee for refuge to any relevant historical-development and documentary considerations that will permit a resolution of the problem. This does not necessarily mean that this is done automatically or even consistently, but only *characteristically,* for there are times when the internal evidence will show unambiguously that a scribal error or some other transmissional phenomenon — whether intentional or unintentional — lies at the root of the reading in one's "best" MS or group; in that case, as an eclectic, he or she will choose another reading. Yet the textual critic of this type has a prevailing predilection — though hardly a whimsical or haphazard one — for the supremacy of external evidence and usually for external evidence of a particular brand. Obviously, not all such eclectic specialists will lean toward the Alexandrian

---

31. See Epp 1974: 393-96 for a statement on the status of the Caesarean text in current criticism.

text-type or its members as determinative; some few may prefer, for instance, the so-called Western witnesses.

The major difficulty with an eclectic approach that specializes in external evidence emerges precisely at this point, that is, with the uncertainty as to which historical-development scheme to adopt as normative. Is it to be the basic Westcott-Hort conception as modified by new developments and discoveries, or some other reconstruction of the earliest history of the NT textual transmission? This inconclusiveness, of course, is no fault of the eclectic method, but is rather a weakness — perhaps *the* weakness — of modern NT textual theory in general (cf. Epp 1974: 390-401). As a matter of fact, far from being at fault in this circumstance, the eclectic method is merely a reflection or a symptom of this fundamental problem. If there were any reasonable certainty about this very earliest history of the NT text and if reasonably confident assertions could be formulated as to precisely how our extant MSS are related to that history of transmission, these difficulties in the eclectic method would disappear — and perhaps also the eclectic method as we know it would itself disappear! Such basic solutions, however, appear not to be close at hand, though certainly some significant advances in methodology, coupled with the extraordinary discoveries of early papyri during the past generation or two, are a source of optimism (cf. Epp 1974: 387, 406-14). In the meantime, most NT textual critics doubtless will follow some form of this moderate or reasoned eclecticism that we have designated the eclectic-specialist approach.

(Observe that genealogists, while they are "specialists" who emphasize external evidence, are not *eclectic* specialists, for internal considerations play virtually no role in their establishment of a text.)

On the left wing of the eclectic-specialist class are those who rely largely, primarily, or even exclusively on internal criteria for resolving text-critical problems and for establishing the original NT text. Obviously, scholars of this persuasion overcome the external-internal polarity by granting to internal evidence the determinative role. This dominance of internal factors, notably the author's style and contextual considerations, was operative, for instance, in the work of Bernhard Weiss, whose editions of the Greek NT appeared between 1894 and 1905,[32] in C. H. Turner's "Notes" (consisting of 100 pages!) on "Marcan Usage" (1923-28), and in M.-J. Lagrange's "critique rationnelle" (1935: esp. 17-40). Both Weiss and Lagrange in effect depart, however, from their proclaimed reliance on internal criticism and move instead to a practical dependence on a "best MS" criterion, and in both cases Codex B is employed as the touchstone of purity. Though customarily mentioned as the leading exponent of "rational criticism" (e.g., Klijn 1949: 170), it can be said of Lagrange that "in almost Hortian terms he pleads for following codex Vaticanus even where the evidence is not clear — on the grounds of its general excellence" (Colwell 1969: 6; cf. n. 26 above).

C. H. TURNER opened his series of studies on Marcan usage by altering Westcott and Hort's famous dictum, "Knowledge of documents should precede final

---

32. See Metzger 1968a: 137-38 for a succinct description of Weiss's procedures, and pp. 175-79 for a general summary of this kind of eclectic methodology.

judgement upon readings" (2.ix, 31), to "Knowledge of an author's usage should precede final judgement" (1923-24: 377), thereby indicating in a striking fashion the need to take internal evidence most seriously, particularly stylistic and philological features, and that these are crucial if not conclusive in text-critical decisions.

Turner's description of grammatical usages in Mark bore fruit in the work of GEORGE D. KILPATRICK, whose views developed from their rather cautious beginnings in 1943 and 1944 (q.v.) until the present time, when they represent what justly may be called the far left of the eclectic-specialist emphasis on internal criteria. Kilpatrick's early views were expressed in statements such as, "We cannot accept or reject textual types or manuscripts as wholes," for each segment of text is only a collection of variants, "each of which is to be judged on its own merits," and by calling for scholars to apply a "rigorous eclecticism" in the Gospels and Acts and to "pursue an impartial eclecticism" also in the Epistles, but to do so in a consistent way everywhere.[33] By eclecticism he apparently meant, at this time, the serious application of text-critical criteria additional to those that tried to move "from the textual families and types to the original text" (1943: 36), that is, criteria additional to external evidence. In other words, for the establishment of the original text, he was urging that all mechanical application of "best MS" and "best text-type" criteria cease and that in addition to the normal criteria arising from knowledge of MSS and palaeographic principles the textual critic should employ also — and with great seriousness — those criteria concerned with harmonization, style, language, theology, and a reading's fitness to account for all others (internal evidence), but with special emphasis on the assertion that in this eclectic method "the decision rests ultimately with the criteria as distinct from the manuscripts, and that our evaluation of the manuscripts must be determined by the criteria" (1943: 25-26). Kilpatrick claimed that his proposals entailed no disparagement of external evidence (1943: 36) (of none, that is, except claims for a normative "best text" or "best MS"), yet in a real sense external criteria were seriously undermined. Whereas he seemed to be asking only that external evidence be removed from its seemingly exclusive position of supremacy in textual decisions, that critics lay aside their predispositions in its favor, and that all criteria be allowed to stand on an equal plane, in actuality external criteria were negatively affected to a much greater extent than these statements would imply, for how can external criteria play a role when "each reading has to be judged on its merits and not on its supports" (1943: 33)? How, for example, can the date or geographical provenance of a reading be relevant when "the decision rests ultimately with the criteria *as distinct from the manuscripts*" [italics added]? The effect of this presumed eclecticism of internal *and* external evidence is that the external evidence virtually is ruled out of court in advance, for this particular presiding judge will allow no evidence along the lines of "general opinions about the value of the manuscripts or textual types" (1943: 26), nor any, presumably, about the date or provenance of a MS containing a given reading or its place in any reconstruction of the history of

---

33. Kilpatrick 1943: 33-34, 36; 1944: 65; see also Kilpatrick 1963b: 136: "At each point the text must be decided impartially on the merits of the readings involved." Similar statements appear inevitably in his many articles on the subject.

NT textual transmission; that leaves little if anything on the external side of the case.[34]

To be fair to Professor Kilpatrick, it must be added that his two earliest articles on this subject encompassed as possibly original only those readings from text-types and witnesses that were acknowledged to be early (notably the Alexandrian and Western texts and their witnesses) (1943: 36); nevertheless, the principles established there by Kilpatrick for evaluating these *early* readings were thereafter applied by him to *all* readings. This becomes explicit when in 1963 he repeated his conclusion that "no manuscript or type of text is uniformly right or wrong" and then affirmed that "this conclusion applies as much to the Byzantine text . . . as to the Western text and the old Uncials," adding that the "outright condemnation" of the Byzantine text was one of Westcott and Hort's greatest errors (1963a: 76). In 1965, Kilpatrick supported and illustrated this conviction from scores of variation-units where he felt that the Byzantine witnesses preserved the original text, and he concluded by saying:

> We have to pursue a consistent eclecticism. Readings must be considered severally on their intrinsic character. Further, contrary to what Hort maintained, decisions about readings must precede decisions about the value or weight of manuscripts. (1965: 205-6)

It is, then, this assessment and judgment of individual readings, inevitably on internal grounds and in complete detachment from any value or weight that may be assigned to the MSS or groups that contain them, that is the heart of this form of the eclectic-specialist approach, though this characterization, as pointed out earlier, does not adequately convey the degree to which external evidence has been excluded by this method; in fact, for all practical purposes it has been eliminated from the text-critical decisions on the original text.

The accuracy of our estimation of the true character of this form of eclecticism is confirmed by the handling of the method in the work of J. K. ELLIOTT, who calls for a "thoroughgoing eclecticism," in which "the cult of the best manuscripts gives way to the cult of the best reading" and which "devotes its main attention to the individual variants themselves and very little attention to external evidence" (1972c: 340-41). The phrase "very little attention to external evidence" is actually, however, an understatement, for nowhere in either of his brief but recent expositions of "thoroughgoing eclecticism" does Elliott mention, much less approve, any external criterion among his extensive listing of critical canons; rather, external criteria are excluded, for his approach "is concerned with finding plausible explanations based on internal considerations to justify the choice of one reading as original and the others as secondary" (1972c: 341; 1974: 349-53), or again, ". . . We are concerned with which reading is likely to represent what our original author wrote. We are not concerned with the age, prestige, or popularity of the manuscripts supporting the readings we would adopt as original" (1972c: 352). In an earlier exposition of the method, a reference presumably to external evidence — stated in terms of palaeo-

---

34. Kilpatrick does speak of assessing the "antiquity of the tradition in a certain manuscript" from its spelling, abbreviations, script, number of columns, and errors (1943: 26).

graphic phenomena and manuscript characteristics — seems to refer only to aids in recovering scribal habits and peculiarities, in actuality internal evidence.[35] Elliott, furthermore, is quite explicit about the antithesis between external and internal criteria, for which he often uses the designations (respectively) of "documentary" and "eclectic" methods, and he is equally explicit about his clear preference for the latter: ". . . It is reasonable to depart from a documentary study and to examine the N.T. text from a purely eclectic standpoint," and "The eclectic method, by using different criteria and by working from a different standpoint, tries to arrive at the true reading, untrammeled by discussion about the weight of MS support."[36]

One of the difficulties with the eclectic approach that specializes in internal criticism may be only a terminological inconsistency, but it should be obvious that those who insist most strongly on an "eclectic" approach actually are the least eclectic, for their partiality toward internal criteria virtually excludes the external. Moreover, since the critical principles of these eclectics are focused for the most part rather narrowly on the style of the author (including language and grammar, and how scribes are likely to have treated what the author wrote),[37] the term "eclectic" loses much of its appropriateness. It is not clear either what the adjectives "rigorous," "impartial," or "thoroughgoing" signify when they modify "eclecticism," for the method's self-imposed limitation to internal criteria surely makes it less "impartial" and less "thorough" than an eclectic-generalist approach or than that of the specialist emphasizing external evidence, for these latter methods utilize both external and internal criteria. Moreover, the term "rigorous" is ambiguous here, for it is not evident whether it means "strict," "severe" in the sense of "narrow," "restricted" (an appropriate designation), or has the sense of "inflexible," that is, rigidly conforming to the eclectic principle (which this school seems not to do); since the latter meaning is close to "thoroughgoing" and since Kilpatrick calls for a "consistent eclecticism" (1965: 205; cf. 1943: 34), it would appear that "rigorous" is meant to refer to thoroughness and consistency in being eclectic (traits that seem not to be the possession of this school).

This semantic problem could more likely be solved, however, by taking "eclectic" to specify the open choice, not of criteria, but of readings from any extant MSS; if so, this kind of eclecticism would be "impartial" in the sense that it shows no favoritism toward any particular MS and has no predilection for any specific text (which is true); it would be "thoroughgoing" in the sense that it considers all readings candidates for the original reading until some internal test rules them out; and it would be "rigorous" and "consistent" in that it never swerves from this openness to every extant reading. The only difficulty here is that nearly all the contexts, in both Kilpatrick and Elliott, that characterize or describe "eclecticism" suggest that "eclectic" is concerned primarily with the open and wide choice of criteria and not of

---

35. Elliott 1968a: 10. There are some ambiguous references to "weak" and "strong" support (p. 11).

36. Elliott 1968a: 5-6, 11; cf. also p. 12: "Often such a study serves as further ammunition against the documentary method"; and 1972c: 341: ". . . internal rather than on documentary criteria."

37. Cf., e.g., Kilpatrick 1963a: 77; Elliott 1968a: 8, who calls conformity to the author's style and usage the eclectic method's "basic rule of thumb."

readings, though the latter also is certainly a prominent feature of this branch of eclecticism.

More substantive criticisms of this eclecticism of internal criteria arise from the side of the evolution and history of NT textual transmission — a tangled history, one must add. Yet there *was* such a history and there *is* such a history to be reconstructed, even though exactly how it is to be done is by no means clear; however, eclectic specialists on the side of internal evidence have pushed their partiality for internal criteria — and also their aversion to external evidence — to such an extent that it is doubtful whether even a definitive reconstruction of the history of early NT transmission (if by some miracle it should appear) would occasion any alteration in their procedures for determining the original NT text. Everyone, I think, will recognize that to utilize history judiciously is always difficult, and most will acknowledge that to ignore history is always perilous. In the case of the NT text, to ignore its external history and the relevant historical factors of its transmission — with or without a definitive reconstruction — and to follow instead an exclusively internal eclecticism may be the surest path to what A. F. J. Klijn already has called the "complete chaos" attendant upon the application of the eclectic method to the recovery of the original NT text.[38] This is not to deny, of course, the very considerable and stimulating methodological contributions and the continuing new insights into textual criteria that flow from this eclecticism that is restricted to internal evidence, though the appropriateness of the particular limitation to one kind of criteria is called into question.

III. Conclusion

The extended, though not devious, path that has taken us all the way from the early "canons of criticism" to contemporary eclectic emphases on internal criteria alone, including the several broader forms of eclectic procedure along the way, provides an answer to the question posed at the outset in the title, "the eclectic method — solution or symptom?" Each exponent or practitioner of an eclectic method feels assured, naturally, that his or her method, given the present circumstances, is the best available solution to NT text-critical problems, though only a very few are willing to assert that eclecticism is anything like a final solution, and it is precisely the finality expressed by those few that is the most questionable of all. This widespread caution, if not always humility, among at least the majority of eclectics should indicate that every eclectic method is at best a temporary "solution" to our basic problems in NT textual criticism, and if such a method really is a solution at all, it is of the most tentative kind. It would appear, rather, that the eclectic method —

---

38. Klijn 1966: 104; cf. 108. Klijn makes this highly critical judgment while affirming at the same time that "the eclectic method seems to be the only adequate method to regain the original text" (104). Observe, however, that, while Klijn's attribution of chaos to the eclectic method explicitly encompasses Kilpatrick's work, Klijn's own views on external evidence are radically different from Kilpatrick's, for Klijn, while approving the "rational criticism" of readings (mainly on grounds of intrinsic probability) states that textual criticism must attempt to render this approach superfluous, mainly by grouping MSS into families and texts (external evidence) (1949: 170).

regardless of type — is more certainly a highly visible symptom of those basic problems. After all, the most fundamental and longest-standing problem of the entire discipline and one that encompasses virtually all others (as this study has attempted to show) is the problem of the criteria for originality of readings; in the foregoing pages, the alternating history of cooperation and antithesis between the two classes of criteria, external and internal, has been sketched in an effort to show (as this study's further purpose) not only how eclecticism has developed within and from this context but where the discipline of NT textual criticism stands today on this central issue. One result is that the eclectic method is seen most clearly as symptomatic of this severe and crucial problem. Yet, eclecticism is not more than this, for it is unable to find a conclusive way to overcome the "crisis of criteria"; indeed, the very name "eclectic" (if — as seems likely — it refers to the choice of appropriate criteria from among many) discloses the fact that the method does not have the solution. Yet, symptoms are extremely useful and important; no disease should be without them, lest there be no warning of trouble and no efforts toward remedy. Certainly the eclectic method provides us with detailed indications of the difficulties in NT textual theory and method, and thereby it assists us greatly both in clarifying those problems and in exploring appropriate solutions. We must, however, beware of treating symptoms rather than the disorder itself.

CHAPTER 9

MODERN TEXTUAL CRITICISM AND THE SYNOPTIC PROBLEM: ON THE PROBLEM OF HARMONIZATION IN THE GOSPELS

Gordon D. Fee

That there is an interrelationship between textual criticism and the Synoptic Problem is the presupposition of most Synoptic studies.[1] Nonetheless the specific nature of that relationship, especially as it affects the finding of solutions, is seldom spelled out, and, it would seem, is frequently neglected. This relationship, it should be noted, goes both ways. On the one hand, Synoptic parallels and one's view of the Synoptic Problem will often be a factor in making textual choices; on the other hand, the establishment of the "original" text of each Gospel is a mandatory prerequisite to the discussion of Synoptic relationships at its basic level, namely the comparison of the Gospels pericope by pericope.[2]

The purpose of this paper in its present form[3] is a modest one. First, I want to explore the single most significant area of interrelationship between the two disciplines, the matter of harmonization/assimilation, and offer some illustrations as to the nature of the problem and directions for solutions; second, I would like to remind those working in Synoptic studies of the necessity of using basic text-critical principles in looking for a solution to the Synoptic Problem.

I. Harmonization

The first, and most obvious, area where the two disciplines overlap is that of harmonization. The problem here is especially complex, for we are dealing both with *authors* who used the text of one (or two) of the others in varying degrees of exactness

---

1. Indeed, the fact that Griesbach's own work is foundational *both* for NT textual criticism *and* for Synoptic studies perhaps highlights the reality of the interrelatedness that exists between the two disciplines.

2. One cannot assume, of course, that any of the Gospel writers used the "original" text of his predecessor. But such a factor is hidden and will be forever unknown to us.

3. This chapter is part of a much larger paper that was distributed and read at the Johann Jakob Griesbach Bicentenary Colloquium 1776-1976, held at Münster (Westphalia), 26-31 July 1976. Since that paper was much too large for publication in the centennial volume, it appeared in publication in two parts, the first part in the centennial volume (see Fee 1978e), part of which is reproduced here, the second part in *NovT* (see Fee 1980a). Only the second half of the first part is reproduced here, since the first part was an overview of "where we are" in the discipline, and would have constituted considerable repetition for this volume.

and with *scribes* who in a variety of ways made parallel passages conform, but who also, by intent or otherwise, could disharmonize passages.

My more immediate concern in this study is with textual criticism. How does one make textual choices where Synoptic parallels are involved? Before looking at a few examples, several preliminary considerations should be noted.

(1) Harmonizations can be of four kinds: (a) between, or among, the Gospels, (b) within a single Gospel, (c) to the LXX, or (d) to a well-known phrase or idea quite apart from any immediate parallel. The addition of ἄρτον μὴ λίθον ἐπιδώσει αὐτῷ; ἢ καί at Luke 11:11 by the majority of MSS is an example of the first kind (despite the split decision of the UBS committee); the addition of ὅπου ὁ σκώληξ αὐτῶν οὐ τελευτᾷ καὶ τὸ πῦρ οὐ σβέννυται at Mark 9:44 and 46 under the influence of 9:48 is an example of the second; the addition of θρῆνος καί at Matt 2:18 by the majority illustrates the third; and the addition (probably) of τοῦ θεοῦ in Matt 6:33 is an example of the fourth. This problem is especially complex when two or three of these kinds can be active at any variation unit. However, the second and fourth of these types, because they are more immediate to the scribe, are more likely to have occurred in "minor harmonizations" (see below) than the first type.

(2) One must be careful not to presuppose automatically what an author or scribe would have done. The problem with the authors here is probably greater than with the scribes. As is well known, Synoptic relationships are sometimes extremely close. For example, in the standard text of the Matthew/Luke account of John's preaching of repentance, Luke has sixty-four words and Matthew sixty-three; they have sixty-two words in common, without a single change of word order and only one difference between a singular and a plural. Although this level of agreement occurs infrequently and is almost exclusively limited to the double tradition between Matthew and Luke, it is evidence that it can occur. For the most part, however, the writers tend to rewrite in varying degrees of exactness.

Copyists, on the other hand, show extremely strong tendencies to make passages conform to one another. Yet not every possible harmonization must be adjudged to be so. Harmonization is far more likely to have occurred in the sayings of Jesus than in the Evangelists' narratives; similarly it is far more likely to have occurred in major additions/omissions or with significant words (= "major harmonizations") than with add/omit pronouns, conjunctions, articles, etc, or with word order (= "minor harmonizations"). These latter especially may be due to all kinds of other factors. Those of us who are aware of "harmonizations" *only* because we have a Gospel synopsis before us cannot presume that early copyists worked from synopses (!) or that their memories of parallels were so keen as to recall the jots and tittles.

(3) By the very historical fact of the greater use of Matthew in the early Church as compared with Mark or Luke, the manuscript traditions of the latter two have far more variants that could be attributed to harmonization than does Matthew, and between them, Mark far more so than Luke. It is almost inevitable that this factor will weigh heavily in making textual choices in Matthew and Mark.

(4) Similarly, although no MS or manuscript tradition has escaped some degree of harmonizing corruption to its text, this phenomenon is a hallmark of the Western and Byzantine traditions, whereas the earlier Alexandrians are relatively pure at this point. Again, this factor simply cannot be lightly put aside when making

textual choices. How great a role it plays will undoubtedly vary from scholar to scholar. Its influence on the editors of the UBS[3] can be seen in two "D" readings in Luke 11:33 and 12:27. In 12:27 they retained a harmonization where only D and the Old Syriac have a disharmonized reading; in 11:33 they retained the harmonized reading in brackets, probably because the early Alexandrians were split.

(5) It should candidly be admitted that our predilections toward a given solution of the Synoptic Problem will sometimes affect textual decisions. Integrity should cause us also to admit to a certain amount of inevitably circular reasoning at times. A classic example of this point is the well-known "minor agreement" between Matt 26:67-68 and Luke 22:64 (‖ Mark 14:65) of the "addition" τίς ἐστιν ὁ παίσας σε. B. H. Streeter (1924: 325-29), G. D. Kilpatrick (1943: 29-30), and W. R. Farmer (1964: 325-28) each resolve the textual problem of Mark in a different way. In each case, a given solution of the Synoptic Problem has affected the textual decision.

At this point one could offer copious illustrations. The four given here were chosen partly because in each case they illustrate in a different way the complexity of the textual problems involved and partly because in some instances I disagree with the conclusions of some of my colleagues.

(a) The choice between ὑποκάτω and ὑποπόδιον at Matt 22:44 ‖ Mark 12:36 ‖ Luke 20:43, in their respective citations of Ps 110:1, especially illustrates the complexities involved. First, there is similar textual variation in all three Gospels; second, all known Greek MSS of the LXX read ὑποπόδιον, as do all MSS of Heb 1:13; third, although the critical editions disagree among themselves, they all agree that the Synoptists do not all have the same reading. The variations in the Synoptic accounts have the following support:

Matt 22:44	ὑποκάτω	ℵ B D G L U Z Γ Θ 047 λ 22 472 2145
	ὑποπόδιον	E F H K M S U V W Δ 33 1241 pler
Mark 12:36	ὑποκάτω	B D W 28
	ὑποπόδιον	ℵ L rell
Luke 20:43	ὑποκάτω	D
	ὑποπόδιον	ℵ B L W rell

In Matthew and Luke the text is certain. The widespread disharmonized form ὑποκάτω must be the original in Matthew (the harmonized ὑποπόδιον is just as likely to the LXX as to Luke); on the other hand, the fact that D's singular readings are generally suspect, plus its proclivities toward harmonization (in this case to Matthew), indicates that ὑποπόδιον is original in Luke. The text of Mark is less certain. Here one's judgment of the MSS as well as one's disposition toward a Synoptic solution play a role. For those, as myself, inclined toward Marcan priority, then the ὑποκάτω is original with Mark, which Matthew copied, but Luke "corrected." For those inclined toward Matthean priority, the textual choice in Mark is less certain. Did Mark copy Matthew or Luke (more likely) in this case? If Luke, then B D W 28 represent conformity to Matthew by early scribes.[4]

4. There is always the possibility, of course, that the Gospel writers had access to a Greek text of the LXX which read ὑποκάτω.

(b) The next illustration is taken from the parallel passages: Matt 4:17 and Mark 1:14b-15. The text reads as follows:

Matt 4:17	Mark 1:14b-15
Ἀπὸ τότε ἤρξατο ὁ Ἰησοῦς	
κηρύσσειν	κηρύσσων τὸ εὐαγγέλιον τοῦ
καὶ λέγειν·	θεοῦ καὶ λέγων, ὅτι πεπλήρωται
μετανοεῖτε· ἤγγικεν γὰρ	ὁ καιρὸς καὶ ἤγγικεν
ἡ βασιλεία τῶν οὐρανῶν.	ἡ βασιλεία τοῦ θεοῦ· μετανοεῖτε
	καὶ πιστεύετε ἐν τῷ εὐαγγελίῳ

The variant add/omit μετανοεῖτε and γάρ in Matt 4:17 illustrates both the complexity of the possibilities of harmonization (internal and external) and the need for greater care in using patristic evidence. The "omission" here made the margin of WH and has been opted for by Kilpatrick (1943: 27) and J. N. Birdsall (1970: 330), where, apart from any Greek evidence, Codex Bobbiensis *(k)* and the Old Syriac, allegedly supported by some early Fathers (Justin, Clement, Origen, Eusebius, Victor-Antioch), are said to preserve the original dissimilated reading. Kilpatrick further argues that this is supported by Matthew's tendency to dissimilate John the Baptist and Jesus.

The alleged patristic support of this omission is totally deceiving:

(i) Justin's "citation" is a loose adaptation (καὶ αὐτὸς λέγων ὅτι ἐγγύς ἐστιν ἡ βασιλεία τῶν οὐρανῶν, *Dial.* 51). This is an *argumentum e silentio* of the worst kind, since there is no hint in Justin either that he was trying to reproduce all the words of Matthew or that in context he had any interest in "repentance."

(ii) So with Clement (*Protr.* IX.87.3): βοᾷ γοῦν ἐπείγων εἰς σωτηρίαν αὐτός· ἤγγικεν ἡ βασιλεία τῶν οὐρανῶν. Furthermore, both of these could just as easily be citations of Mark, conforming to Matthew's use of τῶν οὐρανῶν (cf. W).

(iii) The partial support by Origen, of which Kilpatrick says "the reading seems at least to have been known to Origen," is completely in error. In his commentary on John at the beginning of book X, Origen cites Matt 4:17 in full, and includes the disputed words. Likewise a little later (X.11), in a comment on Heracleon's exegesis of John 2:12, he cites from μετανοεῖτε on. In two closely following citations, where his interest is only in this clause, he then cites ἤγγικεν κτλ. without μετανοεῖτε. Origen, therefore, knew nothing of a text of Matthew which omitted these words, a conclusion further attested in the catenae fragments of his commentary on Matthew.

(iv) Eusebius's evidence is scarcely more certain. In Ps 84:13 he has a citation similar to Clement's. In the *Demonstratio* (IX.8) he has a long citation of Matt 4:12-25. Most of the citation seems to follow the text with care. However, at v. 17 he writes: ἀπὸ τότε γοῦν ἤρξατο ὁ Ἰησοῦς κηρύσσειν καὶ λέγειν, ὅτι ἤγγικεν ἡ βασιλεία τῶν οὐρανῶν. This is adapted just enough to give doubts as to the Greek text Eusebius actually knew.

(v) Among the Fathers, that leaves only the evidence of Victor of Antioch in his commentary on Mark.[5] But his reference is completely puzzling in that he cites the full text in one paragraph, while in the next paragraph he seems to deny

---

5. Preserved in J. A. Cramer, *Catenae in evangelia Matthaei et Marci* (Oxford, 1840) 273.

the preaching of repentance to Jesus.[6] The explanation of this, however, lies *not* in his text of Matthew, but in his attempt to reconcile Matthew with Mark as to what Jesus preached *after* he went to Capernaum. In any case, this is the *only* patristic evidence for the "omission," and it is flimsy indeed.[7]

The point, then, is that we have here not a widespread early witness to Matthew's original, but the coincidence of omission in two versional texts, the omissions of which at other points do not inspire confidence in their originality here. It is these traditions, either dependent on an earlier source or more likely independently but typically, which dissimilate John the Baptist and Jesus. Here, then, is an example of an author's redaction effecting an internal assimilation, which probably for theological reasons was disharmonized by scribes.

(c) The next example is taken from the parallel texts of Matt 3:1-2 and Mark 1:4 (cf. also Luke 3:2-3). These verses read as follows:

Matt 3:1-2	Mark 1:4
παραγίνεται	ἐγένετο
Ἰωάννης ὁ βαπτιστὴς κηρύσσων	Ἰωάννης ὁ βαπτίζων
ἐν τῇ ἐρήμῳ τῆς Ἰουδαίας,	ἐν τῇ ἐρήμῳ
λέγων· μετανοεῖτε·	κηρύσσων βάπτισμα μετανοίας
ἤγγικεν γὰρ ἡ βασιλεία τῶν	εἰς ἄφεσιν ἁμαρτιῶν.
οὐρανῶν.	

The choice between ὁ βαπτίζων and βαπτίζων in Mark 1:4 is related to a whole set of variants in Mark where either internal, cross-Synoptic, or common-idiom harmonization has taken place. The evidence:

Mark 1:4	ὁ βαπτίζων	ℵ B L Δ 33 892 bo
	βαπτίζων	rell
(‖ Matt 3:1 ὁ βαπτιστής — no variation)		
Mark 6:14	ὁ βαπτίζων	ℵ A B pler
	ὁ βαπτιστής	D
(‖ Matt 14:2 ὁ βαπτιστής — no variation)		
Mark 6:24	τοῦ βαπτίζοντος	ℵ B L Δ Θ 28 pc
	τοῦ βαπτιστοῦ	A C D W Byz pler
(no Synoptic parallel)		
Mark 6:25	τοῦ βαπτίζοντος	L 700 892
	τοῦ βαπτιστοῦ	ℵ A B C D Byz rell

6. His text reads: καὶ μετὰ ὀλίγα· ἀπὸ τότε ἤρξατο ὁ Ἰησοῦς κηρύσσειν καὶ λέγειν, μετανοεῖτε, ἤγγικε γάρ. . . . In the following paragraph he says, citing Matthew: καὶ ἀπὸ τότε ἤρξατο κηρύσσειν, καὶ λέγειν, οὐχί, τὸ μετανοεῖτε, καὶ τὰ ἑξῆς, ἀλλὰ μόνον τό, ἤγγικεν ἡ βασιλεία τῶν οὐρανῶν.

7. All of these together offer solid affirmation of R. M. Grant's dictum that "patristic citations are not citations unless they have been adequately analyzed" (1950: 124). They further illustrate the need to use utmost caution when citing patristic "evidence" on the basis of our critical editions and the need for that evidence to appear in some evaluated form [see below, Chapter 17].

(‖ Matt 14:8 τοῦ βαπτιστοῦ — no variation)

Mark 8:28   τὸν βαπτίζοντα   28 565

                 τὸν βαπτιστήν   ℵ A B D Byz rell

(‖ Matt 16:14; Luke 9:19 τὸν βαπτιστήν — no variation)

Besides these, Matthew has three other instances and Luke two of ὁ βαπτιστής without variation. J. K. Elliott, arguing from internal evidence alone, has opted for ὁ βαπτίζων as Mark's style and therefore to be read in each instance (1973: 295). But this seems to be doing textual criticism by means of a Procrustean bed. Almost surely Mark did indeed use the substantive participle at 6:14 and 24, which is probably also to be preferred at 1:4 (this was never made to conform to ὁ βαπτιστής because the other "correction" of dropping the article came to predominate). Furthermore, the normal direction of harmonization is to the more common ὁ βαπτιστής. But in 6:25 another kind of harmonization was carried out by two scribes (700 and an earlier exemplar of L and 892) — to the more immediate context of 6:24 (they are among the first to believe that an author must be consistent!). That factor should also decide in favor of βαπτιστής at 8:28, but here because it is otherwise difficult to explain how 28 and 565 alone among their immediate and more distant relatives both escaped corruption. Thus, we have examples of what is often found in the textual tradition — a scribe making an author's text conform to his own, albeit sometimes more unusual, style.

(d) In his article on Atticism, Professor Kilpatrick has argued that wherever there is a variant between the ἀποκριθεὶς εἶπεν idiom and ἔφη, the former is to be preferred as original because the latter is an Atticistic "improvement." Professor Kilpatrick maintains: "No Greek at any period, left to himself, would say or write ἀποκριθεὶς εἶπεν" (1963b: 126).

I have already responded to this argument at some length and have shown that biblical scribes were not "left to themselves." Especially in the Gospel of John, the manuscript evidence demonstrates the exact opposite, that scribes tended more often toward the full Semitic idiom than away from it. Even John Chrysostom does it in two places where there is no manuscript support![8]

The textual variation at Mark 9:38 ‖ Luke 9:49 presents another interesting case of this variation in terms of Synoptic relationships:

Mark 9:38	**Luke 9:49**
ἔφη αὐτῷ ὁ Ἰωάννης	ἀποκριθεὶς δὲ ὁ Ἰωάννης εἶπεν

In Luke's Gospel the *only* known variation is in codex 16, which reads καὶ ἀποκριθείς for ἀποκριθεὶς δέ. However, in Mark there are the following variations:

---

8. See Fee 1976: 189-91. I have now discovered a third example from Chrysostom. In *hom. 52 in Jo. 2* (M. 59.289) he cites John 8:13, ἀπεκρίθησαν καὶ εἶπον αὐτῷ, where all others read εἶπον οὖν αὐτῷ. It is also noteworthy that Chrysostom not only has the septuagintal idiom, but in each case has the Johannine form of it! Thus he is also conforming to an author's style.

ἔφη . . .		אB Δ Θ Ψ 33 579 892 1071
ἔφη . . . λέγων		L
ἀποκριθεὶς δὲ ἔφη . . .		C 1573 a
ἀποκριθῆ δὲ . . .	λέγων	A Γ Π Byz pler
ἀποκριθῆ . . .	λέγων	D 21 517 954 1012 1574 1675 pc
ἀποκριθῆ δὲ . . . καὶ	λέγει	fam 1 544 b r i
ἀποκριθῆ δὲ . . . καὶ εἶπεν		28
καὶ ἀποκριθεὶς . . .	λέγει	565 700
καὶ ἀποκριθεὶς . . .	εἶπεν	W fam 13pl

Several other data are significant here: (1) Matthew and Luke fluctuate regularly between these two idioms (ἔφη and ἀποκριθεὶς εἶπεν), but with much less textual variation than one finds in Mark. This is clear evidence that both can be used by first-century Greek writers. (2) Wherever ἔφη appears in Mark in NA[26], there is always this multiple variation. (3) In Mark such variation occurs irregularly either with ἀποκριθεὶς εἶπεν or with εἶπεν by itself. But when variation does occur, it can go either way. (4) The other occurrences of ἔφη in Mark are all in Synoptic parallels, but in no case does the parallel read ἔφη. On the other hand, as in this case, the parallel sometimes reads the ἀποκριθεὶς εἶπεν idiom.

The best explanation of all these data, and of the multiple variation in this passage, is *not* the Atticizing of Mark's text, but rather its harmonization either to Mark's more common idiom or to its Synoptic parallel (less likely). If this is so, then either Luke "Semitizes" Mark or Mark "Atticizes" Luke!

These are but a few of thousands of such variations in the Synoptic tradition. There can be little question either (1) that harmonization is a very strong tendency among the scribes in copying the Synoptic Gospels, or (2) that harmonization is always a secondary process in the transmission of the text. But these few examples, and scores of others like them, also illustrate that there is not always a simple answer as to how, and in what direction, that harmonization took place. But a careful analysis of hundreds of such variation-units suggests two conclusions, one about textual criticism and one about the Synoptic Problem:

First, here is another place where the evidence points decidedly in the direction of the "relative purity" of the type of text found in P[75] and B. When all other things are equal, as to which direction the assimilation might have taken place, one is never far wrong in going with the text found in these witnesses. Indeed, so seldom does their text reflect this tendency that, whenever it does, it is a particularly noticeable phenomenon (cf. א B D et al. on Luke 15:21).

Second, when one works with these kinds of variations over many, many instances, and in many different kinds of Gospel settings, the clear direction in which the textual solution tends to lie is also a direction that calls for the priority of Mark. If one were to posit the priority of Matthew, then the resolution of the textual harmonization almost always requires a solution that is either more circuitous or that is less satisfactory in answering the basic question of textual criticism: which text best explains how the other(s) came about? And that leads me to a few final observations about bringing a text-critical mind-set to the resolution of the Synoptic Problem.

II. Textual Principles and the Synoptic Problem

It was Griesbach who first spelled out clearly the first principle of textual criticism: that reading is to be preferred as the original which best explains the existence of all the others. It is always under this rubric that the further questions of scribal tendencies and author's style must be asked. Consciously or unconsciously, this is also the *sine qua non* in resolving the Synoptic Problem: given that there is a direct literary dependence among our Gospels, that Gospel is to be preferred as having priority which best explains how the others came into existence. It seems to this textual critic that this must include *both* the arrangement of the materials (order, form, etc.) *and* the close study of the parallels.[9]

In this instance, of course, there are crucial differences: (1) we are dealing with more complex issues, since we have three known documents plus unknown hidden factors, such as the possibility of written fragments and the tenacity of oral tradition. (2) Whereas copyists (apart from some early expressions in the Western tradition) are trying basically to reproduce an exemplar, Gospel writers are doing the precise opposite. The Gospels they are using are not adequate for them (or their community), and they are *rewriting* the story of Jesus, not merely copying it. For this reason, as E. P. Sanders has demonstrated (1969), one cannot speak of tendencies in the Synoptic tradition with the same sense of confidence one has about scribal tendencies. One who is rewriting, and who also has access to many other sources (either written or oral) unknown to us, may do things which from our perspective are inexplicable. It is for these reasons that J. A. Fitzmyer said at the Pittsburgh Festival: "The history of Synoptic research reveals that the problem is *practically insoluble*" (1970: 132).

With Fitzmyer's judgment I tend to agree. Nonetheless there must be some kind of solution — either one of the existing ones or one yet to come. Our problem is that we have not yet reached agreement on the known, whereas the real problems most likely lie with the unknown. The consensus of even fifteen years ago is less certain today. The Griesbach Hypothesis is receiving a new and full hearing, and gaining converts. Although some have felt it could be "falsified" (Talbert 1972), others have doubted whether it has been so in fact (Buchanan 1974). But the real question is not whether it can be falsified, any more than whether the two-source theory can (if indeed either could be; then of course we must look elsewhere). *The real question is, Which theory best explains the phenomena?* Here we have competing theories, the two most common of which can give reasonable explanations, but which are likewise mutually exclusive. And here it must be insisted upon that *although all things are theoretically possible, not all possible things are equally probable.* The question is not, But is it not possible that . . . ? To which the answer usually must be, Yes. The question is, Is that more probable? In the final analysis, text critics and Synoptic critics are historians and must ultimately come down on the side of what they think is most probable, given all the data now in possession.

---

9. B. Orchard has recently argued that this latter is less significant because the material is often so ambiguous (Orchard 1976). I would here argue that this matter cannot be easily dismissed. I am using these data here as Orchard himself argues we must, namely "for the confirmation of the investigation" (352).

At this point textual criticism may yet have a contribution to make to the historical task. If we allow, as the majority of scholars on both sides do, that there is a *direct* literary relationship between any two of the Synoptists, then the kinds of questions textual criticism brings to such literary relationships are a pertinent part of the analytical task.

Indeed, Farmer assumes this to be true in Step XII in his "new introduction." He states: "Assuming that there is direct literary dependence between Matthew and Luke, internal evidence indicates that the direction of dependence is that of Luke upon Matthew" (1964: 223). What Farmer means by "internal evidence" is precisely the kind of textual/literary arguments Streeter used to argue for Matthew's dependence upon Mark (1924: 162-64). And it is this argument of Streeter's which Butler, though in disagreement, candidly recognized as tending "to support the theory of Marcan priority to the exclusion of all other solutions" (1951: 68).

My point, in conclusion, is a simple one. Since both Marcan and Matthean priorists allow (1) that Luke is secondary, and (2) that Mark and Matthew have a *direct* literary relationship, then a crucial part of a Synoptic solution must be the careful pericope-by-pericope, word-by-word analysis of Matthew and Mark (preferably where Luke is absent) to determine the most likely direction of literary dependence. It has recently been argued that such a procedure is irrelevant (see Orchard 1976). I demur. It is a matter of doing redaction criticism at its primary level. If Matthew used Mark, then explanations of his redaction work must be given; but so also is this true if Mark used Matthew. My point is that such questions must be a part of the process in arriving at a solution of the Synoptic Problem, not simply an exercise engaged in after the solution is found; and it is here that textual criticism, by its way of asking questions, has a direct tie to the Synoptic Problem.

CHAPTER 10

THE MAJORITY TEXT AND THE ORIGINAL TEXT
OF THE NEW TESTAMENT[1]

Gordon D. Fee

The vast majority of NT scholars and students use the Greek NT found in one of the two popular hand-editions, the UBS[3] or NA[26], both of which are the work of the same editors and reflect the same text. Although there are occasional demurrers as to whether this is the best possible critical text, it nonetheless serves as the basis for most contemporary exegetical work.

In recent years, however, there has been a revival at the popular level of an advocacy of the *textus receptus* (TR) and the KJV. Much of this is simply the rhetoric of misinformed fundamentalism, although it has recently found some cohesive visibility in the formation of the (tax-exempt) Dean Burgon Society.[2] An attempt at a more informed defense of this text has been offered by Zane Hodges of Dallas Theological Seminary (1970, 1971), although it is not the TR per se but rather the Majority text (= the Byzantine text-type) that he has advocated. In recent years, the newly constituted Nelson Publishers took up the advocacy of this position in a series of three books: W. N. Pickering's *The Identity of the New Testament Text* (1977); a critical edition of the Majority text, edited by Hodges and A. L. Farstad (1982; cf. my review, 1983); and H. A. Sturz's *The Byzantine Text-Type and New Testament Textual Criticism* (1984; cf. my review, 1985). Since these various publications apparently are having considerable influence among translators in the two-thirds world, not to mention the American Bible belt, and since their various arguments may appear convincing to the non-expert, the following critique is offered to show both their flaws in argumentation and their shortcomings in theory and method.

I. Hodges and the Majority Text

The seminal arguments in this modern advocacy of the Majority text were offered by Zane Hodges, for many years professor of Greek and NT at Dallas Theological

---

1. A rewriting of several papers on this subject (Fee 1978a, 1978b, 1978c, 1979). For an explanation, see the Preface.
2. This "society" was formed in Philadelphia, November 3-4, 1978, and publishes a newsletter, "The Dean Burgon News," which began January 1979.

Seminary. Besides the obvious theological drive behind his presentation[3] (and that of most others of this persuasion), his basic arguments are three (and are repeated in the introduction to the critical edition of this text): (1) the inability of scholarship to explain the rise, the comparative uniformity, and the dominance of the Byzantine text; (2) that the Majority text is the result of a "normal" transmission (= uninterrupted by deliberate corruptions) of the NT text, because "the copies nearest the autograph will have the largest number of descendants" (1970: 21); and (3) a kind of subjectivity (= circular reasoning) on the part of scholarship that considers the earliest MSS to be the best because they contain the best readings.

Since the last question will be considered in the critique of Pickering that follows, here I respond only to the first two arguments, which for Hodges are basically two parts of one argument, based on both the quantity and general uniformity of the extant MSS which support the Byzantine text-type. On the one hand, he argues that modern textual criticism, while "denying to the Majority text any claim to represent the actual form of the original text, . . . is nevertheless unable to explain its rise, its comparative uniformity, and its dominance in any satisfactory manner" (1970: 18). On the other hand, he argues that this uniformity and dominance "can be rationally accounted for, . . . if the Majority text represents simply the continuous transmission of the original text from the very first" (1970: 18). He is faced with the problem, however, that this text-form is completely unknown by any of the evidence up to AD 350, the earliest evidence being in some fourth-century Church Fathers, then later in the fifth century in portions of Codices W and A.[4] He counteracts this problem in a twofold way: (1) by arguing that "all of our most ancient manuscripts derive basically from Egypt," thus suggesting that they represent "a local text of Egypt" (1970: 12-13) and are "merely divergent offshoots of the broad stream of transmission [= the Majority text] whose source is the autographs themselves" (1970: 18);[5] and (2) by affirming as a "truism" that "the manuscript tradition

3. In his response (Hodges 1978) to my original article, Hodges protested that I had made too much of this. But any careful reading of these articles, plus the fact that he and Pickering allowed their pieces to be included in the blatantly theological enterprise of David Otis Fuller (1970), indicates that theology is the bottom line. The theology, in this case, is an urgency about Scripture, that the providence of God would not have allowed Protestant Christianity for so much of its existence to have been wrong about the text of the Bible, and that modern textual criticism stems from Westcott and Hort, whose orthodoxy is suspect on other grounds.

4. It must be emphasized that even though quite a few Byzantine readings existed earlier than this, the text-type itself did not exist. The question here is not a matter of readings, but of *these readings all existing together in collocation in the same piece(s) of evidence.* The failure to recognize this crucial point is the Achilles' heel of Sturz's study as well; it does no good to argue that some Byzantine readings can be shown to have existed early. What must be shown is that they existed *together* in this form that early.

5. Hodges never really addresses the question, How is it that only "offshoots" have been found in the first three hundred years, if the Majority text represents the "broad stream" that issues from the autographs? Why are there no MSS even partly representing the Majority text until the 5th century and no full-scale representatives until the 8th? Earlier answers to this, which apparently Hodges endorses, were given by Burgon 1883: 319, and by Hills 1970: 42, to the effect that "they were read so constantly and copied so frequently that finally they wore out and perished"; and conversely that the "offshoots" survived "because they were rejected by the Greek Churches as faulty and so not used." It is hard to imagine a less historical answer to a historical inquiry than this one.

of an ancient book will, under any but the most exceptional conditions, multiply in a reasonably regular fashion with the result that the copies nearest the autograph will normally have the largest number of descendants" (1970: 27).

1. It should be noted first that Hodges's "truism" is simply not true — either theoretically or actually. As a matter of fact, Hodges rests his case on no historical evidence at all, but on the mere theoretical probability of this "truism." But even theoretically there is no good reason to believe that it is true. It does no good to say that Abraham will have more descendants than Isaac or Jacob, not to mention David or Hezekiah. The question is whether the majority of Abraham's descendants, through either Isaac or Esau, continued through the years to look more like their original ancestor than like their more immediate ancestors through the phenomenon of mixed parentage.[6] The point is that there is not a reason in the world to believe that copies "nearest the autograph" will normally have the largest number of descendants — even if these could be allegedly assumed to bear precise family resemblance.

Furthermore, unless one supposes that subsequent copies were regularly checked against known earlier copies, one must also reasonably assume that whatever errors were made in any of the copies would also be transmitted to their offspring as copies became exemplars. What one may reasonably assume, therefore, is the precise opposite of Hodges's presumption. More copies mean more errors, unless there were to be a systematic attempt to correct subsequent copies against earlier ones. But this is precisely not what one would expect in the earliest period, when (a) copies would not have been made by trained scribes in scriptoria, (b) copies were being made for pragmatic reasons, not necessarily with a sense of copying Scripture, and (c) the earliest copies were probably very early carried away from their place of origin (or first destination). Therefore, the proliferation of copies with numerous differences from the autographs would continue until certain factors converged to stop the process of proliferation and diversity. And when such a check occurred, it would freeze the form of text then current — but a text that would most likely be far removed from the original.

When one turns to a variety of historical evidence, including the NT, one finds this to be exactly the case. In fact, what Hodges calls a "truism" turns out to

---

6. For some reason Hodges simply cannot see the rather total illogic of his theory at this point, and offered a considerable rebuttal in his response. But the fact is that in both human and manuscript lineage the further away one gets from the original "parent(s)" the more the lineage picks up cross-fertilization, especially when one throws in the clear geographic changes brought about by easy mobility.

Thus in response (1978b: 158 n. 2) I suggested the following analogy: Let us assume that two very Swedish parents (tall, blond, blue eyes, and so forth), Olaf and Helga Olson, have two boys, Karl and Sven. These two sons also marry Swedish young women, and each has two children. One of Karl's sons emigrates to the United States and marries a very Italian young woman (short, black hair, dark eyes, and so on), and this son happens to be prolific and has twelve children. Of these children seven marry Italians, one marries a Swede, and four marry American "mixtures." Meanwhile in Sweden, catastrophe has struck the house of Olson and the two children of Sven are killed in an accident. The other son of Karl had one child, a daughter, who turned out to be barren. Thus the only descendants of Olaf Olson are in America, and the vast majority are now assuming very Italian features.

That something very much like this happened to the NT manuscript tradition is precisely why the argument from numbers is so totally irrelevant.

be based on some form of theoretical "logic" not on hard data, since the "truism" does not exist anywhere in antiquity in the data themselves. He uses the Latin Vulgate, for example, as an illustration to support his view of transmission. The enormous diversity and cross-contamination of the more than 8,000 Vulgate MSS amply demonstrates, Hodges argues, the inability of an "official" edition to arise out of diversity and uniformly claim the field (1970: 18). But this is a poor choice of illustration, for what the MSS of the Vulgate do demonstrate is that Hodges's view of transmission does not work out. If it is true that the later hundreds of medieval copies of the Vulgate lacked the uniformity one finds in the Greek MSS, it is also true that they are *far more like one another than they are like Jerome's original*.[7] This is precisely as with the Greek NT, except for greater uniformity of the latter, which has another explanation.[8]

2. In contrast to this theoretical (and unrealistic) view of the transmission of the NT proposed by Hodges, the actual historical data show an enormous fluidity in the earliest period, which disappears in later decades.[9] Hodges's contention that *all* the early evidence derives basically from Egypt is patently false. What we theorized above about the earliest copies (not made by trained scribes, made for practical purposes, and each book transmitted independently over a widely scattered geography) seems in fact to have been the case.

From AD 150-225 we have firm data from all over the ancient world that a variety of text forms were in use, but in all these materials there is not a single illustration of the later Majority (= Byzantine) text *as a text form*. The evidence from Egypt is indeed basically singular. The earliest Greek MSS (P66 P75 P46 P72; ca. 175-250), the citations of Clement (ca. 190-215) and Origen (ca. 215-245), and the earliest translations (Sahidic and Bohairic Coptic) all bear witness to a single text-type. There are indeed some scattered readings in Clement and P66 from the so-called Western tradition and a few readings in P66 where it now has the earliest evidence for Byzantine readings, but these are so few as to alter the basic text of these witnesses only slightly (see Fee 1968b).

The point is that the Byzantine text simply did not exist in Egypt in the early period. P75 is therefore not a reject; it represents the only "broad stream" that existed there. This is further evidenced by Origen, who apparently used several different Bibles, and P66, which was corrected against a second MS. In none of these does one find evidence for the existence of the Majority text.

The same is true elsewhere in the Christian world in the second and third centuries. The other type of text that existed in the second century is commonly

---

7. Hodges also responded that this statement is "wildly untrue." But here he does not seem to have checked the actual data for himself. One might try collating any ten late-medieval Vulgate MSS with Wordsworth and White's edition and see the results. After all, the Sixtine and Clementine editions, for all their differences, agree more often with one another than either does with Wordsworth and White.

8. In the original article I also noted here that the same holds true with all critical editions of the works of the Church Fathers. A good critical edition of a Father's text, or the discovery of early MSS, *always* moves the Father's text of the NT *away from* the TR and *closer to* the text of our modern critical editions.

9. For the best recent attempt to write a history of the text, see Birdsall 1970.

called "Western" because variants peculiar to it are firmly established in texts found in North Africa (Tertullian, Cyprian, some OL), Italy (Novatian, some OL), and southern France (Irenaeus). "Western," however, is something of a misnomer, for many of its peculiar variants are also found in the East (Tatian and the OS) and occasionally in Egypt (some quotations in Clement, John 6–7 in P66).

But despite this early and widespread attestation, these various witnesses lack the homogeneity found in Egypt and in the later Byzantine text. The textual relationships are not consistently sustained over large portions of text; rather, "Western" describes a group of witnesses, obviously related by hundreds of unusual readings, sometimes found in one or several, sometimes in others, but apparently reflecting an uncontrolled, sometimes "wild" tradition of copying and translating. Again, however, in none of these areas does one find a single witness to the Majority text as a text form, but only sporadic attestation to the existence of some of the Byzantine readings.

One might argue, of course, that *all* the early translations (Latin, Syriac, Coptic) and early Fathers (Justin, Irenaeus, Tatian, Clement, Tertullian, Origen, etc.) had the misfortune to use only the "rejected offshoot" MSS. But if so, who represents the "broad stream" that "wore out" the copies more like the autographs? The obvious answer is that the Byzantine text-form simply did not exist in the second and third centuries, although many of the variants that were to be found in it had already come into existence.

The Majority text as a full-fledged form of text, distinguishable from the Egyptian and "Western," does not appear in history until about AD 350. NT citations that are closer to the TR than to the Egyptian and "Western" texts first appear in a group of writers associated with the church of Antioch: Asterius the Sophist, the Cappadocians, Chrysostom, Theodoret of Cyrus. But even so, these Fathers had a NT only about ninety percent along the way to the full Byzantine text of the later Middle Ages. The earliest Greek MS to reflect this text is from Alexandria (Codex W, ca. 400 — Luke 8:14–14:53 only) and is only about eighty-five percent Byzantine, while the earliest full witnesses to it are uncials from the eighth and ninth centuries (Codices E F G H M Ω) — and even these reflect a slightly earlier stage of the text finally found in the TR.[10] The fact is that even this text, as generally homogeneous as it is from 400 to 1500, has clearly evolved from an earlier form, where the kinds of readings peculiar to it become more thoroughgoing at a later stage.

These are the historical data. They are "objectively verifiable" and incontrovertible. It is true that the actual origins of the Byzantine text as a text-type are shrouded in mystery, but that is scarcely an argument in its favor. If it were indeed closer to the autographs, the same "mystery" would prevail for the origin of the Egyptian text. In either case one has to argue for recensional activity at its beginning. But this has been demonstrated not to be true of the Egyptian text (see Fee 1974 [Chapter 13]), whereas the Byzantine text has all the earmarks of a recension — of a kind for which there is firm evidence of its existence (1974: 30-31).

The idea that the Majority text of the Middle Ages reflected the "broad stream" of the transmission of the text going back to the autographs is simply a myth.

10. For the full display of the data demonstrating these judgments, see Fee 1974 and Fee 1971a [now Chapters 13 and 15].

But the question still must be answered: How does one account for its dominance and general uniformity?

3. It was suggested above that one would expect a proliferation and diversity among copied texts until certain factors would combine to stop that process. But that would not at the same time guarantee that one of these texts should emerge as dominant and thereby become the uniform text of all Greek Christendom. Such in fact did nevertheless happen — but *only* with regard to the Greek text. The Latin, Armenian, and Syrian churches, among others, developed their own dominant and generally uniform text, which did not coincide with the Greek text. But our interest is with the Greek. How did the Byzantine text become dominant? The answer lies in a combination of several factors that converge between the fourth and seventh centuries.

(a) By the fourth century all of the factors that led to diversity had been superseded by their opposites. First, instead of untrained scribes who copied parts of the Bible for pragmatic purposes, there had emerged the trained Christian scribe, whose work was being produced in scriptoria. This began early in Alexandria, as the Egyptian MSS bear abundant witness, and probably was thoroughgoing after Constantine.

Second, the concept of canon brought in an ecclesiastical concern over the wording per se, which did not exist among the copyists of the second century, as the NT citations in all the Church Fathers of this century bear ample witness. The origins of the Latin Vulgate are to be explained precisely for this reason.[11] This will not guarantee uniformity, of course, but it will surely lessen the amount of "new variation" and, conversely, will add to the process of cross-checking and "correcting" existing MSS (note the several times this happened to Codex Sinaiticus, always away from its Egyptian standard and in greater conformity to the Byzantine [see Fee 1968a: 43-44]).

Third, instead of copies being made to be carried off to some other center, copies were now being made to remain where they were — for study purposes. Herein lies one of the most significant factors both for "dominance" and uniformity. After all, it is not by accident that the vast majority of extant Greek MSS were found in large quantities in monastery and university libraries!

(b) One can scarcely underestimate the influence of Chrysostom in the history of the Greek church. As Quasten notes, "None of the Eastern writers has won the admiration and love of posterity to such a degree as he" (1960: 3.429). Prime evidence of this influence is both the abundant quantity of extant MSS of his own writings (by far greater than for any other Greek Father) and the great number of extant spurious writings attributed to him, whose authors sought immortality for their writings under the prestige of Chrysostom's name. It is almost inevitable that the text-form Chrysostom used first at Antioch and then later carried to Constantinople should become the predominant text of the Greek church.[12]

11. Damasus of Rome asked Jerome to make a new translation because of the great diversity that existed in the Latin Bibles.

12. For reasons not easy to decipher, Hodges chose to refute this reality, arguing that studies showed that Chrysostom did not in fact witness to a Byzantine text. But his argument only underscored a point made above, that Chrysostom simply had an early expression of the Byzantine text that was about ninety percent along the way to its full medieval expression.

Furthermore, Hodges chose to cite an earlier study by Geerlings and New (1931) that seemed to dispute this reality about Chrysostom's text. But my own sampling of work on Chrysos-

(c) The most important factor for the dominance and general uniformity of the Byzantine text is directly related to (b) above. By the end of the seventh century, the Greek NT was being transmitted in a very narrow sector of the Church — namely, the Greek Orthodox Church with its dominant patriarchate in Constantinople. By the time of Chalcedon, Greek was almost unknown in the West,[13] and after Chalcedon the decline of Alexandria and the subsequent rise of Islam narrowed Greek-speaking Christendom still further.

All of these factors together ensure both the dominance and general uniformity of a text-form properly called Byzantine.[14]

II. Pickering's "Identity" of the New Testament Text

By all counts, Wilbur Pickering's *The Identity of the New Testament Text* (1977) is the most substantial presentation of the case against the modern critical text and for the Majority text. Unfortunately, the book suffers throughout from misrepresentations of scholarly research, the use of rhetoric in the place of argument, and an apparent lack of first-hand acquaintance with many of the primary data. It is tempting in such a case to go through the book *seriatim* and to point out its many errors, hoping that the cumulative effect of such a display will tell its own story. However, I shall limit myself here to three of the more substantial matters, which taken together seem totally to negate Pickering's arguments: (1) his understanding of text-critical methodology; (2) his understanding of the causes of textual corruption; and (3) his understanding and use of the Church Fathers. But before we examine each of these in turn, an attempt should be made to understand what Pickering is trying to do.

An Overview of the Argument

The urgency behind *Identity* is clearly a theological one. From Pickering's point of view, the great fault of contemporary NT textual criticism is that it cannot offer us total certainty as to the original NT text (17-18, with emphasis on uncertainty in italics). Therefore, in its place he hopes to establish a new theory of textual transmission (or at least to restate an old one in a new way), which in turn will lead to a different methodology (actually an adoption of a methodology spelled out by Dean Burgon).

To get at this new theory of transmission and different method, he begins by trying to show the bankruptcy of the present situation. Thus, in his first full chapter

---

tom's text made me realize that something was desperately wrong with that study. The result of this interchange with Hodges caused me to go back over the work of Geerlings and New. It turned out that the failure was methodological. The results of that inquiry were published as Fee 1979 and demonstrated that Chrysostom's text of the NT was consistent throughout.

13. Another point Hodges took exception to. But to say that someone like Augustine knew Greek is a far cry from saying that he used a Greek NT, which he did not.

14. The rest of the original article responded to Hodges's final argument as to the "subjectivity" and "circularity" of the reasoning of modern textual criticism. Since most of that response was a summary of some arguments presented in Fee 1974 [Chapter 13], and the rest of it can be found in the critique of Pickering that follows, I chose to omit it from the present presentation.

(2), he offers a critique of contemporary eclecticism. What is urgent for him here is (a) to define eclecticism strictly in terms of its use of "the canons of internal criticism," and (b) to tie this bankrupt method to Westcott-Hort. The tie with Westcott-Hort is especially crucial, since the largest section of the book (chapters 3–4, comprising one-half of the actual text) is the author's attempt to discredit their methodology and theory of text. These chapters are crucial to Pickering's enterprise, because he feels that by discrediting Westcott-Hort he has thereby also discredited contemporary eclecticism; this in turn opens the door to a whole new way of looking at the history of transmission, which is offered in chapter 5, the other crucial chapter in the book. Chapter 6 (understandably) anticipates three objections to this new way of looking at the text, and chapter 7 very briefly discusses the "new" method under Burgon's seven "Notes of Truth."

Although there are several places in Westcott-Hort where Pickering would apply the scalpel, he has great urgencies about four in particular: (1) What Pickering calls their "basic approach." The problem here is that Westcott-Hort were willing to treat the NT as they would any other book. This is not right, he argues, because textual corruption in "any other book" was basically accidental; for the NT, textual corruption was basically deliberate and theologically motivated. (2) Their genealogical method. From Pickering's point of view, this suffers from Westcott-Hort's failure to reckon with deliberate alteration and from their failure to establish genuine text-types and recensions.[15] (3) Their assertion that Majority text readings did not exist before Chrysostom. Here especially Pickering uses the Church Fathers to suggest otherwise. (4) The use of internal evidence. This is a real *bête noire* for Pickering throughout the book. Indeed, much of the rhetoric comes into play whenever this evidence is mentioned.

Pickering's own theory is essentially that of Hodges, and can be very simply put: The original text of the NT is that which is found among the majority of extant Greek MSS. To get to this position there are basically two lines of reasoning: (1) Although the majority of Greek MSS show substantial agreement, enough differences exist among them to suggest that very few are direct copies of each other. Therefore, all of the available MSS in all traditions offer *independent* witness to the original text. (2) Most corruption to the NT text was deliberate (for Pickering this equals "theologically motivated"). It can be shown, he argues, that most early Christians (= the orthodox) had a high view of Scripture; therefore they would *not* have deliberately corrupted the text. Thus, "normal" transmission (= basically errorless) would have been carried on by the majority (= orthodox) of early Christians, which would have resulted in the majority of MSS being very similar and bearing witness together to the original text.

For anyone with first-hand knowledge of the data, the flaws in much of this reasoning will be immediately apparent. For the sake of those without that knowledge, I offer the following critique.

15. This is an area that will not be examined in this paper, although it is another place where Pickering has misunderstood the data and misrepresented scholars, including myself. Had Pickering read my entire monograph on P[66] with care and checked the same statistics in Fee 1971a [Chapter 15], his rhetoric (56) might have been more subdued.

The Question of Methodology

In some ways Pickering's disagreement with contemporary text-critical methodology is difficult to pin down. In the chapter on eclecticism his argument has four stages. (1) He notes that eclecticism is "a major, if not controlling, factor on the textual scene today" (23). (2) He attempts a definition of eclecticism, but he does so only in terms of a very limited expression of that method, namely "an eclecticism based solely on internal considerations" (25). (3) He then rejects such eclecticism as "unreasonable," because it has "no principled basis for rejecting conjectural emendations" and "no history of the transmission of the text"; and he calls other scholars in as supporting witnesses. (4) Finally, he argues that the real source of this method is Westcott-Hort, who only appeared to follow external evidence, but in fact made the prior choice of their favorite text-type "on internal (subjective) considerations" (27). The actual rise of eclecticism, Pickering argues, is due to the conflicts and confusion that followed Hort. He concludes this chapter by asserting, finally, that although "most scholars do not practice pure eclecticism" (= that based solely on internal principles), all modern textual criticism, including the so-called pure eclectics (!), are under "the psychological grip of W-H" (29).

Although some of this is an accurate assessment of things, for the most part it presents a hopelessly confused understanding of the present scene. The problem lies in Pickering's understanding and use of the term "eclecticism." For example, he inveighs against "an eclecticism based solely on internal considerations," because "it is unreasonable," it "has no principled basis for rejecting conjectural emendations," and it "has no history of the transmission of the text" (25). Precisely! All of this has been seen by other scholars and has been argued against with considerable vigor (see especially Martini 1974; cf. Fee 1976 [Chap. 7]). But this is an eclecticism that is practiced by only two known scholars, G. D. Kilpatrick and J. K. Elliott.[16] Indeed, I have argued elsewhere that this is not eclecticism at all in its classical sense but rather an *eclectic use of internal evidence* (1978e: 157). But this is *not* the eclecticism that is the method of contemporary textual criticism — not even close. To see this, all one has to do is to read the *Textual Commentary* (Metzger 1971) that accompanies the UBS[3] and see how often choices have been made on the basis of the manuscript evidence. And it is precisely because the editors have done this so often that Elliott and Kilpatrick have regularly written articles against this Greek text.[17]

For Pickering to define eclecticism solely in terms of Kilpatrick and Elliott, and then to lump such scholars as Metzger, Epp, and Colwell together with Kilpatrick and Elliott, is a serious distortion. An even greater error is for him to argue that Elliott's method is under "the psychological grip of W-H" (29). As a matter of fact, in terms of method per se, Kilpatrick and Elliott are at the opposite end of the spectrum from WH, while Hodges and Pickering are themselves on the same end as Westcott-Hort. Let me demonstrate.

---

16. See Fee 1976 [Chapter 7]; a bibliography for both scholars appears on p. 175 n. 7 [now n. 2].

17. See Elliott 1973, 1975a, 1975b; cf. Kilpatrick 1966, 1978.

At the present moment the real methodological difference among textual critics has to do with how much weight, if any at all, one gives to *external* evidence in making textual decisions. It is well known that Westcott-Hort gave an extraordinary amount of weight to external evidence, just as do Pickering and Hodges. The differences — and these are considerable indeed! — lie in *which* external evidence one places confidence in, and *how* one comes to value that evidence more highly than others. The crucial difference between them is that Westcott-Hort were simply better historians, in that they took into consideration the probable causes of corruption as a part of the procedure to evaluate the evidence.

On the other hand, Kilpatrick and Elliott abandon the external evidence almost altogether. What is of interest here is that both Kilpatrick/Elliott and Hodges/Pickering have Westcott-Hort as their common foe! Elliott is against Westcott-Hort because they used "purely documentary criteria";[18] and now Pickering is against them for fathering an eclecticism based solely on internal criteria. Neither has properly understood Westcott-Hort or eclecticism.

Modern textual criticism, the "eclecticism" of the UBS[3], RSV, NIV, NASB, etc., stands over against both Kilpatrick/Elliott and Hodges/Pickering. Such eclecticism recognizes that Westcott-Hort's view of things was essentially correct, but it is not nearly so confident as they that the early text of Alexandria is "neutral."

All of this can be presented numerically. On a scale of 1 to 50 (1 = internal evidence; 50 = external evidence), textual critics can be rated according to the relative weight they give to one or the other. The following ratings, of course, are arbitrary, but they reflect what in fact is going on. (WH is given in parenthesis because they arrived at their preference for one kind of external evidence partly on the basis of internal questions.) Ratings: Elliott — 2; Kilpatrick — 4; NEB — 20; UBS[3] — 30; (WH) — 43; Hodges/Pickering — 50.

Pickering's failure to note these crucial methodological differences causes him to muddy the waters at several places in his argument:

1. He notes that "eclectics" are themselves uneasy about eclecticism. Some of this is indeed legitimate uneasiness — especially the apparent lack of a new textual theory to replace Westcott-Hort.[19] But in nearly every case that Pickering cites, the unrest is being expressed by someone in the middle (= the true eclectic) who decries the "eclecticism" on the extreme left.

2. Although Pickering acknowledges that not all eclectics practice the eclecticism of Kilpatrick and Elliott (28), he nonetheless tries to tie all contemporary scholars to Westcott-Hort. In so doing, he seems to make some confusion between methodology and textual theory. As one reads through the whole book, it is clear that Pickering's *methodological* concern is with *any kind of use of internal evidence* —which he styles "subjective." It is here that all contemporary NT textual critics do indeed have something in common; but it is something they have in common with scholarship long before Westcott-Hort and with textual scholarship in every

18. See esp. Elliott 1968a. This is an irresponsible charge on Elliott's part, but he continues to make it.

19. See Fee 1976: 177-81, where Kilpatrick's and Elliott's method has been subjected to severe criticism on this point.

field of classical study. But the use of internal evidence, which may indeed have a degree of subjectivity to it — as all historical study does — is nothing more or less than another way of expressing the causes of corruption. To this item we shall turn in a moment.

3. In terms of method, Pickering should simply have gone after the use of "internal evidence," since this is the clear methodological failure of the so-called rigorous eclectic. Instead he spends the larger part of his book going after Westcott-Hort's textual theory as a whole. The reason for this almost certainly is *not* their use of internal evidence and its subsequent influence on textual criticism. Pickering in fact gives only ten pages to this question. The real reason would seem to be their dismissal of the TR as a secondary textual development, which is another matter on which all modern textual scholars are in agreement. It is Westcott-Hort's *textual theory*, which allowed them to make this judgment, that is the ultimate urgency for Pickering. But as a matter of fact this judgment has little or nothing at all to do with eclecticism as a method.

4. When Pickering begins to make this imperceptible move from methodology to textual theory, he notes that several scholars have expressed uneasiness over the fact that Westcott-Hort's methodology has been rejected, on the one hand, while contemporary texts continue to look like WH, on the other. It should also be noted that this dilemma was the cause of a certain amount of the unrest over classical eclecticism. This unrest has two foci: (a) Westcott-Hort's use of genealogy; (b) their confidence in the text of B, which had come to be seen as a "recension," not a "neutral" expression of the original text. What Pickering fails to note is that in recent years both of these causes for unrest have been laid to rest.[20] Thus, when contemporary NT textual critics use such terms as "the earliest and best MSS," or "early and independent support," they are not under some kind of psychological commitment to Westcott-Hort. Such terms are used because they are believed to be accurate descriptions of the evidence, which are based on a thoroughly historical understanding of the causes of corruption to the text.

The Causes of Corruption

In a more recent rebuttal, Pickering once again reiterated the importance, for him, of his alleged dismantling of Westcott-Hort (1978). Their theory, he says, "is like the floors in a multistoried building: Each level depends on the one below it." He then repeats his contention that he has demolished each floor, including the foundation. Assuming for the moment that this is an adequate analogy, one should note that the opposite might also be true. That is, if the "foundation" is found to be secure, then the superstructure may only need some reinforcing, not demolition. And it is at the foundation, what Pickering calls their "basic approach," where his own misunderstandings are so thoroughgoing as to render much of the rest of his book without great value.

The problem begins for him with his confused use of the word "normal"

---

20. See esp. my discussion of this in Fee 1978e. For the second item, cf. Martini 1978.

as it refers to textual transmission. On the one hand, his whole case rests on the assumption that the transmission of the NT text was "normal" (104-10); yet at the same time he condemns Westcott-Hort for treating the NT as one would any other book (41). One would think that "normal" means that the NT in fact has had a transmission very much like any other book. Obviously, this cannot be what Pickering means. What then?

For Pickering, Hort's crucial, and basic, mistake was his assertion that "there are no signs of deliberate falsification of the text for dogmatic purposes" (WH 1881: 2.282). That this is not correct is something on which all subsequent scholarship is agreed. Pickering, however, seems to have missed the point here, for he has taken the concepts of "deliberate falsification" and "dogmatic purposes" to be coterminous. That is, he understands deliberate or intentional change introduced into the NT text as always theologically motivated. "Malicious changes," he calls such variation, made by "persons lacking in integrity" (104). His argument (93-104) makes it clear that the bad theology involved is in fact a low view of Scripture. Thus, he argues that anyone who really believed these texts to be God's Word would not have deliberately altered them — only heretics would have done that. He assumes, therefore, that if he can show that the early Christians had a "high view" of Scripture, then it automatically follows that they would not have deliberately altered the text. This is bold argumentation indeed, given the actual nature of the data from the first four Christian centuries!

The most obvious flaw in Pickering's argument here is his confusion of the terms "deliberate" and "theological." Hort, of course, well knew that all kinds of corruptions were "deliberate." The clear proof of this is simply to read his "Notes on Select Passages" (1881: 2. "Appendix," 1-140) or his analysis of conflate readings, or his discussion of the "internal evidence of readings" (1881: 2.93-107, 19-30). These reveal that Hort recognized that most significant variation to the NT text was not accidental.

By "dogmatic purposes," however, Hort meant that there is little evidence that deliberate changes were made to the text for the sake of some theological axe to grind. He was wrong in this, of course, as subsequent studies have revealed.[21] But this is what he meant, and what most textual critics today mean when they speak of a theologically motivated variant.

To be sure, E. C. Colwell once used the term in a way more like Pickering's.[22] But Colwell clearly said that the "theological" motivation had to do with the church's *love* for its Scripture. This is a far cry from Pickering's equation of "dogmatic reasons" with "malicious changes" made by persons lacking integrity. Pickering's case fails at two points:

1. The view that most corruption to the text was deliberate, theological, and malicious stands almost as the antithesis to what actually appears to have been the case. The alternative view, which will be supported by the evidence given below, can be stated as follows: Although most corruption to the NT text was probably

21. See, among others, Williams 1951: 25-53, 56-58, and Epp 1966a [see now Chapter 2: 34].

22. Colwell 1952: 53, cited by Pickering: 42.

"deliberate," it was seldom theologically motivated in the sense of trying to score a theological point; furthermore, although *deliberate,* it was *not malicious* in the sense of trying to alter the *meaning* of the text (in fact "deliberate," as a way to distinguish such variation from inadvertent error, does not even need to mean "thoughtful" or "purposeful"). Rather, such changes were ordinarily made in the interest of the readability or *completeness* of the text, that is, in the interest of clarifying its meaning. For the early Christians, it was precisely because the meaning was so important that they exercised a certain amount of freedom in making that meaning clear.

This view of things can easily be supported simply by analyzing the variants for any given piece of text of the NT.

First, it should be noted that all textual corruption can be objectively set out. If one collates any two or more MSS, for any given section of text, all variation may be classified into one of six kinds, without first trying to establish one of the MSS as a base. Variation is either:

(a) add/omit (words, phrases, sentences, or large sections)
(b) substitutions (of words, tense, number, etc.)
(c) word order (transpositions of words or phrases)
(d) any combination of (a), (b), and (c) in a single variant
(e) transpositions (of a large section of text from one place to another)
(f) major rewriting of a sentence or paragraph.

Apart from careless errors, most of which could also be placed in the above categories, these are the only kinds of variations to a text that are possible. Of these (f) is always deliberate, (d) and (e) ordinarily so, and (a), (b), or (c) may or may not be so. That is, the add/omit of a nominative personal pronoun in John may be due (1) to the scribe's awareness of John's habits vis-à-vis standard Greek and thus a deliberate conformation to one or the other, or (2) to his own personal Greek usage, resulting in a careless add/omit of the pronoun.

Now my point: If one were to take any five to ten verses from anywhere in the NT and collate all the available textual evidence, the vast majority of variants among the MSS belong to categories (a), (b), and (c), and of these the substantial majority simply do not fit in any meaningful way the concept of theologically motivated alteration. One may take, for example, the first five verses in John 13, for which my own collations include all the data from Tischendorf and von Soden, plus the papyri. For these five verses, there are twenty-seven different variation-units: fourteen are add/omit; ten are substitutions; two are word order; and one is a combination of add/omit and substitution.

Many of these are probably not deliberate at all (e.g., the "addition" of τοῦ before θεοῦ by Family 1 in v. 3, or its "omission" by Δ Θ a few words later, or the change in v. 1 by P[66] from τοῦ κόσμου τούτου to τούτου τοῦ κόσμου). But many were almost certainly deliberate. Let us take, for example, the change γενομένου/γινομένου (v. 2), which places the footwashing either after or during the meal. Although only a single letter is involved, the change was probably deliberate one way or the other. Some kind of theological understanding of the Supper may even have been involved. But how is this variation "malicious"? Or take further the change in v. 2 with reference to Judas's "surname." Did John say, "Judas son of Simon Iscariot," or "Judas Iscariot son of Simon"? It makes scarcely any difference in meaning whether the father or the son bears the family name (or geographical designation), and surely nothing theological is involved. Yet someone (or several someones) changed it from one to the other.

Take still further the complex word order change in v. 2, where at least seven different alternatives are found. Essentially it is a choice between ". . . into the heart of Judas . . . that he might betray him" or ". . . into the heart that he might betray him, Judas. . . ." This can only have happened intentionally — but maliciously? or for dogmatic purposes? Here is where one can also see the *why* of change, for the second form is as awkward in Greek as it is in English. Who would purposely have done something like that to the text, when there is not a single thing to be gained by such awkwardness (the meaning is the same, whatever the order of the words)? But if John wrote the second as the original, one can easily see what happened. He wrote: "The devil had already put it in his heart to betray him," and then added the nominative "Judas, son of Simon" in order to clarify his pronouns. Later copyists simply helped him out further by changing the word order and also by putting "Judas" in the genitive. The result was exactly what John intended, but without the awkwardness.

Similarly, there are two variations between aorists and perfects (v. 1 ἦλθον/ἐλήλυθα; v. 3 ἔδωκεν/δέδωκεν). In both cases the sense of the perfect is required. However, it is well known that John sometimes uses the aorist in a perfective sense (e.g., Abbott 1906: 324-28), so either could have come from him. But when a copyist made a change, again deliberately, it almost surely would have been because there was an aorist in the MS being copied and it was changed to the perfect that the sense required. A deliberate change in the other direction is well-nigh impossible to account for. And again, this is neither malicious nor theological, unless it is theological in Colwell's sense — out of love for the Bible.

One can go anywhere in the NT, and the profile will be the same. The vast majority of textual corruptions, though deliberate, are *not* malicious, nor are they theologically motivated. And *since* they are not, Pickering's view of "normal" transmission (which is the crucial matter for his theory) simply disintegrates.

2. Pickering's unhistorical view of the causes of textual corruption is almost certainly what also causes him to slight the matter of "the internal evidence of readings," for after all, most of the canons of internal criticism (at least those under the rubric "transcriptional probability") are merely other ways of speaking about the causes of variation.

Thus, the canon of "the shorter reading," though less useful than others, simply means that in most cases of "deliberate" variation scribes were more likely to have added words (pronouns, conjunctions, etc.) than they were to have deleted them. The canon of "the more difficult reading" means that since a copyist changed the text one way or the other, the change usually was made toward a more "readable," or clearer, understanding of the text. Similarly, the canon "harmonization" simply means that a scribe who knew his texts well is far more likely to have conformed one text to another than vice versa.

All of this has placed Pickering in something of a dilemma. On the one hand, because modern textual criticism relies heavily on such canons, he must of necessity at some point address himself to them. On the other hand, because he believes most corruption to be theologically motivated, he seems to have difficulty coming to terms with the real nature of this evidence. Thus, he makes two pleas: (1) agnosticism: "No twentieth century man confronting a set of variant readings can know or prove what actually took place to produce the variants" (78; cf. 24); (2) a kind of reverse domino theory, which suggests that if one of the canons can ever be shown not to be true at any point, then the canon is never true — or at least no sure guide.[23]

A word about both of these: First, Pickering's agnosticism is unworthy of historical research. *All* historical investigation proceeds by framing hypotheses on the basis of limited data, then testing the hypotheses against all the possible data. Conclusions are then drawn on the basis of probabilities. Pickering's own view of transmission in fact is based partly on a (albeit *non sequitur*) hypothesis framed on the basis of certain sayings in early Church Fathers. But to say that because we cannot prove what actually took place, we must therefore cash in our historical sense is something we are frankly unwilling to do. I may have been mistaken as to how any one of the variants noted above from John 13 actually happened, but Pickering cannot throw over the whole enterprise with the swipe of his hand. Instead, he must show why *another* explanation is a better one in each case.

Second, the exception to a rule does not prove the rule false or useless; hopefully it causes all of us to proceed with due caution. But Pickering would throw them all out, even the possibilities of harmonization, although he does so in this latter case only by throwing in a red herring.[24]

One hesitates to try to illustrate all of this, because in the final analysis it is the cumulative force of the data that brings conviction. Nonetheless, I have chosen two passages from Mark, two among hundreds like these, to illustrate the concept of "the more difficult reading" and "harmonization"; to show how off target Pickering's objections really are; and to insist that if he and Hodges do not like these explanations, they must give good *historical reasons* for their Majority text alternative (or at least show how the universal choice of textual criticism is in fact a theologically motivated variant from the second century).

a) *Mark 1:2.* In a context where Mark cites from both Malachi and Isaiah — in that order — there are the following two variants:

(1) ἐν τῷ Ἠσαίᾳ τῷ προφήτῃ ("in Isaiah the prophet"). This is the reading in all Church Fathers before Photius (d. 895), except for one citation in Irenaeus, who elsewhere also cites this reading.[25] It is the reading of all the early versions

---

23. See esp. the conclusion of his discussion of "the more difficult reading" (84).

24. In one of the more extraordinary arguments in the book, Pickering (86) starts by attacking the notion that "in the synoptic Gospels the 'Byzantine' text is characterized by harmonizations." In a total *non sequitur* he appeals to Colwell's evidence that in three early papyri the scribes "were much more addicted to *harmonization to the immediate context,*" a kind of harmonization, he (Colwell) suggests, that often is scarcely noted in the manuals. Because of this lack of discussion, Pickering would have us throw out the whole notion! [See now Chapter 9].

25. Since this one citation stands alone in all of the early Greek and Latin evidence, and since Irenaeus himself clearly knows the other text, this "citation" is especially suspect as a later corruption.

(Latin, Coptic, most Syriac, Gothic, Georgian), except the Harclean Syriac (ca. 615) and the Armenian (ca. 405). This latter in fact is the earliest known evidence for reading (2). This is also the reading of the earliest MSS East (א B) and West (D OL), as well as several others.

(2) ἐν τοῖς προφήταις ("in the prophets"). The earliest Greek evidence for this reading is the Codex Alexandrinus (A) and the Codex Washingtonianus (W), both fifth century; thereafter it is found in several MSS of the ninth century; and finally it predominates in almost all the later medieval MSS.

Reading (1) is a clear example of "the more difficult reading being preferred as the original." There is simply no devious theological motivation imaginable for one to have changed reading (2) to (1). In fact, the only possible explanation of a deliberate change in that direction would have been by someone who was trying to be more precise and failed to recognize that the first part of the quote came from Malachi. Here again the "theology" could scarcely have been "malicious." But surely the opposite is the more likely. Purely in the interest of precision, someone, who recognized that the citation was a collation from two prophets, simply "corrected" the text to reflect that precision.

Pickering argues that the canon of "the harder reading" is "simply inapplicable" (84). Why? Because "we have no way of knowing what factors influenced the originator of a variant" (agnosticism again) and because the canon is vulnerable "to the manipulation of a skillful and determined imagination." But what is so "skillful" about the above reasoning? And if one cannot *know*, surely one can talk about historical probabilities. The point is that this example can be multiplied a thousand times over; and *in the vast majority of cases the "easier" reading (= the corruption) is that of the Majority text.*[26] What Pickering must explain is how the more difficult reading became so immediately popular that it is the only known reading in the church for three centuries, and so predominated in the West, in Egypt, and in Syria that it is the only reading translated into the earliest versions and the only reading known to every Church Father who cites the text.

b) *Mark 13:14‖Matt 24:15*. The variant that concerns us here is an example of harmonization, a matter wherein Pickering apparently realizes he is hurting, since he offers such specious reasoning. His only argument against this canon is that since harmonization of more than one kind took place, therefore all alleged harmonizations are suspect! But it is simply not true that scholarship has ignored other kinds of harmonization except those in parallel passages;[27] and even if it had done so, to discover another kind hardly invalidates the former.

With regard to harmonization in the Synoptic Gospels, some data are incontrovertible: (1) The Gospel of Matthew was the most cited and used of the Synoptic Gospels.[28] (2) Mark's text has almost twice as many variants involving harmonization as does either Matthew or Luke, probably because Mark was the

---

26. Pickering (83) asks for a "statistical demonstration" to support this canon. All one need do is go through the apparatus of Tischendorf and count!

27. See my discussion in Fee 1978e [Chapter 9].

28. This can now be most forcefully demonstrated simply by counting the references in the available volumes of *Biblia Patristica* (Allenbach 1975-87).

least used of the Gospels. These data simply cannot be ignored in making textual decisions.

In our passage, all known witnesses of Matthew of every kind (Greek, versions, Fathers, etc.) read τὸ ῥηθὲν διὰ Δανιὴλ τοῦ προφήτου ("spoken of through the prophet Daniel"). In Mark, however, these words are missing in the earliest Greek evidence (ℵ B D pc), in most of the Latin evidence (*c k* are the only exceptions), in the Coptic, and in the Armenian. The only early Church Father to mention the Marcan passage is Augustine, who explicitly says these words are missing in Mark.

What Pickering must answer is, Why did some early copyists choose to omit this phrase in Mark? And why *only* in Mark but never in the more frequently used Matthew? And why, with regard to this matter in general, would anyone go about trying to *dis*harmonize the Gospels, when all the known evidence (Tatian, Church Fathers, versions, etc.) demonstrates conclusively the harmonistic bent of the early church?

Once more, these examples can be multiplied, and, whatever else, all of this can hardly be dismissed as so much subjectivity.

3. The final and fatal flaw in Pickering's understanding of textual corruption is found in his use of the second-century Fathers to support his view of "normal" transmission. Pickering sets up his case this way: (a) All kinds of evidence can be adduced from the early period (apostolic through the second century) to show that these writers considered the NT documents as authoritative Scripture.[29] (b) There are good reasons to believe that they were also especially careful with regard to the wording of these texts. (c) Therefore, we must also assume that these same concerned Christians exercised similar care in the copying and transmitting of their texts.

The basic flaw in this argument is step (b). Here Pickering's "good reasons" are limited to a variety of citations, from the NT through Tertullian, which evidence concern for false teachers and show awareness of those who "twist" Scripture. Typical of Pickering's argument is his rhetorical comment on Rev 22:18-19: "Faced with such a sanction, would any true believer dare to tamper with the text, or transcribe it carelessly?" (101). Then sayings of the Fathers are brought in as support, e.g., Polycarp 7:1, "Whoever perverts the sayings of the Lord . . . that one is the firstborn of Satan."

There are two things that invalidate this argument. First, this is simply bad exegesis of the NT and the Fathers. Polycarp, for example, was not talking about the perversion that comes through the *transmission* of the text, but rather with the *interpretation* of the text.

Second, Pickering's argument is based on *sayings* from these various sources. When one looks at these Fathers' actual *citations* of the NT, his argument totally disintegrates.

Pickering's argument demands the following logic: (1) Since each of these Fathers mentioned belongs to the orthodox stream of Christianity, where the normal (= no deliberate changes), *especially* careful, transmission of the text was taking place, and (2) since the deliberate changes were made by those who did *not* hold to

---

29. This is in itself a moot point, but for now it is conceded.

orthodox theology (including a high view of Scripture), therefore, (3) the text of the NT found in these Fathers should itself evidence this special care, or at least should reflect the readings of the Majority text, the true descendants of these orthodox Fathers.

But what we find is precisely the opposite. First of all, there is absolutely *no* evidence that these Fathers cited the NT as a text demanding their special care ("special care" meaning concern for the precise wording). Indeed, the NT writers themselves regularly cite the OT loosely, although there is no question that they considered the OT as Scripture. In fact, in one place (Eph 4:8) Paul's point rests upon his new wording of the text, which is otherwise unknown in the entire textual tradition of the OT.

In the case of Clement of Rome we have a Father who generally cites the OT with special care;[30] yet for the NT there is not a single "citation" or allusion that is even closely verbatim. The closest is *1 Clem.* 36:2‖Heb 1:3-4, where Clement has *five* variants from the common NT text. (The most any known MS has is three.) The same holds true for Polycarp and Justin.

The final two Fathers, Irenaeus and Tertullian, are even more instructive, for here at last we have evidence of real citations of the NT text. Despite Pickering's assertion that Irenaeus "heavily" supports the Majority text,[31] the fact is that his text differs from the Majority even more than Pickering's hated Egyptian MSS do. But how could it have been otherwise? For even though he tends to cite the text with more care than does Tertullian, his mature years were lived out in southern France, and he used a Greek text very much like those lying behind the OL.

To show the total disregard for the actual data one finds in Pickering, I will illustrate a little more fully from Tertullian. For this purpose, I went to *adversus Praxean,* because (1) Praxeas was a heretic, (2) Praxeas did not distort the words of the text, but misinterpreted them, and (3) in such a work Tertullian's arguments are regularly based on the very wording of the text itself. Yet does he cite with care? Hardly.

I checked his Johannine citations in chapter 22. There is scarcely a citation (and none, when the citation is at least a full sentence long) in which Tertullian does not differ both with the Greek text and with the Latin, not to mention those several other places where he agrees with the OL (especially *e*) against the Greek evidence. For example, in 22.12 he cites John 10:34-38, where he has eleven variations from the Greek and Latin, plus one (v. 38, omit καὶ γινώσκητε [or πιστεύσητε]) that he shares with several OL MSS. A little later, in chapters 26 and 27, he has occasion to cite Luke 1:35 three different times. Each of these differs from the others and one of them reads the *ex te* with *a c e r*[1] and many others. Thus, he not only does *not* exercise care, but his own text is a far cry from Pickering's "orthodox" Majority text.

---

30. See the conclusion by Hagner 1973: 35: "If there is anything that distinguishes the manner of quotation in Clement . . . it is . . . the large number of quotations which agree closely with the LXX."

31. This is so far off target that one wonders whether Pickering ever consulted a single item in a somewhat modest bibliography on this subject.

My point is that Pickering has made use of some *statements* from these Fathers to argue that those *copying* the Bible would have done so with extraordinary care. Yet for each of the Fathers whose statements he has used: (1) they do not themselves exhibit care in using the very words of the NT, and (2) when they do "cite" the NT text they reveal abundant evidence of the "deviant" text of the NT that Pickering argues was the result of "abnormal" or "malicious" transmission!

To conclude: Pickering has not only failed to take seriously, or even to understand, the causes of corruption, but he has also disregarded the nature of the very data he would use to establish the case for his "normal" transmission. All of this seems fatal to his enterprise.

The Use of Patristic Evidence

Besides these more crucial failures, there are several other areas where Pickering has dealt loosely with the data. In fact, one may reasonably wonder whether he has ever seriously wrestled either with the primary sources or with the secondary literature. For this paper I will note only one of these additional deficiencies, his use of patristic evidence, because this is an area where I have been active over several years. We have just noted something of his failure in this regard in the immediately preceding section. Here I want to take issue with his discussion of the biblical texts used by the Fathers before Chrysostom, where he tries to demonstrate the existence of the Byzantine text-type in these Fathers (62-76). This discussion is profuse with errors, chiefly due to his reliance on unreliable secondary information and to his neglect of literally scores of scholarly studies that contravene his assertions.[32]

But before examining just a few of these, a very important preliminary word about text-types and manuscript relationships is in order.

Pickering regularly talks about Byzantine readings as being earlier than Chrysostom — and he is right. That is, readings that eventually became the text of the majority can often be shown to have existed as early as the second century. For example, the majority of harmonizations found in the Majority text vis-à-vis the text of Egypt et al. are already found in the OL MSS in the West. But this was not Hort's point, or mine, or that of others who have labored in this area.

P[66], for example, is said to have Byzantine readings. In a sense this is correct in that P[66] — and even P[75] on rare occasions — is now the earliest evidence for a variant *away from* the Egyptian text-type that is later to be found in the Majority text. But in comparison with places where P[66] reads with the Egyptians *against* the Byzantines, these "Byzantine" readings are of little consequence; and above all else they do not render P[66] a Majority text MS.[33]

Our point here has *not* to do with readings. After all, Hort himself saw that only the "conflations" and a few others were readings actually *created* by the "Byzantine recensor." Rather, it is all of these readings *together,* in *combination,* that

---

32. The overlooked bibliography here is so large that it can hardly be given in a footnote. For example, I know of eleven different studies on Origen alone that contradict all of Pickering's discussion, and not one of them is even recognized to have existed.

33. All of this has been carefully set forth in my monograph on P[66] (Fee 1968b).

distinguishes the later MSS from the earlier — and the later Fathers from the earlier.[34] Thus, when one speaks of the texts of the Fathers, the question is not whether any given Father before Chrysostom has some Byzantine *readings;* the question is whether any Father before Chrysostom shows evidence for all these readings in combination in the same way the Majority text MSS do.

Pickering partially recognizes this problem and thus uses data from Edward Miller to support his contention that "the Byzantine text not only is to be found in the writings of the early fathers, but that in fact it *predominates*" (68). He then asserts that in this matter "no one has ever taken up Miller's challenge." But the reason for no direct response to Miller on the part of scholarship is that for over seventy years scholarly examinations of the texts of most early Fathers have been appearing, all of which stand as the thorough refutation of Miller, and all of which Pickering completely ignores.

Now about the Fathers themselves. One of the problems with patristic evidence is that it must be carefully analyzed before it can be used. That is, one must be sure (a) that a given Father's work has been faithfully transmitted, (b) that the Father was actually quoting (= copying), not merely "remembering" his NT, and (c), especially in the Gospels, that it was one Gospel and not another that was being quoted.

Pickering brushes off item (a) by calling it a "quibble" (69). But one may be assured that this is not a quibble; it is crucial. Unfortunately, all of Burgon's data that Miller used is suspect because of his use of uncritical editions, especially Migne. This will be noted several times in the following discussion.

Item (c) is also an area where Burgon and Miller were indiscriminate in their use of Fathers' texts. It is simply a maxim in the citation of patristic evidence for the Gospels that a Father can be cited in support only (a) if he tells us he is citing one Gospel, not the others (including specific commentaries and homilies, of course), or (b) the citation is unique to one of the Gospel writers, or (c), when there are parallels, the language of one Gospel is so unique as to make identification probable. The problem here is a simple one: Early Fathers were as prone as we are today to harmonize and collate, and therefore to speak of the "rich young ruler," although all three of these designations appear in no single Gospel.

Burgon's and Miller's data are simply replete with useless supporting evidence; and Pickering apparently cites Burgon or Miller without ever checking their data. Thus, in his one "concrete definition" of the idea of "antiquity," Pickering (130) cites Burgon's data on the appearance of "vinegar" in Matt 27:34, an article which Burgon considered to be his finest hour (1896b: 253-58). I took the trouble to check over three-quarters of Burgon's seventeen supporting Fathers and *not one of them* can be shown to be citing Matthew.

In another place Pickering accuses F. G. Kenyon of not being "precisely

---

34. Pickering seems quite in error here, or else he is using the concept of "strictly Byzantine" readings in a rather loose way, when he asserts (68) that "to disprove Hort's assertion, it is only necessary to find *some* 'strictly Byzantine' readings." It would do no such thing, since the question is *not* readings, but *all these readings together.* After all, it is this — and this alone — that makes a Byzantine MS differ from any other. Cf. n. 3 above.

fair" with Miller because he neglected Miller's evidence for Byzantine readings in several passages. I checked the evidence for the first of these, the variant "to repentance" in Matt 9:13 and Mark 2:17 for which Miller cites Barnabas, Justin, Irenaeus, Origen, Eusebius, Hilary, and Basil as in support. Here is the actual evidence:

First, it should be noted that this saying is parallel in all three Gospels (Matt 9:13‖Mark 2:17‖Luke 5:32); in the UBS[3] Matthew and Mark are exactly parallel (except for a γάρ in Matthew); in Luke the verb has been changed from ἦλθον ("I came") to ἐλήλυθα ("I have come"), he has added εἰς μετάνοιαν ("to repentance"), and there is no known evidence of any kind for Luke in which these words are missing. But they are missing in Matthew and Mark in all the early Greek and most of the early Latin and Coptic evidence.

As to the "supporting" Fathers:

(1) *Barn.* 5:9: Not only does "Barnabas" not mention any Gospel, but in the critical edition (Funk-Bihlmeyer) the disputed words are not even found (in this case supported by the "majority text" S H L against V).

(2) Justin, *apol.* 1.15: Again, there is no mention of any Gospel. In fact, as A. J. Bellinzoni (1967) has shown, almost all of the Jesus sayings in Justin are pre-Tatianic harmonizations,[35] and this is one of them.

(3) Irenaeus, *haer.* 3.5.2: Again, there is no mention of any Gospel; but in this case the citation includes the preceding verse, which makes it certain that Luke is being cited. The Latin translation of Irenaeus here is nearly identical with a few OL MSS of Luke; Matthew is out, because of a long omission; and the only OL codex of Mark that has Irenaeus's wording is Palatinus *(e),* and that MS does not have "to repentance" in Mark.

(4) Origen, *Jo.* 28.16 (Pickering has the wrong book number): Although Origen does not refer to a Gospel, this citation is most likely from Luke because of the ἐλήλυθα. On the other hand, that he knew a Gospel *without* εἰς μετάνοιαν is made clear by his reference to this saying in *Jo.* 6.42.

(5) Eusebius, *Ps. 146:3:* Again, there is no mention of any Gospel. The "citation" includes the preceding verse and altogether is a nicely harmonized version of Mark and Luke. Precisely the same "citation" is also found in *Demonstratio* 4.10.11.

(6) Basil: The citation in *ep.* 46.6 is exactly like the two in Eusebius. In *hom. Ps. 48:1,* there is only an allusion, with no possible way to identify it as from one or the other of the Gospels. The "citation" in *poenit.* 3 in fact belongs to Eusebius Emesenus and is so loose as to defy identification with a Gospel.

(7) Hilary, *comm. Matt (ad loc.),* does indeed have these words in his text. But this evidence is modified by the fact that he also cites Mark *without* the disputed words.

The only certain patristic support for the Majority text of Matthew, therefore, is the one citation from Hilary and one in Epiphanius *(haer.* 51.5.1), which Miller

---

35. This has recently been disputed by Strecker 1978, but Strecker has scarcely refuted the harmonistic character of nearly all of Justin's Gospel citations.

overlooked. On the other hand, certain evidence for this saying in its shortened form (whether from Matthew or Mark) is found in *Barnabas, 2 Clem.* 2:4, Origen, and pseudo-Justin (*res.* 7.23). All of this could have been discovered by Pickering himself had he used primary, or more adequate secondary, sources.

Pickering's dependence on inadequate sources finally pushes his argument beyond credibility when he concludes by listing twenty-nine Fathers who allegedly "recognize" Byzantine readings. Among these, he lists Clement of Alexandria, Tertullian, the Clementines, Hippolytus, and Origen and says they all "heavily" support the Byzantine text (75). While this is not true of any of these Fathers, nor of most of those on his list, I will give the evidence only for Hippolytus and Origen, since Pickering has made a special point of both (63-65).

Hippolytus. Pickering cites with approval the remarks by H. C. Hoskier on Hippolytus's citations of 1 Thess 4:13-17 and 2 Thess 2:1-12, where he concluded: "*Hippolytus'* early third-century MS is found generally on the side of what Turner would call the 'later' MSS" (1914: 427). But Hoskier, who usually works with better data, is simply all wrong here.

For these two paragraphs in Paul, I collated the Byzantine text against the UBS[3]. Not counting orthography, there are eleven variations between them. Then I collated Hippolytus (Achelis's edition in the GCS series) against these eleven variants, as well as against the common text of Byz/UBS[3], which turned up seven further variants in Hippolytus. Here are the data:

(a) Hippolytus has two singular readings (2 Thess 2:4 ἑαυτόν + ὡς; 2:6 *om.* ἐν).

(b) Of the eleven variants between Byz/UBS[3], he agrees with the UBS[3] nine times, and with the Byz two, both of which are also read by the Western witnesses D F G OL (1 Thess 4:13 κεκοιμημένων; 2 Thess 2:3 ἁμαρτίας *l.* ἀνομίας).

(c) The five other variants from the common text are all supported by the Western witnesses (D F G OL, sometimes E Tertullian Hilary).

(d) In all sixteen nonsingular variants, Hippolytus has the same reading as at least two, and usually all five, of the Western witnesses (D E F G OL).

This is precisely what one should expect of someone living in Rome in the early third century. Whatever else, there is nothing Byzantine about his text whatsoever [see now Osburn 1982].

Origen. Origen's text is of considerable interest — and importance — because he changed residence in the middle of his life (AD 231), from Alexandria to Caesarea. Parts of his NT text in fact have been shown to reflect this change. It is not possible to list all the ramifications of all the data here. But some notations on the NT citations found in his commentary on John will be instructive, because this work was actually begun in Alexandria (Books 1-5) and completed in Caesarea (Books 6-39?). Here are the data:

His text of John itself is thoroughly Egyptian, both in the Alexandrian and Caesarean sections. Apparently he took his copy of John with him, a copy he used all his life; for in all his works his text of John hardly varies from its basically Egyptian form. For example, for chapters 1, 4, 8, and 13 I recently analyzed his text (1980b) in a manner similar to that of Hippolytus in the preceding section. For these chapters of John there are 109 variants between Byz/UBS[3], where Origen also has text. Of these he sides with the UBS[3] ninety-seven times and with the Byzantines only seven! In those few variants where he differs from both the Byz/UBS[3] he is almost always joined by one or more of the early Egyptian witnesses.

The same phenomenon, but just slightly less thoroughly so, is also true of his text of Luke, the Pauline Epistles, and the Revelation. He used an Egyptian text for each in both cities. The text of Matthew is also consistent throughout the commentary, but reflects a much greater degree of mixture in variants also supported by the MSS in von Soden's I class (D W Θ f[1] f[13] 28 565 700 etc.).

His text of Mark used in this commentary is where so much interest lies. For during the Alexandrian and earlier Caesarean parts of the commentary, that is, in Books 1-10, his text is Egyptian in precisely the same percentages as with John. Of forty-two variants between Byz/UBS[3] where Origen has text, he sides with the UBS[3] thirty-seven times and with the Byzantines only four, and in two of these latter he has the Egyptian reading — which the UBS[3] did not take as its text. In the five variants where he differs from the Byz/UBS[3] common text, he is supported in each instance by א and/or C.

At some point, however, in the writing of this commentary Origen ceased using the copy of Mark he brought with him from Alexandria and began to use a local text;[36] for in a long series of citations from Mark 12–15 in Books 20, 28, and 32 (the others are lost) his Marcan text ceases altogether being Egyptian and becomes a witness to the so-called Caesarean MSS (esp. Θ and 565). This is clearly demonstrated by three phenomena: (a) Of the sixteen Byz/UBS[3] variants, he reads nine with the Byzantines and seven with the Egyptians. But more significantly he reads with some combination of D W Θ 28 565 700 in all but two of the sixteen. (b) His text has an enormous increase in variants from the common text, nineteen in all, and in seventeen cases he reads with Θ W 565 etc., most of which variants are peculiar to these MSS. (c) He cites Mark 14:60-61 both in Book 10 and in 28, that is, on each side of the change of Bibles. The citation in Book 10 has two readings with א B against D Θ 565 700, whereas in Book 28 he reverses himself.

What is of crucial significance here is that in this clear example of Origen's using a different copy of Mark, and presumably one he found in Caesarea where one might have expected the Majority text to be found if it were available this early, Origen in no way reflects this text. Of thirty-five variants he agrees with the "Caesareans" thirty-one times; and only nine of these eventually come to be shared with the Byzantines as well. Therefore, Pickering's statement that Origen "heavily" favors the Majority text is *totally false* [see also Fee 1982a].

It must be repeated in conclusion that what is true of Hippolytus and Origen can also be shown to be true for most of the other Fathers Pickering cites. Hort had previously argued that purely Byzantine readings are unknown before AD 250. Subsequent discoveries have demonstrated that although this needs some qualification, it is still true. He also suggested that the first Father to have Byzantine readings in combination, that is, actually to use a predominantly Byzantine text, was Chry-

---

36. This was first noted by Streeter 1924: 77-78, 91-102. It was considerably refined, and made certain, by Lake et al. 1928: 259-77.

sostom. This, too, now needs to be modified, since the heretical Asterius the Sophist (d. 341) used such a text.[37] But he is the *only* Father before Chrysostom known to have done so. Pickering (62) accuses scholarship of "still widely believing" Hort's judgments about the nature of the ante-Nicene patristic evidence. But they do so with good cause. Hort was right, and this crucial step in his argument still holds, notwithstanding Pickering's accusations based on the use of poor secondary evidence and his misrepresentations of the papyrus evidence.[38]

Conclusion — A Test Case

We may conclude with certainty that Pickering has altogether failed to identify the original NT text. Furthermore, his own proposal simply eliminates textual criticism altogether. What need is there of scholarship when a computer can be programmed to identify the majority reading at every point?

The evidence that Pickering's method renders him incapable of doing textual criticism is found in the fact that he offers only one example in the entire book as to how his method works in actual practice. This one example is the variant "God" or "he who" ($\overline{\Theta\Sigma}$ or OΣ) in 1 Tim 3:16, of which he says:

> Fully 300 Greek MSS read "God" while only eight read something else. Of these eight, three have private readings and five agree in reading "who." So we have to judge between 97% and 2%, "God" versus "who." It is really hard to imagine any possible set of circumstances in the transmissional history sufficient to produce the cataclysmic overthrow in statistical probability that is required by the claim that "who" is the original reading. (112)

There we have it: 97% to 2% wins, so we have no need to look at the evidence or examine the causes of corruption, because they could never overturn "statistical probabilities." But let us examine the evidence anyway. First the external evidence:

1. I do not know how many Vulgate MSS of 1 Timothy there are, but surely more than a thousand. In any case, there is not a single Latin-speaking Christian in the entire history of the church who knew the reading that emerged as that of the Majority text.

2. The same thing is true of every other ancient version: Syriac, Coptic, Armenian, Ethiopic, Gothic — none of them reads "God." And all of these versions eventually go back to Greek texts from every sector of the empire from the second to the fifth centuries. Thus, the 97% deals only with a very narrow section of Christianity: the Greek Orthodox Church.

---

37. I hope eventually to publish the evidence for this conclusion. In Acts alone, e.g., there are ten variants between Byz/UBS[3], and Asterius supports the Byzantine text in seven. Random samplings in Matthew and Romans revealed the same kind of text.

38. This is another item where Pickering has quite misinterpreted the data. His statements about P[75] are so far wrong that he has either never read, or has refused to acknowledge, the evidence from studies by Martini, Porter, and myself. P[75] has a closer relationship to B than most of the MSS within Family 13 have to one another! Yet Pickering questions the "assignment of . . . P[75] to the 'Alexandrian text-type' " as something not truly reasonable (p. 56).

3. Despite Burgon's attempt to show otherwise, the variant reading "God" is unknown among the Greek Fathers before the last part of the fourth century. The earliest certain witnesses for this reading are Gregory of Nyssa (d. 394) and Didymus (d. 398). Given the significance this reading could have had in the christological controversies of the third and fourth centuries, the argument from silence in this case is an especially telling one.

Thus, the reading ΟΣ ("He who") or the slight corruption Ο ("that")[39] is read everywhere in Egypt, all through the West, and elsewhere in the East until the late fourth century. (The earliest Greek MS to read "God" dates from the eighth century!)

The real question, then, is not Pickering's — how did "God" succeed in the majority if not original? — but rather, if "God" were the original, (a) how did the other reading (with its variation) come into existence at all? and (b) how did this inexplicable "corruption" disseminate so thoroughly at such an early stage that the "original" reading could not make its appearance anywhere, at any stage in the process, outside the Greek evidence?

The answer is simple. The variation could only have occurred to someone reading a Greek text and only after the true original ("he who") had been thoroughly disseminated throughout Christian antiquity. Furthermore, the corruption in Greek could only have gone one way, from ΟΣ to $\overline{\Theta\Sigma}$ because the line of abbreviation above the ΘΣ would never have made it possible for this reading to have been confused with ΟΣ. That, plus the fact that ΟΣ has no antecedent, makes the change to ΘΣ a logical one as well. That the reading "God," once it made the textual stream, should finally predominate should surprise no one!

The final evidence is internal. Early Christian hymns tended to take two forms: a doxology with a ὅτι-clause (praise, and the reason for it), or with ὅς-clauses, where the antecedent was understood to be Christ. Paul uses this latter form in another instance in which he appears to be citing a hymn (Col 1:15, 18b). Therefore, the allegation that a change from "God" to "he who" was done by theological tampering is simply not true. The text "he who" clearly refers to Christ, and all the christological import is there in the original.

Thus, Pickering's book fails on all counts: in his understanding of the present scene, in his argumentation, in his understanding and use of the data, and in his own methodology, as well as in the very thing he was at least hoping to do — to open up the discussion anew as to the value of the Byzantine text. In contrast to Burgon, whose erudition at least made him a doughty warrior, this book falls short all along the line.

His "new" method for identifying the NT text is the wholesale adoption of Burgon's seven "notes of truth," all of which are simply seven different ways of saying that the majority is always right (although he never tells us why it is the majority at the end of the fifteenth century, rather than that at the end of the eighth

---

39. It must be noted that the versional evidence that appears to read the neuter relative pronoun is all evidence for ΟΣ; this is a typical "versional" variant, in which the translation "corrects" the Greek of the original.

or of the fourth). Perhaps it could be wished that we could obtain certainty so easily — simply by means of a computer printout. Unfortunately, the computer cannot be programmed to deal with the human variables that Pickering regularly mentions. Textual criticism is a historical science, subject to the various weaknesses of those human beings who first copied the texts, as well as of those of us who spend countless hours gathering, sifting, and evaluating the sources. Computers will be of immense value for storing the data, but unfortunately they cannot be relied upon to identify which of the variants may have been theologically motivated.

PART IV

ESTABLISHING TEXTUAL RELATIONSHIPS

CHAPTER 11

THE CLAREMONT PROFILE METHOD FOR GROUPING NEW TESTAMENT MINUSCULE MANUSCRIPTS[1]

Eldon Jay Epp

New Testament textual critics have always welcomed with enthusiasm the discovery of a Codex Sinaiticus or of each new series of biblical papyri, such as the Chester Beatty or the Bodmer, and with each such discovery they welcome also the accompanying labors of analysis, the difficult reassessment of previously known material, and the often painful revisions in method and theory which must be faced. In a similar way, textual critics invariably are delighted to find an early versional MS or that of a Church Father containing a portion of NT text, and they accept with pleasure the riches which are thereby added to the store of materials. But, I dare say, few indeed are the textual scholars who are elated by an additional Greek *minuscule* MS or who view the many hundreds of NT minuscules as comprising anything less than a formidable mass of vexing and insoluble problems.

Sheer quantity accounts for part of the problem. While there are presently eighty-one Greek papyri of the NT and 266 uncial MSS, there are at last count 2,754 Greek minuscules.[2] The difficulty of this minuscule problem may be indicated also in the following comparative figures: in 1909, only fourteen papyri were known, but these have increased in number nearly 600%, and the extensive energy devoted to their analysis in recent years is not surprising; likewise, uncial MSS have increased by nearly 60%. This means that textual critics have for generations been confronted by this burdensome mass of MSS, and yet — with one notable exception — they have failed or been unable to prosecute a broad-scale methodological effort directed toward the sorting and classification of this massive and intractable complex.[3]

---

1. A paper first read before the SBL, Pacific Coast Section, in May, 1967, with the kind permission of Messrs. McReynolds and Wisse and the other members of the staff of the IGNTP at Claremont, where the present writer served as consultant during the academic year 1966/67. The writer's debt to these staff members and to President Colwell, Chairman of the American Executive Committee of the Project, will be obvious to all.

2. These figures are the latest given by Kurt Aland 1967: 183. The figures below for the year 1909 are from Kenyon 1912: 57, 128-29. [For more current figures, see Chapter 1: 3-6 and Chapter 2: 31.]

3. The current work on "1000 minuscules examined in 1000 passages" at the Münster Institut für neutestamentliche Textforschung can hardly qualify as classification of the minuscules,

The one exception, of course, was the work of Hermann von Soden, which appeared between 1902 and 1910 as part of the voluminous prolegomena to his critical edition of the NT. It is well known that von Soden classified all the textual witnesses under one of three recensions or text-forms, I, H, or K. Beyond this broad grouping, von Soden further subdivided the K and I forms into such groups as K^1, K^i, K^x, and K^r; I^α, I^η, with further subgroups, I^ι with subgroups, I^ϕ with subgroups, I^β with subgroups, I^o, I^π, I^σ, I^x with subgroups, and I^r. The details of these classifications and subclassifications for the Gospels may be found in some 500 large and closely packed pages of volume two in the three-volume prolegomena (712-893 [= K]; 1041-1358 [= I]), and the enormity of von Soden's achievement can be grasped when it is recognized that he classified, under the K and I text-forms, more than 1260 minuscules of the Gospels out of the nearly 1350 known to him. A count of Gospel minuscules known as of 1963 comes to about 2000, which means that von Soden classified approximately sixty-three percent of all the minuscules of the Gospels available to us now. Yet, as will appear presently, von Soden's specific classifications did not always have a sufficient basis, nor were they always determined by a uniform or consistent method. In spite of this qualification and regardless of what may be said of the details of von Soden's group-classifications, it is nonetheless abundantly clear that his work has, since his day, formed the basis for all classification of minuscule MSS, and his groupings and their symbols have, almost without exception, been employed whenever a new MS has been classified; moreover, it may also be stated that, in general terms, von Soden's groupings, wherever tested, have held up remarkably well in the face of analysis. This statement, as already intimated, needs to be qualified in precise terms later, and it is essential also to emphasize that this affirmation of the general validity of von Soden's judgments on *groups* should by no means be understood as approval of his broader textual theory involving the I-H-K text, or as approval of the symbols by which he designated the smaller groups, if these symbols are understood as he intended them — that is, within the context of and in accordance with his textual theory. In other words, what has stood the test of time is the general integrity of the individual, smaller groups, and only that; the identifications with certain text-forms or recensions, or the indications of intra- and inter-group relationships which the group designations convey, are open to serious question at many points, but the isolation, homogeneity, and independent existence of most of his small groups and often also of his subgroups as individual groups have become contributions of abiding value.

When this has been said, several questions immediately come to the forefront: What precisely is von Soden's system or method for arriving at groups? On the basis of von Soden's work, could suitable representatives of each group, and thus suitable representative minuscule MSS of the NT as a whole, be selected quickly and conveniently from the mass of MSS for use in a critical apparatus? Do his

for its aim is to show which MSS belong to the Byzantine text so that they "may be henceforth neglected" in establishing the original text [see K. Aland 1965: 342-44; 1967: 194-96]. The publication of these data could aid a later process of classification, but it may be that the variants chosen will be unsuitable for the detailed analysis demanded.

groupings readily lend themselves to testing at any desired point, and do they provide for the easy classification of newly found and previously unclassified MSS?

The answer to the first question carries with it the answer to the other two: apparently von Soden began to investigate, in a systematic fashion, the text of the μοιχαλίς (= μ) or *pericope adulterae,* and he produced a stemma consisting of seven textual forms derived from the original of the pericope. This analysis may well have provided the clue for his procedure in grouping MSS,[4] but only a very few groups which were arrived at on the basis of the μοιχαλίς fall into the same groupings under his I or K text-forms.[5] Apart from the μοιχαλίς, then, von Soden apparently had neither a systematic nor a consistent means for arriving at his groupings; certainly he did not have a *rigidly* consistent or a *rigidly* systematic method, or if he did it is no longer obvious in his work, for even a superficial examination of his data shows at once that MSS were collated in varying places and with various degrees of completeness. For instance, some MSS were collated word for word and completely; some only in one Gospel or two (and not always the same one or two); some only in one chapter of one or more Gospels, others in several chapters; some closely related MSS were collated in entirely different passages; some groups were identified on the basis of a few selected chapters in Mark (as was the Iᵠ group), but other groups on the basis of broader or different samplings; and, finally, some MSS were collated only "cursorily" in longer or shorter passages. Indeed, if there was any consistent system of collation and sampling in von Soden's study, it is perhaps now only to be seen in the fact that certain chapters of the Gospels appear frequently in the lists of collated passages, for example, Matthew 1, 5, 15, 21; Mark 10, 11, 12; Luke 7, 8; John 6, 7, and so forth.

Thus, while von Soden left us with a series of groups and with lists of MSS which were strong and pure or weak and mixed members of those various groups, he did not leave us with either clear-cut principles or precise means for understanding, describing, or identifying the distinctive characteristics of a given group, nor did he leave with us a ready and convenient method for classifying any given additional minuscule MS. (If it should be suggested that the critical apparatus of his text-volume provides such a means for identifying group-readings and then classifying further MSS, it is sufficient, in reply, merely to point to the incompleteness and inconsistency in the citation of manuscript evidence and to the extensive inaccuracy of his apparatus. Moreover, von Soden's apparatus in the Gospels contains the evidence of only about 100 minuscule MSS representing the numerous I groups, of merely five minuscules of the K¹ group, and of no specific minuscules of the Kⁱ, Kˣ, or Kʳ groups.)

A rigid consistency in choosing his sample passages for collation would have been a step in the right direction, but his lack of this consistency and the sheer mass of his data leave us frustrated, bewildered, and without an easily accessible stepping stone to further progress. Those, like E. C. Colwell, David Voss, Kirsopp

---

4. Von Soden also used lectionary apparatus as an aid in classification.
5. Iᵝ is one example, though even here the weaker half of the group has variant forms of μ. See von Soden: 1159-60; cf. 504-5, 1152.

and Silva Lake, Jacob Geerlings, and others,[6] who have tested the integrity of some of von Soden's groups or made further group identifications, have done so only by taking von Soden's data as a mere starting point and working out a systematic and consistent testing procedure. But perhaps we are ungrateful if we expect von Soden to have given us more than the data for a starting point, for the provision of a base and a place to begin is itself a significant contribution.

Recently the IGNTP has also taken its starting point from von Soden, for one of the critical problems facing the Project — and one which confronts every *apparatus criticus* — is what to do with the mass of minuscule MSS. To cite them all *and* completely could be defended as an ideal, but there are also weighty theoretical considerations against such a procedure, to say nothing of the time-consuming task of accumulating hundreds and hundreds of full collations and the problems of editing and printing the volumes of additional data thereby produced. Clearly some other procedure must be adopted. To eliminate from the critical apparatus all of the estimated 2400 minuscules which represent the Byzantine text, as Professor Kurt Aland proposes for his edition (a more extreme measure than von Soden adopted), makes little if any contribution to the study of the history of the text in the Byzantine period (see n. 3 above). No, the answer to the problem of the minuscule MSS in a critical apparatus must be *selection in the interest of providing appropriate representation.* Such appropriate representation could involve the use of several criteria, such as the age of MSS, place of origin and geographical distribution, and the inclusion of dated MSS, but the most obvious primary consideration should be adequate representation of all known groups of MSS as determined by their textual character. Certainly a collection of suitable examples of minuscule MSS selected for their date, provenance, and textual complexion, each cited in full in the *apparatus criticus,* would constitute a gold mine of information for the historian of the Byzantine text and would also provide a reasoned, balanced, and adequate sampling of this wide-ranging late text of the Greek NT. (This selection of minuscules for the critical apparatus would, of course, be additional to the full citation of all Greek papyri and uncials, and additional to an adequate selection of lectionary,[7] patristic, and versional evidence, which together would constitute the full *apparatus criticus* proposed by the International Project.)

The general history of the IGNTP is well known — alas! perhaps too well known, for the optimistic hopes expressed in 1945 before the Society of Biblical Literature, when the project was approved by this Society, indicated that an "exhaustive" "critical apparatus to the four Gospels" was to be prepared and "ready for publication within the period of a decade."[8] Such prospects, renewed and updated

---

6. See, e.g., Lake, Blake, and New 1928; Silva New 1932; Colwell 1936, vol. I, on Fam. 2327 and Fam. 574; Silva Lake 1937 on Fam. Π; Voss 1938 on K^r; Kirsopp Lake 1941; Geerlings 1961a, 1961b, and 1962a on Fam. 13; 1962b, 1963, 1964 on Fam. Π.

7. The Greek lectionaries, incidentally, may pose a problem similar in many ways to that of the minuscules, for there are now 2135 lectionaries of the NT (see n. 2 above), and these need to be sorted and classified. Indeed, this appears to be the next major task facing the staff of the Project, and such work is now under way. [See Colwell, Parks, Wisse, and McReynolds 1968: 188-91 and American and British Committees of the IGNTP 1984-87: 1.vi, xi.]

8. *JBL* 65 (1946) ii.

from time to time, unfortunately have not been realized, nor is the first volume on Luke ready to be published now some twenty years after the formal launching of the Project.[9] Prospects of material support and enthusiastic cooperation by many scholars largely justified the early optimism. Subsequently, however, financial and other problems have seriously impeded progress, but I would venture to say that the failure to find a way to untie the Gordian knot of the minuscule complex of MSS has perhaps as much as any other single factor — and surely more than any other *methodological* factor — prevented the desired progress in completing the new apparatus.

While the adjectives "exhaustive," "complete," and "comprehensive" in early descriptions of the proposed critical apparatus obviously were hyperbolic, by at least 1950 it was clear that, in addition to the full citation of all papyri and all uncials, "enough minuscule manuscripts [would be cited] to give an adequate representation to every known text-type, family or subfamily, as well as to any such groups as may be discovered in the course of our work" (Parvis 1950: 307). By the middle 1950s, two principles had been stated for the selection and inclusion of minuscule data: the apparatus would take account of (1) "the Greek manuscripts which belong to some already established family or subfamily"; and (2) "the Greek manuscripts which show relevant divergence from the late Byzantine text."[10] Following the lines of these earlier statements, three principles for the selection of minuscules were approved in the autumn of 1966 at a joint meeting of the British and American Committees of the Project: (1) all known groups should be adequately represented; (2) some MSS should be included which throw light on the history of the text in the Byzantine period; and (3) some minuscules should be selected which are akin to early witnesses.[11] It was subsequently estimated that 300 minuscules would be the highest number feasible for inclusion.

But how is it to be determined which minuscules best or adequately represent the known groups? What, indeed, is adequate representation of a group — are only the purest or strongest members to be included, or also some weak, peripheral, and mixed members? Are the so-called known groups in fact demonstrable as groups? How is it to be decided which MSS throw light on the history of the Byzantine text? And how, except by full collation, are minuscules which show kinship to early witnesses to be isolated? Questions such as these faced the staff of the Project in the autumn of 1966, and we found ourselves in a most difficult — indeed, an impossible — situation; we were expected, in order to produce an *apparatus criticus,* to answer in advance the very questions which the *apparatus criticus* was designed to answer; we were required to determine *in advance* the very groupings from which appropriate and representative examples could be selected for an apparatus which was designed,

9. Others might date the Project from 1942 rather than 1945; others from 1948, when it was endorsed by the American Textual Criticism Seminar and (again) by the SBL; see *JBL* 68 (1949) xxv; 69 (1950) ii-iii, xxv-xxvi; and Parvis 1950: 302-3. [The two-volume critical apparatus of Luke finally was published in 1984-87: American and British Committees of the IGNTP.]

10. Parvis, *The Emory Alumnus* (December, 1955) 9.

11. Minutes of the joint meeting held at Selwyn College, Cambridge, September 5-7, 1966.

in part, to provide a basis for such a determination of groupings; we were expected to delve into the history of the Byzantine text in order to provide materials suitable for the eventual understanding of its complex history. In short, we were preparing a critical apparatus which was designed to be a halfway house toward the solution of numerous textual questions, including the vexing minuscule problem, but we were being forced, by the impossibility of including all the data, to draw conclusions that could properly be drawn only from the material of our own completed project!

Nevertheless, the Claremont staff of the Project turned its attention to the various criteria for the selection of minuscule MSS, in the hope that, by happenstance, an adequate representation would emerge. Dated MSS were deemed important for unraveling the history of the Byzantine text, as were MSS which could be identified with specific localities or scriptoria, and certain wild, independent, mixed, or otherwise unusual MSS were considered for inclusion in the select list of perhaps 300 minuscule MSS for Luke. But more important and more difficult was the examination of von Soden's groups — and of the work of scholars building upon his classifications — in an effort to isolate the most appropriate representatives of each. The method here was basically that employed by von Soden but much more clearly exemplified in the work of the Lakes, of Voss, and others, namely the identification of distinctive group-readings for each suspected group and, on the basis of such an analysis, the isolation of the best representatives.

Early in November 1966, when this work was substantially complete for most groups, President Colwell and Professor Clark reported, as they had been requested to do by the American and British Committees, on proposed criteria for the selection of minuscules *outside* of established groups and of minuscules which are akin to early witnesses. They suggested that a single criterion would be sufficient — a simple "quantitative measurement of the amount of variation from the *Textus Receptus*."[12] President Colwell had earlier published several methodological treatises on quantitative measurement (two with Ernest W. Tune),[13] and thus the Claremont staff prepared to test various MSS to determine their distance from the TR.

Claremont's answer to the minuscule problem arose, it seems to me, out of the confluence of these two procedures: (1) the search for the best representatives of known groups, with the accompanying identification of group-readings, and (2) the quantitative measurement of minuscules in terms of their distance from the TR. First, the three graduate students working with the Project investigated the various known groups under procedure one, with procedure two in the background. Paul McReynolds, a Graduate Assistant in the Project, had undertaken the study of the K groups of von Soden, and, by good fortune, was compiling information concurrently on all four K groups; since the collation-base for the Project is the TR (Oxford, 1873 edition), McReynolds placed in juxtaposition the information for the four groups as they were related to the TR, and this provided ready ground for the observation by Frederik Wisse, a graduate student who had volunteered a consider-

12. Letter of President Colwell to Members of the Executive Committee of the Project, dated 7 November 1966.
13. E.g., Colwell 1958, 1959; Colwell and Tune 1963, 1964.

able amount of time to the Project, that the group-readings, as determined for von Soden's groups and subgroups, revealed distinctive patterns in terms of their relationship to or distance from the TR. Wisse had himself worked extensively on several of the I groups, and he and McReynolds had observed that the older procedure of identifying distinctive readings for each group was helpful but, by itself, not adequate as a grouping methodology, for distinctive readings — where they existed at all — were generally few and far between for most groups, and any random sampling technique, even though the sample consisted of a long passage, was likely to be inconclusive. If, on the other hand, a group pattern of readings, not necessarily unique to but characteristic of each group, could now be determined from a selected sample passage consistently examined in numerous MSS, perhaps a usable method could be fashioned. Thus, they devised a series of test-readings in Luke 1, which took into account all of the variant readings of all of the uncials and some 180 minuscule MSS of Luke. To qualify as a test-reading, a variant from the TR had to have the support of a two-thirds majority of the members of some known group (i.e., some previously identified group, usually one of von Soden's). Admittedly, there is a certain arbitrariness in this method of selecting the test-readings; for one thing, the test-readings were taken from variants in perhaps only nine or ten percent of the total number of minuscules of the Gospels. Is it not possible, then, that some variation-units which would be significant for such a testing have been overlooked because they do not happen to occur in this small portion of MSS?

In reply, two things can be said: (1) First, the previous assessment of the holdings of the Project in terms of adequate representatives of all known groups gave assurance that the Master File of the Project contained a satisfactorily representative selection, at least insofar as the earlier methods could ascertain. (2) Second, the Byzantine MSS together form, after all, a rather closely knit group, and the variations in question within this entire large group are relatively minor in character. It is possible, of course, that some group-readings have been missed in the ten percent sampled; but the danger is nothing like that of selecting, say, ten percent of the papyri or of the uncials and basing a methodology of grouping on these selected few, for in that case it is probable that MSS like P[75] ℵ B D Θ or W might one or even all be overlooked. The minuscules, however, stand in a different situation; if von Soden is generally correct in his isolation of groups (as we have affirmed earlier), then the vast majority of minuscules are of the K^x and K^r type (which stand nearest to the TR), and the percentage of MSS in the I group and in the other K groups which are in the files of the Project is proportionately very, very much greater than for the vast K^x and K^r groups. This is added assurance that hardly any readings which stand at any considerable distance from the TR are likely to have been overlooked in the selection of test-readings. Subsequently, in fact, the actual investigation of MSS not already in the Master File demonstrated that very few new readings were uncovered by adding full collations of new MSS.

A further aspect of arbitrariness could be found in the fact that von Soden's groupings provided the general limits for the selection of test-readings: only those readings were retained which were supported by at least two-thirds of the MSS in our files which belonged to some identifiable group, and these identifiable groups were usually von Soden's; is it not possible, then, that additional or different groupings exist which will now be even further obscured? Again, it is possible but unlikely, in view of what has been said above, that such additional group-readings have been missed; nor does the use of previously identified groups as a base preclude the discovery, from these test-readings, of new groups or of new arrangements of groups, for the test-readings measure relative distance from the TR.[14] Thus, from the data which the test-readings provide, it should be possible to arrive at any actually existing pattern of groupings, for broadly representative test-readings, even though derived from previous groupings, do not predetermine the groups themselves. Furthermore, unlike many sampling procedures, the density of test-readings per sentence or verse is very high — so high that it is inconceivable that a group as yet unknown could exit without eventually silhouetting itself in an identifiable pattern against these test-readings.

Finally, in defense of the test-readings, it should be emphasized that the method about to be described is itself to some considerable extent self-sharpening and self-corrective, especially with reference to determining primary and secondary readings for specific groups; that is to say that, as more and more MSS are examined, the ever increasing data reveal that certain test-readings lose their status as primary readings for a given group and become secondary readings for that group (though remaining primary reading for other groups), or move from secondary readings to primary, or in another group may lose entirely their position as characteristic readings for that particular group.

McReynolds and Wisse found that in the first chapter of Luke, sixty-one variants qualified as test readings. The reading of each collated MS in the Project's files was then checked at these sixty-one places, and each agreement or disagreement was recorded on a tally sheet by a simple "X" mark, producing for each MS a pattern of its agreement and disagreement with these test-readings, and soon it was possible to plot a configuration or profile of the readings characteristic of each of the various groups which emerged. Some fourteen distinct groups finally appeared, each with a distinctive profile of readings.

It is important to emphasize that the profile method is based not on the determination of *distinctive* readings for each group, but upon the identification of *characteristic* readings for each group; that is, each group reveals a distinctive profile which is formed by the readings characteristic of but not necessarily distinctive to that group. Thus, some of the test-readings are shared by many or by nearly all groups, others by several or by two or three, and still others are found only in the MSS of a single group (and then are distinctive readings for that group), but it is the overall, distinctive *profile* or configuration emerging from the characteristic readings which is the genius of the method.

A method now had been born which appeared promising indeed, for if it could be validated it would mean that any given MS could be examined in a relatively small number of predetermined and systematically selected places, and its resulting textual profile — and therefore its textual character — could, in most cases, be al-

---

14. Any objection to the use of the TR as a standard in this process will not be well founded, for the same relative patterns should emerge regardless of the standard, although the use of something like Codex Vaticanus would unduly complicate matters, for the standard in this case would be unnecessarily remote from the text whose characteristics are being examined.

most instantly identified with that of an established group, or, if its profile did not match or show a close relationship to a known group, manageable data would be in hand for further group classification as the body of information expanded.

The developing method was carefully scrutinized by the full Claremont staff of the Project, namely, President Ernest C. Colwell, who is Chairman of the American Executive Committee of the Project, Mr. Alan Sparks, a graduate student and Administrative Assistant for the Claremont branch, Messrs. McReynolds and Wisse, and the present writer, as a member of the Committee on Straight-Text Greek Manuscripts and special consultant to the Project. It was the consensus of the group that not one chapter of Luke but three should be employed, so as to give the sampling procedure a broader base and also to allow to each MS a threefold verification of a group identification. In addition to Luke 1, chapters 10 and 20 were selected. Chapter 10 produced sixty-seven test-readings, while seventy-nine appeared in chapter 20, and profiles for each of the fourteen groups so far identified were constructed for each of the additional test chapters. It is sufficient here to say that the use of chapters 10 and 20 quite strikingly confirms the results reached on the basis of chapter 1; or, to put it differently, individual MSS, except where they contain block or boxcar mixture, quite consistently receive the same group designation in each of the three test chapters, and the same MSS quite consistently fall together into the same groups in each of the three chapters. In those cases where a MS conforms to one group in one chapter, but to some extent moves away from that group in another, the third test area is available as a deciding factor. It should be noted also that while some fourteen groups have clearly and decisively emerged, there still are some MSS which defy classification at this time. When sufficient instances have come to light and can be analyzed, it is to be hoped that some further group classifications will be feasible.

It has not been my intention to expose the details of this rather sophisticated profile method, for that privilege must be reserved for the two young scholars who developed the method, who did all the detailed and exacting work, and who endured the tedium of such an investigation. Rather, it has been my aim only to set down something of the broad background out of which the method arises, to place the method in its more immediate context of the IGNTP, to describe ever so briefly the instrument itself, and, finally now, to emphasize some facets of its immediate and practical usefulness as well as its more far-reaching significance.

First of all, it should be obvious enough that the Claremont profile method has important implications for and applications to the Project's proposed *apparatus criticus,* for it should now be possible to examine, in the space of perhaps two hours, any MS or microfilm of a MS containing Luke (and later of other portions of the NT[15]) and to determine with relative ease and considerable certainty its group identity. Hundreds of MSS can now be scanned, and the entire minuscule mass should

---

15. Appropriate series of test-readings will presumably be drawn up for Matthew, Mark, John, and eventually other sections of the NT as the Project moves to these areas. If the group designations resulting from the application of the method in Luke are generally borne out in, say, one test chapter in John, then perhaps only a rather limited further testing — such as a single chapter in each Gospel — will be necessary for the Gospels. The implicit assumption is that in most cases the results in Luke will be valid at least for the Gospels in any minuscule, but this is an assumption whose correctness needs to be demonstrated.

become amenable to a long-overdue sorting process. As a result, much of the log-jam of minuscules should break up, clearing the way not only for speedier completion of the proposed critical apparatus, but providing also a significantly less fortuitous selection of minuscules for that apparatus.

The method has other practical applications. For instance, the K^x and K^r types of MSS, which stand nearest to the TR, are doubtless already represented adequately in the files of the Project, and the profile method allows those who are searching for and microfilming additional MSS to use shortcuts in identifying these K^x and K^r MSS, which can then be passed by in favor of MSS which will be of greater immediate interest. Thus, it can be determined from the K^x and K^r profiles that if a MS has more than six of the test-readings in Luke 1, or more than ten in Luke 10, it is not K^x or K^r and should be microfilmed; or, if a MS lacks a specified test-reading in Luke 1, it should be microfilmed regardless of other readings, and so forth. On the other hand, if it should at any time be deemed a necessary or desirable task, the profile method will readily allow for determining the "best" K^x or K^r MSS and lends itself also to determining further inner groupings or finer distinctions within these groups (or any other).

But what of the more far-reaching significance? For one thing, the profile method has already called for certain adjustments, on solid grounds, in von Soden's classifications. The specific conclusions must await an official presentation of the method by its originators, but the following generalizations may be offered here: to date, two of von Soden's (minor) groups have been eliminated, since they reveal no distinctive pattern; also, one subgroup has disappeared because four-fifths of its members fall into other groups; the subgroups in another group were not sustained, for subgrouping was found to be superfluous within the closely knit larger, original group; and a number of individual MSS have been reclassified. On the other hand, many of von Soden's groupings and classifications have been strikingly confirmed, including designations of groups, subgroups, and individual MSS.

In broader terms, finally, it would appear that the Claremont profile method for grouping NT minuscule MSS may well mark the turning point in the study of this class of Greek witnesses to the NT text, for it offers, as has nothing previously, a consistent and systematic method for classifying minuscules and, in addition, recognizes the all-important methodological principle that both agreements and disagreements between MSS, as well as between groups, must be fully taken into account and measured. If the optimism expressed here needs to be tempered with caution, it should be understood, naturally, that the profile method requires further and final testing and possibly refinement, calls for detailed explication and defense, invites the provocation of every possible criticism, and in the end, of course, must stand the test of further scholarly judgment. Nevertheless, when the method's practical usefulness and immediate application are added to its wide-ranging and long-term methodological significance, any description other than "major breakthrough" would appear to be less than adequate.[16]

16. In the years following the completion of this journalistic report, McReynolds and Wisse published brief reports (Wisse and McReynolds 1970; McReynolds 1972, 1979) and Wisse published a full explication of the method (1982). Refinements and critiques of the "Claremont Profile Method" (now a well-established designation) include Richards 1977a: esp. 131-36, 207-9; 1977b, 1979, 1980; Ehrman 1986, 1987a: 468-71; 1987b: 40-44; 1989: 379-81.

CODEX SINAITICUS IN THE GOSPEL OF JOHN: A CONTRIBUTION TO METHODOLOGY IN ESTABLISHING TEXTUAL RELATIONSHIPS

Gordon D. Fee

In his important study on the origin of text-types, Ernest C. Colwell concludes with ten suggestions for further investigation and criticism. The ninth of these suggestions reads: "The textual history of the New Testament differs from corpus to corpus, and even from book to book; therefore the witnesses have to be regrouped in each new section" (1961: 138). A corollary to this suggestion is the fact that certain MSS also differ from book to book — and even within books — as to the type of text they represent. Codex W, which makes a distinct change from a Neutral[1] to a Byzantine type of text at Luke 5:12 and is Western in Mark 1:1–5:30, is an example of this kind of "divided" MS (see Sanders 1912). Therefore, in the latest manuals text-type groupings which both regroup from corpus to corpus and recognize the "divided" nature of certain MSS, appear as a matter of course (e.g., Metzger 1968a: 213-16; Greenlee 1964: 117-18).

With Colwell's suggestion in view, this study proposes to add another chapter to the already stormy career of Codex Sinaiticus (א), by re-examining the MS in the Fourth Gospel as to the possibility of its being "divided" rather than simply "mixed." Since one of the problems such an investigation faces is the use of an adequate methodology, this study also offers an analysis and proposal of method for establishing textual relationships.

I. The Problem of Codex Sinaiticus in John

The secondary character of א as a witness to the Neutral text-type, especially in the Gospel of John, has long been noted. Hort himself had observed (1881: 2.151):

> The Western readings are specially numerous in St John's Gospel, and in parts
> of St Luke's: they belong to an early and important type, though apparently not
> quite so early as the fundamental text of D, and some of them are the only
> Greek authority for Western readings which, previous to the discovery of א,
> had been known only from versions.

1. The terms Western, Neutral, and Byzantine will be used without quotations marks to refer to the three major text groups. It is to be understood that the terms always mean "so-called."

In his *Die Schriften des Neuen Testaments,* Hermann von Soden (1902-3) made a detailed study of the peculiarities of ℵ. His twelfth and final "peculiarity" was an analysis of ℵ D agreement, in which he concluded that there was little significant agreement between them in Matthew, Mark, and Luke. But for John the picture was different. Here he included a list — by no means complete[2] — where ℵ and D agreed against all other Greek witnesses. This analysis tended to strengthen Hort's observation about ℵ in John; but it was still considered to be a Neutral witness with a mixture of Western readings.

The Western elements in ℵ were also brought into prominence in the work of H. C. Hoskier (1914). But his primary concern lay in separating ℵ from B as a chief ally. He did note the frequent affinities of ℵ with the versions, but did little with its affinities with D. He therefore failed to provide anything constructive in view of these relationships.

Over the years the various manuals have consequently tended to qualify the association of ℵ and B by some such statement as: "The type of text witnessed by Sinaiticus belongs in general to the Alexandrian group, but it also has a definite strain of the Western type of readings."[3] But at all times ℵ has been considered to be basically Neutral, with Western readings.

In 1957, M.-E. Boismard offered a study of P66 in John 7–9, in which he indicated displeasure with the prevailing textual groupings. Among other suggestions, he maintained that in John 1–8 ℵ had closer textual affinities with D than with B. In fact he called one of his own textual groups S D (S for Sinaiticus).[4]

This proposal of Boismard has been virtually ignored by text critics. The reasons for this are not difficult to find. In the first place, he has found little or no following as to the main thesis of the paper, namely, that the scribe of P66 copied alternately, in sections of five verses to a half chapter, from an exemplar of one text-type and then from another. Second, there is probably a great deal of uneasiness about Boismard's methodology, since the second of his five newly proposed "text-types," whose principal witness is Tatian (!), has absolutely no Greek witnesses (the secondary witnesses are sys.c a b e georg, pers, aeth).[5]

Moreover, the details on which his conclusion about ℵ D rests are limited chiefly to the analysis of P66 in chapters 7 and 9 (although this indeed is quite

---

2. For example, in chapter 4 alone he includes but five occurrences and leaves out the following six: 4:11 om. οὖν; 4:14 δὲ πίνων l. ὃς δ᾽ ἂν πίῃ; 4:17 ἔχεις l. ἔχω; 4:27 add. αὐτῷ post εἶπεν; 4:38 ἀπέσταλκα l. ἀπέστειλα; 4:42 μαρτυρίαν l. λαλιάν.

3. Metzger 1968a: 46; cf. Gregory 1907: 337, and Greenlee 1964: 116.

4. One should note at this point how close Colwell came to this conclusion, before rejecting it, in samplings of variants in John 7 (see 1959: 766-67). His final conclusion that in terms of "gross statistics . . . S [ℵ] is closer to B than to D" in John 7 is worthy of note, inasmuch as this is both contrary to the conclusions of Boismard's coincident analysis, and was based on an insufficient methodological principle in an article whose main force was methodological. It should be further noted, however, that Colwell was using this as an illustration to warn against partial comparisons. The present paper, and Colwell himself, in collaboration with E. W. Tune in a later paper on method (1963), argue that there is also danger in "gross statistics," which frequently tend to distort actual textual affinities.

5. [See the longer critique of Boismard's methods and conclusion in Chapter 16 of the present volume.]

convincing). He does offer four important examples at the beginning of the paper to support his category S D, but they scarcely amount to full-scale justification, and could just as easily be fitted into a scheme which sees ℵ as Neutral with Western readings.

Codex Sinaiticus therefore needs to be re-examined in the Gospel of John in the light of Boismard's conclusion. If in fact ℵ is, in John 1–8, a Western MS with Neutral readings rather than *vice versa*, then this should be clearly spelled out; for such a conclusion may affect in no small measure what one may further say about textual relationships in the Gospel of John.

The problem now is how one is to conduct such an investigation with proper methodological principles.

II. The Problem of Methodology

The method used in the following analysis is not to be considered a new proposal; it is rather an attempt to carry out, and thereby further to refine, some methodological suggestions already made by E. C. Colwell and E. W. Tune (1963). But before outlining the steps of this method, a word is in order as to those concerns which led to its adoption.[6]

The single most important factor in establishing textual relationships of any kind is the determination of the criteria by which such relationships should be measured. Colwell (1959: 757) has suggested that ideally the only proper method is to compare a given MS completely with all other MSS. Until some refinement of computer analysis is available, however, one will have to settle for a partial method somewhere below the ideal. Nevertheless, by careful controls one should be able to derive results which would approximate those of the ideal.

Since the time of Lachmann the most common approach to textual relationships has been to count the number of "agreements in error" or "peculiar agreements" against an external standard. In the case of NT criticism this external standard has, until recent times, been the TR. The statistical data from this method usually took the form of "the total number of agreements in variation from the TR."

For some years, however, and with increasing frequency, the adequacy of a method using variations from an external standard has been called into question. In 1945 Bruce M. Metzger concluded his summary study of the Caesarean text by asking two important questions about method. First, "Is it licit to reconstruct the ancient 'Caesarean text' from ofttimes late documents merely by pooling the non-Byzantine variants?" Second, "Is it possible to analyze the textual complexion of a given document merely by utilizing all variants, large and small?"[7]

His first question raised the problem of the validity of analyses which failed to take total variation into account instead of some form of partial variation from an

---

6. For a more detailed examination of the history of method, see Hills 1949. The greater part of this paper deals with the history of method. Hills's divisions as to what constitutes differences of method seem open to question; and his conclusion in favor of sampling from variations from the TR stands directly opposite the position taken in this paper. For a more recent survey of this history, see Porter 1961: 98-104, and Metzger 1968a: 179-81.

7. 1945: 486, 488. This article now appears with some updating in 1963b, 42-72. The words enclosed in brackets in the succeeding quotations indicate the changes found in the later edition.

external standard. As he cogently observed: ". . . obviously it is of slight value in determining family relationship to know only that in a certain area a given manuscript agrees with, say, B and ℵ ten times in differing from the Textus Receptus. If B and ℵ should differ from the Textus Receptus in ninety [other] instances, the Neutral element in the given manuscript would be slight indeed" (488). This problem was also noted, and a more thorough procedure pleaded for, by Harold S. Murphy in his study of Eusebius's *Demonstratio Evangelica* (1954: 167-68).

Metzger's second question, and one which for the most part has been all too often neglected, urges discrimination as well as tabulation of variants. He noted that "the possibility of [mere] chance coincidence among manuscripts in agreeing in small variations (involving, *inter alia,* word order, common synonyms, the presence or absence of the article, the aorist for the imperfect or historical present) has not been sufficiently taken into account" (489). In a similar vein, Heinrich Zimmermann argued against K. Aland's tabulation of P66 that "die Lesarten wollen nicht nur gezählt, sondern auch gewogen werden."[8]

In spite of these objections, however, a count based on variations from an external standard has persisted. One may note, for example, the objections raised against Victor Martin's edition of P66 in 1956, where he used Souter's text as a basis for collation. Those who objected continued the same methodology; they merely substituted a modern TR (Nestle) for Souter (cf. Aland 1957).

The steps toward analyses of manuscript relationships on the basis of total variation rather than agreement in variation from an external standard have been forthcoming only in the past decade. An initial probe in this direction was attempted by Calvin L. Porter (1961). After a survey of various methods used or suggested in the past, he related of his own: "The method of analysis used here is based not upon the calculation of agreements between manuscripts, but upon the calculation of disagreements. The computation of disagreements takes into consideration the individuality of each MS involved" (104-5). His method simply consists of collating disagreements in all of the MSS chosen for analysis (in his case all Greek MSS of the Gospel of John through the fourth century), and tabulating the percentage of disagreement each has with all the rest.

It is to Porter's credit that he chose a method which compared each MS totally with the others; and as a preliminary step in indicating possible close relationships it may have permanent value. But as a total method it seems to suffer in at least three particulars.

1. One needs a surer guide to demonstrate *agreements* between MSS. Porter's analysis of Sinaiticus is particularly telling at this point; for ℵ has such an inordinate number of singular readings in John that it tended to have a similar and very high percentage of disagreements with all the early MSS. Whatever relationship it does have with these MSS, therefore, must be determined in the area of agreements.

Porter, to be sure, recognized this difficulty, but his analysis of agreements generally took the form of "the agreement of two against the rest." Whereas such tabulations are a valid part of looking at agreements, it would seem to be *only* a part.

8. 1958: 219. Aland's collation appeared as 1957: 161-84.

What is needed is a way of seeing the *percentage of agreements between all the MSS over a total area of variation*.

2. One's method must be flexible enough to have perspective for all manuscript traditions. The objection to Porter here stems from the limitations imposed by his choice of MSS. In the first place, there may be a fallacy in the basic assumption as to what constitutes the "earliest" MSS. He was correct in choosing those which actually date from the first four centuries. But he apparently did not consider the possibility that the text found in a later MS may itself date within the earlier period. The case in point, of course, is Codex Bezae. Without a doubt some of its text reflects a later tradition (e.g., where, as in John 4:42, it sides with A and the Byzantine tradition against the early Greeks and most of the OL); but for the most part its basic text has been long acknowledged to be much earlier than the date of the actual MS itself. This failure to reckon fully with the Western tradition could easily lead to partial conclusions, even about the relationship of the early witnesses to each other.

3. One's method needs to be able to see relationships in sections of a book, as well as over the whole book. This is the opposite of the error which Porter argued against. He correctly observed (19 n. 25) that manuscript relationships usually have been established by examining test sections, and that while this is helpful for clues or hypotheses, the more comprehensive efforts to check and establish findings are seldom forthcoming. On the other hand, statistics such as Porter's, which are based on an entire book, may overlook Colwell's principle noted above, that MSS must also be examined section by section within a given book.

One may therefore perhaps use with profit Porter's preliminary step of tabulating disagreements, but the total method must move in another direction. This direction has been pointed out by Colwell and Tune in their contribution to the Casey Festschrift (1963).

They establish as a basic premise that sound method should take into account the total amount of variation, not simply the variants from an external text used as a "norm." They further argue that one should exercise discrimination in regard to what is counted. What this means in terms of method is that singular readings are not included in the counting,[9] and that only those places of variation are counted where *at least two* of the MSS involved in the computation agree against the rest. This means, of course, that one must exercise care in the choice of MSS to be tabulated and in the extent of the text which is included.

After the units of variation in the given section are isolated, then the numbers of agreements involved between all the MSS at each unit of variation are tabulated. For convenience this count is finally put into percentages.

Basically, this is the procedure followed in the present analysis, with the following differences from Colwell and Tune:

1. In their explanation of "discrimination before counting," Colwell and Tune note that they have "eliminated readings which occur *commonly* in MSS as the

---

9. Their presentation of two tables (30-31), one showing percentages with singular readings included and the other without, is sufficient demonstration that they are correct in the exclusion of singulars from the tabulation.

result of scribal error or habit, even if supported by more than one MS, since such agreement was probable as coincidence" (26). While I agree to eliminate such items as spelling, I have, on the other hand, included all variations in the counting. The present study suggests that "weighing" may be done *after* counting. Such a process of weighing will look at the number and kinds of significant agreements which are involved in the count. This writer discovered that there was significant correlation between the percentage of total agreement between two MSS and the number of *significant readings* which were peculiar to the two against all the rest. Conversely, both the number and significance of peculiar agreement between two MSS which did not have a high percentage of agreement were negligible.

It was felt proper therefore, as a part of the total method, to analyze such items as peculiar agreements, and agreements with or against certain textual traditions, as well as the number and kinds of singular readings, in order to gain a full perspective of the relationships one is seeking.

2. The most significant difference between the present study and that of Colwell and Tune is in the choice of MSS to be tabulated. Their choice was based on an attempt to show relationships between text-types; therefore, they included the following broad cross-section of MSS: P45 P66 P75 ℵ A B D W Θ Ψ Ω CR 565 TR.

Since the present interest is more specifically that of determining the relationship of ℵ to other MSS, the choice for tabulation has been narrowed to P66 P75 ℵ A B C D W TR. It will be observed that this is simply a list of the major MSS up to the sixth century. Moreover, any singular agreement between the TR and only one of the others was not included in the number of variation-units counted.[10] Whereas this may not appear to go beyond my second criticism of Porter, it is believed that it does for the following reasons:

(a) A certain knowledge of MSS is already assumed. The close relationship of P75 and B has already been clearly demonstrated.[11] D is the well-known leader of a quite different type of text. And A has been recognized as being at the beginning of the process called the Byzantine text-type. The selection, therefore, includes at least the earliest witnesses of the major textual groupings, excluding Caesarean, whose text has never been defined in John.

(b) The addition of one or more later MSS increases the number of variation-units to be counted, but it *always* does so in favor of a higher percentage of agreement of all the earlier MSS with one another. Moreover, as a simple mathematical phenomenon, the percentage of increase is much higher at the lower end of the spectrum than at the higher. One may illustrate this from the findings of the following analysis (cf. the first table given below).

In chapter 4 of John, 61 variation-units were counted, based on the MSS chosen for this study. The inclusion of the other MSS of Colwell-Tune's analysis increased the number to 81. At 61 points of variation B and D agreed only 10 times,

---

10. The term "variation-unit" is defined by Colwell and Tune as "referring to a length of the text wherein our MSS present at least two variant forms; it is that passage in which differences occur" (1964: 254).

11. See especially Porter 1962: 363-76. Cf. my unpublished doctoral dissertation (1966: 192-222).

or 16.4 percent; the agreement of P[75] and B was 52, or 85.2 percent. These were the lowest and highest percentages of agreement between the MSS tabulated. The inclusion of Θ Ψ Ω C[R] 565 and TR increased the agreement between B and D to 27, or up to 33.3 percent. By the same token the agreement between P[75] and B was increased by 20 up to 72, or 88.8 percent. Among all the early MSS the slightest increase in agreement was between D and W; and their number of agreements was increased by 14.

It may be granted that 33 percent agreement is still low, and that the basic agreements are still reflected when the later MSS are added. But the point of view taken in this study is that the clearer picture among the earlier MSS is afforded by the present selection. The increased agreement when later MSS are added seems to indicate that there is a certain relationship which the early MSS have simply because they are early. This is probably significant when other relationships are being sought, but not for the relationship of the early MSS among themselves.

III. Codex Sinaiticus in John 4

When the suggested method is applied to the fourth chapter of the Gospel of John,[12] the following results are obtained:

1. The tabulation of the number of agreements in John 4 over 61 units of variation is found in Table 12.1 (see p. 228).[13]

It will be noted that the three highest sets of relationships are between P[75] and B, P[66c] and C, and A and TR. The significant thing for Codex ℵ is the much higher percentage of agreement it has with D than with any other MS. When D is used as a base, its highest percentage of agreement is also with ℵ. However, it should be noted further that ℵ has a consistently poor relationship with all other MSS. D, on the other hand, has a similar poor relationship with the others, except for A and TR.

Colwell and Tune suggest that "the quantitative definition of a text-type is a group of MSS that agree more than 70% of the time and is separated by a gap of about 10% from its neighbours" (1963: 29). With this definition, P[75] and B in John 4 clearly fit into the category of text-type, as do A and TR. D and ℵ do not fit the first percentage, but they do the second, that is, they have a 57 percent agreement, and for ℵ the next closest is 34 percent (P[66c]) and for D 44 percent (TR). This would mean that even if one may not classify ℵ D as a text-type, each has a significantly closer relationship to the other than to any other MS.

This relationship seems strong enough to classify ℵ as a basically Western text in John 4. A further look at the nature of its agreement with D strengthens the statistical analysis.

2. Of the 61 units of variation in John 4, 16 are the result of two of the

---

12. Chapter 4 was chosen as the test section for very practical reasons. It is the first chapter where D is complete, and one of the few chapters where C is complete. Moreover, P[75] begins to have considerable lacunae after this chapter. Whereas the chapter division is rather arbitrary, this chapter does include two independent pericopes, and perhaps a third, if one wishes to divide the "harvest sayings" from "the Samaritan woman."

13. The full collation of these 61 variation-units, as well as the singular readings in John 4, may be found as Appendix 1 in my unpublished dissertation (1966: 273-81).

TABLE 12.1

AGREEMENTS IN JOHN 4 WHERE AT LEAST TWO MSS (Not Including TR) AGREE AGAINST THE REST

	TR	p66*	p66c	p75	B	ℵ*	ℵc	A	C	D	W
TR	—	37/60.6	40/65.6	32/52.5	31/50.8	19/31.0	31/50.8	51/83.6	34/55.7	27/44.3	39/64.0
p66*	37/60.6	—	—	40/65.6	37/60.6	21/34.4	30/49.2	34/55.7	42/68.9	20/32.8	37/60.6
p66c	40/65.6	—	—	43/70.5	41/67.2	19/31.0	30/49.2	37/60.6	46/75.4	20/32.8	42/68.9
p75	32/52.5	40/65.6	43/70.5	—	52/85.2	19/31.0	28/45.7	36/59.0	42/68.9	12/19.7	34/55.7
B	31/50.8	37/60.6	41/67.2	52/85.2	—	20/32.8	29/47.5	38/62.3	43/70.5	10/16.4	37/60.6
ℵ*	19/31.0	21/34.4	19/31.0	19/31.0	20/32.8	—	—	17/27.9	20/32.8	35/57.4	17/27.9
ℵc	31/50.8	30/49.2	30/49.2	28/45.7	29/47.5	—	—	32/52.5	30/49.2	31/50.8	30/49.2
A	51/83.6	34/55.7	37/60.6	36/59.0	38/62.3	17/27.9	32/52.5	—	36/59.0	25/41.0	37/60.6
C	34/55.7	42/68.9	46/75.4	42/68.9	43/70.5	20/32.8	30/49.2	36/59.0	—	16/26.2	38/62.3
D	27/44.3	20/32.8	20/32.8	12/19.7	10/16.4	35/57.4	31/50.8	25/41.0	16/26.2	—	24/39.3
W	39/64.0	37/60.6	42/68.9	34/55.7	37/60.6	17/27.9	30/49.2	37/49.2	38/62.3	24/39.3	—

NOTE: The first figure represents the number of agreements at 61 units of variation. The second figure represents the percentage of agreement.

MSS agreeing almost alone against all other Greek MSS. There are two other places (4:42, 51) where the unit of variation is the result of two sets of two agreeing alone against all others. Thirteen of these 20 instances of singular agreement are between א and D, and in the majority of these they have OL support:

4:9   א* D a b e j om. οὐ γὰρ συγχρῶνται Ἰουδαῖοι Σαμαρίταις

4:11   א D 472 a b e ff² j l syᶜ om. οὖν post πόθεν

4:14   א* D ὁ δὲ πίνων l. ὃς δ' ἂν πίῃ

4:17   א D aur b c e ff² j l r¹ ἔχεις l. ἔχω

4:24   א* D* ff² om. αὐτόν

4:24   א* D a j r¹ προσκυνεῖν δεῖ l. δεῖ προσκυνεῖν

4:27   א* D bo ἐν τούτῳ l. ἐπὶ τούτῳ

4:27   א D 1093 a b ff² j r¹ syˢ·ᶜ add αὐτῷ post εἶπεν

4:38   א D ἀπέσταλκα l. ἀπέστειλα

4:42   א* D b l r¹ σὴν μαρτυρίαν l. σὴν λαλιάν

4:45   א* D ὡς l. ὅτε

4:51   א D ἤγγειλαν l. ἀπήγγειλαν (or omit)

4:51   א D b r¹ om. λέγοντες

A casual check of these agreements reveals that the majority are much more than merely coincidental scribal errors. One seems to be dealing here with a genuine textual tradition, supported by two major Greek MSS and often by the OL (especially a b j r¹).

The only other clear pairing off such as this in the remaining seven instances of singular agreement is between P⁷⁵ and B:

4:11   P⁷⁵ B syˢ om. ἡ γυνή

4:42   P⁷⁵ B τὴν λαλιάν σου l. τὴν σὴν λαλιάν

4:52   P⁷⁵ B ἐκείνην l. παρ' αὐτῶν

These, too, are clearly "related" readings, not simply the coincidence of scribal error. It is worthy of note at this point that P⁷⁵ has now eliminated what once were the three most significant singular readings of B in John 4.

The remaining four of the singular agreements are of the "scribal error" type and probably are not significant in demonstrating textual relationships (4:15 P⁶⁶* D διψήσω l. διψῶ; 4:23 P⁶⁶* א* 124ᶜ 254 αὐτῷ l. αὐτόν; 4:42 B W 80 b f r¹ syᶜ om. ὅτι; 4:54 א W a b ἐποίησεν σημεῖον l. σημεῖον ἐποίησεν). Besides these agreements there are the following instances where א and D are joined by a scattering of Greeks against all the rest:

4:1   Ἰησοῦς l. κύριος

4:14   add. ἐγώ ante δώσω

4:17   ἄνδρα οὐκ ἔχω l. οὐκ ἔχω ἄνδρα

4:25   ἀναγγέλλει l. ἀναγγελεῖ

4:46   ἦν δέ l. καὶ ἦν

4:51   om. αὐτοῦ post οἱ δοῦλοι

Except for 4:1 these are less significant than the former list, but they do point up the number of agreements ℵ and D have together against the Neutral tradition.

One other significant reading should be noted at this point. In 4:42 there are the following variants:

αὐτοὶ γὰρ ἀκηκόαμεν	P66 P75 A B C W Byz pl
αὐτοῦ γὰρ ἀκηκόαμεν	D a
αὐτοὶ γὰρ ἀκηκόαμεν παρ' αὐτοῦ	ℵ Π2 565 λ φ pc

While the readings of ℵ and D are not identical, they do seem to represent what one might call "an independent witness to a common textual tradition." It could be argued, of course, that D merely reflects a scribal error in terms of the reading of P66 et al. But since this same phenomenon occurs in the succeeding chapters of John, it is very likely that they are here related to a common textual tradition. If this be true, such "agreement" will be an important factor in one's considertion as to the homogeneity of this textual tradition.[14]

In contrast to these readings, one should also investigate the agreement of ℵ with the Neutral tradition against D. Such agreement appears to be negligible in this chapter of John. I note the following instances:

4:5   ℵ B P66 P75 add. τῷ ante Ἰωσήφ

4:15   ℵ* B P66 P75 διέρχωμαι (-ομαι) l. ἔρχωμαι (-ομαι)

4:21   ℵ B P66 P75 C* L W pc b j l q sa πίστευέ μοι γύναι l. γύναι πίστευέ μοι (A Byz read πίστευσόν).

4:25   ℵ B P66 P75 C* W 053 565 λ ἅπαντα l. πάντα

4:39   ℵ B P75 C* L bo b e ff2 l q r1 ἅ l. ὅσα

4:42   ℵ B P66 P75 C* W 083 aur a b c ff2 l r1 vg om. ὁ χριστός

4:51   ℵ B P66* P75 A C W παῖς αὐτοῦ l. υἱός σου (TR παῖς σου)

4:53   ℵ* B P75 C 053 0125 λ itpl om. ἐν ante ἐκείνη

4:53   ℵ B P66 P75 A C L pc aur a b c ff2 vg om. ὅτι

Something further should be said about this list. First, only two of these (4:42, 51) are significant readings, in the sense of indicating possible close textual relationships. Second, in each of these instances except 4:51 the reading of D is also supported by the entire Byzantine tradition and the TR. Moreover, in these remaining eight, where its Greek text may be determined, the more important MSS of the OL version also support the so-called Neutral reading.

What this seems to suggest, therefore, is not so much that ℵ is joining the Neutral tradition, as that D is here conforming to the Byzantine. The fact that there are similar readings where ℵ and D read with the Neutral tradition against most of

14. Another reading of a similar nature, but less important, is at 4:33, where the majority of MSS read οὖν after ἔλεγον. Here ℵ* (as the only Greek MS) sides with d (against D) e syc in omitting the conjunction. D, on the other hand, reads δέ with a b q r1. One wonders whether D, by adding the "wrong" conjunction, is witnessing to a "Western" tradition which originally omitted it. The fact that it is only a conjunction, where most MSS tend to be quite independent, lessens the strength of such a suggestion.

the later MSS (4:46 om. ὁ Ἰησοῦς; 4:47 om. αὐτόν; 4:50 om. καί or δέ) would seem also to point to such a conclusion. Here, then, we have instances of "early" against "late" readings, rather than Western against Neutral; and ℵ has the "early" reading, while D has the "late."

It is true that in this chapter there are two places in which ℵ fails to join D in what has been called a Western reading (4:3 add γῆν; 4:49 om. μου); but what one is to classify as Western in this section of John now becomes a problem. For example, what does one call the omission of οὕτως in 4:6, where neither ℵ nor D joins a aur b e ff² j l r¹, supported by λ 69 124 565 788 pc?

What this all seems to say is that ℵ and D are definitely related, but that the textual tradition to which they belong lacks the homogeneity that is found in the tradition of P⁷⁵ B (or that ℵ or D, or both, have suffered conformation to another textual tradition). This is further demonstrated when one investigates the singular readings of our chief MSS in this chapter.

3. The one other point at which ℵ and D show marked similarity, though not exact agreement, is the number of singular readings each has. In chapter 4 of John there are the following number of singular (or nearly singular) readings as far as Greek MSS are concerned:

P⁶⁶	5
P⁷⁵	6
B	2
ℵ	25 (12 have OL or OS support)
A	1
C	3
D	21 (12 have OL or OS support)
W	16 (5 have OL or OS support)

What is significant here is the number of readings where ℵ and D are the only Greek witnesses to read with the Old Latin or Old Syriac MSS.

This does not say too much in terms of direct relatedness, but it would seem to indicate that ℵ and D both are members of an uncontrolled textual tradition and are under the same influence as, or have been influenced by, the older versions. Moreover, if one has been accustomed to speaking of D and OL agreement as Western, one perhaps should be prepared to do the same with ℵ and OL agreement, at least in John 4.

It would seem clear, therefore, that on the basis of counting and of weighing variants, one must agree with Boismard that, in this chapter of John at least, ℵ is a Western text. The problem now is, what is the extent of ℵ as a Western text in John?

IV. Codex Sinaiticus in John 1–9

A chapter-by-chapter application of our method over the remainder of the first nine chapters of John indicates that a similar relationship between ℵ and D exists through chapter 8. At chapter 9 the picture alters completely. The graphic demonstration of this is found in Tables 12.2 and 3.

Table 12.2 (see p. 233) shows the percentage of agreement over chapters 1–8 at 320 points of variation. Because D has a large lacuna at 1:16–3:26, no statistics are included from this section (the significance of א for this section will be suggested below). It will be noted that the percentage of total agreement between א and D is somewhat lower than in chapter 4. But it is also true that its percentage of agreement with B is likewise considerably lower. The reasons for this are that in chapter 5 א temporarily lacks its close relationship with D (dropping to 37.8 percent at 45 units of variation), whereas א happens to be closer to B in chapter 4 than in any other of the first eight chapters (dropping to 21.4 percent in chapters 6 and 7 at 150 units of variation). Over the entire section א has a *28 percent higher agreement with D than with B.*

Table 12.3 (see p. 234) shows the percentage of agreement in chapter 9 at 51 units of variation. There is no doubt that here א is once again basically in the Neutral tradition. A chapter-by-chapter analysis for the remainder of John reveals that א stays in the Neutral tradition throughout, in the sense that it is more closely related to the Neutral witnesses than to D.[15] To be sure, it still has some Western readings, but they are now the exception rather than the rule. What is important, however, is that א is never as closely related to B as is P[75], and often it is not as closely related to P[75] B as is C or L. For the most part its departure from P[75] B is less in the direction of D than in that of those witnesses which compose the Byzantine tradition.[16]

John 1–3

In this section D has a large lacuna, but on each side of that lacuna א and D are clearly related. In 1:1-16, at nine points of variation, there are the following numbers of agreement.

	TR	P66	P75	B	א*	אc	A	C	D	W
TR	—	7	7	5	1	6	8	7	2	6
P66	7	—	7	5	3	6	6	7	5	4
P75	7	7	—	7	1	6	8	7	3	4
B	5	5	7	—	1	5	6	7	2	2
א*	1	3	1	1	—	—	0	2	7	2
אc	6	6	5	5	—	—	5	8	4	4
A	8	6	8	6	0	5	—	6	2	5
C	7	7	7	7	2	8	6	—	3	4
D	2	5	3	2	7	4	2	3	—	3
W	6	4	4	2	2	4	5	4	3	—

15. See, e.g., the statistics for John 9 in Colwell and Tune 1963:31.

16. In chap. 8, e.g., א has a 41.4 percent relationship with B, 43.2 percent with D, 48.3 percent with TR, and 51.7 percent with A. Almost all of its readings are also shared by A and the Byzantine tradition. C, on the other hand, has a 72.5 percent relationship with B and a 43.1 percent with A; and L has a 69 percent relationship with B and a 41 percent with A.

TABLE 12.2

PERCENTAGE OF AGREEMENTS IN JOHN 1–8, BASED ON 320 VARIATION-UNITS, WHERE AT LEAST TWO MSS (Not Including TR) AGREE AGAINST THE REST

	TR	𝔓66*	𝔓66c	𝔓75	B	ℵ*	ℵc	A	C	D	W
TR	—	50.9	56.3	56.5	52.5	35.0	51.6	80.1	63.8	37.5	58.4
𝔓66*	50.9	—	—	51.1	54.3	43.7	48.5	54.0	55.6	35.8	46.7
𝔓66c	56.3	—	—	58.2	58.7	43.0	52.2	58.3	61.9	34.8	51.5
𝔓75	56.5	51.1	58.2	—	81.0	25.5	42.1	56.2	72.8	22.9	58.5
B	52.5	54.3	58.7	81.0	—	26.6	41.6	57.6	68.7	22.2	60.3
ℵ*	35.0	43.7	43.0	25.5	26.6	—	—	25.5	36.2	54.1	31.3
ℵc	51.6	48.5	52.2	42.1	41.6	—	—	57.3	53.1	46.6	42.2
A	80.1	54.0	58.3	56.2	57.6	25.5	57.3	—	58.9	38.3	52.0
C	63.8	55.6	61.9	72.8	68.7	36.2	53.1	58.9	—	30.0	60.0
D	37.5	35.8	34.8	22.9	22.2	54.1	46.6	38.3	30.0	—	34.4
W	58.4	46.7	51.5	58.5	60.3	31.3	42.2	52.0	60.0	34.4	—

TABLE 12.3

PERCENTAGE OF AGREEMENTS IN JOHN 9, BASED ON 51 VARIATION-UNITS, WHERE AT LEAST TWO MSS (Not Including TR) AGREE AGAINST THE REST

	TR	$\mathfrak{p}^{66*}$	$\mathfrak{p}^{66c}$	$\mathfrak{p}^{75}$	B	ℵ*	ℵᶜ	A	D	W
TR	—	35.3	39.2	47.1	45.1	33.3	52.9	82.4	47.1	52.9
$\mathfrak{p}^{66*}$	35.3	—	—	51.0	49.0	45.1	54.9	45.1	35.3	29.4
$\mathfrak{p}^{66c}$	39.2	—	—	49.0	51.0	49.0	58.8	47.1	35.3	33.3
$\mathfrak{p}^{75}$	47.1	51.0	49.0	—	78.4	62.7	56.9	45.1	25.2	66.7
B	45.1	49.0	51.0	78.4	—	62.7	66.7	41.2	31.4	58.8
ℵ*	33.3	45.1	49.0	62.7	62.7	—	—	31.4	35.3	58.8
ℵᶜ	52.9	54.9	58.8	56.9	66.7	—	—	47.1	41.2	54.9
A	82.4	45.1	47.1	45.1	41.2	31.4	47.1	—	35.3	45.1
D	47.1	35.3	35.3	25.5	31.4	35.3	41.2	35.3	—	37.3
W	52.9	29.4	33.3	66.7	58.8	58.8	54.9	45.1	37.3	—

In 3:26-36, at seven points of variation, there are these agreements (C reads at only one place and is not included):

	TR	P⁶⁶	P⁷⁵	B	ℵ*	ℵᶜ	A	D	W
TR	—	4	2	4	2	3	7	3	5
P⁶⁶	4	—	5	6	1	2	4	1	5
P⁷⁵	2	5	—	4	3	2	2	1	3
B	4	6	4	—	1	2	4	1	5
ℵ*	2	1	3	1	—	—	2	4	2
ℵᶜ	2	1	3	1	—	—	3	3	3
A	7	4	2	4	2	2	—	3	5
D	3	1	1	1	4	3	3	—	3
W	5	5	3	5	2	2	5	3	—

This indicates that on both sides of the lacuna, ℵ is the closest companion to D, and *vice versa*. The extent and nature of singular agreement against all other Greek witnesses over these 16 units of variation is similar to that of chapter 4.

> 1:4   ℵ D it syᶜ·ᵖ ἐστίν l. ἦν
> 1:13 ℵD om. ἐκ²
> 1:15 ℵ* D b om. λέγων
> 3:31 ℵ* D a b j l q ὁ δὲ ὢν l. ὁ ὢν

Besides these are four other significant variants where ℵ and D are joined by a few Greek witnesses against all the rest.

> 1:3   ℵ* D P⁶⁶ λ 71 οὐδέν l. οὐδὲ ἕν
> 1:6   ℵ* D* W add. ἦν ante ὄνομα
> 3:31 ℵ* D P⁷⁵ λ 565 a b e f ff² l r¹ syᶜ sa om. ἐπάνω πάντων ἐστίν
> 3:32 ℵ D λ 22 28 565 pc a b e ff² j l r¹ syˢ·ᶜ om. τοῦτο

At only one point (3:34 om. ὁ θεός) in these sections does ℵ join what appears to be the strictly Neutral tradition against D. And again ℵ is joined by the strength of the OL (b e f l), while D reads with A and the entire Byzantine tradition.

One should be prepared, therefore, to regard ℵ as the leading Greek witness to the Western tradition in the section 1:16–3:26, where D is lacking. The following readings seem to be significant in this regard:

> 1:18 ℵ a δ om. ὁ ὢν
> 1:20 ℵ e l sa om. καὶ ὡμολόγησεν
> 1:21 ℵ W a b e ff² l r¹ add. πάλιν post αὐτόν
> 1:25 ℵ a e syᶜ om. καὶ ἠρώτησαν αὐτόν
> 1:28 ℵ P⁶⁶ a b e r¹ ἐγένετο ἐν Βηθανίᾳ l. ἐν Βηθανίᾳ ἐγένετο
> 1:28 ℵ syᶜ add. ποταμοῦ post Ἰορδάνου

1:32   ℵ a b e r¹ sy^s.c ὡς περιστερὰν καταβαῖνον l. καταβαῖνον ὡς περιστεράν

1:32   ℵ* e om. λέγων

1:32   ℵ W b e q r¹ μένον l. ἔμεινεν

1:34   ℵ* 77 218 b e ff² sy^s.c (a sa) ὁ ἐκλεκτός l. ὁ υἱός

1:47   ℵ 124 aur a b ff² l r¹ ἰδών . . . καὶ l. εἶδεν

1:47   ℵ* a τοῦ Ναθαναήλ l. αὐτοῦ

2:3   ℵ* a b ff² j r¹ (e l sy^hmg) οἶνον οὐκ εἶχον ὅτι συνετελέσθη ὁ οἶνος τοῦ γάμου· εἶτα l. ὑστερήσαντος οἴνου

2:6   ℵ* 13 346 a e r¹ arm om. κείμεναι

2:11   ℵ* (P⁶⁶* f q) add. πρώτην post Γαλιλαίας (P⁶⁶* f q ante ἀρχήν)

2:12   ℵ 245 249 440 1010 aur a b e ff² l cop^ach2 om. καὶ οἱ μαθηταὶ αὐτοῦ

2:14   ℵ a f q καὶ τὰ πρόβατα καὶ βόας l. βόας καὶ πρόβατα

2:15   ℵ* a b e ff² j l q r¹ ἐποίησεν . . . καὶ l. καὶ ποιήσας

2:15   ℵ* a e l q om. τε

3:1   ℵ* aur b c f ff² l vg ὀνόματι l. ὄνομα αὐτῷ

3:5   ℵ* pc e τῶν οὐρανῶν l. τοῦ θεοῦ

3:8   ℵ aur a b e ff² r¹ sy^s.c add. τοῦ ὕδατος καὶ ante τοῦ πνεύματος

The full extent of this witness is lessened somewhat when one considers that ℵ lacks at least one important Western reading in this section (3:6 add. ὅτι ἐκ τῆς σαρκὸς ἐγεννήθη and ὅτι ἐκ τοῦ πνεύματός ἐστιν), and that it joins the Neutral tradition without Western support in three significant readings (1:18 θεός l. υἱός; 3:13 om. ὁ ὢν ἐν τῷ οὐρανῷ; 3:16 om. αὐτοῦ). But the nature of many of the readings in the above list indicates that ℵ is basically a member of the Western tradition, so much so that perhaps its agreements with B just noted should be considered Western support for these readings.

John 5–8

The percentage of agreement for ℵ and D in this section is as follows:

| | Chapter 5 | | Chapter 6 | | Chapter 7 | | Chapter 8 | |
	ℵ*	D	ℵ*	D	ℵ*	D	ℵ*	D
TR	31.1	40.0	35.2	34.1	30.6	33.9	54.2	39.6
P⁶⁶*	35.6	20.0	52.5	36.1	61.3	45.2	35.4	41.7
P⁶⁶c	35.6	20.0	50.8	34.4	58.9	40.3	41.7	43.8
P⁷⁵	30.2	16.3	29.9	26.0	19.7	13.1	35.4	33.3
B	28.9	15.5	23.9	25.0	17.8	20.9	37.5	33.3
ℵ*	—	37.8	—	51.1	—	58.1	—	58.3
ℵc	—	33.3	—	44.3	—	51.6	—	52.1
A	17.8	44.4	29.0	32.3	lac.	lac.	lac.	lac.
C	lac.	lac.	28.9	34.2	lac.	lac.	46.7	30.0
D	37.8	—	51.1	—	58.1	—	58.3	—
W	35.6	33.3	31.6	29.5	19.4	33.9	41.7	37.5

As indicated above, the relationship between ℵ and D is less in chapter 5 than elsewhere in John 1–8. However, a glance at the above percentages shows that the decrease in ℵ D agreement is not in favor of agreement with another MS or textual tradition. The percentage of agreement between ℵ and the others remains much the same, and it continues to agree more with D than with others, though not by as much.

An examination of the variants in this chapter indicates that many of the phenomena noted in chapter 4 are found here as well, but not in such quantity. D and ℵ have only four singular agreements:

> 5:13 ℵ* D* ἔνευσεν l. ἐξένευσεν
> 5:18 ℵ D 053 a b e f l om. οὖν
> 5:19 ℵ D a b l ποιεῖ ὁμοίως l. ὁμοίως ποιεῖ
> 5:32 ℵ* D aur a e q syᶜ οἴδατε l. οἶδα

Besides these there are two other readings where ℵ and D reflect a common textual tradition.

5:2. The name of the pool where the impotent man was healed has three basic variations, with some spelling difference within the three:

> Βηθζαθά   ℵ 33 b l ff²
> Βελζεθά   D a r¹
> Βηζαθά   L e
>
> Βηθεσδά   A C Byz pler f q TR
> Βησθεσδά   N
>
> Βηθσαϊδά   P⁷⁵ B W 0125 aur c vg bo
> βηδσαϊδά   P⁶⁶ sa

This is a case of "triple variation," where there is a clear Western, Neutral, and Byzantine tradition.

5:9. After the καί which begins the second clause, ℵ a b e syˢ add ἠγέρθη καί and D λ φ ff² add the participle ἐγερθείς. Again, one has agreement in witness without identical readings.

On the other hand, there are only two readings where ℵ joins the Neutral tradition against D, and without the support of the early versions:

> 5:12 P⁶⁶ P⁷⁵ B ℵ C* L sa om. τὸν κράβατόν σου
> 5:17 P⁷⁵ B ℵ W 1241 om. Ἰησοῦς

Clearly, therefore, ℵ is not leaving its relationship with D in favor of the Neutral tradition. The real cause of this lessened relationship appears to lie in three factors: (1) It will be noted that in this chapter alone, of the first eight chapters of John, D is closer to another MS (A) than to ℵ. D appears to have been influenced more by the Byzantine tradition in this chapter than elsewhere, and this accounts in part for the decrease in its relationship to ℵ. (2) ℵ is simply less Western here than elsewhere. D, for example, reads almost alone with the OL at the following significant places:

5:3   add. παραλυτικῶν post ξηρῶν
5:9   om. ἐν ἐκείνῃ τῇ ἡμέρᾳ
5:13 ἀσθενῶν l. ἰαθείς
5:20 ἀγαπᾷ l. φιλεῖ
5:20 δείκνυσιν l. δείξει
5:37 μαρτυρεῖ l. μεμαρτύρηκεν

א, on the other hand, has only one significant reading of this type (v. 25 א* a b om. καὶ νῦν ἐστιν). (3) A look at the 45 variation-units in this chapter reveals that the majority are of the "less significant" type (word order, add/omit the article, conjunctions, pronouns, etc.). Moreover, within these less significant variants there is a greater mixture of agreement among the early witnesses than one finds at those places which appear to be more significant.

It has seemed to the purpose of this study to find reasons for the decrease in א D agreement in John 5, because it is immediately clear that in chapters 6 and 7 one has again a relationship similar to that found in chapters 1–4. The statistics alone seem strong enough to demonstrate this;[17] an examination of select readings confirms it.

In the following list of variants, א and D have singular agreement, or are joined by a very few Greek witnesses against all the rest. It will be noted that many of the readings (e.g., 6:11, 17, 19) clearly indicate textual relatedness, not simply the result of coincidental scribal errors.

6:3   א* D 124 565 pc aur a ff[2] l ἀπῆλθεν l. ἀνῆλθεν
6:3   א* D P[66] φ 63 71 ἐκαθέζετο l. ἐκάθητο
6:5   א D P[66]* Θ aur a b c f ff[2] l r[1] vg ὄχλος πολύς l. πολὺς ὄχλος
6:7   א* D 1424 ἀποκρίνεται l. ἀπεκρίθη
6:11 א D a b e q r[1] sy[c.p] εὐχαρίστησεν καὶ ἔδωκεν l. εὐχαριστήσας διέδωκεν
6:14 א D Θ M aur a b ff[2] l r[1] εἰς τὸν κόσμον ἐρχόμενος l. ἐρχόμενος εἰς τὸν κόσμον
6:17 א D κατέλαβεν δὲ αὐτοὺς ἡ σκοτία l. καὶ σκοτία ἤδη ἐγεγόνει
6:17 (א) D 80 a sy[pal] (ὁ) Ἰησοῦς πρὸς αὐτούς l. πρὸς αὐτοὺς ὁ Ἰησοῦς
6:19 א* D 106 1321 2145 (= latt) στάδια l. σταδίους
6:22 א D P[28] 42 b c ff[2] r[1] vg εἶδεν l. εἶδον (or ἰδών)
6:22 א D φ a sy[c] τοῦ Ἰησοῦ l. αὐτοῦ (or omit)
6:27 א D e ff[2] j sy[c] δίδωσιν ὑμῖν l. ὑμῖν δώσει (φ pc a b f l q r[1] δώσει ὑμῖν)
6:33 א D Θ add. ὁ post ἄρτος
6:37 א* D 280 (a e) b sy[s.c] om. ἔξω

---

17. The sudden increase in agreement between P[66] and א is the result of a change in P[66], not א.

6:46 ℵ* D a b e r¹ θεόν l. πατέρα

6:64 ℵ D 1604 a b e q r¹ ἐξ ὑμῶν εἰσίν τινες l. εἰσὶν ἐξ ὑμῶν τινες

6:66 ℵ D P⁶⁶ Θ φ pc aur b c f ff² j l r¹ add. οὖν post τούτου

6:71 ℵ* D K λ om. τόν ante Ἰούδαν

7:1 ℵ* D P⁶⁶ pc aur a b c e f ff² l r¹ sy^s.c om. καί

7:3 ℵ* D Θ G U λ pc it vg om. σου

7:6 ℵ* D W 047 106 1200 e sy^c.p om. οὖν

7:8 ℵ D K M Π pc aur a b c e ff² vg sy^c bo οὐκ l. οὔπω

7:10 ℵ D pc a b e r¹ sy^s.c om. ὡς

7:12 ℵ D P⁶⁶ 33 it vg sy^c τῷ ὄχλῳ l. τοῖς ὄχλοις

7:17 ℵ D P⁶⁶ om. τοῦ

7:26 ℵ D 49 108 aur a b e f q r¹ vg sy^c.p μήτι l. μήποτε

7:29 ℵ D P⁶⁶ 131 ἀπέσταλκεν l. ἀπέστειλεν

7:31 ℵ D P⁶⁶ πολλοὶ δὲ ἐπίστευσαν ἐκ τοῦ ὄχλου l. ἐκ τοῦ ὄχλου δὲ
πολλοὶ ἐπίστευσαν (Byz TR πολλοὶ δὲ ἐκ τοῦ ὄχλου ἐπίστευσαν)

7:31 ℵ D Θ φ a c e ff² vg sy^c.p ποιεῖ l. ἐποίησεν

7:32 ℵ D P⁶⁶ pc c e add. δέ post ἤκουσαν

7:32 ℵ D P⁶⁶ ὑπηρέτας οἱ φαρισαῖοι καὶ οἱ ἀρχιερεῖς l. οἱ ἀρχιερεῖς καὶ
οἱ φαρισαῖοι ὑπηρέτας

7:35 ℵ D 249 aur a b c e ff² l r¹ vg sy^s.c om. ἡμεῖς

7:37 ℵ D P⁶⁶*vid Θ λ 69 pc it vg ἔκραζεν l. ἔκραξεν

7:37 ℵ* D P⁶⁶* b e om. πρός με

7:46 ℵ* D P⁶⁶* οὕτως ἄνθρωπος ἐλάλησεν l. ἐλάλησεν οὕτως ἄνθρωπος
(Byz TR οὕτως ἐλάλησεν ἄνθρωπος)

7:47 ℵ D λ 33 pc a c e ff² sa om. οὖν

7:48 ℵ D πιστεύει l. ἐπίστευσεν

The full extent of this relatedness is further reflected in the small amount of agreement ℵ has with the more strictly Neutral tradition against D. I note the following:

6:10 P⁷⁵ B ℵ L N a sy^c om. δέ or οὖν post εἶπεν

6:47 P⁶⁶ P⁷⁵ B ℵ C L T W j om. εἰς ἐμέ post πιστεύων

6:58 P⁶⁶ P⁷⁵ B ℵ C L T W bo om. ὑμῶν post πατέρες

7:20 P⁶⁶ P⁷⁵ B ℵ L T W X 33 213 1241 om. καὶ εἶπεν

7:49 P⁶⁶ P⁷⁵ B ℵ T W λ 33 ἐπάρατοι l. ἐπικατάρατοι

Again, as in chapter 4, all of the data point to a relatedness within an uncontrolled, or nonhomogeneous, textual tradition. Besides the fact that in chapter 6, where ℵ and D have so many significant unique agreements, they have only a 51% total agreement, there are three other important factors which point to "relatedness within an uncontrolled tradition."

1. There are at least five instances in chapter 6 where ℵ and D reflect the same textual tradition, but not with identical readings:

6:1. D Θ 249 2145 b e j r¹ add εἰς τὰ μέρη after Γαλιλαίας, reflecting a textual tradition which placed the feeding of the five thousand on the western side of the lake, near the city of Tiberias. This same tradition, though not read by ℵ in verse 1, is picked up in 6:23 only by ℵ. In place of τοῦ τόπου, it reads οὔσης, which results in a reading: "Other boats came from Tiberias, *which was near* where they ate. . . ."[18]

6:23. ℵ and D alone read a genitive absolute for the indicative of the rest of the MSS.

ἐπελθόντων οὖν τῶν πλοίων	ℵ
ἄλλων πλοιαρίων ἐλθόντων	D } = b j r¹ syᶜ
ἄλλα (δὲ) ἦλθεν πλοῖα (-άρια)	Pler

6:25. ℵ D and 28 alone of the Greeks change γέγονας to a form of ἔρχομαι (ℵ 28 ἦλθες; D ἐλήλυθας). It is possible for this to be coincidental; but the difficulty among the versions in rendering γέγονας here without resorting to the verb "to come" seems to indicate that ℵ and D are a part of this tradition. This looks strongly like versional influence on the Greek here.

6:61.	ἔγνω οὖν . . . καί	ℵ* (Θ) φ
	ὡς οὖν ἔγνω	D
	εἰδὼς δέ	Rell
	ἰδὼν δέ	C

6:71. The "surname" of Judas has the following variations:

Ἰσκαριώτου	P⁶⁶ P⁷⁵ B C G L W Ψ 33 892 1241 pc sa
Ἰσκαριώτην	Byz pler TR
Σκαριώθ	D aur a b ff² r¹
ἀπὸ Καρυώτου	ℵ* Θ φ syʰᵐᵍ

There is no textual relatedness between ℵ and D at this point, where Codex Bezae apparently is under the influence of the Latin spelling. But ℵ* Θ φ indicate that the name is not a surname but a town from which Judas came, as in "Philip of Bethsaida." What is significant is that ℵ here appears to reflect a Western tradition; for in the four other occurrences of this name in the Fourth Gospel (12:14; 13:2, 26; 14:22) D alone (joined by e at 13:2) reads ἀπὸ Καρυώτου. Since it is argued in this paper that ℵ is no longer Western somewhere after 8:38, it seems clear that it is reflecting the Western tradition here, a tradition reflected by D in every other occurrence of the name in the Gospel.

2. The number of instances in which each is the only Greek witness (or nearly so) to read with the OL or OS remains at a very high level. ℵ has 18 in chapter 6, and 8 in chapter 7; D has 19 in chapter 6, and 6 in chapter 7. Many of these are quite significant readings (e.g., 6:15 ℵ aur a c ff² j l vg syᶜ φεύγει l.

---

18. This is one of the readings selected by Boismard (1957: 369) to substantiate his ℵ D text-type.

ἀνεχώρησεν; 6:24 D b ff² l r¹ ἔλαβον ἑαυτοῖς πλοιάρια l. ἐνέβησαν (καὶ) αὐτοὶ εἰς τὰ πλοιάρια).

3. The witness of P⁶⁶ in these chapters also seems significant at this point. Through chapter 5, there are only four places where P⁶⁶ might be considered to be picking up a Western reading (1:3 οὐδέν l. οὐδὲ ἕν; 1:28 ἐγένετο ἐν Βηθανίᾳ l. ἐν Βηθανίᾳ ἐγένετο; 2:11 add. πρώτην; 4:1 Ἰησοῦς [P⁶⁶*ᵛⁱᵈ] l. κύριος).¹⁹ In chapters 6 and 7 there is a sudden increase in this strain (see 6:3, 5, 66; 7:1, 12, 17, 29, 31, 32, 37, 37, 46). What is significant for the Western text here is that along with these there is also a sudden increase in the number of instances where P⁶⁶ reads alone, or almost alone, with either ℵ or D. In chapters 6–7 there are fourteen such agreements with ℵ, and nine with D.²⁰ The fact that such agreement should increase at the very point where its number of Western readings also increases, seems strongly to suggest that the textual tradition to which P⁶⁶ is here witnessing lacks homogeneity.

The importance of noting this lack of homogeneity in the Western tradition is that one must broaden one's perspective for finding this tradition in John. Although D is undoubtedly its leading representative, it is not necessarily a "pure" representative. If the long addition by D a ff² in 6:56 is Western, so also is the φεύγει of ℵ aur a c ff² j l vg syᶜ in 6:15. Moreover, singular agreements between ℵ and P⁶⁶ (e.g., 6:64 ἦν ὁ μέλλων αὐτὸν παραδιδόναι l. ἐστιν ὁ παραδώσων αὐτόν; cf. a e q) probably also represent this tradition — at least in these two chapters.

The End of the Western Text in ℵ

As noted above, there is no question that in chapter 9 ℵ is no longer a witness to the Western tradition (except perhaps at infrequent readings). This is demonstrated not only by the statistics of agreements (Table 12.3), but also by its sudden lack of singular agreements with D. There are but three in chapter 9:

9:19 ℵ* D syᵖ add. εἰ ante οὗτος
9:35 ℵ* D syˢ·ᵖ add. καὶ ante ἤκουσεν
9:40 ℵ* D 63 253 aur b c e f ff² l r¹ syˢ bo om. ταῦτα

P⁶⁶, by way of contrast, has six such readings with D, and only one with ℵ, where it is also joined by W (9:9 om. ὅτι). Moreover, there is a sudden *decrease* in singular readings in ℵ (10, with only two having OL support); at the same time there is a like *increase* of such readings in D (35, with 15 having OL support).

But since this analysis has been using the rather arbitrary device of chapter

19. The reading of ὁ Ἰησοῦς for P⁶⁶* in 4:1 is not self-evident; it is not so noted in the *editio princeps,* nor in the the articles calling attention to corrections missed in the edition (see Boismard 1963: 120-33; Aland 1957-76: 10.62-64; and Fee 1965: 66-72). But the correction seems quite certain. One may observe how unlike every other kappa on this page is the kappa of the κ̅ς̅. (Note also the kappa in the κ̅ε̅ on the following page in 4:11.) Moreover, the downstroke of what is now a kappa is identical to the iota of the ι̅ς̅ directly beneath it.
20. P⁶⁶ ℵ 6:7, 58, 64, 64; 7:3, 13, 23, 28, 30, 32, 39, 45, 46, 50. P⁶⁶ D 6:10, 40, 53, 56, 62; 7:12, 14, 35, 42.

divisions, the question remains as to whether one can locate the exact place where ℵ drops its close relationship with D. In spite of the continued high percentage of agreement between ℵ and D in chapter 8, there are indications that the break takes place within this chapter. The following considerations seem to point to some place after verse 38 as this point of departure.

There are six places of singular, or nearly singular, agreement in the chapter, but they all occur between verses 12 and 28:

8:16 ℵ* D sys.c om. πατήρ
8:19 ℵ (D) pc b add. καὶ εἶπεν post Ἰησοῦς
8:24 ℵ D φ e om. μοι
8:25 ℵ D pc εἶπεν οὖν l. καὶ εἶπεν or εἶπεν
8:27 ℵ D 64 aur c e ff² l add. τὸν θεόν post ἔλεγεν
8:28 ℵ D 28 106 add. πάλιν

Beyond this point there are a number of instances where ℵ and D agree with the Byzantine tradition against most of the early MSS. The last significant place where this occurs is in verse 38, where it happens three times.

ℵ D Byz it	μου
P⁶⁶ P⁷⁵ B C L W X Ψ 070 1	omit
ℵ* D P⁶⁶ N Byz it vg	ἑωράκατε
P⁷⁵ B C L K W X Θ φ λ 33 pc f bo	ἠκούσατε
ℵ D C N Byz it vg	ὑμῶν
P⁶⁶ P⁷⁵ B L W Ψ 070	omit

Finally, D has twenty-three singular readings in this chapter, nine of which have OL and/or OS support; however, seven of these latter occur after verse 38. ℵ, on the other hand, has fifteen singular readings, with two having OL support; but none of the latter and only two of the former occur after verse 38.

This evidence, coupled with that of chapter 9, suggests that even though one may not have certainty as to the exact point, the end of ℵ as a Western witness in John is around 8:39.

There is one further factor which points to the conclusion that ℵ is a Western text in John 1:1–8:38, and that is the nature of the corrections of ℵ. Without regard to which, or how many, correctors are involved, the direction of the corrections is quite significant.

It will be noted from the various tables presented above that the correctors in chapters 1–8 *always decrease* the amount of agreement between ℵ and D, while at the same time they *always increase* — and substantially so — the agreement between ℵ and every other MS. On the other hand, in chapter 9 the correctors increase the agreement with D as well.

This clearly indicates that the first hand of ℵ in chapters 1–8 is closely related to D and that the direction of correction is almost always away from D rather than toward it.

V. Conclusions

From the evidence presented above, the following conclusions about textual relationships are singled out because of their significance for future study.

1. Although it was not the major emphasis of the paper, the statistics alone confirm the very important conclusion of Porter, that the Neutral text-type existed in a relatively pure form in P^{75} at least by AD 200. Not only do P^{75} and B have a consistently high relationship to each other, but it is also consistently higher than any other two MSS have with each other (including A and TR). To speak of P^{75} as a "mixed" text would seem to press the definition of that term beyond recognizable limitations (as, e.g., Metzger 1968a: 155).

2. Codex Sinaiticus is a leading Greek representative of the Western textual tradition in John 1:1–8:38. The evaluation of its witness at any point of variation in this section of John should have this conclusion in view. Moreover, any further study of textual relationships in John, in which א is a part of the consideration, should also proceed with this conclusion in view.

3. Perhaps the most important thing about the Western character of א in John 1–8 is that it points up the lack of homogeneity which exists within this tradition. The facts here presented seem to indicate that there is an uncontrolled tradition to which certain MSS bear common witness, but that this tradition is not fully represented by any single MS or combination of MSS in the way in which P^{75} and B represent the Neutral.

PART V

PAPYRI AND TEXT-CRITICAL METHOD

CHAPTER 13

P75, P66, AND ORIGEN: THE MYTH OF EARLY TEXTUAL RECENSION IN ALEXANDRIA

Gordon D. Fee

The dilemma of contemporary NT textual criticism relates directly to the labors of Westcott and Hort (WH). On the one hand, there has been an open disavowal — one might call it debunking — of WH's methodology and textual theory, while at the same time critical texts since WH have generally continued to have a clearly "Hortian" face. In fact, the recent United Bible Societies' *Greek New Testament* (UBS3), which was produced by the so-called eclectic method, has moved even closer to WH than other subsequent critical texts.

Although it is often suggested that the debunking of WH stems from the failure of their genealogical method, that is scarcely true. As E. C. Colwell has pointed out,[1] and as anyone can see for oneself by a careful reading of Hort's *Introduction*, Hort used genealogy only to be rid of the Byzantine MSS. Once genealogy had led him back to the second century, to the texts represented in the great uncials B and D, Hort frankly admitted that "the genealogical method ceases to be applicable, and a comparison of the intrinsic general character of the two texts becomes the only resource" (1881: 2.42).

At this point Hort's theory of textual transmission became the crucial factor, and this is the real cause of subsequent unrest. Although he apparently was open to the possibility that both of his two ancient texts might have suffered corruption, his analysis of the texts of B and D led him to conclude differently. He therefore argued, on the basis of "the internal evidence of readings,"

> where then one of the documents is found habitually to contain these morally certain or at least strongly preferred readings, and the other habitually to contain their rejected rivals, we can have no doubt that the text of the first has been transmitted in comparative purity, and that the text of the second has suffered comparatively large corruption. (32)

His conclusion that B thus represented a "neutral" text, that is, a text that had been transmitted in "comparative purity," is well known:

---

1. 1968: 141-42 [158]. All of Colwell's articles cited in this paper may now be found in *Studies* (1969); however, they will be cited here according to their original publication, followed by the corresponding page numbers from *Studies* in brackets.

> It will be evident . . . that B must be regarded as having preserved not only a very ancient text, but a very pure line of very ancient text, and that with comparatively small depravation either by scattered ancient corruptions otherwise attested or by individualism of the scribe himself. (250-51)

On the basis of such a textual theory, Hort applied his own kind of rational eclecticism to the recovery of the original NT text. First, "where the two ultimate witnesses agree, the text will be as certain as the extant documents can make it" (41); and second, where these disagree, one should generally follow B, for "the superiority of [B] must be as great in the variations in which Internal Evidence of Readings has furnished no decisive criterion as in those which have enabled us to form a comparative appreciation of the two texts" (32). Thus the only places where the WH text did not correspond to B were (1) where B had obvious scribal errors, (2) where B had occasionally picked up a corruption also attested in other ancient witnesses, and (3) in those few instances where the other text, D, had the better of it on the basis of the internal evidence of readings, most notably in the so-called Western noninterpolations.

It was this appraisal of the "neutral," that is, "unmixed," quality of their Neutral text-type which was to be the most disturbing factor in their theory. In contrast to their judgment of B, one of the "assured results" of subsequent criticism was that Hort's Neutral (= Egyptian) text-type, rather than representing a text transmitted in comparative purity, was itself a scholarly recension created in Alexandria in the last third/early fourth century. In 1954, K. W. Clark went so far as to call this "the most influential factor in recent criticism" (1954: 37).

Such a recension associated with the name of Hesychius had been proposed as early as the eighteenth century,[2] but it was first taken seriously when advocated by W. Bousset (1894: 74-110). The leading cause for the acceptance of the theory during this century was the papyrus discoveries, up to and including the discovery of P^{66} in 1956. All of these discoveries showed a much more fluid and "mixed" state of textual transmission than Hort had proposed. In fact, the mixture was of such a nature that none of the fourth-century text-types was found in these MSS in a "pure" state. This led to such expressions as "pre-recensional" and "proto-Alexandrian."

Typical of this "new" attitude elicited from the papyri were Kenyon's remarks in the *Introduction* to his edition of the Chester Beatty Papryi:

> This much . . . may be said without hesitation. On the one hand, it [the Chester Beatty discovery] is not an out-and-out supporter of the 'Neutral' or Vatican type of text; but neither is it, on the other hand, an out-and-out supporter of the 'Western' type. . . . For the moment it must suffice to point out that the occurrence of this type of text in a manuscript from Egypt contemporaneous with, or at least not much later than, Origen . . . points, perhaps decisively, to the conclusion that the Vatican MS does not represent a text of original purity dominant in Egypt throughout the second and third centuries; . . . and that the Vatican text represents the result, not of continuous unaltered tradition, but of skilled scholarship working on the best available authorities. (1933b: 16)

---

2. See the excellent survey in Martini 1966: 1-41.

Along with the papyrus finds, plausible hypotheses of the recensional process in Alexandria were also forthcoming. In his article in the Lagrange Festschrift, Kenyon proposed:

> During the second and third centuries, a great variety of readings came into existence throughout the Christian world. In some quarters, considerable license was shown in dealing with the sacred text; in others, more respect was shown to the tradition. In Egypt this variety of texts existed, as elsewhere; but Egypt (and especially Alexandria) was a country with a strong tradition of scholarship and with a knowledge of textual criticism. Here, therefore, a relatively faithful tradition was preserved. About the beginning of the fourth century, a scholar may well have set himself to compare the best accessible representatives of this tradition, and so have produced a text of which B is an early descendant. (1940: 250)

Kenyon suggested further that the homogeneous character of B throughout the NT also pointed to "scholarly recension." Since the books of the NT originally traveled as individual units and then probably in various corpuses, these units and corpuses quite naturally have different textual histories. In the Gospels, for example, Mark has the largest amount of variation per page of text, while John has the least. Moreover, the Western text exhibited in D has much greater variation in Luke-Acts than it does in Mark or John. Kenyon therefore concluded that the character of B, which is so homogeneous throughout the NT, implies "the exercise of editorial selection" across the various textual histories, as well as the internal editing of the various texts (1949: 208).

Whereas such a recension was usually thought to be the work of one hand, Günther Zuntz proposed that it might be the result of a long process. His reconstruction of this process is worth noting in full:

> Its beginnings were inconspicuous, and roughly 150 years passed before it culminated in the 'Euthalian' edition. Prior to this final achievement, the Alexandrian correctors strove, in ever repeated efforts, to keep the text current in their sphere free from the many faults that had infected it in the previous period and which tended to crop up again even after they had been obelized. These labours must time and again have been checked by persecutions and the confiscation of Christian books, and counteracted by the continuing currency of manuscripts of the older type. None the less they resulted in the emergence of a type of text (as distinct from a definite edition) which served as a norm for the correctors in provincial Egyptian scriptoria. The final result was the survival of a text far superior to that of the second century, even though the revisers, being fallible humans rejected some of its correct readings and introduced some faults of their own. (1953: 271-72)

Zuntz, however, was candid to observe that "even so, it must be admitted that no direct evidence attests the philological endeavours which we have inferred" (272). He finally rested his argument on the acknowledged philological skill of Origen and on Clement's apparently intimate acquaintance with grammatical terminology. He concludes that "the Greek grammatical tradition and technique was among the pagan achievements by which Alexandria enriched the Christian tradition" (273).

Perhaps the most significant part of Zuntz's hypothesis is his answer to the question as to *how* the Alexandrian copyists achieved the high quality of their texts. Against Lietzmann, who had suggested that it was the result of expert collation and editing of "wilder" texts, Zuntz correctly observed that such a process could only result in the "emergence of an average text of that very type." Rather, he maintained, "this indeed is the essential fact: somehow the Alexandrian collators must have been enabled to use manuscripts superior to those current in the second century" (274).[3] The preservation of such texts as these, Zuntz further noted, "bespeaks the conscious appreciation of the original wording as a value *per se*. . . . This is not the attitude of the believer or the theologian as such: it requires at least a touch of the philological mind" (275).

It should be noted here that these hypotheses add a considerable dimension of ambiguity to the term "recension." Whereas the term ordinarily means "the text created according to specific principles, for use in one segment of the church,"[4] and thereby implies a revision of the text, for Zuntz at least — and for Kenyon as well — the Egyptian "recension" was not so much a revising of the text as it was the producing of a text very much in accord with modern textual criticism. That is, this editor

> would be a trained scholar, whose guiding principle would be accuracy, not edification, who would be thinking of the author rather than of the reader. He would be careful to consult the oldest manuscripts accessible to him, and would compare their variant readings in the light of critical science, considering which was most likely to give the author's original words. He would tend to omit superfluities or insufficiently attested words or passages, and to prefer the more difficult reading to the easier, as more likely to have been altered. (Kenyon 1949: 248-49).

Thus the term "recension" may mean a "revision," implying both the creation of variants and the selection of similar readings where variation already exists, or it may mean an "edition," implying not emendation of the text but selection from good and bad manuscripts and/or good and bad readings.

But whether as a "revision" or an "edition," the recensional nature of B has become a byword in NT textual criticism. The recent text-critical handbooks[5] and NT introductions,[6] as well as articles on "trends"[7] and on text-types,[8] are almost unanimous in their concurrence with Kenyon's conclusion that the Egyptian text "is

---

3. It should be noted that by the text "current in the second century" Zuntz basically means the ancestors of the Western tradition.

4. This is the definition used by Porter 1962: 364. It appears to be a translation of Duplacy's translation (1959: 33) of Sacchi 1956: 35.

5. E.g., Taylor 1961: 54; Greenlee 1964: 86-87; Metzger 1968a: 215-16.

6. Most recently in Kümmel 1966: 384.

7. E.g., Clark 1954:37; Aland 1959: 730.

8. Colwell 1961: 137 [47-49].

now generally regarded as a text produced in Egypt and probably at Alexandria under editorial care" (1949: 208).

Hence our dilemma, for as long as our critical texts continue to look very much like a text that is generally acknowledged to be edited, we seem merely to be "pursuing the retreating mirage of the 'original text.'"[9] To be sure, some critics such as Kenyon have not been distressed. Kenyon candidly admitted with regard to Hort's Neutral text-type: "Even if it is an edited text, it may be a well-edited text; and in the case of all ancient literature a well-edited text is the best we can hope for" (1949: 210). Understandably, most textual critics have not been able to accommodate themselves so easily to this state of affairs. In 1947 E. C. Colwell wrote, "No patching will preserve the theory of Westcott and Hort. . . . A new theory and method is needed. . . . Our dilemma seems to be that we know too much to believe the old; we do not yet know enough to create the new" (133 [83]). Seven years later, in a "where we are now" article, K. W. Clark similarly spoke of the currently reigning eclectic method as "secondary and tentative" and incapable by itself to "create a text to displace Westcott-Hort and its offspring. . . . By its very nature," he added, "it belongs to a day like ours in which we know only that the traditional theory of text is faulty but cannot yet see clearly to correct the fault" (1954: 37). In a similar article, K. Aland declared it "alarming" that after seventy-five years we are still in the era of WH (1959: 721-22), and more recently likened this situation to crossing the Atlantic in a ship constructed in 1881 (1965: 346).

I

The publication in 1961 of P[75], a late-second/early-third-century MS containing substantial portions of Luke and John, has put this whole question into a new perspective. The studies by C. L. Porter of its text of John (1961, 1962) and by C. M. Martini (1966) of its text of Luke, where Martini was especially pursuing the question of the recensional character of B, have demonstrated such a close relationship between this papyrus and B that there is no longer any possibility that B reflects a late-third/early-fourth-century recension in *any* sense of that term. My own work on the quantitative method of establishing textual relationships[10] has completely verified and more carefully defined Porter's conclusions about the text of John. The following application of the method to the text of Luke 10 further substantiates the conclusions of Martini.

In order to get as broad a spectrum of textual relationships as possible, I collated the following MSS, choosing at least three from each of the already known text-types: P[45] P[75] ℵ A B C D E G L W Θ Ψ Ω 1 13 33 579 1241 b e TR. There are 105 variation-units in Luke 10 where at least two of these agree against the rest. Since there are occasional lacunae in some of the MSS and since Greek variants which are not translatable must also be treated as lacunae in the versions, the number of agreements has been translated into percentages. The results may be found in Table 13.1.

9. The words are from Clark 1966: 15.
10. 1968b; 1968a: 23-44 [See now Chapter 12].

TABLE 13.1

PERCENTAGES OF AGREEMENTS IN LUKE 10 AT 105 VARIATION-UNITS WHERE ANY 2 OF THE CONTROL MSS AGREE AGAINST THE REST

	P45	P75	ℵ	A	B	C	D	E	G	L	W	Θ	Ξ	Ω	1	13	33	579	1241	b	e	TR
P45	—	69	61	44	63	45	54	47	47	60	44	42	65	47	51	53	53	49	64	59	40	51
P75	69	—	72	44	94	59	39	46	47	70	42	47	66	44	52	47	65	66	67	46	41	46
ℵ	61	72	—	50	74	63	49	52	52	78	50	56	72	51	60	54	68	69	73	35	33	53
A	44	44	50	—	42	57	32	89	89	54	80	78	55	89	60	81	70	56	58	41	40	86
B	63	94	74	42	—	57	41	44	45	74	40	45	75	42	52	46	66	75	65	48	40	42
C	45	59	63	57	57	—	44	80	83	70	78	72	69	75	66	73	74	66	63	47	40	78
D	54	39	49	32	41	44	—	36	36	44	35	40	50	34	42	43	40	37	52	57	67	36
E	47	46	52	89	44	80	36	—	98	55	88	83	57	91	67	84	74	56	64	49	40	95
G	47	47	52	89	45	83	36	98	—	55	88	81	60	91	67	80	71	57	65	49	38	93
L	60	70	78	54	74	70	44	55	55	—	52	58	95	53	64	58	80	76	72	51	43	53
W	44	42	50	80	40	78	35	88	88	52	—	78	56	84	63	77	67	54	61	47	35	84
Θ	42	47	56	78	45	72	40	83	81	58	78	—	60	79	63	83	72	56	64	46	35	82
Ξ	65	66	72	55	75	69	50	57	60	95	56	60	—	55	66	56	85	76	74	53	43	56
Ω	47	44	51	89	42	75	34	91	91	53	84	79	55	—	62	80	68	55	62	43	37	93
1	51	52	60	60	52	66	42	67	67	64	63	63	67	62	—	64	71	56	67	58	50	67
13	53	47	54	81	46	73	43	84	80	58	77	83	56	80	64	—	70	56	67	41	37	81
33	53	65	68	70	66	74	40	74	71	80	67	72	85	68	71	70	—	70	74	49	44	70
579	49	66	69	56	75	66	37	56	57	76	54	56	76	54	56	56	70	—	61	46	43	54
1241	64	67	73	58	65	63	52	64	65	72	61	64	74	62	67	67	74	61	—	57	44	66
b	59	46	35	41	48	47	57	49	49	51	47	46	52	43	58	41	49	46	57	—	51	40
e	40	41	33	40	40	40	67	40	38	43	35	35	43	37	50	37	44	43	44	51	—	33
TR	51	46	53	86	42	78	36	95	93	53	84	82	56	93	67	81	70	54	66	40	33	—

NOTE: P45 has text at 73 variants; P75 at 104; ℵ at 104; Ξ at 94; b at 81; e at 82.

Although these percentages are evidence enough of the very close relationship between P[75] and B, the following observations indicate the full extent of that relationship.

1. There are only twelve disagreements between P[75] and B in this chapter, six of which are singular (or nearly so) to P[75] or B:

10:19 B add την post δυναμιν
10:24 P[75] U 998 sy[c] om. γαρ
10:27 B* H om. σου post θεον
10:31 B 1 579 om. εν ante τη οδω
10:37 B* om. ο ante Ιησους
10:39 P[75] om. του

There is one further reading where each has a nearly singular reading against the rest:

10:18	P[75] 472	ως αστραπην πεσοντα εκ του ουρανου
	B 254 579	εκ του ουρανου ως αστραπην πεσοντα
	א A C D W rell	ως αστραπην εκ του ουρανου πεσοντα

It will be observed that these variants are basically textual trivia, of the scribal error variety, not the stuff of genetic relationships.

There are five other disagreements between them where each has a reading supported by one or more of the early MSS:

10:39	P[45] P[75] א L Ξ 579	και
	B* A C W Byz TR	η και
	D	η
10:39	P[45] P[75] A W Byz b TR	Ιησου
	B* א D L Ξ 579 892 it[pl] bo sy[c]	κυριου
10:40	P[45] P[75] א D Byz TR	κατελιπεν
	B A C L Ψ pm	κατελειπεν
10:42	P[45] P[75] A C W Byz TR	ενος δε εστιν χρεια
	B	ολιγων δε χρεια εστιν η ενος
	א[c] L 1 33 579	ολιγων δε εστιν χρεια η ενος
	א*	ολιγων δε εστιν η ενος
	38 sy[pal]	ολιγων δε εστιν χρεια
10:42	P[45vid] P[75] A C W Byz TR	απ' αυτης
	א* B D L 579	αυτης

Of these variants only the first one in 10:42 is textually significant,[11] and at this point B et al. seem to preserve the reading of the text-type. B also preserves

---

11. 10:39 Ιησου/Κυριου may be so, but each is abbreviated in the MSS to ΙΣ and ΚΣ, which makes it an easy place for error.

the Egyptian text at 10:39 (κυριου) and 10:42 (om. απ), while P[75] preserves the text-type reading at 10:39 (om. η). It may be of interest to note further that P[75] and B read together without any variation whatever for the first eighteen verses, covering two distinct pericopes, and that the five nonsingular disagreements all occur in a single pericope.

In order to indicate how minimal the amount of disagreement between P[75] and B actually is, a comparison of the disagreements in Luke 10 between some of the MSS in Family 1 may be noted. According to Kirsopp Lake, the closest textual relationship in this family exists between Codices 118 and 209. The relationship is such that Lake could argue: "Either 118 209 have common archetype X, or 118 is a copy of 209" (1902: xxiii). The next level of relationship in this family is between 1 and 209. In chapter 10 of Luke, 118 and 209 have eight disagreements, none of which is a singular reading to either codex, and 1 and 209 have fourteen disagreements. This means that in terms of disagreements, P[75] and B in Luke 10 are within the same range of relationship as exists within the "inner circle" of Family 1.

2. The closeness of this relationship is further demonstrated by the agreements between P[75] and B. There are four variants where P[75] and B are the only uncials to support one of the readings:

10:1	P[75] B 579 700 713 e	απεστειλεν
	ℵ A C D L N W Θ rell	απεστειλεν αυτους
10:6	P[75] B 433 1012 it[pl] Or	εχει η
	ℵ A C L W Byz c e sy	η εχει
	1604 pc TR	μεν η εχει
	Θ	η
10:21	P[75] B aur vg	τω πνευματι τω αγιω
	ℵ D Ξ 1241 a b l	εν τω πνευματι τω αγιω
	C K Π 1	τω πνευματι τω αγιω ο Ιησους
	L X 33 c e ff[2] r[1]	ο Ιησους εν τω πνευματι τω αγιω
	Θ 579	ο Ιησους τω πνευματι τω αγιω
	N φ	ο Ιησους τω πνευματι
	A W Byz TR	τω πνευματι ο Ιησους
	P[45]	εν τω πνευματι
10:27	P[75] B	καρδιας σου
	ℵ A C D L W rell	καρδιας σου και

There are six other variants where P[75] and B are joined by only one or two of the Egyptian uncials:

10:5	P[75] B ℵ 1241 e	εισελθητε οικιαν πρωτον
	A W Θ Byz sy[s] bo TR	οικιαν εισερχεσθε πρωτον
	D a	εισελθητε πρωτον οικιαν
	C L X Ξ λ aur c f vg	οικιαν εισελθητε πρωτον

10:6	P75 B ℵ* 579	επαναπαησεται
	rell	επαναπαυσεται
10:15	P75 B L 0115 157 726 1375 bo	του αδου
	rell	αδου
10:24	P75 B 0124 sa	ακουσαι μου
	rell	ακουσαι
10:27	P75 B Ξ 0124 472	καρδιας
	ℵ A C W Θ Byz aur e f vg	της καρδιας
	D a b c ff² i l q r¹	τη καρδια
10:30	P75 B ℵ* C* sy^{c.p}	υπολαβων
	rell	υπολαβων δε

and four others where they are supported by D or P45 (with very little other support) against the rest:

10:2	P75 B D 0180 700 e	εργατας εκβαλη
	rell	εκβαλη εργατας
10:15	P75 B D 579 sy^{s.c}	καταβηση
	rell	καταβιβασθηση
10:35	P45 P75 B sa	εδωκεν δυο δηναρια
	D c e	δηναρια δυο εδωκεν
	rell	δυο δηναρια εδωκεν
10:38	P45 P75 B sa	omit
	P3 ℵ* C 579	εις την οικιαν
	L Ξ 33	εις την οικιαν αυτης
	A D W Θ Ψ Byz it vg TR	εις τον οικον αυτης

They further agree in eleven Egyptian readings against D and the Byzantine MSS (10:3 om. εγω; 10:19 δεδωκα l. διδωμι; 10:20 εγγεγραπται l. εγραφη; 10:21 ευδοκια εγενετο l. εγενετο ευδοκια; 10:25 om. και 2⁰; 10:32 . . . ελθων l. γενομενος . . . [P45 D] or γενομενος . . . ελθων [A C W Byz TR]; 10:36 om. ουν; 10:38 om. εγενετο; 10:39 προς l. παρα; 10:39 παρακαθεσθεισα l. παρακαθισασα; 10:41 κυριος l. Ιησους), as well as two others where D joins the Egyptian MSS against ℵ and the rest (10:1 [10:17] add δυο; 10:35 om. αυτω).

Although matters of orthography are ordinarily omitted from any quantitative method of establishing manuscript relationships, it may be noted in conclusion that P75 and B agree with very few others at four such places in this chapter:

10:7	P75 B D 579	εσθοντες
	rell	εσθιοντες
10:13	P75 B A D 579 a	Βηδσαιδα
	C L R X Ξ Byz TR	Βηθσαιδα
	P45 ℵ E U W	Βηθσαιδαν

10:35	P45 P75 B	εαν
	rell	αν
10:42	P3 P75 B 1 579	μαριαμ
	rell	μαρια

It remains only to be stated that a similar analysis for the rest of Luke has shown that this same relationship is maintained throughout.

The verdict is clear. The discovery of P75 now makes it certain that *the text of B existed in the second century across two separate textual histories both in its main features and in most of its particulars.* If the Egyptian text-type is a recension in either sense of that term, it is *not* a recension of the late third/early fourth century. P75 has forever laid to rest the "Hesychian hypothesis."

However, the discovery of P75 has not solved the problem of the recensional nature of the Egyptian text-type. It has, as E. J. Epp noted recently (1974: 393 [now Chap. 5]), simply pushed the problem back into the second century. In other words, the question must now be asked whether this text-type is recensional at all. If so, there are only two alternatives. Either it was a recension *created* in the second century (= a revised text), or else it was the *culmination of a process* (= Zuntz's "Euthalian" edition), but a process which had very little time to develop.

The question to which this study is addressed is whether historical probability favors either of these two alternatives, or whether it favors a third — viz., that Hort was basically correct, that the Egyptian text-type is a *carefully preserved* tradition (= careful copying) and not a recension at all. To answer this question a new look at P75 is required. This paper proposes a methodology for such a study. But before that, the texts of Origen and P66, in a negative way, offer answers as to the probability of the presence in second-century Alexandria of the kind of recensional activity necessary to have *created* the text of P75 B.

II

It has been frequently posited, as noted above, chiefly because of his well-known mastery of the philological tradition, that Origen was the philological mind behind the production of the Egyptian recension (= edition) in the church of Alexandria. Dean Burgon, in fact, accused Origen of being the culprit who created the Egyptian text (= revision).

There are several converging factors, however, which demonstrate quite decisively that Origen not only did not create this text, but also did not have the kind of concern for the NT text that would make him representative of the "philological mind" necessary for such a recension.

1. As I have shown elsewhere (1971a), Origen's text of John is a primary witness to the Egyptian text-type (along with P75 B and P66 C). Since both P66 and P75 antedate Origen, he could not have created this text. Furthermore, Origen's citations of the Gospel of John are not affected by his move to Caesarea in 231. This means, in all probability, that he carried such a text with him when he moved. This indeed might indicate his preference for this text as over against others.

The same is *not* true, however, of his citations of Mark. As Lake, Blake, and New have conclusively shown (1928), Origen's text of Mark, as it is reflected in the citations in his *Commentary on John,* underwent a decided change *away from the Egyptian text-type* at Book X. This indicates that, even though Origen tended to cite his current NT text with remarkable precision,[12] he did not seem to care especially whether that text was "pure" or not. That is, for some NT books Origen changed texts and for others he did not. But his was not a question of a search for the original wording per se; it was simply a matter of geography and convenience.

2. Even more significant are the results of the studies of Frank Pack and Bruce M. Metzger as to Origen's general attitude toward textual variation in the NT. Pack's dissertation (1948), entitled "The Methodology of Origen as a Textual Critic in Arriving at the Text of the New Testament," analyzed two kinds of evidence: (1) places where Origen specifically commented on variant readings, and (2) multiple variants within Origen's own citations. His conclusion is most remarkable: Although Origen was aware of variation, offered suggested causes for variation, and even at times engaged in cautious correction of his copies, his "handling of the text closely parallels the work done by later editors and textual workers in shaping the stylized Byzantine text." Pack adds, "The process that ended with the Byzantine text-type finds its beginnings in Origen's methodology, for it was a process of 'correction' of the knowledge, use and conflation of different textual traditions, and the handling of the text with the interests of teaching and preaching in mind" (346-47).

Metzger (1963a) has recently analyzed the "Explicit References in the Works of Origen to Variant Readings in New Testament Manuscripts." His conclusions are important to the argument of this study:

> He was an acute observer of textual phenomena but was quite uncritical in his evaluation of their significance. In the majority of cases he was content merely to make the observation that certain other copies present a different reading, without indicating his preference for one or the other variant. This tantalizing nonchalance is so unlike his careful procedure in dealing with the Greek text of the Old Testament that some special explanation must be sought. . . . *On the whole his treatment of variant readings is most unsatisfactory from the standpoint of modern textual criticism.* He combines a remarkable indifference to what are now regarded as important aspects of textual criticism with a quite uncritical method of dealing with them. (93-94; italics mine)

We may conclude the following, therefore, regarding Origen and the Egyptian text-type: (1) In the Gospel of John he is a witness to this text-type; but as such he represents its preservation by means of careful transmission, not its "recension." The philological tradition capable of *creating* such a text had to have been a part of

---

12. One is accustomed to reading the opposite about Origen's habits of citation. See, e.g., Metzger 1968: 87: "Origen is notorious in this regard, for he seldom quotes a passage twice in precisely the same words." Cf. the similar opinion of Zuntz 1953: 82-83. But in comparison with other Fathers, his citing of John makes theirs look like the work of a backwoods preacher who never consults his text.

the church of Alexandria before Origen. (2) In contrast to his work on the OT, Origen never shows a concern for a "critical text" of the NT writings. Furthermore, where editorializing *may* be shown to exist, he does not edit *toward* the text of P75 B on the basis of Alexandrian philological know-how, but rather *away* from that text on principles later to be found in the Byzantine tradition.

The question may well be asked: If such an acknowledged "textual expert" as Origen in the early third century showed no particular interest in "scholarly recensional activity" that would have produced a text like P75 B, does historical probability favor the existence either of the person or the incentive to create a text on such principles in the second century? The evidence seems rather to point to "careful preservation," probably with occasional stylistic changes, as the true product of the Alexandrian philological *expertise*.

III

These conclusions as to the textual concerns of Origen are similar to those that have already been made about the scribe of P66, who antedates Origen probably by a generation. The primary importance of this MS to our question lies in the corrections which the original scribe made to his text, for herein is our earliest piece of actual historical evidence in which recensional activity is clearly present. But the scribe's habits and textual relationships of his uncorrected text also have relevance.

Furthermore, E. C. Colwell has suggested that "P66 gives the impression of being the product of a scriptorium" (1965: 382 [118]). There are two features about the MS which point to this conclusion: the scribe's excellent calligraphy and the changes to the text made against a second *Vorlage*. If this is true, then P66 offers us firsthand evidence of a kind of official editorial activity going on in the church in Alexandria in the time of Clement. And almost everything the scribe does points away from recensional activity of a kind that would produce the Egyptian text-type.

1. Quite in contrast to P75, of whose scribe Colwell says, "[His] impulse to improve style is for the most part defeated by the obligation to make an exact copy" (1965: 386 [121]), the scribe of P66 is a careless workman. In the extant MS he has 482 variants which are unsupported by Greek witnesses, and over 200 of these are simply nonsense readings. Granted that such readings are frequently corrected, they nevertheless demonstrate the basic inefficiency of the scribe. This is further substantiated by the scribe's frequent — and inconsistent — itacisms. He has 432 such readings and frequently spelled the same word two different ways in the same sentence. Colwell's judgment is the correct one: "Wildness of copying is the outstanding characteristic of P66" (386 [121]). Such carelessness, however, is scarcely the product of such recensional activity as Zuntz called for in order to produce the Egyptian text-type.

2. This MS has a close relationship — much closer than ℵ, for example — to the text of P75 B. Since P75 B has a remarkable homogeneity with regard to certain stylistic features of John's Gospel, P66 can be tested as to its faithfulness in preserving these features. Although it is not invariably the case, and although the MS far more often preserves Johannine style than otherwise, in the vast majority of those places where P66 varies from P75 B it does so by abandoning Johannine style in the interest

of more common Greek (see Fee 1968b: 36-56). That, of course, may be due simply to his *Vorlage*. It might also be noted that such revision — if indeed this scribe is responsible for any of it — is perhaps a reflection of scholarly interests. But if so, then P[75] B reflect a nonscholarly tradition, for they consistently have readings in John which are neither good classical nor koine idiom, but reflect the *ungriechisch* Johannine idiom. Again, the text of P[66] is not moving toward P[75] B but away from it.

3. There are two areas where the scribe of P[66] may be tested with greater certainty as to his own peculiar editorial idiosyncrasies: his singular readings and his corrections.

a. Colwell has analyzed the singular readings of all three early Johannine papyri — P[45] P[66] P[75] — as to the editorializing on the part of scribes which such readings reveal. Although Colwell's method needs to be used cautiously,[13] my own work on P[66] has validated his conclusions:

> P[66] editorializes as he does everything else — in a sloppy fashion. He is not guided in his changes by some clearly defined goal which is always kept in view. If he has an inclination toward omission, it is not "according to knowledge," but is whimsical and careless, often leading to nothing but nonsense. (1965: 387 [123])

b. Similarly, I have subjected the approximately 450 corrections of P[66] to the closest scrutiny (1968b: 57-75). What is of major significance here is that the original scribe himself has corrected his text against a second *Vorlage* (59-60). Here, then, is unquestioned recensional activity. The conclusion of that study was that in matters of style, as well as in more substantial variations, this scribe-turned-recensor was interested neither in manuscript purity (i.e., preserving one type of text over against another because it was more likely the original) nor in "scholarly" recension of the kind one might expect in Alexandria. Rather, he was interested in presenting a good, readable text, which smooths out grammar and tends to remove difficulties. Such editorializing, it should be noted in conclusion, is precisely the opposite of that which both Kenyon and Zuntz theorized to have produced the Egyptian text-type.

IV

This evidence from Origen and P[66], of course, does not mean that recensional activity of another kind did not exist. The point is that at present we have no certain evidence[14] that points to *recensional activity* of another kind. For when we turn to P[75], we find

---

13. For example, when a MS such as P[75] is shown to be basically transmitting his exemplar and has such close relationships with another MS, it may be that some of its singular readings are genuine to the text-type, while all subsequent variants are deviations. This is especially true when the singular reading is in harmony with other readings of the same kind in the text-type.

14. There are two possible exceptions. Zuntz (1953: 252-62) has argued that the corrections of P[46] are of this kind. While on the whole his argument appears convincing, it is based on such a scanty amount of material that the conclusions are tentative at best. There is also a series of deletions in P[66] in John 7 and 14, which seem to be made by a second hand and which bring the text into conformity to the Egyptian text-type. See Fee 1968b: 60n10.

nothing that resembles recensional activity at all, but rather a scribe who is carefully preserving his original text.

The fact that P75 is not itself a recension is demonstrated by two factors: (1) The nature and number of the individualisms of the scribe, both nonsense readings and otherwise, as well as the paucity of corrections to the text makes it almost certain that this MS itself is *not* a recension. In comparison with any of the other early papyri, this scribe produced a remarkably error-free copy. As Colwell noted, "The control had been drilled into the scribe before he started writing" (1965: 382 [117]). However, the presence of at least seventy-six uncorrected nonsense readings in the MS (almost as many as have been corrected) indicates that there was no serious checking or revising taking place. It is not an "edition" of Luke and John, but as Colwell again has correctly concluded:

> In P75 the text that is produced can be explained in all its variants as the result of a single force, namely the disciplined scribe who writes with the intention of being careful and accurate. (381 [117])

To be fair, it should be noted that this conclusion stands quite in contrast to that of K. W. Clark (1966). After a brief — too brief, it would seem, to bear the weight of his conclusion — examination of three singular readings in P75, Clark concluded that

> in general, P75 tends to support our current critical text, and yet the papyrus vividly portrays a fluid state of the text at about A.D. 200. Such scribal freedom suggests that the gospel text was little more stable than an oral tradition and that we may be pursuing the retreating mirage of the 'original text'. (15)

Perhaps it is true, after all, that everything is relative — that our judgments are obscured by our points of comparison or by our perception of things. Yet Clark's choice of three variants from Luke to portray "vividly" the "fluid state of the text" is not a very happy one. The marginal addition of θέλω καθαρίσθητε καὶ εὐθέως ἐκαθαρίσθησαν at 17:14 is clearly the work of a later hand. (Clark is quite misleading at this point in saying that "the scribe of P75 borrows. . . ."). Moreover, the "unique reading heretofore unreported" of ἰσχύν for ἰχθύν at 11:11 is a "nonsense" reading pure and simple, since the ἰσχύν is immediately followed by μὴ ἀντὶ ἰχθυός. This error is surely a form of "mental metathesis" and not a case of "scribal freedom." Clark's third reading, ἤρξατο for ἤρξαντο at 11:24, is not singular to P75 as Clark suggests. It is also read by Π 1 579 1200 1375. But in spite of later support, this reading looks like a case of independent error pure and simple, rather than of scribal freedom. The exact thing occurs in P75 at Luke 14:18, where the accompanying πάντες makes the reading impossible. One might compare also Luke 9:42 εἰσῆλθεν l. εἰσῆλθον; Luke 11:53 ἐξέλθοντες l. ἐξέλθοντος; Luke 17:4 ἀφήσει l. ἀφήσεις; and Luke 23:29 ἔρχεται l. ἔρχονται, all of which are uncorrected — and impossible Greek.

Such readings have nothing to do with textual fluidity. One does indeed find such in P45 and P66, but in P75 one has a careful copyist, who made occasional errors which he failed to correct.

(2) That P75 is not a recension but a careful copy is also illustrated by its textual relationships, especially with B and ℵ (see Table 13.1, above). We have

already noted the very close relationship P[75] has with B. The number of differences between them, however, also indicates that B is not a copy of P[75]. Either they are related through a common ancestor (step-brothers or uncle-nephew), or B is a direct descendant (grandson or great-grandson) with slight corruption through the intermediate source(s).

A careful analysis of the disagreements between the two MSS suggests a common ancestor as the most plausible explanation of the relationship. The disagreements between them in Luke and John are presented in Tables 13.2-7 catalogued according to types of variation. In order to detect any possible tendencies in "editorializing," the singular and subsingular readings in each MS have also been isolated.[15]

It should be noted that there are no patterns or directions of "editorializing" in B that are not already anticipated by its earlier — and closest — relative, which simply underscores a point made above as to the nonrecensional character of B. Thus in Luke, B tends to omit the preposition in partitive phrases (10:42; 12:58), but so also does P[75] (17:17). B was once accused by H. C. Hoskier of reading simple words for compound forms (1914: 1.248-49), which it does singularly at Luke 6:38 and 15:24. But in the four examples from Luke which Hoskier used, P[75] also reads the simple form, and does so singularly at 11:22, 13:25, and 15:22. In other words, these phenomena belong to the text-type, not to the idiosyncrasies of either scribe.

But even more significant for our present argument is the fact that for several types of variants the two MSS individually witness to phenomena to which they more often bear witness together — and that frequently against the majority. For example, P[75] lacks a possessive pronoun found in B in five subsingular readings in Luke and one singular reading in John. B has the same thing once in Luke. Where they divide and have substantial support, P[75] more often lacks the possessive. But there are numerous instances in both Gospels where they agree in such "omissions," usually with a small minority of supporting witnesses, against the majority (e.g., Luke 12:22; John 2:12; 3:16, 17; 6:58; 8:38 2x; 10:29). Similarly, P[75] has ten instances in Luke and three in John where it singularly (or nearly so) omits the article; B has five such in Luke and ten in John. But these two MSS also have several such cases of unique agreement (Luke 8:6, 35; 14:1; John 8:12; 12:30 [in their word order]) as well as many others where they are joined by one or a few other MSS against the rest (e.g., Luke 5:3, 5 2x; 6:30; 8:41; John 6:45; 7:14; 8:19, 25, 34, 58; 9:35, 41; 11:44). And these are but two of several examples.

This dual phenomenon of a very high percentage of agreement over all textual variation both in Luke and John and of a clear pattern of agreement in type of variant even where they disagree points to common ancestry, not to intermediate corruption between P[75] and B. That is, both MSS are faithfully preserving textual phenomena which are anterior to them, which in turn means that P[75] is not itself the recension.

One final datum also supports this conclusion, namely the relationship of ℵ to P[75] and B. Table 13.1 shows that ℵ is a member of the same text-type, but as

---

15. The lists for B include only those variants where P[75] also has text.

TABLE 13.2

SINGULAR AND SUBSINGULAR READINGS OF P⁷⁵ IN LUKE
LISTED ACCORDING TO TYPES OF VARIATION FROM CODEX B

Pronouns	Conjunctions	Add/Omit Article	Verb Forms	Word Order	Prepositions	Compound Words	Other "Nonsignificant" Variants	"Significant" Variant
8:22 –S	v 5:1	– 3:22	11:23	7:6	– 14:32	+ 12:42	v 8:21	– 13:34
9:9 –D	– 9:42	– 10:39	14:28	14:10		– 13:25	– 11:31 C	– 14:8
9:34 –O	+ 9:48	– 13:1	15:13	14:28			v 11:42	+ 16:19
11:7 +PC	v 11:39	– 15:18	16:22	24:27			v 12:45	v 16:30
11:27 –D	v 12:28	– 22:55	23:8				v 15:17	v 24:26
13:1 –O	– 12:39 C	– 24:28	24:21				v 24:18 C	
	– 13:14 C							
	– 14:21							
	– 15:12							
	– 15:30							
	v 16:27							
	– 22:24							
	– 23:11							
(line — below are subsingular)								
8:7 vO	– 6:41	+ 13:30	4:41	10:18	v 4:35	– 11:22	v 16:31	
9:29 –P	+ 9:28	– 15:6	11:18 C		+ 13:13	– 15:22	v 22:47	
12:18 +PC	– 10:24	– 16:18	12:29		v 24:47		v 23:46	
12:24 –S	– 13:29	– 17:1	23:12					
12:31 –P	– 14:26	– 22:26 C						
12:45 vP	– 16:22							
12:53 –PC	– 24:17							
14:8 –P								
14:25 –P								
23:3 –O								
23:12 vD								

NOTE: The readings listed above the line are singular readings in P⁷⁵; those below the line have isolated support from one or a few late MSS. The following symbols are used:

– The reading is "omitted" in P⁷⁵
+ The reading is "added" in P⁷⁵
v P⁷⁵ has a variant wording
S Subject
O Object or indirect object
P Possessive
D Demonstrative
C The listed reading has been corrected to conform to B

TABLE 13.3

SINGULAR AND SUBSINGULAR READINGS OF B IN LUKE LISTED ACCORDING TO TYPES OF VARIATION FROM P[75]

Entries listed above the line in each column are singular readings in B; entries below the line have isolated support.

Pronouns	Conjunctions	Add/Omit Article	Verb Forms	Word Order	Prepositions	Compound Words	Other "Nonsignificant" Variants	"Significant" Variant
	− 23:50	− 9:58	23:23	8:27	− 22:19 C		− 13:11 C	− 11:42 C
	− 24:15 C	+ 10:19	23:26	16:17			− 13:14 C	v 16:15
	+ 24:39	− 10:37 C					v 16:1 C	v 17:23 C
		− 15:10					v 16:15 C	v 22:9
		− 22:51					− 22:40 C	
							− 24:44	
							− 24:52 C	
(line)	*(line)*	*(line)*	*(line)*	*(line)*	*(line)*	*(line)*	*(line)*	*(line)*
10:27 −PC	v 22:61	− 8:9	13:17	9:1	v 8:29	− 6:38 C	v 8:13 C	v 13:7 C
23:2 vO		+ 11:30	23:45		− 10:31	− 15:24	+ 13:32	− 23:35
					+ 11:36	+ 17:12	v 16:12	
					− 12:58		− 17:34	
							− 23:39	

NOTE: The readings listed above the line are singular readings in B; those below the line have isolated support from one or a few late MSS. The following symbols are used:

− The reading is "omitted" in B
+ The reading is "added" in B
v B has a variant wording
S Subject
O Object or indirect object
P Possessive
D Demonstrative
C The listed reading has been corrected to conform to P[75]

TABLE 13.4

DISAGREEMENTS BETWEEN P75 AND B IN LUKE WHERE EACH HAS IMPORTANT MS SUPPORT LISTED ACCORDING TO TYPES OF VARIATION

Pronouns	Conjunctions	Add/Omit Article	Verb Forms	Word Order	Prepositions	Compound Words	Other "Nonsignificant" Variants	"Significant" Variant
6:25 +O	+ 3:20	+ 6:3	8:22	5:2	v 4:35	+ 13:21	– 8:28	v 10:42
6:28 vO	+ 7:22 C	+ 6:49	9:62	9:18	+ 9:62	– 23:11	v 9:12	– 11:25
8:5 vR	+ 11:24	+ 9:1	10:40	9:28	+ 10:42	– 24:49	v 9:39	+ 11:33
8:20 –P	v 12:29	– 11:11	11:2	9:48	– 17:7		+ 9:59	v 11:48
10:39 –R	– 12:48	– 11:13	11:50	9:59			v 10:39	– 12:39
11:22 –P	+ 13:7	– 11:44	12:8	12:43			v 11:15, 18, 19	v 13:33
11:31 vO	– 14:34	+ 12:53	13:15	12:56			v 11:41	– 15:21
12:22 –P	+ 22:39	+ 14:35	13:27 C	13:31			v 13:5	
13:2 vD	– 23:5	+ 15:22	14:13	13:35			– 23:29	
14:23 +PC	– 23:11	+ 18:10	14:17	14:26			v 24:1	
14:27 vP	– 23:50	– 23:6	15:4 C	16:27			v 24:39	
15:22 vP		+ 23:25	15:24	22:50			v 24:47	
16:4 vP		– 23:29	17:22				– 24:49	
17:6 –D		+ 23:31	22:41				– 24:53	
17:30 vD								
23:53 vO								
24:39 –P								

KEY:

– P75 lacks a reading found in B
+ P75 has a reading not found in B
v P75 and B have variant wording
O Object or indirect object
P Possessive pronoun
R Relative pronoun
D Demonstrative pronoun
C The reading of P75 has been corrected to conform to B

TABLE 13.5

SINGULAR AND SUB-SINGULAR READINGS OF P75 IN JOHN LISTED ACCORDING TO TYPES OF VARIATION FROM CODEX B

Pronouns	Conjunctions	Add/Omit Article	Verb Forms	Word Order	Prepositions	Compound Words	Other "nonsignificant" Variants	"Significant" Variant
5:12 −O	v 5:13	+ 2:1	4:17	1:18 C	v 7:13	− 10:2	− 5:25	− 4:47
6:57 +P	− 6:39	− 7:33	4:18	4:54			v 6:17	v 6:50
8:55 +O	+ 9:30 C	− 11:13	6:5	5:34			v 6:19	v 8:38
9:6 vC	+ 11:31	− 14:22	6:39	7:18			− 7:17	v 10:7
10:17 −P			8:24	7:23			+ 8:52	v 11:12
10:29 vP			9:39	8:17			− 9:8	− 12:38
				14:19			− 11:13	v 14:21
2:18 −O	− 4:50	+ 10:12	5:16	2:10			v 1:51	
2:24 −O	− 6:40	+ 12:15	5:20	4:9			v 9:34	
8:22 −S	+ 8:15		8:46				+ 14:9	
8:34 −O	− 9:41		14:12					
	+ 11:25							

NOTE: The readings listed above the line are singular readings in P75; those below the line have isolated support from one or a few later witnesses. The following symbols are used:

− The reading is "omitted" in P75
+ The reading is "added" in P75
v P75 has a variant wording
S Subject
O Object or indirect object
C The listed reading has been corrected to conform to B

TABLE 13.6
SINGULAR AND SUB-SINGULAR READINGS OF B IN JOHN LISTED ACCORDING TO TYPES OF VARIATION FROM P[75]

Pronouns	Conjunctions	Add/Omit Article	Verb Forms	Word Order	Prepositions	Compound Words	Other "Nonsignificant" Variants	"Significant" Variant
12:28 vP		+ 3:25	13:27 C	1:21	- 2:19	- 7:6	- 1:4 C	v 4:40
		- 5:14		10:1	- 2:23		- 1:14 C	+ 5:45
		- 7:1		10:7			7:34	
3:28 +P	- 5:29	- 8:39	10:25	10:32			v 9:7	- 11:21
	- 8:59	- 8:42	10:40				v 10:24	v 8:56
		- 10:7		2:17				
		- 10:25 C		4:16			- 1:13 C	
		- 1:47		13:9			v 4:52	
		- 4:46						
		- 6:46						
		- 10:18						

NOTE: The readings listed above the line are singular readings in B; those below the line have isolated support from one or a few later witnesses. The following symbols are used:

- The reading is "omitted" in B
+ The reading is "added" in B
v B has a variant wording
P Possessive
C The listed reading has been corrected to conform to P[75]

266

TABLE 13.7

DISAGREEMENTS BETWEEN P⁷⁵ AND B IN JOHN WHERE EACH HAS IMPORTANT MS SUPPORT LISTED ACCORDING TO TYPES OF VARIATION

Pronouns	Conjunctions	Add/Omit Article	Verb Forms	Word Order	Prepositions	Compound Words	Other "Nonsignificant" Variants	"Significant" Variant
1:22 +S	+ 1:42	+ 1:18	1:19	1:37	v 3:16 C	− 11:33	− 1:26	v 1:15 C
1:27 −S	− 2:4	− 3:5	1:26	2:1	− 6:44		+ 1:27	+ 1:19
5:10 +P	+ 3:18	− 3:23	2:15	2:13			− 1:35	+ 2:15
5:45 vOC	+ 3:31	+ 3:24	3:12	3:20			+ 2:17	v 3:31
7:47 +O	+ 5:12	− 6:23	4:12	5:6			+ 3:28	v 7:4
8:28 −P	v 6:18	− 6:29	6:39	6:52			+ 4:1	− 7:39
8:54 vPC	− 8:36	+ 6:53	7:19	6:60			+ 4:3	v 8:57
9:4 vO	+ 8:41	− 7:28 C	8:31	9:17			v 4:29	v 9:6
9:17 vO	+ 8:52	− 9:11	8:39 C	9:22			− 4:35	− 9:21
14:10 v	− 9:16	+ 10:34	8:41	9:31			v 4:46	− 9:38
14:11 −O		+ 11:21	10:27	10:39			v 6:24	− 10:8
		+ 11:24	10:29				+ 7:40	v 10:29
		− 12:9	12:13				v 8:14 C	
		− 12:18	14:17				− 9:11	
		+ 12:36					v 10:10	
							− 12:34	
							v 12:40	
							+ 12:46	

KEY:
− P⁷⁵ lacks a reading found in B
+ P⁷⁵ has a reading not found in B
v P⁷⁵ and B have variant wording
S Subject
P Possessive pronoun
O Object or indirect object
C The reading of P⁷⁵ has been corrected to conform to B

a more distant relative. A similar relationship to the text-type is sustained in John 9–21. There are several variants of genealogical significance where ℵ, sometimes with other early support, agrees with P75 against B and the rest (Luke 12:39; John 8:57; 9:21, 38-39). Such genealogical agreement between MSS which are otherwise more distant relatives also argues for common ancestry further upstream from P75.

We may conclude, then, that Hort was correct about B on both counts: it preserves "not only a very ancient text, but a very pure line of very ancient text" (1881: 2.250-51). But, of course, by "very pure line" Hort meant "with regard to the original text." Up to this point we mean only with regard to its text-type. The final question is whether the ancestor(s) of P75 B is recensional in the sense of a revised or produced text; and the problem here is methodological. How does one judge what is recensional and what is not, especially when the MS one is investigating is *not* a recension?

The only possible option is to follow Hort: our conclusion must be based on an examination of the "internal evidence of readings." But whereas Hort's case was based on samplings of evidence, the full statement of such a case must be based on a thorough examination of all the variations in all the MSS in any given book.

I suggest the following method for such an examination (cf. Zuntz 1953: 160-215):

1. Variants should be listed according to various types: add/omit the article, add/omit conjunctions, word order, harmonizations, etc. But such lists also need flexibility. A special designation for the possibility of *homoeoteleuton* is needed. What may appear to be harmonization may also be due to other factors. Add/omit the article must be listed with distinctions between proper, abstract, and common nouns, as well as between nominative and oblique cases. Furthermore, for many of these items one should keep a companion list of all occurrences without variation, so as to have a cross-check both for an author's style and for the frequency of variation. Finally, singular and subsingular readings need to be isolated from those variants with substantial support.

2. The tendencies of textual groupings as well as individual MSS should then be analyzed for each classification of variants. Without making any value judgments at this point, one can simply catalogue manuscript and text-type idiosyncrasies. Such tendencies should always be noted of one MS or group against another, *not* against some external standard such as the TR or UBS3/NA26. For example, in John Codex B lacks the definite article some eighty times where the combination of E G Ω has it; the opposite never occurs. Thus one may say that B and its closest allies P66 and P75 have a tendency to be anarthrous in John as over against the Byzantine MSS.

3. Whether these tendencies can be judged as recensional or a preservation of the original will finally be based on three other factors: (a) conformity to or deviation from an author's established style, (b) known scribal habits, (c) cross-checking of tendencies across the various NT books and *corpora*. A further word about each of these is in order, lest one become so rigid as to neglect other options or so flexible as to appear temperamental or circular.

(a) No fixed rules may be established as to whether a reading is original or recensional by its relationship to an author's style, for a reading may be regarded as original *because it conforms* to that style or recensional *because a scribe may have conformed* it to the author's style. Nonetheless, some general judgments hold, especially where, as in the case of John, certain stylistic features are peculiar to him in the NT or where he has an abundance of a koine idiom otherwise less often attested. Thus his abundance of asyndeton, the frequent omission of the article with personal names in the nominative, the abundance of ὅτι-*recitativum*, the redundant nominative personal pronoun, the frequency of the "vernacular possessive," etc. are Johannine peculiarities in the NT.

This does not arbitrarily mean, however, that any variation from such stylistic features is therefore recensional. For example, any variation without the connective in John must not be automatically assumed to be original. For some MSS (e.g., P⁶⁶ ℵ D) reflect random carelessness with regard to conjunctions. Furthermore, the absence of καί in 7:1 and the fourfold variation at 9:28 involve parataxis, and in such cases the removal of parataxis seems far more likely than its addition by later scribes under Semitic influence. Moreover, it must always be left open that John himself occasionally varied his normal usage, and that a later scribe conformed the deviation to the norm. Thus, for example, John is regularly asyndetic with the two formulae for direct discourse, ἀπεκρίθη Ἰησοῦς καὶ εἶπεν αὐτ(ῷ) and λέγει αὐτ(ῷ) ὁ Ἰησοῦς; but there are just enough cases where a connective is certain so as to add an element of uncertainty where variation occurs.

But despite the variables, it is possible to subject the manuscript tradition to rigorous examination as to its tendencies with regard to these Johannine peculiarities. And in general it may be assumed that tendencies *away from* John toward either a more common *or* a more classical idiom are recensional in nature.

(b) "Known scribal habits" is where much of the difficulty lies, for in spite of our asseverations to the contrary, scribes may be shown to go in many directions (see esp. E. Sanders 1969) and no MS or text-type is without some ambiguity in this regard. G. D. Kilpatrick has repeatedly argued that any variant that can be classified as atticistic is thereby secondary (see 1963a, 1963b, 1967). But this argument has for the most part fallen on deaf ears, because the opposite seems as likely to be true; that is, that scribes may have preferred koine, and especially septuagintal, idioms to classical ones.

But again, in spite of the variables, patterns and tendencies on the part of scribes in general, and MSS and text-types in particular, may be ascertained. In the Synoptic tradition, for example, certain MSS and text-types have a much higher frequency of harmonization than others, although no MS is completely guiltless and not every apparent "harmonization" may be assumed to be so. So also with other features which cross NT books and *corpora* such as add/omit possessives, subjects, and object pronouns, or certain features of word order.

(c) Both of the above need to be regularly cross-checked across the NT, for it is precisely here that one at times can best discover an author's style and/or scribal habits. The point is, that what is to be regarded as recensional must be consistently so throughout the NT. This may be stated best by way of illustration.

In my study of the use of the definite article with personal names in John (1970a), I noted that the anarthrous Ἰησοῦς in John had often been considered the peculiarity of Codex B, for the idiom is deeply entrenched in the Egyptian text-type and partly so in other MSS as well. The fact that the idiom is rare in the Synoptic Gospels, even in P75 and B, should serve as a cross-check to demonstrate that the idiom goes back to John, not to an Egyptian recension. Otherwise one *must* ask, Why only here in the NT did this recensor do such an *ungriechisch* thing? Similarly, against Kilpatrick (1963b: 132-33), one must ask why *only* in John the Egyptian MSS abandon the septuagintal (and koine) future *middle* of ζῆν for the "atticistic" *active*.

When this method is applied to the textual variation in Luke and John with an eye toward the possible recensional character of the ancestor of P75 B, the results are strongly against such a likelihood. This, of course, assumes that "scholarly recension" will remove Johannine idiosyncrasies, not create them; that it will tend to harmonize passages, not remove or change such wordings; and that it will tend to alleviate difficulties, not engender them. The full justification of this conclusion will require a volume of considerable size filled with lists of data. Here we can offer only a sample illustration with the further note that the complete data will vary little from the sampling.

In Luke 10 and 11 there are at least eighty-five variants in the total manuscript tradition which might be related to the question of harmonization. Not all of these, of course, are necessarily so, since they include variations of many kinds and therefore may reflect other scribal errors or idiosyncrasies. Furthermore, the probability of true assimilation of one gospel to another is far greater in the words of Jesus than in the evangelist's narrative. With these variables taken into account, several tendencies emerge.

On the one hand, the Western tradition, especially Codex D, has a profusion of such readings. The following list gives only the more substantial of these, where D and/or the OL read almost alone against the rest:

10:14	(= Mt 11:22) εν ημερα κρισεως l. εν τη κρισει f13 c f r1 syc
10:23	(= Mt 13:16) add και ακουοντες α ακουει D c e f
10:27	(= LXX) om. και εν ολη τη διανοια σου D Γ 1241 itpl
11:2	(= Mt 6:7) add μη βαττολογειτε ως οι λοιποι δοκουσιν γαρ τινες οτι εν τη πολυλογεια αυτων εισακουσθησονται αλλα προσευχομενοι D
11:3	(= Mt 6:11) δος l. διδου D ℵ 28 71 1675 pc
11:3	(= Mt 6:11) σημερον l. το καθ' ημεραν D 28 71 1071 2141 itpl
11:4	(= Mt 6:12) τα οφειληματα l. τας αμαρτιας D 131 b c ff2 r2
11:4	(= Mt 6:12) ως και ημεις l. και γαρ αυτοι D itpl
11:4	(= Mt 6:12) τοις οφειλεταις ημων l. παντι οφειλοντι ημιν D b c ff2 r l syp
11:30	(= Mt 12:40) add και καθως Ιωνας εν τη κοιλια του κητους εγενετο τρεις ημερας και τρεις νυκτος. ουτως και ο υιος του ανθρωπου εν τη γη D a e ff2
11:35-36	Replace with Matt 6:23 D a b e ff2 i
11:39	(= Mt 23:25) add υποκριται D b
11:43	(= Mt 23:6) add και τας πρωτοκλισιας εν τοις δειπνοις D (C) f13 it
11:49	(= Mt 23:34) om. και η σοφια του θεου ειπεν D b

11:51 (= Mt 23:35) υιου βαραχαιου ον εφονευσαν αναμεσον του
θυσιαστηριου και του ναου l. του απολομενου μεταξυ του
θυσιαστηριου και του οικου D a sy^c

In 43 of the 85 alleged harmonizations there is substantial manuscript
support for the harmonizing variant. D joins others in 14 of these. More significantly,
the Byzantine tradition here shows the same harmonizing tendencies, picking up 27
of these variants. Again, many of them are substantial:

10:22 (= Lk 10:23) add και στραφεις προς τους μαθητας ειπεν
10:27 (= LXX [Mk 12:30]) εξ . . . l. εν . . . (three times)
11:2   (= Mt 6:9) add ημων ο εν τοις ουρανοις (+D)
11:2   (= Mt 6:10) add γενηθητω το θελημα σου ως εν ουρανω και επι
γης (+D)
11:4   (= Mt 6:13) add αλλα ρυσαι ημας απο του ουρανου (+D)
11:11 (= Mt 7:9) add αρτον, μη λιθον επιδωσει αυτω η και (+D)
11:29 (= Mt 12:39) add του προφητου
11:33 (= Mt 5:15; Mk 4:21) add ουδε υπο τον μοδιον (+B, D)
11:44 (= Mt 23:27) add γραμματεις και φαρισαιοι υποκριται (+D)

P75 and/or B, on the other hand, have only one instance of subsingular
harmonization (11:31 [= Mt 12:43] P45 P75 αυτην l. αυτους) and five other places
where they are joined by others in such a reading.

10:7 (= Mt 10:10) omit P75 ℵ B D L X Ξ 579 892 1241 pc
εστιν A C R W Θ Ψ Byz TR

10:15 (= LXX; Mt 11:23) καταβηση P75 B D sy^c.s
καταβιβασθηση rell TR

10:22 (= Mt 11:26) ευδοκια εγενετο P75 B C L X Ξ Ψ 070 1 33 579 pc
εγενετο ευδοκια P45 ℵ A D W Byz TR

11:20 (= Mt 12:28) εγω P75 B C D L R f13 33 pc
omit P45 ℵ A W Byz TR

11:24 (= Mt 12:44) τοτε P75 B L X Θ Ξ 0124 33 892 1071 1241 b l sa bo
omit P45 ℵ* A C D W Byz rell TR

It will be easily noted that, except for καταβηση in 10:15 and perhaps τότε
in 11:24, these are far less substantial than those noted above for the Western and
Byzantine MSS. Finally, it should be noted that (in addition to 11:33 above) P75 and
B disagree in two other such readings (the second reading is the harmonization):

11:25 (= Mt 12:44) omit P75 ℵ A D W Byz TR
σχολαζονται B C L Ξ Ψ f1 f13 33 892 pc

11:50 (= Mt 23:35) εκκεχυμενον P45 B 33 69 1241
εχχυνομενον P75 ℵ A C D W Θ Byz rell TR

While not all of these harmonizations are necessarily secondary, it is surely true that the large majority are. And while it is also true that no MS has escaped corruption at this point, it is likewise true that P75 and B are "comparatively pure" when compared with either the Western or Byzantine traditions.

This conclusion is similar to that already established for the variations of add/omit the article with personal names in John (see Fee 1970a). For this present study I also did a sampling of variations of asyndeton, ὅτι-*recitativum,* and various kinds of word order in John. With regard to asyndeton, the results were very close to the above sampling of harmonizations, although D did not have such notable singularity. But again, in comparison with the Western and Byzantine MSS, P75 and B had a very high record in maintaining this Johannine feature. This is all the more remarkable when one considers that scholarly recension would almost certainly go in the other direction.

All MSS and text-types showed remarkable ambiguity with variations of the ὅτι-*recitativum.* But generally, MSS tended to reject it rather than to add it, and P75 B tended to preserve (add?) it more than others.

Likewise also with word order: P75 B far more often preserved Johannine features than other MSS; and in one list of "word order variants tending toward more logical juxtaposition," P75 B invariably had the *lectio difficilior.*

V

The conclusion to which all of these data point is that the concept of a scholarly recension of the NT text in Alexandria either in the fourth century *or* the second century, either as a created or a carefully edited text, is a myth. The leading MSS of the Egyptian text-type (P75 B) are not themselves recensional — at least not in any meaningful sense of that word. Where one MS of this tradition (P66) is clearly recensional, it is so toward a Byzantine type of recension, not Alexandrian. Furthermore, the one man skilled in such textual matters (Origen) showed no concern for such a recension; and it is doubtful that someone earlier than he would have had such a concern. Finally, an analysis of the textual character of P75 B *when compared with other manuscript traditions* indicates that there is little evidence of recensional activity of any kind taking place in this text-type. These MSS seem to represent a "relatively pure" form of preservation of a "relatively pure" line of descent from the original text.

This further means that one of the horns of our current dilemma has been eliminated, namely the concern over the "Hortian" face of our critical texts. We have not simply returned to Hort, nor have we fully revived his theory of text. If he could talk about the "comparative purity" of B, we prefer to put far more emphasis on "comparative" than Hort did. If our resultant text looks much like Hort's, that is perhaps irrelevant. It only means that Hort was essentially on the right path.

Furthermore, this conclusion has considerable consequence for text-critical methodology. We are not returning to genealogy, nor do we begin with one text (P75 B) and follow it except where it is in obvious error. The eclectic method, that is, deciding the original NT text variant by variant, is a valid one. But proper eclecticism plants its feet firmly on the manuscript evidence, including an adequate theory of textual transmission and an evaluation of the relative merits of the witnesses.

If all of this means that we still appear to be crossing the Atlantic in an 1881 ship, it may be that they built them better in those days. But more likely the point of wonder is not that we still follow WH, but that they, without our discoveries and advances, revealed such remarkable judgments.

CHAPTER 14

THE SIGNIFICANCE OF THE PAPYRI FOR DETERMINING THE NATURE OF THE NEW TESTAMENT TEXT IN THE SECOND CENTURY: A DYNAMIC VIEW OF TEXTUAL TRANSMISSION[1]

Eldon Jay Epp

This is largely an exercise in historical-critical imagination. It is an attempt to discover some things we do not know about the earliest stages of NT textual transmission by applying creative imagination to what we do know. The question, to be more specific, is whether we can take our limited knowledge of the earliest textual witnesses, combine it with the data we have about our later textual witnesses, and then think creatively about the process that must — or at least might — have produced it all. The approach proposed involves: first, exploring the dynamic relationships and movements (both secular and Christian) that must have occurred in the earliest centuries of textual transmission; second, utilizing textual complexions — commonly called text-types — to sort out the MSS; and, third, bringing into view the early textual spectrum that results from, and is reflected in, the array of manuscript witnesses. In pursuing the first of these tasks, it will be instructive to offer two brief sketches, one of the general situation in the first few centuries of Christianity, and another of the specific environment of the earliest NT manuscripts and papyri.

I. The Dynamic Historical Situation of the Early Church

In looking at the earliest centuries of Christianity, that period when the NT text originated and began its odyssey of transmission, the word "dynamic" is constitutive. For too long the text of the NT has been conceived in static terms. It has often been assumed that one type of text existed only in one place and other types existed only somewhere else; or that one of these types on a rare occasion made its way solely to some other location; or that distinctive and persistent "local texts" existed at a number of discrete localities; or that revisions and refinements of certain texts took

1. This chapter was prepared for an international conference at the University of Notre Dame (15-17 April 1988) on "Gospel Traditions in the Second Century" and was published in a volume under that title edited by William L. Petersen (Notre Dame, IN: University of Notre Dame Press, 1989), though with an added subtitle of "Origins, Recensions, Text, and Transmission." The eight participants (in addition to the editor) were Barbara Aland, Tjitze Baarda, J. Neville Birdsall, Sebastian P. Brock, Joël Delobel, Helmut Koester, Frederik Wisse, and the present writer.

place in isolated fashion in insulated locations. To be sure, all of these things probably happened, but much, much more was happening also — and simultaneously.

We focus, of course, on those first centuries when Christianity was expanding with rather phenomenal rapidity and in all directions within the vast Greco-Roman world until, already by the end of the second century, Christian centers existed from Edessa and Antioch and Caesarea in the East to Spain and Lyon and Rome in the West, and from Britannia and Sinope in the North to Carthage and Alexandria in the South.[2] This was not a static, but a dynamic world. And this was not an eastern world or a western world — it was both eastern and western; this was not a northern world or a southern — but both northern and southern. And things were happening: from its Judaean and Galilean origins, Jewish Christianity quickly spread to places like Antioch of Syria and Damascus, thence to Asia Minor and Macedonia, and to Greece and Rome (Koester: 2.86-94). As Mithraism spread to virtually every outpost of the Roman army, so — in the earliest generations — Christianity spread to innumerable Jewish settlements throughout that Greco-Roman world, and, of course, to non-Jewish centers as well.

The writings that were later to constitute the "New Testament" were in circulation, along with other Christian documents. For example, Jewish-Christian Gospels (later to be designated "noncanonical") were appearing around the middle of the second century in Syria-Palestine and Egypt, and during that same period and in the same areas Christian gnostic groups were flourishing and came into conflict with the mainstream church.[3] In Rome in 144 CE, Marcion — soon to be considered the arch-heretic of the church — was excommunicated by the church of Rome. Even before this, early doctrinal definitions were underway, including — among a wide range of emerging issues — questions concerning the nature of Christ and his relation to God, the definition of church authority and organization, as well as liturgical practices and eschatological views, and the relation of church to empire. Differences in understanding these issues are reflected already in the NT writings and occur with increasing specification, for example, in *1 Clement, Didache, Epistle of Barnabas, Polycarp,* the *Letters* of Ignatius, the *Apocalypse of Peter,* the *Shepherd of Hermas,* as well as in Montanus, Tatian, Celsus, Hegesippus, and Irenaeus. The general heterodoxy of this initial period of Christianity is now well recognized, as is the early dominance in many areas of what the orthodox church would later call "heresies."[4] Certainly heterodoxy — "a syncretistic situation conducive to speculative thought without hierarchical control"[5] — was the mark of the earliest Egyptian

---

2. Compare the endpaper maps in Frend 1984. For much of the summary of early Christianity that follows, I have used this volume as a general resource. In addition, I have relied upon the more cautious — and, for the earliest period, undoubtedly more accurate — work of Helmut Koester (1982, vol. 2) and J. Neville Birdsall (1970), whose discussion is always in full awareness of the church-historical context.

3. Koester 1982: 2.201-3, 219-33, esp. 232; and also 236.

4. For a convenient summary of these points, see Wisse 1986.

5. Wisse 1983: 142; see also Klijn 1986; note the following statement: "Egypt is a fine example of burning questions dealing with orthodoxy and heterodoxy, and with Jewish Christianity and gnosis" (175).

period, which encompassed a variety of practices in Christianity, including gnostic forms of the young faith.

Meanwhile, forces outside Christianity were affecting it as well. Pliny the Younger, Governor of Bithynia in Asia Minor, wrote to Emperor Trajan around 112 CE about "the contagious disease of this superstition" (10.96), and Christian apologists, beginning with Quadratus and Aristides, soon issued their "invitations to a philosophical way of life" (Koester 1982: 2.338-40). Justin also sought to demonstrate the truth of the Christian faith, and died around 165 CE for confessing it, as did the aged Polycarp.

Then, by the end of the second century, the Greek NT was being translated into Latin, undoubtedly also into Syriac, and possibly into Coptic.[6] It is both of interest and of considerable significance to observe that "in the first two centuries all the theologians who achieved fame in the West were themselves from the East (from Marcion and the Apologists through Irenaeus and Hippolytus)," and, therefore, that "all the significant theologians of any influence in the West in the early period came from Eastern church backgrounds, bringing their New Testament texts with them" (K. and B. Aland 1987: 68).

With the coming of the third century, issues of Christian theology and philosophy were pursued in increasingly sophisticated fashion by Clement of Alexandria, Tertullian, Origen, Cyprian, and others, involving, for example, controversies over rebaptism, penance, Easter, the trinity, and christology. Influential centers of Christian scholarship existed, for example, in Alexandria and Caesarea, and Origen was influential in both. Manichaeism was a threat, but the greater threat in the middle of the third century was the brief Decian persecution, affecting Christians in cities throughout the empire, followed by a similar period under Valerian several years later.

In the midst of these varied activities, both positive for the church's development as well as negative, and occurring variously in the East and the West and from North to South, the earliest Christian writings were continuing to circulate. This can be documented in a number of ways. Colossians (4:16) shows that letters were exchanged between churches and read, and 2 Peter (3:15-16) confirms a knowledge of "all" of Paul's letters, indicating that they were in movement. The Apostolic Fathers (ca. 90-130) quoted from the earlier Christian writings. Justin (ca. 150) knows two or more of our four Gospels. Marcion not only limited his canon to the Gospel of Luke and ten letters of Paul, but edited them critically. Tatian produced his Diatessaron in Syria around 175, beginning a competition between a single, harmonized Gospel and the four separate Gospels. Succeeding Church Fathers quoted from a wide range of writings, many of which were to become canonical. Final settlement of the NT canon was to come more than two centuries after the days of Justin and Marcion, though the collection and authority of the fourfold Gospel and of the Pauline corpus were clear enough by Irenaeus's time (ca. 180).

Though we can never know the actual extent of the circulation of Christian writings throughout the Roman world, the process was dealt a severe blow during

---

6. Birdsall 1970: 345-47; cf. Metzger 1977: 8, 287-90.

the Diocletian persecution at the outset of the fourth century, when — beginning perhaps in 303 — copies of Christian Scripture were confiscated and destroyed. Over the following two decades, events significant for the church — both positive and negative — continued, culminating in Constantine's opening of the Council of Nicaea in 325 and his establishment of the "new Rome" at Constantinople in 330, and, of course, in the achievement by Eusebius of an *Ecclesiastical History*.

The point of this hasty and quite inadequate survey of activities and movements in the first few centuries of Christianity is simply to recall the multifarious interactions in these tumultuous times and to suggest that copies of NT books — as well as those of other early Christian writings — were circulating within these complex situations and were interactive with the circumstances described and with innumerable others like them. Unfortunately, we cannot with certainty link any specific early MS with any specific event or person. Yet we can imagine — quite legitimately — the importance of biblical MSS again and again in this early Christian world. We can well envision their role in worship and homily, in teaching and polemic, in church consultations, and in times of persecution; and we can postulate their certain transfer from congregation to congregation, from church leader to church leader, and from scholar to scholar, within both orthodox and heterodox Christianity.

It is within this background of dynamic movement, development, and controversy that the earliest NT MSS must be examined, for — as has long been asserted but too little exercised — the text of the NT in its earliest stages was a vibrant, living text that functioned dynamically within the developing church. Textual criticism, therefore, can never be understood apart from the history of the church.[7]

II. The Environment of the Earliest New Testament Manuscripts

In addition to this ecclesiastical background, we need also to sketch not only the situation with respect to the earliest MSS, including something of the environment they shared in the places where they were found, but also their general life setting in Christianity's dynamic first centuries. There are innumerable difficulties attending these tasks, as everyone recognizes, yet this is a crucial step if we are to make progress. One of the difficulties is that we know almost nothing about the specific provenance of our early MSS, except — of course — that the forty-five earliest ones all come from Egypt and that twenty of these (as well as seven others) were unearthed at Oxyrhynchus. Very little, however is known about Christianity at Oxyrhynchus at the time these MSS were used and finally discarded — although this general area of Egypt is known to have been a center of Christian activity at a later time, that is, in the fourth and fifth centuries (E. G. Turner 1968: 28).

Of the provenance of the other earliest papyri, such as the famous Chester

---

7. On the study of NT textual criticism in the context of church history, see especially Birdsall 1970: 311-16, 328-77; see also n. 1, above. See also K. and B. Aland 1987: 49-54, 67-71. The latter work, however, exaggerates the lack of attention to church history by NT textual critics, for viewing textual variants as products of the church's tradition is a theme that has been pursued by a number of scholars over the past sixty years, though most notably by American and British textual critics; for a summary, see Epp 1966: 15-21.

Beatty (P[45], P[46], P[47]) and the Bodmer papyri (P[66], P[72], P[75]), still less is known, though it was reported at the time of their purchase that the Chester Beatty papyri were discovered in a pitcher in a ruined church or monastery near Atfih (Aphroditopolis) in the Fayyûm (Roberts 1979: 7), about one-third of the way down the Nile River from Oxyrhynchus toward Alexandria. A similar statement accompanied the purchase of P[52], the earliest NT fragment of all, which was assumed to have come either from the Fayyûm or from Oxyrhynchus (Roberts 1935: 24-25; Bell and Skeat 1935: 7). It has also been surmised that Beatty and Bodmer codices may have come from the same church library, though there is no proof (Roberts 1970: 56). Among the famous uncial MSS, it has been suggested on occasion that Codices Vaticanus (B) and Sinaiticus (ℵ) represent two of the fifty parchment MSS that, according to Eusebius, were ordered by Constantine around 331 for his new churches in Constantinople, but this identification is based, most tenuously, on Eusebius's reference to "volumes of threefold and fourfold forms," which could, of course, fit the respective three-column and four-column formats of the two codices. However, Eusebius's words can be interpreted in other ways, and there are some reasons to think that Codex Vaticanus may have originated in Egypt.[8] Likewise, though Codex Alexandrinus (A) is usually assumed to have originated in Alexandria, it might have come from Constantinople or Caesarea (Streeter 1924: 120 n. 1). All of this is to suggest that our knowledge of the provenance of early NT MSS is scant.

Accordingly, these sparse data would seem to offer precious little assistance in an effort to link our early MSS in some direct way with early church history. Difficult as the process is, the fact that all of the earliest MSS come from Egypt makes worthwhile any and every conceivable form of investigation of the Egyptian environment. Artifacts and MSS from Alexandria certainly would help, but papyri from Alexandria and the Delta region have not survived, and the ancient city of Alexandria is now below sea level (Bell 1948: 10), raising several critical questions. For instance, were the cities in the Fayyûm or those farther removed from Alexandria, like Oxyrhynchus, Antinoe, or Hermopolis, in close touch with Alexandria or largely isolated from it? With what ease or difficulty did letters and literature circulate in these areas? What was the general level of cultural and literary activity in such places? Information on these matters will help us assess the role that the papyrus books originating in these localities might have played in society and the extent to which such books circulated within Egypt and in the Greco-Roman world generally.

We begin, then, by asking what we know of Christianity in Egypt in this period. Statements about our lack of knowledge are classic,[9] but the beginnings of Christian faith in Alexandria and in other parts of Egypt must reach back to the first half of the second century, even though that cannot easily be documented. One might, however, argue for that conclusion from our earliest NT MS, P[52]. This tiny fragment of the Fourth Gospel was written in the first quarter of the second century, but

8. See Metzger 1968a: 7-8; see also Birdsall 1970: 359-60.
9. For statements from Adolf Harnack and B. H. Streeter, see Klijn 1986: 161; from C. H. Roberts, see the opening sentence of 1979: 1, also quoted by Pearson 1986: 132.

probably nearer 100 than 125;[10] the same may be said for the "Sayings of Jesus" fragment from Oxyrhynchus[11] and of Papyrus Egerton 2, usually referred to as "the Unknown Gospel."[12] The precise provenance of neither P[52] nor Egerton 2 is known, but doubtless they are from the Fayyûm or Oxyrhynchus (Roberts 1935: 24-25), and the "Sayings of Jesus" fragment is from Oxyrhynchus. In fact, certain affinities between the latter papyrus and P[52] suggest to some that they could have come from "the same early Christian community in Middle Egypt" (Roberts 1935: 25).

Looking at the early date of these papyrus fragments and their likely provenance in the Fayyûm or Oxyrhynchus — that is, in Middle Egypt 150 to 200 miles up the Nile of Alexandria — suggests that Christianity was well established in those areas by around 100 CE. In addition, the very likelihood that a number of the very early Oxyrhynchus Christian papyri were private copies — copies belonging to individual Christians rather than to communities or churches[13] — reinforces the early presence of Christianity in Egypt, for the following reason: though possibly debatable, it is logical to assume that copies of authoritative books would first be in the possession of a church or community (for liturgical and instructional use) and only later be copied for private use. If so, the existence of private copies so far from Alexandria at so early a period suggests the early origin, rapid expansion, and significant saturation of Christianity in at least the lower third of Egypt at an early time.

Though this scenario is the most likely one, a *caveat* is in order. It is possible — following the line of argument to be presented below — that one or even all of these early Christian papyri could have been written elsewhere and brought into Egypt for use there, and such an event could have occurred immediately after the production of a papyrus MS or considerably thereafter. Should this have taken place many decades or as much as a century or more after their writing, these MSS could not so easily be used to document the presence of Christianity in Egypt in the early second century.

Yet it must be remembered that virtually all of the papyri are from Egyptian rubbish heaps and presumably, therefore, were in extended use — most likely in Egypt — prior to being discarded. Nevertheless, the possibility that MSS like P[52] could have been produced elsewhere and imported into Egypt is a further complicating factor and gives the whole matter an ironic twist: In determining the presence of Christianity in Egypt, the date that a papyrus MS was discarded may be more important than the date of its copying.[14] If, for example, it could be determined that

---

10. Roberts 1935. Though at an earlier time dated 125-150, recent opinion moves it back into the 100-125 period, perhaps very early in that quarter century. See Roberts 1935: 12-16; B. and K. Aland 1987: 85.

11. Grenfell and Hunt (1898: 1-3 and plate) gave it the first position in their first published volume of *The Oxyrhynchus Papyri*.

12. Bell and Skeat; Koester 1982: 2.222. Roberts 1970: 62 dates it "about the middle" of the 2d century.

13. Roberts 1979: 9. He says "many, but not all" of our papyri may have belonged to individual Christians. For more on the nonprofessional quality of these papyri, see Roberts 1970: 62-63.

14. I owe this point to Frederik Wisse, in discussion at the conference.

P[52] was discarded in 175 or 200 or 250, and if we knew more about how long MSS were used in early Christian congregations before they were "retired" and replaced, we could work backward from the date of discard to the date of a probable presence of Christianity in Middle Egypt. Unfortunately, much less is known about when the MSS were cast on the rubbish heaps than about the date and provenance of writing — which is itself precious little — and the useful life of a papyrus MS in a liturgical setting is something I have not seen discussed.[15]

The non-Christian Egyptian papyri in general, however, provide information on two other factors highly relevant to our discussion, and here there is greater clarity: first, the papyri attest extensive and lively interactions between Alexandria and the outlying areas, and also between the outlying areas and other parts of the Roman world, including Rome itself; and, second, they provide evidence of the wide circulation of documents in this early period. The following are a few examples. Papyri indicate that Jews were in touch with each other in the provinces.[16] One papyrus shows that of 325 Philadelphians registered as resident outside that village, sixty-four were resident in Alexandria (Roberts 1979: 4). Tax registers from Karanis suggest a population of five or six thousand there and "a small minority of Alexandrian citizens, who are probably absentee landlords," as well as Greeks from Alexandria and Roman veterans; and literary texts there include Homer's *Iliad* and Chariton's romance, *Chaereas and Callirhoe* (E. G. Turner 1968: 80-81). Hermopolis (up the Nile from Oxyrhynchus) yielded an official letter of congratulation to a certain Plution upon his return from Rome, including quotations from Euripides and *Poimandres* (Turner 1968: 85-86). A number of members of the Museum at Alexandria are connected by the papyri with estates in the outlying country. One prominent member of this scholarly group, around 200 CE in Philadelphia, can also be connected with Rome, leading E. G. Turner to remark that he was "a person therefore who might have carried books from Rome to Philadelphia" (1968: 86). Other members of this Museum elite can be documented in Antinoe (near Hermopolis) and in Oxyrhynchus. Documents from Oxyrhynchus, dating from around 173 CE, involve people who were obviously Alexandrian scholars (one of whom is known otherwise) and who discuss the procurement of books. Turner's conclusion on this is of interest:

> Here, for Oxyrhynchus at least, we tread firm ground: a circle of persons exchanging notes on how to procure and get copies made of works of scholarship, who are themselves professional scholars. (1968: 87)

In addition, there is extensive papyrus evidence that documents and letters were brought to Egypt from a wide range of localities and from considerable distances, including Ravenna, Macedonia, Seleucia, Ostia, Rome, and Constantinople, eliciting Turner's rhetorical question, "What books or Christian texts might not have been carried in?" He adds that these data serve to "alert the searcher to the possibility

---

15. Contrary to common opinion, papyrus is a durable substance: see Epp 1989b: 262-66 for a summary of the issue.
16. Roberts 1979: 4 (who refers, of course, to Tcherikover and Fuks 1957-64: vols. 1 and 2).

that other literary (and religious) books, Latin or Greek, found in Egypt were the products of scriptoria outside Egypt," though he admits that a desideratum in the field is a criterion for identifying MSS copied outside Egypt (1968: 50-51, 96).[17]

SITES OF PAPYRUS FINDS IN EGYPT

Oxyrhynchus also yielded an account of fees paid to a scribe for copying MSS. There were letters asking friends in Alexandria to buy paper for them, or telling family members that inkwells and pens had been left for their use, or revealing fine expression and writing style. An interesting papyrus scrap lists subjects for student declamations which would require the reading of Thucydides or Euripides (Turner 1968: 83-84, 87). In the villages in the Fayyûm generally, Homer, Plato, Sophocles, and other Greek

17. See also Roberts and Skeat 1983: 35.

authors are well represented (Turner 1971: 96). Moreover, the papyrus texts of the "Acts of the Alexandrian Martyrs," stemming from the first three centuries, represent a "pamphleteering literature, probably passed from hand to hand" (Turner 1971: 96; cf. Roberts 1979: 3); and there is evidence of wide circulation since specimens have been found as far as 200 miles apart, beginning more than 150 miles from Alexandria at Arsinoe, then at Oxyrhynchus, and perhaps also at Panopolis, 160 miles up the Nile from Oxyrhynchus (Roberts: 3). From these data, C. H. Roberts concludes:

> With this analogy in mind, we shall not be inclined to accept the view of some scholars that until the third century Christianity was confined to Alexandria when Christian manuscripts of second century date have been found in Middle and Upper Egypt. . . . There is abundant evidence of a close and continuous relationship between the Greeks of Alexandria and the Greek middle class in the provincial towns and villages at all levels — economic, cultural, and personal. (1979: 4)[18]

It is not easy, however, to determine precisely what economic, cultural, and personal life was actually like in a district capital such as Oxyrhynchus, where archaeological finds were minimal. It is, however, of interest — as we have already observed — how much can be discerned from "philological archaeology," that is, from the papyrus documents. We know something of the number of public buildings from records of a night watchman's rounds — including temples and two Christian churches; we have evidence, actually, of twenty temples, of gymnasia, of courts for playing ball and a race course, of a theater — seating 8,000 to 12,000 people — as well as a script on papyrus for a play of Euripides; and we have records of money allocated for a new street, of residents' addresses in named quarters of the city, and of soldiers stationed in Oxyrhynchus.[19] This is in addition to the correspondence and literary activity alluded to earlier, all of which adds up to a city full of cultural and intellectual pursuits, not to mention, of course, the everyday activities of life.

Similar data could be compiled for other cities in the Fayyûm or farther up the Nile, where papyri have been found, but what we have outlined will be sufficient to make the point that these were places not only of literacy but of literary activity and that they were in frequent and relatively easy communication — both through travel and letter writing — with Alexandria and other major areas in the Greco-Roman world. As further documentation, reference might be made, for example, to *P. Mich. Zenon* 10, a letter dated 257 BCE, which reports a two-month adventure by ship from Alexandria to southern Asia Minor; but the letter itself which told of the trip "took only nineteen days to get back to the village of Philadelphia in the Arsinoite nome, some 250 kilometers up-river from Alexandria" (Lewis 1986: 12). In addition, mundane commercial documents on papyrus show that the business dealings of the Philadelphian banker, Zenon, reached not only nearby Memphis, but all the way into the Nile Delta to places

---

18. See also Roberts and Skeat 1983: 35.
19. Roberts 1979: 81-82; see also 78-88 for other localities and cultural information.

like Athribis, about seventy miles from Philadelphia, and Mendes, forty miles farther into the Delta near the Mediterranean Sea.[20]

Though one would not hastily equate the Christian production and use of books with the cultural literary activity of the Greco-Roman world, yet the Christian papyri — in our case the NT papyri — must be viewed within this active, vibrant world, and viewed with every degree of legitimate historical and creative imagination that can be brought to bear on the subject.

III. Textual Clusters and the Early Spectrum of the New Testament Manuscripts

It is time, now, to look at the early NT text within this twofold background of the church-historical context and the Egyptian cultural setting as revealed through the papyri. We must explore how our knowledge of the NT MSS might be combined with the information gained from their historical-cultural environment and then break through, if possible, to new insights into the earliest period of textual transmission. Should that elude us, we may hope at least for greater clarity on the issues that confront us in the early formative period.

A. Designations for the Textual Clusters

A first step (though by no means an indispensable one) is to take seriously the clarion call from the early post–World War II era that we abandon the anachronistic terminology used in the period prior to the discovery of the Chester Beatty and Bodmer papyri. Kenneth W. Clark issued that call already in 1948, before the Bodmer papyri were known, by saying that "the only studies made thus far [of the Chester Beatty papyri] seem to approach these texts by reversing the centuries. We require a new mental attitude, wherein we . . . approach these earliest materials *de novo*," adding that "we should study the third-century witnesses in their own right" (1950: 20-21). More widely quoted — and rightly so — has been the statement of J. Neville Birdsall in 1958, who pointed out the fault "common to many contemporary scholars who attempt to discuss and define such early evidence as this by standards of later witnesses," adding specifically:

> Beyond the fourth century the divisions of "Neutral," "Western," "Caesarean," "Byzantine" (or corresponding terms) are apposite: but in the early period, which such a papyrus as p^{66} reveals to us, these concepts are out of place. The task of present-day criticism is to inaugurate an era in which we begin from the earliest evidence and on the basis of its interpretation discuss the later. (1960: 7)

So, we shall abandon the long-standing but largely anachronistic and par-

---

20. Lewis 1986: 53-54. Note, incidentally, that the Zenon correspondence refers to the acquisition of papyrus rolls from the Delta region (54). [See now Epp 1991, esp. 52-55, and n. 25, below.]

tially misleading designations of the past when discussing the earliest textual period, especially the terms "Neutral," "Western," and "Caesarean," and we shall try some new terms. Departure from the old categories is particularly important when dealing with the papyri, but we should go a step further and abandon also, at least for the moment, the term "text-type," since the existence of such entities in the early centuries has been questioned in some quarters.[21] We shall substitute "textual group" or "textual cluster," assuming that these terms lack the offensive implications of a rigidly fixed form or a tightly integrated character and that they avoid the attribution to textual groups of an officially conveyed status. Then, if and as appropriate, we may bring back the term "text-type" in the course of the investigation.

It will be obvious to all that proposing new symbols in the field of NT textual criticism is an extremely hazardous venture, as witnessed by the fate accorded the schemes of Westcott-Hort, or von Soden, or F. G. Kenyon — all of which seemed appropriate enough in their respective periods of research, but, as scholarship passed them by, were soon out of date. Nor do I wish to suggest that proposing new terminology is either the burden of this paper or, for that matter, of any intrinsic importance. Yet, reluctance to start anew is, by default, to permit the perpetuation of anachronistic labels and to necessitate the repeated explanation of terms that already are used by all of us only with surrounding quotation marks.

In forming new designations, ideally we should begin with terms or symbols that are both simple and unbiased, or — alternatively — with terminology that has a genuine historical basis. On the latter approach, natural designations for NT textual clusters, for example, would be "the P75 text," "the P45 text," etc., but the obvious danger here is the same as that which brought about our present terminological crisis: who can say that even MSS like P75 will remain either the earliest or the most distinctive representative of that particular textual cluster?[22] Rather, the use of arbitrary symbols is preferable, though it would be advantageous if we could employ some symbols that, at the same time, would also recognize and recall certain aspects of our past scholarship that are generally recognized as valid. That would make the symbols both more meaningful and easier to remember. So, rather than merely selecting in an arbitrary fashion the numbers 1, 2, 3, 4 or the Greek letters alpha, beta, gamma, delta (as Westcott-Hort and Kenyon did, though with different mean-

21. Most prominently Kurt Aland; see 1965: 334-37 (and the updated German version, 1967: 188-89); more recently, see K. and B. Aland 1987: 59-64, 103, who distinguish between "different forms" of the text (which they say did exist prior to the 3d/4th century) and "text types" (which they say existed only in the 4th century and after); cf. Colwell 1969: 55: "Very few, if any, text-types were established by that time [AD 200]."

22. As to the likelihood of discovering additional NT papyri of importance, see the pessimistic statement in K. and B. Aland 1987: 75: "After the impressive growth in the number of manuscripts recorded in the nineteenth century by Gregory and in the twentieth century by the Institute for New Testament Textual Research, it is unlikely that the future will bring any comparable increases," though they go on to allow that recent finds at St. Catherine's Monastery on Mt. Sinai "could change the situation." Of course, the rising water table throughout Egypt, as a result of the high dam at Assuan, threatens the survival of any buried papyri; yet, the long-standing pessimism in the past about new finds in Egypt was repeatedly falsified by fresh discoveries (see E. G. Turner 1968: 40).

ings[23]), I would suggest that we keep matters as simple as possible and use the letters A, B, C, and D when probing for the basic NT textual groups of the early period. These are symbols that will easily justify themselves, and yet will remain essentially unbiased regardless of future discoveries and developments. In this way we can make a fresh start — at least in appearances — with respect to our terminology, and yet retain connections that are sufficiently reminiscent of certain significant scholarly achievements in our evolving history of the text as to give the system immediate credibility. The four proposed groups are set forth in what follows.

Textual Group "A" — On this scheme, "A" would designate what is variously called the Majority text, or the Koine, or the later Byzantine; with the letter "A" suggesting such words as the "average" text (in the sense of ordinary or common), or the "accepted" text (with affinities to "textus receptus"), or the "ascendant" text (since it became the text that prevailed, though wrongly so), but also calling to mind Codex Alexandrinus (A), which is the oldest representative of this textual group — though only in the Gospels — and of course recalling Westcott-Hort's designation "Antiochian" (1881: 2.142-46). (We could use "K" for Koine, or "M" for Majority, but there is a nice symmetry in using four consecutive letters of the alphabet.)

Textual Group "B" — The symbol "B" would be used to represent the character and quality of the text found in P[75] and Codex Vaticanus (B), which are the major representatives of this textual cluster. Of the close relationship of the texts in these two specific MSS there can be no doubt. The symbol "B," while it may appear to perpetuate anachronistic procedures of the past — in that it appears to use a later manuscript name for an earlier textual phenomenon — is in reality quite neutral when it is seen simply as one of several consecutive letters of the alphabet. Yet, it has the advantage of easy recognition.

Textual Group "D" — The letter "D" (to skip group "C" for the moment) would designate the kind of text found in P[29], P[48], and P[38], which in a later form is found in Codex Bezae (D). The use of "D" would rid us of the largely misleading term "Western," but would leave us with a well-established symbol for this textual cluster and — again — place it in a more unbiased setting.

Textual Group "C" — Finally, the letter "C," which conveniently stands between "B" and "D," would represent the "in-between" text that occurs, for example, in P[45] and in parts of Codex Washingtonianus (W). The letter "C," of course, recalls the term Caesarean," though this is a name that should no longer be perpetuated; yet no harm will be done if, for some, it serves to recall the general kind of text found in this cluster.

Before offering further explanations of this scheme, it should be observed that those who eschew the identification of text-types in the early period of NT textual transmission (see n. 21 above) will object to the entire enterprise; but such an approach appears to reflect more an obscurantism than a realistic attempt to come to terms with the early data, limited though it is. It seems to me that we should use as judiciously and as creatively as possible the data we have and venture boldly

---

23. See Taylor 1963: 6-7; Kenyon 1949: 197.

toward some scholarly progress — we should take risks, forge new paths — rather than close off the future by preemptive decisions or through judgments that by their very nature preclude advances in our knowledge of the past.

B. Definitions of Textual Clusters

The next steps are to define these textual clusters in greater detail (using the fresh symbols) and then to show how they are to be viewed dynamically within their general life-setting in those earliest centuries of Christianity. Naturally, there is a fair measure of tentativeness in all of this, but that — as we say — "goes with the territory." Though textual criticism has shown itself to be — by its very nature — a highly conservative discipline, an overly cautious attitude when exploring theoretical issues will forestall the progress so urgently required in the field. We need to open some new windows, and — if possible — a few doors as well! A general survey of the situation of the text in the earliest known period will set the stage for these closer definitions of textual groups.

The forty-five earliest NT MSS which are currently known, that is, those dating up to and including the turn of the third/fourth centuries, present us with a number of differing textual complexions. Everyone recognizes this, though not all agree on how they are to be differentiated or what to call them or what the range of difference means. These and other difficulties abound as we try to interrogate these aged witnesses and as we attempt to use them in theorizing procedures. Perhaps the most obvious difficulty is that most are highly fragmentary in nature. Yet, the first principle to be adopted in assessing the fragmentary papyri is clear enough: "If a fragment preserves a passage where there is any variation in the tradition, it is quite sufficient to signal the textual character of the whole manuscript," as Kurt Aland and Barbara Aland affirm in their recent book (1987: 58).[24]

A second difficulty is that all forty-five of these earliest MSS — as well as all the other NT papyri — are from Egypt, and Egypt only. Does this mean that the array of textual complexions they present all originated in Egypt? In answering that question, we should resist the temptation to look to later NT MSS that may represent other places and draw any conclusions; rather — at least at this stage of investigation — we should stay with the earliest MSS only and restrict our analysis to them alone. But does that not preclude the possibility of offering any sort of answer as to whether all the NT texts found on papyri originated in Egypt? No, for it seems to me that we do have a path toward an answer, though — by the nature of the case — it cannot be decisively demonstrated.

The answer as to whether the varying textual complexions of the earliest papyri all originated in Egypt — and, therefore, the answer to the more substantive question as to whether Egypt is representative of the entire early history of the NT text — that answer was implicit in our description of the movement of population and the circulation of letters and literature in Egypt in the first centuries of the

---

24. They support the principle with the everyday analogy that "there is no need to consume a whole jar of jelly to identify the quality of its contents — a spoonful or two is quite enough!"

Christian era. That is, if — as we have shown — there existed a lively and vigorous movement of people back and forth between Alexandria and the Greco-Roman world to the east and west and north, and also between Alexandria and the upper regions of Egypt, especially the Fayyûm and centers like Oxyrhynchus, and if — as we have shown — there was a brisk circulation of letters and of literature in these same areas, then we are compelled to give up, first, the notion that all of these textual complexions necessarily originated in Egypt, and, second, that they remained in or were confined to Egypt. In fact, the evidence from the non-NT papyri which reveals dynamic interchanges of people, letters, and books to and from Egypt, as well as within Egypt, actually would permit us to go to the logical extreme — if we wished — of asserting that *none* of the NT textual complexions necessarily originated in Egypt, though there is no reason to carry the matter that far. Suffice it to say that the breadth and intensity of the intellectual commerce between Egypt — even Middle and Upper Egypt — and the rest of the vast Mediterranean region between 30 and 300 CE[25] supports the strong possibility — indeed the strong probability — that *the various textual groups presented by our Egyptian papyri represent texts from the entire Mediterranean region* (including, of course, those texts that might have originated in Egypt itself).

A dynamic view of NT textual transmission, then, envisions considerable movement of NT MSS to and from Egypt and within Egypt, at least in the period up to the Diocletian persecution beginning around 303. It also permits us, by inference, to put to rest the question as to whether Egypt adequately represents the textual spectrum of earliest Christianity — we may presume that it does.

Another line of argument can be employed to support the same conclusion

25. The case for the widespread and speedy transfer of letters in the Greco-Roman world has now been presented, with detailed documentation, in Epp 1991, especially in the section on "The Speed of Transferring Letters" (52-55). Here it is shown, from dated and docketed papyrus letters — i.e., letters containing both the date of writing and the date of receipt — that letters could travel some 800 miles in two months; or some 350 miles in thirty-six days; or 125 miles in three weeks, or some 400 miles in fourteen days; or 150 miles in four, six, or seven days; or fifteen miles in the same day, to cite several actual examples. The study concludes that:

> The evidence sampled here — and there is much more — documents . . . the prompt transfer of letters throughout the Greco-Roman world. This lively activity occurred not only within Egypt (i.e., between the Delta, the Fayyum, and upper Egypt), but between Egypt and places as far removed as Ostia in Italy, Cilicia in Asia Minor, Sidon in Syria, and Arabia — to mention only a few specific examples cited above. These data can be combined with other evidence of brisk "intellectual commerce" and dynamic interchanges of people, literature, books, and letters between Egypt and the vast Mediterranean region during the broad NT period to permit at least two claims about the early NT manuscripts: (1) the various textual complexions (usually called "text-types") represented by the earliest NT papyri — all of which were found in Egypt — did not have to originate there, but could easily, in a matter of a few weeks, have moved anywhere in the Mediterranean area. Moreover, if some of these textual complexions did originate in Egypt, the dynamic situation meant that they would not — could not — have been confined to Egypt. Therefore, (2) it is not only theoretically possible, but quite probable that the present array of text-types represented in the Egyptian NT papyri do, in fact, represent text-types from the *entire* Mediterranean region, and, furthermore, that they could very likely represent *all* of the existent text-types in that large region in the early period of NT textual transmission. (55-56)

in a more explicit fashion. Recently C. H. Roberts (with T. C. Skeat) has made a case that the *nomina sacra* (the uniform abbreviations of divine names and sacred terms in MSS) were a Christian creation established either by the church at Jerusalem before 70 CE, or by the church at Antioch slightly later — as a kind of "embryonic creed" of the first church — and that from there they "spread to Egypt and everywhere where Greek was written." This system, Roberts says, "was too complex for the ordinary scribe to operate without either rules or an authoritative exemplar" — because without one or the other it would have been difficult, even in a small Christian community, to determine which usages (of the secondary *nomina sacra*) were secular and which were sacred.[26] In addition, a case can be made that the *nomina sacra* and the codex form of book not only were both Christian inventions, but that both came into existence at the same place at about the same time. Moreover, both phenomena share the same characteristic: each serves effectively to differentiate Christian books from both Jewish and secular books (Roberts and Skeat: 57-58).

The presence in Egypt of "this remarkably uniform system of *nomina sacra*" in the earliest Christian MSS (all of which were codices) only slightly more than a century after their invention calls for explanation. Roberts's conclusion is that already "at an early date there were standard copies of the Christian scriptures" (1970: 64). On this theory, such standard copies would have to have been established in Jerusalem or Antioch and transmitted, either directly or through other centers, to Egypt. Others think that the *nomina sacra* (and also the codex form) might have originated at Alexandria or even Rome.[27] The point is that a highly technical, rigidly practiced *Christian* procedure was well established in Middle Egypt prior to the time of our earliest NT papyri, which in a rather striking fashion, regardless of its place of origin, attests to the active movement of NT MSS within the eastern Greco-Roman world — and at the very least attests to early and active textual transmission within Egypt itself.

Though no one yet is asserting that the *nomina sacra* procedures and practices suggest that Christian scriptoria existed prior to 200, that is at least a possibility. What these practices do suggest with more certainty, however, is that the churches in this earliest period, at least in the East, were perhaps not as loosely organized as has been assumed,[28] and, therefore, they also were not as isolated from one another as has been affirmed. Indeed, at least one "program of standardization"[29] — the *nomina sacra* —was certainly functioning with obvious precision and care. Moreover, the exclusive use of the codex by Christians for biblical books in the earliest period (Roberts and Skeat 1983: 42) evidences a second standardization program — the very form that the books assumed appears to have been a matter of

---

26. The basic case is made in Roberts 1979: 44-46, where he argued for Jerusalem, but it is revised and supplemented in Roberts and Skeat 1983: 57-61, where Antioch is favored.

27. See Roberts 1979: 42-44; for arguments against Alexandria especially, see Roberts and Skeat 1983: 54-57.

28. These two points are made against views taken in K. and B. Aland 1987: 55-56, 59.

29. The phrase is from K. and B. Aland 1987: 59, where, in their discussion of P[45], P[46], and P[66], they do at least allow for the possibility that the MSS could have been "imported from elsewhere."

policy. We should not, then, "rule out of court" the likelihood that additional standard textual procedures were in operation at this very early time.

When — at long last — we now analyze the textual characteristics of our earliest NT witnesses, noting differences among readings that are sufficient to distinguish separate textual complexions, and when we subsequently trace lines of connection with later MSS of similar textual complexions, we must take these factors into account. Other significant observations will arise in the process of sketching the composition of the various textual clusters, to which we now turn.

Members of the "A" text group — The "A" text cluster, that is, the "accepted" text or the Koine or later Byzantine textual group, need not be further considered here, for the early papyri are not involved (although a few papyri of the sixth and seventh centuries do represent the "A" text). Furthermore, everyone recognizes that this textual group exists, though not until the fourth century — that is, after the period of the earliest papyri. Moreover, everyone also acknowledges that this can actually be called a "text-type."[30] The recognized constituent members can be found in the standard handbooks.[31]

Members of the "B" text group — The place to begin a description of the "B" textual cluster is with the striking and highly significant fact that the texts of P[75] and Codex Vaticanus (B) are almost identical, a fact which demonstrates that there is virtually a straight line from the text of a papyrus dated around 200 to that of a major, elegant MS of 150 years later.[32] Does this permit us to expect — or to require — that similarly direct connections will be found between other early papyri and certain later MSS? Not necessarily, for both the discovery of the NT papyri and the survival of later MSS are random phenomena, and no uniform or complete representation of the textual spectrum can be expected to have been preserved for us. So we take what we have, both of the early papyri and the later witnesses, and attempt a creative reconstruction of the transmission process, recognizing that it will always be partial and less than fully satisfying. Precisely because this is the situation, the close affinity of P[75] and B is all the more striking, for it demonstrates that an early papyrus can stand very near the beginning point of a clearly identifiable and distinctive textual group that has been preserved with a high degree of accuracy over several generations and through a period that often has been assumed to have been a chaotic and free textual environment.

If we had several pieces of evidence like the P[75]-B relationship, it would be plausible to argue that the situation was not chaotic, but quite orderly. Although that evidence eludes us due to the randomness of the survival of papyrus, the evidence we have does, to a certain extent, move in that direction. For it was more likely a semblance of standardization, rather than accident, that permitted the text of Vaticanus — over several generations — to maintain its close affinity to that represented in P[75]. Vaticanus was not copied from P[75] — they had a common ancestor (Fee 1974: 33-40) — so one must ask about the transmission process that would have produced

30. See, e.g., K. and B. Aland 1987: 51, 64-69.
31. E.g., Metzger 1971: xxx-xxxi; Metzger 1968a: 213.
32. This hardly requires documentation, but both references and evidence may be found in Fee 1974: 24-28 [now Chapter 13].

this very similar resultant text. To answer that P[75] is a MS with a "strict" text (K. and B. Aland 1987: 64, 93, 95) may be descriptive, but it does not answer the question *"why?"* Indeed, the very employment of the term "strict" in describing some early NT papyri implies — though it does not prove — that a form of standardization was operative in the transmission process already at an early time.

As a matter of fact, the discovery of P[75] nullified an older view of standardization, for the close affinity of P[75] with Codex Vaticanus swept away the cobwebs of a long-standing and commonly held notion that Codex Vaticanus reflects only a third/fourth-century recension. On the contrary, it can be demonstrated that the P[75]-B textual tradition represents a relatively pure form of preservation of the text of a common ancestor,[33] and that P[75], therefore, is not itself an editorial adaptation or recension.[34] We are left, then, with the undoubted fact that a distinctive kind of text, *with both antecedents and descendants,* existed in the very early period of NT textual transmission. That text actually exists in an extant document from around 200 CE. It also had earlier antecedents, although it is difficult to specify their dates. However, a dynamic view of textual transmission — combined with the *nomina sacra* evidence — would suggest that not only the text of P[75] and its antecedents, but also other early NT papyri have a significantly earlier history in Judaea or Syria, as well as in Egypt. Moreover, there are enough hints that some early procedures of standardization were involved in the process to warrant calling the P[75]-B cluster a "text-type." Therefore, I would not hesitate to affirm the existence of at least one text-type — which we can designate the "B text-type" — *in the second century.*

The slightly earlier P[66] is usually associated with P[75] and the later Vaticanus in this textual group. It has been argued that P[66] is the product of a scriptorium.[35] Whether or not this is the case, the papyrus was produced by a "scribe-turned-recensor," who (though a careless workman) was himself correcting his text against a second exemplar and, in addition, appears intent on producing a more readable, common Greek style by abandoning Johannine style on numerous occasions (Johannine style, that is, as it is found in P[75] and B). Thus, his text moves away from that of P[75] (and toward the kind of readings later seen in the "A" type of text), though overall the text of P[66] still is closer in character to that of P[75] (and B) than it is to other MSS,[36] though it falls short (by at least ten percentage points) of the seventy percent agreement required by current practice to demonstrate textual affinity (see below). Yet, to place a text like P[66] in a "text-type" like "B" does not diminish "B" as an actual text-type, for the motivations of the scribe of P[66] — both his efforts to make the text readable and his quasi-scholarly activity in comparing and correcting his copy to a second exemplar — can be adequately recognized, providing thereby

33. See the compelling series of arguments that lead to this conclusion in Fee 1974; on the recension view, see 20-24; on the view that there is a common ancestry of the MSS, see 33-40.

34. Fee 1974: 32-33; cf. K. and B. Aland 1987: 64, 93, 95, where the term "strict" implies the same conclusion.

35. E.g., by Ernest C. Colwell and Gordon D. Fee; for documentation and arguments, see Fee 1974: 30-31. On the "impossibility" of Christian scriptoria before 200 (except perhaps in Alexandria "about 200"), see K. and B. Aland 1987: 70.

36. Fee 1974: 30-31; cf. Fee 1968b: 9-14, 35, 76-83.

an explanation for his departures from his text-type norm. It may be a "wild" member of the group, but it is a group member nonetheless.[37]

If this is an adequate analysis of P[66] and of its relationship to P[75] and Vaticanus, then we learn something significant about "text-types." A text-type is not a closely concentrated entity with rigid boundaries, but it is more like a galaxy — with a compact nucleus and additional but less closely related members which range out from the nucleus toward the perimeter. An obvious problem is how to determine when the outer limits of those more remote, accompanying members have been reached for one text-type and where the next begins. We shall return to this issue in a moment.

To these witnesses for the "B-text" — P[75], Vaticanus (B), and P[66] — can be added others, both among the papyri and among later MSS that share a similar textual complexion. These identifications necessarily must be quite tentative with respect to the fragmentary papyri. In addition, the classifications for all MSS should really be structured separately for various sections of the NT, particularly for the Gospels, for the Pauline letters, for Acts and the General Epistles, and for Revelation, because many MSS confine their contents to one of these groups. The matter is more complex, however, for "the textual history of the New Testament differs from corpus to corpus, and even from book to book; therefore the witnesses have to be re-grouped in each new section" (Colwell 1961: 138 = 1969: 55). This is primarily the result of the way in which books were grouped in the transmission process, for the makeup of MSS varies vastly and many different combinations of books are to be found as one moves from MS to MS.[38] In addition, a number of MSS show "block mixture," that is, they contain sections reflecting one distinctive kind of text, and other sections reflecting another. Thus, any classification of MSS will lack the desired precision and neatness.

By definition, textual clusters, and especially text-types, can only become visible and be identified when lines of connection can be drawn between and among a number of MSS which share a similar textual complexion. Furthermore, standards must be established both to determine relationships between MSS and to differentiate distinctive textual groups from one another. These standards cannot be impressionistic or based on random samples, but must be grounded in a scientific and full comparison of agreement/disagreement in variation-units (or in test readings, when large numbers of MSS are under consideration). The isolation of the variation-units (or test readings) must then be followed by quantitative measures of textual similarities and differences. These methods have been extensively explored and utilized, as well as substantially refined, in the current generation of NT textual criticism.[39] As to the definition of "text-type," no one yet has surpassed that offered by Ernest C. Colwell:

---

37. A. F. J. Klijn's description of P[66] as "Neutral in a non-pure way" is accepted and confirmed by Fee 1968b: 35.

38. See K. and B. Aland 1987: 78-79 for statistics.

39. See the important theoretical work, and its application, by Gordon D. Fee, especially 1968a [now Chapter 12].

The quantitative definition of a text-type is a group of manuscripts that agree more than 70 percent of the time and is separated by a gap of about 10 percent from its neighbors. (Colwell-Tune 1963: 29 = Colwell 1969: 59)

Although highly fragmentary MSS do not lend themselves readily to this process, yet the readings within their variation-units can be fully compared with those of any other MS. To such results the criterion earlier quoted must be applied (see n. 24 above): the textual character of a whole MS can be signalled even by a fragment's agreement with a variation in the textual tradition; therefore significant agreement with other MSS should qualify even a fragmentary witness as a member of a textual cluster. The randomness of the fragmentary papyri raises additional questions, however. For example, in these situations is seventy percent agreement still the minimum to qualify as a "fellow member" of a textual group?

In spite of all these contingencies, the process of assessing textual complexions can go forward and relationships can be established. In the case of the B-text, the later "trajectory" of transmission would include — beyond P75, Vaticanus (B), and P66 — the fourth-century Codex Sinaiticus (ℵ) (though not in John 1–8), Codex L (eighth century), and minuscules 33 (ninth century), 1739 (tenth century) (except in Acts), and 579 (thirteenth century), to mention only the most obvious.

Members of the "C" text group — In line with our stated principle of beginning at the beginning, we start with one of the early papyri that clearly differs in its textual complexion from that represented in the "B" text, namely, P45. Since textual groupings can be defined only when lines of connection can be drawn to other similar MSS, we want to know if such connections exist for P45. Since the time of its discovery and initial analysis, its most interesting connections have been found to be with Codex Washingtonianus (W) of the fifth century, but only in Mark 5:31–16:20 (since W is a classic example of block mixture). Elsewhere in the Gospels, its text has been described as "intermediate" between the Alexandrian (= "Neutral") and "Western," to use the usual designations (Metzger 1968a: 37) and the usual methods,[40] or — to use our designation — its text stands between the "B" and "D" textual groups. Thus, P45 was linked to a textual group called "Caesarean," a text-type considered, until recently, as a well-established one standing midway between "B" and "D." This is not the place to review the exigencies of the so-called "Caesarean" text (see Hurtado 1981), but it is sufficient to say that the P45-W kind of text cannot be described as either "Caesarean" or "pre-Caesarean" in Mark. Rather, it constitutes its own group, with further developments evident in f13, but with no significant connections with its previously regarded "Caesarean" fellow members, chief among which were Codex Koridethi (Θ) and minuscule 565 (Hurtado: 88-89). Yet the affinity of variation-units between P45 and W in Mark virtually reaches the seventy percent mark (68.9%), with P45 and f13 registering 55.3% agreement, but no other MS reaching more than 44% agreement with P45 (Hurtado 63; cf. 86-87). Hence, the line or "trajectory" of the P45 or "C" text, to the extent that it can be recognized at present, extends from P45 to W (in Mark) and secondarily to f13. Codex

40. See Epp 1989b, where the treatment of the papyri in the history of NT textual criticism is treated in detail.

W, by the way, appears to have been written in Egypt,[41] but — on the basis of principles earlier enunciated — it would be premature and unwarranted to draw the conclusion that it might represent a text-type of Egyptian origin.

In the case of the "C" text, we cannot readily refer to the standard handbooks to find its constituent members. This is due to the fact that so much has changed in the discipline in the past decades.

Members of the "D" text group — Finally, four or five MSS (including one uncial) from the third or fourth century form another early cluster: P[29], P[48], P[38], 0171, and perhaps P[69]. These have a connection with Codex Bezae (D) of the fifth century. The reality of a D-text (long known as the "Western" text) is not doubted, although it has recently been asserted that its existence "as early as the second century" is "quite inconceivable."[42] Admittedly, the chronological gap between the earliest representatives and the major MS that connects with them is greater than the gap between P[75] and Vaticanus (B), yet it is no greater than that between P[45] and Washingtonianus (W). Of course, no one will claim that if we had extensive portions of P[29] or P[48], or of the other early MSS in this group, they would be virtually identical to Codex Bezae. This later MS, Codex Bezae, has a complex history of its own, and the text

---

41. H. A. Sanders 1912: v, though he gives no reason or explanation for the fourth century date.

42. K. and B. Aland 1987: 55. However, their conception of the D-text is not clear, as appears from their several statements on the subject: (1) The claim that "it is quite inconceivable that the text of Codex Bezae Cantabrigiensis could have existed as early as the second century" (55). (2) The assertion that Codex Bezae's "tendentious revision (or more probably that of its ancestor of the third/fourth century) is based on a papyrus with an 'early text' of this kind" (51). (3) The reference to "the phantom 'Western' text" (55). (4) The statement, while speaking of the "Early Text" (prior to the third/fourth century), that "we also find manuscripts, although only a few, which approach the neighborhood of the D text" (64). (5) The affirmation that these pre-third/fourth-century MSS include "some which anticipated or were more closely akin to the D text, but not until the fourth century . . . did the formation of text types begin" (64). (6) Finally, the claim that "the text found in Codex Bezae . . . represents (in its exemplar) the achievement of an outstanding early theologian of the third/fourth century" (69).

Apparently the Alands wish to differentiate between the "D text" and the "Western" text (as a geographical designation) (67-69), insisting that the latter is a "phantom" [yet for generations no one has seriously suggested that the "Western" text was western]. A curiosity, therefore, is their repeated emphasis that there could be no early "Western" text because "no important personality can be identified at any time or place in the early Western church who could have been capable of the singular theological achievement represented by the text of the Gospels and Acts in the ancestor of Codex Bezae Cantabrigiensis (D)" (69; cf. 54). Indeed, if one wanted to make the case (though no one does) that the "Western" text was western, it would not be essential to identify a specific, known individual capable of producing it; after all, the canonical Epistle to the Hebrews was produced by someone not only unknown to us now, but also unidentified in antiquity (witness Origen). In the final analysis, the Alands affirm that "only the Alexandrian text, the Koine text, and the D text are incontestably verified" (67; cf. 243), but this apparently means the D text only after the second century (if we take seriously the strong statement on p. 55). Of these six statements (in the preceding paragraph), it seems that numbers 2, 4, and 6 are correct.

At the Notre Dame conference, Barbara Aland appeared to accept the term "proto" or "pre-D-Text" to describe the kind of text in MSS like P[29] and P[48], implying that the D-text (though in her view not in existence until the beginning of the third century) represents a *process*, developing from a "proto D-Text" to a later, established "D-Text." In their book (p. 93), the Alands do refer to P[29], P[38], and P[48] as "precursors or branches of the D text." Yet, note their caution about using the prefix "pre-" for any textual group (67).

it contains has evolved over more time and perhaps through greater exigencies than did the text of Vaticanus, though it has been almost impossible to determine the nature and scope of those situations. Yet — and this is crucial — lines of connection can be drawn from the four or five early MSS to Codex Bezae, and a further "trajectory" can be traced into the tenth century in minuscule 1739 (Acts only) and to the thirteenth century with minuscules 614 and 383.

It is significant that all five of the early MSS placed in this category contain portions of Luke-Acts (0171 also contains a portion of Matthew), and that three of them contain only portions of Acts (P[29], P[38], P[48]). It is well known that the textual distinctives of Codex Bezae are more prominent in Luke-Acts (and especially in Acts) than in Matthew, Mark, or John. Though accidental, it is nonetheless extraordinary that it is precisely the most noteworthy portions of the later representative, Codex Bezae, that — relatively speaking — are so numerously represented by very early MSS. Certainly that lends more credibility to the connection with Codex Bezae than would otherwise be the case, and just as certainly it lends greater credibility to the identification of a "text-type" that includes Codex Bezae as a prominent member.

The preceding is simply a sketch of the constituent members of each group; many more could be added to the "A," "B," and "D" clusters (though not so easily to the "C" cluster [but see below]). However, our interest lies in the NT *papyri* and whether more of them can be fitted into the textual scheme outlined above. It would be premature — and presumptuous — for me to imply that independent judgments permit me to place the various remaining papyri into these groups, but many of them have been categorized by other individuals according to their textual complexions, and the following is at least suggestive of the result (though new assessments and measurements undoubtedly are in order).[43]

1. *The "A" group:* P[84] (6th); P[68], P[74]? (7th); P[42] (7th/8th)
2. *The "B" group:* P[52] (2d); P[46], P[64+67], P[66] (2d/3d); P[1], P[4], P[15], P[20], P[23], P[28], P[39], P[40], P[47], P[49], P[53], P[65], P[75], P[91] (3d); P[13], P[16], P[72] [in Peter], P[92] (3d/4th); P[10], P[62], P[71], P[86] (4th); P[50], P[57] (4th/5th); P[14] (5th); P[56] (5th/6th); P[33+58] (6th); P[3], P[43], P[44], P[55] (6th/7th); P[11], P[31], P[34] (7th); P[60], P[61]? (7th/8th).
3. *The "C" group:* P[45] (most of Mark). In addition, though fresh assessments must be made, the following papyri are identified as mixed, with elements of "B" and "D": P[27] (3d); P[37]? (3d/4th); P[8], P[35] (4th); P[36] (6th).
4. *The "D" group:* P[5], P[29], P[48], P[69]? (3d); P[37]?, P[38], P[72] [Jude], 0171 (3d/4th); P[25]? (4th); P[19]? P[21]? (4th/5th); P[41] (7th/8th).

Though the placement of each papyrus in these categories is subject to review and possible revision, this is a beginning. These lists take into account the papyri through number 76, with the addition of P[84], P[86], P[91], and P[92], for decisions on textual groupings are not readily available for the rest. Yet, sixty-one of these

43. I simply rely on Metzger 1971: xxix-xxx, and his earlier groupings in 1968a: 247-55, with modifications from other sources. I have consulted the original publications of the most recently available papyri and have adopted the editors' judgments when given.

eighty papyri can be placed into various textual groupings, or seventy-six percent of them. If their respective categorizations can be sustained, then seventy-six percent is a significant proportion. The textual complexion of the remaining ones will need to be clarified or initially determined (if possible). An obvious difficulty is that the procedure of classifying textual fragments really works only when there is a later comparative basis in larger bodies of surviving text that permits us to identify the kind or character of text that a particular papyrus represents. Small fragments that issue in no clear lines of connection to later materials are difficult to classify.

Can this proposal on early textual groupings be buttressed in any other way? Certainly the quotations of Church Fathers from the same period are essential aspects of the data and should be utilized in the process of discriminating among early textual groups, and — though more complex and difficult — the early versions should be employed in the same way. The standard handbooks will indicate the textual groups that the various early Fathers and versions support, but such a discussion would take us well beyond the reasonable scope of the present paper.

IV. Conclusion

Did "text-types" exist in the first two centuries of Christianity? If so, how early and where? Though exact answers cannot be given to the latter questions, I have established reasonable grounds for concluding that three identifiable text-types were in existence around 200 CE or shortly thereafter: a "B" text-type, a "C" text-type, and a "D" text-type. I have also furnished reasons for justifying the existence of these text-types already in the second century. Though some may consider the "reasonable grounds" to be "speculative," I would rather call them "creative." Essentially, I have argued as follows:

(1) The dynamism of the early Christian environment in the first three centuries stimulated the movement of Christian writings (whether later to become "canonical" or "noncanonical") over wide areas of the Greco-Roman world and encouraged their use in various aspects of the liturgical and theological/intellectual life of the church.

(2) The dynamism of life in the Greco-Roman world — even in the outlying areas of Egypt (where most of the NT papyri were discovered) — permitted relatively easy travel and rather free transmission of letters and documents, so that the earliest NT papyri — though they have survived accidentally and randomly — are generally representative of the earliest NT texts used by the Christianity of the time in all parts of the Greco-Roman world. Incidentally, it is of more than passing interest that the NT papyri contribute virtually no new substantial variants, suggesting not only that virtually all of the NT variants are preserved somewhere in our extant manuscript tradition, but also that representatives of virtually all textual complexions have been preserved for us in the papyri.

(3) Several hints, found in the NT (and in other Christian) papyri themselves, suggest that standardization procedures were in existence already in the late first or early second century for the transmission of Christian texts, such as the codex form, the *nomina sacra* techniques, and the possible presence of scriptoria. These standardization procedures permit us to claim that our very earliest NT papyri had

antecedents or ancestors as much as a century earlier than their own time. This point is supported by the demonstration that the P75-B text had a common ancestor earlier than the third-century P75 itself.

(4) By tracing lines of connection from the earliest papyri to later MSS with similar textual complexions, the broad *spectrum* of the early NT text can be viewed, revealing a range of differing textual complexions, which — at their extremes — merge with or blend into one another. To employ another model alluded to earlier, a number of distinctive textual *trajectories* present themselves. This model has the advantage of envisioning, in a chronological, developmental fashion, extended series of related MSS in distinctive groups. Such trajectories not only begin with one or more papyri and extend forward for several — and sometimes many — centuries, but they also extend backward to the hypothetical antecedent manuscripts/texts that preceded the earliest papyri. As we have observed, P75 had an antecedent whose existence can be established even though that MS itself is not extant, and the same kind of text appears later in Codex Vaticanus. The result is that a genuine trajectory can be drawn from a very early (though non-extant) MS to P75, and then to Codex Vaticanus, and on to later witnesses. Moreover, since no canonical NT books were authored in Egypt, the texts had to travel to Egypt; hence, MSS copied anew in Egypt have trajectories reaching back to their antecedents in other parts of the very early Christian world.

What is striking in this process is that one or more of the earliest papyri almost immediately can be connected with an early major uncial MS that has a similar textual complexion. The major, nonfragmentary uncials from the fourth and fifth centuries are Sinaiticus (א), Vaticanus (B), Alexandrinus (A), Ephraemi (C), Washingtonianus (W), and Bezae (D). Four of these connect with papyri to form our distinctive early textual groups: Vaticanus and Sinaiticus for the "B" text-type; Washingtonianus for the "C" text-type; and Bezae for the "D" text-type. Another uncial, Alexandrinus, represents the later "A" text-type and, not surprisingly, connects with some sixth- and seventh-century papyri; the remaining uncial, Ephraemi, is a mixed, composite MS. If such lines of connection could not be drawn, the claim for early "text-types" would be less credible, though by no means discredited.

If all the groups presented as neat a picture as the B-text trajectory described earlier, the trajectory model would be the most appropriate one, especially if the MSS representative of each text-type showed the requisite seventy percent agreement among themselves and also the required ten percent difference in the percentage of agreements with the members of the adjacent text-types. Such a ten percent gap can generally be shown when measuring MSS that have extensive portions of text (whether papyri, uncials, or minuscules), but such measurements are difficult and less significant when attempted with the fragmentary papyri. Therefore, unless measurements of the latter can be refined, it may be preferable to employ the "spectrum" model when describing the early text-types.

On the spectrum model, the primary colors (distinct text-types) can be seen immediately, namely, the B, C, and D text-types in the earliest period. As we look further along in time, the A text-type presents itself as an identifiable hue on the textual spectrum. Many of the fragmentary papyri (as specified in the lists for the various textual groups above) will reveal the same strong colors that identify a text-type, but others will appear as shades of the brighter hues, and the early papyri will range broadly across the spectrum. Yet a spectrum is a spectrum: it has concentrations of primary and secondary colors, with gradations of merging and blending hues between them. This very well portrays the early textual situation, with three (or four) primary concentrations that represent clearly identifiable early text-types and a spread of MSS between them.

(5) Therefore, (a) since clear concentrations of MSS with similar textual character existed in the earliest period of transmission accessible to us, and — to change the figure — since lines of connection can be drawn from the papyri to major MSS with recognizable textual complexions, and (b) since these concentrations or lines of trajectory identify clusters that in turn differentiate themselves sufficiently from other clusters, the claim that at least three "text-types" existed in the dynamic Christianity of the second century may be made with considerable confidence.

PART VI

METHOD AND USE OF PATRISTIC EVIDENCE

CHAPTER 15

THE TEXT OF JOHN IN ORIGEN
AND CYRIL OF ALEXANDRIA:
A CONTRIBUTION TO METHODOLOGY
IN THE RECOVERY AND ANALYSIS
OF PATRISTIC CITATIONS

Gordon D. Fee

New Testament textual criticism has tended to view patristic citations with consid-erable ambiguity. On the one hand, because the Fathers so often quoted from memory and thus tended toward imprecision and conflation, we are told that their evidence "must be treated with extreme caution" (Markham and Nida 1966: 23). On the other hand, because they are generally earlier than most of the manuscript evidence, patristic citations are viewed by some as the royal road to the original NT text.[1] Unfortunately, extreme caution has often led to total neglect; however, their elevation as primary evidence seems to be due to lack of proper caution.

The thesis of this study is that in order to rescue patristic citations from oblivion (or neglect, due to uneasiness about ambiguity) and to allow them their proper hearing as textual data, two urgent tasks are before us: 1) To collect, evaluate, and present all the data of each Father's NT text, and, as much as possible, to attempt a critical reconstruction of that text. 2) On the basis of such reconstructed texts, to evaluate (in some cases, re-evaluate) each Father's text as to his place in the history of the NT text.

The present study, therefore, is an attempt to offer methodology for both of these tasks and to illustrate the methodology with the reconstructed text of John 4 in Origen and Cyril of Alexandria.

I

A few years ago in a study dealing with the use of the Fathers in NT textual criticism, Professor Jack Suggs suggested: "More ambitiously [than merely presenting all the data], we might aim at publishing 'critically reconstructed' texts of these patristic

---

1. See esp. the work of M.-E. Boismard, in a series of articles in *Revue biblique* (1948, 1950, 1951, 1952, 1953, 1957). Boismard's principles and resultant text have been adopted by D. Mollat in his translation of John in the *Jerusalem Bible* (Paris, 1960). For a critique of Boismard's and Mollat's use of patristic evidence see Fee 1971b [now Chapter 16].

witnesses" (1957: 147). I would urge that such critical reconstructions, especially of the biblical texts of the early Greek Fathers, are currently the most urgent need for the study of patristic citations in NT textual criticism.

The most obvious demonstration of this judgment is that there are presently available reconstructed texts, or at least presentations of the full textual data, for most of the key Latin Fathers,[2] while on the Greek side we have *only* the full NT text of Clement of Alexandria[3] and Nonnus,[4] and the Gospel of Mark in Chysostom.[5]

We are not lacking studies of the other Greek Fathers' texts, but such studies give results only, usually in the form of variants from the TR, or simply statistics based on these variants. This is understandable, in that "results" are the end-products of such studies, and the limitations imposed by publication tend to be prohibitive. Therefore, many reconstructions, or at least collections and presentations of all the data, which have been made in the past twenty years continue to lie in general inaccessibility in American universities in the form of unpublished Ph.D. dissertations.[6]

The needs here are several: 1. Presentations of a Father's text in the form of variants from the TR usually mean that one cannot discover a Father's *agreements* with the TR when some part of the manuscript tradition varies. What this means further is that *one can never collate the Father's text with any other text.* Therefore, the amount of agreement or disagreement of a Father with the whole manuscript tradition is based on an arbitrary — albeit at times useful — outside factor. It is precisely this methodological failure which is the weakness of many attempts to place the text of a Father within the history of textual transmission.

2. It is difficult to assess the results of studies where only lists of variants are presented. My own efforts in trying to reconstruct the texts of Origen and Cyril

2. AMBROSE: (Luke and John) Rolando and Carigliano 1945; (full NT) Muncey 1959.
AUGUSTINE: (Gospels) C. H. Milne (Cambridge, 1926).
CYPRIAN: (Acts) P. Corssen (Berlin, 1892); (full NT) P. Heidenreich (Bamberg, 1900); (full NT) H. von Soden (TU 33; 1909).
IRENAEUS: (full NT) W. Sanday and C. H. Turner (Oxford, 1923); (Gospels) B. Kraft (Freiburg, 1924).
LUCIFER CAGLIARI: (Gospels) A. M. Coleman (Amsterdam, 1932).
TERTULLIAN: (full NT) H. Roensch (Halle, 1870); (Matt, John) G. J. D. Aalders (Amsterdam, 1932).

3. Mees 1970. Although this supersedes Barnard 1899, it must be used with care. Cf. *infra,* n. 16.

4. Janssen 1903. This must be used with extreme caution.

5. Geerlings and New 1931: 121-42. This has the disadvantage of having been collected from Migne. [See now Fee 1979a for a critique and new presentation of the data.]

6. I am aware of the following:
ATHANASIUS: (Gospels) G. Zervopoulos (Boston U., 1955).
BASIL: (Gospels in *Moralia*) H. H. Oliver (Emory, 1961).
CLEMENT ALEX.: (Gospels) R. J. Swanson (Yale, 1956); (Paul in *Stromata*) J. A. Brooks (Princeton, 1965).
CYRIL ALEX.: (Gospels) L. H. Witherspoon (Boston U., 1962).
DIDYMUS: (Gospels) W. C. Linss (Boston U., 1955).
EUSEBIUS CAES.: (NT in *Demonstratio*) H. S. Murphy (Yale, 1951); (full NT) M. J. Suggs (Duke, 1954); (Gospels) D. Volturno (Boston U., 1956).
ORIGEN: (Matt in *comm. in Matt.*) K. W. Kim (Chicago U., 1946).

for this study have taught me a new caution about lists of variants. Too often there has been an uncritical acceptance of a reading which can clearly be shown to be secondary to the Father. Two examples will suffice:

    a. In Tasker's study of the text of John in Origen's commentary on John, he includes as Origen's text the ὡς before φραγέλλιον at 2:15 (1936: 149). This happens to be the reading of a non-Origenic *lemma* put at the beginning of Book 10 by another hand.[7] Three times in the commentary (including his real *lemma* at 10.20) Origen cites this passage, besides four adaptations which include the words ποιήσας φραγέλλιον ἐκ σχοινίων. In none of these does ὡς occur. Therefore, in spite of its now early contemporary support in P[66] and P[75], ὡς φραγέλλιον simply is not the text of Origen.

    b. In Kim's study of Origen's text of John in his *On Prayer, Comm. on Matt.,* and *Against Celsus,* he lists Origen as allegedly supporting the alleged Caesarean group (f[1] 124 565 et al.) in the omission of ἰδοὺ λέγω ὑμῖν at 4:35 (1950: 74). But this "omission" stands at the beginning of the cited portion (covering vv. 35-36), which reads: ". . . ὑπὸ τοῦ κυρίου λέγεται: ἐπάρατε τοὺς ὀφθαλμοὺς κτλ." This is an argument from silence of the weakest kind. In the *Comm. on John* Origen does in fact five times cite the passage only from ἐπάρατε to ἤδη, but these are interspersed among four full citations of the verse (at least from οὐκ on), in none of which is the clause missing. One surely is not prepared, on the basis of the shortened form of citation, to argue that Origen is using two different texts, one with and one without the clause!

    The point here is that a full presentation of the data, and a critical assessment of it, would tend to eliminate such dubious "variants." And even if one feels that my criticisms are in error, it is only the full textual data that will help one to make *that* judgment.

    3. If the texts of the Fathers are going to have general usefulness in the various *apparatus critici,* it is important to eliminate as much ambiguity as possible when a Father has more than one citation of a passage. This problem has been most recently highlighted by the UBS edition of the Greek NT. For example, in the first 100 variants in the Gospel of John, the evidence of Origen is cited in 48 instances, in 32 of which he is listed as supporting two or more readings! Although it is true, as the editors acknowledge, that "a Church Father not infrequently quotes the same passage in more than one form, often from memory rather than consulting a manuscript, and may therefore appear in support of different readings" (Aland et al. 1966: xxx), it is also true that much of the uncertainty is due to the (necessary) use of uncritical editions, or to the uncritical evaluation of the Father himself, that is, his citing habits, the kind of work in which the citation is found, etc.

    Such ambiguity will often be eliminated when a Father's biblical text has been critically reconstructed. For example, in UBS[3] Origen is cited as supporting both ἔμεινεν and ἔμειναν at John 2:12. It is true that in the Commentary at 10.3 and 13.39 extant MSS of Origen read ἔμεινεν. But at 10.1, in a passage which has the

---

7. Not only is such a long *lemma* at the beginning quite unlike anything else in the *Commentary,* but it fails also when collated with the *lemmata* and text of the commentary that follows. This is also Preuschen's judgment (*GCS* 4.170) [See now Fee 1973a].

effect of a *lemma,* Origen's text reads ἔμειναν.[8] That the plural is his correct text is made clear in a comment at 10.9; there he affirms that *not only* Jesus, *but also* his mother, brothers, and disciples ἐκεῖ ἔμειναν.

Given the need, however, there is still a question of method in presenting such a text. Ideally the presentation should attempt to *reconstruct* the text that a Father used, either across a lifetime, or in a given work. Therefore, *evaluation* of cited material is a must, especially an evaluation of the Father's accuracy. But the presentation must also be *complete,* including all known citations and adaptations from all available sources.

There are two alternative methodologies which can do both. The common one is followed by Sanday and Turner's edition of Irenaeus's NT text (1923), and more recently by Mees in his study of Clement of Alexandria (1970). Here every citation or adaptation is listed separately, and the apparatus lists textual data, including agreements/disagreements with the MS tradition. In such editions the evaluation takes place either in footnotes or in the discussion of the text itself.

The alternative is the one offered in this paper, where the texts of John 4 in Origen and Cyril are given. Here there is a running text of the Father, as much as one can reconstruct it from his literary remains. With the text there are two, sometimes three, apparatuses. The first is a list of citations/adaptations available only in translation. These are *not* used in the reconstruction of the text because, at least in Origen's case, they are not always trustworthy representations of Origen's Greek text and need to be evaluated on their own.[9] The second apparatus includes the references to all citations, the extent of text of each citation, and the complete text of all adaptations with *verbal* significance. The third apparatus lists, and frequently discusses, all variations, including MS variations to a single citation and any variations in the Father's citing of a passage.[10]

A word is necessary here about the terms "citation" and "adaptation." In a forthcoming article in the *Journal of Biblical Literature* (1971b [Chapter 16]) I have offered the following definitions for patristic evidence:

Allusion: Reference to the *content* of a biblical passage in which *verbal* correspondence to the NT Greek text is so remote as to offer no value for the reconstruction of that text.

Adaptation: Reference to a biblical passage, which has clear *verbal* correspondence to the Greek NT, but which has been adapted to fit the Father's discussion and/or syntax.

Citation: Those places where a Father is consciously trying to cite, either from memory or by copying, the very words of the biblical text. Anyone who works closely with a given Father's text will probably make a further distinction in this category by noting citations at times to be "strict" or "loose."

---

8. Preuschen (*GCS* 4) edited the text to read ἔμεινεν against all manuscript evidence and against the obvious text of Origen.

9. This is the judgment of Bardy 1920, for the Pauline citations at least.

10. Well after this work was completed I discovered that this is very similar to the method of Rolando and Carigliano 1945. A comparison of their work with Muncey 1959, which also offers a running text, can be very instructive in some "how-to's" and "how-not-to's."

For critically reconstructed texts such categories are not only useful, but imperative. Furthermore, for this study it seemed wise to err on the side of completeness, and thereby to include some significant allusions. However, for the sake of keeping the apparatus as uncluttered as possible, both allusions and adaptations have been included after the siglum "ADAPT."

The real danger with such reconstructions as these — and it is a real danger — is that one may be crossing not only oranges and lemons, but also oranges and apples; that is, an eclectic text of Origen's Johannine citations, including citations from the commentary, as well as the practically useless catenae fragments,[11] not to mention works written in Alexandria and Caesarea, runs the risk of trying to mix texts that simply will not mix. Not only may he have used different texts of John at different times, but his own manner of citing in a work such as *contra Celsum* may differ from that in the Commentary. Futhermore, each of his works has suffered its own textual fate. (It is surely not accidental that the vast majority of Byzantine variants from Origen's usual Neutral text of John are found in citations where Migne is the best edition available!)

Such difficulties may generally be overcome if the editor makes his priorities clear. For example, with Origen's text I have yielded to the following priorities: First in importance is the text found in the Commentary on John, particularly *ad loc.* citations and adaptions. Second, the *lemmata* of the commentary, which in Origen's text are remarkably free from later modifications (these, by the way, are often the only citations available). Third, citations from the commentary at places other than *ad loc.*, under the supposition that he would be more likely to "look up" a passage here than elsewhere. Fourth, citations from other works, where geographical distinctions were always kept in view. Since this tends to present Origen's Alexandrian text, readings likely to be the result of his Caesarean residence are called out in the text with a superscript (caes) and discussed in the apparatus.

The same general priorities hold true for Cyril. In his case, however, one is dealing with a Father whose citing habits are much less exact. It is doubtful whether he ever consulted his biblical text when citing. He frequently — even in his Johannine commentary — introduces a citation ἔφη δέ που καὶ αὐτὸς ὁ σωτήρ (and he really means "somewhere"). Where one might expect him to have consulted his text, such as the catenae of proof texts in the *Thesaurus,* only Migne's edition is available, and there the text has been thoroughly conformed to the Byzantine text-type. Furthermore, he habitually cites some passages in conflation,[12] which are separated in the commentary *ad loc.*, thus indicating that they are habits of memory and certainly do not reflect any available copy of John. Therefore, I have yielded to the text of the commentary as having first priority, with *lemmata* second, and variants from elsewhere in the commentary and from all other works a distant third.

---

11. My experience with the Johannine text in these fragments confirms the judgment of Brooke 1896: 1.xxv: "They are practically useless for textual purposes."

12. For example, he conflates John 6:51 and 33 as ἐγώ εἰμι ὁ ἄρτος ὁ ζῶν ὁ ἐκ τοῦ οὐρανοῦ καταβὰς καὶ ζωὴν διδοὺς τῷ κόσμῳ (*ador.* 9, *ador.* 12, *apol. orient* 97, *apol. Thdt.* 39, *Chr. un., glaph. Lev., Is.* 3.2, *Is.* 3.5, *Is.* 5.6, *Joel* 1.15, *Amos* 8.11, *Mic.* 7.14, *Lc.* 12.10, *Lc.* 22.14, *Jo.* 1.6, *Jo.* 4.4, *hom. div.* 15, *synous.* 3, *thes.* 11). He does the same with John 14:10 and 12:49; John 14:9, 10:30, and 14:10; and several others.

The texts here given, of course, are not suggested to be absolute. One can use only the materials at hand. Emendations are a tenuous procedure at best. Because of the clear proclivities of Origen, I have been tempted to emend his citations at times, especially those preserved only in the catenae fragments. The closest thing to emendation, therefore, occurs in an occasional bracketed reading, and the discussion is given in the textual notes.[13]

The point is, finally, that not only is this an attempt to *recover* Origen's and Cyril's texts of John, but also to *present* all the available data for such a recovery. The advantages to such a presentation are not simply to be found in the saving of space. One now has a text which is easily collated with the MS tradition, as long as such collating is done judiciously. Furthermore, the text of John from any single work can be quickly recovered from the apparatus, if this kind of study is desirable.

II

According to Kirsopp Lake, the chief value of patristic citations "consists in the opportunity which they afford us of localising and dating various kinds of text in mss. and versions" (1928: 48). For this reason, the great majority of studies of Fathers' texts have been efforts to show their textual relationships with the Greek and versional evidence. However, as noted above, few of these studies have escaped the secondary methodology based on agreements in variants from the TR. Although this method might work accidentally — when a Father's text is particularly close to a given MS or text-type — it is especially inadequate in texts with an appreciable amount of "mixture."[14]

The obvious faults of the method may be illustrated from Cyril's text of John 4. In this chapter his text varies from the TR 35 times, three of which are singular and one subsingular (4:37, word order with 579). In the remaining 31 his text has the following agreements: B 22, L 22, ℵ 21, D 19, Origen 18. However, by simply adding one other factor, one may see how totally misleading such "agreements" are. Cyril's text has the following number of agreements *with the TR against these MSS:* B 19, L 11, ℵ 46, D 35, Origen 18. This should mean that ultimately his text will be more like that of Codex L than the others. But even these figures will not tell the whole story until the various agreements among these MSS *vs.* Cyril and the TR are noted. The final absurdity of all this is that in the first set of figures, Origen has extant text only at 25 points of variation, so that apart from the giving of percentages even the number of agreements *vs.* TR is misleading.[15]

13. See, e.g., Origen's text at John 4:10.

14. Although not put quite in these terms, this methodological failure was noted first by Murphy (1954: 167-68) in his study of Eusebius's *Demonstratio Evangelica*.

15. This methodological failure renders almost valueless a large portion of several of the unpublished dissertations on Fathers' texts. This is especially true of L. H. Witherspoon's study of Cyril, G. Zervopoulos's of Athanasius, and W. Linss's of Didymus. Zervopoulos, for example, shows Origen in agreement with Athanasius in John an incredibly low 23%, while D has a 27% and ℵ a 46% agreement, and the highest agreement is with B (47%). Witherspoon's statistics are about as useless. His method "accidentally" shows the highest relationship with L, but other relationships, compared with those in this study, are quite out of line.

What is needed, therefore, is a method based on direct comparisons of texts which can effectively show the relationships of a Father's text with all known MSS and text-types. There are two ways of doing this, depending essentially on the *amount* of extant text recoverable from the Father's writings, or on the *variable nature* of extant text.

When a Father has a small amount of text, usually in the form of short, random citations from a Gospel, such as Clement of Alexandria, Athanasius, and Didymus in John, then the method used by Mees in his recent study (1970) is excellent. With complete disregard to the TR, he has analyzed the text of Clement by direct comparison with the MSS themselves. For each NT book he discusses variants under kinds of relationships, depending on the witnesses available. For example, he discusses Matthean citations first in relation to each of the available papyri, then to the "so-called Western text," then to the "Eastern textgroup" (relationships with B and ℵ are presented individually), and finally to "other groups." Under these groups he also notes *kinds* of variations, such as "short text" and various kinds of grammatical variants. In John's Gospel he does much the same, except that the major analysis consists of the various relations with and against P66 and P75. Although Mees's work has too many errors in details to be used without caution,[16] his methodology is basically sound and should correct the rather too easy inclusion of Clement's text amoung "Western" witnesses.

When a Father has a larger amount of text, such as Origen and Cyril in John, the method used in the following paragraphs shows not only a profile of general relationships but also the details of relationships with individual MSS.[17]

The first step of this method is to collate the Father's text with "control" MSS, selected to give a broad cross-section of the various textual traditions. For this study I have collated Origen and Cyril with the following:

P66 P75 B C — "primary" Neutrals (proto-Alexandrian)
L W Ψ 33 579 892 1241 — "secondary" Neutrals (later Alexandrian)
ℵ D b e — Westerns
Θ 1 13 — Caesareans
A E G Δ Ω TR — Byzantines

16. Mees does not always use care in his listing of Clementine readings; nor does he properly distinguish between citations, adaptations, and allusions. For example, he lists the citation ὁ πιστεύων ἔχει ζωὴν αἰώνιον (*Str.* V.85.1) under John 3:15, with an apparatus of variations and a discussion in his section on Clement's text "gegen *Pap.* 66, *Pap.* 77"! Barnard was more nearly correct in listing it under John 3:36. But surely this is a citation of John 6:47, since it only approximates the other passages, but is in fact an exact citation of the clearly prevailing Egyptian text of 6:47. Further, under John 3:29 a loose adaptation from *Exc. Thd.* 65.1 is listed (correctly), but to list variants from such an adaptation (Clement's reading of ἑστώς as an alleged agreement with D) seems to be a questionable procedure. Cf. further the review by Swanson 1970, who notes similar errors, as well as many others in the citing of supporting evidence.

17. With slight modifications, this is essentially the method worked out by Colwell and Tune 1963, which I have used elsewhere on straight text MSS (1968a). H. H. Oliver's unpublished dissertation (Emory Univ., 1961) on the Gospel text of Basil's *Moralia* follows such a method. See also the recently published study of the text of Epiphanius by Eldridge 1969.

TABLE 15.1

PERCENTAGES OF AGREEMENT BETWEEN MSS. AT 97 VARIATION-UNITS IN JOHN 4

	p^{66*}	p^{66c}	p^{75}	ℵ	A	B	C	D	E	G	L	W	Δ	Θ	Ψ	Ω	1	13	33	579	892	1241	b	e	TR	Or	Cyr
p^{66*}	—	—	79.2	54.6	67	79.4	85.3	48.5	66	63.9	68	72.2	61.9	66	70.1	58.8	64.9	59.8	72.2	57.7	66	63.5	41.9	45.9	66	83.3	71.9
p^{66c}	—	—	80.2	51.5	67	80.4	85.3	48.5	67	67	72.2	74.2	63.9	62.9	72.2	59.8	66	62.9	77.3	59.8	69.1	66.7	43.2	44.6	68	80.6	76.2
p^{75}	79.2	80.2	—	51	64.6	89.6	80.9	39.6	60.4	62.5	70.7	64.6	61.5	59.4	67.7	57.3	62.5	55.2	67.7	63.5	64.6	60.4	39.7	32.9	60.4	84.5	70.5
ℵ	54.6	51.5	51	—	43.3	52.6	52.6	59.8	39.2	38.1	45.7	42.3	39.2	38.1	41.2	36.1	45.4	38.1	44.3	35.1	48.5	40.6	64.9	48.6	40.2	45.8	48.9
A	67	67	64.6	43.3	—	68	66.3	46.4	81.4	82.5	69.1	59.8	83.5	80.4	81.4	79.4	69.1	68	73.2	82.5	78.4	57.3	37.8	33.8	82.5	66.7	69.8
B	79.4	80.4	89.6	52.6	68	—	83.2	38.1	59.8	61.9	73.2	69.1	62.9	57.7	74.2	55.7	62.9	51.5	70.1	66	64.9	57.3	41.9	35.1	58.8	91.7	71.9
C	85.3	85.3	80.9	52.6	66.3	83.2	—	43.2	62.1	63.2	74.7	71.6	63.2	63.2	72.6	58.9	59.5	61.1	77.9	63.2	65.3	67	46.6	45.2	64.2	85.7	75.5
D	48.5	48.5	39.6	59.8	46.4	38.1	43.2	—	45.7	41.2	52.6	47.4	45.7	48.5	45.4	43.3	45.4	48.5	50.5	42.3	51.5	49	56.8	54.1	47.4	38.9	51
E	66	67	60.4	39.2	81.4	59.8	62.1	45.7	—	93.8	61.9	55.7	93.8	79.4	77.3	90.7	71.1	75.3	67	77.3	81.4	62.5	39.2	40.5	90.7	62.5	64.6
G	63.9	67	62.5	38.1	82.5	61.9	63.2	41.2	93.8	—	64.9	56.7	91.8	79.4	78.4	88.7	71.1	56.7	71.1	78.4	79.4	66.7	37.8	37.8	90.7	62.5	66.7
L	68	72.2	70.7	45.7	69.1	73.2	74.7	52.6	61.9	64.9	—	66	64.9	82.5	78.4	66	67	56.7	79.4	67	72.2	70.7	39.2	43.2	67	69.4	77.1
W	72.2	74.2	64.6	42.3	59.8	69.1	71.6	47.4	55.7	56.7	66	—	58.8	80.4	82.5	56.7	58.8	54.6	68	58.8	63.9	59.4	40.5	39.2	60.8	70.8	67.7
Δ	61.9	63.9	61.5	39.2	83.5	62.9	63.2	45.7	93.8	91.8	67	58.8	—	80.4	82.5	92.8	75.3	74.2	71.1	80.4	83.5	65.6	37.8	37.8	92.8	66.7	68.8
Θ	66	62.9	59.4	38.1	80.4	57.7	63.2	48.5	79.4	79.4	82.5	80.4	80.4	—	77.3	81.4	77.3	73.2	71.1	80.4	74.2	62.5	40.5	41.9	78.4	58.9	65.6
Ψ	70.1	72.2	67.7	41.2	81.4	74.2	72.6	45.4	77.3	78.4	82.5	82.5	82.5	77.3	—	77.3	73.2	62.9	78.4	78.4	77.3	63.5	37.8	41.9	76.3	73.6	75.0
Ω	58.8	59.8	57.3	36.1	79.4	55.7	58.9	43.3	90.7	88.7	66	56.7	92.8	81.4	77.3	—	71.1	71.1	68	75.3	77.3	65.6	35.1	40.5	87.6	56.9	64.6
1	64.9	66	62.5	45.4	69.1	62.9	59.5	45.4	71.1	71.1	67	58.8	75.3	77.3	73.2	71.1	—	70.1	72.2	72.2	71.1	66.7	47.3	48.6	73.2	66.7	62.5
13	59.8	62.9	55.2	38.1	68	51.5	61.1	48.5	75.3	56.7	56.7	54.6	74.2	73.2	62.9	71.1	70.1	—	62.9	68	69.1	71.9	36.5	41.9	75.3	54.2	62.5
33	72.2	77.3	67.7	44.3	73.2	70.1	77.9	50.5	67	71.1	79.4	68	71.1	71.1	78.4	68	72.2	62.9	—	70.1	71.1	76	43.2	43.2	70.1	69.4	77.1
579	57.7	59.8	63.5	35.1	82.5	66	63.2	42.3	77.3	78.4	67	58.8	80.4	80.4	78.4	75.3	72.2	68	70.1	—	77.3	63.5	28.4	37.8	78.4	65.3	68.8
892	66	69.1	64.6	48.5	78.4	64.9	65.3	51.5	81.4	79.4	72.2	63.9	83.5	74.2	77.3	77.3	71.1	69.1	71.1	77.3	—	71.9	44.6	45.9	86.6	65.3	67.7
1241	63.5	66.7	60.4	40.6	57.3	57.3	67	49	62.5	66.7	70.7	59.4	65.6	62.5	63.5	65.6	66.7	71.9	76	63.5	71.9	—	38.4	41.1	66.7	59.2	67.4
b	41.9	43.2	39.7	64.9	37.8	41.9	46.6	56.8	39.2	37.8	39.2	40.5	37.8	40.5	37.8	35.1	47.3	36.5	43.2	28.4	44.6	38.4	—	60.8	29.9	58.5	32.9
e	45.9	44.6	32.9	48.6	33.8	35.1	45.2	54.1	40.5	37.8	43.2	39.2	37.8	41.9	41.9	40.5	48.6	41.9	43.2	37.8	45.9	41.1	60.8	—	33	65.0	38.9
TR	66	68	60.4	40.2	82.5	58.8	64.2	47.4	90.7	90.7	67	60.8	92.8	78.4	76.3	87.6	73.2	75.3	70.1	78.4	86.6	66.7	29.9	33	—	56.9	64.6
Or	83.3	80.6	84.5	45.8	66.7	91.7	85.7	38.9	62.5	62.5	69.4	70.8	66.7	58.9	73.6	56.9	66.7	54.2	69.4	65.3	65.3	59.2	58.5	65.0	56.9	—	71.4
Cyr	71.9	76.2	70.5	48.9	69.8	71.9	75.5	51	64.6	66.7	77.1	67.7	68.8	65.6	75.0	64.6	62.5	62.5	77.1	68.8	67.7	67.4	32.9	38.9	64.6	71.4	—

All variants are listed where any two of these agreed against the rest. There are 97 such variants in John 4, which yield the percentage of agreements found in Table 15.1.

The relationships of these MSS to Origen and Cyril are found in Table 15.2, grouped in descending order of agreement.

Table 15.2 Percentages of Agreement in John 4 between Origen and Cyril and the Control MSS Selected for This Study

Origen		Cyril	
B	91.7	L	77.1
C	85.7	33	77.1
P75	84.5	P66c	76.0
P66*	83.3	C	75.5
P66c	80.6	Ψ	75.0
Ψ	73.6	P66*	71.9
Cyr	71.4	B	71.9
W	70.8	Orig	71.4
L	69.4	P75	70.5
33	69.4	A	69.8
A	66.7	Δ	68.8
Δ	66.7	579	68.8
1	66.7	W	67.7
579	65.3	892	67.7
892	65.3	1241	67.4
e	65.0	G	66.7
E	62.5	Θ	65.6
G	62.5	E	64.6
1241	59.2	Ω	64.6
Θ	58.9	TR	64.6
b	58.8	1	62.5
Ω	56.9	13	62.5
TR	56.9	D	51.0
13	54.2	ℵ	48.9
ℵ	45.8	e	38.9
D	38.9	b	32.9

This table clearly shows Origen to be a strong Neutral witness in John 4, with a very distant relationship to the basic Western witnesses. On the other hand, while Cyril appears to be more Neutral than Western, and is "secondary" within that tradition, his profile is far less sharp than Origen's. The basic reason for this lies in the methodology: there were simply too many cases of otherwise non-related MSS having apparently accidental agreements against the rest, thus raising the percentage of agreement of all the others.

Therefore, a refinement was worked out to clarify the profile, in which variants were classified on the basis of known text-types. Apart from singular readings, they were divided into the following classes: (N = Neutral, W = Western, etc.; the figure in parenthesis is the number of such variants in John 4).[18]

N1 At least 3 of the primary Neutrals, with little other support (9)

N2 P[75] B alone against all others (3)

N3 One or a few Neutrals, with little other support (4)

W1 ℵ D with at least 2 OL against all others (8)

W2 ℵ D or W with OL or OS support against all others (29)

W3 ℵ and/or D with OL and/or OS, with some Caes. against most of the rest (6)

W4 ℵ D alone (or with one OL) against all others (6)

W5 Most OL with some Caes. against most of the rest (3)

W6 OL with little support against all others (11)

C Isolated Caes. with little or no support, against all others (9)

NW1 The majority of Neutrals, with ℵ and/or D and most OL, against most of the rest (14) [This category = "early" vs. "late"]

NW2 Same as NW1 but with more "late" support (8)

NW3 A few Neutrals, with ℵ and/or D and some OL, against most of the rest (4)

NB1 The majority of Neutrals, with some Caes. and Byz. against most of the rest (4) [The Westerns read with the majority of Byzantines]

NB2 A few Neutrals, supported by a few Byz. against the rest (1)

NWB A few Neutrals, Western (sometimes Caes.), and Byz. against most of the rest (17)

MISC A few, mostly non-related, MSS against all the rest (18).

When Origen's and Cyril's texts were collated against these classifications, their textual character became immediately clear. Neither of them has been influenced in any way by either the Western or Caesarean MSS. Cyril shares no readings of 63 in the Western categories, nor any of the nine Caesareans. Origen has a single, although somewhat doubtful, Western reading in class W3 (om. εἰς αὐτόν at 4:39 with ℵ* a e 482), and a single Caesarean reading from his clearly Caesarean period (om. ἰδοὺ λέγω ὑμῖν at 4:35 with fam. 1 124 565 1241 in his *Comm. on Romans*).

The best way to discover the true nature of their Neutral relationships is from variants in N1, N2, NW1, NW2, and NB1. The following table puts these relationships into clear focus (in a descending scale, the figures in the first column are numbers of agreement in 9 variants in class N1; in the second column are agreements in 26 variants in classes NW1, NW2, and NB1):

18. In the interest of space, these lists could not be included in the paper. The complete list, with supporting witnesses, may be obtained from the author.

Table 15.3 Manuscript Agreements with Classes of Variants

N1 (9 variants)		NW1, NW2, NB1 (26 variants)	
B	- 9	B	- 24
P75	- 8	C	- 24
Origen	- 6 (of 7)	P75	- 23 (of 25)
P66	- 7	Origen	- 17 (of 20)
C	- 7	P66	- 22
W	- 4	W	- 20
L	- 3	Cyril	- 20
A	- 2	L	- 19
Ψ	- 2	33	- 19
33	- 2	1241	- 14
579	- 2	Ψ	- 13
892	- 2	579	- 9
1241	- 2	892	- 8
Cyril	- 1	Chrys	- 7 (of 25)
Chrys	- 1	A	- 6
E	- 0	E	- 2
Δ	- 0	Δ	- 2
TR	- 0	TR	- 1

Of two extant readings in category N2 Origen alone supports P75 B in one (4:42 τὴν λαλιάν σου. l. τὴν σὴν λαλιάν); Cyril reflects support of P75 B in another.[19]

The verdict is clear: Origen's text of John 4 is a "primary" Neutral. This is true not only of the commentary on John, but in general of Johannine citations from all periods. The chief reason for his failure to have a higher percentage of agreement with the early Neutrals (P66 P75) than he does (see Table 15.2) is that in categories N3 and NWB, he supports now one and then the other, when they are divided.

Finally, it should be noted about Origen's Johannine text that his move to Caesarea has scarcely affected it — at least in the Commentary at John 4. The significance of this is that this part of the Commentary is in Book 13, which was written during his Caesarean period. As Lake has clearly shown, Origen began to use a Caesarean text of Mark at least from Book 10 on, and used it the rest of his life (1928). This simply does not hold true for his text of John 4, although further judgments must wait until this study is completed for the whole of John.

Cyril, on the other hand, is just as clearly "secondary" Neutral as Origen is "primary." This is attested both by his failure to read more of the purely Neutral variants (N1, N2) and by his high level of agreements (with W L 33) where variants may be classified as "early" and "late."

19. At 4:52 there are the following variants (Cyril's conflation is probably a reflection of the text of P75 B):

παρ' αυτων την ωραν	E G H L Δ Ψ Ω 1241 pler TR
την ωραν παρ' αυτων	P66 א C D W Θ f1 f13 33 579 892 pc
την ωραν εκεινην	P75 B
παρ' αυτων την ωραν εκεινην	Cyril

It is precisely this secondary character of Cyril, L, and 33 to B that led Hort to distinguish between his Neutral and Alexandrian text-types (WH 1881: 2.130-32). Although it is not a primary purpose of this paper, one may, on the basis of Tables 15.1 and 3, make some preliminary suggestions as to the nature of the Egyptian text, and show thereby Origen's and Cyril's place in the "history of transmission."

In the first place, there are two levels of "primary" Neutrals:

1) P75 B Origen, which have approximately 90% agreement among themselves, about 80% with the second level (P66 C), about 70% with the third level (L 33 Cyril), and from 70% to 55% with the fourth level (Ψ 892), at the lower end of which there is a similar agreement with the Byz and TR.

2) P66 C, which have approximately the same agreement with each other as with P75 B Origen (about 80%), but a 10% spread to the next level (L 33 Cyril), with whom they agree at about the same percentage as do P75 B Origen. All other percentages are about the same as those of level 1, except for slightly higher agreements with the Caesareans and the TR. Therefore, they are second level because they tend to fluctuate slightly from the basic text of P75 B Origen.

There are also two levels of "secondary" Neutrals:

3) L 33 Cyril. The first characteristic of this level is that they have their *highest* percentage of agreement with each other and Ψ. There is not a great spread to the next level of agreements (both levels of "primaries"). After that they agree about the same with the fourth level of Neutrals *and* with the Byzantines. This means, therefore, that while still basically Neutral texts, they have begun to absorb a good number of readings which later became standardized in the Byzantine text. From Table 15.3, W also clearly belongs to this level. The percentages of W in Table 15.1 are misleading because it tends to go its own way so often, and it is one of the only Neutral MSS which has had a generous amount of Western influence in John 4.

4) Finally, there is a group of MSS (Ψ 579 892 1241 A) which may be yet distinguished from the full Byzantines as having about a 15-20% spread between their highest agreements and the "primary" Neutrals, which in turn is about 10% higher than the full Byzantines have with P75 B. A glance at Table 15.3 defines these yet more sharply in terms of "Neutral" relationships.

It will be also noted that codices E G Δ Ω and the TR clearly form a text-type, in the same percentage categories as P75 B. Codex Δ, therefore, is in *no* way a Neutral MS in John (at least in chap. 4).

Furthermore, it will be noted that the above "levels" are *only* meaningful for MSS which are in these two text-types. All other relationships must be investigated individually, although this may be done with reference to the Neutral and Byzantine text.[20]

---

20. For example, I did a quick check on Chrysostom's text in the *Homilies on John*. In Table 15.3 he has one reading in column 1, and seven of twenty-five in column 2. This would seem to place him at level 4 above. However, this is quite misleading; for the one omission in column 1 is the *only* reading he shares with the Neutrals; however, he reads 9 of 63 Western variants, and *none* of the Caesarean. His text therefore appears to be "on the way" toward the Byzantine text-type. Where he reflects earlier readings they are *predominantly* Western, quite often in agreement with the Old Syriac. Is there a possible hint here as to the nature of the text of Antioch?

Finally, whatever other role may be assigned to the texts of Origen and Cyril, one can make some rather positive claims about their place in the history of the NT text. Certainly neither was the *creator* of a text; each simply reflects the predominant text of Alexandria in his day. Furthermore, the Neutral text-type is almost certainly *not* recensional in any traditional sense of the word. If it existed *prior* to Origen (P75 and his own exemplar), then who in Alexandria either could have, or would have, cared to create it? The relationship of the Alexandrian text 200 years later (Cyril) to the Byzantine is a more complicated problem. I have shown elsewhere that a Byzantine type of textual transmission (smoothing out the text) goes on as early as P66 (1968b). The origin of this text as a text-type is still one of the knotty problems of our discipline.

In any case, a full presentation and thorough investigation of all the Fathers' texts, including such men as Asterius the Sophist, who quite early (before 340) has an abundance of Byzantine readings, is necessary before the history from 200 to 500 can be written with greater accuracy.

The Texts

The rationale for these texts is given in the body of the paper. A few words about sigla are necessary.

The works and abbreviations follow Lampe's *Patristic Lexicon.* Since the majority of Origen's citations are from the *GCS* series, locations are given by vol. no., page, and line. In other instances the abbreviation for the edition is also given (e.g., M for Migne). The same holds true for Pusey's first five volumes of Cyril's works. Most of the works in Pusey's volumes 6 and 7 are now found in a much better edition by E. Schwartz, *Acta Conciliorum Oecumenicorum (ACO)*.

In the text itself items in parenthesis are *not* found in the Father's text, but are given to provide context to the reconstruction. Usually these are reconstructions based on adaptations. Brackets have a twofold use: 1) to indicate doubt in my mind as to whether the true text of the Father is ever recoverable, because of his own and/or manuscript ambiguity, and 2) to indicate readings which are suspect because they differ from his ordinary text-type, and which are available only in poor editions or generally useless sources. The *siglum* (caes) in the body of the text of Origen means that a variant noted in the apparatus may possibly be a reading resulting from his Caesarean residence.

In the reference apparatus the *lemma,* when extant, is always given first, followed by full citations, then partial citations (with extent of text), and finally adaptations/allusions, which are given in full.

In each instance the references from the Commentary appear first; citations from other works follow in alphabetical order. When an adaptation includes several verses, it is given in full in the first verse, with diagonal lines indicating approximate verse divisions. In the second and following verses, a cross reference is given.

In the adaptations, the words, or parts of words, reflecting the Father's biblical text are in italics, for convenience' sake.

ORIGEN

1 (ως ουν εγνω ο κυριος οτι ηκουσαν) οἱ Φαρισαῖοι ὅτι Ἰησοῦς πλείονας μαθητὰς ποιεῖ καὶ βαπτίζει [ἢ][a] Ἰωάννης. 2 — (καιτοι γε) Ἰησοῦς αὐτὸς οὐκ ἐβάπτιζεν, ἀλλ' οἱ μαθηταὶ αὐτοῦ — 3 ἀφῆκεν τὴν Ἰουδαίαν καὶ ἀπῆλθεν εἰς τὴν Γαλιλαίαν. 4 ἔδει (δε) αὐτὸν διέρχεσθαι διὰ τῆς Σαμαρείας. 5 (ερχεται ουν εις πολιν της Σαμαρειας λεγομενην Συχαρ) πλησίον τοῦ χωρίου ὃ ἔδωκεν Ἰακὼβ τῷ Ἰωσὴφ (τω υιω αυτου· 6 ην δε εκει) πηγὴ τοῦ Ἰακώβ. ὁ (ουν) Ἰησοῦς κεκοπια-

---

6 ADAPT. [6-7] ... et ibi invenies *puteum*, *supra* quem Salvator noster *sedebat* requiescens post *itineris laborem* tunc / cum *veniente muliere Samaritana et volente haurire aquam* de puteo. *hom.* 12.1 *in Num.* (7.94.13); Ipse Dominus cum *ex itinere fatigatus* fuisset. *hom.* 10.5 *in Gen.* (6.100.5).

---

1 ADAPT. [1,3,4,6] και φαινεται δια το εγνωκεναι τους Φαρισαιους οτι Ιησους πλειονας μαθητας ποιει και βαπτιζει ⟨η⟩ Ιωαννης / αφιεις την Ιουδαιαν και απερχομενος εις την Γαλιλαιαν, / οτε εδει αυτον διερχεσθαι δια της Σαμαρειας, / και γενομενος παρα τη πηγη του Ιακωβ φησι το· *Jo.* 13.39 (4.264.23); [1,2] και ο μεν παρα τω Ιωαννη Ιησους γινωσκεται παρα τοις Φαρισαιοις βαπτιζων, / εν τοις μαθηταις αυτου βαπτιζων ... *Jo.* 10.8 (4.178.7).

2 ADAPT. [1,2] see. v. 1; ο γαρ Χριστος, Ιησους ων, καν μη βουλησθε αυτος ουκ εβαπτιζεν, αλλ' οι μαθηται αυτου, αυτος ων ο προφητης, *Jo.* 6.23 (4.133.23); Χριστος ουν εν υδατι ου βαπτιζει, αλλ' οι μαθηται αυτου· *Jo.* 6.23 (4.133.33).

3 ADAPT. [1,3,4,6] see v. 1; [3-6] προειπων γουν τινα τροπον αφιησιν την Ιουδαιαν και απεισιν εις την Γαλιλαιαν ο κυριος, / διηγησαμενος τε, επει εδει αυτον διερχεσθαι δια της Σαμαρειας τα λεγομενα / πλησιον του χωριου ο εδωκεν Ιακωβ τω Ιωσηφ / παρα τη πηγη του Ιακωβ, ... *Jo.* 13.54 (4.284.16).

4 ADAPT. [1,3,4,6] see v. 1; [3-6] see v. 3; [4,6] ως οτε απο Ιεροσολυμων διηρχετο δια της Σαμαρειας ⟨εις την Γαλιλαιαν και⟩ / φθασας επι το φρεαρ κοπιασας εκ της οδοιποριας εκαθεσθη παρ' αυτω, ... *comm. in Mt.* 21:1 (10.520.12).

5 ADAPT. [3-6] see v. 3.

6 ADAPT. [1,3,4,6] see v. 1; [3-6] see v. 3; [4,6] see v. 4; ειπερ δε μη εγινετο τι χρησιμον εκ του πιειν απο της πηγης, ουτ' αν εκαθεζετο επι τη πηγη ο Ιησους, ... *Jo.* 13.4 (4.229.25); η δε της Σαμαρειτιδος ουκ ουσα ωρα

---

[a] PREUSCHEN, *GCS*, p. 264: "⟨ἢ⟩ Rasur an d. St., von d. Ausgg. erg."; BROOKE, I, p. 289: "ἢ] om. ut videtur".

κὼς ἐκ τῆς ὁδοιπορίας ἐκαθέζετο (ουτως) ἐπὶ τῇ πηγῇ·[b] ὥρα ἦν (ως) ἕκτη.

7 Ἔρχεται γυνὴ (εκ της Σαμαρειας) ἀντλῆσαι ὕδωρ. (λεγει) αὐτῇ ὁ Ἰησοῦς, Δός μοι πιεῖν· 8 οἱ (γαρ) μαθηταὶ αὐτοῦ ἀπεληλύθεισαν εἰς τὴν πόλιν, ἵνα τροφὰς ἀγοράσωσιν. 9 (....) οὐ γὰρ[c] συγχρῶνται Ἰουδαῖοι Σαμαρείταις. 10 ἀπεκρίθη [ὁ][d] Ἰησοῦς καὶ εἶπεν αὐτῇ, Εἰ ᾔδεις τὴν δωρεὰν τοῦ θεοῦ καὶ τίς ἐστιν ὁ λέγων σοι, Δός μοι πιεῖν, σὺ ἂν ᾔτησας αὐτὸν καὶ ἔδωκεν ἄν[e] σοι ὕδωρ ζῶν. 11 καὶ λέγει αὐτῷ ἡ γυνή, Κύριε, οὔτε ἄντλημα ἔχεις καὶ τὸ φρέαρ ἐστὶν βαθύ· πόθεν οὖν

---

7 ADAPT. [6-7] see v. 6; Da mihi bibere. *hom.* 10.3 *in Gen.* (6.96.10).

εκτη αφιεται. Jo. 13.29 (4.254.8); *εκτον εν τη Σαμαρεια παρα τη* πηγη *του Ιακωβ εδιδαξεν.* Jo. 13.64 (4.297.22); *πως το μεν· εκαθεζετο επι πηγης ο Ιησους. fr.* 74 *in Jo.* (4.541.16); *εκτη γαρ ωρα της ημερας ην. fr.* 52 *in Jo.* (4.526.18); [6,8] *εκτης ωρας της ημερας ουσης ο Ιησους εν τη* πηγη *καθεσθεις διελεχθη τη Σαμαρειτιδι,* / *των μαθητων επι τω αγορασαι τροφας απεληλυθοτων· fr.* 59 *in Jo.* (4.532.4).

7 ADAPT. *οιον επι την Σαμαρειτιδος οτι ειπων αυτη ο Ιησους, δος μοι πιειν.* Jo. 20.41 (4.384.1); *αμα προνοουμενος ωφελειας της μελλουσης επι το αντλησαι υδωρ εκ της πηγης ερχεσθαι γυναικος. fr.* 52 *in Jo.* (4.526.20); *ουτ' αν ελεγεν τη Σαμαρειτιδι, δος μοι πιειν.* Jo. 13.4 (4.229.27).

8 *fr.* 53 *in Jo.* (4.527.3). ADAPT. [6,8] see v. 6; *οι δε μαθηται ... απεληλυθοτων εις την πολιν, ινα τροφας αγορασωσιν.* Jo. 13.32 (4.256.9).

9 Jo. 13.9 (4.233.32), Jo. 20.35 (4.373.25). ADAPT. *ισως δ' αν επιζητησειε τις την αιτιαν δι' ην Ιουδαιοι ου συγχρωνται Σαμαρειταις. fr.* 53 *in Jo.* (4.526.24).

10 *fr.* 74 *in Jo.* (4.541.19); [10-11] *ει ... ζων* Jo. 20.41 (4.384.2); Jo. 13.1 (4.226.15); *συ ... ζων* Jo 13.7 (4.231.28), Jo. 13.8 (4.233.12).

11 [10-11] Jo. 20.41 (4.384.4); *κυριε ... βαθυ* Jo. 13.7 (4.231.24); *ουτε ... βαθυ* Jo. 13.9 (4.233.34), [Heracl.] Jo. 13.35 (4.260.20).

---

b Two *catenae* mss. for *fr.* 74 read επι της γης. Cf. P[66]* 1241.

c omit γαρ Jo. 13.9.

d The ὁ is in the present text of *fr.* 74. However, Origen's text of John in the *catenae* has been notoriously conformed to a later textual tradition. Since Origen's text is most like that of B and P[75], and since these two mss. are consistently anarthrous with this idiom, the appearance of the article is highly suspect. Cf. the commentary at 2,19; 8,49; 54; 13,7,8. However, the article is found at 4,13; 8,14,19.

e αν Jo. 13.1, Jo. 13.7] omit Jo. 13.8, Jo. 20.41, *fr.* 74 *in Jo.*

ἔχεις τὸ ὕδωρ τὸ ζῶν; **12** μὴ σὺ μείζων εἶ τοῦ πατρὸς ἡμῶν Ἰακώβ, ὃς δέδωκεν ἡμῖν τὸ φρέαρ καὶ αὐτὸς ἐξ αὐτοῦ ἔπιεν καὶ οἱ υἱοὶ αὐτοῦ καὶ τὰ θρέμματα αὐτοῦ; **13** ἀπεκρίθη ὁ Ἰησοῦς καὶ εἶπεν αὐτῇ, Πᾶς ὁ πίνων ἐκ τοῦ ὕδατος τούτου͡ διψήσει πάλιν· **14** ὃς δ᾽ ἂν πίῃͤ ἐκ τοῦ

---

13 [13-14] omnis, qui biberit ex hac aqua, iterum sitiet. *hom. 7.5 in Gen.* (6.76.4).

13 [13-14] omnis enim qui biberit ex aqua ista, sitiet rursum. *hom. 13.4 in Ezech.* (8.450.3).

14 [13-14] qui autem biberit ex aqua, quam ego dedero, non sitiet in aeternum, sed erit fluvius in eo fons aquae salientis in vitam aeternam. *hom. 13.4 in Ezech.* (8.450.4).

14 [13-14] qui autem biberit de aqua, quam ego do ei, non sitiet in aeternum. *hom. 7.5 in Gen.* (6.76.5).

14 Qui autem biberit de aqua, quam ego do ei, fiet in eo fons aquae salientis in vitam aeternam. *hom. 19.4 in Jos.* (7.413.14).

14 Quicumque biberit ex hac aqua, quam ego do ei, non sitiet in aeternum. *Cant.* (8.66.13).

14 ADAPT. Qui credit inquit in me, *fiet in eo fons aquae salientis in vitam aeternum. hom. 7.5 in Gen.* (6.76.7); *Qui ab Jesu aquam sibi datam*

---

12 *Jo.* 13.14 (4.238.31);μη ... Ιακωβ *fr.* 53 *in Jo.* (4.528.1). ADAPT. ... εις τον της Σαμαρειτιδος λογον περι του λεγομενου υπ᾽ αυτης φρεατος, ως ο Ιακωβ εδωκει αυτο και αυτος εξ αυτου επιεν και οι υιοι αυτου και τα θρεμματα αυτου, ... *Jo.* 13.1 (4.226.5), ει γαρ επιεν Ιακωβ εξ αυτης και οι υιοι αυτου και τα θρεμματα αυτου ... *Jo.* 13.6 (4.231.10), ταχα δε ουκ αληθες και το· Ιακωβ εκ του φρεατος επιεν και οι υιοι αυτου και τα θρεμματα αυτου· *Jo.* 13.9 (4.234.1).

13 *lemma* [13-14] *Jo.* 13.1 (4.226.10); πας ... παλιν *Jo.* 13.2 (4.227.13), *Jo.* 13.3 (4.228.7), *Jo.* 13.4 (4.229.24), [13-14] *comm. in Mt. 12:8* (10.79.9). ADAPT. [13-14] ... καν νοηθωσιν ακριβως, εκ του τον μεν πιοντα απο της πηγης του Ιακωβ διψην παλιν / τον δε πιοντα εκ του υδατος, ου διδωσιν ο Ιησους, πηγην υδατος εν εαυτω ισχειν αλλομενου εις ζωην αιωνιον. *Jo.* 13.5 (4.230.1); και γαρ εκ τουτου, φησι, του υδατος ο πινων διψησει παλιν· *fr.* 54 *in Jo.* (4.528.11); διο ο πινων εκ του υδατος του νομικου διψησει παλιν. *fr.* 56 *in Jo.* (4.529.11).

14 *lemma* [13-14] *Jo.* 13.1 (4.226.11); ος ... αιωνιον *Jo.* 13.3 (4.228.12); ος ... αιωνα [13-14] *comm. in Mt. 12:8* (10.79.10), *fr.* 54 *in Jo.* (4.528.12), *comm. in Mt. 12:8* (10.79.12), *Ps. 106:5* (*AS* 3, p. 216). ADAPT. [13-14]

ͭ του υδατος τουτου *lemma Jo.* 13.1, *Jo.* 13.2, *Jo.* 13.4, *comm. in Mt. 12,8*] τουτου του υδατος *Jo.* 13.3.

ͤ ος δ᾽ αν πιη *lemma Jo.* 13.1, *Jo.* 13.3, *fr.* 54 *in Jo.*, *comm. in Mt. 12,8 (bis)*] ο πινων *Ps. 106,5*; cf. adapt. in *exp. in Pr.* 24. This is almost certainly an adaptation to context, not an isolated support of ℵ D.

ὕδατος οὗ ἐγὼ δώσω αὐτῷ, [οὐ μὴ διψήσει[h] εἰς τὸν αἰῶνα, (αλλα το
υδωρ ο δωσω αυτῳ)][i] γενήσεται πηγὴ ἐν αὐτῷ[j] ὕδατος ἀλλομένου εἰς

---

biberunt et haec *facta* est *in iis fons aquae vivae salientis in vitam aeternam.*
Cant. 3 (8.206.16); *Qui bibit, non sitiet in aeternum. hom.* 1 *in Ps.* 36 (M.
12.1326); ... *fiet in te fons aquae salientis in vitam aeternam*... *hom.*
12.5 *in Gen.* (6.113.3); ... per affluentiam doctrinae *fons aquae vivae*
salientis in vitam aeternam. Cant. 3 (8.206.21);... ubi in corde uniuscuius-
que credentium *fons aquae vivae fit salientis in vitam aeternam. Cant.* 3
(8.221.10); ... flumina de ventre eius fluent *fons aquae salientis in vitam*
aeternam. hom. 7.3 *in Is.* (8.283.19); ... flumina de ventre suo educat
aquae vivae salientis in vitam aeternam. hom. 1.2 *in Gen.* (6.3.26).

---

see v. 13; τοτε δε ο πιων εκ του υδατος, ου δωσει ο Ιησους, εξει την γενομενην
εν αυτω πηγην υδατος αλλομενου εις ζωην αιωνιον, ... *Jo.* 13.4 (4.229.11);
[Heracl.] και εις το· *ου μη διψηση δε εις τον αιωνα· Jo.* 13.10 (4.234.20);
... καθως αυτος ο Χριστος φησιν· *ο πινων εκ του υδατος τουτου ου μη διψηση*
εις τον αιωνα. exp. in Pr. 24 (M.17.229); το δε· *ου μη διψηση εις τον αιωνα.*
fr. 54 *in Jo.* (4.528.16); ... *απο πηγης υδατος αλλομενου εις ζωην αιωνιον*
φανερουμενα ... *Jo.*13.6 (4.230.32); ... ιν' ουν ημιν χαρισηται *πηγην του*
αλλομενου υδατος εις ζωην αιωνιον. Jo. 13.6 (4.231.8); ... εν τω κρειττονι
της υδριας λαβουσα εκ του υδατος του γενομενου *εν αυτη αρχες υδατος αλλομενου*
εις ζωην αιωνιον· Jo. 13.29 (4.253.26); οιον δε εχουσα τι ηδη *του αλλομενου εις*
ζωην αιωνιον υδατος δια το ειρηκεναι· *Jo.* 13.8 (4.233.10); ... και *πηγας υδατος*
αλλομενου εις ζωην αιωνιον. Cels. 6.20 (2.91.5); ... ινα *πηγη υδατος αλλομενου*
εις ζωην αιωνιον η εν αυτοις *hom.* 19.4 *in Jos.* (7.413.14); ... αλλον εχοντα
ποταμους εν αυτω *αλλομενους εις ζωην αιωνιον. fr.* 22 *in Jer.* (3.208.16); ...
αφ' ης *ποταμοι ρευσουσιν υδατος αλλομενου εις ζωην αιωνιον. fr.* 165 *in Lc.*
(9.294.22); επαν εχωσιν εν εαυτοις *ποταμους υδατος αλλομενου εις ζωην αιωνιον.*
or. 30.3 (2.395.8).

---

[h] διψησει *comm. in Mt. 12,8 (bis), Ps. 106,5*] διψηση *fr.* 54 *in Jo.*
(bis), exp. in Pr. 24; cf. Heracleon's text, *Jo.* 13.10.

[i] The words ου μη διψησει etc. apparently had fallen out of Origen's
exemplar for the commentary due to *homoioteleuton* (cf. C* 13 477 543
726 1200 1375 1573 cop). Not only are these words missing from the
lemma and the one full citation in the commentary, but also from the
adaptation at 13.4. However the six citations in other works which include οὐ μὴ διψήσει εἰς τὸν αἰῶνα indicate that Origen did know the normal text. Cf. the discussion in E. HAUTSCH, *Die Evangelienzitate des*
Origenes (TU 34²; 1909) 130-31.

[j] πηγη εν αυτω *lemma Jo.* 13.1, *Jo.* 13.3] εν αυτω πηγη is supported
only by the adaptation at *Jo.* 13.4 (4.229.11). The contemporary P⁶⁶
is the only other Greek witness to this word order.

ζωὴν αἰώνιον. **15** λέγει πρὸς αὐτὸν ἡ γυνή, Κύριε, δός μοι τοῦτο τὸ ὕδωρ, ἵνα μὴ διψῶ, μηδὲ διέρχωμαι ἐνθάδε ἀντλεῖν.

16 λέγει αὐτῇ, Ὕπαγε φώνησόν σου τὸν ἄνδρα[k] καὶ ἐλθὲ ἐνθάδε. **17** ἀπεκρίθη ἡ γυνὴ καὶ εἶπεν, Οὐκ ἔχω ἄνδρα. λέγει αὐτῇ ὁ Ἰησοῦς, Καλῶς εἶπας ὅτι Ἄνδρα οὐκ ἔχω.[l] **18** πέντε γὰρ ἄνδρας ἔσχες, καὶ νῦν ὃν ἔχεις οὐκ ἔστιν σου ἀνήρ· τοῦτο ἀληθὲς εἴρηκας. **19** λέγει αὐτῷ ἡ γυνή, Κύριε, θεωρῶ ὅτι προφήτης εἶ σύ. **20** οἱ πατέρες ἡμῶν ἐν τῷ ὄρει τούτῳ προσεκύνησαν· καὶ ὑμεῖς[m] λέγετε ὅτι[n] ἐν Ἱεροσολύμοις

---

15 Da mihi Domine hanc aquam, ut non sitiam, neque veniam huc haurire, *hom.* 7.5 *in Gen.* (6.76.5).

20 Patres nostri omnes in hoc monte adoraverunt, et vos dicitis quia in Hierosolymis est locus, ubi oportet adorare. *princ.* 1.1 (5.19.20).

---

15 *lemma Jo.* 13.7 (4.231.21); κυριε ... αντλειν *Jo.* 20.41 (4.384.6); δος ... αντλειν *Jo.* 13.10 (4.235.11); δος ... υδωρ *Jo.* 13.1 (4.227.1), *Jo.* 13.7 (4.231.29), *Jo.* 13.8 (4.233.11), [Heracl.] *Jo.* 13.10 (4.235.8).

16 *lemma* [16-17] *Jo.* 13.8 (4.232.7); υπαγε ... ενθαδε *Jo.* 13.4 (4.229.30), *Jo.* 13.8 (4.233.9), *Jo.* 13.11 (4.235.34); φωνησον ... ενθαδε *Jo.* 13.11 (4.235.26). ADAPT. [Heracl.] ετι δε ο Ηρακλεων προς το· λεγει αυτη, φησι, δηλον οτι τοιουτο τι λεγων, ει θελεις λαβειν τουτο το υδωρ υπαγε φωνησον τον ανδρα σου· *Jo.* 13.11 (4.235.16).

17 *lemma* [16-17] απεκριθη ... ανδρα *Jo.* 13.8 (4.232.8); *lemma* [17-18] λεγει ... εχω *Jo.* 13.9 (4.233.15); ουκ εχω ανδρα *Jo.* 13.8 (4.233.14), *Jo.* 13.9 (4.233.28); καλως ... ανδρα *Jo.* 13.9 (4.233.29). ADAPT. [Heracl.] ειτα προς τουτο· αληθες ειρηκας οτι ανδρα ουκ εχεις φησιν· *Jo.* 13.11 (4.235.34); ... φησιν, καλως λεγεις ανδρα μη εχειν. *fr.* 57 *in Jo.* (4.530.14).

18 *lemma* [17-18] *Jo.* 13.9 (4.233.16); πεντε ... ανηρ [om. γαρ] *Jo.* 13.62 (4.296.6); πεντε ... εσχες *fr.* 57 *in Jo.* (4.530.19), [om. γαρ] *Jo.* 13.11 (4.236.3); και ... ανηρ *fr.* 57 *in Jo.* (4.531.6); τουτο αληθες ειρηκας *Jo.* 13.9 (4.233.30).

19 *lemma* [19-20] *Jo.* 13.12 (4.236.16); θεωρω ... συ *Jo.* 13.12 (4.236.29), *Jo.* 13.63 (4.296.7).

20 *lemma* [19-20] *Jo.* 13.12 (4.236.17), *Jo.* 13.13 (4.237.16); οι ... προσεκυνησαν *Jo.* 13.14 (4.238.33), [Heracl.] *Jo.* 13.15 (4.239.22); οι πατερες ημων *Jo.* 13.12 (4.236.30).

---

[k] σου τον ανδρα *lemma Jo.* 13.8, *Jo.* 13.8, *Jo.* 13.11] τον ανδρα σου *Jo.* 13.4, *Jo.* 13.11; cf. Heracleon's text.

[l] ανδρα ουκ εχω *lemma Jo.* 13.9] ουκ εχω ανδρα *Jo.* 13.9 (4.233.29). Heracleon supports the Western reading ανδρα ουκ εχεις.

[m] In the citation at 4.237.16, Origen reads υμεις δε, which is a contextual adaptation. After προσεκυνησαν he has added a parenthetical δεικνὺς τὸ Γαριζεῖν.

[n] οτι *Jo.* 13.13] omit *lemma Jo.* 13.12.

ἐστὶν ὁ τόπος ὅπου προσκυνεῖν δεῖ. **21** λέγει αὐτῇ ὁ Ἰησοῦς, Πίστευέ
μοι, γύναι, ὅτι ἔρχεται ὥρα ὅτε οὔτε ἐν τῷ ὄρει τούτῳ οὔτε ἐν Ἱεροσο-
λύμοις° προσκυνήσετεp(caes) τῷ πατρί. **22** ὑμεῖς προσκυνεῖτε ὃ οὐκ
οἴδατε· ἡμεῖς προσκυνοῦμεν ὃ οἴδαμεν, ὅτι ἡ σωτηρία ἐκq τῶν Ἰουδαίων
ἐστίν. **23** ἀλλ'ἔρχεται ὥρα, καὶ νῦν ἐστιν, ὅτε οἱ ἀληθινοὶ προσκυνηταὶ

---

21 Venit hora ut veri adoratores neque in Hierosolymis neque in
hoc monte adorent patrem. *princ.* 1.1 (5.19.25). ADAPT. uti iam *neque
in monte* Garizim *neque in Hierosolymis* sit locus, ubi oporteat adorare.
hom. 17.1 *in Jos.* (7.401.3).

23 ADAPT. *Nunc* enim illud *est* tempus *quando veri adoratores
adorant patrem* neque in Hierosolymis neque in monte Garizim, sed *in
spiritu et veritate. hom.* 13.3 *in Gen.* (6.118.9); ... sed *veri adoratores, qui
adorant patrem, in spiritu et veritate* adorent. *hom.* 17.1 *in Jos.* (7.401.4).

---

21 *lemma Jo.* 13.16 (4.239.26); [21,24] οτι ... πατρι *Cels.* 6.70
(2.140.21); ουτε[1] ... πατρι *Jo.* 13.14 (4.238.27), *Jo.* 13.16 (4.240.11,14);
[Heracl.] πιστευε μοι, γυναι *Jo.* 13.16 (4.239.30). ADAPT. πας γουν ῳ Χριστος
επιδεδημηκεν ουτε εν Ιεροσολυμοις ουτε εν τω των Σαμαρειτων ορει προσκυνει
τῳ θεῳ, .. *Jo.* 1.6 (4.11.14); οσον μεν ουν ουδεπω εληλυθεν η υπο του κυριου
ειρημενη ωρα, οτε ουτε εν τῳ ορει τουτῳ ουτε εν Ιεροσολυμοις προσκυνησουσιν τῳ
πατρι, ... *Jo.* 13.13 (4.238.2); οτε μεντοι γε ουτε εν τῳ ορει τουτῳ ουτε εν
Ιεροσολυμοις τις προσκυνει, ... *Jo.* 13.16 (4.240.23); διοπερ ουκ ειρηται, ουτε
εν Ιεροσολυμοις προσκυνησετε τῳ θεῳ, αλλα ουτε εν Ιεροσολυμοις προσκυνησετε
τῳ πατρι. *Jo.* 13.16 (4.240.25).

22 *lemma Jo.* 13.17 (4.240.28); οτι ... εστιν *Jo.* 13.17 (4.241.28);
[Heracl.] *Jo.* 13.19 (4.243.15). ADAPT. πως ου σαφες τινα τροπον η σωτηρια
εκ των Ιουδαιων γινεται; *Jo.* 13.17 (4.242.3).

23 *lemma* αλλ' ... αληθεια *Jo.* 13.18 (4.242.8); *lemma* και γαρ ...
αυτον *Jo.* 13.20 (4.244.1); αλλ' ... εστιν *Jo.* 13.13 (4.238.19); ερχεται

° The word order ουτε εν Ιεροσολυμοις ουτε εν τῳ ορει τουτῳ occurs
in the allusion in *Jo.* 1.6, in *Cels.* 6.70, and in the Latin translation of
de Princ. 1.1. This word order is attested elsewhere in cod. 28 and the
lemma of Cyril of Alexandria's commentary (although not so twice in
the comm. *ad loc.*).

p (caes) In the citation in *Cels.* 6.70 Origen reads προσκυνησουσι.
This may be a "Caesarean" reading (cf. fam. 13). However, it is probably
nothing more than an adaptation to context (cf. *Jo.* 13.13, which is
followed by the rather confirming adaptation in 13.16 [4.240.25], "Therefore it is *not* said 'neither in Jerusalem shall *you* worship *God*' but 'neither
in Jerusalem shall *you* worship *the Father*'."). Since the *Cels.* reading
comes in a citation combining verses 21 and 24, προσκυνησουσι may simply
be a reflection of verse 23. In any case it is a doubtful Caesarean reading.

q εκ *lemma Jo.* 13.17, adapt. *Jo.* 13.17 (4.242.3)] απο *Jo.* 13.17
(4.241.28).

προσκυνήσουσι τῷ πατρὶ ἐν πνεύματι καὶ ἀληθείᾳ· καὶ γὰρ ὁ πατὴρ τοιούτους ζητεῖ τοὺς προσκυνοῦντας αὐτόν. 24 πνεῦμα ὁ θεός, καὶ τοὺς προσκυνοῦντας αὐτὸν ἐν πνεύματι καὶ ἀληθείᾳ δεῖ προσκυνεῖν. 25 λέγει αὐτῷ ἡ γυνή, Οἶδα‧ ὅτι Μεσσίας ἔρχεται, ὁ λεγόμενος Χριστός· ὅταν ἔλθῃ ἐκεῖνος, ἀναγγελεῖ‧ ἡμῖν ἅπαντα.‧ 26 λέγει αὐτῇ ὁ Ἰησοῦς, Ἐγώ εἰμι, ὁ λαλῶν σοι.

27 Καὶ ἐπὶ τούτῳ ἦλθον οἱ μαθηταὶ αὐτοῦ, καὶ ἐθαύμαζον ὅτι μετὰ γυναικὸς ἐλάλει· οὐδεὶς μέντοι γε εἶπεν, Τί ζητεῖς; ἤ, Τί λαλεῖς

---

24 Deus spiritus est, et eos qui adorant eum, in spiritu et veritate oportet adorare. *princ.* 1.1 (5.17.2), *idem.* (5.19.26).

24 Spiritus Deus est, et qui adorant eum, in spiritu et veritate oportet adorare. *hom.* 26 *in Lc.* (9.153.5).

24 Deus spiritus est. *princ.* 1.1 (5.18.3), *idem.* (5.19.12,17), *hom.* 4.1 *in Lev.* (6.316.16).

... εστιν *Jo.* 13.14 (4.238.26). ADAPT. εξεστιν ουν και εν τω πνευματι και αληθεια προσκυνειν τω πατρι οτε ου μονον ερχεται ωρα αλλα και νυν εστιν, ... *Jo.* 13.14 (4.238.23); τηρητεον δε οτι οι αληθινοι προσκυνηται ου μονον εν μελλουση ωρα αλλα και ενεστηκυια προσκυνουσι τω πατρι εν πνευματι και αληθεια *Jo.* 13.18 (4.242.29); ... εν τω πνευματι και αληθεια προσκυνησεις τω θεω. *Ps. 64:2* (*AS* 3, p. 74).

24 *lemma Jo.* 13.21 (4.244.17); *Cels.* 2.71 (1.193.20), [21,24] *Cels.* 6.70 (2.140.23); *Cels.* 7.27 (2.178.17); πνευμα ο θεος *Jo.* 13.21 (4.244.25), *Jo.* 13.23 (4.247.12), *Cels.* 6.70 (2.140.11), *idem.* (2.140.19). ADAPT. αλλα μαθων οτι πνευμα ο θεος, πνευματικως λατρευων αυτω πνευματι και αληθεια ουχετι δε τυπικως προσκυνει τον των ολων πατερα και δημιουργον. *Jo.* 1.6 (4.11.16), [Heracl.] προς τουτοις το· εν πνευματι και αληθεια προσκυνεισθαι τον θεον. *Jo.* 13.19 (4.243.25); [Heracl.] εις μεντοι γε το· πνευμα ο θεος. ο Πρακλεων φησιν ... το δε τους προσκυνουντας εν πνευματι και αληθεια δει προσκυνειν σαφηνιζειν νομιζων φησιν· *Jo.* 13.25 (4.248.28); ... δι' ων εδιδαξεν οτι ουκ εν σαρκι δει προσκυνειν και σαρκιναις θυσιαις τον θεον αλλ' εν πνευματι, ... αλλα και ουκ εν τυποις προσκυνειν δει τω πατρι αλλ' εν αληθεια. *Cels.* 6.70 (2.140.24).

25 *lemma Jo.* 13.26 (4.250.4); οιδα ... απαντα *Jo.* 1.5 (4.10.15), *Jo.* 1.21 (4.26.6); οταν ... απαντα *Jo.* 13.27 (4.251.11), *idem.* (4.251.22).

26 *lemma* [26-27] *Jo.* 13.27 (4.251.28); εγω ... σοι *Jo.* 1.21 (4.26.8). *Jo.* 13.27 (4.251.24), [Heracl.] *Jo.* 13.28 (4.252.33).

27 *lemma* [26-27] *Jo.* 13.27 (4.251.28); εθαυμαζον ... ελαλει *Jo.* 13.28 (4.252.31).

ʳ οιδα *lemma Jo.* 13.26. *Jo.* 1.5] οιδαμεν *Jo.* 1.21. The comment immediately following the *lemma* supports the singular as Origen's true text. It begins: ἄξιον ἰδεῖν πῶς ἡ Σαμαρεῖτις ... τὴν παρουσίαν Χριστοῦ προσδοκᾷ. So also HAUTSCH, *op. cit.*, p. 131.

ˢ αναγγελει *lemma Jo.* 13.26, *Jo.* 1.21, *Jo.* 13.27 (*bis*)] απαγγελει *Jo.* 1.5.
ᵗ απαντα *lemma Jo.* 13.26, *Jo.* 1.5, *Jo.* 13.27 (*bis*)] παντα *Jo.* 1.21.

μετ' αὐτῆς; **28** ἀφῆκεν οὖν τὴν ὑδρίαν αὐτῆς ἡ γυνὴ καὶ ἀπῆλθεν εἰς τὴν πόλιν καὶ λέγει τοῖς ἀνθρώποις, **29** Δεῦτε ἴδετε ἄνθρωπον ὃς εἶπέν μοι πάντα [ἃ]ᵘ ἐποίησα· μήτι οὗτός ἐστιν ὁ Χριστός; **30** ἐξῆλθον ἐκ τῆς πόλεως καὶ ἤρχοντο πρὸς αὐτόν.

31 'Εν τῷ μεταξὺ ἠρώτων αὐτὸν οἱ μαθηταὶ λέγοντες, 'Ραββί, φάγε. **32** ὁ δὲ εἶπεν αὐτοῖς. 'Εγὼ βρῶσιν ἔχω φαγεῖν ἣν ὑμεῖς οὐκ οἴδατε. **33** ἔλεγον οὖν οἱ μαθηταὶ πρὸς ἀλλήλους, Μή τις ἤνεγκεν αὐτῷ φαγεῖν; **34** λέγει αὐτοῖς ὁ 'Ιησοῦς, 'Εμὸν βρῶμά ἐστιν ἵνα ποιήσω τὸ

---

34 Meus cibus est, ut faciam voluntatem eius, qui me misit, et

---

28 *lemma* [28-29] *Jo.* 13.29 (4.253.7); αφηκεν ... γυνη [om. ουν] *Jo.* 13.31 (4.255.21). ADAPT. [28-30] εως αφεισα την υδριαν αυτης η γυνη απελθουσα εις την πολιν ειπη τοις ανθρωποις· *Jo.* 13.28 (4.252.19); της Σαμαρειτιδος καταλιπουσης την υδριαν και απεληλυθυιας εις την πολιν υπερ του ευαγγελισασθαι τα περι του σωτηρος. *Jo.* 13.51 (4.279.14).

29 *lemma* [28-29] *Jo.* 13.29 (4.253.8), [28-30] *Jo.* 13.28 (4.252.21), *Jo.* 13.63 (4.296.8); παντα α εποιησεν *Jo.* 13.29 (4.253.17), *idem.* (4.253.30); [Heracl.] μητι ... Χριστος *Jo.* 13.31 (4.255.28).

30 [28-30] *Jo.* 13.28 (4.252.22), *Jo.* 13.30 (4.254.33); εξηλθον [+ δε] ... πολεως *Jo.* 13.31 (4.255.29). ADAPT. ... επειπερ και αυτοι εξηλθον ευ ποιουντες εκ της πολεως και ηρχοντο προς αυτον. *Jo.* 13.30 (4.254.29).

31 *lemma Jo.* 13.32 (4.256.1), *Jo.* 13.32 (4.256.20). ADAPT. και ουχι ... εγεγραπτο· εν δε τω μεταξυ ελεγον αυτω οι μαθηται, ραββι, φαγε. *Jo.* 13.32 (4.256.22).

32 *lemma Jo.* 13.33 (4.257.20); εγω ... οιδατε *Jo.* 13.34 (4.259.8), *idem.* (4.259.11), *idem.* (4.259.14), *idem.* (4.259.17). ADAPT. ... εως ταχα φθασομεν επι το την αυτην βρωσιν φαγειν τω υιω του θεου, ην επι του παροντος οι μαθηται ουκ οιδασιν. *Jo.* 13.34 (4.260.11).

33 *lemma Jo.* 13.35 (4.260.14); μητις ... φαγειν *fr.* 59 *in Jo.* (4.531.18). ADAPT. ... μηποτε βλεποντες τι θειοτερον οι μαθηται φασιν προς αλληλους· μη τις ηνεγκεν αυτω φαγειν; *Jo.* 13.35 (4.260.21).

34 *lemma Jo.* 13.36 (4.260.27); εμον ... εργον *comm. in Mt.* 16:7 (10.487.2); εμον ... με *Jo.* 13.36 (4.261.19), [Heracl.] *Jo.* 13.38 (4.263.14); τελειωσω ... εργον *Jo.* 13.36 (4.261.33). ADAPT. οπερ γαρ και επραττεν ο Ιησους ποιων το θελημα του πεμψαντος αυτον και τελειων αυτου το εργον, ... *Jo.* 13.34 (4.259.9); ... πρωτον μεν ινα ποιηση το θελημα του πεμψαντος αυτον. *Jo.* 13.37 (4.262.22); [Heracl.] ... οτι μειζον εστιν ο ειχεν βρωμα φαγειν, οπερ ην ποιησαι το θελημα του πεμψαντος αυτον και τελειωσαι το εργον αυτου. *Jo.* 13.35 (4.260.24); ... καθα λεγει, εμον βρωμα εστι του ποιησαι το θελημα

ᵘ α *Jo.* 13.28, *Jo.* 13.29 (*bis*)] οσα *lemma Jo.* 13.29, *Jo.* 13.63. Although the reading of the *lemma* is supported by the later citation, the text of the commentary reads α three times in the immediate context of v. 29.

θέλημα τοῦ πέμψαντός με καὶ τελειώσω αὐτοῦ τὸ ἔργον. 35 οὐχ ὑμεῖς λέγετε ὅτι ["Ετι]ᵛ τετράμηνός ἐστιν καὶ ὁ θερισμὸς ἔρχεται; ἰδοὺ λέγω

---

perficiam opus eius. *hom.* 7.3 *in Lev.* (6.381.20). *Cant.* 2 (8.120.9), *hom.* 14.2 *in Ezech.* (8.453.13).

34 Meus cibus est, ut faciam voluntatem eius, qui me misit. *hom.* 17.6 *in Num.* (7.165.24).

34 Meus cibus est, ut faciam voluntatem eius, qui me misit, et consummem opus eius. *hom.* 3.3 *in Is.* (8.257.1).

34 Mea est esca, ut faciam voluntatem eius, qui me misit, et perficiam opus ipsius. *comm. in Mt. 16:7* (10.487.2).

34 Mea esca est, ut faciam voluntatem eius, qui me misit, et perficiam opus eius. *comm. ser.* 86 *in Mt.* (11 198.1)

του πεμφαντος με. *sel. in Num.* (M. 12.584); ... ον τροπον Χριστος κεχωρηκεν, ο ελθων ποιησαι το θελημα αυτου του πατρος και παν αυτο τελειωσας. *or.* 26.3 (2.360.28).

35 *lemma Jo.* 13.39 (4.263.32); *lemma* ιδου ... ηδη *Jo.* 13.42 (4.267.28); ουχ ... ηδη *Jo.* 13.40 (4.265.22); *idem* (4.266.25); *Jo.* 13.45 (4.271.21), *comm. in Rom.* (*JTS*, 13, p. 221), *idem.* (*JTS*, 14, p. 12); ουχ ... ερχεται *Jo.* 13.39 (4.263.36), *idem.* (4.264.27), *Jo.* 13.40 (4.267.3); ετι ... ερχεται *Jo.* 13.40 (4.266.14); επαρατε ... ηδη *Jo.* 13.40 (4.265.27), *idem.* (4.266.35), *Jo.* 13.42 (4.269.1), *Jo.* 13.47 (4.273.16), *Jo.* 28.4 (4.393.33), *hom.* 5.13 *in Jer.* (3.43.9), *or.* 13.5 (2.329.21); επαρατε ... υμων *Jo.* 13.42 (4.267.30); θεασασθε ... ηδη *Jo.* 13.44 (4.271.7). ADAPT. ου γαρ εχρην φασκειν το ᾿ ουχ υμεις λεγετε οτι ετι τεσσαρες ημεραι και ο θερισμος ερχεται, ἤ ετι τεσσαρα ετη και ο θερισμος ερχεται. *Jo.* 13.40 (4.266.8); ... απιοντα εις την Γαλιλαιαν οτε ετι τετραμηνος ειπεν εις τον θερισμον. *Jo.* 13.39 (4.265.6); ... λεγειν οτι τετραμηνος εστιν και ο θερισμος ερχεται. *Jo.* 13.40 (4.265.33); επαρατε τους οφθαλμους υμων διοπερ ο τοιουτος ουδε θεασεται τας χωρας καν ωσιν λευκαι προς θερισμον ηδη. *Jo.* 13.42 (4.268.11); ... ινα θεασωνται τας χωρας οτι λευκαι εισιν προς θερισμον ηδη. *Jo.* 13.44 (4.271.13); ... τους επαραντας τους οφθαλμους κατα τας υποθηκας του σωτηρος ημων Ιησου, ινα θεασωνται τας χωρας πως ησαν λευκαι προς θερισμον ηδη, ... *Jo.* 13.49 (4.276.11); και οτε λευκη εστιν ηδη προς θερισμον εξεστι μοι λοιπον λαβειν ... *comm. I Cor.* 41 (*JTS*, 9, p. 512).

ᵛ ετι *lemma Jo.* 13.39, *Jo.* 13.39 (4.264.27), *Jo.* 13.40 (4.267.3); cf. adapt. *Jo.* 13.40 (4.266.8), *Jo.* 13.39 (4.265.7)] omit *Jo.* 13.40 (4.265.22), *Jo.* 13.40 (4.266.25), *Jo.* 13.39 (4.263.36), *comm. in Rom.* (*bis*); cf. adapt. *Jo.* 13.40 (4.265.33)] omit οτι *Jo.* 13.45 (4.271.21). The adaptation at 13.40 (4.266.8), "not, *yet* four days or *yet* four years...", seems to verify ετι as Origen's true text. However, there is an unusually high incidence of omission, which is the text of P⁷⁵ D L *et al.*

ὑμῖν, ʷ⁽ᶜᵃᵉˢ⁾ ἐπάρατε τοὺς ὀφθαλμοὺς ὑμῶν καὶ θεάσασθε τὰς χώρας
ὅτι λευκαί εἰσιν πρὸς θερισμὸν ἤδη. 36 ὁ θερίζων μισθὸν λαμβάνει καὶ
συνάγει καρπὸν εἰς ζωὴν αἰώνιον, ἵνα ὁ σπείρων ὁμοῦ χαίρῃ καὶ ὁ θερίζων.
37 ἐν γὰρ τούτῳ ὁ λόγος ἐστὶνᵏ ἀληθινὸς ὅτι "Ἄλλος ἐστὶν ὁ σπείρων καὶ
ἄλλος ὁ θερίζων. 38 ἐγὼ ἀπέστειλα ὑμᾶς θερίζειν ὃ οὐχ ὑμεῖς κεκοπιά-
κατε· ἄλλοι κεκοπιάκασιν, καὶ ὑμεῖς εἰς τὸν κόπον αὐτῶν εἰσεληλύθατε.
39 Ἐκ δὲ τῆς πόλεως ἐκείνης πολλοὶ ἐπίστευσαν [εἰς αὐτὸν]ʸ τῶν

---

38 alii laboraverunt et vos in laborem eorum introistis *hom.* 6.11
in Ex. (6.202.19).

---

36 *lemma Jo.* 13.43 (4.269.9), *Jo.* 13.47 (4.274.2); ο θεριζων ...
αιωνιον *Jo.* 13.43 (4.270.6), *Jo.* 13.43 (4.270.12), [Heracl.] *Jo.* 13.46
(4.272.4), *or.* 13.5 (2.329.22); ο θεριζων μισθον λαμβανει *Jo.* 13.47 (4.274.9);
συναγει ... αιωνιον *Jo.* 13.45 (4.271.34); ινα ... θεριζων *Jo.* 13.46 (4.272.18),
Jo. 13.48 (4.275.15), [Heracl.] *Jo.* 13.49 (4.276.18). ADAPT. πας ο θεριζων μισθον λαμβανει και συναγει καρπον εις ζωην αιωνιον ινα πας ο σπειρων ομου
χαιρη και πας ο θεριζων *Jo.* 13.47 (4.274.10); ... ο σπειρων ομου χαιρει και ο
θεριζων ... *Jo.* 13.46 (4.272.32); ενα μεν οτε λαμβανει μισθον, ετερον δε οτε
συναγει καρπον εις ζωην αιωνιον. *Jo.* 13.45 (4.271.27).
37 *lemma Jo.* 13.49 (4.276.3), [Heracl.] *Jo.* 13.49 (4.276.29); αλλος¹
... θεριζων *Jo.* 13.43 (4.270.16), *idem.* (4.270.25). ADAPT. ... αληθες το·
αλλος ο σπειρων, και αλλο θεριζων· *Jo.* 13.41 (4.267.19); και ουτω δηλον πως
αλλος ο σπειρων και αλλος ο θεριζων. *Jo.* 13.49 (4.276.11).
38 *lemma Jo.* 13.50 (4.277.3), [om. εγω] *Jo.* 13.41 (4.267.20), *Jo.*
13.47 (4.274.6); αλλοι ... εισεληλυθατε *Jo.* 13.50 (4.278.28), [Heracl.] υμεις
... εισεληλυθατε *Jo.* 13.50 (4.279.2).
39 *lemma Jo.* 13.51 (4.279.11), [39-40] *Jo.* 13.30 (4.254.34). ADAPT.
... επαναλαμβανει η γραφη τα περι των εληλυθοτων εκ της πολεως προς αυτον
και πιστευσαντων δια την μαρτυριαν της γυναικος λεγουσης οτι· ειπεν μοι παντα

ʷ ⁽ᶜᵃᵉˢ⁾ Omit ιδου λεγω υμιν *comm. in Rom.* (*bis*). Cf. fam. 1 124 565 1241.
Although this citation is from a *catena*, its interesting double history seems
to make it a genuine reflection of Origen's Johannine text during his later
Caesarean period. A whole paragraph from Origen's commentary has
been preserved in the *catenae* under two different passages in Romans
(under Rom. 3,21 and 7,7), and this Johannine citation appears in the
middle of the paragraph. In both places the clause is missing, and this
has been confirmed now by the Tura fragment (J. SCHERER, Le Caire
1957).
ˣ The citation from Heracleon has the word order of D: εστιν ο λογος.
ʸ εις αυτον *Jo.* 13.30] omit *lemma Jo.* 13.51; cf. adapt. *Jo.* 13.51,
Jo. 13.52. Probably the omission here represents Origen's text. If so, it
is one of his very few Western readings (= ℵ* 482 a e).

Σαμαρειτῶν διὰ τὸν λόγον τῆς γυναικὸς μαρτυρούσης ὅτι Εἶπέν μοι πάντα [ἃ]ᶻ ἐποίησα. **40** ὡς οὖν ἦλθον πρὸς αὐτὸν οἱ Σαμαρεῖται, ἠρώτων αὐτὸν μεῖναι παρ' αὐτοῖς· καὶ ἔμεινεν ἐκεῖ δύο ἡμέρας. **41** καὶ πολλῷ πλείους ἐπίστευσαν διὰ τὸν λόγον αὐτοῦ. **42** τῇ δὲ γυναικὶ ἔλεγον, Οὐκέτι διὰ τὴν λαλιάν σουᵃᵃ πιστεύομεν· αὐτοὶ γὰρ ἀκηκόαμεν, καὶ οἴδαμεν ὅτι ἀληθῶς οὗτός ἐστινᵇᵇ ὁ σωτὴρ τοῦ κόσμου.

οσα εποιησα. *Jo.* 13.51 (4.279.20); η μεν ουν αρχη των απο της Σαμαρειας πιστευοντων πολλων ην ο λογος της γυναικος μαρτυρουσης οτι, ειπεν μοι παντα α εποιησα. *Jo.* 13.52 (4.281.2); [Heracl.] ο δ' Ηρακλεων το μεν εκ της πολεως αντι του· εκ του κοσμου εξειληφεν· το δε· δια τον λογον της γυναικος. *Jo.* 13.51 (4.279.31).

40 lemma [40-41] *Jo.* 13.52 (4.280.5); [39-40] ως ... αυτοις *Jo.* 13.30 (4.255.2); ηλθον ... Σαμαρειται *Jo.* 13.30 (4.255.4); εμεινεν ... ημερας *Jo.* 13.52 (4.280.10). ADAPT. ... οι Σαμαρειται ερωτωσιν τον Ιησουν, ουχ ινα μεινη εν τη πολει, αλλα παρ' αυτοις. *Jo.* 13.30 (4.254.26); ... και πρωτων αυτον μειναι παρ' αυτοις. ου γεγραπται δε μετα τουτο, οτι εισηλθεν εις την πολιν, αλλ' εμεινεν εκει δυο ημερας. *Jo.* 13.30 (4.255.6); ... ο Ιωαννης ου πεποιηκεν το· ηρωτων αυτον οι Σαμαρειται εισελθειν εις την Σαμαρειαν, η εισελθειν εις την πολιν, αλλα μειναι παρ' αυτοις. *Jo.* 13.52 (4.280.21); ... ου φησι· και εμεινεν εν τη πολει εκεινη δυο ημερας η εμεινεν εν τη Σαμαρεια, αλλ' εμεινεν εκει. *Jo.* 13.52 (4.280.25); ... οτι δυο ημερας μεινας εκει παρα τοις Σαμαρευσιν ... *Jo.* 13.39 (4.264.32); ... καταλιπων τους ερωτησαντας αυτον μειναι παρ' αυτοις. *Jo.* 13.56 (4.287.13).

41 lemma [40-41] *Jo.* 13.52 (4.280.6). ADAPT. [41-42] η δε αυξησις και ο πληθυσμος των πολλῳ πλειονων πιστευοντων / ουκετι δια τον λογον της γυναικος / αλλα δια τον λογον αυτον. *Jo.* 13.52 (4.281.4).

42 lemma *Jo.* 13.53 (4.281.27); ουκετι ... κοσμου *Jo.* 13.30 (4.254.13). ADAPT. [41-42] see v. 41; αρνουνται την δια την λαλιαν της γυναικος πιστιν, κρειττον εκεινης ευροντες το ακηκοεναι αυτου του σωτηρος, ωστε και ειδεναι οτι αληθως ουτος εστιν ο σωτηρ του κοσμου. *Jo.* 13.53 (4.281.30); αλλα γε αναγκαιοτατα προς την διαφοραν του λογου των Σαμαρειτων εστιν ουκετι δια την λαλιαν πιστευοντων της γυναικος αλλ' ακηκοοτων και ειδοτων οτι ουτος εστιν ο σωτηρ του κοσμου. *Jo.* 13.53 (4.283.16); [Heracl.] Ηρακλεων δε απλουστερον εκλαβων το· ουκετι δια την σην λαλιαν πιστευομεν φησι λειπειν το μονην. ετι μεν γαρ προς το· αυτοι γαρ ακηκοαμεν, και οιδαμεν οτι ουτος εστιν ο σωτηρ του κοσμου φησιν. *Jo.* 13.53 (4.283.22).

ᶻ α *Jo.* 13.30. *Jo.* 13.52] οσα lemma *Jo.* 13.51; cf. adapt. *Jo.* 13.51.

ᵃᵃ Origen's text is that of P⁷⁵ B; Heracleon reads την σην λαλιαν with the majority.

ᵇᵇ αληθως ουτος εστιν lemma *Jo.* 13.53, *Jo.* 13.53 (4.281.32)] ουτος εστιν αληθως *Jo.* 13.30] omit αληθως *Jo.* 13.53 (4.283.18) and Heracleon.

43 Μετὰ δὲ τὰς δύο ἡμέρας ἐξῆλθεν ἐκεῖθεν εἰς τὴν Γαλιλαίαν· 44 αὐτὸς γὰρ Ἰησοῦς ἐμαρτύρησεν ὅτι προφήτης ἐν τῇ ἰδίᾳ πατρίδι τιμὴν οὐκ ἔχει. 45 ὅτε οὖν ἦλθεν εἰς τὴν Γαλιλαίαν, ἐδέξαντο αὐτὸν οἱ Γαλιλαῖοι, πάντα ἑωρακότες ὅσα^cc ἐποίησεν ἐν Ἱεροσολύμοις ἐν τῇ ἑορτῇ, καὶ αὐτοὶ γὰρ ἦλθον εἰς τὴν ἑορτήν.

46 Ἦλθεν οὖν πάλιν εἰς τὴν Κανὰ τῆς Γαλιλαίας, ὅπου ἐποίησε τὸ ὕδωρ οἶνον. καὶ ἦν τις βασιλικὸς οὗ ὁ υἱὸς ἠσθένει ἐν Καφαρναούμ. 47 (.... απηλθεν) πρὸς αὐτὸν καὶ ἠρώτα ἵνα καταβῇ καὶ ἰάσηται αὐτοῦ τὸν υἱόν, ἔμελλεν γὰρ ἀποθνήσκειν.

48 (....) Ἐὰν μὴ σημεῖα καὶ τέρατα ἴδητε, οὐ μὴ πιστεύσητε.

---

43 *lemma* [43-44] Jo. 13.54 (4.283.30). ADAPT. αλλα και εν τοις εξης ουκ ειρηται μετα δε τας δυο ημερας εξηλθεν εκ της πολεως αλλα και εξηλθεν εκειθεν. Jo. 13.30 (4.255.8).

44 *lemma* [43-44] Jo. 13.54 (4.283.31), Jo. 13.54 (4.284.1), *idem.* (4.284.5), *idem.* (4.284.8), Jo. 13.55 (4.284.30); προφητης ... εχει *fr.* 60 *in* Jo. (4.532.14).

45 *lemma* Jo. 13.56 (4.286.1), Jo. 13.39 [om. ουν] (4.265.2); παντα ... εορτη Jo. 13.56 (4.286.8). ADAPT. εις γαρ τινα τοπον της Γαλιλαιας εδεξαντο αυτον εωρακοτες παντα οσα εποιησεν εν Ιεροσολυμοις εν τη εορτη. Jo. 13.54 (4.284.12); ... μαρτυρουμενους δια τουτο αυτον δεδεχθαι, επει ελθοντες εις την εορτην εν Ιεροσολυμοις παντα εωρακασιν α εποιησεν εκει ο Ιησους. Jo. 13.56 (4.286.18); ... ελθοντα αυτον εις την Γαλιλαιαν εδεξαντο παντα εωρακοτες οσα εποιησεν εν τοις Ιεροσολυμοις. Jo. 13.56 (4.286.24).

46 *lemma* ηλθεν ... οινον Jo. 13.57 (4.287.25), *lemma* και ... Καφαρναουμ Jo. 13.58 (4.288.10). ADAPT. [46-47] ο δε βασιλικος περι υιου ως ετι νοσουντος και αποθνησκειν μελλοντος ... *comm. in Mt. 15:21* (10.62.3); ... οτι παραγενομενος εις την Γαλιλαιαν ηλθεν εις την Κανα της Γαλιλαιας οπου προτερον πεποιηκεν το υδωρ οινον. Jo. 13.39 (4.265.10); αλλα και μετα τουτο οτι ηλθεν εις την Κανα της Γαλιλαιας ανεγραψε. Jo. 13.54 (4.284.13).

47 ADAPT. [46-47] see v. 46; ... γενομενος προς αυτον και ερωτων, ινα καταβη και ιασηται αυτου τον υιον· εμελλεν γαρ αποθνησκειν. Jo. 13.58 (4.289.28); ... τον δε ασθενησαντα αυτου υιον εν Καφαρναουμ και μελλοντα αποθνησκειν. Jo. 13.58 (4.289.17); ... ο βασιλικος γενομενος προς αυτον, οπως καταβη εις το χωριον της νοσου του παιδιου και ιασηται τον νενοσηκοτα. Jo. 13.59 (4.291.14); [Heracl.] ειτα το· εκ της Ιουδαιας εις την Γαλιλαιαν ... ημελλεν αποθνησκειν. Jo. 13.60 (4.291.29).

48 εαν ... πιστευσητε Jo. 13.59 (4.291.12), Jo. 13.63 (4.296.18), Jo. 13.64 (4.297.5), *fr.* 179 *in Mt.* (12.86.4), [Heracl.] Jo. 13.60 (4.292.5), εαν ... ιδητε Jo. 13.59 (4.289.31). ADAPT. ... ινα οι μη αλλως πιστευοντες εαν μη ιδωσι σημεια και τερατα πιστευσωσι. *comm. in Mt. 15:21* (10.62.9).

---

cc οσα Jo. 13.39, Jo. 13.56 (4.286.8), adapt. Jo. 13.54, Jo. 13.56 (4.286.25)] α *lemma* Jo. 13.56, adapt. Jo. 13.56 (4.286.18). The *lemma* appears to be secondary in this instance. The citations in the immediate context read οσα.

49 (....) [κατάβηθι πρὶν ἀποθανεῖν τὸ παιδίον μου.]ᵈᵈ

50 Πορεύου· ὁ υἱός σου ζῇ.

51 ἤδη (δε) αὐτοῦ καταβαίνοντος οἱ δοῦλοι ἀπήντησαν αὐτῷ λέγοντες ὅτι ὁ παῖς αὐτοῦ ζῇ.ᵉᵉ

52 (.... οτι εχθες) ὥραν ἑβδόμην ἀφῆκεν αὐτὸν ὁ πυρετός.

53 (....) καὶ ἐπίστευσεν αὐτὸς καὶ ἡ οἰκία αὐτοῦ ὅλη. **54** τοῦτο δὲ πάλιν δεύτερον σημεῖον ἐποίησεν ὁ Ἰησοῦς ἐλθὼν ἐκ τῆς Ἰουδαίας εἰς τὴν Γαλιλαίαν.

---

49 [Heracl.] *Jo.* 13.60 (4.292.8).

50 *Jo.* 13.59 (4.290.10); ο υιος σου ζη *Jo.* 13.39 (4.265.13), *Jo.* 13.59 (4.291.17), *Jo.* 13.62 (4.295.17), [Heracl.] *Jo.* 13.60 (4.292.14).

51 ADAPT. εμφαινεται δε αυτου το αξιωμα και εκ του *ηδη αυτου κατα-βαινοντας τους δουλους αυτω απηντηκεναι, λεγοντας οτι ο παις αυτου ζη. Jo.* 13.58 (4.288.20); ουτοι [οι δουλοι] ... και απαντωσιν τω πατρι ευαγγελιζομενοι την ζωην του θεραπευθεντος δια του· ο παις σου ζη. *Jo.* 13.59 (4.290.13); [Heracl.] ο παις σου ζη. *Jo.* 13.60 (4.292.23).

52 ADAPT. ου ματην δε ωραν εβδομην αφιησιν αυτον ο πυρετος. *Jo.* 13.59 (4.290.17).

53 *lemma* και ... ολη *Jo.* 13.58 (4.288.11); [Heracl.] επιστευσεν ... ολη *Jo.* 13.60 (4.292.31). ADAPT. ... και η οικια αυτου ολη πεπιστευκετω *Jo.* 13.58 (4.288.25).

54 *lemma Jo.* 13.62 (4.294.9); τουτο ... Ιησους *Jo.* 13.63 (4.296.15), *idem.* (4.296.35); [Heracl.] εκ ... Γαλιλαιαν *Jo.* 13.60 (4.291.29). ADAPT. κατελθων δε εκ της Ιουδαιας εις την Γαλιλαιαν πως τουτο δευτερον σημειον πεποιηκεν ο Ιησους. *Jo.* 13.59 (4.290.23).

ᵈᵈ This is from Heracleon.

ᵉᵉ The reconstruction of this verse relies chiefly on the adaptation at *Jo.* 13.58. The only variation from this in the second adaptation is the reading σου for αυτου. For the same reconstruction see HAUTSCH, *Die Evangelienzitate*, pp. 131-32.

CYRIL

1 Ὡς οὖν ἔγνω ὁ κύριος ὅτι ἤκουσαν οἱ φαρισαῖοι ὅτι Ἰησοῦς πλείονας μαθητὰς ποιεῖ καὶ βαπτίζει[a] ἢ Ἰωάννης 2 — καίτοι γε αὐτὸς Ἰησοῦς οὐκ ἐβάπτιζεν, αλλ' οἱ μαθηταὶ αὐτοῦ — 3 ἀφῆκε τὴν Ἰουδαίαν καὶ ἀπῆλθε πάλιν εἰς τὴν Γαλιλαίαν. 4 ἔδει δὲ αὐτὸν διέρχεσθαι διὰ τῆς Σαμαρείας, 5 ἔρχεται οὖν εἰς πόλιν τῆς Σαμαρείας λεγομένην Συχάρ, πλησίον τοῦ χωρίου ὃ ἔδωκεν Ἰακὼβ Ἰωσὴφ τῷ υἱῷ αὐτοῦ· 6 ἦν δὲ ἐκεῖ πηγὴ τοῦ Ἰακώβ· ὁ οὖν Ἰησοῦς κεκοπιακὼς ἐκ τῆς ὁδοιπορίας ἐκαθέζετο οὕτως ἐπὶ τῇ πηγῇ· ὥρα ἦν ὡς[b] ἕκτη.

7 Ἔρχεται γυνὴ ἐκ τῆς Σαμαρείας ἀντλῆσαι ὕδωρ. λέγει αὐτῇ ὁ Ἰησοῦς, Δός μοι πιεῖν· 8 οἱ γὰρ μαθηταὶ αὐτοῦ ἀπεληλύθεισαν[c] εἰς

---

1 *lemma* [1-3] *Jo.* 2.4 (3.261.13). ADAPT. το γορ ως ουν εγνω λεγειν τον αγιον ευαγγελιστην ... *Jo.* 2.4 (3.261.20); εντευθεν τοιγαρουν εγνωκεναι φησιν ο ευαγγελιστης τον κυριον οτι ηκουσαν οι φαρισαιοι οτι Ιησους πλειονας μαθητας ποιει η Ιωαννης. *Jo.* 2.4 (3.262.24).

2 *lemma* [1-3] *Jo.* 2.4 (3.261.14).

3 *lemma* [1-3] *Jo.* 2.4 (3.261.15).

4 *lemma* [4-5] *Jo.* 2.4 (3.263.1), *Jo.* 2.4 (3.263.20).

5 *lemma* [4-5] *Jo.* 2.4 (3.263.1).

6 *lemma* ην ... τη πηγη *Jo.* 2.4 (3.264.22), *lemma* ωρα ... εκτη *Jo.* 2.4 (3.266.20). ADAPT. ... ηδη γεγονως ο σωτηρ επι τη πηγη καταλυει του Ιακωβ. *Jo.* 2.4 (3.264.25); καταλυει δε κεκοπιακως εκ της οδοιπορίας, ως γεγραπται, ... *Jo.* 2.4 (3.265.6); ιδου κεκοπιακεν (κεκοπιακως B) εκ (απο B) της οδοιπορίας. *Jo.* 2.4 (3.265.17); ... καιτοι και κεκμηκως εκ της οδοιπορίας, ως γεγραπται ... *Jo.* 2.4 (3.291.19); αλλα και οτε την των Σαμαρειτων διεθει χωραν, κεκμηκε δε εκ της οδοιπορίας, καθα γεγραπται, εκαθεζετο επι τη πηγη. *Jo.* 10.2 (4.573.31); αλλ' ως εκτην ειναι την ωραν φησιν, ... *Jo.* 2.4 (3.266.28); ... τινα τροπον κεκοπιακεν εκ της οδοιπορίας ο τω ιδιω πνευματι στερεων ουρανους. *Nest.* 5.2 (*ACO* I.1.6 p. 97); ... και οτι ουχ ο θεος εκοπιασεν εν τη οδοιπορία, αλλ' ο αναληφθεις ανθρωπος. *resp.* 5 (5.586.4).

7 *lemma* [7-9] *Jo.* 2.4 (3.267.4); δος μοι πιειν *Jo.* 2.4 (3.268.1).

8 *lemma* [7-9] *Jo.* 2.4 (3.267.5); απεληλυθησαν ... αγορασωσιν *Jo.* 2.5 (3.292.1).

---

[a] και βαπτιζει is lacking in the adaptation (3.262.24). Cf. cod. 71 1194 sy[s].

[b] ως B, Pusey] ωσει D, E, Aub, Migne. Cf. the adaptation (3.266.28) for Cyril's true text.

[c] απεληλυθεισαν *Jo.* 2.4] απεληλυθησαν *Jo.* 2.5 (B, Pusey), απελυθησαν (D, E, Aub, Migne).

τὴν πόλιν, ἵνα τροφὰς ἀγοράσωσι. 9 λέγει αὐτῷ ἡ γυνὴ ἡ Σαμαρεῖτις,
Πῶς σὺ Ἰουδαῖος ὢν παρ' ἐμοῦ πιεῖν αἰτεῖςᵈ γυναικὸς Σαμαρείτιδος
οὔσης;ᵉ οὐ γάρᶠ συγχρῶνται Ἰουδαῖοι Σαμαρείταις.ᵍ 10 ἀπεκρίθη
Ἰησοῦς καὶ εἶπεν αὐτῇ, Εἰ ᾔδεις τὴν δωρεὰν τοῦ θεοῦ καὶ τίς ἐστιν ὁ
λέγων σοι, Δός μοι πιεῖν,ʰ σὺⁱ ἂν ᾔτησας αὐτὸν καὶ ἔδωκε [ἄν]ʲ σοι
ὕδωρ ζῶν. 11 λέγει αὐτῷ ἡ γυνή, Κύριε, οὔτε ἄντλημα ἔχεις καὶ τὸ
φρέαρ ἐστὶ βαθύ· πόθεν οὖν ἔχεις τὸ ὕδωρ τὸ ζῶν; 12 μὴ σὺ μείζων
[εἶ]ᵏ τοῦ πατρὸς ἡμῶν Ἰακώβ, ὃς ἔδωκεν ἡμῖν τὸ φρέαρ τοῦτοˡ καὶ
αὐτὸς ἐξ αὐτοῦ ἔπιε καὶ οἱ υἱοὶ αὐτοῦ καὶ τὰ θρέμματα αὐτοῦ; 13 ἀπε-

---

9 *lemma* [7-9] λεγει ... Σαμαρειτις *Jo.* 2.4 (3.267.6), *lemma* [9-10]
πως ... Σαμαρειταις *Jo.* 2.4 (3.268.3), πως ... ουσης *Jo.* 2.5 (3.286.2),
ου ... Σαμαρειταις *Jo.* 6 (4.108.21).

10 *lemma* [9-10] απεκριθη ... αυτη *Jo.* 2.4 (3.268.5), *lemma* [10-
11] ει ... ζων *Jo.* 2.4 (3.268.11), *glaph.* Gen. 4.4 (M. 69.197), *hom. pasch.*
18.5 (M. 77.817); ει ... αυτον *Jo.* 2.4 (3.269.1). ADAPT. αποθαυμαζειν
γαρ αναπειθων την του θεου δωρεαν, ταυτης εαυτον εισφερει χορηγον. *Jo.* 2.4
(3.268.26).

11 *lemma* [10-11] λεγει ... γυνη *Jo.* 2.4 (3.268.13), *lemma* κυριε ...
... ζων *Jo.* 2.4 (3.269.27).

12 *lemma* [12-13] *Jo.* 2.4 (3.270.7); μη ... τουτο *Jo.* 2.4 (3.270.20),
Jo. 3.6 (3.474.12); μη ... Ιακωβ *Jo.* 2.4 (3.271.12).

13 *lemma* [12-13] απεκριθη ... αυτη *Jo.* 2.4 (3.270.9); *lemma* [13-15]
πας ... παλιν *Jo.* 2.4 (3.271.7); πας ... παλιν *Jo.* 2.4 (3.271.19); [13-14]
πας ... παλιν *Jo.* 3.6 (3.470.10), *Jo.* 3.6 (3.474.16), *Jo.* 5.1 (3.689.22),
glaph. Ex. 2 (M. 69.445), Is. 1.2 (M. 70.96), Is. 4.4 (M. 70.1060), Is. 5.2
(M. 70.1217), Is. 5.4 (M. 70.1296), I Cor. 5.1 (5.290.26), *hom. pasch.* 18.5
(M. 77.817).

ᵈ πιειν αιτεις *Jo.* 2.5, *Jo.* 2.4 *lemma* (D, E, Aub, Migne)] ζητεις πιειν
υδωρ *Jo.* 2.4 *lemma* (B, Pusey). Although the readings of Codex B are
generally superior, the evidence for πιειν αιτεις in the later citation
in the commentary makes this singular reading of B suspect.

ᵉ Σαμ. ουσ. *Jo.* 2.4 *lemma* (D, E, Aub, Migne, Pusey), *Jo.* 2.5] ουσης
Σαμ. *Jo.* 2.4 *lemma* (B). Cf. P⁷⁵ *pc.*

ᶠ γαρ *Jo.* 2.4 *lemma*] omit *Jo.* 6.

ᵍ Cod. B concludes the *lemma* with ουσης. However, this ms. regularly shortens *lemmata*.

ʰ δος μοι πιειν *Jo.* 2.4 *lemma*, *glaph.* Gen. 4.4, *hom. pasch.* 18.5]
omit *Jo.* 2.4 (3.269.1).

ⁱ The citation in *hom. pasch.* 18.5 reads ουκ for συ.

ʲ αν *glaph.* Gen. 4.4, *hom. pasch.* 18.5] omit *Jo.* 2.4 *lemma*

ᵏ ει *Jo.* 2.4 *lemma* (D, E, Aub, Migne), *Jo.* 2.4 (3.270.20) [D, E,
Aub, Migne], *Jo.* 2.4 (3.271.12), *Jo.* 3.6] omit *Jo.* 2.4 *lemma* (B, Pusey),
Jo. 2.4 (3.270.20) [B, Pusey].

ˡ τουτο *Jo.* 2.4 *lemma*, *Jo.* 2.4 (3.270.20)] omit *Jo.* 3.6.

κρίθη Ἰησοῦς καὶ εἶπεν αὐτῇ, Πᾶς^m ὁ πίνων ἐκ τοῦ ὕδατος τούτου διψήσει πάλιν· **14** ὃς δ' ἂν πίῃ ἐκ τοῦ ὕδατος οὗ ἐγὼ δώσω αὐτῷ,^n οὐ μὴ διψήσει εἰς τὸν αἰῶνα, ἀλλὰ τὸ ὕδωρ ὃ δώσω^o αὐτῷ γενήσεται ἐν αὐτῷ^p πηγὴ ὕδατος ἀλλομένου εἰς ζωὴν αἰώνιον. **15** λέγει πρὸς αὐτὸν ἡ γυνή, Κύριε,^q δός μοι τοῦτο τὸ ὕδωρ, ἵνα μὴ διψῶ μηδὲ ἔρχωμαι ἐνθάδε ἀντλεῖν.

16 Λέγει αὐτῇ ὁ Ἰησοῦς, Ὕπαγε φώνησον τὸν ἄνδρα σου^r καὶ ἐλθὲ ἐνθάδε. **17** λέγει αὐτῷ ἡ γυνή, Ἄνδρα οὐκ ἔχω. λέγει αὐτῇ ὁ Ἰησοῦς, Καλῶς εἶπες ὅτι ἄνδρα οὐκ ἔχω·^s **18** πέντε γὰρ ἄνδρας^t ἔσχες, καὶ νῦν ὃν ἔχεις οὐκ ἔστι σου ἀνήρ· τοῦτο ἀληθὲς εἴρηκας. **19** λέγει

---

14 *lemma* [13-15] *Jo.* 2.4 (3.271.7), [13-14] *Jo.* 3.6 (3.470.10), *Jo.* 3.6 (3.474.17), *Jo.* 5.1 (3.689.23), *Is.* 1.2 (M. 70.96), *Is.* 4.4 (M. 70.1060), *Is.* 5.2 (M. 70.1217), *Is.* 5.4 (M. 70.1296), *I Cor.* 5.1 (5.290.21); [13-14] ος ... αιωνα *glaph. Ex.* 2 (M. 69.445), *hom. pasch.* 18.5 (M. 77.817). ADAPT αλλ' εξει πηγην εν εαυτω προς ζωην αιωνιον αποτρεφειν ισχυουσαν. *Jo.* 2.4 (3.271.22).

15 *lemma* [13-15] λεγει ... γυνη *Jo.* 2.4 (3.271.10), *lemma* [15-16] δος ... αντλειν *Jo.* 2.4 (3.272.7); κυριε ... αντλειν *Jo.* 3.6 (3.470.17).

16 *lemma* [15-16] λεγει ... Ιησους *Jo.* 2.4 (3.272.8), *lemma* υπαγε ... ενθαδε *Jo.* 2.4 (3.272.15), *Jo.* 2.5 (3.289.8).

17 *lemma* [17-19] *Jo.* 2.4 (3.273.1). ADAPT. αποδεχεται δε χρησιμως ανδρα λεγουσαν ουκ εχειν, ... *Jo.* 2.4 (3.273.11).

18 *lemma* [17-19] *Jo.* 2.4 (3.273.2).

19 *lemma* [17-19] λεγει ... γυνη *Jo.* 2.4 (3.273.4); *lemma* κυριε ... συ *Jo.* 2.4 (3.273.15).

---

^m και πας *glaph. Ex.* 2] omit *I Cor.* 5.1] πας *rell.*

^n ου μη διψησειε εις τον αιωνα, αλλα το υδωρ ο δωσω αυτω *lemma Jo.* 2.4, *Jo.* 3.6 (3.470.10) [B, Pusey], *Jo.* 5.1, (*glaph. Ex.* 2, *hom. pasch.* 18.5)] omit *Jo.* 3.6 (3.470.10) [D, E, Aub, Migne], *Jo.* 3.6 [3.474.17), *Is.* 1.2, *Is.* 4.4, *Is.* 5.4, *I Cor.* 5.1. The omission here is scarcely due to *homoioteleuton* as it probably is in C* 13 477 543 1200 *et al.* Nor did Cyril probably ever have a ms. with this "short text." This is another example of the fact that Cyril has one text in his Bible, but tends to follow shortened and/or combined forms when citing from memory.

^o δωσω *lemma Jo.* 2.4] δωσω εγω *Jo.* 3.6 (3.470.12 in B)] εγω δωσω *Jo.* 5.1. Again this fluctuation is typical of Cyril when citing from memory, which he is probably doing in the latter two instances.

^p εν αυτω *lemma Jo.* 2.4, *Jo.* 3.6 (*bis*), *Is.* 1.2, *Is.* 5.2, *Is.* 5.4, *I Cor.* 5.1] αυτω *Jo.* 5.1, *Is.* 4.4.

^q κυριε *Jo.* 3.6] omit *lemma Jo.* 2.4.

^r τον ανδρα σου *Jo.* 2.4] σου τον ανδρα *Jo.* 2.5.

^s οτι ανδρα ουκ εχω *lemma Jo.* 2.4 (D, E, Edd.)] omit B.

^t ανδρας B, Pusey] omit D, E, Aub, Migne.

αὐτῷ ἡ γυνή, Κύριε, θεωρῶ ὅτι προφήτης εἶ σύ. **20** οἱ πατέρες ἡμῶν ἐν τῷ ὄρει τούτῳ προσεκύνησαν· καὶ ὑμεῖς λέγετε ὅτι ἐν Ἱεροσολύμοις ἐστὶν ὁ τόπος ὅπου προσκυνεῖν δεῖ. **21** λέγει αὐτῇ ὁ Ἰησοῦς, Πίστευέ[u] μοι, γύναι, ὅτι ἔρχεται ὥρα ὅτε οὔτε ἐν τῷ ὄρει τούτῳ οὔτε ἐν Ἱεροσολύμοις· προσκυνήσετε τῷ πατρί. **22** ὑμεῖς προσκυνεῖτε ὃ οὐκ οἴδατε· ἡμεῖς[w] προσκυνοῦμεν ὃ οἴδαμεν, ὅτι ἡ σωτηρία ἐκ τῶν Ἰουδαίων ἐστίν. **23** ἀλλ' ἔρχεται ὥρα καὶ νῦν ἐστιν, ὅτε οἱ ἀληθινοὶ προσκυνηταὶ προσκυνήσουσι τῷ πατρὶ ἐν πνεύματι καὶ ἀληθείᾳ· καὶ γὰρ ὁ πατὴρ τοιούτους ζητεῖ τοὺς προσκυνοῦντας αὐτόν. **24** πνεῦμα ὁ θεός, καὶ τοὺς προσκυ-

---

20 *lemma* [20-21] *Jo.* 2.4 (3.274.1), *Jo.* 2.5 (3.286.6); οι ... προσεκυνησαν *Jo.* 2.5 (3.274.25).

21 *lemma* [20-21] λεγει ... Ιησους *Jo.* 2.4 (3.274.3), *lemma* πιστευε ... πατρι *Jo.* 2.4 (3.275.1), *Jo.* 6.1 (4.202.23), [21-24] *ador.* 1 (M. 68.136).

22 *lemma Jo.* 2.5 (3.276.4); [21-24] *ador.* 1 (M. 68.136); *Arcad.* 113 (*ACO* I.1.5 p. 90), *Chr. un.* (*SC* 97, p. 472), *dial. Trin.* 6 (M. 75.1061), *Pulch.* 11 (*ACO* I.1.5 p. 31); υμεις ... οιδαμεν *Jo.* 2.5 (3.284.1), *inc. unigen.* (*SC* 97, p. 262), *schol. inc.* 2 (*ACO* I.5.1 p. 230), *Thds.* 32 (*ACO* I.1.1 p. 63), *thes.* 9 (M. 75.117); οτι ... εστιν *Abac. 3,3* (2.128.5).

23 *lemma* [23-25] *Jo.* 2.5 (3.284.14), [23-24] *Jo.* 6.1 (4.202.25). [21-24] *ador.* 1 (M. 68.136). ADAPT. αληθινοι δε οντες προσκυνηται, προσκυνουμεν εν πνευματι και αληθεια τω θεω και πατρι. *Jo.* 2.5 (3.282.7); ... καθ' ον οι αληθινοι προσκυνηται την εν πνευματι λατρειαν προσοισουσι τω θεω και πατρι. *Jo.* 2.5 (3.285.6); και τινες μεν οι αληθινοι προσκυνηται, τινες δε ... *Zach. 11,13* (2.467.1).

24 *lemma* [23-25] *Jo.* 2.5 (3.284.16), *Jo.* 4.5 (3.588.16), [23-24] *Jo.* 6.1 (4.202.29), *Jo.* 10.2 (4.557.10), [21-24] *ador.* 1 (M. 68.136), *dial. Trin.* 7 (M. 75.1085), † *Ps. 114,4* (M. 69.1269), *Is.* 1.5 (M. 70.236), *Is.* 4.1 (M. 70.857). *Is.* 4.1 (M. 70.912), *Is.* 4.5 (M. 70.1108), *Zach. 8,7* (2.387.18), *hom. pasch.* 6.6 (M. 77.516), *hom. pasch.* 10.4 (M. 77.629), *hom. pasch.* 20.3 (M. 77.845), *hom. pasch.* 29.2 (M. 77.965), *Juln.* 4 (M. 76.696), *Juln.* 10 (M. 76.1029), *thes.* 35 (M. 75.652); πνευμα ο θεος *Jo.* 2.5 (3.284.25), *Jo.* 4.3 (3.552.16), *dogm.* (5.550.11), *ep. Calos.* (5.604.4), *Lc. 12,10* (M. 72.732), *resp.* 2 (5.577.20), *resp.* 10 (5.593.4); και[1] ... προσκυνειν *ador.* 9 (M. 68.589); ADAPT. χαιρει τη αληθεια και τους προσκυνουντας αυτον, εν αληθεια και πνευματι βουλεται προσκυνειν. *Jo.* 6 (4.104.11).

---

[u] πιστευε *lemma Jo.* 2.4 (D, E, Aub, Migne), *Jo.* 6.1, *ador.* 1] πιστευσον *lemma Jo.* 2.4 (B, Pusey).

[v] *hoc. ord. Jo.* 6.1, *ador.* 1] εν Ιεροσολυμοις ουτε εν τω ορει τουτω *lemma Jo.* 2.4. The word order of the *lemma* is attested elsewhere, as far as I know, only in cod. 28 and in three citations by Origen (*Jo.* 1.6 [allusion]; *Cels.* 6.70; *princ.* 1.1 [Latin]).

[w] Part of the ms. tradition of *schol. inc.* 2 and *Thds.* 32 add δε; all others lack the conjunction.

νοῦντας αὐτὸνˣ ἐν πνεύματι καὶ ἀληθείᾳʸ δεῖ προσκυνεῖν. 25 λέγει αὐτῷ ἡ γυνή, Οἴδαμεν ὅτι Μεσίας ἔρχεται, ὁ λεγόμενος Χριστός· ὅταν ἔλθῃ ἐκεῖνος, ἀναγγελεῖᶻ ἡμῖν πάντα. 26 λέγει αὐτῇ ὁ Ἰησοῦς, Ἐγώ εἰμι, ὁ λαλῶν σοι.

27 Καὶ ἐπὶ τούτῳ ἦλθον οἱ μαθηταὶ αὐτοῦ, καὶ ἐθαύμαζον ὅτι μετὰ γυναικὸς ἐλάλει· οὐδεὶς μέντοι εἶπε, Τί λαλεῖς; ἤ, Τί ζητεῖς μετ' αὐτῆς;ᵃᵃ 28 ἀφῆκεν οὖν τὴν ὑδρίαν αὐτῆς ἡ γυνὴ καὶ ἀπῆλθεν εἰς τὴν πόλιν καὶ λέγει τοῖς ἀνθρώποις, 29 Δεῦτε ἴδετε ἄνθρωπον ὃς εἶπέ μοιᵇᵇ πάντα ἃᶜᶜ ἐποίησα· μήτι οὗτός ἐστιν ὁ Χριστός; 30 ἐξῆλθονᵈᵈ ἐκ τῆς πόλεως καὶ ἤρχοντο πρὸς αὐτόν.

31 Ἐνᵉᵉ τῷ μεταξὺ ἠρώτων αὐτὸν οἱ μαθηταὶ αὐτοῦ λέγοντες, Ῥαββί, φάγε. 32 ὁ δὲ εἶπεν αὐτοῖς, Ἐγὼ βρῶσιν ἔχω φαγεῖν ἣν ὑμεῖς οὐκ οἴδατε. 33 ἔλεγον οὖν οἱ μαθηταὶ πρὸς ἀλλήλους, Μή τις ἤνεγκεν

---

25 *lemma* [23-25] λεγει ... γυνη *Jo.* 2.5 (3.284.18); *lemma* οιδαμεν ... παντα *Jo.* 2.5 (3.285.3), *Jo.* 2.5 (3.286.15), *Jo.* 5.1 (3.673.21), *Jo.* 6.1 (4.189.23), *Ps. 39,2* (M. 69.981), *Is. 5.4* (M. 70.1312). ADAPT. ... ειτα λεγουσης εκεινης οτε ελθη Μεσιας απαγγελει ημιν παντα. *Lc.* (5.472.31).
26 *lemma Jo.* 2.5 (3.285.17); εγω ... σοι *Jo.* 2.5 (3.286.22), *Lc. 19,15* (M. 72.873), *Lc.* (5.473.1).
27 *lemma Jo.* 2.5 (3.287.4,11,24).
28 *lemma* αφηκεν ... πολιν *Jo.* 2.5 (3.288.5); *lemma* [28-29] και λεγει τοις ανθρωποις *Jo.* 2.5 (3.289.3).
29 *lemma* [28-29] *Jo.* 2.5 (3.289.3); ADAPT. δευτε και ιδετε φησι συνετως *Jo.* 2.5 (3.289.17).
30 *lemma Jo.* 2.5 (3.289.24).
31 *lemma* [31-32] *Jo.* 2.5 (3.291.6).
32 *lemma* [31-32] ο ... αυτοις *Jo.* 2.5 (3.291.7); *lemma* εγω ... οιδατε *Jo.* 2.5 (3.292.4), *ador.* 16 (M. 68.1060), *glaph. Gen.* 3.4 (M. 69.169), *Mic. 5,7* (1.686.19), *Abac. 3,14* (2.159.5), *Lc. 19,15* (M 72.874), *Lc.* (5.473.5).
33 *lemma* [33-34] *Jo.* 2.5 (3.292.13).

ˣ αυτω *Is.* 4.1 (M. 70.912); all others αυτον.
ʸ τη αληθεια *ador.* 1; all others αληθεια.
ᶻ αναγγελει *lemma Jo.* 2.5, *Jo.* 2.5, *Jo.* 5.1, *Jo.* 6.1] απαγγελει *Ps. 39,2*, cf. adapt.] ευαγγελει *Is.* 5.4.

ᵃᵃ τι λαλεις, η τι ζητεις μετ' αυτης (B, E, Pusey)] τι λαλεις η τι λαλεις [ζητεις] μετ' αυτης (D, Aub, Migne).
ᵇᵇ μοι B, D, Pusey] omit E, Aub, Migne. Cf. W ff².
ᶜᶜ α B, Pusey] οσα D, E, Aub, Migne.
ᵈᵈ εξηλθον B, Pusey] +ουν D, E, Aub, Migne.
ᵉᵉ εν B, Pusey] εν δε D, E, Aub, Migne.

αὐτῷ φαγεῖν; **34** λέγει αὐτοῖς ὁ Ἰησοῦς, Ἐμὸν βρῶμά ἐστιν ἵνα ποιήσω[tt] τὸ θέλημα τοῦ πέμψαντός με[ss] καὶ τελειώσω αὐτοῦ τὸ ἔργον. **35** οὐχ[hh] ὑμεῖς λέγετε ὅτι [Ἔτι][ii] τετράμηνός[jj] ἐστι καὶ ὁ θερισμὸς ἔρχεται; ἰδοὺ λέγω ὑμῖν,[kk] ἐπάρατε τοὺς ὀφθαλμοὺς ὑμῶν[ll] καὶ θεάσασθε τὰς χώρας ὅτι λευκαί εἰσι πρὸς θερισμὸν ἤδη.[mm] **36** ὅ[nn] θερίζων μισθὸν λαμβάνει καὶ συνάγει καρπὸν εἰς ζωὴν αἰώνιον, ἵνα ὁ σπείρων ὁμοῦ χαίρῃ καὶ ὁ

---

34 *lemma* [33-34] *Jo*. 2.5 (3.292.14,20); εμον . . . εργον *Jo*. 10.2 (4.574.7), *glaph. Gen*. 3.4 (M. 69.169), *Abac. 3,14* (2.159.6), *Mic. 5,7* (1. 686.21). ADAPT. βρωμα γαρ ειναι λεγων εαυτω θυμηρεστατον το ποιησαι το θελημα του πεμψαντος αυτον και τελειωσαι αυτου το εργον, . . . *Jo*. 2.5 (3.293.1); αυτος τοιγαρουν υπαρχων ο υιος το αγαθον του πατρος θελημα, τελειοι το εργον αυτου, σωτηρια τοις πιστευουσιν εις αυτον αναδεικνυμενος. *Jo*. 2.5 (3.294.13).

35 *lemma Jo*. 2.5 (3.295.14,25), [35-36] *ador*. 3 (M. 68.292), [35-36] *ador*. 17 (M. 68.1093), [35-36] *glaph. Num*. (M. 69.621), [35-36] *Os. 2,23* (1.80.24); ουχ . . . ερχεται *Jo*. 2.5 (3.295.22).

36 *lemma* [36-37] *Jo*. 2.5 (3.296.16), [35-36] ο . . . αιωνιον *ador*. 3 (M. 68.292), [35-36] και ο θεριζων μισθον λαμβανει και ο συναγων *ador*. 17 (M. 68.1096), [35-36] και ο . . . αιωνιον *glaph. Num*. (M. 69.621), [35-36] και ο . . . αιωνιον *Os. 2,23* (1.81.1). ADAPT συναξει γαρ δη παντως αυτοις τον εις ζωην αιωνιον αποτρεφοντα καρπον. *Jo*. 2.5 (3.297.9).

[tt] ποιησω *lemma Jo*. 2.5, *Jo*. 10.2, *Abac. 3,14, Mic. 5,7*] ποιω *glaph. Gen*. 3.4.

[ss] πεμψαντος με *lemma Jo*. 2.5, *glaph. Gen*. 3.4, *Abac. 3,14. Mic. 5,7* (B, D, Pusey); cf. adapt. *Jo*. 2.5 (3.293.1)] πατρος μου *Jo*. 10.2 *Mic. 5,7* (A).

[hh] ουχ *lemma Jo*. 2.5, *ador*. 17, *glaph. Num*., *Os. 2,23, Jo*. 2.5] ουχι *ador*. 3.

[ii] οτι ετι *lemma Jo*. 2.5, (B, Pusey), *Jo*. 2.5 (B, Pusey), *glaph. Num*.] οτι *lemma Jo*. 2.5 (D, E, Aub, Migne), *Jo*. 2.5 (D, E, Aub, Migne), *ador*. 3, *ador*. 17, *Os. 2,23*. This same kind of fluctuation may be found in Origen's several citations of this passage. Cyril tends to cite it *without* ετι. This probably reflects his true text, which at this point would be in agreement with P[75] and L, as well as several others.

[jj] τετραμηνος *lemma Jo*. 2.5, *Jo*. 2.5, *ador*. 3, *ador*. 17, *Os. 2,23*] τετραμηνον *glaph. Num*.

[kk] Codex B omits υμιν in the *lemma*.

[ll] υμων] omit *glaph. Num*.

[mm] The *lemma* places ηδη at the beginning of verse 36. Cyril does not comment on the passage in such a way as to make his text certain, nor does he cite verses 35 or 35 separately; however, he probably understood the adverb to belong to the end of verse 35, as is suggested from the following comment under verse 35: λευκαίνεται δὲ πέπειρός τε καὶ ἕτοιμος ἤδη πρὸς τὸ πιστεύειν γεγενημένος . . . (3.296.7).

[nn] ο *lemma Jo*. 2.5, *ador*. 3] και ο *ador*. 17, *glaph. Num*., *Os. 2,23*.

θερίζων. **37** ἐν γὰρ τούτῳ ὁ λόγος ἀληθινός ἐστιν, ὅτι ῎Αλλος ἐστὶν ὁ σπείρων καὶ ἄλλος ὁ θερίζων. **38** ἐγὼ ἀπέστειλα ὑμᾶς θερίζειν ὃ οὐχ ὑμεῖς κεκοπιάκατε· ἄλλοι κεκοπιάκασι, καὶ ὑμεῖς⁰⁰ εἰς τὸν κόπον αὐτῶν εἰσεληλύθατε.

39 ᾿Εκ δὲ τῆς πόλεως ἐκείνης πολλοὶ ἐπίστευσαν εἰς αὐτὸν τῶν Σαμαρειτῶν διὰ τὸν λόγον τῆς γυναικὸς μαρτυρούσης ὅτι Εἶπέ μοι πάντα ὅσα ἐποίησα. **40** ὡς οὖν ἦλθον πρὸς αὐτὸν οἱ Σαμαρεῖται,ᵖᵖ ἠρώτων αὐτὸν μεῖναι παρ' αὐτοῖς· καὶ ἔμεινεν ἐκεῖ δύο ἡμέρας. **41** καὶ πολλῷ πλείους ἐπίστευσαν διὰ τὸν λόγον αὐτοῦ, **42** τῇ τε γυναικὶ ἔλεγον ὅτι Οὐκέτι διὰ τὴν σὴν λαλιὰν πιστεύομεν· αὐτοὶ γὰρ ἀκηκόαμεν, καὶ οἴδαμεν ὅτι οὗτός ἐστιν ἀληθῶς ὁ σωτὴρ τοῦ κόσμου.ᑫᑫ

43 Μετὰ δὲ τὰς δύο ἡμέρας ἐξῆλθεν ἐκεῖθεν εἰς τὴν Γαλιλαίαν. **44** αὐτὸς γὰρ ᾿Ιησοῦς ἐμαρτύρησεν ὅτι προφήτης ἐν τῇ ἰδίᾳ πατρίδι τιμὴν οὐκ ἔχει.ʳʳ **45** ὅτε οὖν ἦλθεν εἰς τὴν Γαλιλαίαν, ἐδέξαντο αὐτὸν οἱ Γαλιλαῖοι, πάντα ἑωρακότες ὅσα ἐποίησεν ἐν ῾Ιεροσολύμοις ἐν τῇ ἑορτῇ, καὶ αὐτοὶ γὰρ ἦλθον εἰς τὴν ἑορτήν.

46 ῏Ηλθεν οὖν πάλιν εἰς τὴν Κανὰ τῆς Γαλιλαίας, ὅπου ἐποίησε

---

37 *lemma* [36-37] *Jo.* 2.5 (3.296.17).

38 *lemma Jo.* 2.5 (3.297.22).

39 *lemma Jo.* 2.5 (3.298.10). ADAPT. θαυμαζει γαρ λιαν ο ευαγγελιστης *πολλους εις Χριστον πεπιστευκεναι λεγων δια τον λογον της γυναικος.* *Jo.* 2.5 (3.298.15).

40 *lemma* [40-41] *Jo.* 2.5 (3.298.24).

41 *lemma* [40-41] *Jo.* 2.5 (3.298.25). ADAPT. *πολλοι γαρ επιστευσαν δια τον λογον αυτου. Jo.* 2.5 (3.299.13).

42 *lemma Jo.* 2.5 (3.299.18). ADAPT. *εγνωκεναι δε φασιν, οτιπερ ειη σαφως ο του κοσμου σωτηρ. Jo.* 2.5 (3.299.23).

43 *lemma* [43-44] *Jo.* 2.5 (3.299.26).

44 *lemma* [43-44] *Jo.* 2.5 (3.299.27). ADAPT. ... και φησιν, οτι μεμαρτυρηκεν αυτος (αυτοις B) ο Ιησους (σωτηρ B) οτι προφητης εν τη ιδια πατριδι τιμην ουκ εχει. *Jo.* 2.5 (3.300.10).

45 *lemma Jo.* 2.5 (3.300.26).

46 *lemma* ηλθεν ... οινον *Jo.* 2.5 (3.301.5); *lemma* [46-48] ην ... Καφερναουμ *Jo.* 2.5 (3.301.14).

⁰⁰ υμεις assumptum ex B (Pusey).

ᵖᵖ Codex B οι Σαμαρειται προς αυτον.

ᑫᑫ κοσμου *lemma Jo.* 2.5 (B, Pusey); cf. adaptation] add ο Χριστος *lemma Jo.* 2.5 (D, E, Aub, Migne). Although one cannot make too great a case from omissions in a loose citation, the adaptation here seems to confirm the omission as the true text of Cyril.

ʳʳ τιμην ουκ εχει *lemma Jo.* 2.5 (D, E, Edd.); cf. adaptation] ατιμος *lemma* (B).

τὸ ὕδωρ οἶνον. ἦν δέ τις βασιλικὸς οὗ ὁ υἱὸς ἠσθένει ἐν Καφερναούμ. 47 οὗτος ἀκούσας ὅτι Ἰησοῦς ἥκει ἐκ τῆς Ἰουδαίας εἰς τὴν Γαλιλαίαν, ἀπῆλθε πρὸς αὐτὸν καὶ ἠρώτα ἵνα καταβῇ καὶ ἰάσηται αὐτοῦ τὸν υἱόν, ἔμελλε γὰρ ἀποθνήσκειν. 48 εἶπεν οὖν ὁ Ἰησοῦς πρὸς αὐτόν, Ἐὰν μὴ σημεῖα καὶ τέρατα ἴδετε, οὐ μὴ πιστεύσητε. 49 λέγει πρὸς αὐτὸν ὁ βασιλικός, Κύριε, κατάβηθι πρὶν ἀποθανεῖν τὸ παιδίον μου. 50 λέγει αὐτῷ ὁ Ἰησοῦς, Πορεύου· ὁ υἱός σου ζῇ. ἐπίστευσεν ὁ ἄνθρωπος τῷ λόγῳ ᾧ εἶπεν ὁ Ἰησοῦς καὶ ἐπορεύετο. 51 ἤδη δὲ αὐτοῦ καταβαίνοντος οἱ δοῦλοι αὐτοῦ [ὑπήντησαν]ᵃᵃ αὐτῷ καὶ ἀπήγγειλαν λέγοντες ὅτι ὁ υἱός σου ζῇ. 52 ἐπύθετο οὖν παρ' αὐτῶν τὴν ὥραν ἐκείνην,ᵗᵗ ἐν ᾗ κομψότερον ἔσχε· καὶ εἶπον αὐτῷ ὅτι Χθὲς ὥραν ἑβδόμην ἀφῆκεν αὐτὸν ὁ πυρετός. 53 ἔγνω οὖν ὁ πατὴρ ὅτι ἐν ἐκείνῃ τῇ ὥρᾳᵘᵘ ἐν ᾗ εἶπεν αὐτῷ ὁ Ἰησοῦς,ᵛᵛ ὅτιʷʷ ὁ υἱός σου ζῇ. καὶ ἐπίστευσενˣˣ αὐτὸς καὶ ἡ οἰκία αὐτοῦ ὅλη. 54 τοῦτο πάλιν δεύτερον σημεῖον ἐποίησεν ὁ Ἰησοῦς ἐλθὼν ἐκ τῆς Ἰουδαίας εἰς τὴν Γαλιλαίαν.

---

47 *lemma* [46-48] *Jo.* 2.5 (3.301.14). ADAPT. εμελλε γαρ αποθνησκειν ο παις *Jo.* 2.5 (3.302.20).

48 *lemma* [46-48] ειπεν ... αυτον *Jo.* 2.5 (3.301.17); *lemma* [48-49] εαν ... πιστευσητε *Jo.* 2.5 (3.302.3), *dial. Trin.* 6 (M. 75.1060).

49 *lemma* [48-49] *Jo.* 2.5 (3.302.3,11).

50 *lemma* λεγει ... ζη *Jo.* 2.5 (3.302.22); *lemma* [50-51] επιστευσεν ... επορευετο *Jo.* 2.5 (3.303.3); πορευου ... ζη *Jo.* 2.5 (3.302.28), *Arcad.* 220 (*ACO* I.1.5 p. 118).

51 *lemma* [50-51] *Jo.* 2.5 (3.303.4). ADAPT. απαγγελλουσι δε την του παιδος θεραπειαν υπαντωντες οιχεται ομου ... *Jo.* 2.5 (3.303.11).

52 *lemma* [52-54] *Jo.* 2.5 (3.303.17). ADAPT. αναπυνθανεται παρ' αυτων την ωραν της επι το κρειττον του νοσουντος ροπης. *Jo.* 2.5 (3.303.23).

53 *lemma* [52-54] *Jo.* 2.5 (3.303.19), *Arcad.* 220 (*ACO* I.1.5 p. 118).

54 *lemma* [52-54] *Jo.* 2.5 (3.303.21).

ᵃᵃ υπηντησαν adapt. *Jo.* 2.5] απηντησαν *lemma Jo.* 2.5. Although one may not have certainty in such cases, it seems more likely that Cyril's text is to be found in the adaptation, and that later scribes conformed the *lemma* to their current text.

ᵗᵗ εκεινην *lemma Jo.* 2.5 (B, Pusey)] omit *lemma Jo.* 2.5 (D, E, Aub, Migne).

ᵘᵘ ωρα *lemma Jo.* 2.5, *Arcad.* 220 (VA Schwartz)] ημερα *Arcad.* 220 (SD).

ᵛᵛ ο Ιησους *lemma Jo.* 2.5] omit *Arcad.* 220.

ʷʷ οτι *lemma Jo.* 2.5] omit *Arcad.* 220.

ˣˣ επιστευσεν *lemma Jo.* 2.5] add εις αυτον *Arcad.* 220 (SD read επιστευσαν).

CHAPTER 16

THE TEXT OF JOHN IN *THE JERUSALEM BIBLE:* A CRITIQUE OF THE USE OF PATRISTIC CITATIONS IN NEW TESTAMENT TEXTUAL CRITICISM

Gordon D. Fee

The difficulties in recovering the biblical text of the early Church Fathers are known to all who have worked in the field of textual criticism and may be found in any of the standard manuals. Such difficulties stem both from the Father himself and from copyists and editors.

As to the Church Father: Did he cite Scripture by looking up the passage, or from memory? If, as was usual, it was from memory, can his memory be trusted to reproduce the copy of Scripture he must have possessed? Furthermore, it is perhaps presumptuous to assume that any Father, writing over a thirty-forty-year period, had only one Bible; and perhaps it is folly even to assume he had only one Bible at any given time. (After all, as early as Origen, there is acknowledgment of many copies of Scripture.) Then, too, some Fathers tended to relocate from time to time (Irenaeus, Origen, Athanasius, Chrysostom), so that not only may they have used different Bibles in a lifetime, but also Bibles from different geographical centers with different kinds of texts.

As to scribes and editors: All the scribal questions asked of the NT MSS themselves must also be applied to the Father's biblical text. It has long been recognized that the monks of the Middle Ages, to whom we are indebted for many of the extant copies of the Fathers, often tended to conform biblical passages to a more contemporary text. And editors are not faultless. This is true not only of the older, and sometimes less critical editions (which Migne reproduced, adding his own errors), but also of such editions as E. Pusey's of Cyril of Alexandria[1]

---

1. It was suggested by Nestle (1901:145), without indication of evidence, that "as late as 1872, an Oxford editor, in bringing out Cyril of Alexandria's Commentary on the Gospel according to St. John, wrote down only the initial and final words of the quotations in his manuscript, and allowed the compositor to set up the rest from a printed edition of the Textus Receptus." This is not at all true of the Johannine citations; others I have not checked. But Pusey did make some editorial blunders. For example, he tended to conform many of Cyril's citations to one another, often from work to work, and sometimes even without MS support. E.g., all MSS of the commentary on Zeph 3:16 read his citation of John 15:13 as follows: μείζονα ταύτης τῆς ἀγάπης οὐδεὶς ἔχει (a reading also found in the fragments of his Luke comm. [PG 72.725]). Pusey, however, has conformed it to read ταύτης ἀγάπην with the normal text. At the same place in the commentary he makes Cyril

---

and of some of the editors in the *GCS*.[2]

It is not surprising, therefore, in light of such difficulties, that patristic citations have assumed a supportive role, and are generally relegated to a place of tertiary importance, in the quest for the original NT text.

However, there has been an occasional demurrer. In 1903 F. C. Conybeare confidently predicted that "scores of old readings will be restored in the text of the New Testament" from further careful editing of the Greek and Latin Fathers (1902: 113). About the same time the German philologist F. Blass was actually producing such texts of the Gospels (1901a, 1901b, 1902). Using the combined evidence of the early uncials (with a preference for the Western ones), the OL and/or OS, and the Church Fathers, especially Chrysostom and Nonnus, he edited a Greek text of John quite unlike any other that has ever been published. Its chief characteristic was *lectio brevior potior*, which meant not simply omitting the well-known "long texts" of the TR (e.g., 3:13; 5:4; 6:51; 7:46; 8:59; 11:41; 16:16), but also hundreds of nouns, pronouns, adverbs, and phrases of various kinds, which Blass felt had crept into the Greek tradition as attempts to smooth out John's originally terse prose.[3]

For the most part this work was considered a curiosity — or was not considered at all[4] — until the Dominican M.-E. Boismard gave it a fresh and thorough airing in a series of articles in the *Revue biblique*.

The first of these appeared in 1948 and set the pattern for the rest. With uncommon thoroughness Boismard brought together all available evidence for the text of John 5:39. He then discovered in the versions and Fathers (the only Greek evidence, the Egerton papyrus) two other text forms, differing from the common text. From these he reconstructed the "leçon primitive" — ἐν αἷς δοκεῖτε ζωὴν ἔχειν· αὐταὶ μαρτυροῦσιν περὶ ἐμοῦ.

The role of the Fathers in this article was spelled out in much greater detail in "Critique textuelle et citations patristiques" (1950), where he argued that "there exists a patristic textual tradition differing from the MS tradition, and almost completely unknown by the latter" (388-89). He gives several examples from John (12:32; 14:2; 14:23; 17:5; 17:21), each of which has the common feature of being a "short text."

This paved the way for "Lectio brevior, potior" (1951) where, following Blass's lead, he worked his way through John 7, giving thirty-seven illustrations of a "short text" attested chiefly in the versions and Fathers, Chrysostom and Nonnus again being the most important. In a subsequent discussion he chose several of these

---

read the future ἕξετε in a citation of John 16:33 against all manuscript evidence, because apparently he decided that that was Cyril's usual text (which it probably was; but since ἔχετε *is* found in other citations [*Ador.* 5; *Hom. div.* 7], it is probably best to edit on the basis of MS evidence alone).

2. See Suggs (1958: 141 n. 1), who calls attention to this in Heikel's edition of Eusebius. Examples may also be found in Preuschen's edition of Origen's Commentary on John; e.g., the reading of ἔμεινεν l. ἔμειναν in John 2:12 against all manuscript evidence.

3. A word count in John 4 is interesting: TR 958, WH 912, Blass 856, with 14 more in brackets as doubtful!

4. I found no mention of it at all in the standard manuals: Lake 1928, Vaganay 1937, Souter 1947, Kenyon 1949, Vogels 1955b, Greenlee 1964, Metzger 1968a.

as the original text. The next two articles (1952, 1953) brought the theory to bear on specific passages of John, while the final article on P[66] (1957) actually spelled out a new theory of text-types, the second of which is the "short text" (Tatian, sys.c., geo, pers, eth, Chrys, Non), and the third the Western (‎א D, most of the OL).

The chief implications of this labor appear to be twofold: preference for the shorter text as the primitive text of John,[5] and the use of patristic citations as *primary* evidence in the discovery of the primitive text.

In general, this work has received scarcely more notice than Blass's.[6] However, the advent of D. Mollat's translation of John in *The Jerusalem Bible (JB)* has taken Boismard's theories out of the laboratory into the market place in a permanent form.[7] Mollat offers 185 separate textual notes in the original French edition, seventy-two of which explain the choice of a "short text" variant, while thirty-four others choose a more common reading with the alternative short form left in the notes (although Mollat obviously prefers these at times to the actual text of his translation[8]). Sixty-nine others discuss variant readings not involving addition or omission. Two others are given only because they indicate disagreement with the Vulgate; while one offers a plausible emendation (19:29). There are only seven notes where Mollat chose a "long" text; and this includes the *pericope adulterae,* which is included even though non-Johannine, because "the passage was accepted in the canon and there are no grounds for regarding it as unhistorical" (*JB,* note u). What is significant in these notes is Mollat's overwhelming preference for Boismard's text-types 2 and 3. The chief support for his short text turns out to be, in this order of preference: ‎א, sys, OL, Chrys, D, Nonnus.[9]

While the whole text — and textual theory, which I call "eclectic Western" — has inherent interest for a more detailed critique, my interest in this paper is Boismard's and Mollat's use of patristic citations. Although their work is to be appreciated as a truly original attempt to get back past the third century, there are considerable grounds for doubt as to whether their text really does so.

I

In the first place the basic methodology is open to question. It is one thing to put all the evidence on equal footing and to try to push back through various kinds of

---

5. For Boismard this was not simply an unqualified choice of a short text as original. It was, first of all, a stylistic consideration. "Rough," short prose is for him a part of Johannine style. Cf. 1951: 164-66, and Mollat 1960: 62-64.

6. The exceptions: Suggs 1958: 144-45; Duplacy 1959b: 48-51; Birdsall 1957a: 200-205, 1957b: 61-63; Mees 1968: 116-18; Klijn 1969: 36 n. 4.

7. Mollat 1960; ET, *The Jerusalem Bible* (1966). The nature of this text has been briefly noted by Rhodes 1970.

8. E.g., see the notes on 1:12, 7:26, 11:50, 12:32, and many others.

9. Cf. the author's own statement of preference for a short text based on stylistic considerations: "Le Sinaïticus nous est apparu comme un témoin souvent très probe de ce style, en accord fréquent avec le codex de Bèze dans une partie notable de l'évangile. Il nous a semblé représenter dans l'ensemble 'une tradition moins contaminée que le Vaticanus' (M.-E. Boismard). L'accord du texte de saint Jean Chrysostome avec la tradition syro-latine nous a également servi de base pour la restitution de leçons qui nous semblaient primitives" (65).

conflations and omissions to a primitive text which best explains all others. But it is quite another to reconstruct this primitive reading on a purely eclectic basis, so that by a process of picking and choosing one "creates" an original reading that is supported *in toto* by *no* single piece of evidence. Yet this is precisely the nature of Boismard's resultant text for such passages as John 1:12-13 (1950: 401-8); 1:18 (1952); 6:22-24 (1953: 359-70); and 11:48-50 (1953: 350-53).[10]

For example, Boismard's resultant text of 1:12-13 is:

ὅσοι δὲ ἐπίστευσαν εἰς αὐτόν,
ἔδωκεν αὐτοῖς ἐξουσίαν τέκνα θεοῦ κληθῆναι·
ὃς οὐκ ἐξ αἱμάτων οὐδὲ ἐκ σαρκός,
ἀλλ' ἐκ θεοῦ ἐγεννήθη.[11]

But one wonders whether his evidence is really evidence at all. The first two lines are derived from two very "loose" citations by Tertullian (where he appears to have been influenced by 1 John 3:1) and from the alleged "omission" by several Fathers of τοῖς πιστεύουσιν εἰς τὸ ὄνομα αὐτοῦ. This "omission," unknown to the entire manuscript tradition, is supposed to reflect the earlier, short form of the text, before ἐπίστευσαν was corrupted to ἔλαβον.

The third line has a similar lineage. First, various MSS and/or Fathers drop one of the phrases of the common text (thereby showing its "fluidity"); second, Boismard's reading is said to be found in Justin, Epiphanius, Babai the Great, the *Acta Archelai,* some MSS of the Ethiopic, and (indirectly!) in Augustine and Ambrose. But this is an improper use of patristic evidence. Justin's "citation," for example, which gives "proof of its antiquity," is such a distant allusion that one is hard pressed to discover it (*Dial.* 135.6: "Even so it is necessary for us here to observe that there are two seeds of Judah, . . . the one *begotten by blood and flesh,* the other by faith and the Spirit"). The other patristic evidence is equally as allusive, for in no instance can it be demonstrated that the Father was actually trying to cite John 1:13, nor is it even clear that the passage was in mind at all.

To use such evidence as a primary source for reconstructing original readings seems to be a doubtful procedure.

II

The second charge that can be leveled against Boismard's and Mollat's use of the Fathers is their neglect of the Hortian rule: Knowledge of documents should (indeed, for the Fathers *must*) precede final judgment upon readings.[12] This is most apparent in their heavy reliance upon Chrysostom and Nonnus.

---

10. Cf. also 2:12 and 9:24 in *JB*.

11. Although this is not the text of *JB,* it is suggested by Mollat as perhaps original: "La leçon originale est peut-être représentée par le texte plus court encore, que l'on trouve chez plusieurs Pères et dans plusieurs Mss de la vers. éthiopienne: 'ni sang ni chair.' Comme dans le v. précédent, la leçon courante est probablement une 'leçon confluente'" (69).

12. This was briefly noted by Birdsall 1957a: 205.

The text of the Fourth Gospel known to Nonnus is recoverable only from his remarkable paraphrase of the entire Gospel, composed in hexameters sometime after 431. But despite R. Janssen's attempt to reconstruct his Johannine text (1903), and despite Boismard's arguments as to what certain words in the paraphrase *must* have reflected of the original (1948: 13), Nonnus's text simply cannot be used as a *primary* source for the recovery of the text of John, especially for a short text. Two things militate against it: (1) it is a *paraphrase* in the fullest sense of that word; scarcely a word recalls the actual language of John itself.[13] (2) It is a *metrical paraphrase,* which means that many of his "omissions" may very well be in the interest of meter.

The text of Chrysostom fares just a little better. In the first place, most Johannine citations are found in his homilies on John, where there is a rich, but as yet poorly edited textual tradition.[14] Furthermore, as Bebb suggested long ago, citations may be expected to be less exact in homilies than in "controversial treatises" (1890: 216). The fact is, Chrysostom's biblical quotations are imprecise to a fault. For example, at John 4:49 there are the following variants in the manuscript tradition:

αποθανειν το παιδιον μου	P⁶⁶ P⁷⁵ B C L N W Θ Byz pler TR
αποθανειν το παιδιον	D f¹ 565
αποθανειν τον παιδα μου	ℵ q
αποθανειν τον υιον μου	A f¹³ pc

In the homily *ad loc.* Chrysostom cites the passage three times in a short span. They read:

πριν αποθανειν τον υιον μου
πριν η αποθανειν το παιδιον μου
πριν αποθανειν το παιδιον

Are we to argue that Chrysostom knew three different text forms? Does omission of μου in the third instance constitute support for the Western "short text"? Is παιδιον his true text on the basis of two to one? Probably *no* to the first two questions and *yes* to the third, but on other grounds than count; and this is only one example of the enormity of the problem (cf. the three consecutive citations of 7:17 *ad loc.*).

Furthermore, there is an extremely high incidence of singular readings in Chrysostom's text, which also points to imprecision. In the text of the homilies, I

---

13. John 5:39, for example, reads:

Γραπτὰ θεορρήτων μαστεύετε Θέσφατα βιβλίων,
ᵉΗσιν ἔχειν ἔλπεσθε χρόνου παλιναύξει κύκλῳ.
Ζωὴν οὐ μινθοῦσαν· ἐνὶ Γραφίδεσσι δὲ κεῖναι,
Μαρτύριην βοόωσιν ἐμὴν ὑποφήτορι μύθῳ
᾿Αθαναΐῳ σάλπιγγι.

Janssen's reconstruction: ἐρευνᾶτε τὰς γραφάς, ἐν αἷς δοκεῖτε ζωὴν αἰώνιον ἔχειν καὶ ἐκεῖναί εἰσιν αἱ μαρτυροῦσαι περὶ ἐμοῦ.

14. Harkins 1958: 404-12 promised an edition which has not yet appeared.

counted nine singulars (one is supported by cod. 544) in the first seventeen verses of John 7 alone. If such readings indicate poor copying on the part of a scribe (see Colwell 1965), how much more do they represent loose citing habits on the part of a Father.[15]

The point is, as R. M. Grant argued some years ago, that "patristic citations are not citations unless they have been adequately analyzed" (1950: 124). Such an analysis should attempt at least two things: (1) to gather all the data from the literary remains of each Father and, as much as possible, *reconstruct* his biblical text;[16] and (2) to *evaluate* the Father's citing habits in various kinds of works for accuracy of quotation. And this should be done *before* the evidence of that Father is brought to court.

A further word is in order here about item (1) and our general need to use greater semantic precision when referring to a Father's text. Since not all "citations" are truly citations, one must not only be aware of the differences, but must also insist on them when reconstructing a Father's text, or when citing his text as evidence. In a review of Muncey's presentation of the text of Ambrose, J. Duplacy indicated four categories: reminiscence, allusion, citation adapted to context, true citation (1959a: 393). I would offer three categories, combining two of Duplacy's, with the following definitions:

Allusion. Reference to the *content* of a biblical passage in which *verbal* correspondence to the NT Greek text is so remote as to offer no value for the reconstruction of that text. This is probably what Duplacy means by "reminiscence."

Adaptation.[17] Reference to a biblical passage, which has clear *verbal* correspondence to the Greek NT, but which has been adapted to fit the Father's discussion and/or syntax. This is probably Duplacy's "allusion" and "citation adapted to context."

Citation. Those places where a Father is consciously trying to cite, either from memory or by copying, the very words of the biblical text. Anyone who works closely with a given Father's text will probably make a further distinction in this category by noting citations at times as "strict" or "loose."

It should be noted at this point that *allusion, adaptation,* and *citation* are

---

15. It may also be of interest to note that for Blass, Boismard, and Mollat, Chrysostom does not become a textual hero until John 7; but it is somewhere from homily 48 (on John 7:1-8) and following that the homilies grow decidedly less detailed. Thus the first twenty homilies are on the first chapter of John, but chs. 18–21 have only six homilies altogether. It is at least possible, although I have not had opportunity to investigate it fully, that his "short text" citations are part of this tendency toward less detail.

16. Suggs 1958: 147 has suggested: "More ambitiously [than simply presenting all the data *à la* P. M. Barnard's text of Clement], we might aim at publishing 'critically reconstructed' texts of these patristic witnesses." I would argue that for patristic citations to become fully useful such reconstructions are imperative. For a methodology, along with the reconstructed text of John 4 in Origen and Cyril of Alexandria, see Fee 1971a [Chapter 15]. For the Latin Fathers, cf. the excellent work on Ambrose in Luke and John by Rolando and Corigliano 1945. This is superior in every way to Muncey 1959. Muncey's incompleteness, as well as his failure adequately to evaluate the data, generally negates the usefulness of his study.

17. I am indebted to J. N. Birdsall for this happy choice of words to describe this kind of citation.

not in themselves value words. Indeed, it may be clearly demonstrated that adaptations and allusions at times have more "value" than citations in discovering the Father's true text.[18] However, anyone working closely with a Father's text, and trying to reconstruct that text, *should* make some value judgments, based on his knowledge of the Father's citing habits, or on the condition of the preservation of his works. Thus a citation from memory from a Father like Cyril of Alexandria, where he introduces the biblical text ἔφη δέ που καὶ αὐτὸς ὁ σωτήρ (which he does regularly, and he really means "somewhere"), is not of the same textual value as a citation in his commentary on John, where he cites the passage and makes a point of the very words used.

III

The third weakness of Boismard's and Mollat's use of the Fathers is related to the problem of "short text." I note three items:

1. There are several instances where their *brevior* conflicts with *difficilior* (cf. Mees 1968: 116-18). In fact, a random sampling of the notes in *JB* suggested that the "short text" preferred by Mollat was a smoothing out of some rather awkward Johannine expressions. For example, given an "original" text of John 7:42 that read καὶ ἀπὸ Βηθλέεμ τῆς κώμης Δαυίδ (sy^s, Blass) or καὶ ἀπὸ Βηθλέεμ τῆς κώμης (eth, Chrys, Cyril, Mollat), what scribe anywhere would *add* ὅπου ἦν [Δαυίδ] after κώμης? Yet this clause, awkward and therefore "more difficult" though it is, is typically Johannine (cf. 1:28; 10:40; 11:32; 12:1; 20:19). Therefore, it is clearly original on all counts.

This, too, is a good example of how *not* to use versional and patristic evidence — especially for "short text." The "omission" in sy^s may be easily explained as a "translational" omission, not the reading of its Greek exemplar.[19] The translation is a bit free, to be sure, but one suspects that this is part of the character of the *Vetus syra*.

The evidence from the Fathers is even less convincing. Chrysostom's only citation of this passage is in his homily *ad loc.*, where he is suggesting the reason for Christ's not having cited Scripture at 7:38. The reason, he says, is that "their understanding [of Scripture] was corrupt," which he then illustrates with a catena of Johannine passages, of which portions of vv. 40-42 are a part: οἱ μὲν γὰρ ἔλεγον: οὗτός ἐστιν ὁ προφήτης [7:40], ἄλλοι δὲ ἔλεγον, ὅτι πλανᾷ τὸν ὄχλον [7:12]: ἄλλοι δὲ ἔλεγον, οὐκ ἐκ τῆς Γαλιλαίας ἔρχεται ὁ Χριστός, ἀλλὰ ἀπὸ Βηθλέεμ τῆς κώμης [7:41-42! cf. 7:52]: ἄλλοι δὲ ἔλεγον, ὁ Χριστὸς ὅταν ἔρχεται, οὐδεὶς γινώσκει πόθεν ἐστί [7:27] (*PG* 59.785). One may as well argue from such "evidence" that Chrysostom's text of John also "omits" οὐχ ἡ γραφὴ εἶπεν ὅτι ἐκ τοῦ σπέρματος Δαυίδ from v. 42.

---

18. For example, see Origen's text of John 2:15. In two citations of the passage (*lemma Jo.* 10.20; *Jo.* 13.56) the verb ἀνέστρεψεν (ἀναστρέφω) appears. But in five adaptations, four of which occur in the commentary *ad loc.*, the verb appears in modified forms and always as a form of ἀνατρέπω. Origen's text, therefore, is almost certainly ἀνέτρεψεν, which has been conformed by copyists in the two citations. Cf. the discussion by Hautsch 1909: 128.

19. Cf. the text of the NEB (Tasker 1964: 42) with the translation: ". . . from David's village of Bethlehem"!

Cyril, on the other hand, cites the passage three different times (*Jo.* 5.2; *Is.* 5.4; *Nest.* 3.3). In the Isaiah commentary he does indeed omit ὅπου ἦν Δαυίδ, but in the other two instances the phrase is included. One has three choices: either (1) Cyril knew two different text forms, and cited now one and then the other; or (2) later scribes added the missing clause in *Jo.* and *Nest.;* or (3) Cyril knew only one text form — the "long" one — and omitted the clause himself in a *memoriter* citation in the Isaiah commentary. A complete study of Cyril's citations will reveal that number 3 is the only viable choice; for examples of this kind of "omission" in Cyril may be multiplied, where we have more than one extant citation of a passage.

2. This leads one to note further that the exactness, or lack of it, on the part of a Father must also be reckoned with when he has only one extant citation of a passage. Two or more citations, all identical, tend to reinforce one's conclusions about a Father's text. And even when the citations differ, there are usually some bases for decision (context, kind of work, geography, etc.).[20] But to place heavy emphasis on a single citation with an "omission" from a Father like Chrysostom or Cyril seems to be a case of bad judgment.

3. A short text based on a Father's citation is a particularly precarious argument from silence. This is especially true of "silence" either at the beginning or end of the cited portion. A case in point is Boismard's alleged omissions by the Fathers of τοῖς πιστεύουσιν εἰς τὸ ὄνομα αὐτοῦ in John 1:12. Among those listed as supporting the omission are Origen (in a citation preserved in Pamphilus), Athanasius, Chrysostom, and Cyril. While it is true that for each a citation of v. 12 may be found which concludes with γενέσθαι, it is further true that these Fathers elsewhere cite the passage by including v. 13, and in every instance the disputed words are also included. The point is obvious: All these Fathers knew a Greek text which contained the concluding words of v. 12, but sometimes they simply stopped citing at γενέσθαι.

In the same vein one wonders about Mollat's curious omission of κύριε at 11:21 (*cum* B sy[s] [he erroneously includes Chrys]) and 13:37 (ℵ* 33 565 sy[s] cop Chrys Non). This vocative occurs thirty times in John, and there is textual evidence (of sorts) for the omission of it in twenty-two instances. One could at least hope for consistency. Sinaiticus omits κύριε three other times (4:19; 13:6, 9), sy[s] two others (4:11; 21:17), and Chrysostom, when one uses his evidence *e silentio,* twelve others (4:15, 49; 6:34, 68; 11:3, 27, 34, 39; 12:21; 13:6 [1/2]; 14:28; 20:15). If this seems unfair, it should be pointed out that the patristic evidence at 13:37 is of the same kind as all the others — "silence" at the beginning of a cited portion.[21]

The only places where such omissions may be regarded as valid evidence are those where it would seem to be highly unusual for a Father to have omitted the

---

20. One wonders, e.g., about the value of Boismard's including Cyril's three citations as supporting the omission of ἐκ τῆς γῆς from John 12:32 (1950: 391), when he cites the passage twenty-eight other times *with* the phrase, including the fragment from the commentary *ad loc.*

21. Blass omits κύριε eight times, with three more in brackets as doubtful. Even he is not fully consistent: On the combined evidence of Chrys and Non alone, he omits it at 11:34, puts it in brackets at 11:3, and keeps it at 6:68.

disputed words, had he known them. Thus Hort says of some patristic citations of John 3:13: "It is morally certain that most of them would have included ὁ ὢν ἐν τῷ οὐρανῷ, if it had stood in the texts used by the writers" (1881: Appendix 75). But even here one must use caution about this "moral certainty."

IV

What shall we say, then, finally of the use of the Church Fathers in the recovery of the original NT text?

1. As primary evidence they offer little help. In spite of much that is of great worth — Mollat's translation I find particularly excellent — Boismard's textual theory is not likely to hold up under careful scrutiny.

It must be granted, however, that there are some unusual readings in the Fathers not found in the manuscript tradition which deserve special attention. One such is the variant at John 14:2, πολλαὶ μοναὶ παρὰ τῷ πατρί. This is not simply a short text because of omission; it is a reading so widely attested,[22] and almost always in the same form, that one rightly suspects that here something has been lost in the MS tradition which is available only in patristic evidence.

However, it should be noted that some of the Fathers who cite the shorter form, clearly know the long form as well (Chrysostom and Cyril). Does this mean that they knew two text forms? Perhaps; but I would hazard a guess that the short form *never* existed in any MS, but rather became the popular form of citation in a kind of oral tradition.[23]

2. As supportive evidence they are of great value, and not simply as a matter of counting noses. For example, Chrysostom's clear Antiochene support, with W (from Egypt) and the OL codices a b ff[2] l r[1] (from Europe), of the reading εἶχεν ἐξουσίαν for ἤθελεν of John 7:1 *is of the same value as any of the* MSS. Indeed, he felt strongly enough about the theological implications of his text (presumably his only one, since he does not "emend" or argue for a variant) that he took considerable pains to explain why the divine Son "had no authority" to go about in Judea.

Whether the original text or not — it certainly looks like the *lectio difficilior* —such evidence must have its full hearing. Therefore, the appeal of this paper is not that we relegate patristic citations to a place of relative insignificance. On the contrary, the appeal is that we continue the tasks of editing patristic texts and gathering and reconstructing their biblical texts until all the evidence is fully available and carefully analyzed. Only then can it have its proper hearing.

22. Boismard lists Irenaeus, Athanasius, Eusebius of Caesarea, Epiphanius, Basil, Gregory of Nyssa, Gregory of Nazianzus, Cyril of Alexandria, Mark the Hermit, Nilus, Theodoret, Theodore of Mopsuestia, Procopius of Gaza, Maximus Confessor, and perhaps Clement of Alexandria among the Greeks. He could have included Chrysostom (*Thdr.* 1.21 [*SC* 117, 1966, p. 214]). Among the Latins are Tertullian, Hilary, Augustine, as well as others, such as Cyprian, Origen (Latin), Jerome, etc., who add either the verb or the possessive.

23. I have a perfect example of this from my own denominational background, where there is a geographically well-distributed oral tradition of John 17:3, "that they may know thee, whom to know aright is life eternal." To some people this is a sacred text and they are nonplussed when one suggests that it cannot be found in their Bibles.

CHAPTER 17

THE USE OF GREEK PATRISTIC CITATIONS IN NEW TESTAMENT TEXTUAL CRITICISM: THE STATE OF THE QUESTION

Gordon D. Fee

In NT textual criticism, patristic citations have ordinarily been viewed as the third line of evidence, after the Greek MSS and Early Versions. Along with the Early Versions, they are considered as indirect, or supplementary, evidence for the text of the NT,[1] and often therefore are also thought to be of tertiary importance. In fact, however, patristic evidence is often of *primary* importance, both in the task of reconstructing the history of the text and in that of recovering the original. F. J. A. Hort, for example, used the Fathers as one of three criteria in determining the secondary character of the Byzantine text-type;[2] and his use of the Fathers in his debate with Ezra Abbot on John 1:18 (1876: 30-42) is still a model for evaluating the data, despite his use — born of necessity — of some uncritical texts of the Fathers.

I. The Problems

The problems with the use of this evidence are three, reflecting in turn the Father himself, the transmission of his evidence, and our own need to discriminate carefully what is truly primary and what is not.

1. The Church Father and His Bible

The problems created by the Fathers themselves and their citing habits are several, and are frequently noted. Basically, they cover four areas:

    1. The question of copying or citing from memory. Did the Father cite Scripture by looking up the passage and copying his text or did he simply cite from

---

    1. Such judgments are regularly found in the manuals on textual criticism, most recently those by Metzger 1968a: 86-88, and K. and B. Aland 1987: 166-69. The latter is particularly instructive, inasmuch as a whole chapter is devoted to the Early Versions, while the Greek patristic evidence receives less than three pages, mostly bemoaning the difficulties and lack of valid or definitive studies of the Fathers' texts. Cf. also the overview articles by Suggs 1958, who calls this evidence "supplemental," and Metzger 1972:379-400, who speaks of it as "indirect."
    2. 1881: 2.107-15. Cf. the use of this evidence by Streeter 1924: chap. 4.

memory? If, as appears to be most common, it was from memory, can his memory be trusted to reproduce the copy of Scripture he must have possessed?

2. The question of citing habits. The citing habits of the Fathers range from rather precise (e.g., Origen) to moderately careful (e.g., Eusebius) to notoriously slovenly (e.g., Epiphanius); therefore, the habits of each Father himself must be carefully studied before his citations can be fully useful.

3. The character/type of work involved. In many Fathers the care with which they cite varies from work to work.[3] For the most part, they tend to be more accurate in commentaries and controversial treatises, the latter especially so if the meaning of the biblical text is involved; whereas they cannot necessarily be expected to be as precise in letters and sermons.

4. The number of Bibles used by the Father. It is perhaps presumptuous to assume that any Father, writing over a thirty- to forty-year period, had only one Bible; and perhaps it is folly even to assume he had only one Bible at any given time. After all, as early as Origen there is acknowledgment of many copies of Scripture. Furthermore, some Fathers tended to relocate from time to time (Irenaeus, Origen, Athanasius, Chrysostom), so that they may not only have used different Bibles in a lifetime, but Bibles from different geographical centers with differing kinds of texts.

2. Scribes and Editors

All the scribal questions asked of the NT MSS themselves must also be applied to the Father's texts, and especially to that portion of their texts where they cite Scripture. It has long been recognized that the monks of the Middle Ages, to whom we are indebted for many of the extant copies of the Fathers, sometimes tended to conform biblical passages to a more contemporary text — although as Suggs has pointed out (1958: 140), this problem can be overstated, since there is also good evidence that the trained copyist normally aimed at verbal accuracy.

Unfortunately, neither are editors faultless. This is true not only of the older, and sometimes less critical editions (which Migne reproduced in his *Patrologia Graeca,* sometimes adding his own errors), but also of such editions as E. Pusey's of Cyril of Alexandria[4] and of some of the editors in the magisterial *Die griechischen christlichen Schriftsteller der ersten drei Jahrhunderte* [see below]. The net result is that even though critical editions are a must, and greatly increase our access to the Fathers' NT texts, they must also be used critically by those seeking to recover those texts.

3. The Need to Discriminate

The problem here rests with the judgments, or lack thereof, on the part of those who use these data. This is often true of individual authors, whose use of patristic evidence

---

3. My own work with the Fathers confirms this judgment first made by Bebb 1890: 216, and repeated by Suggs 1958: 143 and Metzger 1972: 379-80.
4. [On this question see n. 1 in the preceding chapter.]

sometimes belies failure to have worked carefully with a Father's citation in context.[5] But it is also — and especially — true of the *apparatus critici* of our standard critical editions, which in turn leads to any number of misjudgments on the part of those who use such editions, usually because they lack the time and resources to investigate every patristic citation of a given passage.

This problem is well illustrated in the apparatus of the UBS[3] *Greek New Testament,* where for the most part the evidence was derived from the apparatuses of Tischendorf and von Soden.[6] In this text for the first time, even though limited in its selection, the working scholar has available a handy, reliable list of Greek and versional evidence for most of the (translationally) significant variants in the NT. But the patristic evidence in the majority of instances is either incomplete, ambiguous, or unreliable. This evidence can *never* be implicitly trusted, as one can the Greek and versional evidence, and the close study of any of these passages always requires personal, firsthand analysis of the patristic data.[7]

The problem, it must be quickly pointed out, is not the fault of the editors of the UBS text; rather, it is the result of a great lacuna in NT studies, namely, the collection and presentation of the NT text(s) used by the Greek Fathers,[8] based on a careful analysis and evaluation of the available data. Hort himself lamented this problem over one hundred years ago: "It is unsatisfactory that so much of the patristic testimony remains uncertain in the present state of knowledge; but such is the fact. Much of the uncertainty, though not all, will doubtless disappear when the Fathers have been carefully edited" (1876: 5). It is the unfortunate reality of this science that over one hundred years later, the Alands can make a similar lament about the condition of this evidence, to the effect that the vast majority of work in this area still remains to be done (1987: 168-69).

This is not to say that some work has not been done. In fact, analyses of Greek patristic texts can be found scattered throughout the literature and in several unpublished dissertations.[9] Unfortunately, most of these studies suffer from substantial methodological failures;[10] and the published portions of these analyses present only lists of variants and statistics. As of this writing, the only Greek Fathers for whom we have a complete published text are Clement of Alexandria (Mees 1970) and Gregory of Nyssa (Brooks 1991). In addition, there is available the text of the

---

5. A case in point is the use of Origen's discussion of Luke 10:42 in catena fragment 78 in John by M. Augsten and A. Baker, discussed below (section V).

6. See the Introduction to the UBS[3], p. xxxvi.

7. For example, in my study of Luke 10:41-42 in the Metzger Festschrift (1981) the analysis of the patristic evidence, which is highly important primary evidence for this passage, demonstrated the UBS[3] to be unreliable on six counts (Basil in var. 1; Clement and Basil in var. 2; Origen in var. 5; Clement and Augustine in var. 6) and incomplete on several others (Evagrius, Nilus, Augustine, for var. 2; Cassian, Olympiodorus for var. 4). Such a problem occurs again and again in this edition.

8. The evidence for the pre-Vulgate Latin Fathers is both more readily accessible, from the Vetus Latina Institut at Beuron, and of limited value, since for the most part the text represented in these Fathers is that of the Old Latin version(s). For an account of these data, see Frede 1971.

9. For a list of these see n. 6 in Chapter 15.

10. The Alands have rightly judged "that there is not one of them which would not be worth doing over" (1987: 168).

Gospels in Didymus of Alexandria (Ehrman 1986), the text of the Pauline corpus in Hippolytus of Rome (Osburn 1982), plus the reconstructed text of John 4 in Origen and Cyril (Fee 1971a) and the available text of Mark in Chrysostom (Fee 1980b). As long as such a situation prevails, the usefulness of Greek patristic data will lie outside the reach of most working scholars.

However, we are currently at a point in history where great progress can be made. In an extensive paper on patristic citations presented twenty years ago at a special consultation on NT textual criticism,[11] I noted that there were six tasks before us: (1) continued publication of good critical editions of the Fathers; (2) an index of NT citations from all Fathers for each NT book; (3) the critical reconstruction, or otherwise full and critical presentation, of each Father's NT text; (4) the evaluation of each Father's textual relationships, or placing the Father's evidence in the history of the transmission of the text; (5) the presentation of such evidence in the various *apparatus critici;* and (6) the evaluation and use of patristic citations in the recovery of the "original" NT text. For the present study these are regrouped under four heads — gathering, presenting, evaluating, and using the evidence — with some "where we are" or "should be" comments on each.

II. Gathering the Evidence

Getting access to the patristic data is probably the most frustrating part of any scholar's attempt to deal in detail with a given textual variant. Fortunately, some of that frustration is now being relieved. My purpose here is simply to report on the present state of affairs, to the time of this writing.

1. The Index to the Fathers

The four-volume *Clavis Patrum Graecorum,* published in the Greek series of the Corpus Christianorum (Turnhout), is now the absolutely indispensable guidebook to the Greek Fathers and their works.[12] The *Clavis* alerts one to all the works of a given Father, the best critical editions, discussions about authenticity, the availability of a work in early versions, and the more significant bibliography. It should also help to standardize nomenclature.

2. The Critical Editions

Although much work remains yet to be done,[13] a random look through the *Clavis* reveals that the publication of critical editions continues apace. Besides the two major series, *Die griechischen christlichen Schriftsteller der ersten drei Jahrhunderte* (1897--) and *Sources chrétiennes* (1941--), critical editions also appear in a great

---

11. Called by the SBL at its 90th annual meeting, held in New York, October 22-27, 1970. The paper was subsequently published in two parts (1971a, 1971b) [now Chapters 15 and 16].

12. For the Latin Fathers, see *Clavis Patrum Latinorum* (Brugge: Karel Beyaert, 1961).

13. The single most glaring need continues to be the lack of a critical edition of the majority of the works of Chrysostom.

variety of other places. One needs always to consult the *Clavis* for the latest edition of a given Father's work(s).

The necessity and usefulness of these editions can scarcely be overestimated. Take, for example, the NT citations in Hippolytus of Rome. On the basis of J. W. Burgon's large collection of patristic evidence,[14] all gathered from uncritical editions, H. C. Hoskier argued that Hippolytus's citations of 1 Thess 4:13-17 and 2 Thess 2:1-12 (in his *On Christ and Antichrist*) are "generally found on the side of [the Byzantine MSS]" (1914: 427). But a check of these citations in the Achelis edition of *GCS* demonstrates that Hippolytus's text is consistently in agreement with D F G and the OL (cf. Fee 1979: 419-20 and Osburn 1982), which is precisely what one would expect of someone living in Rome in the early third century.

However, as already noted, for NT textual criticism a note of caution must also be struck, since the editors of these editions are not always sensitive to the special nature of the NT citations or to the citing habits of the Father.[15] One must therefore never simply take the edition at face value, but must always be ready to rethink with the editor as to which variant in the Father's own manuscript tradition most likely represents the actual text of the Father.

3. The Index of Patristic Citations

In order to find the patristic evidence for any given NT text, the first volumes of the much needed and very welcome index of patristic quotations are now available from the Centre d'Analyse et de Documentation patristique of the Faculty of Protestant Theology of Strasbourg (Allenbach 1975-87). The first four volumes include all of the Fathers of the second and third centuries, plus three Palestinian Fathers from the fourth (Eusebius of Caesarea, Cyril of Jerusalem, Epiphanius of Salamis). Happily, this index is of all biblical citations, not just the NT. Also happily, but for *textual* purposes somewhat frustratingly, allusions, as well as citations and adaptations, are included. Frequently one must sift through a large number of inconsequential listings in order to realize a minimal net gain of textual data. Nonetheless, such a thorough index is a giant step forward.

4. The IGNTP Luke

The International Greek New Testament Project (IGNTP), now over forty years old, has finally published its edition of the available evidence for the Gospel of Luke.[16] The patristic apparatus in this edition is a significant advance over anything heretofore available for Luke's Gospel. Nonetheless, for all its value, there still remain

14. For this collection, see Metzger 1972: 171.

15. All who have worked closely with these data have their stories to tell. Cf., e.g., Fee 1971b: 164 n. 2 (on Preuschen's edition of Origen); Suggs 1958: 141 n. 1 (on Heikel's edition of Eusebius); and K. and B. Aland 1987: 167 (on the CSEL edition of Cyprian).

16. *The New Testament in Greek. The Gospel According to St. Luke. Part One, chapters 1–12* (Oxford: Clarendon, 1984); *Part Two, chapters 13–24* (1987). For a history of the patristic data in this volume, see Duplacy and Suggs 1971.

some imperfections in this edition,[17] particularly because the apparatus lacks a way of being sensitive to the evaluating process.

With these various tools, one now has access to the critical editions of the Fathers' works and to all of their biblical references. But the greater task still remains, that of presenting these data within the framework of a full evaluation.

III. Presenting the Evidence

Unfortunately, despite the good progress over the past twenty years, convenient access to reliable patristic data is still many years away. Here the needs are two: (1) the full presentation, with careful evaluation, of the NT texts used by individual Fathers, Father by Father, and where necessary, work by work; (2) the production of an apparatus for patristic evidence in our critical editions that can be used with a similar measure of confidence as with the manuscript and versional evidence.

What is needed in the first instance is a full presentation of the NT text of each of the Greek Fathers, as that text can be culled from his extant works and either presented or in some cases reconstructed, where that is possible or necessary. To this end a series has now been launched under the auspices of the Society of Biblical Literature through Scholars Press, entitled *The New Testament in the Greek Fathers: Texts and Analyses* (NTGF),[18] in which such presentations can now be published in a uniform way, either of a given Father's entire NT,[19] or of portions thereof.[20] The parameters of this series, which are herewith described, should serve as basic guidelines for all such presentations.[21]

1. The Introduction to each volume provides a brief sketch of the Father's life and writings, and discusses the unique problems attendant to the analysis and classification of his citations of the NT text. Normally this also includes (1) a discussion of the problems concerning the authenticity of works commonly attributed to the Father, (2) other circumstances of his life that might complicate a textual

17. Cf., e.g., the review by Petersen (1988), who especially highlights the inadequacies of the patristic evidence. These problems are the result of many factors, mostly related to a lack of proper oversight for the decade between 1955 and 1966. During that period an enormous amount of nearly useless data had been collected, because the collectors (1) did not use critical editions (relying mostly on Migne's *PG*), and (2) even then did not carefully read the Father's text, but relied on Migne's notoriously unreliable references, so that at times it is quite incomplete. The present writer was hired by the Project to spend the summer of 1969 to see what could be done with the material available to that time. I soon discovered that a great deal had not been done at all, and that much that had been done needed to be redone. After several months of labor (continuing on into the Autumn), I turned over to the editors files of cards that were approximately 90 to 95 percent checked or redone altogether. By such a process some errors are bound to have made their way into the apparatus.

18. Currently edited by Gordon D. Fee, Bruce M. Metzger, William L. Petersen, and Bart Ehrman.

19. As with Mees's presentation of Clement of Alexandria (1970); cf. vol. 2 of NTGF by James Brooks, of the whole NT of Gregory of Nyssa.

20. As in vol. 1 of NTGF by Ehrman (1986), of the text of the Gospels in Didymus the Blind.

21. The following sketch combines material from an original proposal by the author at the centennial meeting of the SBL in 1980 with the presentation made by Bart Ehrman at the annual SBL meeting in 1986, announcing the actual appearance of the series.

analysis (e.g., Didymus's blindness, or Origen's or Chrysostom's moves from one locale to another), and (3) comments on the Father's citing habits that may contribute to the formal analysis.

2. The second component is the actual presentation of the text, which in every case is to be based *only on critical editions* of the Father's works. The presentation itself takes one of two forms, depending on the quantity of the evidence and the nature of the Father's citing habits. First, where a Father (a) cites freely, and/or (b) cites infrequently, and/or (c) cites texts in two or more forms, the safest procedure is to list all the various forms in which a text is cited, in a fashion similar to the study of Clement's text by M. Mees (1970). However, in contrast to Mees's work, a more thorough evaluation of the data as to what actually constituted Clement's text is both possible and desirable.

The second method is that proposed by the author some years ago for Origen and Cyril of Alexandria (1971a), in which a carefully reconstructed text of the Father's NT is presented. Such a presentation must be careful not to lose any piece of evidence, including textual variations in the transmission of the Father's work; at the same time a thorough evaluation of the data is made so as to present to the highest degree possible the very text of the Father's NT.

3. At some point, either with the presentation of the text itself or in a full listing elsewhere, an apparatus of the Father's text is included, collated in full against carefully selected control MSS representing the previously established textual groups. No standardized group of witnesses is required, but normally twenty to forty of the most important textual representatives are included. The collations are presented in full for all citations (or usable adaptations).

4. These data are then analyzed so as to ascertain the textual affinities or relationships of the Father's text with the other available witnesses to the NT text. The basic methodology employed here is the quantitative method, pioneered by E. C. Colwell and further refined by G. D. Fee (1968a), in which percentages of agreements are established between the Father's text and all the other MSS used in the collation, where any two of them agree in variation against all the rest.

Since for most Fathers this method only establishes the broader parameters of his textual relationships, some kind of further analysis is also usually needed. This may take the form of group profiles, pioneered by B. Ehrman (1987), or of a profile method I devised for my study of the text of John and Mark in Chrysostom (1980b), in which one isolates a Father's agreements/disagreements with the Majority text and UBS[3], as well all singular readings and subsingular agreements.

5. Finally, each volume will normally conclude with some statement concerning the historical results of the study, especially in terms of how the analysis has contributed to our further understanding of the history of the transmission of the NT. The significance of these conclusions will vary, but their potential for helping us write the history of the NT text is great, since they afford us firm evidence for the condition of the text at some datable, geographical point.[22]

---

22. Ehrman also suggested, and in his volume included, an appendix of the results of the study that could become a part of the UBS apparatus.

It can scarcely be emphasized enough how useful such collections and presentations of patristic evidence will be for the future of this discipline; it is hoped that many scholars will find some time to engage in this effort, or at least to direct younger scholars toward dissertations that might eventually be included in the series.[23]

IV. Evaluating the Evidence

Over forty years ago R. M. Grant rightly argued that "patristic citations are not citations unless they have been adequately analyzed" (1950: 124). Indeed, the unfortunately numerous examples of careless or completely invalid usage demand that this must become an inviolable axiom in our discipline. The needs here are two: First, there is a need to devise *a set of criteria, or guidelines, by which to assess the degrees of certainty or doubt with regard to any patristic citation.* Second, for the sake of those who regularly use the NA[26] or UBS[3] editions, a means is needed whereby these degrees of certainty or doubt can be expressed in the *apparatus criticus,* thus enabling the user to move toward the same degree of confidence with regard to these data as with the manuscript and versional evidence.

The following guidelines are offered as a preliminary working list toward such a set of criteria, beginning with certainty and working toward extremely doubtful materials. At the same time suggestions are made as to how such certainty and doubt might appear in an apparatus, including a sample reworking of the apparatus of Luke 10:42.

1. A Father's name could be listed in **bold type** when there is absolute certainty as to the actual text used by that Father (as much as historians may speak of "absolute certainty"). Such cases include:

1.1 *When in his subsequent discussion the Father makes a point of the very words used by the biblical author.*

> [e.g., Chrysostom's evidence for εἶχεν ἐξουσίαν in John 7:1. In his *hom. 48 in John* he says, "What are you saying blessed John? Did he not εἶχεν ἐξουσίαν, who was able to do all that he wanted to? . . . For when he says that he εἶχεν ἐξουσίαν, he speaks of him as to his being man, . . ."; cf. Basil's interpretation of the ὀλίγων and ἑνός of Luke 10:42 in *reg. fus.* 20.3.]

1.2 *When in a commentary or homily the subsequent discussion confirms the wording of a citation.*

> [e.g., Origen's considerable discussion of the text of the Lord's Prayer in both Luke and Matthew in *On Prayer;* cf., as an example of "omission" in a Father's text, Cyril of Jerusalem's homily on the story of the healing of the invalid in John 5, where it is certain from his discussion in the homily itself that he knew nothing of the gloss in vv. 3b-4.]

---

23. Cf. the appeal by the Alands (1987: 169): "This is a field ripe for innumerable doctoral dissertations and learned investigations. Any volunteers?"

1.3 *When the Father actually cites a known variation to his own text.*[24] (In this case, of course, the Father becomes certain evidence for two readings; but one reading is that of the Father's own text, which is the first interest in the use of his materials. His evidence for the second reading should continue to be designated ORIGEN[mss].)

> [E.g., Origen, in *hom. 6.40 in John,* mentions that other MSS known to him have Βηθαβαρᾷ in John 1:28, which he prefers to the Βηθανίᾳ of his text.]

1.4 *When in a commentary, homily, or controversial treatise, the Father repeats the text in the same way again and again.*

> [Editors must use proper caution here, because this could simply be a case of consistent faulty memory. But in many cases one can arrive at the highest level of certainty. E.g., in his *Commentary on John,* Book X, Origen cites or alludes to the text of John 2:15 five times in which the words τὰ κέρματα occur; in Book XIII he has occasion to refer back to this event and twice more cites it with τὰ κέρματα. Since this reading is consonant with Origen's textual relationships elsewhere, one can have the highest degree of certainty that this is the reading of his text.]

For all other kinds of citations it is absolutely imperative that a Father's citing habits be known (i.e., his degree of concern for verbal accuracy, his tendencies to adapt, cite loosely, paraphrase, or toward omissions or substitutions, etc.). For example, Origen demonstrates a very high degree of verbal accuracy (at least when he cites John's Gospel), whereas Epiphanius shows practically none at all,[25] while Asterius the Sophist, although demonstrating a generally high degree of verbal accuracy, shows clear proclivities toward the omission of words and phrases in the interest of his homiletic style. This kind of information is especially important for the next categories.

2. We should include a Father's name in CAPITALS in those cases where there is a high degree of probability that we have the Father's actual text, but not with the same degree of certainty as in category 1. These include the following:

2.1 *A citation of several verses in length, especially so when the biblical author or book is also singled out.*

> [This assumes that an author is more likely to have consulted his text at such points than otherwise. However, one must use great care here; for this is also a place where a copyist of the Father's work may have unconsciously conformed the text to his own standard (e.g., the full citation of the Matthean version of the Lord's Prayer in Origen's *On Prayer* has been conformed to the prevailing text by the addition of ὅτι in v. 5 and τῆς in v. 10, as the subsequent discussion by Origen makes clear). And, of course, in a Father like Epiphanius, who does *not* consult his text, this criterion is of no value (see, e.g., his "citations" of Mark 5:2-14 in the *Panarion.*)]

---

24. See, e.g., the useful collections of such notes in Origen and Jerome gathered by Metzger (1963a: 1979).

25. This phenomenon in particular mars the study by Eldridge 1969; cf my review (1971c).

2.2 *An isolated citation with a text form that shows clear affinities with a Father's otherwise well-established textual relationships.*

[E.g., in his homily on the sinful woman in Luke 7:36-50, Amphilochius in a short space twice cites v. 37 in the word order of the Majority text; since his textual proclivities are clearly in this direction, one can be reasonably certain that this represents his actual NT. So also Origen's many single citations of the Gospel of John that are in harmony with P[75] and B.]

2.3 *In most of the isolated citations of a Father whose citing habits reflect a rather high degree of verbal accuracy.*

[Although this must be used with some degree of caution, and usually in conjunction with 2.2, Origen serves as a case in point. Since the majority of his isolated citations of the Gospel of John scattered throughout his works generally conform to the Egyptian text found in his Commentary, one can have reasonable certainty about his isolated citations of other NT books as well.]

2.4 *When a Father alludes to the language of a passage in such a way that it is virtually impossible for him to have done so without knowledge of the biblical text.*

[This criterion has especially to do with large additions/omissions. The operative word is "language." E.g., one can assume by the *language* he uses that Tertullian knew a text of John 5 that carried the gloss of vv. 3b-4. But one can be equally dubious as to whether Ps-Didymus *(de Trinitate)* or Amphilochius knew a text of John with these words. Even though they refer to an angel stirring the water, in both cases the rest of their comments not only do not reflect the "language" of the gloss, but in fact offer a different understanding of the tradition. Here one can be sure only that they knew about the tradition reflected in the Western gloss; but it is doubtful whether they knew a biblical text with these words.[26]]

2.5 *Where in various unsuspecting ways* [e.g., verb inflections where the root is changed in allusions or adaptations] *the Father reveals his text where subsequent scribes are most highly likely to have tampered with it.*

[E.g., despite the occurrence of ἀνέστρεψε in two citations of John 2:15 in the Commentary, Origen elsewhere refers back to this passage in five different adaptations, and in each case the verb appears as an inflected form of ἀνατρέπω.[27]]

2.6 *In Synoptic parallels when a Father actually notes the usage in another Gospel.*

[E.g., in *hom. 58 in Matt*, Chrysostom notes that in contrast to Matthew, the disciples in Mark (9:33) οὐκ ἠρώτησαν, ἀλλ᾿ ἐν ἑαυτοῖς διελογίζοντο (repeated a few lines later). This is a typically free rendering by Chrysostom of the Byzantine text of this verse. One is well advised to use caution here,

---

26. For a fuller analysis of these texts, see Fee 1982b.
27. For the data here see Fee 1973a: 78-81.

however, since most such allusions are from memory and some Fathers have notoriously poor memories in this regard.[28]]

3. In most other citations, the Father should be simply listed in regular lower case. This is not to throw unnecessary doubt on a patristic citation; rather, it is to inform the user that some degree of caution is necessary, since the editors do not have the two higher kinds of certainty about the citation. In most cases these citations probably reflect the actual text used by the Father, but one simply cannot be as sure as in the cases noted above.

4. There is one category of citations that needs further comment, and which may appear in our apparatuses in any of the above forms, depending on the other criteria. It is well known that Fathers in two or more citations often reflect two or more text forms. In such cases the following guidelines should prevail:

4.1 Many times a careful analysis of all the data reveals that in fact the Father knew and used only one form of text and that the second citation reflects either (a) a fault of memory, or (b) inconsequential omissions or adaptations in a new context. This is especially true when the two citations reflect a "long" or "short" form of text (i.e., the addition/omission of adverbs, adjectives, pronouns, or prepositional phrases). In most such cases the "long" form reflects the Father's actual text, while the "short" form is an abbreviated version made by the Father himself.[29] I would argue that such "short form" variants have no business in our apparatuses.

4.2 On the other hand, sometimes it can be shown beyond reasonable doubt that the Father knew and used two different forms of text (e.g., Origen's Mark citations in the Commentary on John; Hesychius's two homilies on the presentation of Jesus). In such cases the Father should be listed twice, as reasonably certain evidence that he knew and used two different texts.

4.3 In many instances no clear decision can be made as to 4.1 or 4.2. In such cases one must use the Father's evidence with utmost caution, perhaps list it twice, but in parentheses. For the most part it is far less likely that a Father actually knew and used two different texts than either that he is guilty of carelessness or that an error has made its way into his own textual tradition. This means that we usually must admit to our not knowing his text rather than to suggest that he knew both forms.

5. Finally, in the following situations one must exhibit the greatest caution in including or using a Father's text as supporting evidence. If one were to choose to include them in an apparatus, then they should be enclosed with parentheses, indicating to the reader the highest form of doubt that this is good evidence:

5.1 Synoptic parallels are especially treacherous waters.[30] With most Fathers there is a strong tendency for *memoriter* citations to become intricately, but probably not purposefully, harmonized. Therefore, such evidence can be used with confidence in only three categories of citations: (a) Where the text is part of a commentary or

---

28. E.g., in his *hom. 44 in Matt.*, Chrysostom says, "Therefore, another evangelist also says," and then "cites" Mark 4:13 as follows: πῶς οὖν ἔγνωτε τὴν παραβολήν;

29. Cf. the similar judgments by Metzger 1972: 396.

30. See some of the suggestions in this regard in Fee 1978e [now Chapter 9].

homily on the Gospel in question; (b) where the Father explicitly tells us from which Gospel he is citing; (c) where the material cited or referred to is unique to one of the Gospels.

5.2 It is generally a doubtful procedure to place much confidence in the "short text" of a Father, when one is dealing with an isolated quotation and the alleged "omission" is at the beginning or end of the citation.[31]

> [Examples of this dubious practice abound in the UBS[3] apparatus; e.g., the alleged "omission" of καὶ ἡ ζωή by Origen and Titus of Bostra in John 11:25 is patently mistaken, as is the "omission" of ἢ ἑνός by Origen or of the whole clause by Clement and Augustine in Luke 10:42; and a significant portion of the patristic evidence for John 3:13 and 1 Cor 2:14 is highly suspect. Here in particular our apparatuses need to be "cleaned up" by omitting all such dubious, or patently incorrect, "evidence."]

5.3 *Lemmata* of commentaries and homilies are notoriously poor risks; in the catenae they are even worse. In the former case, unless the *lemmata* can be demonstrated to have been generally carefully preserved (as in Origen's Commentary on John), they are only as useful in establishing a Father's text as they are supported by the ensuing commentary.

5.4 In an isolated citation of a single verse one can almost never use a Father's evidence for the presence or absence (or substitution) of connective particles and conjunctions.[32] In most cases such conjunctive signals have either been omitted or conformed to the Father's own context. Unfortunately, a much too high incidence of these nearly useless "variants" occurs in the IGNTP Luke. Except for those instances where a citation is of several verses in length, it should be universally agreed to eliminate such items from all quantitative analyses; they should also be eliminated from our apparatuses.

5.5 In a Father with a notorious number of singular readings (e.g., Chrysostom's homilies; Epiphanius's *Panarion*), one must be especially cautious in finding any significance in his subsingular readings, that is, isolated agreements with one or a few other witnesses. Usually such agreements mean nothing as to the Father's text, but rather reflect independently created singular readings. If such data are ever to be included in an apparatus (on the principle of not losing any piece of datum), then they must appear in parentheses.

Since these are programmatic suggestions, it is hoped that they might be subjected to careful scrutiny and further refinement. The use of such criteria, of course, assumes a certain amount of knowledge of the Fathers and their texts; those who gather and present these texts are in the best position to offer this kind of service. Hopefully, the presentations of the future will attempt to aid others in this way.

---

31. This is one of several problems with the attempt by Boismard, following the earlier lead of F. C. Conybeare, to use the Fathers (along with the versions) to discover an earlier, independent, and more likely original text than that found in the early Greek MSS. [See Chapter 16 above.] Cf. the critique by Metzger 1972: 387-95 (who notes earlier critiques by F. Neirynck in *ETL* 53 [1977] 383-99, and M. Roberge in *LTP* 34 [1978] 275-89).

32. This was first noted by Suggs 1958: 142. My own work with these data over many years has confirmed absolutely the validity of this judgment.

On the basis of such criteria the *apparatus critici* of the future could also be designed so as to reflect the degrees of certainty or doubt involved. Such apparatuses should be guided by two principles: on the one hand, no single datum should be lost or discarded; on the other hand, not all data should be implied to have equal value (as is now the case).

To illustrate such an apparatus, I have reworked that of UBS[3] for Luke 10:41-42, on the basis of the rather thorough study of each of the Father's texts for my contribution to the Metzger Festschrift (1981):

μεριμνᾶς καὶ θορυβάζῃ (or τυρβάζῃ) περὶ πολλά, ἑνὸς δέ ἐστιν χρεία P[45,75] A C* Κ Ρ Δ Θ Π Ψ f[13] 28 565 700 892 1009 1010 1071 1079 1195 1216 1230 1241 1242 1253 1344 1365 1546 1646 2148 2174 *Byz Lect* it[aur,f,(q)] vg syr[c,p,h] cop[sa] CHRYSOSTOM Evagrius Nilus PS-BASIL PS-MACARIUS JOHN-DAMASCUS AUGUSTINE ‖ μεριμνᾶς καὶ θορυβάζῃ περὶ πολλά, ὀλίγων δέ ἐστιν χρεία ἢ ἑνός P[3] ℵ B C[2] L 1 33 579 2193 syr[hmg] cop[bo] eth it[m] **Origen Basil** CYRIL-ALEXANDRIA OLYMPIODORUS JEROME CASSIAN ‖ μεριμνᾶς καὶ θορυβάζῃ περὶ πολλά, ὀλίγων δέ ἐστιν χρεία 38 cop[boms] arm geo ‖ μεριμνᾶς καὶ θορυβάζῃ περὶ πολλά it[c] ‖ θορυβάζῃ D it[d] ‖ *omit* it[a,b,e,ff2,i,l,r1] syr[s] AMBROSE POSSIDIUS

When all of our *apparatus critici* can so distinguish between Fathers' certain and less certain citations, and leave the dubious ones out altogether, then the users of our Greek critical texts can have far more confidence in their own ability to make textual decisions.

V. Using the Evidence

The final step in the process is the use of this evidence in the twofold task of finding the original NT text and writing the history of its transmission. The Fathers have long played a significant role in each of these tasks, as can be seen from the following illustrations. Hopefully, when much more of the evidence has been presented and evaluated in the manner outlined here, we will be able to do these two tasks with even greater precision.

1. The Fathers and the Original NT Text

To illustrate the significance of carefully evaluated patristic evidence, where one has the highest degree of certainty as to the Father's text, we might examine in greater detail two texts from the previous discussion: Luke 10:42 and John 7:1.

a) Luke 10:42[33]

In some of the discussions on this text, it had been argued (1) that the so-called "conflate" reading ("Martha, Martha, you are concerned and troubled over many

---

33. For the full display of evidence and more complete discussion, see Fee 1981.

things; few things are needed, indeed only one") was the creation of Origen, and (2) that the reading was basically an Egyptian phenomenon. A careful analysis of the patristic evidence makes it clear that neither of these is true.

First, Origen's evidence is preserved in two catenae fragments: one from John's Gospel, in which he mentions and interprets only the "few things" (= Judaism); the other from Luke's Gospel, where he cites and interprets both the "few things" (= Judaism) and the "one thing" (= Christianity). This evidence has been treated in two ways. On the one hand, A. Baker (1965) argued that since Origen "knew" a text only with ὀλίγων and since P75 was equally early evidence in Egypt for a text only with ἑνός, Origen himself was the source of the "conflate" reading found in the rest of the Egyptian evidence. On the other hand, Monika Augsten (1968) argued on the basis of the Johannine fragment that Origen was early evidence for the variant that reads only ὀλίγων, which she considered to be the Lukan original.

But this is questionable use of patristic evidence, especially with regard to the confidence both scholars place on Origen's knowing a text only with ὀλίγων. Two things militate against it: (1) In this fragment, Origen does not in fact "cite" the text. Rather, in a passage in which his interest is in Martha alone, he adapts the Lukan passage and concludes by "citing" only her portion ("Martha, Martha, about many things you are troubled and distracted [περισπᾶσαι], but few things are needed"), which he then proceeds to interpret as referring to Judaism and the "few things" needed in the Law for salvation. This is a clear case where criterion 5.2 prevails (a "short text" where the "omission" lies at the end of a citation). (2) This is further confirmed by the catena fragment from Luke's Gospel, where Origen interprets *both portions* of the text. The interpretation of ὀλίγων is not only the same in both cases, but is clearly dependent on the contrast with ἑνός. One can be sure, therefore, that the longer text is the only one Origen knew and used. Not only did he not create the longer reading, he is the certain evidence that this reading existed very early in Egypt.

Second, that this is not simply an Egyptian reading is also made certain by other patristic evidence. Jerome cites this text in a letter written from Rome in 384. Whether this reading was available in Rome or came from Jerusalem, in either case it clearly existed outside Egypt. So too with Basil, who, like Origen, not only knew only this text, but also offered an interpretation of the two parts. Thus, even though the rest of the evidence from the East reads ἑνὸς δέ ἐστιν χρεία, Basil and Jerome offer evidence that is not easily traceable to Egypt for the existence of this reading elsewhere. That it is probably the original text can be shown on other grounds.

b) John 7:1

Here the "standard text" reads: οὐ γὰρ ἤθελεν ἐν τῇ Ἰουδαίᾳ περιπατεῖν ("For he did not *wish* to go about in Judea"). But another reading found very early in the OL codices a b ff2 l r1, as well as in Codex W, is also the only reading known to Chrysostom: οὐ γὰρ εἶχεν ἐξουσίαν ἐν τῇ Ἰουδαίᾳ περιπατεῖν ("For he did not have authority to go about in Judea"). On all counts, this latter reading is the *lectio difficilior*, so much so that Chrysostom felt compelled to explain why the Son of God did not have such authority — it had to do with the self-imposed limitations of his humanity.

The evidence from Chrysostom is especially noteworthy. Even though he is the only witness to this reading in the geographical area from which the Byzantine text emerged, and to which he is one of the early witnesses, he shares a reading in this case with the early and best of the OL evidence, as well as with one MS from Egypt. It is possible, of course, that this is merely a "Western" reading that found its way to Antioch and Egypt and influenced Chrysostom and W; but it is equally likely (more likely, I would argue) that here we have early and independent witnesses to the original text, which was suppressed very early for theological reasons. In any case, Chrysostom serves in this instance as the equivalent of any MS, and as datable (391 CE) and geographically certain (Antioch) evidence.

The value of such evidence, of course, is that Chrysostom antedates by several centuries the actual Greek MSS with which he otherwise shares textual affinities.

Discussions such as these can be found scattered throughout the literature; in each case the text of the Fathers plays a role of primary significance, right alongside the Greek MS tradition. Hence the need for a full presentation and evaluation of this evidence.

2. Writing the History of Transmission

Although there are still several lacunae in the data, and several places where precision is not easy to come by, what we now know about the texts of the earliest Fathers gives us considerable confidence in outlining the history of transmission with some broad strokes. What we learn from this evidence confirms what has been known for a long time — despite some demurrers from the twentieth century based on early judgments from the evidence of the papyri and from inadequate presentations of the patristic evidence.

It is now certain that two distinct forms of the NT existed in the East and West. The last authors in the West to write in Greek (Hippolytus of Rome and Irenaeus of Lyons) both used Greek texts that looked very much like those that lay behind the earliest Latin versions. Tertullian, and all subsequent writers in Latin, are clearly dependent on these Latin versions.

A different picture emerges in Egypt, where the basic text, such as that found in Origen and the earliest Greek MSS from this area (P75 P46 P72 B, and to a lesser degree P66), looks very much like a good, but not perfect, preservation of the original texts themselves. When Origen moved to Caesarea (230 CE), he appears to have taken along his Alexandrian copy of John's Gospel; however, for much of the rest of the NT he began to use texts that differed considerably from those in Alexandria. Similar, somewhat mixed texts can also be found in other early writers from this area (e.g., Eusebius, Epiphanius, Cyril of Jerusalem, Basil). In the meantime the later writers in Alexandria (Didymus, Cyril) exhibit texts that have begun to be modified toward a text that emerges about the same time in Antioch and elsewhere. The earliest Father with extant text, who used this emerging text, is Asterius the Sophist. This text was also that used by Chrysostom in Antioch and then in Constantinople; although it looked very much like Basil's, it had been modified considerably, so that it was about seventy-five percent along the way to the text that would eventually dominate in the Greek church — probably very much under the influence of Chrysostom himself.

These broad outlines seem clear; the difficulties lie with the evidence from the Fathers in Palestine and Asia Minor, where there seem to have been various degrees of textual mixture — of more than one kind. Although this is the area where much work has formerly been done, the results of these labors are for the most part of little usefulness, since so many of them represent faulty methodology. Once these studies have been redone, with full presentations and evaluations, it is still possible that some of the details of the text(s) in these areas can be written with more precision.

All of this is to say, then, that much has been done; but there is still much that needs doing. The studies of the future will be of much greater usefulness to all, if they take seriously the suggestions put forth in this overview.

BIBLIOGRAPHY

Abbot, Ezra
  1888   *The Authorship of the Fourth Gospel and Other Critical Essays.*
          Boston: Ellis.

Abbott, Edwin A.
  1906   *Johannine Grammar.* London: A. & C. Black. [Reprinted Farn-
          borough, England: Gregg, 1968]

Aland, Barbara
  1976   "Neutestamentliche Textkritik Heute." Pp. 3-22 in *Verkündigung
          und Forschung: Neues Testament.* BEvT 2. Munich: Kaiser.

  1985   "Die neuen neutestamentlichen Handschriften vom Sinai." Pp. 76-
          89 in Kunst 1985.

  1988   "A New Instrument and Method for Evaluating the Total Manu-
          script Tradition of the New Testament." Pp. 33-50 in Kunst 1988.
          [Now pp. 317-32 in 2d ed. (1989) of K. and B. Aland 1987]

  1989   "Die Münsteraner Arbeit am Text des Neuen Testaments und ihr
          Beitrag für die frühe Überlieferung des 2. Jahrhunderts: Eine
          methodologische Betrachtung." Pp. 55-70 in Petersen 1989.

  1990   "Neutestamentliche Textforschung und Textgeschichte: Erwägun-
          gen zu einem notwendigen Thema." *NTS* 36 (1990) 337-58.

Aland, Kurt
  1957-76 "Neue Neutestamentliche Papyri." *NTS* 3 (1956/57) 261-86; 9
          (1962/63) 303-16; 10 (1963/64) 62-79; 11 (1964/65) 1-21; 20
          (1973/74) 357-81; 22 (1975/76) 375-96. Parts 1 and 2 in Aland,
          1967 91-136, 137-54.

  1957   "Papyrus Bodmer II, ein erster Bericht." *TLZ* 82: 161-84.

  1959   "The Present Position of New Testament Textual Criticism." *SE* 1:
          717-31.

  1963   *Kurzgefasste Liste der griechischen Handschriften des Neuen
          Testaments: I: Gesamtübersicht.* ANTF 1. Berlin: De Gruyter.
          [Continued in "Die griechischen Handschriften des Neuen Testa-
          ments: Ergänzungen zur 'Kurzgefassten Liste' (Fortsetzungsliste
          VII)." Pp. 1-53 in Aland 1969.]

  1964   ed. *Synopsis quattuor evangeliorum.* Stuttgart: Württembergische
          Bibelanstalt. Reissued in 1972 as *Synopsis of the Four Gospels:*

Greek-English Edition of the Synopsis quattuor evangeliorum with the Text of the Revised Standard Version. London: United Bible Societies.

1965   "The Significance of the Papyri for Progress in New Testament Research." Pp. 325-46 in Hyatt 1965.

1966a   "Der heutige Text des griechischen Neuen Testaments: Ein kritischer Bericht über seine modernen Ausgaben." Pp. 44-71 in *Die Bibel in der Welt. Band 9: Jahrbuch des Verbandes der Evangelischen Bibelgesellschaften in Deutschland 1966.* Ed. Robert Steiner. Halle. Revision in Aland 1967: 58-80. [Cited from the latter]

1966b   "Bemerkungen zu Probeseiten einer grossen kritischen Ausgabe des Neuen Testaments." *NTS* 12 (1965/66) 176-85. Reprinted in Aland 1967: 81-90.

1967   *Studien zur Überlieferung des Neuen Testaments und seines Textes.* ANTF 2. Berlin: De Gruyter. [Twelve studies]

1969   ed. *Materialien zur neutestamentlichen Handschriftenkunde I.* ANTF 3. Berlin: De Gruyter.

1970   "Novi testamenti graeci editio maior critica: Der gegenwärtige Stand der Arbeit an einer neuen grossen kritischen Ausgabe des Neuen Testamentes." *NTS* 16 (1969/70) 163-77.

1972   ed. *Die alten Übersetzungen des Neuen Testaments, die Kirchenväterzitate und Lektionare: Der gegenwärtige Stand ihrer Erforschung und ihre Bedeutung für die griechische Textgeschichte.* ANTF 5. Berlin/New York: De Gruyter.

1975-83 ed. *Vollständige Konkordanz zum griechischen Neuen Testament: Unter Zugrundelegung aller modernen kritischen Textausgaben und des Textus Receptus.* ANTF 4. 2 vols. in 3. Berlin/New York: De Gruyter.

1976   ed. for the Patristischen Arbeitsstelle of Münster: *Repertorium der griechischen christlichen Papyri. I: Biblische Papyri: Altes Testament, Neues Testament, Varia, Apokryphen.* Patristische Texte und Studien 18. Berlin/New York: De Gruyter.

1979a   "The Twentieth-Century Interlude in New Testament Textual Criticism." Pp. 1-14 in Best and Wilson 1979. Reprinted as "Die Rolle des 20. Jahrhunderts in der Geschichte der neutestamentlichen Textkritik," pp. 28-42 in Kunst 1979.

1979b   "Neutestamentliche Textforschung und elektronische Datenverarbeitung." Pp. 70-82 in Kunst 1979.

1981   "Der neue 'Standard Text' in seinem Verhältnis zu den frühen Papyri und Majuskeln." Pp. 257-75 in Epp and Fee 1981.

1982   "Ein neuer Textus Receptus für das griechische Neue Testament?" *NTS* 28 (1982) 145-53.

1985   "Die Grundurkunde des Glaubens: Ein Bericht über 40 Jahre Arbeit an ihrem Text." Pp. 9-75 in Kunst 1985.

1987   ed., in collaboration with Annette Benduhn-Mertz and Gerd Mink,

Text und Textwert der griechischen Handschriften des Neuen Testaments. I: Die Katholischen Briefe. Vol. 1: Das Material. Vol. 2.1: Die Auswertung (P23-999). Vol. 2.2: Die Auswertung (1003-2805). Vol. 3: Die Einzelhandschriften. ANTF 9; 10: 1-2; 11; 3 vols. in 4. Berlin/New York: de Gruyter.

Aland, Kurt, and Barbara Aland.

1979   ed. *Novum Testamentum Graece post Eberhard Nestle et Erwin Nestle, communiter ediderunt Kurt Aland, Matthew Black, Carlo M. Martini, Bruce M. Metzger, Allen Wikgren.* 26th ed. Stuttgart: Deutsche Bibelstiftung. [11th printing, 1987]

1982   *Der Text des Neuen Testaments: Einführung in die wissenschaftlichen Ausgaben sowie in Theorie und Praxis der modernen Textkritik.* Stuttgart: Deutsche Bibelgesellschaft. [Eng. tr. 1987]

1987   *The Text of the New Testament: An Introduction to the Critical Editions and to the Theory and Practice of Modern Textual Criticism.* Tr. Erroll F. Rhodes. Grand Rapids: Eerdmans; Leiden: Brill. 2d ed., 1989. [1987 ed. is cited — page numbers usually are identical in 1989 ed.] [German original, 1982]

Aland, Kurt, Matthew Black, Carlo M. Martini, Bruce M. Metzger, and Allen Wikgren

1966   ed. *The Greek New Testament.* 1st ed. New York/London/Edinburgh/Amsterdam/Stuttgart: United Bible Societies.

1975   ed. *The Greek New Testament.* 3d ed. New York/London/Edinburgh/Amsterdam/Stuttgart: United Bible Societies. 3d ed., corrected, 1983.

Alford, Henry

1883   *The Greek Testament.* 4 vols. New ed. Boston.

Allenbach, J., et al.

1975-87   *Biblia Patristica: Index des citations et allusions bibliques dans la littérature patristique.* Centre d'Analyse et de Documentation patristiques. Paris: Centre National de la Recherche Scientifique.

American and British Committees of the International Greek New Testament Project

1984-87   ed. *The New Testament in Greek: The Gospel according to St. Luke: Part One: Chapters 1–12. Part Two: Chapters 13–24.* Oxford: Clarendon Press.

Augsten, Monika

1968   "Lukanische Miszelle." *NTS* 14 (1967/68) 581-83.

Baarda, Tjitze

1975   *The Gospel Quotations of Aphrahat the Persian Sage. I: Aphrahat's Text of the Fourth Gospel.* 2 vols. Akademisch Proefschrift, Free University. Amsterdam: Krips Repro B. V. Meppel.

1980   "Op weg naar een standaardtekst van het Nieuwe Testament? Enkele opmerkingen bij de verschijning van de 26ste druk van 'Nestle.'" *Gereformeerd Theologisch Tijdschrift* 80: 83-137.

1983   *Early Transmission of Words of Jesus: Thomas, Tatian and the Text of*

the New Testament: A Collection of Studies. Ed. J. Helderman and
S. J. Noorda. Amsterdam: VU Boekhandel [Free University Press].

Baker, Aelred
1965   "One Thing Necessary." *CBQ* 27: 127-37.

Barbour, Ruth
1981   *Greek Literary Hands* A.D. *400-1600.* Oxford: Clarendon Press.

Bardy, Gustave
1920   "Le texte de l'épître aux Romains dans le commentaire d'Origène-
            Rufin." *RB* 29: 229-41.

Barnard, P. M.
1899   *The Biblical Text of Clement of Alexandria in the Four Gospels
            and the Acts of the Apostles.* TextsS 5/5. Cambridge: Cambridge
            University Press.

Barrett, Charles Kingsley
1979   "Is There a Theological Tendency in Codex Bezae?" Pp. 15-27 in
            Best and Wilson.

Bartsch, Hans-Werner
1981   "Ein neuer Textus Receptus für das griechische Neue Testament?"
            NTS 27 (1980/81) 585-92.

Bebb, L. J. M.
1890   "The Evidence of the Early Versions and Patristic Quotations on
            the Text of the Books of the New Testament." *Studia biblica et
            ecclesiastica* 2: 195-240.

Becker, Ulrich
1963   *Jesus und die Ehebrecherin: Untersuchungen zur Text- und Über-
            lieferungsgeschichte von Joh. 7,53–8,11.* BZNW 28. Berlin: Töpel-
            mann.

Bell, H. Idris
1948   *Egypt from Alexander the Great to the Arab Conquest: A Study in
            the Diffusion and Decay of Hellenism.* Oxford: Clarendon Press.

Bell, H. Idris, and T. C. Skeat
1935   *Fragments of an Unknown Gospel and Other Early Christian
            Papyri.* London: Oxford University Press.

Bellinzoni, Arthur J.
1967   *The Sayings of Jesus in the Writings of Justin Martyr.* NovTSup
            17. Leiden: Brill.

Bengel, Johann Albrecht
1855   *Gnomon Novi Testamenti* 3d ed., ed. by J. Steudal; Tübingen.
            [Original 1742]

Benoit, André, and Pierre Prigent
1971   ed. *La Bible et les Pères: Colloque de Strasbourg (1ᵉʳ-3 octobre
            1969).* Bibliothèque des centres d'études supérieurs spécialisés.
            Paris: Presses universitaires de France.

Bentley, Jerry H.
1983   *Humanists and Holy Writ: New Testament Scholarship in the Re-
            naissance.* Princeton, NJ: Princeton University Press.

Best, Ernest, and R. McL. Wilson, eds.

1979   *Text and Interpretation: Studies in the New Testament Presented to Matthew Black.* Cambridge/New York: Cambridge University Press.

Birdsall, J. Neville

1957a   "The Text of the Fourth Gospel: Some Current Questions." *EvQ* 29: 195-205.

1957b   "Photius and the Text of the Fourth Gospel." *NTS* 4 (1957/58) 61-63.

1957c   "Current Trends and Present Tasks in New Testament Textual Criticism." *Baptist Quarterly* 17 (1957/58) 109-14.

1960   *The Bodmer Papyrus of the Gospel of John.* Tyndale New Testament Lecture, 1958. London: Tyndale.

1965   "How the New Testament Came to Us." Pp. 121-44 in *Understanding the New Testament.* Ed. O. Jessie Lace. Cambridge: Cambridge University Press.

1970   "The New Testament Text." Chap. 11, pp. 308-77 in *The Cambridge History of the Bible: Volume 1: From the Beginnings to Jerome.* Ed. P. R. Ackroyd and C. F. Evans. Cambridge: Cambridge University Press.

1976   "Rational Eclecticism and the Oldest Manuscripts: A Comparative Study of the Bodmer and Chester Beatty Papyri of the Gospel of Luke." Pp. 39-51 in Elliott 1976.

1988   Review of K. and B. Aland 1987. *BT* 39: 338-42.

1989   "The Western Text in the Second Century." Pp. 3-17 in Petersen 1989.

1990   "Manuscripts," "Texts of the Bible," and "Textual Criticism (New Testament)." Pp. 419-22, 678-84 in *A Dictionary of Biblical Interpretation.* Ed. R. J. Coggins and J. L. Houlden. London: SCM; Philadelphia: Trinity Press International.

Birdsall, J. Neville, and Robert W. Thomson

1963   ed. *Biblical and Patristic Studies in Memory of Robert Pierce Casey.* Freiburg/Basel/New York: Herder.

Black, Matthew

1967   *An Aramaic Approach to the Gospels and Acts.* 3d ed. Oxford: Clarendon Press.

1972   "The Syriac Versional Tradition." Pp. 120-59 in K. Aland 1972.

1974   "Notes on the Longer and Shorter Text of Acts." Pp. 119-31 in *On Language, Culture, and Religion in Honor of Eugene A. Nida.* Ed. M. Black and W. A. Smalley. The Hague/Paris: Mouton.

1981   "The Holy Spirit in the Western Text of Acts." Pp. 159-70 in Epp and Fee 1981.

Black, Matthew, and Robert Davidson

1981   *Constantin von Tischendorf and the Greek New Testament.* Glasgow: University of Glasgow Press.

Blackman, Edwin Cyril

1948   *Marcion and His Influence.* London: SPCK.

Blake, Robert P.
1974   ed. *The Old Georgian Version of the Gospel of Mark from the Adysh Gospels with the Variants of the Opiza and Tbet' Gospels.* PO 20: 3. Turnhout, Belgium: Brepols.
1976   ed. *The Old Georgian Version of the Gospel of Matthew from the Adysh Gospels with the Variants of the Opiza and Tbet' Gospels.* PO 24: 1. Turnhout, Belgium: Brepols.
Blake, Robert P., and Maurice Brière
1950   ed. *The Old Georgian Version of the Gospel of John from the Adysh Gospels with the Variants of the Opiza and Tbet' Gospels.* PO 26: 4. Paris: Firmin-Didot.
Blass, Friedrich Wilhelm
1895   *Acta Apostolorum sive Lucae ad Theophilum liber alter. Editio philologica apparatu critico . . .* Göttingen: Vandenhoeck & Ruprecht.
1896   *Acta Apostolorum sive Lucae ad Theophilum liber alter, secundum formam quae videtur Romanam.* Leipzig: Teubner.
1897   *Evangelium secundum Lucam sive Lucae ad Theophilum liber prior, secundum formam quae videtur Romanam.* Leipzig: Teubner.
1898   *Philology of the Gospels.* London: Macmillan.
1901a   *Evangelium secundum Lucam cum variae lectionis delectu.* Leipzig: Hinrichs.
1901b   *Evangelium secundum Matthaeum cum variae lectionis delectu.* Leipzig: Hinrichs.
1902   *Evangelium secundum Iohannem cum variae lectionis delectu.* Leipzig: Hinrichs.
Boismard, M.-E.
1948   "A propos de Jean V,39: Essai de critique textuelle." *RB* 55: 5-34.
1950   "Critique textuelle et citations patristiques." *RB* 57: 388-408.
1951   "Lectio brevior, potior." *RB* 58: 161-68.
1952   " 'Dans le sein du Père' (*Jo.,* 1,18)." *RB* 59: 23-39.
1953   "Problèmes de critique textuelle concernant le quatrième évangile." *RB* 60: 347-71.
1957   "Le Papyrus Bodmer II." *RB* 64: 363-98.
1981   "The Text of Acts: A Problem of Literary Criticism?" Pp. 147-57 in Epp and Fee 1981.
Boismard, M.-E., and A. Lamouille
1984   *Le texte occidental des Actes des Apôtres: Reconstitution et réhabilitation. Tome I: Introduction et textes. Tome II: Apparat critique, Index des caractéristiques stylistiques, Index des citations patristiques.* Synthèse 17. Paris: Editions Recherche sur le Civilisations.
Borse, Udo
1966   "Der Kolosserbrieftext des Pelagius." Inaugural dissertation, Bonn. Bonn.
Bousset, Wilhelm
1894   *Textkritische Studien zum Neuen Testament: Die Recension des Hesychius.* TU 11/4. Leipzig: Hinrichs.

Bover, Joseph M., S.J.
1968   ed. *Novi Testamenti biblia graeca et latina.* 5th ed. Madrid: Consejo superior de investigaciones científicas.

Bover, Joseph M., and José O'Callaghan
1977   ed. *Nuevo Testamento trilingüe.* BAC 400. Madrid: La editorial católica.

Bray, William D.
1959   *The Weekday Lessons from Luke in the Greek Gospel Lectionary.* Studies in the Lectionary Text of the Greek New Testament 2: 5. Chicago: University of Chicago Press.

Brière, Maurice
1955   ed. *La version géorgienne ancienne de l'Evangile de Luc d'après les Evangiles d'Adich avec les variantes des Evangiles d'Opiza et de Tbet'.* PO 28: 3. Paris: Firmin-Didot.

Brock, Sebastian
1981   "The Resolution of the Philoxenian/Harclean Problem." Pp. 325-43 in Epp and Fee 1981.

Brooke, A. E.
1896   *The Commentary of Origen on S. John's Gospel.* Cambridge: Cambridge University Press.

Brooks, James A.
1991   *The New Testament Text of Gregory of Nyssa.* SBLNTGF 2. Atlanta, GA: Scholars Press.

Browne, Gerald M.
1979   ed. *Michigan Coptic Texts.* Studia et textus 7. Barcelona: Papyrologica Castroctaviana.
1982   *Griffith's Old Nubian Lectionary.* Studia et textus 8. Barcelona: Papyrologica Castroctaviana.

Bruce, Frederick Fyvie
1950   *The Books and Parchments: Some Chapters on the Transmission of the Bible.* Westwood, NJ: Revell.

Buchanan, George W.
1974   "Has the Griesbach Hypothesis Been Falsified?" *JBL* 93: 550-72.

Buck, Harry Merwyn
1958   *The Johannine Lessons in the Greek Gospel Lectionary.* Studies in the Lectionary Text of the Greek New Testament 2: 4. Chicago: University of Chicago Press.

Burgon, John William
1871   *The Last Twelve Verses of the Gospel according to S. Mark.* Oxford. Reprinted (with an introduction by Edward F. Hills), n.p.: Sovereign Grace Book Club, 1959.
1883   *The Revision Revised.* London: John Murray. Reprinted, Paradise, PA: Conservative Classics, n.d.
1896a   *The Causes of the Corruption of the Traditional Text of the Holy Gospels.* Ed. Edward Miller. London/Cambridge: Bell.

1896b   *The Traditional Text of the Holy Gospels Vindicated and Established.* Ed. Edward Miller. London: Bell.

Butler, B. C.
1951   *The Originality of St Matthew: A Critique of the Two-Document Hypothesis.* Cambridge: Cambridge University Press.

Carigliano, T.
1946   "Restitutio critica textus latini evangelii secundum Iohanneum ex scriptis S. Ambrosii." *Bib* 27: 30-64, 210-40.

Casson, Lionel, and Ernest L. Hettich
1950   *Excavations at Nessana. Volume 2: Literary Papyri.* Colt Archaeological Institute. Princeton, NJ: Princeton University Press; London: Oxford University Press.

Cavallo, Guglielmo
1967   *Ricerche sulla maiuscola biblica.* 2 vols. Studi e testi di papirologia 2. Florence: Le Monnier.

Champlin, Russell
1966   *Family E and Its Allies in Matthew.* SD 28. Salt Lake City, UT: University of Utah Press.

Clark, Kenneth Willis
1950   "The Manuscripts of the Greek New Testament." Pp. 1-24 in Parvis and Wikgren 1950.
1953   "Textual Criticism and Doctrine." Pp. 52-65 in De Zwaan 1953.
1954   "The Effect of Recent Textual Criticism upon New Testament Studies." Pp. 27-50 in *The Background of the New Testament and Its Eschatology.* Ed. W. D. Davies and D. Daube. Cambridge: Cambridge University Press. Reprinted, pp. 65-89 in Clark 1980.
1962a   "The Textual Criticism of the New Testament." Pp. 663-70 in *Peake's Commentary on the Bible.* Ed. M. Black and H. H. Rowley. London/New York: Thomas Nelson.
1962b   "The Text of the Gospel of John in Third-Century Egypt." *NovT* 5: 17-24. Reprinted, pp. 157-64 in Clark 1980.
1966   "The Theological Relevance of Textual Variation in Current Criticism of the Greek New Testament." *JBL* 85: 1-16. Reprinted, pp. 104-19 in Clark 1980.
1968   "Today's Problems with the Critical Text of the New Testament." Pp. 157-69 in Rylaarsdam 1968. Reprinted, pp. 120-32 in Clark 1980.
1980   *The Gentile Bias and Other Essays.* Selected by John L. Sharpe III. NovTSup 54. Leiden: Brill.

Clemons, James T.
1968   *An Index of Syriac Manuscripts Containing the Epistles and the Apocalypse.* SD 33. Salt Lake City, UT: University of Utah Press.

Cocroft, Ronald E.
1968   *A Study of the Pauline Lessons in the Matthean Section of the Greek Lectionary.* SD 32. Salt Lake City, UT: University of Utah Press.

Colwell, Ernest Cadman

1936   *The Four Gospels of Karahissar.* 2 vols. Chicago: University of Chicago Press.

1947   "Genealogical Method: Its Achievements and Its Limitations." *JBL* 66: 109-33. Reprinted, pp. 63-83 in Colwell 1969.

1952a   *What is the Best New Testament?* Chicago: University of Chicago Press.

1952b   "Text and Ancient Versions of the New Testament." *IB* 1.72-83.

1958   "The Significance of Grouping of New Testament Manuscripts." *NTS* 4 (1957/58) 73-92. Reprinted as "Method in Grouping New Testament Manuscripts," pp. 1-25 in Colwell 1969.

1959   "Method in Locating a Newly-Discovered Manuscript within the Manuscript Tradition of the Greek New Testament." *SE* I: 757-77. Reprinted, pp. 26-44 in Colwell 1969.

1961   "The Origin of Texttypes of New Testament Manuscripts." Pp. 128-38 in *Early Christian Origins: Studies in Honor of Harold R. Willoughby.* Ed. A. Wikgren. Chicago: Quadrangle. Reprinted as "Method in Establishing Quantitative Relationships between Text-Types of New Testament Manuscripts," pp. 56-62 in Colwell 1969.

1965   "Scribal Habits in Early Papyri: A Study in the Corruption of the Text." Pp. 370-89 in Hyatt 1965. Reprinted as "Method in Evaluating Scribal Habits: A Study of P45, P66, P75," pp. 106-24 in Colwell 1969.

1967   "External Evidence and New Testament Criticism." Pp. 1-12 in Daniels and Suggs 1967.

1968   "Hort Redivivus: A Plea and a Program." Pp. 131-56 in Rylaarsdam 1968. Reprinted, pp. 148-71 in Colwell 1969.

1969   *Studies in Methodology in Textual Criticism of the New Testament.* NTTS 9. Leiden: Brill. [Eleven of his text-critical essays]

Colwell, Ernest C., Irving Alan Sparks, Frederik Wisse, and Paul R. McReynolds

1968   "The International Greek New Testament Project: A Status Report." *JBL* 87: 187-97.

Colwell, Ernest C., and Ernst W. Tune

1963   "The Quantitative Relationships Between MS. Text-types." Pp. 25-32 in Birdsall and Thomson 1963. Reprinted as "Method in Establishing Quantitative Relationships between Text-Types of New Testament Manuscripts," pp. 56-62 in Colwell 1969.

1964   "Variant Readings: Classification and Use." *JBL* 83: 253-61. Reprinted as "Method in Classifying and Evaluating Variant Readings," pp. 96-105 in Colwell 1969.

Conybeare, Frederick Cornwallis

1902   "Three Early Doctrinal Modifications of the Text of the Gospels." *Hibbert Journal* 1: 96-113.

Cramer, J. A.

1838-44   *Catenae Graecorum Patrum in Novum Testamentum.* 8 vols. Oxford: Oxford University Press.

Dain, A.

1964   *Les Manuscrits.* Rev. ed. Collection d'études anciennes. Paris: Les Belles Lettres. [1st ed., 1949]

Daniels, Boyd L., and M. Jack Suggs

1967   ed. *Studies in the History and Text of the New Testament in Honor of Kenneth Willis Clark, Ph.D.* SD 29. Salt Lake City, UT: University of Utah Press.

Daris, Sergio

1967   ed. *Un nuovo frammento della prima lettera di Pietro (1 Petr 2,20–3,12).* Papyrologica Castroctaviana 2. Barcelona: Papyrologica Castroctaviana.

Darlow, T. H., and H. F. Moule

1903   *Historical Catalogue of the Printed Editions of Holy Scripture in the Library of the British and Foreign Bible Society.* 2 vols. in 4. London: Bible House.

Davies, Margaret

1968   *The Text of the Pauline Epistles in Manuscript 2344 and Its Relationship to the Text of Other Known Manuscripts, in Particular to 330, 436 and 462.* SD 38. Salt Lake City, UT: University of Utah Press.

Dearing, Vinton A.

1959   *A Manual of Textual Analysis.* Berkeley/Los Angeles: University of California Press.

1967   "Some Notes on Genealogical Methods in Textual Criticism," *NovT* 9: 278-97.

1974a   *Principles and Practice of Textual Analysis.* Berkeley/Los Angeles: University of California Press.

1974b   "Determining Variations by Computer," SBLSP 1974, 14-35. Cambridge, MA: Society of Biblical Literature.

1979   "New Objections to the Genealogical Method of Textual Criticism Propounded by Dom Henri Quentin." Pp. 115-19.

Dekkers, E.

1961   *Clavis Patrum Latinorum.* Brugge, Belgium: Beyaert.

Delebecque, Edouard

1980   "Les deux prologues des Actes des Apôtres." *RevThom* 80: 628-34.

1982a   "Ascension et Pentecôte dans les Actes des Apôtres selon le codex Bezae." *RevThom* 82: 79-89.

1982b   "De Lystres à Philippes (Ac 16) avec le *codex Bezae.*" *Bib* 63: 395-405.

1982c   "Paul à Thessalonique et à Bérée selon le text occidental des Actes (XVII,4-15)." *RevThom* 82: 604-16.

1983   "Les deux versions du voyage de saint Paul de Corinthe à Troas (Ac 20,3-6)." *Bib* 64: 556-64.

1986   *Les deux Actes des Apôtres.* EBib ns 6. Paris: Gabalda.

Delobel, Joël

1982   "The Sayings of Jesus in the Textual Tradition: Variant Readings in the Greek Manuscripts of the Gospels." Pp. 431-57 in *Logia: Les paroles de Jésus — The Sayings of Jesus: Mémorial Joseph Coppens.* Ed. J. Delobel. BETL 59. Louvain: Peeters; Leuven: Leuven University Press.

1984   "Jean Duplacy: Sa contribution à la critique textuelle du Nouveau Testament." *ETL* 60: 98-108.

1985   "Luke 6,5 in Codex Bezae: The Man Who Worked on Sabbath." Pp. 453-77 in *A cause de l'évangile: Mélanges offerts à Dom Jacques Dupont.* LD 123. Paris: Cerf.

1989a   "Extra-Canonical Sayings of Jesus: Marcion and Some 'Non-Received' Logia." Pp. 105-16 in Petersen 1989.

1989b   "The Lord's Prayer in the Textual Tradition: A Critique of Recent Theories and Their View on Marcion's Role." Pp. 293-309 in *The New Testament in Early Christianity: La réception des écrits néotestamentaires dans le christianisme primitif.* BETL 86. Leuven: Leuven University Press/Peeters.

De Zwaan, Johannes

1953   *Studia Paulina in honorem Johannis De Zwaan septuagenarii.* Haarlem, The Netherlands: Bohn.

Duplacy, Jean

1959a   "Citations patristiques et critique textuelle du Nouveau Testament." *RSR* 47: 391-400.

1959b   *Où en est la critique textuelle du Nouveau Testament?* Paris: Gabalda. [Originally *RSR* 45 (1957) 419-41; 46 (1958) 270-313, 431-62; continued in *RSR* 50 (1962) 242-63, 564-98; 51 (1963) 432-62; 53 (1965) 257-84; 54 (1966) 426-76; then with C. M. Martini, in *Bib* 49 (1968) 515-51; 51 (1970) 84-129; 52 (1971) 79-113; 53 (1972) 245-78; 54 (1973) 79-114; 58 (1977) 259-70, 542-68.]

1966   "Histoire des manuscrits et histoire du texte du N.T.: Quelques réflexions méthodologiques." *NTS* 12 (1965/66) 124-39. Reprinted in Duplacy 1987: 39-54.

1968   "Une tâche importante en difficulté: L'édition du Nouveau Testament grec." *NTS* 14 (1967/68) 457-68. Reprinted in Duplacy 1987: 69-80.

1970   "Les lectionnaires et l'édition du Nouveau Testament grec." Pp. 509-45 in *Mélanges bibliques en hommage au R. P. Béda Rigaux.* Ed. A. Descamps and A. de Halleux. Gembloux: Duculot. Reprinted in Duplacy 1987: 81-117.

1975   "Classification des états d'un texte, mathématiques et informatique: Repères historiques et recherches méthodologiques." *Revue d'Histoire des Textes* 5: 249-309. Reprinted in Duplacy 1987: 193-257. [With a bibliography from 1881 to 1974]

1981   "La préhistoire du texte en Luc 22:43-44." Pp. 77-86 in Epp and Fee 1981.

1987   *Etudes de critique textuelle du Nouveau Testament.* Ed. Joël

Delobel. BETL 78. Leuven: Leuven University Press/Peeters. [Twenty of his text-critical articles]

Duplacy, Jean, and M. Jack Suggs

1971   "Les citations grecques et la critique du texte du Nouveau Testament: Le passé, le présent et l'avenir." Pp. 187-213 in Benoit and Prigent 1971. Reprinted in Duplacy 1987: 123-49.

Ehrman, Bart D.

1986   *Didymus the Blind and the Text of the Gospels.* SBLNTGF 1. Atlanta: Scholars Press.

1987a   "The Use of Group Profiles for the Classification of New Testament Documentary Evidence." *JBL* 106: 465-86.

1987b   "Methodological Developments in the Analysis and Classification of New Testament Documentary Evidence." *NovT* 29: 22-45.

1988   "1 Joh 4$_3$ and the Orthodox Corruption of Scripture." *ZNW* 79: 221-43.

1989   "A Problem of Textual Circularity: The Alands on the Classification of New Testament Manuscripts." *Bib* 70: 377-88.

Eldridge, Lawrence Allen

1969   *The Gospel Text of Epiphanius of Salamis.* SD 41. Salt Lake City, UT: University of Utah Press.

Elliott, J. Keith

1968a   *The Greek Text of the Epistles to Timothy and Titus.* SD 36. Salt Lake City, UT: University of Utah Press.

1968b   "ΔΙΔΩΜΙ in 2 Timothy." *JTS* 19: 621-23.

1969   "The Use of ἕτερος in the New Testament." *ZNW* 60: 140-41.

1970   "Nouns with Diminutive Endings in the New Testament." *NovT* 12: 391-98.

1972a   "Κηφᾶς: Σίμων Πέτρος: ὁ Πέτρος: An Examination of New Testament Usage." *NovT* 14: 241-56.

1972b   "Phrynichus' Influence on the Textual Tradition of the New Testament." *ZNW* 63: 133-38.

1972c   "Rational Criticism and the Text of the New Testament." *Theology* 75: 338-43.

1973   "The United Bible Societies' Greek New Testament: An Evaluation." *NovT* 15: 278-300.

1974   "Can We Recover the Original New Testament?" *Theology* 77: 338-53.

1975a   "The United Bible Societies' Textual Commentary Evaluated." *NovT* 17: 130-50.

1975b   "A Second Look at the United Bible Societies' Greek New Testament." *BT* 26: 325-32.

1975c   "Ho baptízōn and Mark i.4." *TZ* 31: 14-15.

1976   ed. *Studies in New Testament Language and Text: Essays in Honour of George D. Kilpatrick on the Occasion of His Sixty-fifth Birthday.* NovTSup 44. Leiden: Brill.

1977   "Plaidoyer pour un éclectisme intégral appliqué a la critique tex-
            tuelle du Nouveau Testament." *RB* 84: 5-25.
1978   "In Defense of Thoroughgoing Eclecticism in New Testament Tex-
            tual Criticism." *ResQ* 21: 95-115.
1981   "An Eclectic Textual Commentary on the Greek Text of Mark's
            Gospel." Pp. 47-60 in Epp and Fee 1981.
1982   *Codex Sinaiticus and the Simonides Affair: Examination of the
            Nineteenth Century Claim That the Codex Sinaiticus Was Not an
            Ancient Manuscript.* Analecta Vlatadon 33. Thessaloniki: Patriar-
            chal Institute for Patristic Studies.
1983a   "The International Project to Establish a Critical Apparatus to
            Luke's Gospel." *NTS* 29: 531-38.
1983b   "Review of Aland and Aland 1982." *TZ* 39: 247-49.
1987   *A Survey of Manuscripts Used in Editions of the Greek New Testa-
            ment.* NovTSup 57. Leiden: Brill.
1989   *A Bibliography of Greek New Testament Manuscripts.* SNTSMS
            62. Cambridge/New York: Cambridge University Press.

Ellis, Arthur A.
1862   *Bentleii critica sacra: Notes on the Greek and Latin Text of the
            New Testament, Extracted from the Bentley MSS. in Trinity College
            Library.* Cambridge: Deighton, Bell.

Epp, Eldon Jay
1962   "The 'Ignorance Motif' in Acts and Anti-Judaic Tendencies in
            Codex Bezae." *HTR* 55: 51-62.
1965   "Some Important Textual Studies." *JBL* 84: 172-75.
1966a   *The Theological Tendency of Codex Bezae Cantabrigiensis in Acts.*
            SNTSMS 3. Cambridge/New York: Cambridge University Press.
1966b   "Coptic Manuscript G67 and the Role of Codex Bezae as a Western
            Witness in Acts." *JBL* 85: 197-212.
1967   "The Claremont Profile-Method for Grouping New Testament
            Minuscule Manuscripts." Pp. 27-38 in Daniels and Suggs 1967.
            [Chapter 11]
1974   "The Twentieth Century Interlude in New Testament Textual Criti-
            cism." *JBL* 93: 386-414. [Chapter 5]
1975   Review of Metzger 1971. *CBQ* 37: 134-36.
1976a   "The Eclectic Method in New Testament Textual Criticism: Solu-
            tion or Symptom?" *HTR* 69: 211-57. [Chapter 8]
1976b   "Textual Criticism, NT." *IDBSup*, 891-95.
1976c   "Toward the Clarification of the Term 'Textual Variant.'" Pp.
            153-73 in Elliott 1976. [Chapter 3]
1978   "A Textus Receptus Continuus?" Pp. 18-23 in *Protocol of the
            Thirty-Second Colloquy,* The Center for Hermeneutical Studies in
            Hellenistic and Modern Culture. Ed. Edward C. Hobbs. Berkeley,
            CA: Center for Hermeneutical Studies. [Cf. Kilpatrick 1978]
1979   "New Testament Textual Criticism in America: Requiem for a
            Discipline." *JBL* 98: 94-98.

1979-84   Review of Aland 1975-83. *CBQ* 41 (1979) 148-51; 42 (1980) 258-61; 46 (1984) 778-80.

1980   "A Continuing Interlude in New Testament Textual Criticism." *HTR* 73: 131-51. [Chapter 6]

1981   "The Ascension in the Textual Tradition of Luke-Acts." Pp. 131-45 in Epp and Fee 1981.

1989a   "Textual Criticism." Chapter 4, pp. 75-126 in *The New Testament and Its Modern Interpreters.* Ed. Eldon Jay Epp and †George W. MacRae, S.J. Philadelphia, PA: Fortress; Atlanta, GA: Scholars Press. [Chapter 2]

1989b   "New Testament Textual Criticism Past, Present, and Future: Reflections on the Alands' *Text of the New Testament.*" *HTR* 82: 213-29.

1989c   "The Significance of the Papyri for Determining the Nature of the New Testament Text in the Second Century: A Dynamic View of Textual Criticism." Pp. 71-103 in Petersen 1989. [Chapter 14]

1989d   "The New Testament Papyrus Manuscripts in Historical Perspective." Pp. 261-88 in *To Touch the Text: Studies in Honor of Joseph A. Fitzmyer, S.J.* Ed. Maurya P. Horgan and Paul J. Kobelski. New York: Crossroad.

1990   Review of K. and B. Aland 1987. *Int* 44: 71-75.

1991   "New Testament Papyrus Manuscripts and Letter Carrying in Greco-Roman Times." Pp. 35-56 in *The Future of Early Christianity: Essays in Honor of Helmut Koester.* Ed. Birger A. Pearson in collaboration with A. T. Kraabel, G. W. E. Nickelsburg, and N. R. Petersen. Minneapolis, MN: Fortress.

1992a   "Textual Criticism (NT)." Pp. 412-35 of vol. 6 in *The Anchor Bible Dictionary.* 6 vols. Garden City, NY: Doubleday.

1992b   "Western Text (NT)." Pp. 909-12 of vol. 6 in *The Anchor Bible Dictionary.* 6 vols. Garden City, NY: Doubleday.

1993   "The Greek Fragments of Qumran Cave 7." *The Dead Sea Scrolls: Hebrew, Aramaic, and Greek Texts with English Translations.* Princeton Theological Seminary Dead Sea Scrolls Project. Ed. James H. Charlesworth. Tübingen: Mohr-Siebeck; Louisville, KY: Westminster/John Knox [forthcoming].

Epp, Eldon Jay, and Gordon D. Fee

1981   ed. *New Testament Textual Criticism: Its Significance for Exegesis: Essays in Honour of Bruce M. Metzger.* Oxford: Clarendon Press.

Eshbaugh, Howard

1979   "Textual Variants and Theology: A Study of the Galatians Text of Papyrus 46." *JSNT* 3: 60-72.

Farmer, William Reuben

1964   *The Synoptic Problem: A Critical Analysis.* New York: Macmillan.

1974   *The Last Twelve Verses of Mark.* SNTSMS 25. Cambridge/New York: Cambridge University Press.

Fascher, Erich
  1953   *Textgeschichte als hermeneutisches Problem.* Halle (Salle): Nie-
              meyer.
Fee, Gordon D.
  1965a   "Corrections of Papyrus Bodmer II and the Nestle Greek Testa-
              ment." *JBL* 74: 66-72.
  1965b   "The Corrections of Papyrus Bodmer II and Early Textual Trans-
              mission." *NovT* 7: 247-57.
  1966   "The Significance of Papyrus Bodmer II and Papyrus Bodmer XIV-
              XV for Methodology in New Testament Textual Criticism." Unpub-
              lished Doctoral Dissertation. University of Southern California.
  1968a   "Codex Sinaiticus in the Gospel of John: A Contribution to Meth-
              odology in Establishing Textual Relationships." *NTS* 15 (1968/69)
              23-44. [Chapter 12]
  1968b   *Papyrus Bodmer II (P66): Its Textual Relationships and Scribal
              Characteristics.* SD 34. Salt Lake City, UT: University of Utah Press.
  1970a   "The Use of the Definite Article with Personal Names in the Gospel
              of John." *NTS* 17 (1970/71) 168-83.
  1970b   Review of Elliott 1968a. *JBL* 89: 505-6.
  1971a   "The Text of John in Origen and Cyril of Alexandria: A Contribu-
              tion to Methodology in the Recovery and Analysis of Patristic
              Citations." *Bib* 52: 357-94. [Chapter 15]
  1971b   "The Text of John in *The Jerusalem Bible:* A Critique of the Use
              of Patristic Citations in New Testament Textual Criticism." *JBL*
              90: 163-73. [Chapter 16]
  1971c   Review of Eldridge 1969. *JBL* 90: 368-70.
  1973a   "The *Lemma* of Origen's *Commentary on John,* Book X — an
              Independent Witness to the Egyptian Textual Tradition?" *NTS* 20
              (1973/74) 78-81.
  1973b   "Some Dissenting Notes on 7Q5 = Mark 6:52-53." *JBL* 92: 109-12.
  1974   "P75, P66, and Origen: The Myth of Early Textual Recension in
              Alexandria." Pp. 19-45 in *New Dimensions in New Testament
              Study.* Ed. Richard N. Longenecker and Merrill C. Tenney. Grand
              Rapids, MI: Zondervan. [Chapter 13]
  1976   "Rigorous or Reasoned Eclecticism — Which?" Pp. 174-97 in
              Elliott 1976. [Chapter 7]
  1978a   "A Critique of W. N. Pickering's *The Identity of the New Testament
              Text.*" *WTJ* 41: 397-423.
  1978b   "Modern Textual Criticism and the Revival of the Textus Recep-
              tus." *JETS* 21: 19-34.
  1978c   "Modern Textual Criticism and the Majority Text: A Rejoinder."
              JETS 21: 157-60.
  1978d   "The Textual Criticism of the New Testament." Pp. 127-55 in
              Biblical Criticism: Historical, Literary, and Textual, by R. K. Har-
              rison, B. K. Waltke, D. Guthrie, and G. D. Fee. Grand Rapids, MI:
              Zondervan. [Chapter 1]

1978e "Modern Textual Criticism and the Synoptic Problem." Pp. 154-69 in Orchard and Longstaff 1978. [Chapter 9]

1979 "A Critique of W. N. Pickering's *The Identity of the New Testament Text,* a Review Article." *WTJ* 41: 397-423.

1980a "A Text-Critical Look at the Synoptic Problem." *NovT* 22: 12-28.

1980b "The Text of John and Mark in the Writings of Chrysostom." *NTS* 26 (1979/80) 525-47.

1981 " 'One Thing is Needful?' Luke 10:42." Pp. 61-75 in Epp and Fee 1981.

1982a "Origen's Text of the New Testament and the Text of Egypt." *NTS* 28 (1982) 358-64.

1982b "On the Inauthenticity of John 5:3b-4." *EvQ* 54: 207-18.

1983 Review of Hodges 1982. *Trinity Journal* 4: 107-13.

1985 Review of Sturz 1984. *JETS* 28: 239-42.

1987 *The First Epistle to the Corinthians.* NICNT. Grand Rapids, MI: Eerdmans.

1992a "The Use of Greek Patristic Citations in New Testament Textual Criticism: The State of the Question." *ANRW* II/26/1: 246-65. [Chapter 17]

1992b "Textual-Exegetical Observations on 1 Corinthians 1:2, 2:1, and 2:10." Pp. 1-15 in *Scribes and Scripture: New Testament Essays in Honor of J. Harold Greenlee.* Ed. David Alan Black. Winona Lake, IN: Eisenbrauns.

Finegan, Jack

1974 *Encountering the New Testament Manuscripts: A Working Introduction to Textual Criticism.* Grand Rapids, MI: Eerdmans.

Fischer, Bonifatius

1970 "The Use of Computers in New Testament Studies, with Special Reference to Textual Criticism." *JTS* 21: 297-308.

1972 "Das Neue Testament in lateinischer Sprache: Der gegenwärtige Stand seiner Erforschung und seine Bedeutung für die griechische Textgeschichte." Pp. 1-92 in K. Aland 1972.

1985 *Lateinische Bibelhandschriften im frühen Mittelalter.* Vetus Latina: Aus der Geschichte der lateinischen Bibel 11. Freiburg: Herder.

1986 *Beiträge zur Geschichte der lateinischen Bibeltexte.* Vetus Latina: Aus der Geschichte der lateinischen Bibel 12. Freiburg: Herder. [Eight text-critical articles]

Fitzmyer, Joseph A.

1970 "The Priority of Mark and the 'Q' Source in Luke." Pp. 131-70 in *Jesus and Man's Hope.* A Perspective Book. Pittsburgh: Pittsburgh Theological Seminary.

1976-85 Review of Aland 1975-83. *JBL* 95 (1976) 679-81; 97 (1978) 604-6; 100 (1981) 147-49; 102 (1983) 639-40; 104 (1985) 360-62.

Fox, Adam

1954 *John Mill and Richard Bentley: A Study of the Textual Criticism of the New Testament 1675-1729.* Oxford: Blackwell.

Fox, Douglas J.
1979   The "Matthew-Luke Commentary" of Philoxenus: Text, Transla-
            tion and Critical Analysis. SBLDS 43. Missoula, MT: Scholars
            Press.
Frede, Hermann Josef
1961   Pelagius der irische Paulustext Sedulius Scottus. Vetus Latina: Aus
            der Geschichte der lateinischen Bibel 3. Freiburg: Herder.
1962-1971   ed. Vetus Latina: Die Reste der Altlateinischen Bibel. Vol. 24.
            Epistula ad Ephesios; Epistulae ad Philippenses et ad Colossenses.
            Freiburg: Herder. [See 1975-91 below; also Thiele]
1971   "Bibelzitate bei Kirchenvätern: Beobachtungen bei der Heraus-
            gabe der 'Vetus Latina.'" Pp. 79-96 in Benoit and Prigent.
1973   Ein Neuer Paulustext und Kommentar. 2 vols. Vetus Latina: Aus
            der Geschichte der lateinischen Bibel 7. Freiburg: Herder.
1975-91   ed. Vetus Latina: Die Reste der Altlateinischen Bibel. Vol. 25.
            Epistula ad Thessalonicenses, Timotheum, Titum, Philemonem,
            Hebraeos. Freiburg: Herder. [See 1962-71 above; also Thiele]
1981   Kirchenschriftsteller: Verzeichnis und Sigel. 3d ed. Vetus Latina
            1/1. Freiburg: Herder.
1984   Kirchenschriftsteller: Aktualisierungsheft 1984. Vetus Latina 1/1a.
            Freiburg: Herder.
1988   Kirchenschriftsteller: Aktualisierungsheft 1988. Vetus Latina 1/1b.
            Freiburg: Herder.
Frend, W. H. C.
1984   The Rise of Christianity. Philadelphia: Fortress.
Friedrichsen, George W. S.
1961   Gothic Studies. Medium Aevum Monographs 6. Oxford: Black-
            well.
Froger, J.
1968   La critique des texts et son automatisation. Initiation aux nou-
            veautés de la science 7. Paris: Dunod.
Fuller, David Otis
1970   ed. Which Bible? Grand Rapids, MI: Grand Rapids International
            Publications. 3d ed. rev. and enlarged, 1972.
1973   ed. True or False? The Westcott-Hort Textual Theory Examined.
            Grand Rapids, MI: Grand Rapids International Publications.
1975   ed. Counterfeit or Genuine: Mark 16? John 8? Grand Rapids, Mi:
            Grand Rapids International Publications.
Gallagher, J. Tim
1970   "A Study of von Soden's H-Text in the Catholic Epistles." AUSS
            8: 97-119.
Gamble, Harry Y., Jr.
1977   The Textual History of the Letter to the Romans: A Study in Textual
            and Literary Criticism. SD 42. Grand Rapids, MI: Eerdmans.
Garitte, Gérard
1955   L'ancienne version géorgienne des Actes des Apôtres d'après deux

manuscrits du Sinaï. Bibliothèque du Muséon 38. Louvain: Publications Universitaires.

Geer, Thomas C., Jr.

1988   "Codex 1739 in Acts and Its Relationship to Manuscripts 945 and 1891." *Bib* 69: 27-46.

1989   "The Two Faces of Codex 33 in Acts." *NovT* 31: 39-47.

1990   "The Presence and Significance of Lucanisms in the 'Western' Text of Acts." *JSNT* 39: 59-76.

Geerard, M.

1983-87   *Clavis Patrum Graecorum.* 4 vols. CChr. Turnhout, Belgium: Brepols.

Geerlings, Jacob

1961a   *Family 13 — The Ferrar Group: The Text according to Matthew.* SD 19. Salt Lake City, UT: University of Utah Press.

1961b   *Family 13 — The Ferrar Group: The Text according to Luke.* SD 20. Salt Lake City, UT: University of Utah Press.

1962a   *Family 13 — The Ferrar Group: The Text according to John.* SD 21. Salt Lake City, UT: University of Utah Press.

1962b   *Family Π in Luke.* SD 22. Salt Lake City, UT: University of Utah Press.

1963   *Family Π in John.* SD 23. Salt Lake City, UT: University of Utah Press.

1964   *Family Π in Matthew.* SD 24. Salt Lake City, UT: University of Utah Press.

1968a   *Family E and Its Allies in Mark.* SD 31. Salt Lake City, UT: University of Utah Press.

1968b   *Family E and Its Allies in Luke.* SD 35. Salt Lake City, UT: University of Utah Press.

Geerlings, Jacob, and Silva New

1931   "Chrysostom's Text of the Gospel of Mark." *HTR* 24: 121-42.

Globe, Alexander

1980   "Some Doctrinal Variants in Matthew 1 and Luke 2, and the Authority of the Neutral Text." *CBQ* 42: 52-72.

1983   "*The Dialogue of Timothy and Aquila* as Witness to a Pre-Caesarean Text of the Gospels." *NTS* 29 (1983) 233-46.

1984   "Serapion of Thmuis as Witness to the Gospel Text Used by Origen in Caesarea." *NovT* 26: 97-127.

Grant, Frederick Clifton

1946   "The Greek Text of the New Testament." Pp. 37-43 in *An Introduction to the Revised Standard Version of the New Testament.* Ed. Luther A. Wiegle. Chicago: International Council of Religious Education, American Standard Bible Committee.

Grant, Robert McQueen

1950   "The Citation of Patristic Evidence in an Apparatus Criticus." Pp. 117-24 in Parvis and Wikgren.

Greenlee, J. Harold
1955   *The Gospel Text of Cyril of Jerusalem.* SD 17. Copenhagen: Munksgaard.
1964   *Introduction to New Testament Textual Criticism.* Grand Rapids, MI: Eerdmans.
1968   *Nine Uncial Palimpsests of the Greek New Testament.* SD 39. Salt Lake City, UT: University of Utah Press.

Greeven, Heinrich
1981   *Synopse der drei ersten Evangelien mit Beigabe der johanneischen Parallelstellen/Synopsis of the First Three Gospels with the Addition of the Johannine Parallels.* 13th rev. ed. of Albert Huck, *Synopse.* Tübingen: Mohr-Siebeck.

Gregory, Caspar René
1900-1909   *Textkritik des Neuen Testament.* 3 vols. Leipzig: Hinrichs.
1907   *Canon and the Text of the New Testament.* International Theological Library. Edinburgh: T. & T. Clark. Eng. tr. of 1902 ed.

Grenfell, Bernard P., and Arthur S. Hunt
1898   *The Oxyrhynchus Papyri: Part I.* London: Egypt Exploration Fund.

Griesbach, Johann Jakob
1796-1806   *Novum Testamentum Graece.* 2d ed. 2 vols. London: Elmsly; Halle: Haeredes.

Griffith, John G.
1969   "Numerical Taxonomy and Some Primary Manuscripts of the Gospels." *JTS* 20: 389-406.
1973   "The Interrelations of Some Primary MSS of the Gospels in the Light of Numerical Analysis." *SE* 6: 221-38.
1984   "A Three-Dimensional Model for Classifying Arrays of Manuscripts by Cluster-Analysis." *Studia Patristica* 15: 79-83.

Grunewald, W., ed. with Klaus Junack
1986   *Das Neue Testament auf Papyrus: I. Die Katholische Briefe.* ANTF 6. Berlin/New York: de Gruyter.

Hagner Donald A.
1973   *The Use of the Old and New Testaments in Clement of Rome.* NovTSup 34. Leiden: Brill.

Hammond, C. E.
1880   *Outlines of Textual Criticism Applied to the New Testament.* 3d ed. rev. Oxford: Clarendon Press.

Hammond Bammel, Caroline P.
1985   *Der Römerbrieftext des Rufin und seine Origenes-Übersetzung.* Vetus Latina: Aus der Geschichte der lateinischen Bibel 10. Freiburg: Herder.

Harkins, Paul W.
1958   "The Text Tradition of Chrysostom's Commentary on John." *TS* 19: 404-12.

Harms, Ray
1966   *The Matthean Weekday Lessons in the Greek Gospel Lectionary.*

Studies in the Lectionary Text of the Greek New Testament 2: 6. Chicago: University of Chicago Press.

Hatch, William Henry Paine

1951   *Facsimiles and Descriptions of Minuscule Manuscripts of the New Testament.* Cambridge, MA: Harvard University Press.

Hautsch, E.

1909   *Die Evangelienzitate des Origenes.* TU 34/2. Leipzig: Hinrichs.

Henss, Walter

1967   *Das Verhältnis zwischen Diatessaron, christlicher Gnosis und "Western Text."* BZNW 33. Berlin: Töpelmann.

Higgins, A. J. B.

1986   "The Arabic Diatessaron in the New Oxford Edition of the Gospel according to St Luke in Greek." *JTS* 37: 415-19.

Hills, Edward F.

1949   "The Inter-Relationship of the Caesarean Manuscripts." *JBL* 68: 141-59.

1956   *The King James Version Defended! A Christian View of the New Testament Manuscripts.* Des Moines, IA: Christian Research Press. 2d ed. rev.: *The King James Version Defended! A Space-Age Defense of the Historic Christian Faith,* 1973. 3d ed. rev., 1978.

1970   "The Magnificent Burgon." Pp. 34-53 in Fuller 1970; pp. 86-105 in 3d ed. (Fuller 1972).

Hintze, Fritz, and Hans-Martin Schenke

1970   ed. *Die Berliner Handschrift der Sahidischen Apostelgeschichte (P. 15 926).* TU 109. Berlin: Akademie-Verlag.

Hirunuma, Toshio

1987   *New Testament Textual Studies: The Process and Development of the Discipline.* Tokyo: Yamamoto Shoten. [Text in Japanese; treats more than 100 individual scholars *seriatim* since the Gutenberg Bible]

Hodges, Zane C.

1968   "The Greek Text of the King James Version." *BSac* 125: 334-45.

1970   Reprint of 1968 in Fuller 1970: 9-22; pp. 25-38 in 3d ed. (Fuller 1972).

1971   "Rationalism and Contemporary New Testament Criticism." *BSac* 128: 27-35.

1978   "A Rejoinder." *JETS* 21: 143-56.

Hodges, Zane C., and Arthur L. Farstad

1982   ed. *The Greek New Testament according to the Majority Text.* Nashville/Camden/New York: Thomas Nelson.

Hofmann, Josef

1967   ed. *Die äthiopische Übersetzung der Johannes-Apokalypse.* CSCO 281-82, Scriptores Aethiopici 55-56. Louvain: CSCO.

1969   ed. *Die äthiopische Johannes-Apokalypse kritisch untersucht.* CSCO 297, Subsidia 33. Louvain: CSCO.

Holmes, Michael W.
1983   "The 'Majority Text Debate': New Form of an Old Issue." *Theme-lios* 8 (January 1983) 13-19.
1985   Review of Sturz 1984. *TrinityJ* 6: 225-28.
1989   Review of K. and B. Aland 1987. *JBL* 108: 139-44.
1990   "The Text of the Matthean Divorce Passages: A Comment on the Appeal to Harmonization in Textual Decisions." *JBL* 109: 651-64.

Horsley, G. H. R.
1981-87   ed. *New Documents Illustrating Early Christianity: A Review of the Greek Inscriptions and Papyri Published in 1976. . . . 1977. . . . 1978. . . . 1987.* 5 vols. to date. North Ryde, N.S.W., Australia: Ancient History Documentary Research Centre, Macquarie University.

Hort, Fenton John Anthony
1876   *Two Dissertations.* Cambridge: Macmillan.

Hoskier, Herman Charles
1914   *Codex B and Its Allies: A Study and an Indictment.* 2 vols. London: Quaritch.

Howard, Wilbert Francis
1949   *The Romance of New Testament Scholarship.* London: Epworth.

Hug, Johann Leonhard
1836   *Introduction to the New Testament.* Tr. from 3d German ed. by D. Fosdick, Jr., with notes by M. Stuart. Andover.

Hug, Joseph
1978   *La finale de l'évangile de Marc (Mc 16,9-20).* EBib. Paris: Gabalda.

Hulbert-Powell, C. L.
1938   *John James Wettstein 1693-1754: An Account of His Life, Work, and Some of His Contemporaries.* London: SPCK.

Hulley, K. K.
1944   "Principles of Textual Criticism Known to St. Jerome." *Harvard Studies in Classical Philology* 55: 87-109.

Hurtado, Larry W.
1973   "Codex Washingtonianus in the Gospel of Mark: Its Textual Relationships and Scribal Characteristics." Ph.D. dissertation. Case Western Reserve University. [Cf. 1981a]
1981a   *Text-Critical Methodology and the Pre-Caesarean Text: Codex W in the Gospel of Mark.* SD 43. Grand Rapids, MI: Eerdmans.
1981b   "The Doxology at the End of Romans." Pp. 185-99 in Epp and Fee 1981.

Husselman, Elinor M.
1962   ed. *The Gospel of John in Fayumic Coptic (P. Mich. Inv. 3521).* University of Michigan, Kelsey Museum of Archaeology Studies, 2. Ann Arbor, MI: Kelsey Museum of Archaeology.

Hyatt, J. Philip
1965   ed. *The Bible in Modern Scholarship: Papers Read at the 100th*

Meeting of the Society of Biblical Literature, December 28-30, 1964. Nashville/New York: Abingdon.

Jacquier, Eugène-Jacques

1913   *Le Nouveau Testament dans l'église chrétienne. II: Le Texte du Nouveau Testament.* 2d ed. Paris: Gabalda.

Janssen, R.

1903   *Das Johannes-Evangelium nach der Paraphrase des Nonnus Panipolitanus.* TU 23/4. Leipzig: Hinrichs.

Joussen, Anton

1969   *Die Koptischen Versionen der Apostelgeschichte (Kritik und Wertung).* BBB 34. Bonn: Hanstein.

Jülicher, Adolf

1954-72   *Itala: Das Neue Testament in altlateinischer Überlieferung.* Ed. Walter Matzkow and Kurt Aland. *Matthäus-Evangelium,* 2d ed. 1972; *Markus-Evangelium,* 2d ed. 1970; *Lucas-Evangelium,* 1954; *Johannes-Evangelium,* 1963. Berlin: de Gruyter.

Junack, Klaus

1972   "Zu den griechischen Lektionaren und ihrer Überlieferung der Katholischen Briefe." Pp. 498-591 in K. Aland 1972.

1981   "Abschreibpraktiken und Schreibergewohnheiten in ihrer Auswirkung auf die Textüberlieferung." Pp. 277-95 in Epp and Fee 1981.

Kasser, Rodolphe

1958   ed. *Papyrus Bodmer III: Evangile de Jean et Genèse I–IV,2 en Bohaïrique.* CSCO 177-78, Scriptores coptici 25-26. Louvain: CSCO.

1961   ed. *Papyrus Bodmer XVII: Actes des Apôtres, Epîtres de Jacques, Pierre, Jean et Jude.* Cologny-Genève: Bibliotheca Bodmeriana.

1962   ed. *Papyrus Bodmer XIX: Evangile de Matthieu XIV,28–XXVIII,20, Epître aux Romains I,1–II,3 en sahidique.* Cologny-Genève: Bibliotheca Bodmeriana.

1966   *L'Evangile selon Saint Jean et les Versions coptes de la Bible.* Bibliotheque théologique. Neuchâtel: Delachaux et Niestlé.

Kenyon, Frederic George

1926   *Handbook to the Textual Criticism of the New Testament.* 2d ed. London: Macmillan. 1st ed. 1912.

1933a   *Recent Developments in the Textual Criticism of the Greek Bible.* Schweich Lectures, 1932. London: British Academy.

1933b   *The Chester Beatty Biblical Papyri: Fasciculus I: General Introduction.* London: Emory Walker.

1938   "The Text of the Greek New Testament." *ExpTim* 50: 68-71.

1940   "Hesychius and the Text of the New Testament." Pp. 245-50 in *Mémorial Lagrange.* Uppsala: Seminarium Neotestamentium Upsaliense.

1949   *The Text of the Greek Bible.* Rev. ed. London: Duckworth. [Cf. 1975]

1958   *Our Bible and the Ancient Manuscripts.* Rev. by A. W. Adams. New York/Evanston, IL: Harper & Row.

1975   *The Text of the Greek Bible.* 3d ed. rev. and augmented by A. W. Adams. London: Duckworth. [Cf. 1949]

Kerschensteiner, Josef

1970   *Der altsyrische Paulustext.* CSCO 315, Subsidia 37. Louvain: CSCO.

Kieffer, René

1968   *Au delà des Recensions? L'evolution de la tradition textuelle dans Jean VI,52-71.* ConBNT 3. Lund: Gleerup.

Kilpatrick, George Dunbar

1942   Review of Legg 1940. *JTS* 43: 33.

1943   "Western Text and Original Text in the Gospels and Acts." *JTS* 44: 24-36. Reprinted in Kilpatrick 1990: 113-27.

1944   "Western Text and Original Text in the Epistles." *JTS* 45: 60-65.

1956   "Some Notes on Marcan Usage." *BT* 7: 2-9, 51-56, 146. Reprinted in Kilpatrick 1990: 128-33.

1958   ed. *Η ΚΑΙΝΗ ΔΙΑΘΗΚΗ.* 2d ed., with revised critical apparatus. London: British and Foreign Bible Society.

1960a   "διαλέγεσθαι and διαλογίζεσθαι in the New Testament." *JTS* 11: 338-40. Reprinted in Kilpatrick 1990: 189-90.

1960b   "Some Notes on Johannine Usage." *BT* 11: 173-77. Reprinted in Kilpatrick 1990: 345-50.

1963a   "An Eclectic Study of the Text of Acts." Pp. 64-77 in Birdsall and Thomson 1963. Reprinted in Kilpatrick 1990: 358-69.

1963b   "Atticism and the Text of the Greek New Testament." Pp. 125-37 in *Neutestamentliche Aufsätze: Festschrift für Prof. Josef Schmid zum 70. Geburtstag.* Ed. J. Blinzler, O. Kuss, and F. Mussner. Regensburg: Pustet. Reprinted in Kilpatrick 1990: 15-32.

1965   "The Greek New Testament Text of Today and the *Textus Receptus.*" Pp. 189-208 in *The New Testament in Historical and Contemporary Perspective: Essays in Memory of G. H. C. MacGregor.* Ed. H. Anderson and W. Barclay. Oxford: Blackwell. Reprinted in Kilpatrick 1990: 33-52.

1966   Review of the UBS[3]. *JBL* 85: 479-81.

1967a   "Style and Text in the Greek New Testament." Pp. 153-60 in Daniels and Suggs 1967. Reprinted in Kilpatrick 1990: 53-62.

1967b   "The Aorist of γαμεῖν in the New Testament." *JTS* 18: 139-40. Reprinted in Kilpatrick 1990: 187-88.

1969   "Some Problems in New Testament Text and Language." Pp. 198-208 in *Neotestamentica et Semitica: Studies in Honour of Matthew Black.* Ed. E. E. Ellis and M. Wilcox. Edinburgh: T. & T. Clark. Reprinted in Kilpatrick 1990: 229-40.

1970   "Language and Text in the Gospels and Acts." *VC* 24: 161-71.

1978a   "A Textus Receptus Redivivus?" Pp. 1-15 in *Protocol of the Thirty-Second Colloquy,* The Center for Hermeneutical Studies in Hellenistic and Modern Culture. Ed. Edward C. Hobbs. Berkeley, CA: Center for Hermeneutical Studies.

1978b "Griesbach and the Development of Text Criticism." Pp. 136-53 in Orchard and Longstaff 1978.

1981 "Conjectural Emendation in the New Testament." Pp. 349-60 in Epp and Fee 1981. Reprinted in Kilpatrick 1990: 98-109.

1990 *The Principles and Practice of New Testament Textual Criticism: Collected Essays of G. D. Kilpatrick.* Ed. J. K. Elliott. BETL 96. Leuven, Belgium: Leuven University Press/Peeters.

Kim, K. W.

1949 "The Matthean Text of Origen in His *Commentary on Matthew.*" *JBL* 68: 125-39.

1950 "Origen's Text of John in His *On Prayer, Commentary on Matthew, and Against Celsus.*" *JTS* ns 1: 74-84.

Kim, Young Kyu

1988 "Palaeographical Dating of P46 to the Later First Century." *Bib* 69: 248-57.

Klijn, Albertus Frederik Johannes

1949 *A Survey of the Researches into the Western Text of the Gospels and Acts.* Utrecht: Kemink.

1966 "In Search of the Original Text of Acts." Pp. 103-10 in *Studies in Luke-Acts: Essays Presented in Honor of Paul Schubert.* Ed. L. E. Keck and J. L. Martyn. Nashville/New York: Abingdon.

1969 *A Survey of the Researches into the Western Text of the Gospels and Acts: Part Two 1949-1969.* NovTSup 21. Leiden: Brill.

1986 "Jewish Christianity in Egypt." Pp. 161-75 in *The Roots of Egyptian Christianity.* Ed. B. A. Pearson and J. E. Goehring. Studies in Antiquity and Christianity. Philadelphia: Fortress.

Koester, Helmut

1982 *Introduction to the New Testament. Volume Two: History and Literature of Early Christianity.* Philadelphia: Fortress; Berlin/New York: de Gruyter.

1985 "The Text of 1 Thessalonians." Pp. 219-27 in *The Living Text: Essays in Honor of Ernest W. Saunders.* Ed. D. E. Groh and R. Jewett. Lanham/New York/London: University Press of America.

Kubo, Sakae

1965 *P72 and the Codex Vaticanus.* SD 27. Salt Lake City, UT: University of Utah Press.

1976 "Textual Relationships in Jude." Pp. 276-82 in Elliott 1976.

Kümmel, Werner G.

1955 "New Testament Research and Teaching in Present Day Germany." *NTS* 1 (1954/55) 229-34.

1966 *Introduction to the New Testament.* 14th rev. ed. of P. Feine and J. Behm. Nashville: Abingdon.

1972 *The New Testament: The History of the Investigation of Its Prob-*

lems. Tr. by S. McLean Gilmour and Howard C. Kee. Nashville/New York: Abingdon.

Kunst, Hermann

1979   ed. *Bericht der Hermann Kunst-Stiftung zur Förderung der neutestamentlichen Textforschung für die Jahre 1977 bis 1979.* Münster/W.: Hermann Kunst-Stiftung.

1985   ed. *Bericht der Hermann Kunst-Stiftung zur Förderung der neutestamentlichen Textforschung für die Jahre 1982 bis 1984.* Münster/W.: Hermann Kunst-Stiftung.

1988   ed. *Bericht der Hermann Kunst-Stiftung zur Förderung der neutestamentlichen Textforschung für die Jahre 1985 bis 1987.* Münster/W.: Hermann Kunst-Stiftung.

1992   ed. *Bericht der Hermann Kunst-Stiftung zur Förderung der neutestamentlichen Textforschung für die Jahre 1988 bis 1991.* Münster/W.: Hermann Kunst-Stiftung.

Lachmann, Karl

1830   "Rechenschaft über seine Ausgabe des Neuen Testaments von Professor Lachmann in Berlin." *TSK* 3: 817-45.

Lagrange, Marie-Joseph

1935   *Critique textuelle. II: La critique rationnelle.* EBib. Paris: Gabalda.

Lake, Kirsopp

1902   *Codex 1 of the Gospels and Its Allies.* TextsS 7: 3. Cambridge: Cambridge University Press.

1928   *The Text of the New Testament.* Oxford Church Text Books. 6th ed. rev. by Silva New. London: Rivingtons.

Lake, Kirsopp, Robert P. Blake, and Silva New

1928   "The Caesarean Text of the Gospel of Mark." *HTR* 21: 207-404.

Lake, Kirsopp, and Silva Lake

1941   *Family 13 (The Ferrar Group): The Text according to Mark, with a Collation of Codex 28 of the Gospels.* SD 11. London: Christophers.

Lake, Silva

1937   *Family Π and the Codex Alexandrinus: The Text according to Mark.* SD 5. London: Christophers.

Legg, S. C. E.

1935   ed. *Nouum Testamentum graece secundum textum Westcotto-Hortianum: Euangelium secundum Marcum.* Oxford: Clarendon Press.

1940   ed. *Nouum Testamentum graece secundum textum Westcotto-Hortianum: Euangelium secundum Matthaeum.* Oxford: Clarendon Press.

Leloir, Louis

1953-54   *Saint Ephrem: Commentaire de l'Evangile concordant, version arménienne.* 2 vols. CSCO 137, 145, Scriptores armeniaci 1-2. Louvain: CSCO.

1958   *L'Evangile d'Ephrem d'après les oeuvres éditées: Recueil des Textes.* CSCO 180, Subsidia 12. Louvain: CSCO.

| 1962 | *Le Témoignage d'Ephrem sur le Diatessaron.* CSCO 227, Subsidia 19. Louvain: CSCO. |

1962   *Le Témoignage d'Ephrem sur le Diatessaron.* CSCO 227, Subsidia 19. Louvain: CSCO.

1963   *Saint Ephrem: Commentaire de l'Evangile concordant, texte syriaque (Manuscrit Chester Beatty 709).* Chester Beatty Monographs, 8. Dublin: Hodges Figgis.

1967   *Citations du Nouveau Testament dans l'ancienne tradition arménienne.* 2 vols. CSCO 283-84, Subsidia 31-32. Louvain: CSCO.

Lewis, Naphtali

1974   *Papyrus in Classical Antiquity.* Oxford: Clarendon Press.

1986   *Greeks in Ptolemaic Egypt: Case Studies in the Social History of the Hellenistic World.* Oxford: Clarendon Press.

Lo Bue, Francesco

1963   ed. *The Turin Fragments of Tyconius' Commentary on Revelation.* TextsS ns 7. Cambridge: Cambridge University Press.

Luck, Georg

1981   "Textual Criticism Today." *AJP* 102: 164-94.

Lyonnet, Stanislas, S.J.

1950   *Les origines de la version arménienne et le Diatessaron.* BibOr 13. Rome: Biblical Institute Press.

McReynolds, Paul R.

1972   "The Value and Limitations of the Claremont Profile Method." SBLSP 1.1-7.

1979   "Establishing Text Families." Pp. 97-113 in O'Flaherty.

Manson, Thomas William

1942   Review of Legg 1940. *JTS* 43: 88-89.

Markham, Robert P., and Eugene A. Nida

1966   *An Introduction to the Bible Societies' Greek New Testament.* New York: United Bible Societies.

Martin, Victor

1956   ed. *Papyrus Bodmer II: Evangile de Jean chap. 1–14.* Cologny-Genève: Bibliotheca Bodmeriana.

1962   ed. *Papyrus Bodmer II: Supplement: Evangile de Jean chap. 14–21.* New ed. (with Facsimiles). Cologny-Genève: Bibliotheca Bodmeriana.

Martin, Victor, and Rodolphe Kasser

1961a   ed. *Papyrus Bodmer XIV: Evangile de Luc chap. 3–24 (P75).* Cologny-Genève: Bibliotheca Bodmeriana.

1961b   ed. *Papyrus Bodmer XV: Evangile de Jean chap. 1–15 (P75).* Cologny-Genève: Bibliotheca Bodmeriana.

Martini, Carlo M.

1966   *Il problema della recensionalità del codice B alla luca del papiro Bodmer XIV.* AnBib 26. Rome: Biblical Institute Press.

1974   "Eclecticism and Atticism in the Textual Criticism of the Greek New Testament." Pp. 149-56 in *On Language, Culture, and Religion: In Honor of Eugene A. Nida.* Ed. M. Black and W. A. Smalley. The Hague/Paris: Mouton.

1976   "Text, NT." *IDBSup:* 884-86.

1978   "Is There a Late Alexandrian Text of the Gospels?" *NTS* 24 (1977/78) 185-96.

1980   *La parola di Dio alle origini della Chiesa.* AnBib 93. Rome: Biblical Institute Press.

1981   "The 'Harder Reading' in Textual Criticism: An Application of the Second Law of Thermodynamics." *BT* 32: 101-7.

Mastricht, Gerhard von

1711   ed. *Η ΚΑΙΝΗ ΔΙΑΘΗΚΗ, Novum Testamentum . . . ac tandem Crisis Perpetua, qua singulas Variantes earumque valorem aut originem ad XLIII. Canones examinate G. D. T. M. D.* [Gerhardus de Trajecto Mosae Doctor]. Amsterdam: ex officina Wetsteniana.

Mees, Michael

1968   "Lectio brevior in Johannesevangelium und ihre Beziehung zum Urtext." *BZ* 12: 111-19.

1970   *Die Zitate aus dem Neuen Testament bei Clemens von Alexandrien.* Quaderni di "Vetera Christianorum" 2. Bari: Istituto di Letteratura Cristiana Antica.

1975   *Ausserkanonische Parallelstellen zu den Herrenworten und ihre Bedeutung.* Quaderni di "Vetera Christianorum" 10. Bari: Istituto di Letteratura Cristiana Antica.

Menoud, Philippe Henri

1951   "The Western Text and the Theology of Acts." *Studiorum Novi Testamenti Societas, Bulletin* 2: 19-32. Reprinted in *Bulletin of the Studiorum Novi Testamenti Societas I-III.* Cambridge: Cambridge University Press, 1963. Also pp. 61-83 in Menoud, *Jesus Christ and the Faith: A Collection of Studies.* PTMS 18. Pittsburgh: Pickwick, 1978.

Merk, Augustinus, S.J.

1964   ed. *Novum Testamentum graece et latine.* 9th ed. Rome: Biblical Institute Press.

Messina, Giuseppe, S.J.

1951   *Diatessaron Persiano.* BibOr 14. Rome: Biblical Institute Press.

Metzger, Bruce Manning

1945   "The Caesarean Text of the Gospels." *JBL* 64: 457-89. Reprinted in Metzger 1963: 42-72.

1955a   *Annotated Bibliography of the Textual Criticism of the New Testament 1914-1939.* SD 16. Copenhagen: Munksgaard.

1955b   "A Survey of Recent Research on the Ancient Versions of the New Testament." *NTS* 2 (1955/56) 1-16.

1959   "Recent Discoveries and Investigations of New Testament Manuscripts." *JBL* 78: 13-20.

1963a   "Explicit References in the Works of Origen to Variant Readings in New Testament Manuscripts." Pp. 78-95 in Birdsall and Thomson 1963. Reprinted in Metzger 1968: 88-103.

1963b   *Chapters in the History of New Testament Textual Criticism.* NTTS 4. Leiden: Brill. [Seven text-critical essays]

1965   "Recent Contributions to the Study of the Ancient Versions of the New Testament." Pp. 357-69 in Hyatt 1965.

1966   "The Textual Criticism of the New Testament." *ExpTim* 78: 324-27, 372-75.

1968a   *The Text of the New Testament: Its Transmission, Corruption, and Restoration.* 2d ed. Oxford/New York: Oxford University Press. 1st ed., 1964; 3d ed., 1992.

1968b   *Historical and Literary Studies: Pagan, Jewish, and Christian.* NTTS 8. Leiden: Brill. [Includes six text-critical studies]

1971   ed. (for the Editorial Committee) *A Textual Commentary on the Greek New Testament: A Companion Volume to the United Bible Societies' Greek New Testament (Third Edition).* London/New York: United Bible Societies.

1972   "Patristic Evidence and the Textual Criticism of the New Testament." *NTS* 18 (1971/72) 379-400. Reprinted in Metzger 1980: 167-88.

1975   "The Practice of Textual Criticism among the Church Fathers." *Studia Patristica* 12: 340-49. Reprinted in Metzger 1980: 189-98.

1977   *The Early Versions of the New Testament: Their Origin, Transmission, and Limitations.* Oxford: Clarendon Press.

1979   "St. Jerome's Explicit References to Variant Readings in Manuscripts of the New Testament." Pp. 179-90 in Best and Wilson 1979. Reprinted in Metzger 1980: 199-21.

1980   *New Testament Studies: Philological, Versional, and Patristic.* NTTS 10. Leiden: Brill. [Includes eight text-critical studies]

1981   *Manuscripts of the Greek Bible: An Introduction to Greek Palaeography.* New York/Oxford: Oxford University Press.

Michaelis, J. D.

1802   *Introduction to the New Testament.* Tr. H. Marsh. 2d ed. London.

Miller, Edward

1894   ed. *A Plain Introduction to the Criticism of the New Testament,* by F. H. A. Scrivener. 4th ed. 2 vols. New York: Bell.

Moir, Ian A.

1956   *"Codex Climaci Rescriptus Graecus": A Study of Portions of the Greek New Testament Comprising the Underwriting of Part of a Palimpsest in the Library of Westminster College, Cambridge (Ms. Gregory 1561, L).* TextsS ns 2. Cambridge: Cambridge University Press.

1968   "The Bible Societies' Greek New Testament." *NTS* 14 (1967/68) 136-43.

1976   "The Text of Ephesians Exhibited by Minuscule Manuscripts Housed in Great Britain — Some Preliminary Comments." Pp. 313-18 in Elliott 1976.

1981a   "Can We Risk Another 'Textus Receptus'?" *JBL* 100: 614-18.

1981b "Orthography and Theology: The Omicron-Omega Interchange in Romans 5:1 and Elsewhere." Pp. 179-99 in Epp and Fee 1981.

Molitor, Joseph
1965 *Synopsis latina evangeliorum Ibericorum antiquissimorum secundum Matthaeum, Marcum, Lucam desumpta e codicibus Adysh, Opiza, Tbeth necnon e fragmentis biblicis et patristicis quae dicuntur Chanmeti et Haemeti.* CSCO 256, Subsidia 24. Louvain: CSCO.
1968 *Grundbegriffe der Jesusüberlieferung im Lichte ihrer orientalischen Sprachgeschichte.* Kommentare und Beiträge zum Alten und Neuen Testament. Düsseldorf: Patmos.

Mollat, D.
1960 *L'Evangile et les Epîtres de S. Jean.* La Saint Bible. 2d ed. Paris. 1st ed., 1954.

Morgan, Richard S.
1970 "Optical Readers: 1970." *Computers and the Humanities* 5 (1970/71) 75-78.

Muncey, R. W.
1959 *The New Testament Text of Saint Ambrose.* TextsS 4. Cambridge: Cambridge University Press.

Murphy, Harold S.
1954 "Eusebius' NT Text in the *Demonstratio Evangelica*." *JBL* 73: 162-68.

Nellessen, Ernst
1965 *Untersuchungen zur altlateinischen Überlieferung des ersten Thessalonicherbriefes.* BBB 22. Bonn: Hanstein.

Nestle, Eberhard
1901 *Introduction to the Textual Criticism of the Greek New Testament.* London: Williams and Norgate. [Tr. from 2d German ed.]

New, Silva [later, Silva Lake]
1932 "A Patmos Family of Gospel Manuscripts." *HTR* 25: 85-92.

O'Callaghan, José, S.J.
1970 *"Nomina Sacra" in papyris graecis saeculi III neotestamentariis.* AnBib 46. Rome: Biblical Institute Press.

O'Flaherty, Wendy Doniger
1979 ed. *The Critical Study of Sacred Texts.* Berkeley, CA: Berkeley Religious Studies Series. Graduate Theological Union.

Oliver, Harold H.
1962 "Present Trends in the Textual Criticism of the New Testament." *JBR* 30: 308-20.

Omanson, Roger L.
1983 "A Perspective on the Study of the New Testament Text." *BT* 34: 107-22.

Orchard, Bernard
1976 "J. A. T. Robinson and the Synoptic Problem." *NTS* 22 (1975/76) 346-52.

Orchard, Bernard, and Thomas R. W. Longstaff
1978   ed. *J. J. Griesbach: Synoptic and Text-Critical Studies 1776-1976.* SNTSMS 34. Cambridge/New York: Cambridge University Press.

Orlandi, Tito
1974   ed. *Papiri della Università degli Studi di Milano (P. Mil. Copti). Volume Quinto: Lettere di San Paolo in Copto-Ossirinchita.* Milan: Istituto Editoriale Cisalpino-La Goliardica.

Ortiz de Urbina, Ignatius, S.J.
1967   ed. *Vetus Evangeliorum Syrorum et exinde excerptum Diatessaron Tatiani.* Biblia Polyglotta Matritensia 6. Madrid: Consejo Superior de investigaciones científicas.

Osburn, Carroll D.
1981   "The Text of 1 Corinthians 10:9." Pp. 201-12 in Epp and Fee 1981.
1982   "The Text of the Pauline Epistles in Hippolytus of Rome." *SecCent* 2: 97-124.

Ott, Wilhelm
1973   "Computer Applications in Textual Criticism." Pp. 199-223 in *Computer and Literary Studies.* Ed. A. J. Aitken, R. W. Bailey, and N. Hamilton-Smith. Edinburgh: Edinburgh University Press.

Pack, Frank
1948   "The Methodology of Origen as a Textual Critic in Arriving at the Text of the New Testament." Unpublished Dissertation. University of Southern California.
1960   "Origen's Evaluation of Textual Variants in the Greek Bible." *ResQ* 4: 139-46.

Parker, David C.
1977   "The Development of Textual Criticism since B. H. Streeter." *NTS* 24 (1977/78) 149-62.
1990   "The International Greek New Testament Project: The Gospel of John." *NTS* 36 (1990) 157-60.

Palmer, Humphrey
1968   *The Logic of Gospel Criticism: An Account of the Methods and Arguments Used by Textual, Documentary, Source, and Form Critics of the New Testament.* London: Macmillan; New York: St. Martin's Press.

Parvis, Merrill M.
1947   "New Testament Criticism in the World-Wars Period." Pp. 52-73 in *The Study of the Bible Today and Tomorrow.* Ed. H. R. Willoughby. Chicago: University of Chicago Press.
1950   "The International Project to Establish a New Critical Apparatus of the Greek New Testament." *Crozer Quarterly* 27: 301-8.
1962   "Text, NT." *IDB* 4.594-614.

Parvis, Merrill M., and Allen P. Wikgren
1950   ed. *New Testament Manuscript Studies: The Materials and the Making of a Critical Apparatus.* Chicago: University of Chicago Press.

Pearson, Birger
    1986   "Earliest Christianity in Egypt: Some Observations." Pp. 132-59 in *The Roots of Egyptian Christianity*. Ed. B. A. Pearson and J. E. Goehring. Studies in Antiquity and Christianity. Philadelphia: Fortress.

Pervo, Richard I.
    1985   "Social and Religious Aspects of the 'Western Text.'" Pp. 229-41 in *The Living Text: Essays in Honor of Ernest W. Saunders*. Ed. D. E. Groh and R. Jewett. Lanham/New York/London: University Press of America.

Petersen, William Lawrence
    1985   *The Diatessaron and Ephrem Syrus as Sources of Romanos the Melodist*. CSCO 475, Subsidia 74. Louvain: CSCO/Peeters.
    1988   Review of IGNTP, *The New Testament in Greek: The Gospel according to Luke. JBL* 107: 758-62.
    1989   ed. *Gospel Traditions in the Second Century: Origins, Recensions, Text, and Transmission*. Christianity and Judaism in Antiquity 3. Notre Dame, IN: University of Notre Dame Press.

Petzer, Jacobus Hendrik = Kobus
    1986   "The Papyri and New Testament Textual Criticism: Clarity or Confusion?" Pp. 18-31 in *A South African Perspective on the New Testament: Essays by South African New Testament Scholars Presented to Bruce Manning Metzger*. Ed. J. H. Petzer and P. J. Hartin. Leiden: Brill.
    1988   "Shifting Sands: The Changing Paradigm in New Testament Textual Criticism." Pp. 394-408 in *Paradigms and Progress in Theology*. Ed. J. Mouton, A. G. van Aarde, and W. S. Vorster. Pretoria: Human Sciences Research Council.
    1990a   *Die teks van die Nuwe Testament: 'n Inleiding in die basiese aspekte van die teorie en praktyk van die tekskritiek van die Nuwe Testament*. Hervormde Teologiese Studies, Supplementum 2. Pretoria: Universiteit van Pretoria.
    1990b   "A Survey of the Developments in the Textual Criticism of the Greek New Testament since UBS[3]." *Neot* 24: 71-92.
    1990c   "Author's Style and the Textual Criticism of the New Testament." *Neot* 24: 185-97.
    1991a   "Eclecticism and the Text of the New Testament." Pp. 47-62 in *Text and Interpretation: New Approaches in the Criticism of the New Testament*. Ed. P. J. Hartin and J. H. Petzer. NTTS 15. Leiden: Brill.
    1991b   "Style and Text in the Lucan Narrative of the Institution of the Lord's Supper (Luke 22.19b-20)." *NTS* 37 (1991) 113-29.

Pickering, Wilbur N.
    1977   *The Identity of the New Testament Text*. Nashville: Thomas Nelson.
    1978   "'Queen Anne . . .' and All That: A Response." *JETS* 21: 165-68.

Porter, Calvin L.

1961   "A Textual Analysis of the Earliest Manuscripts of the Gospel of John." Unpublished Doctoral Dissertation. Duke University.

1962   "Papyrus Bodmer XV (P75) and the Text of Codex Vaticanus." *JBL* 81: 363-76.

1966   "John IX. 38, 39a: A Liturgical Addition to the Text." *NTS* 13 (1966/67) 387-94.

Quasten, Johannes

1960   *Patrology.* 3 vols. Utrecht: Spectrum.

Quecke, Hans

1972   ed. *Das Markusevangelium saïdisch: Text der Handschrift PPalau Rib. Inv.-Nr. 182 mit den Varianten der Handschrift M 569.* Studia et textus 4. Barcelona: Papyrologica Castroctaviana.

1977   ed. *Das Lukasevangelium saïdisch: Text der Handschrift PPalau Rib. Inv.-Nr. 181 mit den Varianten der Handschrift M 569.* Studia et textus 6. Barcelona: Papyrologica Castroctaviana.

1984   ed. *Das Johannesevangelium saïdisch: Text der Handschrift PPalau Rib. Inv.-Nr. 183 mit den Varianten der Handschrift M 813 und 814 der Chester Beatty Library und der Handschrift M 569.* Studia et textus 11. Barcelona: Papyrologica Castroctaviana.

Quispel, Gilles

1975   *Tatian and the Gospel of Thomas: Studies in the History of the Western Diatessaron.* Leiden: Brill.

Reuss, Joseph

1957   *Matthäus-Kommentare aus der grieschischen Kirche aus Katenen-handschriften.* TU 61. Berlin: Akademie-Verlag.

1966   *Johannes-Kommentare aus der grieschischen Kirche aus Katenen-handschriften.* TU 89. Berlin: Akademie-Verlag.

1984   *Lukas-Kommentare aus der grieschischen Kirche aus Katenen-handschriften.* TU 130. Berlin: Akademie-Verlag.

Rhodes, Erroll F.

1959   *An Annotated List of Armenian New Testament Manuscripts.* Annual Report of Theology, Monograph Series 1. Tokyo: Rikkyo (St. Paul's) University.

1970   "Text of NT in Jerusalem and New English Bibles." *CBQ* 32: 41-57.

1981   "Conjectural Emendations in Modern Translations." Pp. 361-74 in Epp and Fee 1981.

Rice, George E.

1980a   "The Anti-Judaic Bias of the Western Text in the Gospel of Luke." *AUSS* 18: 51-57.

1980b   "Some Further Examples of Anti-Judaic Bias in the Western Text of the Gospel of Luke." *AUSS* 18: 149-56.

1984   "Western Non-interpolations: A Defense of the Apostolate." Pp. 1-16 in *Luke-Acts: New Perspectives from the Society of Biblical Literature Seminar.* Ed. C. H. Talbert. New York: Crossroad.

1985 "Is Bezae a Homogeneous Codex?" Pp. 39-54 in *Perspectives on the New Testament: Essays in Honor of Frank Stagg*. Ed. C. H. Talbert. Macon, GA: Mercer University Press.

Richards, William Larry

1974 "Textual Criticism on the Greek Text of the Catholic Epistles: A Bibliography." *AUSS* 12: 103-11. Continued (under different titles) in *AUSS* 13 (1975) 261-72 and 14 (1976) 301-11.

1977a *The Classification of the Greek Manuscripts of the Johannine Epistles*. SBLDS 35. Missoula, MT: Scholars Press.

1977b "A Critique of a New Testament Text-critical Methodology — the Claremont Profile Method." *JBL* 96: 555-66.

1979 "Manuscript Grouping in Luke 10 by Quantitative Analysis." *JBL* 98: 379-91.

1980 "An Examination of the Claremont Profile Method in the Gospel of Luke: A Study in Text-Critical Methodology." *NTS* 27 (1980/81) 52-63.

1983 "Gregory 1175: Alexandrian or Byzantine in the Catholic Epistles?" *AUSS* 21: 155-68.

Riddle, Donald W.

1936 "Textual Criticism as a Historical Discipline." *ATR* 18: 220-33.

Roberts, Colin H.

1935 *An Unpublished Fragment of the Fourth Gospel in the John Rylands Library*. Manchester: Manchester University Press.

1956 *Greek Literary Hands 350 B.C.–A.D. 400*. Oxford: Clarendon Press.

1970 "Books in the Graeco-Roman World and in the New Testament." Pp. 48-66 in *The Cambridge History of the Bible. Volume 1: From the Beginnings to Jerome*. Ed. P. R. Ackroyd and C. F. Evans. Cambridge: Cambridge University Press.

1979 *Manuscript, Society and Belief in Early Christian Egypt*. Schweich Lectures, 1977. London: Oxford University Press.

Roberts, Colin H., and T. C. Skeat.

1983 *The Birth of the Codex*. London: Oxford University Press.

Robinson, James M.

1990 *The Pachomian Monastic Library at the Chester Beatty Library and the Bibliothèque Bodmer*. Occasional Papers 19. Claremont, CA: Institute for Antiquity and Christianity.

Robinson, James M., et al.

1970 "The Institute for Antiquity and Christianity: International Greek New Testament Project." *NTS* 16 (1969/70) 180-82.

Robinson, James M., and Helmut Koester

1971 *Trajectories through Early Christianity*. Philadelphia: Fortress.

Roca-Puig, Ramon

1962 ed. *Un papiro griego del evangelo de san Mateo*. 2d ed., with a note by Colin Roberts. Barcelona: Gremio Sindical de Maestros Impresores.

Rolando, G. M.
1945   "Ricostruzione teologico-critica del testo latino del Vangelo di S. Luca usato da S. Ambrogio." *Bib* 26 (1945) 238-76; 27 (1946) 3-17.

Royse, James R.
1979   "Scribal Habits in the Transmission of New Testament Texts." Pp. 139-61 in O'Flaherty 1979.
1981   "Scribal Habits in Early Greek New Testament Papyri." Unpublished Doctoral Dissertation. Graduate Theological Union.
1983   "The Treatment of Scribal Leaps in Metzger's *Textual Commentary*." *NTS* 29 (1983) 539-51.

Rylaarsdam, J. Coert
1968   *Transitions in Biblical Scholarship.* Essays in Divinity 6. Chicago: University of Chicago Press.

Sacchi, Paolo
1956   *Alle origini del Nuovo Testamento: Saggio per la storia della tradizione e la critica del testo.* Pubblicazioni della Università degli studi di Firenze Facoltà di Lettere e Filosofia 4 ser.: 2. Florence: Felice Le Monnier.

Salmon, Victor
1976   *The Fourth Gospel: A History of the Textual Tradition of the Original Greek Gospel.* Tr. M. J. O'Connell. Collegeville, MN: Liturgical. [French original, 1969]

Sanday, William, and C. H. Turner
1923   *Novum Testamentum Sancti Irenaei Episcopi Lugdunensis . . . Edited from the MSS with Introductions, Apparatus, Notes, and Appendices.* Old-Latin Biblical Texts 7. Oxford: Clarendon Press.

Sanders, Ed Parish
1969   *The Tendencies of the Synoptic Tradition.* SNTSMS 9. Cambridge/New York: Cambridge University Press.

Sanders, Henry A.
1912   *The New Testament Manuscripts in the Freer Collection. Part I: The Washington Manuscript of the Four Gospels.* New York: Macmillan.
1918   *The New Testament Manuscripts in the Freer Collection. Part II: The Washington Manuscript of the Epistles of Paul.* New York: Macmillan.
1926   "An Early Papyrus Fragment of the Gospel of Matthew in the Michigan Collection." *HTR* 19: 215-26.

Sanz, Peter
1946   ed. *Griechische literarische Papyri christlichen Inhaltes I (Biblica, Väterschriften und Verwandtes).* Mitteilungen aus der Papyrussammlung der Nationalbibliothek in Wien, ns 4. Baden bei Wien: Rohrer.

Schaff, Philip
1903   *A Companion to the Greek Testament and the English Version.* New York/London: Harper.

Schenke, Hans-Martin
1981   ed. *Das Matthäus-Evangelium im mittelägyptischen Dialekt des Koptischen (Codex Scheide)*. TU 127. Berlin: Akademie-Verlag.

Schmid, Josef
1955-56   *Studien zur Geschichte des griechischen Apokalypse-Textes*. Münchener Theologische Studien, Historische Abteilung 1. Ergänzungsband. 3 vols. Munich: Karl Zink.

Scrivener, Frederick Henry Ambrose
1894   *A Plain Introduction to the Criticism of the New Testament*. 4th ed. by E. Miller. 2 vols. London: G. Bell.

Shepherd, Massey Hamilton, Jr., and Sherman Elbridge Johnson
1946   ed. *Munera studiosa*. Cambridge, MA: Episcopal Theological School. [Festschrift W. H. P. Hatch]

Silva, Moisés
1985   "Internal Evidence in the Text-Critical Use of the LXX." Pp.151-67 in *La Septuaginta en la investigacion contemporanea (V Congreso de la IOSCS)*. Ed. N. F. Marcos. Madrid: Consejo superior de investigaciones científicas.
1988   Review of K. and B. Aland 1987. *WTJ* 50: 195-200.

Smyth, Herbert Weir
1956   *Greek Grammar*. Rev. ed. Cambridge, MA: Harvard University Press. 1st ed., 1920.

Souter, Alexander
1947   ed. *Novvm Testamentvm Graece: Textvi retractatoribvs anglis adhibito brevem adnotationem criticam svbiectit*. 2d ed. Oxford: Clarendon Press.

Staal, Harvey
1969   *Codex Sinai Arabic 151: Pauline Epistles*. 2 vols. SD 40. Salt Lake City, UT: University of Utah Press.

Stählin, Otto
1926   "Zur Vorbereitung des neuen Tischendorf." *ZNW* 25: 165-68.

Strecker, Georg
1978   "Eine Evangelienharmonie bei Justin und Pseudoklemens." *NTS* 24 (1977/78) 297-316.

Streeter, Burnett Hillman
1924   *The Four Gospels: A Study of Origins, Treating of the Manuscript Tradition, Sources, Authorship, & Dates*. London: Macmillan.

Strothmann, Werner
1971   *Das Wolfenbütteler tetraevangelium syriacum: Lesarten und Lesungen*. Göttinger Orientforschungen, 1st series: Syriaca 2. Wiesbaden: Harrassowitz.

Strugnell, John
1971   "A Plea for Conjectural Emendation in the New Testament, with a Coda on 1 Cor 4:6." *CBQ* 36: 543-58.

Sturz, Harry A.
1984   *The Byzantine Text-Type and New Testament Textual Criticism.*
            Nashville/Camden/New York: Thomas Nelson.

Suggs, M. Jack
1958   "The Use of Patristic Evidence in the Search for a Primitive New
            Testament Text." *NTS* 4 (1957/58) 139-47.

Swanson, Reuben J.
1970   Review of Mees 1970. *JBL* 89: 519.

Talbert, Charles H., and Edgar V. McKnight
1972   "Can the Griesbach Hypothesis Be Falsified?" *JBL* 91: 338-68.

Tasker, R. V. G.
1936   "The Text of the Fourth Gospel Used by Origen in His Commen-
            tary on John." *JTS* 37: 146-55.

1964   ed. *The Greek New Testament, Being the Text Translated in the
            New English Bible.* London: Oxford University Press; Cambridge:
            Cambridge University Press.

Taylor, Vincent
1963   *The Text of the New Testament: A Short Introduction.* 2d ed. Lon-
            don: Macmillan.

Tcherikover, Victor A., and Alexander Fuks
1957-64   *Corpus Papyrorum Judaicarum.* 3 vols. Cambridge, MA: Harvard
            University Press.

Testuz, Michel
1959   ed. *Papyrus Bodmer VII-IX. VII: L'Epître de Jude, VIII: Les deux
            Epîtres de Pierre, IX: Les Psaumes 33 et 34.* Cologny-Genève:
            Bibliotheca Bodmeriana.

Thiele, Walter
1956-69   ed. *Die Reste der altlateinischen Bibel.* Vol. 26. *Epistulae Catho-
            licae.* Freiburg: Herder. [See also Frede]

1965   *Die lateinischen Texte des 1. Petrusbriefes.* Vetus Latina: Aus der
            Geschichte der lateinischen Bibel 5. Freiburg: Herder.

Thrall, Margaret E.
1981   " 'Putting on' or 'Stripping off' in 2 Corinthians 5:3." Pp. 221-37
            in Epp and Fee 1981.

Tischendorf, Constantin
1869-94   *Novum Testamentum Graece.* 8th major ed. 3 vols. Vols. 1-2: text
            (Leipzig: Giesecke & Devrient, 1869-72); Vol. 3: *Prolegomena*,
            by C. R. Gregory (Leipzig: Hinrichs, 1894).

Timpanaro, Sebastiano
1963   *La genesi del metodo del Lachmann.* Bibliotechina del saggiatore
            18. Florence: Felice Le Monnier. German ed., tr. by D. Irmer: *Die
            Entstehung der Lachmannschen Methode.* 2d rev. ed. Hamburg:
            Buske, 1971.

Tinnefeld, Franz Hermann
1963   *Untersuchungen zur altlateinischen Überlieferung des 1. Timo-*

theusbriefes. Klassisch-philologische Studien 26. Wiesbaden: Harrassowitz.

Tov, Emmanuel
1982   "Criteria for Evaluating Textual Readings: The Limitations of Textual Rules." *HTR* 75: 429-48.

Tregelles, Samuel Prideaux
1854   *An Account of the Printed Text of the Greek New Testament.* London: Bagster.
1860   "Introduction to the Textual Criticism and Study of the New Testament." Vol. 3 of T. H. Horne, *An Introduction to the Critical Study and Knowledge of the Holy Scriptures.* 4 vols. 11th ed. London: Longman, Green, Longman, and Roberts. Also published separately as *An Introduction to the Textual Criticism of the New Testament.* London, 1856.

Treu, Kurt
1966a   *Die griechischen Handschriften des Neuen Testaments in der UdSSR.* TU 91. Berlin: Akademie-Verlag.
1966b   "Neue neutestamentliche Fragmente der Berliner Papyrussammlung." *Archiv für Papyrusforschung* 18: 23-38 + 4 pls.

Turner, Cuthbert Hamilton
1923-28   "Marcan Usage: Notes, Critical and Exegetical on the Second Gospel." *JTS* 25 (1923/24) 377-86; 26 (1924/25) 12-20, 145-56, 225-40, 337-46; 27 (1925/26) 58-62; 28 (1926/27) 9-30, 349-62; 29 (1927/28) 275-89, 346-61.
1928   "The Textual Criticism of the New Testament." Pp. 718-29 in *A New Commentary on Holy Scripture Including the Apocrypha.* Ed. C. Gore, H. L. Goudge, and A. Guillaume. London: SPCK.

Turner, Eric G.
1968   *Greek Papyri: An Introduction.* Oxford: Clarendon Press.
1971   *Greek Manuscripts of the Ancient World.* Oxford: Clarendon Press.
1973   *The Papyrologist at Work.* J. H. Gray Lectures, University of Cambridge, 1971. Greek, Roman, and Byzantine Monograph 6. Durham, NC: Duke University.
1977   *The Typology of the Early Codex.* Haney Foundation Series 18. Philadelphia: University of Pennsylvania Press.

Turner, Nigel
1963   *Syntax.* Vol. 3 of J. H. Moulton, *A Grammar of New Testament Greek.* Edinburgh: T. & T. Clark.

Vaganay, Léon
1937   *An Introduction to the Textual Criticism of the New Testament.* London: Sands. [French original, 1933. See next item]

Vaganay, Léon, and Christian-Bernard Amphoux
1986   *Initiation à la critique textuelle du Nouveau Testament.* 2d ed. rev. by Amphoux. Paris: Cerf. Eng. tr.: *Introduction to New Testament Textual Criticism.* Cambridge/New York: Cambridge University Press, 1992.

Vincent, Marvin R.

1903   *A History of the Textual Criticism of the New Testament.* New Testament Handbooks. New York: Macmillan.

Vogels, Heinrich Joseph

1953   *Evangelium Colbertinum: Codex Lat. 254 der Bibliothèque Nationale zu Paris.* BBB 4-5. 2 vols. Bonn: Hanstein.

1955a   *Untersuchungen zum Text paulinischer Briefe bei Rufin und Ambrosiaster.* BBB 9. Bonn: Hanstein.

1955b   *Handbuch der Textkritik des Neuen Testaments.* 2d ed. Bonn: Hanstein. 1st ed., 1923.

1957   *Das Corpus Paulinum des Ambrosiaster.* BBB 13. Bonn: Hanstein.

Voicu, Sever J., and Serenella D'Alisera

1981   *I.MA.G.E.S.: Index in manuscriptorum graecorum edita specimina.* Rome: Borla.

von Dobschütz, Ernst

1926   "IV. Neutestamentlertagung zu Erlangen am 29. und 30. September 1925." *ZNW* 25: 168-74. "V. Neutestamentlertagung zu Breslau am 4. und 5. Oktober 1926." *ZNW* 25: 315-19.

von Soden, Hermann

1911-13 *Die Schriften des Neuen Testament in ihrer ältesten erreichbaren Textgestalt hergestellt auf Grund ihrer Textgeschichte.* 2d unchanged ed. 2 parts in 4 vols. Göttingen: Vandenhoeck & Ruprecht.

Vööbus, Arthur

1948   *Researches on the Circulation of the Peshitta in the Middle of the Fifth Century.* Contributions of Baltic University 64. Pinneburg: Baltic University.

1951a   *Neue Angaben über die textgeschichtlichen Zustände in Edessa in den Jahren ca 326-340: Ein Beitrag zur Geschichte des altsyrischen Tetraevangeliums.* Papers of the Estonian Theological Society in Exile 3. Stockholm: n.p.

1951b   *Die Spuren eines älteren äthiopischen Evangelientextes im Lichte der literarischen Monumente.* Papers of the Estonian Theological Society in Exile 2. Stockholm, n.p.

1951c   *Studies in the History of the Gospel Text in Syriac.* CSCO 128, Subsidia 3. Louvain: Durbecq.

1953   *Zur Geschichte des altgeorgischen Evangelientextes.* Papers of the Estonian Theological Society in Exile 4. Stockholm, n.p.

1954   *Early Versions of the New Testament: Manuscript Studies.* Papers of the Estonian Theological Society in Exile 6. Stockholm: n.p.

1978   *The Apocalypse in the Harklean Version: A Facsimile Edition of MS. Mardin Orth. 35, fol. 143r-159v, with an Introduction.* CSCO 400, Subsidia 56. Louvain: CSCO.

Voss, David

1936   "Is von Soden's K^r a Distinct Type of Text?" *JBL* 57: 311-18.

Westcott, Brooke Foss, and Fenton John Anthony Hort
1881-82   *The New Testament in the Original Greek.* 2 vols. Cambridge/London: Macmillan. 2d ed. 1896.

Wikenhauser, Alfred, and Josef Schmid
1973   *Einleitung in das Neue Testament.* 6th ed. Freiburg/Basel/Vienna: Herder.

Wikgren, Allen P.
1981   "The Problem in Acts 16:12." Pp. 171-78 in Epp and Fee 1981.

Wilcox, Max
1965   *The Semitisms of Acts.* Oxford: Clarendon Press.

Williams, C. S. C.
1951   *Alterations to the Text of the Synoptic Gospels and Acts.* Oxford: Blackwell.

1953   Revision of A. H. McNeile, *An Introduction to the Study of the New Testament.* 2d ed. rev. Oxford: Clarendon Press.

Wisse, Frederik W.
1982   *The Profile Method for the Classification and Evaluation of Manuscript Evidence as Applied to the Continuous Greek Text of the Gospel of Luke.* SD 44. Grand Rapids, MI: Eerdmans.

1983   "Prolegomena to the Study of the New Testament and Gnosis." Pp. 138-45 in *The New Testament and Gnosis: Essays in Honour of Robert McL. Wilson.* Ed. A. H. B. Logan and A. J. M. Wedderburn. Edinburgh: T. & T. Clark.

1986   "The Use of Early Christian Literature as Evidence for Inner Diversity and Conflict." Pp. 177-90 in *Nag Hammadi, Gnosticism, & Early Christianity.* Ed. C. W. Hedrick and R. Hodgson, Jr. Peabody, MA: Hendrickson.

Wisse, Frederik, and Paul R. McReynolds
1970   "Family E and the Profile Method." *Bib* 51: 67-75.

Witherington, Ben
1984   "The Anti-Feminist Tendencies of the 'Western' Text of Acts." *JBL* 103: 82-84.

Wordsworth, John, Henry Julian White, et al.
1889-1954 *Novum Testamentum Domini Nostri Iesu Christi secundum editionem Sancti Hieronymi.* 4 vols. Oxford: Clarendon Press. Vol. 3, 1954, ed. by H. F. D. Sparks and A. W. Adams.

Wrangham, Franciscus
1828   *Briani Waltoni . . . in biblia polyglotta prolegomena . . .* Cambridge: Deighton.

Wright, Leon E.
1952   *Alterations of the Words of Jesus as Quoted in the Literature of the Second Century.* Harvard Historical Monographs 25. Cambridge, MA: Harvard University Press.

Yoder, James D.
1961   *Concordance to the Distinctive Greek Text of Codex Bezae.* NTTS 2. Leiden: Brill.

Zaphiris, Gérassime

1970   *Le texte de l'Evangile selon saint Matthieu d'après les citations de Clément d'Alexandrie comparées aux citations des Pères et des Théologiens grecs du IIe au XVe siècle.* Gembloux: Duculot.

Zimmermann, Heinrich

1958   "Papyrus Bodmer II und seine Bedeutung für die Textgeschichte des Johannes-Evangeliums." *BZ* 2: 214-43.

1960   *Untersuchungen zur Geschichte der altlateinischen Überlieferung des zweiten Korintherbriefes.* BBB 16. Bonn: Hanstein.

Zuntz, Gunther

1945   *The Ancestry of the Harklean New Testament.* British Academy Supplemental Papers 7. London: Oxford University Press.

1953   *The Text of the Epistles: A Disquisition upon the Corpus Paulinum.* Schweich Lectures, 1946. London: British Academy.

INDEX OF MANUSCRIPTS, VERSIONS, EDITIONS, AND MODERN TRANSLATIONS

A. GREEK MANUSCRIPTS

General, 4-5, 29-32, 86, 111-13, 211 & n.2

Greek papyri

General, 4, 12, 24-25, 30-33, 37, 42-44, 84, 90-96, 110-11, 117-22, 248, 274-97, 358

Bodmer, 24, 30, 44, 84, 110, 278, 283
Chester Beatty, 24, 30, 44, 84, 110, 248, 277-78, 283
Egerton papyrus, 336
Oxyrhynchus, 24, 84, 110, 277-82

P^5, 93-94
P^{29}, 38, 93, 120, 293-94
P^{37}, 93n.24
P^{38}, 38, 93-94, 117-18, 121, 293-94
P^{45}, 24, 38, 90-94, 166, 284, 292-93
P^{46}, 24, 93-94, 127-28, 259n.14
P^{47}, 2
P^{48}, 38, 93-94, 121, 293-94
P^{52}, 32, 278-80
P^{66}, 9, 24, 92-94, 117, 127-29, 132, 136, 166, 186, 201, 222, 247-73, 311-13, 337
P^{69}, 293
P^{72}, 166
P^{75}, 24, 38, 42, 89, 92-94, 105, 114, 120, 128-31, 139, 166, 180, 186, 201, 206n.38, 227, 229, 243, 247, 251-73, 284-85, 289-93, 296, 307, 311-13

Greek uncials

General, 4-5, 31, 87

ℵ (01, Sinaiticus), 5, 21, 32, 103, 114, 129, 136, 161-62, 166, 188, 221-43, 261, 268-69, 278, 292, 296, 337

A (02, Alexandrinus), 18-20, 93, 147, 184, 226-27, 278, 285, 296
B (03, Vaticanus), 5, 32-33, 38, 42, 86, 89, 105n.38, 114, 120, 126-29, 139, 161-62, 166, 168, 180, 193, 206n.38, 222, 229, 236, 243, 247-49, 251-73, 278, 285, 289-93, 296, 311-12
C (04, Ephraemi rescriptus), 296
D (05, Bezae Cantabrigiensis), 18, 38, 55, 65, 89-91, 94, 117, 121, 128-29, 161-62, 176, 222, 225, 227-42, 247-49, 270-71, 285, 293-94, 296, 337
D_p (06, Claromontanus), 18, 93
L (019), 38, 93, 120, 292, 306
W (032, Washingtonianus), 24, 38, 90-91, 93, 121, 184, 187, 221, 285, 292-93, 296
Θ (038, Koridethi), 24, 90-91, 292
0171, 92n.22, 93, 293-94
0220, 93

Greek minuscules

General, 5, 28, 31, 100, 103-4, 211-20
Family 1, 90, 254
Family 13, 90-91, 292
33, 38, 93, 120, 292
383, 38, 93, 121, 294
565, 292
579, 93, 120, 292
614, 38, 93, 121, 294
1739, 38, 93, 120, 292, 294

Greek lectionaries

General, 5, 28, 31, 214n.7

B. VERSIONS

C. CRITICAL EDITIONS OF THE GREEK NT

D. MODERN TRANSLATIONS

INDEX OF BIBLICAL PASSAGES

INDEX OF ANCIENT AUTHORS

INDEX OF MODERN AUTHORS

INDEX OF SUBJECTS